Frank Broughton is a freelance writer and editor whose writing has appeared in *The Face*, *i-D*, *Details*, *Rolling Stone*, *Mixmag* and *Time Out New York*, where he was the founding clubs editor. He was the author of *The Time Out New York Guide* and editor of *The Time Out Book of Interviews 1968-1999*, and deputy editor of *i-D*.

Bill Brewster is a freelance writer specialising in dance music and football. He has been co-editor of *When Saturday Comes*, editor of weekly DJ magazine *Mixmag Update* and editor of New York dance mag *DMC USA*. He is a regular contributor to *IDJ*, and his writing has appeared in many national newspapers. Bill also runs his own label and DJs a mix of everything from funky deep house to crazed psych-rock records all over the UK, Europe and USA.

Together they are authors of *The Manual* (Headline) and *How to DJ (Properly)* (Bantam). They also collaborate on occasional 'Low Life' parties of legendary quality in Harlem and London.

More praise for *Last Night a DJ Saved My Life*:

'Lovingly captures a host of compelling stories from every seminal DJ across the last century . . . The energy which so obviously jumps from the book's pages . . . elevates *Last Night* way above the "trainspotter tome" a book of its ilk could easily have become' *i-D*

'Fascinating, illuminating, thoughtful and insightful' *Muzik*

'[A] superb book . . . essential reading for wannabe DJs or indeed anybody who loves clubbing and popular music' *Time Out*

'If you're a DJ or a dance addict, you'll love it' *Daily Mail*

'An informative, entertaining and immensely likeable book' *Independent*

'The comprehensive clubland history. This will be on a university syllabus by 2010, mark our words' *Jockey Slut*

'You aren't likely to find a better-researched or more wryly humorous look at the history of DJing' *DJ Times*

Also by Bill Brewster and Frank Broughton

Ministry of Sound: The Manual
How to DJ (Properly): The Art and Science of Playing Records

LAST NIGHT A DJ SAVED MY LIFE

The History of the Disc Jockey

Bill Brewster and Frank Broughton

headline

First published in 1999
by HEADLINE BOOK PUBLISHING

Updated edition published in paperback in 2006
by HEADLINE BOOK PUBLISHING

4

Picture research by Kay Rowley

ISBN 978 0 755 31398 3

Printed and bound in the UK by
CPI Mackays, Chatham ME5 8TD

Headline's policy is to use papers that are natural, renewable and recyclable products and made from wood grown in sustainable forests. The logging and manufacturing processes are expected to conform to the environmental regulations of the country of origin.

Typeset in Bembo by Avon DataSet Ltd,
Bidford on Avon, Warwickshire

HEADLINE BOOK PUBLISHING
A division of Hodder Headline
338 Euston Road
London NW1 3BH

www.headline.co.uk
www.hodderheadline.com

'Whosoever knoweth the power of the dance, dwelleth in God.'
— Rumi, Persian dervish poet

'Whosoever danceth not, knoweth not the way of life.'
— Jesus Christ, in a second century gnostic hymn

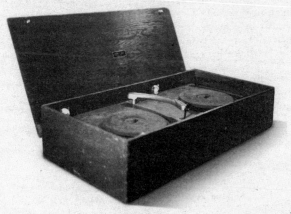

Custom-made double turntable built in 1955 by Edward P. Casey of the Bronx, New York.

CONTENTS

ORIGINAL PREFACE

Original Preface

'A lot of DJs around now, they need to know about this stuff. Someone should put a book together of all this and then we can give it to people and say, "read this before you go DJing".'

– Ashley Beedle, *DJ and producer*

'There's not a problem that I can't fix –
'cos I can do it in the mix.'

– Indeep, *Last Night A DJ Saved My Life*

The story of dance music resides in the people who made it. Or at least played it. And guess what – most of them are alive and well and full of tall tales. We set out to meet as many as possible and start them talking. Some are extremely famous, some we didn't know were still breathing. Some we found in the phone book. Once we started asking questions, the nuggets came flooding out and we were soon brimming with details no one else knew; finding connections that no one had noticed. We were surprised that this story had never been told in full, and along the way felt a sneaking pride that we would be the ones to do it.

Because, sadly, most writing about dance music just hasn't stuck. We keep on reading the same old repeated mistakes, the same well-worn myths, the same poorly researched articles written completely without context. And we're just too thick to deal with the books that have copied all these together and used them as the basis for a lot of abstract nonsense about postmodern intertextuality and Hegelian Gesundfarbensextenkugelschreiber.

So being simple folk, we wrote a simple book. There are a few socio-cultural theories in here, and we like to think we've done a pretty good job of connecting things together and showing where they fit, but what you're about to read is mostly just great stories from people with big egos, explaining what they did to change music.

We aimed to write a biography of dance music's most important figure – the disc jockey. Our story is of how the DJ's job evolved and how the

DJ has been the driving force in popular music. In telling it we've concentrated on his crazier years when he was shaking things up, and given less emphasis to his recent behaviour now that he's settled down and become respectable.

Given this emphasis, this is not a history of dance music itself (although it nearly is). We didn't have time or space to explore the creation of every last sub-genre, so as we followed the evolution of dance music we set our limits with the motto, 'Remember the DJ' and concentrated on the impact of his DJing role rather than the changes he made purely as a producer. And don't be disappointed if your favourite jock doesn't get a whole chapter to himself. We were looking for whoever got there first, not necessarily the ones who were the best. There are plenty of DJs who, while being amazing, talented artists that we know and love and have danced to on many occasions, are only bit players in the big picture.

We had a lot of fun writing this book. If you've got this far you'll probably enjoy reading it. We'll bet a dollar to a dime you'll find things in it which you didn't know. And some of them might even make you laugh.

Hopefully, it can also go some way to counter the ignorance and snobbery which still prevails in grown-up attitudes to dance music. It really is about time. After all, when it comes to the development of music, the dancefloor has always had more influence than the printed word.

Bill and Frank, London 1999

NEW PREFACE

New Preface

DJing is a hundred years old this December, the same age as helicopters, tea bags and cornflakes. To celebrate this auspicious occasion we've completely updated our book, fattened it up, and given it a natty new cover. The initial plan was just to extend its shelf life. Once we got started, however, the project grew and grew. It became a chance, not only to bring things bang up to date, but also to pay more attention to the European side of the story. In 1999 a few critics (well one, thanks Dave) asked, 'Where's German techno? Where's Italian disco? Where's Ibiza?' We tried arguing that we'd written the story of the DJ, not the story of dance music, and that DJing was a fully formed craft as early as the late seventies. We also pointed to a crop of books about acid house and after, which had gone into more depth than we'd ever have space for. Now, though, we've filled those gaps, collected more intriguing tales and can present a much more even-handed and comprehensive volume.

Seen from 2006 it's a neater story, too. DJs are thankfully no longer worshipped quite so preposterously, the big names are struggling a little to pay their mink bills, and most people now understand that DJing is more about collecting great music than doing supernatural things with a mixer. The arc of the DJ's biography has curved elegantly back down to earth.

When *Last Night A DJ Saved My Life* first came out many people were confused by the idea of dance music history. Rock critics are still unlikely to admit to our central thesis – that DJs are more important than bands when it comes to radical shifts in music – but they have had to admit that the guy with the record box has played an important role.

Finally, thanks to all of you who have said such nice things to us about the book. We're proud of how well-loved our baby has been. While it won't exactly secure us a table at The Ivy, it does give us something to talk drunkenly about at parties. Here's to Reginald Fessenden.

Bill and Frank, London 2006
billandfrank@djhistory.com

For more interviews, features, mixes and a lively forum of work-shy trainspotters

www.djhistory.com

THANKS

And this one's for...

Afshin, Vince Aletti, Julian Alexander, Ross Allen, Imogen Aylen, Pauline Barlow, Alexia Beard, Rob Bellars, John Bland, Kool Lady Blue, Mr Blue, Matthew Burgess, Paul Byrne, Bob Casey, Phil Cheeseman, Matthew Collin, Stephanie Collin, Paulette Constable, Lucinda Cook, Michael Cook, DJ Cosmo, Andy Cowan, Jon Dasilva, Fritz and Catherine Delsoin, Drew DeNicola, Ian Dewhirst, Job De Wit, Jeff Dexter, Dave Dorrell, Roger Eagle, Kevin Ebbutt, Mick Eve, Sheryl Garratt, Adam Goldstone, Jolyon Green, Malu Halassa, Donna Halper, David Hills, Omaid Hiwaizi, Nick Hornby, Chris Hunt, Jempi, Danny Krivit, Steve Lau, Dave Lee, John McCready, Jon and Helena Marsh, Mary Maxwell, Paul Noble, Ella Oates, Sean P, Punk Rock Paddington, Elbert Phillips, Dom Phillips, Steve Phillips, Rebecca Prochnik, Sam Pow, Angus Reid, Richard Reyes, Gonnie Rietveld, Toni Rossano, Kay Rowley, Giovanni Salti, Alec Samway, Quinton Scott, Ranj Sehambi, Peter Shapiro, Nicky Siano, Lindsay Symons, Spanky, Dave Swindells, Bruce Tantum, Tracy Thompson, Frank 'Dope' Tope, Koenraad Van Ennerseel, Frie Verhelst, Paul Ward, Emma Warren, Judy Weinstein, Steve and Sylvia Weir, Lesleigh Woodburn, Carl Woodroffe, Doug Young, Mike Zwerin and especially the folks at the DJHistory.com forum for fact-checking and tune-sharing.

And everyone who helped us with interviews and photos
Yoko @ Axis, James @ Plan B, Greg Belson, Barbara @ Boldface Media, Lynn Cosgrave, Jonas @ Electronic PM, DJ Geoffroy, Phli Mison and Clare Woodcock @ Get Involved, Jonathan Green, Sarah @ Groove Connection, Josie James, Peter Kang, Kay-Gee, Lynn Li, JD Livingstone, Catherine Mackenzie, Kevin McHugh, Wayne Pollard, CB Shaw, Justin and Katrina @ 40dB, Nick and Sarah @ MPCE, Liam J. Nabb, Vez and Wendy @ Ninjatune, Louise Oldfield, Mavis Price, Indy @ Radio One, Damian Harris @ Skint, Corinna @ Soul II Soul, Fran @ Strictly Rhythm UK, Tosh @ Tam Tam Books, Matt Trollope, Steve, Jo and Lucy at Twice Is Nice, Shane O'Neill @ Universal, Aurelie and Jody @ Wave Music.

And translations and interpreting
Louise Oldfield and Liam J. Nabb, David Colkett, Peter Hoste

And all at Headline, especially
Emma Tait, Juliana Foster, Lucy Ramsey

Special thanks
Liz, Lola and Imogen

Finally, Bill thanks Frank for being pretentious; Frank thanks Bill for being anal.

ONE
INTRODUCTION

You Should Be Dancing

Back when man was stumbling around the dusty savannahs figuring out the best way to surprise a woolly mammoth, he found his experience divided sharply between night and day. In the light he was a naked animal, prey to those greater than him; but once darkness fell he joined the gods. Under the star-pierced sky, with flaming torches smearing his vision and armies of drummers hammering out a relentless beat, he ate some sacred roots and berries, abandoned the taboos of waking life, welcomed the spirits to his table, and joined his sisters and brothers in the dance.

More often than not, there was somebody at the centre of all this. Somebody who handed out the party plants, somebody who started the action, somebody who controlled the music. This figure – the witchdoctor, the shaman, the priest – was a little bit special, he had a certain power. The next day, as you nursed your hangover, he probably went back to being just your next door neighbour – that guy two huts down who wears a few too many feathers – but when the lights were off and you were heading out into a drum-and-peyote-fuelled trance, he was the don.

Today (no offence to priests and vicars, who try their best) it is the DJ who fills this role. It is the DJ who presides at our festivals of transcendence. Like the witchdoctor, we know he's just a normal guy really – I mean look at him – but when he wipes away our everyday lives with holy drums and sanctified basslines, we are quite prepared to think of him as a god, or at the very least a sacred intermediary, the man who can get the great one to return our calls.

In a good club, and even in most bad ones, the dancers are celebrating their youth, their energy, their sexuality. They are worshipping life through dance and music. Some worship with the heightened levels of perception that drugs bring; but most are carried away merely by the music and the people around them. The DJ is the key to all this. By playing records in the right way the average DJ has a tremendous power to affect people's states of mind. A truly *great* DJ, just for a moment, can make a whole room fall in love.

Because you see, DJing is not just about choosing a few tunes. It is about generating shared moods; it's about understanding the feelings of a group of people and directing them to a better place. In the hands of a master, records create rituals of spiritual communion that can be the most powerful events in people's lives.

This idea of communion is what drives the best musical happenings. It's about breaking the audience/artist boundary, about *being* an event, not just watching one. The hippies in San Francisco knew this when they made the early psychedelic rock shows places to dance. Sid Vicious knew it when he jumped off the stage to pogo in the audience and watch the Sex Pistols. It's the answer to the Happy Mondays' question, 'What's Bez for?' And it's why the twist caused such a dancing revolution: without the worry of having a partner, you were free to be part of the whole room.

The DJ stands at the apex of this idea. If he does his job right, he's down there jumping around in the middle of the dancefloor, even when he's actually locked away behind a lot of electronics in a gloomy glass box.

The lord of the dance

The disc jockey is simply the latest incarnation of an ancient role. As party-starter *par excellence*, he has many illustrious forebears. The shamans were his most resonant ancestors (as no end of misty mystical ravers will tell you); pagan high priests who directed their people by dance to the spirit world and drank drug-filled reindeer piss in order to see god. Since then he has taken many names in many places. He was the music hall's loquacious Master of Ceremonies, he was the jazz age's zoot-suited bandleader, the wrinkled Blue Mountain square dance caller, even perhaps the conductor of symphonies and opera. He may even have been James Brown and George Clinton. For most of our time on the planet, he has been a religious figure. Most older forms of worship are centred around music and dance, their rituals usually focused on some special person who links heaven and earth.

In fact, only recently was dancing ever separated from religion. The Bible tells us 'there is a time to dance'. The Jewish Talmud says the angels dance in heaven. It is a commandment by rabbinical law that Jews *must* dance at weddings, and the Orthodox Hasidim are instructed to dance as an important part of their regular worship. The Shakers, an American nonconformist sect famous for their furniture, lived as celibates with the sexes completely segregated (they expanded by adopting orphans), but their men and women came together to dance in intricate formations as an act of worship.

Shaken and stirred – Shakers conducting an elaborate circular formation dance as an act of religious worship, 1872.

In calling for a greater sense of festivity in the Christian church, sixties theologian Harvey Cox pointed out very sagely that 'some who cannot say a prayer may be able to dance it'. Nevertheless, modern religion has often had problems with dancing, usually because of its obvious connection with sex – 'the perpendicular indication of horizontal desires,' as George Bernard Shaw put it. But people will dance regardless. Islam is fairly unhappy about dancing, but Turkey's cult of whirling dervishes do it to praise Allah. Christianity has regularly outlawed it, only to see outbreaks of dance-desperate people sneaking in a few steps when they can. In Germany in 1374, a time and place where hatred of the body and of dancing was arguably at its peak, after eating some ergot-poisoned bread, great crowds of half-naked people thronged in the streets and did exactly what the church had told them not to: they danced like maniacs. As historian of religious dance ER Dodds wrote, 'The power of the Dance is a dangerous power. Like other forms of self-surrender, it is easier to begin than to stop.'

All this is the DJ's heritage. It is the source of his strength. The DJ is today's lord of the dance.

If you think it's a bit rich to put the disc jockey in such exalted company, consider the status our culture awards him. Things have calmed down a little since the crazed idolatry of the mid nineties, but even so, a top spinner can earn four-, sometimes even five-figure sums for a few hours' work. The DJ has become a millionaire, he has dated supermodels, he has flown between engagements in helicopters and private jets. All this for doing something which is so much fun, as he'll freely admit, that most DJs would do it for free.

If all that doesn't convince you, you'd better have a word with the hundreds of thousands of people worldwide who are involved in the multi-billion-dollar nightclub economy, and certainly the millions of clubbers who dig into their pockets every week to hear the DJ play. In the words of disco-loving Albert Goldman, one of few writers to understand dance music, 'Never, in the long history of public entertainment, have so many paid so much for so little – and enjoyed themselves so immensely!'

So that's why the disc jockey deserves his own history. Even if he's mostly a grumpy, overweight anal retentive who makes a living playing other people's music.

What a DJ actually does

'Anyone who can play chopsticks on the piano and knows how to work a Game Boy can be a DJ,' wrote Gavin Hills when *The Face* sent him to DJ school for the day. 'All you need is some sense of timing and a few basic technical skills and you too could be on a grand a night.'

Is it really that easy, or do DJs come anywhere near *earning* a living?

What exactly does a DJ do?

DJs distil musical greatness. They select a series of exceptional recordings and use them to create a unique performance, improvised to precisely suit the time, the place and the people in front of them. All this looks very much like someone just putting on a few records, and, given an afternoon's introduction to the equipment, the 'anyone could do that' argument seems fairly watertight. Plus of course, any greatness in the music is undeniably the work of the producer and the musicians who made each track. But answer this: how did those spectacular records get into that DJ's box? Where did he find the amazing funk version of that familiar Beatles tune? What was that sixties soul thing with the bassline that turned the dancers to jelly? Or that house record that sounds like The Doors? Or that garage track that's better than anything I've heard in a year of listening to 1Xtra?

What a DJ does is this: he knows music. The DJ knows music better than you, better than your friends, better than everyone on the dancefloor or in the record shop. Some DJs know their chosen genre better than anyone else on the planet. Sure, anyone can play records, but most people only have tunes we've all heard before, songs everyone's bored with. A great DJ will hit a room with musical moments so new and so fresh that it's irrelevant that the music is recorded, and so powerful that they easily surpass your all-time favourites (and here 'fresh' can mean a very old track rescued from complete obscurity as easily as a CDR produced yesterday). The real work of a DJ isn't standing behind some record decks for a couple of hours, looking shifty and waiting for some drinks tickets; the time and effort comes in a life spent sifting through music and deciding if it's good, bad or '*Oh-my-god-listen-to-this!*' A DJ's job is to channel the vast ocean of recorded sound into a single unforgettable evening.

Naturally, few DJs are anything less than obsessive about their music collections. In *The Recording Angel*, Evan Eisenberg tells of Clarence, the heir to a Cadillac salesman's fortune, who sits in poverty in Bellmore, Long Island with an unimaginably vast collection of records. His toilet has stopped working, he can hardly afford to feed himself, but he still collects music obsessively.

'Clarence opens the door and you enter, but just barely. Every surface – the counters and cabinets, the shelves of the oven and refrigerator, and almost all the linoleum floor – is covered with records. They are heavy shellac discs, jammed in cardboard boxes or just lying in heaps; crowning one pile is a plate of rusty spaghetti . . . All he had left was the house – unheated, unlit, so crammed with trash that the door wouldn't open – and three quarters of a million records . . .'

It's not fiction.

To become a good DJ you have to develop the *hunger*. You have to search for new records with the insane zeal of a goldrush prospector digging in a blizzard. You have to develop an excitement for vinyl that verges on a fetish. You shouldn't be able to walk past a charity shop without worrying what classic rarity you might have missed nestling among those Osmonds' LPs. Your blood pressure should jump a little at the thought of slitting open a 12-inch square of shrink-wrap. People will find you boring, your skin will start to suffer, but you will find solace in long, impenetrable conversations with fellow junkies about Metroplex catalogue numbers or Prelude white labels.

Presenting or performing?

Aside from musical knowledge, and the ceaseless research and collecting which supports it, the DJ's skill lies in sharing his music effectively. At its most basic, DJing is the act of presenting a series of records for an audience's enjoyment. So at the simplest level a DJ is a presenter. This is what radio DJs do – they introduce music and intersperse it with chat, comedy or some other kind of performance. However, the club DJ has largely abandoned this role for something more musically creative. Out has gone the idea of *introducing* records in favour of the notion of *performing* them. Today's DJs use records as building blocks, stringing them together in an improvised narrative to create a 'set' – a performance – of their own. By dramatically emphasising the connections between songs, by juxtaposing them or by seamlessly overlaying them, the modern club DJ is not so much presenting discrete records as combining them to make something new. And this kind of patchwork performance, when done well, can be very much greater than the sum of its parts. Consequently the DJ, now no longer merely the host for a revue of other people's recordings, can be considered a true performer.

The essence of the DJ's craft is selecting which records to play and in what order. Doing this better or worse than others is the profession's basic yardstick. The aim is to generate a cohesive musical atmosphere, in most cases, making people dance. But while it might sound simple enough, successfully programming an evening of records (or even just half an hour) is vastly harder than you might think. Try it. Even with a box full of great tunes, choosing songs to keep people dancing – holding their attention without jarring them or boring them – requires a great deal of skill. For some it comes instinctively, for others it's a matter of experience, an ability gained from years of watching people dance.

To really pull it off you need to understand records in terms of their precise effects on an audience – you need to hear music in terms of its energy and feeling. All good DJs can distinguish fine nuances in music; they are sensitive to the complex set of emotions and associations that each song inspires, and they know exactly how each record's style and tempo will impact on the room. This understanding is the foundation of the DJs' improvisation, as they choose which record to play next. This is largely about having an ear for music, about having a critical understanding of what actually makes one song work better than another, and certain songs sound good next to each other. Few DJs are musicians in the sense of playing an instrument, but many display a quite refined musicality.

Even at the purely technical level a DJ's job is fairly demanding. In combining records to create a single, flowing, meaningful (or at least effective) performance, you need to know the structure of each of the songs you're going to play, you must have a reasonably musical ear to hear whether two tunes are in complementary keys, and to seamlessly merge two separate tracks, you must have a quite precise sense of rhythm. To 'beatmatch', to synchronise the beats of two records so you can mix them, you must learn to hear one song in each ear and keep them separate; this cognitive ability involves actually 'rewiring' part of your brain. Other musicians' skills are invaluable. Most good DJs will have a highly reliable musical memory and a firm understanding of song construction. And you obviously need to know the equipment involved: your turntables, your mixer, your amplifier and any other sound processing devices you might be using. A quick glance into any DJ booth should convince you that this can be pretty complex.

The best DJs can even play the sound system itself, using volume and frequency controls, as well as special effects like echo and reverb, to emphasise certain moments or even certain instruments in a song. By 'working the system' a good DJ can make even a single record sound considerably better: more dramatic, more explosive, more danceable. And with production equipment now small enough to bring in to the nightclub, many of today's DJs use studio techniques as well – sampling and looping a passage from a tune, or mixing in some beats or a bassline from their computer, in effect, remixing tracks live to create a unique version for the night.

Most DJs who dare to play outside the security of their bedrooms will have a fairly good technical understanding. But even with a complete mastery of the practicalities you could still be a useless DJ (there are plenty out there). The most fundamental DJ talents are taste and enthusiasm. Taste is key: can you recognise good music and can you separate the great from the merely good? Often of course, taste is as subjective as peach vs avocado for the new bathroom, but it boils down to whether a crowd of people on a dancefloor is at all interested in the same music as you.

If they are, great; but if they're not, how far can you win them over? This is where enthusiasm comes in. The best DJs are evangelists about music. They can make their love for their favourite records completely infectious. You could probably play a hit record and get people to dance, but can you make your crowd love new songs they've never heard before? Can you make them appreciate something which is on the edge of their tastes by recontextualising it and showing them how it fits with an old favourite? The greatest DJs have always been driven by a burning need to share their music. As one DJ puts it, 'DJing is two hours of you showing people what's good.'

The art of DJing

So the DJ is part shaman, part technician, part collector, part selector and part musical evangelist. Doubtless he is a craftsman, the expert at making people dance. But is the DJ an artist? Like the musician, he can be.

Popular understanding of great DJing usually concentrates on the technical aspects: incredibly smooth mixes, fantastically fast changes, mixing with three decks, clever EQing . . . Perhaps the busier a DJ is, the easier it is to believe that he's doing something creative. And many DJs gained their fame from doing astonishing things with record decks, just like many musicians, from Mozart to Hendrix, owe their legend to a godlike mastery of their instruments.

However, a great DJ should be able to move a crowd on the most primitive equipment, and several of history's best DJs have been pretty ropey mixers. Great DJing is not just about tricksy mixing, it's much more about finding amazing new songs and being able to pull them out at just the right moment. More than anything else, it's how sensitively a DJ can interact with a crowd.

The truth about DJing is that it is an emotional, improvisational art form and here the real scope for artistry lies. A good DJ isn't just stringing records together, he's controlling the relationship between some music and hundreds of people. That's why he needs to see them. That's why it couldn't be a tape. That's why it's a live performance. That's why it's a creative act. Music is a hotline to people's emotions, and what a DJ does is use this power constructively to generate enjoyment. Obviously his medium is music, but that's just a means to an end. In a very real sense his primary medium is emotion – the DJ plays the feelings of a roomful of people.

That's a very egocentric way of putting it. More accurately, perhaps, a DJ is *responding* to the feelings of a roomful of people, and then using music to accentuate or heighten them. 'It's communication,' says DJ and producer Norman Cook, aka Fatboy Slim, marking the difference between good DJs and bad. 'It's whether they're communicating to the crowd and whether they're receiving the communication back from the crowd.

'For me, it's whether they look up or not while they're playing,' he adds. 'A good DJ is always looking at the crowd, seeing what they like, seeing whether it's working; communicating with them, smiling at them. And a bad DJ is always looking down at the decks and just doing whatever they practised in their bedroom, regardless of whether the crowd are enjoying it or not.'

David Mancuso, disco's founding father, has always believed very strongly that a DJ is never greater than his audience. His ideal is that the DJ is in equal parts performer and listener. In his view the DJ should be 'a humble person, who sheds their ego and respects music, and is there to keep the flow going – to participate.' On the best nights, he says, he feels like a conduit for the emotions around him, he completes the circuit between the dancers and the music. 'It's a unique situation where the dancer becomes part of the whole setting of the music being played.' In this, the DJ is as much part of the audience as the dancers. 'Basically, you have one foot on the dancefloor and one in the booth.'

DJ and producer David Morales agrees, affirming that a DJ can only do his job properly in the presence of an audience.

'I can't turn it on for myself,' he insists. 'I can't. I got a great sounding studio, but when I make my show tapes for the radio, I can't turn it on. I don't come up with the creative things that come on when I'm playing live to an audience. I can't duplicate it.'

However, when the live feedback is there, he knows he is capable of greatness. And when a night is going well, the feeling is incomparable.

'Ohhh, man, it's like jumping out of my skin,' he says, beaming. 'I dance in the booth. I jump up and down. I wave my arms in the air, you know. It's that feeling of knowing I'm in full control, I can do anything I want.'

When he's on a roll, the feeling is completely sexual.

'Oh, for sure. For me? Absolutely. Pure sex! Absolutely. It's spiritual sex. Classic, spiritual sex. Oh my god, on a great night, man – sometimes I'm on my *knees* in the middle of a mix, just feeling it that way. And then when you play the next record, you can bring it down, you can bring it up, or you can just turn everything off and the people are going *nuts!* And you stand back, you just wipe your forehead and . . . *shiit!* You could play whatever you want. *Whatever you want.* You got 'em from there.'

Sex and DJs are rarely far apart – confirmation, if any is needed, that the act of love and the act of getting people excited through music are close cousins. Francis Grasso, the granddaddy of modern club jocks, was getting blowjobs in the booth back in 1969. 'I bet you can't make me miss a beat,' he'd tell the girl beneath his decks.

Junior Vasquez remembers some drug-crazed Sound Factory clubber dry-humping the speaker stacks in an attempt to get closer to the music. 'He kept yelling, "I'm fucking the DJ",' gleams Junior.

'DJs make love in the same way that they play music,' laughs Matt Black of Coldcut. 'If you think about it, it's got to be true. And also, great DJs are great cooks, my girlfriend reckons.'

Better than a band

The main reason DJs took over from live music was economic. A music lover with a box of 78s could entertain a crowd far more cheaply than a bus full of thirsty musicians. And it also let people hear better music. Imagine yourself in a post-war dance hall. Which would you prefer, a twirl to the local colliery band, with your Uncle Everett on trombone, or Tommy Dorsey captured on record leading one of the world's finest orchestras? Even today a studio recording is usually sonically superior to a live band, even if their amps go up to eleven.

In a 1975 *Melody Maker*, Chris Welch explained the musician's hostility to the discothèque. 'There is nothing worse for a player than to compete with a slick moving conveyor belt of the best product from the world's rock factories, relayed by the finest amplification, with a deejay and lights to inject further doses of adrenalin.'

A musician, however phenomenal, is boxed in by the range of their instrument, the extent of their back catalogue and the scope of their musical style. A DJ has none of these limitations. A DJ is free to play two records next to each other made thirty years apart, or two records from different continents, or to play the one great track from an artist's otherwise hopeless career. Or like the hip hop DJs, they might ignore a band's entire existence save for the forty-five seconds of funkiness in one of their drum breaks.

It's meaningless to argue that a DJ's music is inferior to a live performance. They are simply different things. You can't see the musicians, you can't watch the music being made, but then most of today's music couldn't be played 'live' in any case. For an analogy compare live theatre with the movies. It can be amazing to watch a play where the actor is in the same room with you, a hushed audience hanging on their every breath. But it's also amazing to zoom in on an actor's face, to see them fly, or to watch them jump from the back of a giant exploding lizard.

So you have to compare the DJ and musician carefully. On skill, on talent, on unique artistic abilities, the musician will almost always win. But on scope, on responsiveness, on the ability to go in wildly different directions, the DJ leads the way. The DJ also wins on sheer power, because while a band or a musician can only be themselves, a DJ can distil millions of man-hours of musical genius into a single set. Provided he can find it on eBay and he can justify his kids going without new shoes, a DJ has the potential to play any recording made by anyone, ever. Even the greatest musician only has jurisdiction over a tiny part of the universe of music; the DJ has it all. And since the musicians aren't in the room, after a night of amazing music, who else but the DJ will take the credit?

Back when DJing was about *introducing* records, a DJ's performance was judged mostly on what he did or said in between them. But now that it's about *combining* records, we consider a DJ's performance in much the same way as we do a musician's. Sure, he's playing records made by other people, but he's doing it in a unique and creative way. Even sticking to a single genre there are many thousands of tunes a DJ could choose from to fill an evening, and perhaps several mixes of each. Start doing the maths and you see how a DJ's set is at least as statistically unique as a musician's guitar riff.

The DJ *is* a musician. It just happens that in place of notes he uses songs, in place of piano keys or guitar strings he has records. And like any other musician, the DJ's skill lies in how these are chosen and put together. Think of a DJing performance in a compressed time-frame. Where a guitarist can impress an audience by playing a thirty-second sequence of chords, what a DJ does takes a lot longer – a DJ needs to be judged on a two- or three-hour narrative of tracks.

Imagine a grand tapestry made by stitching together pieces of the finest handmade cloth. Seen up close its beauty comes from the skill of the weavers and embroiderers who made the different fabrics, but seen from a distance it has a beauty of a different scale, a more imposing grandeur that comes from the overall pattern or design. Like the maker of such a tapestry, the DJ is an artist of a different order. The DJ is a musical editor, a *meta*musician, he makes music out of other music.

The industry of dance music is centred on the disc jockey's expertise. As he is the acknowledged expert at making people dance, today the bulk of dance music is produced or remixed by DJs. The DJ's role as the librarian of the world's music puts him in the driving seat now that making music is so often about sampling and combining older records.

And if he's doing his job right, the DJ is enjoying himself just as much as the dancers in front of him. 'Even if I wasn't working, I'd still keep playing records,' says David Morales. 'I enjoy doing what I do. I get a lot of passion from it, and to be paid, and to be put on a pedestal for doing something that I love doing naturally, is mind boggling.'

The postmodern angle

Because his artistry comes from combining other people's art, because his performance is made from other musicians' performances, the DJ is the epitome of a postmodern artist. Quite simply, DJing is all about mixing things together. The DJ uses records to make a musical collage, just like Quentin Tarantino might make a new movie which is just a lot of scenes copied from old movies or Philip Johnson might build a skyscraper shaped like a grandfather clock. This is the essence of postmodernism: nicking forms and ideas and combining them creatively.

Seen on a theoretical level the DJ is fascinating for a number of other reasons. The DJ's role in our culture illustrates very clearly several key themes of postmodern life. As Dom Phillips, former editor of *Mixmag*, puts it, 'The DJ is not an artist, but he is an artist. He's not a promoter, but he is a promoter. He's not a record company man, but he is. And he's also part of the crowd. He's an instigator who brings all these things together.'

Basically, the DJ's job is strange in all the right ways. For a start, is it really a job? It's a way to earn a living, but it's also a lot of fun. DJs provide a service that's obviously worth paying for, but most of them go home and do the same thing in their spare time, and many of them will jump at the chance to play at that special party when the crowd is right, for free, just for the thrill of it.

Another postmodern thing about DJing is that it is both consumption *and* production, and this confuses the hell out of sociologists (as if they needed help). A DJ is a consumer of recorded music: he buys a record and listens to it, just like anyone else might. However, because his audience is listening to it too, he is also, *at the exact same time*, making a product – the performance of the music contained in that record. And the choices he makes as a *consumer* (which records he chooses to buy and listen to) are a defining part of his worth as a *producer* (how creative and distinctive he is). Practising consumption as creativity is a very postmodern thing to do, as we'll demonstrate if you lend us your credit card.

An associated issue is that the DJ is both a performer *and* a promoter. He is entertaining an audience and at the same time he is urging them to go out and buy something – the records that he uses for his performance. Again, people with a PhD find this troubling in the extreme.

Academics are also intrigued by the fact that the DJ makes a living by filtering information; he makes sense of the confusing mass of musical information that bombards us (there are hundreds of dance singles released each week). There's no way that we could find all the great music within our favourite genre, so we rely on DJs to do it for us. They are like personal shoppers who sift through the hundreds of crap records and find the ones we like. These days, fewer and fewer people buy singles; instead, we decide on our favourite DJs and let them buy them for us. Why spend your life obsessively searching for obscure records (in which case you're probably a DJ anyway) when you can buy a DJ-mixed compilation CD made by someone who does that for a living? You could say that these days we don't buy particular records, we buy particular DJs. Another groovy example of post-modernism at work.

Now these are fascinating angles to think about, but there's not much more to them than that, unless of course you introduce some jargon. If you want to write about DJs without leaving the library, or if you want to pretend you're a DJ even though you can't make people dance, we recommend using 'text' or 'found object' whenever you'd normally say 'song' or 'record', and calling the DJ a *bricoleur* (French for 'handyman') whenever you can. Try slipping the words 'signifier' and 'discourse' into your sentences (use them however you like, no one will know) and never say 'slingin' nuff choons' when you could say 'the cutting, sampling and interweaving of discrete media commodities'.

A few 'avant-garde' DJs have successfully pulled such pretentious wool over the eyes of the more academic music critics. We'd argue that New York's DJ Spooky, for example, attracts an audience largely through his writing, by making DJing sound really complicated. It might work on the brains of the chattering classes, but it rarely washes with the bodies on the dancefloor. The DJ should concentrate on 'finding good tunes to play' rather than 'attracting meaning from the data cloud'.

Musical revolutionary

Thanks to his unrivalled freedom to play music of any style and from any time or place, the DJ has long been the central force in the evolution of music. As you'll see, to keep their dancers excited, DJs have been happy to distort, corrupt and combine recordings in ways that would horrify the original artists, and this, more than a few jam sessions, a new bass player or a particularly tragic love affair, is what inspires musical revolution.

As a gun for hire whose reputation depends on the independence of his musical tastes and, above all, on the novelty and distinctness of his performance, the DJ is a far more powerful force for change in music than a band could ever be. Until recently when he was turned into a marketable pop star, the DJ was one of the very few people with any power in the music business who was not subservient to the record industry. His freelance status and his promotional strength let him push back musical boundaries, expose new sounds and synthesise entirely new genres.

So though music historians have largely ignored him, the disc jockey has rarely left the patent office of popular music. Almost every radically new musical form in the last five decades owes its existence to the DJ. He let rhythm and blues and rock'n'roll take their first steps by popularising hidden, localised genres and allowing them to merge. Reggae was totally driven by the needs of the DJ and his sound system. And the DJ was at the very heart of the insurrection which disco wrought on recorded music. Not satisfied with all this, in the last thirty years the DJ really set to work: giving us hip hop, house and their galaxy of satellite genres – musics forged solely by the DJ.

In doing all this, the DJ completely transformed the way music is conceived, created and consumed. While adapting music to better suit the dancefloor he revolutionised the use of studio technology. His power to promote records made him pivotal in the formation of the modern music industry (as well as broadcast advertising). He also greatly advanced the status of recorded music – a record is no longer a representation of some distant 'live' event, it is now a thing in itself, the primary incarnation of a song. And never forget, no band, however radical, would have made much of an impact beyond their back yard without DJs playing their records.

The disc jockey's power has not gone unnoticed by the wider world. The fact that he can wield considerable influence over a large audience has regularly brought him into conflict with establishment forces, and the DJ's history has a rich subtext of power struggles. Perhaps the most dramatic example is that of rock'n'roll propagator Alan Freed, who was hounded to death (literally) by the FBI, ostensibly for taking illegal 'payola' payments – bribes to play certain records. The real reason the US government spent so much energy pursuing him seems to have had more to do with his success in promoting 'degenerate' black music to their impressionable white sons and daughters. More recently, DJ-centred structures like pirate radio and the rave movement have all incurred the wrath of government agencies.

Taking music further

The DJ has been with us for exactly a century. Despite his pivotal role, to this day the established forums of music criticism remain almost completely ignorant of who the DJ is, what he does and why he has become so important. If this book aims to do anything, it is to show the rock historians that the DJ is an absolutely integral part of their subject. As they find space on their shelves for another ten books about The Beatles, perhaps they can spare the time to read this one.

It is probably the fault of our Eurocentricism that dance music's importance has been downplayed for so long. Just as copyright laws protect the western ideals of melody and lyric but largely ignore the significance of rhythm and bassline, musical histories have avoided taking dance music seriously for fear of its lack of words, its physical rather than cerebral nature (hip hop, with its verbal emphasis, is the rule-proving exception). And surprisingly, most writers who *have* explored dance music have written about it as if nobody went to a club to dance before about 1987.

Because of all this, the narrative you are about to read has long existed only as an oral history, passed down among the protagonists, discussed and mythologised by the participants, but rarely set in type, and never before with this kind of scope or rigour.

The desire to dance is innate; it has exerted a constant influence on music. Consequently, the disc jockey has never been far from the very centre of modern popular music. From his origins as a wide-boy on-air salesman to his current resting place as king of globalised pop, the DJ has been the person who takes music further.

TWO BEGINNINGS – RADIO

Make Believe Ballroom

'The entry of broadcasting into the history of music has changed all forms of musical creation and reception. Radio music is a kind of magic and the radio set becomes a magic box.'

– Helmut Reinhold

'I Can't Live Without My Radio.'

– LL Cool J

Who was the very first DJ? Forgetting, for now, the witch doctor, the bandleader and all the disc jockey's other illustrious prototypes, what we're asking is: who first played recorded music to entertain a group of people?

Thomas Edison, who invented the cylinder phonograph in 1877, hardly conceived of putting music on it, and in any case his equipment could only just be heard by a single person, let alone start a party. Emil Berliner, who gave us the flat-disc gramophone in 1887, would still fail on the volume test. A decade later the radio waves were tamed, but it would take another ten years before Marconi's equipment was able to send more than Morse's dots and dashes. However, when the gramophone and radio signal were finally combined, we find our first DJ candidates.

In 1907 an American, Lee DeForest, known as the 'father of radio' for his invention of the triode, which made broadcasting possible, played a record of the William Tell Overture from his laboratory in the Parker Building in New York City. 'Of course, there weren't many receivers in those days, but I was the first disc jockey,' he claimed. DeForest was wrong, however – he had been preceded.

2006 is the centenary of DJing, because at 9pm on Christmas Eve 1906 Canadian engineer Reginald A Fessenden, who had worked with Edison, and who intended to transmit radio waves between the US and Scotland, sent uncoded radio signals – music and speech – from Brant Rock near Boston, Massachusetts, to a number of astonished ships' telegraph operators out in the Atlantic. They would have only ever heard static and beeps before, but Fessenden had equipped a number of United Fruit Company ships with the necessary receivers and told them to listen out for something 'unusual'. He made a short speech explaining what he was doing, read the Bible text 'Glory to God in the highest and on earth peace to men of good will' and played 'Oh Holy Night' on his violin, together with some singing, which he admits 'was not very good'. In between all this, he became the world's first disc jockey, because, using an Ediphone cylinder machine, he also played a record over the airwaves.

What was the very first record played by a DJ?

It was a contralto singing Handel's 'Largo' from *Xerxes*.

Number one – Reginald Fessenden, the world's first DJ.

The power of the DJ

Radio is a unique broadcast medium. It has the power to reach millions, and yet the intimacy to make them each feel they're the most important person listening. Unlike television, which invades the home, dragging in images of the outside world, radio is somehow part of the place in which it is heard, and the voices and music it carries manage to create a strong feeling of community. Sociologist Marshall McLuhan called it the 'tribal drum'. Arnold Passman, in his 1971 book *The Deejays*, wrote, 'The electron tube changed everything, for it returned mankind to spoken communication.'

Because radio can be so seductive, the disc jockey quickly gained adoration, fortune and notoriety. The power of someone playing records across the airwaves was soon noticed and immediately questioned. Musicians saw it as a great threat, and the music business feared it would replace rather than promote their products. The DJ was even viewed with suspicion by government.

The radio DJ was undoubtedly powerful, right from his inception. His promotional might was the bedrock on which the modern music industry was built. He laid the foundations of the broadcast advertising industry, too. And when it came to important developments in music itself, the DJ's influence was unparalleled. As the gatekeeper at the point where music met its audience, able to select and highlight and combine music as he chose, the DJ had more control than anyone over shifting styles and changing tastes. Given the size of the DJ's voice, this cultural power was even broader at times, and the early disc jockeys were also key in fostering understanding between different races and communities.

The disc jockey's influence was soon so strong that it attracted more than just envy and suspicion. America's musicians went on strike for a full year in protest over the rise of the DJ. And before his profession was very old, a radio DJ would be singled out for murderous prosecution by the US government, largely because he was perceived as enjoying too much power.

The age of radio

Radio began in earnest in 1922. Before that there were just scientists and hobbyists dotted around the world toying with the medium and trying to find uses for the new technology. Radio was broadcast to mid-western farmers with coded weather predictions; it was used to boost the morale of the troops of both sides in the First World War trenches; Thomas E Clark in Detroit broadcast to ships plying Lake Erie. In San José in 1909, Charles 'Doc' Herrold saw himself as the first person to realise the entertainment possibilities of the medium, and gave all his neighbours crystal sets so they could receive the music and interviews he broadcast.

In 1911 in New York City, Dr Elman B Meyers started broadcasting a daily eighteen-hour programme which was almost all records. Doc Herrold's wife Sybil (later Sybil True), the world's first recorded female DJ, went on air in 1913 with a show she called 'The Little Ham Programme'. She borrowed records from a local music store and concentrated on young people's music in an effort to encourage youthful interest in radio. Even at this early stage, it was clear that it was a powerful force. Mrs Herrold noted with satisfaction that her programme had a noticeable effect on the store's record sales. 'These young operators would run down the next day to be sure to buy the one they heard on the radio the night before.'

Woman's hour – Eunice Randall at 1XE in Boston, the first woman to be both announcer and engineer.

Radio's advertising potential was soon clear and in 1920 the first commercial stations went on air, Detroit's 8MK (later named WWJ) in August, and KDKA in Pittsburgh in November. KDKA, which gained fame for its coverage of the 1920 presidential election, had grown out of Dr Frank Conrad's experimental broadcasts as station 8XK, which, using wartime equipment, transmitted from his garage. (Canada had beaten all-comers, however, since Marconi's XWA – later named CFCF – was up and running in 1919.)

The story of early radio is a very American one because it was only in the US that radio wasn't immediately seized on as an arm of government. The rest of the world saw the medium as a force to inform and educate their populations and the resulting nationalised broadcasting was paternalistic and staid. America, however, after a brief debate, quickly saw radio as a mass advertising medium. Economic function then dictated its form and, as it looked for ways to gain a large audience, American radio settled firmly on populist entertainment. After 1922, when the first Radio Conference drew up formal proposals for the use of the US airwaves, radio proliferated wildly. In March of that year there were sixty registered stations; by November there were 564.

1922 was also when the BBC took to the air in Britain, with a 15 November news broadcast read by Arthur Burrows. However, given its founding Director General Lord Reith's lofty public service ideals, it took until July 1927 for the BBC to put the needle to the record and give Britain its first DJ. His name was Christopher Stone and he had to work hard to convince the BBC to let him construct a programme around just playing records. However, once on air it was a great success and Stone's dry and disarming manner quickly made him one of the first stars of radio.

Stone groove – Christopher Stone, Britain's first DJ, at the wheels of steel, or at least Bakelite, in 1931.

In a distinct contrast to the corporation's rules of decorum, he was allowed to ad lib his introductions and developed a conversational, almost chatty style as he spun a variety of music. (Stone was also for many years the editor of *Gramophone* magazine, which had been started by his brother-in-law Compton Mackenzie in 1923.) In 1957 *Melody Maker* declared, as it celebrated Stone's seventy-fifth birthday, 'Everyone in Britain who has written, produced or compered a gramophone programme on the air should breathe a prayer, or (if it is in more accord with temperament) raise a glass to salute the man who was the founder of his trade.'

Despite the early triumphs of such pioneers, radio had a long road to travel before it became anything we would recognise. In its seventy-fifth anniversary issue in 1969, *Billboard* described the sleepy nature of the medium in the years before 1935. Explaining that the evening was taken up by broadcasts from ballrooms and symphony halls, the magazine described the rest of the day's schedule:

'Daytime programs were dull and repetitious. A solo pianist was heard sporadically around the clock. Stuffy, pompous staff announcers read the news from the daily press. A singer might have his own hour, accompanied by the solo pianist. Weather and livestock reports, farm produce prices, fruit and citrus warnings, poetry readings and interminable lectures on cultural and scientific subjects by boring local academic figures ate up the clock from sign-on to dusk. Records were played too. The same staff spieler who read poetry announced each disc solemnly, impersonally and formally enough to qualify as an adept funeral director.'

It would be the DJ, with his snappy delivery, his lucrative salesmanship, and all the world's music, who would save radio from this.

The DJ vs the musician

The presence of records on the radio aroused opposition almost immediately. In the US, the Department of Commerce granted preferential licences to stations that didn't use recorded music, since there was a feeling that playing records was a rather inferior style of broadcasting – mainly because live music gave far superior sound reproduction. In 1927 the industry's new governing body, the Federal Radio Commission, re-emphasised that phonograph performances were 'unnecessary'. While the big stations complied, using live music from large orchestras and dance halls, the smaller broadcasters still relied on the gramophone. During the Depression, as belts were tightened, the use of records increased. Soon only the big new radio networks such as NBC and CBS could afford to broadcast only live music.

Musicians called the broadcast of recorded music 'DeForest's prime evil'. Stations paid no performance fee to the artists whose records they used, and every time one was played on the radio it was music that would otherwise have been performed by paid musicians. In 1927 their employment prospects worsened further when *The Jazz Singer* ushered in talking pictures. Thousands of musicians who had performed accompaniment for silent movies were now out of a job. In later years the jukebox would become another rival. Attacked by technology on all sides, it was inevitable that the jobbing musician would fight hard for survival.

The American Federation of Musicians (AFM), a tight-knit closed shop union, declared the DJ to be the enemy of the musician and fought long and hard to prevent records being broadcast on radio. The AFM were aided in this by the Federal Radio Commission who, as Arnold Passman wrote, 'attempted everything this side of public hangings to curb the practice'.

The AFM insisted the music had to be controlled by card-carrying musicians, so for many years DJs at larger stations were given 'record-turners' to play their records as instructed. Then on 1 August 1942 America's musicians actually went on strike over the issue of recorded music. The AFM ordered a ban on members making records, which would be lifted only when the record labels agreed to pay greater royalties to their artists to compensate for income lost through radio's use of records. They also threw in a few demands aimed at curbing the use of jukeboxes in nightclubs. After more than a year during which virtually no new records were made, the record companies relented. In the UK, the Musicians Union and the record companies fought a similar battle against the disc jockey, but this was more about the public performance of records than their broadcast on radio.

The DJ vs the music publishers

Allied to the musicians were the music publishers, then the most powerful part of the music industry. At the time of radio's birth, sheet music was still the dominant popular music commodity and songwriters were the stars of the day. When the world started buying records, however, power shifted away from publishers and songwriters and into the hands of record companies and recording artists. Allowing records on the radio would accelerate this shift, so the publishers fought it every way they could. As early as 1922, the American Society of Composers, Authors and Publishers (ASCAP), the organisation which collects royalties for the music publishing industry, threatened to prosecute radio stations that played records of ASCAP-licensed songs. Eventually, the radio stations agreed to pay ASCAP an annual fee of between $500 and $5,000 each, depending on the size of the station, to play its music.

To counter ASCAP's power, in 1923 the radio stations bonded together and formed the National Association of Broadcasters (NAB). In 1939, hoping to weaken ASCAP's monopoly on the copyright industry, NAB created its own copyright firm, Broadcast Music Incorporated (BMI). While ASCAP aimed to maintain the songwriter's pre-eminence, BMI worked to encourage an industry centred around records and broadcasting. Most established artists were ASCAP members, so BMI's recruits were almost all younger songwriters and musicians, including all the folk and 'race' musicians who ASCAP had not allowed to join. With BMI's close ties to radio and its more ethnic membership, this was great news for the rise of black music.

In 1941 ASCAP demanded a royalty increase of nearly seventy per cent. The stations resisted the increase and ASCAP called a strike which lasted from January to October. During this time, no ASCAP songs could be played on the radio. By the end of the strike, ASCAP had won a significant increase in royalties. However, all the songs played in the meantime had been those licensed by BMI, most of them by upcoming artists signed to independent labels, playing jump-jive, blues, bluegrass, gospel and other less established genres. As a result, strong links had been forged between broadcasters, record retailers and smaller labels, and these ethnic and regional styles of music had gained a lot of exposure.

The DJ vs the record labels

For several years record companies remained unconvinced of radio's overall value as a promotional medium for their products, so they, too, joined the throng in fighting the idea of the disc jockey. They thought people were less likely to buy a record if they could hear it played for free. This fear was borne out by some Depression-era figures which showed that urban areas with popular radio stations were suffering a downturn in record sales (they were actually suffering a downturn in sales of everything). The larger record companies started taking legal steps against selected radio stations and a series of lawsuits ensued. One of these, the infamous Waring case, even reached the US Supreme Court.

'Every label on every record specifically carried the warning that the disk was not to be broadcast,' recalled pioneer DJ Al Jarvis in *Billboard*'s seventy-fifth anniversary issue. 'And so I had to purchase my own records and gamble that the Supreme Court would throw out the Waring case.'

One alternative to records which was successful for a while was the electrical transcription disc, or 'ET', which was in use throughout the forties. This was a monster 16-inch disc pressed not on shellac like the usual 78s but on 'luxurious lightweight vinylite', ie vinyl. It spun at the novel speed of 33rpm, had a playing time of thirty minutes, and contained a whole programme, complete with announcements and a live-sounding orchestra playing the latest hits, all captured using state-of-the-art electronic recording techniques. The transcription disc was aimed at the smaller stations and sold as a monthly subscription service. It lessened the reliance on the announcer/disc jockey and, because it was made specifically for broadcast, it avoided record company litigation.

'Most stations could not afford the orchestras and productions that went into the network radio shows,' explained Ben Selvin, who worked for the leading transcription disc company. 'And so we supplied nearly three hundred stations with transcriptions that frequently – but not always – featured the most popular bands and vocalists.' Selvin recalled that some of the top artists made transcriptions under a phoney name. The money was good, but they had to get round their existing record contracts. Thus Tommy Dorsey became Harvey Tweed, and Ray Noble and Russ Morgan, other big stars of the time, became Reginald Norman and Rex Melbourne respectively.

'A Sure-Fire Audience Builder For Your Station. A Powerful Selling-Vehicle For Your Sponsors' was how the discs, in this case Tiffany Transcriptions, were promoted. Musicians recall the mammoth recording sessions which produced them. In Duncan McLean's book *Lone Star Swing*, Johnny 'Drummer Boy' Cuviello, who played with western swing megastars Bob Wills' Texas Playboys, remembers recording non-stop, all day long – about a hundred songs in a day.

'We never rehearsed a number. Bob would just recall a tune we knew, next second he'd be up on the bandstand: Ready, set, go! One number after another in the can.'

McLean's book also explains how the tiny local stations would use every trick in the book to convince their listeners that the band in question really were broadcasting from nearby. 'Radio stations would usually fake up their own programmes, making on that all twelve or so of the Texas Playboys were crammed into the tiny studio in Slapout, Oklahoma, or wherever. Announcers would come up with effortfully casual links along the lines of, "Well, folks, I hear Eldon Shamblin a-banging on the studio door, so let's have Bob and all the boys play 'Keep Knockin' But You Can't Come In' – and right after that we'll have a message from our friends down at the Slapout feed store." ' Despite optimistic predictions, the booming market in transcriptions died off soon after the war, largely because of the rising popularity of the personality disc jockey.

The professional announcer

The precise origins of the title 'disc jockey' are unclear. Columnist Walter Winchell supposedly coined it to describe DJ Martin Block's pioneering style, though radio historian Ben Fong-Torres cites a record exec Jack Knapp who in 1940 called DJs 'record jockeys' (pointing to their responsibility for 'riding the gain', ie controlling the volume). Certainly on 13 August 1941 *Variety* informed its readers, '. . . Gilbert is a disc jockey, who sings with his records.'

As well as the image of someone 'riding' over the music with his voice, 'jockey' has a number of further associations. It might suggest a skilful manipulator, a man of the people, perhaps a trickster. In Scotland 'Jock' is a man or a fellow; in America a jock is a sportsman, named after his jockstrap, which *protects* his man or fellow. When it was first used it's likely that 'disc jockey' was meant to be a little disparaging. As much as the DJ was jockeying his voice and his records – manoeuvring them with skill – he was also seen as jockeying, as in *hustling*, his place in the world.

The DJ's early years were fraught with such mistrust and he met opposition from all sides. As well as the entire music industry lining up against him, the DJ was held back for many years by a tendency towards ever more neutral announcing. As radio's audience grew, the style of broadcasting was increasingly dictated by the networks: CBS, NBC and numerous others who, in fine American capitalist tradition, had managed to dominate the market. The networks and their advertisers preferred characterless, functional announcing, which they saw as more professional. They provided their local affiliate stations with transcription discs that included clipped, sterile introductions, further reducing the role of the local announcer. It looked as if the DJ would never be much more than a characterless gramophone technician.

However, the disc jockey's star would soon rise. A massive expansion in the market brought competition down to a much more local level, forcing a more intimate style of broadcasting. Advertising was quickly more localised too, especially when TV came along and started stealing the big national sponsors. The new smaller stations were programming to appeal to regional tastes, and they relied mostly on records for their music. This kind of broadcasting definitely needed disc jockeys, not least as persuasive pitchmen to sell up the virtues of chewing tobacco and patent chest tonic. A few talented jocks started to show just how profitable their shows could be.

By the fifties, broadcasters had finally settled most of their disputes with the wider music industry and there were no more legal obstacles to filling airtime with records. The transistor had been invented in 1948, so a radio receiver could now be cheap and portable. And around the same time society invented the teenager. All this could only encourage the rise of the charismatic, fast-talking disc jockey. The post-war world was going to be a very different place, and records on the radio would play a huge part in making it so.

Make Believe Ballroom

Martin Block was the first real star among disc jockeys; one of a handful of successful characters who paved the way for the rapid post-war rise of the DJ. He started as a salesman, advertising various wares and playing records in between, from a loudspeaker truck travelling up and down Broadway, until the police and local store owners shut him up.

In 1934 he found work as the staff announcer on WNEW in New York, reading off courtroom bulletins from the 'Trial of the Century' – the kidnapping and murder of the Lindbergh Baby. During a long break in proceedings, Block decided to play some records, but since the station didn't actually own any, he was forced to buy his own. He rushed out to the Liberty Music shop round the corner, returned with five Clyde McCoy records and played them back to back to make it sound like a live broadcast from a dance hall, complete with introductions that made it seem like he was actually chatting to McCoy, a Louisiana bandleader.

The station's sales department thought it was beneath them to sell ads on a 'disc show', so Block had to go out and seek his own sponsor. Unable to find one who would pay, he arranged to promote Retardo slimming pills, and paid for the product's first commercial himself. A day after Block had been on air imploring overweight women to 'Be fair to your husband, take the reducing pill,' there were 600 letters, each containing a dollar, requesting a box of Retardo. By the end of the week the ad had drawn 3,750 responses.

Block called his show 'The World's Largest Make Believe Ballroom' and concentrated on using records to best effect. In just four months his unscripted, easygoing style, combined with music solely from records, netted him four million listeners, and the show was extended to two-and-a-half hours. Advertisers were now lining up. Over the years, Block's selling prowess grew ever more impressive: one department store reported that his ad-libbed commercials helped it sell 300 refrigerators during a blizzard, and when he made a wartime appeal for pianos to entertain the troops, the United Service Organization were offered 1,500. As his influence grew, he held a contest to come up with a new version of his show's theme song. It was won by a band led by a young man named Glenn Miller.

Block had actually stolen the idea for his show – and even the name – from Al Jarvis, a Canadian disc jockey at KFWB in Hollywood (where Block had been a junior assistant). Though just the staff announcer, Jarvis was an eager student of the music business, and by reading *Billboard* and *Variety* – something none of his colleagues did – he was able to tell his audience a little about each record, while his cosy, friendly style won him plenty of listeners. From the early thirties his 'Make Believe Ballroom' was broadcast six hours a day and became very successful. However, Jarvis enjoyed nowhere near the runaway success of Block, who, with the exact same format, would become number one in radio for nearly a quarter of a century. Surprisingly, Jarvis didn't hold a grudge against Block for the wholesale theft of his idea. 'He was a bright guy who had talent and determination,' he told *Billboard* in 1969.

By 1940, Martin Block was the make-all, break-all of records. If he played something, it was a hit. In 1948, while already under a multi-million-dollar contract with ABC, he was able to syndicate his show for nationwide broadcast. This netted him a massive two million dollars. Block had considerable insight into the power of his profession. In 1942 he told *Billboard* that when he played a record, 'If the platter is a good one, the most effective type of direct marketing has just taken place. And sales are sure to reflect the airing of the disc.'

Block's influence as a disc jockey spawned a new figure in the music industry – the record promoter. In *The Death Of Rhythm And Blues*, Nelson George recounts the story of Dave Clark, a young 'advance man' charged with the job of warming up a particular city for the arrival of numerous touring bands. In 1938 Clark posed as a chauffeur to gain entrance to WNEW's offices (he was black and would have been denied access otherwise) and delivered a record – Jimmy Lunceford's band playing 'St Paul's Walking Through Heaven With You'. Clark sneakily told Block that the disc came direct from the station's owner, who was waiting to hear it on the air. He watched Block put it straight onto the turntable.

Capitol Records formalised this idea of radio promotion in 1942, the first year of the label's existence. With his new company struggling to survive, and unable to press up records because of a wartime shellac shortage (a ship carrying huge amounts of the stuff had just been sunk), Capitol's chairman, Glenn E Wallichs, looked to the DJ to keep the company's music in people's minds. A list was drawn up of the country's fifty most influential jocks and they were each personally delivered a special vinyl sampler of Capitol's output. This was the first example of a label servicing DJs en masse.

'It was a service that created a sensation,' said Wallichs. 'We made the jock a Big Man, an Important Guy, a VIP in the industry. And we published a little newspaper in which we ran their pictures and biographies.'

By the end of the war, radio DJs had started to enjoy much greater respect. And during the fifties and sixties, radio DJing would become a fully accepted profession, an integral part of the music industry. The DJ was a powerful hitmaker and his patronage could start an artist's career overnight. In 1949 Cleveland DJ Bill Randle, who went on to discover Johnnie Ray and Tony Bennett, put it in a nutshell: 'I don't care what it is. I want to make hits.'

Black radio and rhythm and blues

In 1942 *Billboard* introduced a music chart called the 'Harlem Hit Parade'. Three years later it became 'Race Records'. This wasn't meant to refer to any specific musical style, it just meant records made by black people. In 1945, Jerry Wexler, later a partner of Atlantic Records, wrote in the

Saturday Review of Literature suggesting 'a term more appropriate to more enlightened times'. Wexler's suggestion, already used in some quarters, would soon be the recognised catch-all term for black pop. *Billboard* adopted it in 1949. It was 'rhythm and blues'.

The biggest impetus for the rise of black music was the post-war expansion and localisation of radio. In the newly competitive market, smaller stations, independent of the stuffy national networks, had become the norm. These were local broadcasters catering to local advertisers and local music tastes. So a Texas disc jockey might play The Crystal Spring Ramblers and promote animal feed to ranchers, while in New York a DJ would play Red Prysock and Big Mama Thornton and rely for his income on advertising hair oil to Harlem. Together with the jukebox, which was serving a similar localised role, DJs and radio gave a huge boost to the fortunes of less mainstream music and the smaller labels that released it.

It was in this way that the DJ first showed his enduring talent for creating new musical genres. By helping the various splinters of race music reach a much wider audience the DJ had a profound effect on the music's development. By making their music heard far and wide, he fostered pride and ambition in the local folk musicians who played these disparate styles. By letting musicians hear music from other places, he connected different strands, allowing them to coalesce into something more forceful. And by choosing and promoting the music he thought his audience most wanted to hear, the DJ gave the music a direction and a momentum. As the name changed from 'race music' to 'rhythm and blues' the DJ made sure the music changed too.

In 1947 *Ebony* magazine reported that the 'discovery that a voice has no colour has opened new vistas to Negroes in radio'. Black DJs were hurriedly recruited as radio companies looked to target the urban black population. In 1947 *Ebony* could only find sixteen blacks employed in the US as DJs, but by 1955 there were 500, and as Nelson George writes, 'It was the DJs' roles as trendsetters and salesmen, both of themselves and the music, that made them essential to the growth of rhythm and blues.' They talked to their audiences in the slangy 'jive' vernacular, they pitched products aimed specifically at the black consumer, and they were playing artists like Louis Jordan, Etta James and Joe Turner.

It wasn't just their music that was important. Their presence was a beacon for the black communities, important examples of black success in what was then a very white world. Jack Cooper was the first, on the radio as early as 1923. By 1929 he was the smooth-talking host of 'The All Negro Hour', a live variety show on Chicago's multi-lingual, multi-ethnic station WSBC. In 1937 Cooper moved to a record-based format and by 1948 he was on air for more than forty hours a week on four different Chicago stations and earning $185,000 a year (equivalent to nearly $2 million today).

Despite Cooper's lead, a later DJ, Chicago's Al Benson, aka the Ole Swingmaster, is seen as a more influential figure. Speaking at the age of ninety-nine, Richard Stamz – one of the 'Original Thirteen', as a loose collective of America's first black DJs was called – insists Benson was a real inspiration for his listeners, and for any black radio DJ who followed.

'Jack Cooper was the pioneer, but Al Benson was the *godfather*,' says Stamz, explaining that Benson was the first black DJ who didn't adopt a white way of speaking. 'People used to say Al had the worst voice, and he did. But people said, "he sounds like I do". He sounded like the common man.'

'Benson killed the King's English,' recalled another veteran black DJ, Eddie O'Jay. 'He wasn't pretending to be white. He sounded black. They knew he was and most of us were proud of the fact.'

Al Benson grew rich. He bought Chicago's Regal Theater. He built himself a mansion in Michigan. He used his influence to strangle a white-owned nightclub after they refused him a seat. DJs like Benson were very quickly among the richest, most powerful black men in America. They had a huge audience, enormous influence and vast earning potential. Two decades before James Brown declared 'I'm black and I'm proud,' these men were showing black Americans how to hold their heads up high. The world they lived in could be as racist as it liked but if commerce wanted to target the new urban black market, it would have to go through them to get to it.

'Everybody had to see Al if they wanted to sell to the black market in Chicago, whether it was beer or rugs or Nu Nile hair cream,' explained O'Jay, a radio legend through the fifties, who inspired a generation of younger DJs himself (he was so famous the O'Jays named themselves after him).

The DJs were autonomous entrepreneurs. The station sold them the time, and they filled it with whatever would bring in advertisers and an audience. With no restrictions, they took money from advertisers as well as from the record companies directly. For wily salesmen like Benson (who is said to have charged his houseguests for their bed and board), this was the perfect situation. Benson treated the music on his show just like ads, with a certain number of slots for each label. He would play whatever records they'd given him until they brought replacements.

'Al created a dynamic,' explains Billy Learner, Benson's nephew. 'He didn't work for WGES, he worked for himself, because he was brokering time. What he played didn't matter to the station, as long as he brought in the money.'

'Al was making more money than the station owner,' laughs Stamz.

Proving that America's love for green can often overrule its obsession with fleshtones, radio's business model allowed many a black DJ to create an opening for himself, even in the face of appalling racism. Hal Jackson, who started broadcasting in 1939 (and who, amazingly, was still broadcasting weekly on New York's WBLS sixty-five years later), was told, 'No nigger is ever going on the air in Washington,' by the management of WINX in the nation's capital. 'The general manager made a big thing out of it,' Jackson recalls. 'Called all the staff in and said, "Can you imagine? This nigger is talking about going on this radio station. That will never ever happen." ' Jackson wasn't going to let plain old racism stop him, however, so he bought time on the station through a white wholesaler. 'Stations loved him because he'd buy big blocks of time. He never had to tell them what he was going to put in the block. Only the sponsor knew.' Jackson hovered outside the studio until just before his allotted slot, and then used his paid-for airtime to interview two prominent black community leaders. The audience reaction was so good he was hired straight away. 'When I had that first opening I felt that this was the beginning of a whole new era,' says Jackson. Today he is the chairman of a group of US radio stations.

Talking jive

The increased presence of black Americans on radio exposed an entire culture previously closed to whites. There was the music, of course, but the way many of these DJs spoke would also have a huge influence, both on future disc jockeys and on music in general.

'If you want to hip to the tip and bop to the top, you get some threads that just won't stop,' rhymed Lavada Durst on Austin, Texas's KVET. 'Not the flower, not the root, but the seed, sometimes called the herb. Not the imitator but the originator, the true living legend – The Rod,' rapped Baltimore's Maurice 'Hot Rod' Hulbert.

Biggest of them all was Douglas 'Jocko' Henderson, aka TheAce From Outer Space, with his famous '1280 Rocket' rhythm review show, live on WOV from Harlem's Palm Café. Using a rocket ship blast-off to open proceedings, and introducing records with more rocket engines and 'Higher, higher, higher . . .' Jocko conducted his whole show as if he was a good-rocking rhythmonaut. 'Great gugga mugga shooga booga,' he'd exclaim, along with plenty of 'Daddios'.

'From way up here in the stratosphere, we gotta holler mighty loud and clear. *Ee-tiddy-o and a ho*, and I'm back on the scene with the record machine, saying *oo-pap-doo* and how do you do!'

When Yuri Gagarin completed the world's first manned space flight in

1961, Jocko sent him a telegram. This now resides in the Kremlin Museum. It reads: 'Congratulations. I'm glad you made it. Now it's not so lonely up here.' Jocko and similar nutters showed that the radio DJ could be a creative artist in his own right, not just a comedian or a companion but a vocalist, a poet. This aspect of the DJ's craft was to have momentous impact. In Jamaica, the sound system DJs emulated this jive rhyming almost immediately and became superstar deejays as 'toasters' or 'MCs'. In New York twenty years later, there emerged the rapper, the descendant of both traditions.

The other move that the jive-rhyming DJ took was to change colour. Rhythm and blues was too good to remain a black secret for long and as the fifties dawned, certain musically adventurous white DJs started to add it to their playlists. By 1956 a quarter of the best-selling US records would be by black singers. This move was accelerated by the dramatic commercial success of some of the new black stations, exemplified by WDAI in Memphis – since 1948 the first black-owned radio station – which, as well as being the home of DJs BB King and Rufus Thomas (he of the 'Funky Chicken'), was extremely profitable.

In adopting this subversive music, white DJs also started adopting black slang. This 'broadcast blackface', as Nelson George calls it, let them speak (and advertise) to both the black community and younger whites. Dewey Phillips of Memphis's WHBG was so successful at integrating his audience that the wily Sam Phillips of Sun Records chose him to broadcast Elvis Presley's first single.

The idea of the 'white negro' was still born of racism, however. George recounts the amazing tale of Vernon Winslow, a former university design teacher with a deep knowledge of jazz, who was denied a radio announcing job on New Orleans' WJMR simply because he was black. After what seemed like a successful interview, Winslow, who was quite light-skinned, was asked, 'By the way, are you a nigger?' Denied an on-air position merely because of his race, Winslow was hired for a most extraordinary job. He was to train a white DJ to sound black. Winslow had to feed a white colleague – now christened Poppa Stoppa – with the latest local slang, teaching him to say things like 'Look at the gold tooth, Ruth' and 'Wham bam, thank you ma'am'. The show became a smash. One night, frustrated by his behind-the-scenes existence, Winslow snuck a turn at the mic. He was fired immediately. WJMR kept the Poppa Stoppa name and continued using a white man, Clarence Hamman, to provide Poppa's voice. (Winslow had his revenge, though, as Doctor Daddy-O on New Orleans' WEZZ where he would become one of the country's top ten DJs.)

The white negro disc jockey was an extremely successful invention, eventually leading to the zaniness of such star DJs as Murray The K and hundreds of other wacky talkers. Perhaps the most famous white negro was Bob 'Wolfman Jack' Smith, but the Wolfman was a relatively late incarnation. Before him had been Zenas 'Daddy' Sears in Atlanta, George 'Hound Dog' Lorenz in Buffalo, Hunter Hancock in LA, Ken 'Jack The Cat' Elliott in New Orleans, Gene Nobles, John Richbourg and Hoss Allen in Nashville, and, in Cleveland, Alan 'Moondog' Freed.

Alan Freed and rock'n'roll

Rock'n'roll was created by the DJ. The very name comes straight from the title of a radio show. The music itself was simply rhythm and blues under a different name. In a country dramatically divided by race, the term 'rock'n'roll' was just a subtle way of making black music accessible to white kids. Eventually there was a divergence between the two styles, but even this was driven by the DJ. The man who changed the name, and who did more than anyone to popularise the music, aroused such controversy in doing so, that he would be investigated by the US government for much of his professional life – an investigation which eventually drove him to his grave.

Rock'n'roll is said to have been born on the night of 21 March 1952, when Alan Freed, a DJ on Cleveland's WJW, hosted his Moondog Coronation Ball, a huge concert of rhythm and blues. Such was Freed's power as a DJ that, with little advertising except for his on-air announcements, the event drew a phenomenal crowd, almost wholly black. The Cleveland Arena held 10,000 people and Freed had initially worried that he might not recoup his money. However, by 11.30pm, as the *Cleveland Press* reported, there was a 'crushing mob of 25,000 hepcats, jamming every inch of the floor'. Thousands of angry zoot-suited ticket-holders were still outside, and as doors were broken down and fighting broke out, the fire department and police put the house lights up and stopped the show. As a college student of the time commented later, 'It worried the authorities. They'd never seen that many black people in the street.' Following the event, the local press campaigned insistently for Freed to leave town.

On 7 September 1954 Freed broadcast his first show on WINS in New York. Within weeks he was the dominant force on radio there, attracting a huge, racially mixed audience for his uncompromising black music (in Cleveland, his constituency had been overwhelmingly black). Ray Reneri, who worked for Freed, claimed that if he played a record it 'sold ten thousand copies the next day'.

'Rock' and 'roll' were euphemisms for sex, both much used in black music since the twenties, and first used together in 1945. When another

Zooted and suited – on 21 March 1952, Alan Freed's Moondog Coronation Ball drew a crowd of up to 25,000 people, testimony to his great influence as a DJ.

'Moondog' forced him to change the name of his show, Alan Freed's 'Moondog Party' became 'The Rock'n'Roll Party', a term coined by his manager Morris Levy. Ever alert to a business opportunity, Levy even trademarked the term 'rock'n'roll', thinking he'd make money whenever it was used.

Initially at least, rock'n'roll was merely the name of the show and didn't particularly refer to a style of music. Freed used 'rock'n'roll' and 'rhythm and blues' interchangeably, and both *Billboard* and *Variety* continued to refer to the music he played as 'rhythm and blues'. It was only when Elvis Presley's career was launched nationally that the two terms ceased to be synonymous and the music known as rock'n'roll took on a whiter complexion. However, Freed continued to fill his shows with the raw black records he had always played – songs like Hank Ballard's 'Work With Me Annie', The Silhouettes' 'Get A Job' and Buster Brown's 'Fanny Mae'.

The reaction to rhythm and blues/rock'n'roll was damning. Some cities banned it from their concert halls, others insisted that under-eighteens going to a rock'n'roll dance took their parents. The black middle classes thought it would simply reinforce negative stereotypes, with its low-brow, even obscene lyrics promoting an image of black people as sexed-up gamblers and drinkers. White bigots saw it as an attempt at miscegenation, with the Alabama White Citizens Council declaring that rock'n'roll 'appeals to the base in man, brings out animalism and vulgarity . . . It's a plot to mongrelise America'. Most music critics hated it, too. The esteemed jazz writer Leonard Feather wrote that, 'Rock'n'roll appeals to morons of all ages, but particularly young morons.'

Oblivious to such criticisms, Freed ploughed on, using the advantage of his colour to promote this nascent black form on a scale that most blacks had been prevented from doing. By 1957 his show was syndicated across the entire US and could even be heard in Britain on Radio Luxembourg. Alan Freed was not the first person, black or white, to play rhythm and blues on the radio, but he was certainly the most prominent.

Payola

Unfortunately, as well as being known for inventing rock'n'roll, Freed was also famous as the first victim of an intensive government investigation into 'payola', the widespread practice of record labels bribing DJs to play their records. In an era of Cold War paranoia, and following the shattering revelations about the fixing of popular TV quiz shows, the government decided to turn its attention to radio.

The investigations into payola came as a direct result of the rivalry between the two music publishing organisations, ASCAP and BMI. With the rise of broadcasting and the growing profitability of the black and ethnic music which BMI had championed, ASCAP saw its position dramatically eroded. Out of spite, it spurred the government to sniff around the financial workings of radio. At the end of 1959 a Congressional hearing into payola was inaugurated. Naturally, there was plenty to investigate: DJs often accepted money and gifts from record labels. Some even had interests in the publishing companies and labels themselves.

Despite the moralistic outrage, payola was nothing new. It had existed even before records. In Victorian England, songwriter Arthur Sullivan (of Gilbert & Sullivan) succeeded in having a song, 'Thou Art Passing Hence', performed by baritone Sir Charles Santley by giving him a share of the sheet music royalties. This was euphemistically known as 'song plugging'. By 1905, the New York songwriters of Tin Pan Alley were paying out an estimated half a million dollars a year for stage stars to perform certain songs, although the word 'payola' did not appear in print until 1916 when *Variety* described it as 'direct-payment evil'.

The payola investigations coincided neatly with the authorities' increasing concern about rock'n'roll's social effects. FBI Director J Edgar Hoover declared it a 'corrupting influence on America's youth', and the hearings themselves drifted frequently into questions of aesthetics rather than law. The broadcast of forbidden black sounds to excitable white teenagers was seen as revolutionary and profoundly dangerous. In retrospect, the investigation was less an inquiry into financial misdeeds, more a crusade against the unrestricted influence of the disc jockey – here personified by Freed.

He had already been sacked from WINS after a riot during a rock'n'roll concert in Boston. Once the hearings began, and he refused to deny that he'd accepted payola, Freed was fired by his current employers, WABC. A girl interviewed outside one of his shows was in no doubt as to why he had been removed: it was 'the station's way of getting rid of rock'n'roll'. The hearings rumbled on for years, until Freed was eventually convicted on 10 December 1962, fined $500 and given a six-month suspended jail sentence. The *New York Herald Tribune* summed up conservative America's view when it opined that rock'n'roll was 'so bad that it's almost a relief to learn they had to be paid to play it'.

Freed, arrogant and complacent to the last, admitted accepting payments from United Artists, Roulette and Atlantic Records and distributors Cosnat and Superior. Between 1957 and 1959 he made about $50,000 from payola. Intriguingly, some companies had even given him bogus writing credits (and the royalties they generated) for certain records he promoted. To this day, you'll find 'A. Freed' on the credits for Chuck Berry's 'Maybellene'; Berry said until he saw a royalty statement, he had no idea Freed 'had written the song with me'. Importantly, though, Freed never compromised the quality of his shows, and he was certainly not alone in accepting payola.

'It was nothing for the promotion men to keep the disc jockeys in cars and deep freezes and televisions, and fur coats for the little lady,' recalled singer Lou Rawls. 'That was the way business was done, and all of them did it until the Man stepped in and busted Alan Freed.'

It's interesting to compare Freed's treatment with that of an equally prominent DJ. Dick Clark, as host of ABC's syndicated TV dance show *American Bandstand*, was for decades the most powerful figure in American pop. Clark had a financial interest in many of the songs he played on *Bandstand*. He owned a bewildering array of intertwined music companies, and admitted to owning the copyrights to at least 160 songs. However, in comparison to Freed, Clark's obvious conflicts of interest escaped scrutiny. He was hardly pursued, was never charged, and even had his sworn statement reworded so that he could sign it without perjuring himself. Many have suggested that Clark's much whiter taste in music was what saved him from criticism. Freed's music made him a far more appealing target. Congress wanted a scapegoat and if they could discredit rock'n'roll at the same time, so much the better.

'He was playing the black music for the white kids. Next thing you knew they were ganging up on him,' says Hal Jackson, a close friend of Freed's, convinced the DJ's treatment was the result of racism toward the company he kept. 'Alan Freed was friendly with too many black people so they crushed him. They said "Alan, you're with *those* people", but Dick, he was the white saviour. Everything was fixed. They just told him, "Don't you do that again, go back and keep your audience happy." '

Although Freed had brief stints at other radio stations, his career went into steep decline after the hearings. Not satisfied with his payola conviction, the authorities went after him for tax evasion. In response to a constant barrage of investigation and character assassination, his drink problem quickly escalated and he died on 20 January 1965 from complications brought about by alcoholism. The obituaries largely concentrated on his ignominious departure from the public eye rather than his considerable influence on popular music.

In 1973 his arch-rival Dick Clark finally admitted that Freed 'was the man who made rock'n'roll happen' and that 'we owe a great deal to him'. Before Alan Freed, rhythm and blues was unknown to the vast majority of white people. Rock'n'roll not only affected music – in that black artists no longer had to water down their style to achieve widespread success – it also had a profound social impact, bringing many their first experience of black culture. For having such influence, Freed paid dearly. He was a clear example of how much power a DJ can wield, and an even clearer example of the lengths to which the establishment will go to curb that power.

Top 40 and freeform radio

In the long term the payola scandals did little to erode the radio DJ's strength. They did, however, raise the profile of a format known as Top 40. In the wake of payola, the idea of selecting records scientifically and not according to the whims of some corrupt disc jockey had great appeal for station proprietors and their advertisers. In 1961 Murray Kaufman, aka Murray the K, boasted that a Univac computer would select all the music for his show.

The 'invention' of Top 40 is much disputed (in any case, sales charts had existed since the days of sheet music's supremacy). The most popular account relates that in 1950 Todd Storz, station owner of Omaha's KOWH, was one day watching customers choose records from a diner jukebox. He noted that people wanted to hear just a few very popular songs over and over again. With the capacity of the jukebox in mind, Storz named the concept 'Top 40' and applied it to radio programming with great success. WABC in New York adopted it in late 1960 and by 1962 was the city's number one station.

Stacks records – in 1959, as the US raged indignant over payola, New York radio DJ William B Williams illustrated the record companies' 'generosity' by posing amongst the 8,000 free records he received that year.

Mainstream American radio has always put advertising before entertainment. Ratings are all, and anything that ups listening figures is welcomed eagerly. As a result, since the sixties such 'scientific' notions as Top 40 have been taken to extremes. Playlists were trimmed to just twenty-five hit tunes, the most popular of which were 'rapidly rotated' and played as often as hourly. Radio stations were 'formatted', limiting themselves to a very closely defined genre (eg Album Oriented Rock, Top 40, Adult Contemporary, Urban), and only after painstaking market research were new records added to playlists. The DJ's role of selecting records was usurped by a new functionary: the programme director, who was often little more than a market researcher in the service of the ad sales department.

There was a brief backlash against rigid formatting, in the shape of the hippie-driven dream of freeform radio. In the US, FM technology, which allowed hi-fi stereo broadcasts, was first licensed for use in 1961. It was the preserve of 'serious' radio – often broadcast from universities – with academic programmes, jazz and classical music to the fore. But given the rise of sophisticated (or pretentious) rock music, this too found its way onto the FM band, complete with a new intimate style of presentation, and disc jockeys who chose all their own music and who ignored time restrictions and rotation schedules.

The pioneer in this was station KMPX in San Francisco, one of the many music interests of local label owner and concert promoter Tom Donahue. From 1967 Donahue began playing album tracks, avoiding chart hits and promoting the underground bands of the emerging hippie movement, including then unsigned acts Jefferson Airplane and the Grateful Dead. As a postscript, British DJ John Peel had been sneaking album tracks onto the air in a spurious UK chart he compiled on a station in San Bernardino. And in fact, Peel had proposed a format very similar to Donahue's at least six months before freeform was born in San Francisco, though this had been rejected by the station management. In spring 1967, he returned to England and introduced the same ideas on his 'Perfumed Garden' show for pirate station Radio London.

Czar of the world's entertainment

As Marshall McLuhan declared: 'The radio injected a full electric charge into the world of the phonograph.' And it was in the context of radio that the DJ gained his first victories. From humble beginnings as an experimental hobbyist, via his incarnations as quick-witted pitch-man, and jive-talking hipster, the radio DJ showed how much power resides in music and a voice. To this day some of the most influential figures have been found on the dial rather than on the screen: from Murray the K, Gary Byrd, Wolfman Jack, Jimmy Savile and Emperor Rosko, to Howard Stern, Kenny Everett, Annie Nightingale, Steve Barker, Pete Tong, and the late John Peel – the DJ who inspired more people to put music at the centre of their lives than any other.

'The jock rules the roost' proclaimed *Billboard* in 1950. 'He is unbeatable. He is, in short, the Czar of the World's Entertainment. Live with him or join the Merchant Marine. That's the way it is and will be until smarter men devise something better.'

But smart folk had already invented something better – the club DJ.

THREE BEGINNINGS – CLUBS

Night Train

'Mick Mulligan and I were the first people to organise all-night raves. Although today the idea of spending a whole night in a crowded airless basement appears extraordinary, it was very exciting then.'

– George Melly, from 'King Of The Ravers' in *Owning Up*

'Opium? No! Cocaine? No! The Great American Brain Killer Is Dance Music!'

– *Portland Oregonian*, 1932

The revolutionary concept of dancing to records played by a disc jockey was born not in New York, not even in London or Paris, but in the northern English city of Leeds. Here, in a small room in a local mutual society we find the very first example of the club DJ. In 1943 an eccentric young entrepreneur decided the public might pay money to hear recorded music. Why not, if it meant wartime West Yorkshire could swing to big American stars like Glenn Miller and Harry James?

'Today, it's a startling admission,' he says, 'but back then nobody even conceived it. People just didn't think of dancing to records.' Jimmy Savile is nowadays seen as an odd fellow who occasionally appears on TV with a cigar the size of Cuba and a mop of platinum blond hair that hasn't been fashionable since the Crusades. He is a classic British eccentric. He's also a revolutionary DJ.

He grew up in the tough working-class districts of Depression-era Leeds. After war broke out, the teenage Savile was conscripted down the coal mines to assist the Allied effort – though it's hard to imagine him doing anything but hamper it. He was quickly pensioned out of the mines after injuring his back in an underground explosion. As he convalesced, listening to the American Forces Network, he hit upon the bright idea of playing records live, armed only with brittle 78s and a makeshift disco unit.

Still on crutches, he heard that a friend had managed to connect a wind-up gramophone to a valve radio. 'I shuffled round to his house and this was an amazing thing. Here was this record player and he'd contrived to make a pick-up. The fact that the music now didn't come out of the box, it came out of this radio, was unbelievable.'

He borrowed the equipment there and then. 'This. Is. It. A dance! We'll have a dance. And I wrote the tickets out "Grand Record Dance – one shilling".' For ten shillings (which he never got round to paying) Savile hired an upstairs room in the local friendly society on Victoria Terrace, a street away from his house. Six couples turned up and paid to dance to a series of big band records he'd borrowed. The evening itself was not without technical difficulties. 'Installing the equipment was fraught with great dangers,' he wrote in his autobiography, *As It Happens.* 'It was in several pieces connected by wires. These covered the top of a grand piano, glowed red hot when switched on for longer than five minutes, and charred the top of that noble instrument for the rest of its days. By 9pm we had taken eleven shillings, the machine had melted at several soldered points and died quietly, but not before giving a final electric shock to its inventor, causing him to weep openly.'

Savile's mother tried to salvage the evening by performing songs on what was left of the grand piano. 'But it didn't work. Because her music wasn't our music. And she said the burning smell off the top of the piano made her feel ill.' As he records: 'Disaster or not, there can be no doubt that the world's first disco, as they have come to be called, took place in the top room of the Belle Vue Road branch of the Loyal Order of Ancient Shepherds.'

The evening's significance was not lost on Savile. From a fly-by-night scheme to supplement his sick pay had emerged a promising new form of entertainment. 'I didn't think I was an entertainer,' he clarifies. 'What I was doing was creating an atmosphere. An entertainer sings, dances, tells jokes, juggles. I didn't do any of that. I. Was. Creating. An atmosphere.' Even in that small room, with not twenty people present, he felt the thrill of DJing to a live crowd, the same sensation club DJs have enjoyed ever since. 'As I played the records, and I stood there, I felt this amazing . . . power's the wrong word, control's the wrong word. There was this amazing *effect*; what I was doing was causing twelve people to do something. I can make them dance quick. Or slow. Or stop, or start. All this was very heady stuff.'

For his next appearance Savile enlisted the help of another pal, Dave Dalmour, who constructed a sturdier mobile system using an electric record player and a two-and-a-half-inch speaker. 'The beauty of that was you could carry it all on one handle. Terrific,' he says. The volume was about that of a modern transistor radio. 'As long as I set this high enough, so the speaker was level with people's heads.'

This time the venue was a tearoom in nearby Otley. Savile struck an inventive deal that foreshadowed today's norm: 'If he gave me the room for nothing I would bring lots of people in and they would buy his tea and cakes.' Savile's dad was cashier, his brother-in-law collected the tickets. It was less than a roaring success, however, with only about twenty-five people turning up. And at the nine o'clock interval these few patrons defected to a nearby chip shop. Amid uneaten cakes and unwanted pots of tea, Savile did a quick calculation. Playing as advertised till eleven meant a loss as he'd have to shell out a pound for a taxi home. Instead he cannily skipped out and caught the last bus for ninepence.

Sensing the commercial possibilities of a band-less dance, Savile had seen the future. In the following years no one did more, in the UK at least, to move dance culture away from live bands and into the hands of the DJ. From the late fifties he was shaking up the long-established world of the dance halls. He hustled himself into a job as Assistant Manager at Leeds Mecca Locarno in 1961 (where aged thirteen he had once been a drummer in an all-female band), and boosted the takings so much he was given the job of rolling out his 'Teens and Twenties Record Night' format across the nation. 'I finished up running fifty-two dance halls and employing four hundred disc jockeys.'

The northern nightclub world was doubtless a tough arena. Savile

Now then, now then – Jimmy Savile in front of the house which held his first record party.

hinted at his no-nonsense approach in Louis Theroux's TV profile: 'I never threw anybody out. Tied them up in the bloody boiler house until I was ready for them. And then we'd come back and I was judge, jury and executioner.' In his autobiography he even hints at organised crime. Talking of his boss at Manchester's Mecca Plaza he says, 'Jack Binks owned the centre of Manchester above the legal line so I rapidly took control of the town below it.'

Savile applied a series of rules to avoid trouble. 'I made lads wear smart clothes. Because then they wouldn't want to roll about on the floor fighting. No big long sideburns and things like that because they'd want to prove their manliness by cracking somebody.' His DJs also played their part: 'I trained the disc jockeys. No records over thirty-eight bars a minute. Because what you didn't want was exhibitionist dancers, gyrating about and causing a crowd around them.'

As assistant to Mecca boss Eric Morley, Savile would be sent to ailing dance halls to introduce the disc jockey concept. For his first gig in Ilford, he commissioned a proper disco system from Westrex. To cut down on the gaps between records, he had the idea of using two turntables.

'The Westrex lads had only ever installed record players in cinemas. As was the norm there, they put them up in the box for the lighting man to operate. No, no, no, no, it goes on the stage. And, wait a minute, have you got two? I want them next to each other. They said, "You don't need two, Jim, 'cos these are foolproof, they don't break down." No, no, I says. When this record's playing I want to get this one ready. "Bloody hell," he says, "are they in that much of a hurry?" ' His other innovation – not so enduring – was to talk between records. 'Back then,' he says, 'it was the latest gimmick.'

Savile had to overcome resistance from several quarters, not least from the Musicians Union who saw the idea of the disc jockey as an incursion onto their members' turf. In 1934 a group of record labels had successfully sued Cawardine's Tea Rooms in Bristol for playing their records. This led to the creation of Phonographic Performance Limited (PPL), which collects a licence fee from all venues using recorded music. In 1946 there was a ruling that such a licence would only be granted on condition that 'records not be used in substitution of a band or orchestra'. The Musicians Union continued fighting against the incursion of records into live venues; hence those 'Keep Music Live' stickers on guitar cases up and down the land. Savile neatly circumvented MU rules of the day, by the simple expedient of paying some musicians *not* to play. As he says, 'I gave the band full money, but gave them five nights off a week.'

Savile continued to pursue his career as a disc jockey. He was also a professional wrestler for eight years, but by the mid sixties he was a household name in the UK as a DJ on Radio Luxembourg and then as host of the TV institution *Top Of The Pops*, the very first edition of which he presented in 1964. Writer Nik Cohn called him 'our best disc jockey. Come to that, to me, he was our only disc jockey.' Jimmy Savile was the first superstar DJ.

So, as unlikely as it seems, for the idea of inviting people to pay to dance to records in a club we owe a huge debt of gratitude to Sir James Savile OBE. Disc jockeys had long existed on radio, but transposing the idea to a live format required a quantum leap of imagination. As Savile wrote: 'Ideas which are considered wild and foolish when one is penniless suddenly become genius and brilliant in the eyes of the world as soon as one starts to make money.'

How's about that then?

The jukebox

Savile might have been the world's first club DJ, but his experimental evenings were far from the first time people had danced to records. Ironically, the DJ's role was automated even before it came into existence. His clearest predecessor had existed since 1889 and was a machine – the jukebox.

'Juking' is derived from the Gullah dialect of the sea-island slaves of South Carolina and Georgia. It originally meant 'disorderly' or 'wicked' but became a common word in black vernacular for having sex. Like 'rock'n'roll', which also started life as a euphemism for fucking, the verb 'juke' eventually came to mean 'dance'.

So even their name suggests just how important dancing was for these big chrome monsters. The manufacturers, however, were less than keen on the name 'jukebox', since it was obviously both black and lewd. Many operators called them phonographs, and in the American south they were often referred to as piccolos or wurtelisers.

The jukebox was patented in 1889 by San Franciscan Louis Glass, only a couple of years after the record had been invented. The first one was installed in the Palais Royal Saloon in Glass's hometown. Coin-operated and with stethoscope-like ear tubes, it was much like the listening posts in record stores today, except it was the size of a small nuclear reactor. Edison made some similar machines and wheeled them out at state fairs, where up to ten curious folk would plug in and grin at each other. However, these primitive contraptions never grew beyond a novelty.

Only with amplification were the jukeboxes much use and in the twenties, as recording technology progressed, they became fairly widespread. By 1927 an estimated 12,000 were in operation in bars, saloons, speakeasies, roadside rest-stops and cafés across America. In the rural south, black folk partied in 'juke joints' – shacks where booze and music let them escape from their sharecropping drudgery.

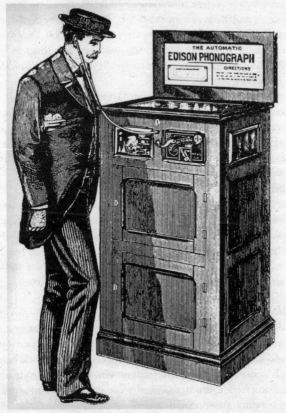

Victorian Walkman – 1891 engraving advertising the Edison Automatic Phonograph, the world's first jukebox.

Jukeboxes were perfect for Depression-era America. Bar owners found the jukebox far cheaper than a band, and the mood was perfect for the nickel-priced escapism they provided. In fact, as the Depression dramatically eroded record sales, the jukebox did much to prevent the music industry reaching bankruptcy. In 1939, keeping jukeboxes stocked with tunes accounted for about sixty per cent of total US record sales.

It was the repeal of Prohibition in 1933 that really caused the jukebox to mushroom. For each illegal speakeasy, five bars, taverns or saloons opened in its place; most had a jukebox. In 1936, Decca alone operated

150,000. By the beginning of the Second World War, there were nearly 500,000 spread across America.

The jukebox was a key instrument of marketing, because it was responsive. By tabulating the number of times each record had been played, its popularity could be accurately gauged. This fact was what inspired the idea of charts; the Top 40 was such because forty records was the standard jukebox capacity. One of the earliest chart-based radio shows was called 'Jukebox Saturday Night'.

Additionally, the jukebox put musical programming firmly in the hands of the venue's owners. Thus records of strictly local appeal were given a chance to shine – an important factor in the commercial rise of rhythm and blues and hillbilly forms. And the jukebox positively encouraged the rude stuff. Dirty blues records, completely unfit for broadcast, were a common feature.

The jukebox's greatest significance came after the war, when its domain extended beyond bars and clubs and into diners and drugstores – places where youngsters hung out. Music to dance to, once inseparable from alcohol, was now something teenagers could share in. Together with the expansion of radio, the jukebox was a crucial force in the musical explosions of rhythm and blues and rock'n'roll. It eroded the reliance on live music and laid the ground for the DJ to take over.

The sock hop

In the US, the first live DJ events were the fifties dances known as 'platter parties' or 'sock hops'. Here, the personality radio DJ stepped out from the studio and took on the role of human jukebox. These sock hops were held in high school gymnasiums (where you removed your shoes to protect the floor, hence the name) and were mainly promotional events for the DJ's radio show. Such events were the basis for *American Bandstand*, the TV programme that made DJ Dick Clark an American institution. Broadcast nationally between 1957 and 1963, *Bandstand* was unsurpassed as a promotional medium until the rise of MTV in the mid eighties.

Almost immediately, amateur disc jockeys took up the idea. Bob Casey, later a Forces DJ in Vietnam and sound engineer on the New York disco scene, ran dances from his first year at high school in 1957.

'A guy would show up, sponsored by 7Up, so you hung up some 7Up posters and you promised to serve 7Up at your dances,' Casey remembers. 'This guy showed up with a little 45 record changer and a little box of fifty records. He'd take the high school gym system, put the microphone in front of his little loudspeaker, he'd have a little microphone. He'd pick it up and say, "Well, that was Brenda Lee and 'I'm Sorry' and now we have

Elvis Presley." He's talking while the record's dropping on the repeater, saying, "OK, drink up your 7Up folks." '

When Bob played his own dances he added an important innovation, the double turntable, custom-built in 1955 by his sound engineer father. 'I had two volume controls and a switch, 'cos I wanted much more music. I wanted to be able to come out of one record and go right into the next record, turn it down and talk over the record and bring it up.'

Wartime Paris

Like food, the discothèque, as the name would suggest, is a French creation; taken from *bibliothèque*, it literally means a record library. Supposedly its origins lie in the Mediterranean port of Marseilles, where sailors would leave their records in café stockrooms while they were away at sea. When shore leave came around, they would return to their favourite bar and listen to records on the phonogram in the corner. Film director Roger Vadim claimed to have coined the word, but a definitive etymology is elusive (the record-lending division of La Bibliothèque Française was called *La Phonothèque*). One interesting point is that it wasn't necessarily a place: *mon discothèque* could mean 'my record collection'. The connotation was of a more intimate, private place than a big-band dance hall, which in France was known as '*le dancing*'.

It was the Nazis who spurred the first disco boom. For the Third Reich, American jazz, with its black and Jewish heritage, ticked all the right boxes as a cultural threat. 'Dubious dance styles that healthy public opinion calls "Nigger music", in which provocative rhythms predominate and melody is violently abused,' declared state broadcasters as they banned it from German airwaves. When America entered the war Goebbels issued further edicts banning the 'rhythms of belly-dancing negroes'. Jazz, already the music of rebellious youth, became nothing less than the soundtrack of resistance.

As war clouds gathered, Hamburg's 'Swing Kids' defied the Nazi Ministry of Propaganda and danced at the Café Bismarck to the music of Count Basie, Duke Ellington and Louis Prima. This was enough to qualify as a crime of 'musical race defilement' and left them open to arrest and Gestapo beatings.

In Paris, too, resistance was played out to jazz, as smoky basements in occupied territory gave the discothèque its lasting reputation as a place where outlaws gathered. Since the First World War Montmartre had hosted a community of black American musicians escaping US racism, most famously Josephine Baker. They had enjoyed star status as they gave Paris a taste for 'le hot jazz', but with the Nazi occupation of June 1940, those who hadn't already fled were banned from playing and then interned. This left native French bands, grudgingly tolerated by the occupying forces, to fill in. Cunning promoter Charles Delaunay co-founder of the Hot Club of France – where jazz violinist Stéphane Grappelli and gypsy guitarist Django Reinhardt rose to fame – staged a dozen large-scale jazz concerts throughout the war to protest the occupation. Collecting the cream of French players, Delaunay disguised US jazz standards as French songs on the programme to sneak them past the censors: 'St Louis Blues' became 'La Tristesse De Saint Louis', 'Honeysuckle Rose' translated to 'La Rose De Chevrefeuille' and 'Take The A-Train' was 'L'Attaque De Train'.

A more vigorous 'fuck you' came from a bizarre youth tribe known as the Zazous, fans of French jazz-swing singer Johnny Hess – their name taken from the Cab Calloway-style scatting in his song 'Je Suis Swing'. These young rebels wore their hair high and long like teddy boys, with zoot-suit trousers cut to the knee to show off coloured socks and shoes with triple-height soles that thirty years later might have done a glam rocker proud. High collars, impossibly tight ties and long sheepskin-lined jackets completed the look, with a curved-handled umbrella carried at all times (copied from British Prime Minister Neville Chamberlain, regarded as quite a style icon). Female Zazous wore short skirts, shabby furs, wooden platform shoes and dark glasses with big lenses, and chose to go hatless to better show off the single lock of hair they had bleached or dyed. These punky youngsters would dance at *les bals clandestines*, smuggling their precious swing records into cafés off the Champs Élysées at places like the Colisée, where it was easy to congregate without alerting the authorities, or in the Latin Quarter where their haunts included Pam Pam, Dupont-Latin, Soufflot, Grand and Petit Cluny. Once gathered, they would throw English slang at each other, swap American novels and jitterbug into the early hours.

The Zazous evolved a complex battle cry. Raising a finger to the world they'd shout 'Swing,' give a little hop, then cry out, 'zazou hey, hey, Hey, Za ZAZOU!,' followed by three slaps on the hip, two shrugs of the shoulder and a turn of the head. To show solidarity with the Jews, as the pogroms began some Zazous took to wearing yellow stars of David, declaring their outlaw musical taste by writing 'SWING' across them. Even stranger, when it was clear that Paris would soon be liberated, female Zazous adopted blackface to show their love for jazz and America. Zazous were regular targets for the boot boys of the collaborationist Vichy government, suffering organised beatings, having their heads shaved and being cast out into the country to sweat in the fields.

They were also responsible for giving Paris a keen taste for dancing in cellars to records.

Liberation

We English speakers like our few French words, and while *discothèque* may well have originally stood for resistance and struggle, its Frenchness grew to suggest sophistication, style, panache, élan. The first place to employ the word is said to have been La Discothèque, a tiny bar in the rue Hachette in occupied Paris where you could order your favourite jazz 78 along with your drink.

Founder of the modern French record industry, the late Eddie Barclay (born Édouard Ruault), spent the war as a nightclub pianist, hanging out with an influential clique of jazz lovers. Barclay claims to have opened the world's first discothèque, Eddie's, after the liberation in 1944. Given that he was a keen record collector, the first major importer of American discs, and the first French producer of vinyl records (vinyl allowed for much louder amplification than shellac 78s), this seems very likely – if anyone had faith in the power of recorded music it was Barclay. He was certainly a party animal, too, clocking up a total of nine wives and throwing parties at his Saint-Tropez villa so lavish they made the rest of the Riviera look like a Blackpool tea-break.

After the war in 1947, another pioneering discothèque was opened in the Rue de Beaujolais by Paul Pacini, a diminutive man of Italian origins from Marseilles, under the name Whiskey-A-Go-Go. Pacini had a bit of a thing for scotch – whisky was then considered an exotic drink in a nation that preferred the grape to the grain. He decorated the walls with tartan, apart from one which was covered in whisky case covers: Ballantine's, Johnny Walker, Dewar's, Cutty Sark and Haig & Haig. The musical menu was equally single-minded; Pacini played jazz, exclusively, on what was reputedly the first jukebox imported into France.

Whiskey-A-Go-Go was soon usurped by another spot. Chez Castel was located on rue Princesse in Saint Germain-des-Prés and was strictly for the invited only. It was the in-crowd's secret hangout, and with only a small address plaque on the door, you may not have found it anyway. Chez Castel was a favoured haunt of the French existentialists, and Jean-Paul Sartre and Simone de Beauvoir could often be found there. A typical evening began with a movie or a show, before people repaired to the discothèque in the basement to dance cheek-to-cheek on the copper and steel chequered dancefloor.

Record producer Henri Belolo, most famously the man behind the Village People and the Ritchie Family, offers a glimpse into these first discos as he recalls another early Parisian discothèque, Jimmy's.

'There was already the glitterball and the banquettes, a big counter where people are drinking; a small DJ booth, with two turntables, on really a table, a pile of vinyls and that's it. The music was not too loud, except on the dancefloor, so people were talking. He was not mixing one record into another. Fade out, fade in with the new, they would never fade one over the other or segué them. The technology of blending records was not available. Everybody was seated, at tables and in the bar, and when the DJ started the record, people had to go from one table to another table to invite the girl.'

This wasn't the only formality. 'Everyone was standing in line – the same dance – when it was called *la bustel*, or the Madison. You had a kind of communication between the people because it was very convivial.'

Like Chez Castell and its other main competitor, Le Privé, Jimmy's was a members' club. 'Private, yes, but of course you can get in. Depends how you dress and if you know already another very important man or woman, the doorman – what you call the physiognomist.'

In 1958 Jean Castel discovered he had another rival. Carrot-topped girl about town Régine Zylberberg came from a family of Belgian-Jewish refugees and had worked her way up the bar business. She had started out as a hostess in her father's joint, Lumière de Belleville, after her mother left them, before landing a job as hatcheck girl at the Whiskey-A-Go-Go in 1953, aged twenty-three. Such was her magnetic charm that when Pacini opened a second club of the same name in Rue Robert-Etienne, the regulars at the original Whiskey started calling it Chez Régine.

'I understood what my own character was to be,' she wrote in her autobiography, 'and what my ambitions were; to make the night sparkle and to become, as far as I could, a sort of high priestess of the here and now.'

When a new Whiskey club in Cannes began to slump, Pacini sent his bright young hostess to save it. Régine knew the value of hype. For a month she would dutifully open the doors at 10.30pm and promptly put up a 'DISCO FULL' sign. People were regularly turned away as the empty cacophony of the club echoed outside. The day she opened for real, the place was mobbed.

In 1958, bankrolled by the Rothschilds, Régine threw open the doors to her own club. She didn't need Jean Castel's existentialists. At Chez Régine she had Jean-Paul Belmondo, Alain Delon and the rest of the *nouvelle vague*. Cocktails were out; patrons bought bottles of spirits for 250F, and the club was designed purely for recorded music: rumbas, tangos, merengues and rock'n'roll. 'We put loudspeakers in every corner, to make the sound carry.' Soon the linoleum dancefloor was bouncing under Brigitte Bardot, Rudolf Nuryev and French Premier Georges Pompidou. 'A lot of ambience on the dancefloor,' recalls Henri Belolo. 'You are taking out your tie and your jacket and you go out dancing.

Everyone dancing. Very wild.' Celebrity observer Robin Leach admitted: 'Working as a journalist covering the jet set in Paris at that time was extremely easy. You'd just go to Régine's every night and wait for the princesses to file in.' Régine spurred them on with themed parties, like her Jean Harlow night where everything was white, down to a lush carpet covering the pavement. 'The moment, the sparkle, the glamour, the sensation,' she wrote. 'The best thing is surprising people, knowing that tomorrow it will all be forgotten.'

Anticipating the glamour of Studio 54 by three years, and beating it hands down for door snobbery, in 1975 Régine took her 800 pairs of shoes to New York and opened a club on the ground floor of the Delmonico Hotel. It was so exclusive that the State Liquor Authority considered suing her for social discrimination. When the plumbing failed in its first week she simply loaded all the dirty glasses into limousines and had them sent to top restaurant Le Cirque to be washed. At the height of her empire there were nineteen Régines around the world. 'I am the person who made the modern way of night-time,' she declared. 'I am the first and only Queen of the Night.'

London

It might have been impossible to buy two ounces of beef or a bag of oranges in post-war London, but there was no shortage of jazz and swing. Club nights would be improvised in underground cellars, smoky back-rooms and illegal speakeasies, and here GIs and hipsters would congregate and dance to music provided by players like Chris Barber, Mick Mulligan and jazz-surrealist George Melly. In fact, the first British all-nighters took place during this period – in Cy Laurie's Jazz Club in Soho.

The scene was wild, even by today's standards. Drugs – principally opium and marijuana – had been smuggled into Britain for many years by African and Chinese sailors, for use within their own communities. However, trade in these substances was moving easily into the clubs. In 1950 it was at one such jazz joint, run by Johnny Dankworth and Ronnie Scott, that the very first British drug bust took place. When the London bobbies raided Club Eleven at 50 Carnaby Street on 15 April 1950 they were suitably appalled. 'There were on the premises between two hundred and two hundred-and-fifty persons,' reported Detective Sergeant George Lyle of Scotland Yard, 'coloured and white, of both sexes, the majority between seventeen and thirty. All these people were searched.' Among the goodies recovered were hemp cigarettes, cocaine and morphine ampoules. The drug conviction Ronnie Scott received prevented Britain's greatest tenor saxophonist from pursuing a career in America.

There were also gigantic trad-jazz raves at the Alexandra Palace, with thousands of kids kitted out in what was then regarded as 'rave gear'. Boys, for example, would wear bowler hats (often with Acker painted on them for jazz clarinettist Acker Bilk), jeans and no shoes; while the girls would wear men's shirts hanging outside black woollen tights, again often accompanied by a bowler hat. The tradsters' dancing had to be seen to be believed, too. It was anti-dancing; a reaction to the liquid moves of the modernists. 'The accepted method of dancing to trad music is to jump heavily from foot to foot like a performing bear, preferably *out of time* to the beat,' wrote George Melly. These elephantine youths were nicknamed 'leapniks' by trad musicians.

The growing immigrant community in London was having an impact, too. West Indians, unaware that one was supposed to be tucked up in bed at ten with a cup of Horlicks, listening to the 'Light Programme', partied all night at places like the Roaring Twenties. The disc jockey here was a hip Jamaican dude called Count Suckle, who introduced the metropolis to bluebeat (named after Ziggy Jackson's ska label Blue Beat). Suckle had already built a considerable reputation among the black community with his sound system parties (usually held on bank holidays) at Porchester Hall, Kilburn Gaumont State, and other venues in west and north-west London. He brought over another Jamaican innovation, the cover-up, whereby the label would be scraped off in order to disguise the identity of the record. Mick Eve, a musician active on the London all-nighter scene, recalls Suckle steaming the label from a pristine copy of Nina Simone's 'My Baby Just Cares For Me'.

New York

Jazz clubs were pretty popular in New York, too. In fact, the city was named 'The Big Apple' by touring jazz musicians, who considered it the most lucrative place to play. The swing of the big bands filled huge ballrooms, but as bebop started to crystallise, the smaller club came into its own. The city's first bebop club, the Royal Roost, grew out of Topsy's Chicken Roost on Broadway. At the start of 1948, a jazz concert was staged by radio DJ Symphony Sid and entrepreneur Monte Kay. Its success spurred the owners on and soon Miles Davis, Charlie Parker and Dexter Gordon were performing there.

The nights were promoted by a savvy Jewish hustler called Morris Levy. Levy's shadow looms large over the history of dance music in the city. At times, it has loomed large *and dark*, since Levy was quite the mobster. 'Morris was a hood. A real hood,' recalls Hal Jackson affectionately. 'People would disappear, and you don't know what happened to them.' (Levy was eventually convicted of extortion conspiracy; he died before he could serve his sentence.) At the behest of Monte Kay, Levy started a new club on 52nd Street and Broadway, its name a homage to the godfather of bebop, Charlie Parker. Birdland opened its doors for business on 15 December 1949. Such was its success that by the fifties Levy was opening clubs on an almost weekly basis. He had the Embers, the Round Table (a favourite haunt of his buddies in the mob), the Down Beat and the Blue Note.

When Alan Freed arrived in the city to take up a radio show at WINS, Levy began to manage the mercurial DJ and promoted Freed's record parties at the Brooklyn Paramount and Fabian-Fox. On 12 April 1955, Freed staged a week-long event under the name Rock'n'Roll Easter Jubilee. By the week's end it had attracted 97,000 kids and broken the twenty-five-year-old box office record at the Paramount with receipts of $107,000.

But Freed's events were more like radio roadshows than nightclubs, and the bebop venues were centred around live music. The first New York spot where all the discernible elements of a modern nightclub were assembled was Le Club. Predictably, considering the discothèque's Parisian origins, it was opened by a Frenchman.

Oliver Coquelin's family owned several grand hotels, including the Meurice and George V in Paris. He had been awarded a purple heart during the Korean War and became an American citizen. After dabbling in ski resorts, he high-tailed it to New York, where, it seems, he arrived at the perfect time. The high society of old money and the social register was on its way out, made obsolete by the dawn of the egalitarian sixties and a new group of the great and good. The jet set had been born and it was landing in New York.

Coquelin knew the right people and found the perfect location: a garage used by a lingerie photographer underneath his apartment in Sutton Place at 416 East 55th Street. He raised the necessary capital from partners Igor Cassini, Michael Butler, the Duke of Bedford and a motor car manufacturer called Henry Ford. He fashioned the club along the lines of a hunting lodge, with Belgian tapestries along the wall, wood-panelling all around the bar, ornate floral arrangements, glass-shaded candles and crisp linen. To one side, an open marble fireplace blazed. The two loudspeakers were so discreet they were barely noticeable. The $150 initiation fee and $35 annual dues ensured the club retained its exclusivity.

Coquelin asked society bandleader Slim Hyatt to find him a DJ, which he duly did. Thus New York's first discothèque DJ was Hyatt's butler, a long-faced, handsome black fellow called Peter Duchin. Coquelin schooled him in the arts of French spinning. Le Club opened on New Year's Eve 1960. The sixties had begun.

The Twist

In the first years of the sixties a revolution took place in the way people danced: a dance that was to have an enormous impact on youth culture. Reviled by critics and commentators as lewd, lascivious and unseemly, it nevertheless captured young imaginations and went some way to crashing the barriers of racial and sexual prejudice. Dance halls would never be the same again, as it destroyed everything that came before. It was the twist.

Russian poet Yevgeny Yevtushenko described a visit to a London nightclub.

'Couples were dancing in a stuffy, packed hall, filled with cigarette smoke. Bearded youths and girls in tight black trousers wriggled and twisted. It was not an especially aesthetic sight. However, among the twisters was a young Negro couple dancing with remarkable lightness and grace, white teeth sparkling in the semi-darkness. They danced full of joy, as if they had been used to the dance since childhood. I suddenly realised why they danced the twist the way they did. The twist is advertised as the miracle of the atomic era. But I remembered Ghana jungles two years ago where I watched African tribal dances. Those dances have existed for thousands of years.'

The twist caused a revolution because of its simplicity. It required no partner, no routine, no ritual, no training. All it needed was the right record and a set of loose limbs. It was an invocation to get on the floor and do your own thing. Because it wasn't a couples' dance, it struck a small blow for sexual equality – destroying the concept of the 'wallflower', a girl awaiting an invitation to dance (coincidentally, the Pill and the twist were launched within months of each other). Most importantly, perhaps, it unified a group of dancers. Dancing the twist you were no longer just focused on your partner, you were partying with a whole roomful of people.

It wasn't particularly new. Ancient variations of it abound. The can-can contains a routine known as the French twist, American slaves from the Congo imported a similar dance, and in the early part of the twentieth century there were many other black dance crazes, such as the mess around and the black bottom, that prefigured the twist. One 1920s song, 'Fat Fanny Stomp', even implored girls to 'twist it a little bit'. Like all good dances, the twist was yet another dancefloor approximation of sex.

The modern twist probably began in Baltimore in 1960 when Hank Ballard recorded the first, and best, version of 'The Twist' after spotting black kids doing it on the *Buddy Dean Show* on local TV. When Ballard's record spread the craze to Philadelphia it began to break nationally, thanks to Dick Clark's *American Bandstand* – the most important TV pop show in America.

Clark divested the twist of all of its sexual connotations, its essential *blackness*, and made it safe for white suburban teenagers. A new version was recorded by a pale-skinned black man called Chubby Checker (whose name was a jokey dig at Fats Domino) for a label, Cameo-Parkway, in which Dick Clark happened to have a financial interest. Clark promoted this new version of 'The Twist' on *Bandstand*, where Checker explained to the audience exactly how it was done: 'Just imagine you're wiping your bottom with a towel as you get out of the shower and putting out a cigarette with both feet.' White dancers, claiming they'd originated it, demonstrated how the dance was done. Checker was soon no.1 in the Hot 100.

Despite the success of Checker's record, the twist had largely died out by the end of 1960. Then, in a curious anomaly, a small wreck of a bar in midtown Manhattan with an occupancy limit of 178 achieved what Clark's nation-wide TV show had failed to do: make the dance into a worldwide fad.

The Peppermint Lounge

At 128 West 45th Street The Peppermint Lounge was hardly the place on which one would expect New York's high society to descend. Adjoined to the Knickerbocker Hotel just off Times Square, the Lounge was originally a gay hustler joint, frequented by sailors, lowlifes and street toughs in leather jackets. It had a long mahogany bar running down one side, lots of mirrors and a tiny dancefloor at the back.

Music was provided by a New Jersey outfit called Joey Dee & the Starliters (who at one stage included actor Joe Pesci on guitar), and here the whole of Manhattan's thrill-seeking in-crowd were to be found twisting. It was especially popular with the acting profession: Marilyn Monroe, Tallulah Bankhead, Shelley Winters, Judy Garland and Noel Coward were all spotted at the Lounge. 'They started twisting in there, so celebrities started mobbing the place,' recalls Terry Noel, a professional dancer at the club. 'Then it got very chic.'

The reaction from most commentators was not favourable, often using thinly veiled racism to damn the dance fad. *Journal-America*'s John McClain described the Peppermint Lounge as having 'the charm, noise, odor, and disorder of an overcrowded zoo'. Arthur Gelb, writing in the *New York Times*, was yet more dismissive: 'The Peppermint Lounge and its surroundings are the scene of a grotesque display every night from 10.30 to 3 o'clock. Café society has not gone slumming with such energy since its forays into Harlem in the twenties. The lure is a tiny dancefloor undulating with the twist where couples gyrate in a joyless frenzy.'

The twist made its transatlantic leap via a couple of routes. One evening in the autumn of 1961, the touring cast of *West Side Story* made an unscheduled stop at Chez Régine in Paris. They brought a stack of new American records with them. In the pile was Chubby Checker's 'The Twist'. At the time, the dance craze in Paris was a rockabilly hybrid called 'yogurt'. One of the yogurt acts, Dick Rivers Et Ses Chats Sauvages, swiftly recorded a twist record: 'Twist À Saint-Tropez'. The twist became hugely popular in France. Even exiled former king and Nazi sympathiser, Edward VIII, the Duke of Windsor, had a go. 'It was amusing, but a bit strenuous,' he reported.

On its arrival in London, the twist caused an outrage. At the Lyceum dance hall a young snake-hipped mod called Jeff Dexter, who'd seen how to do the dance on the cover of the record, was expelled and barred for twisting with a couple of girls. Within a couple of weeks, however, reports had appeared in the press about this dance craze from America and Dexter was a star. 'I got captured on film and it got shown around the cinemas on Pathé newsreels,' he laughs. 'This thing, this *obscenity* that I'd been ejected for, became popular and I got offered a job at the Lyceum. As a dancer!'

Even the BBC had a twist or two. On *Television Dancing Club*, Victor Sylvester's Ballroom Orchestra presented the twist in suitably anodyne form by recasting the Gershwin classic 'Fascinating Rhythm', as 'Fascinating Rhythm Twist'. This sanitised version still drew the ire of appalled suburbanites everywhere. A distressed dance instructor called Mr Stetson told BBC reporters that 'the knees and pelvis are used in such a way that the dancer is making very suggestive movements. I have an extreme objection to the fact that this is not what is called a couple dance. It is a solo dance. A girl can just as easily go out on to the dancefloor without having a partner and exhibit herself in what I consider to be a rather unseemly way for British ballrooms'.

Until the twist came along, Europe had remained impervious to the various fad dances – such as the Madison, the bop and the stroll – that had swept America over the previous decades. In Britain, the jive – a dance imported by American GIs during the Second World War – had been the one routine that all self-respecting dancers knew (with the jitterbug as its less popular and more controversial brother).

Now, released from the constraints of formal steps and partners, the dancer was free to build something completely new. Dancing had returned to the original black styles on which most European formal dances were originally based. You could dance however your imagination suggested.

The popularity of the twist set in train a raft of similarly freeform dances – the frug, the mashed potato, the pony, the hully gully, the monkey. Within a few years, dancefloors had thrown up the freak-outs of the flower power era and the acrobatic flips and spins of northern soul. The twist had dropped an H-bomb on dance conservatism and stripped away the dancefloor's tightly policed rituals. In doing this, it paved the way for a new kind of dance club. It was time for the discothèque to come of age.

Ian Samwell at the Lyceum

Once the jet set got a taste for the low-rent fun of the twist, they poured into the new-fangled discothèques springing up in New York, London and Paris. The tradition of having dance bands as the primary focus of entertainment was being quietly eroded by the ascendancy of vinyl. Up until this point, the DJ had been no more than a minor functionary in the evening's proceedings. He was someone proprietors would rely on to keep the club busy while the next band readied their equipment. But rapidly he would become the focus for the whole night.

It was in Britain that this happened first. Club culture in the UK has almost always been far ahead of its American counterpart, even when musically it may have occasionally lagged behind. The reason for this is largely to do with the way that music is heard. Music in America lives much more on radio than in clubs. The relative freedom of US airwaves has always meant that anyone with a transmitter and a fat wallet could broadcast music. You only had to twiddle the knob to the right frequency to get a dose of your favourite records. In the UK, where radio was still seen largely as an arm of government social policy, the only way to hear the exciting tunes emanating from America was to go out.

At the Lyceum in London the resident DJ was Ian 'Sammy' Samwell, a handsome, bequiffed smoothie with a long history in rock'n'roll. Samwell's entry into the music business had been as guitarist and songwriter with Cliff Richard & the Drifters before he was sacked in preference to Jet Harris. It was Samwell who had penned the first credible British rock'n'roll record, Cliff's 'Move It', as well as committing Georgie Fame and John Mayall to wax for the first time. (Samwell later wrote and produced the Small Faces' 'Watcha Gonna Do About It'.)

As a songwriter signed to a subsidiary of an American publisher, Samwell made regular trips to New York. He brought back coveted rhythm and blues 45s on Atlantic, Chess and Berry Gordy's pre-Motown label Anna, such as Barratt Strong's 'Money'.

In 1961 he was invited to spin records for Tuesday lunchtime dance sessions at the Lyceum, a baroque Edwardian music hall; up until then, such was the disc jockey's status, the records had been played by the electrician. Soon Samwell was asked to fill a Sunday slot. 'The Lyceum's record collection was pretty pathetic,' he recalls. 'So I started to bring my own records. I played a lot of stuff you couldn't hear on the BBC, mostly rhythm and blues because it was hip and great to dance to.' He would spin records for the first three hours and then play in the intervals between the Mick Mortimer Quartet and Cyril Stapleton's Orchestra, who appeared on the Lyceum's giant revolving stage.

Though he never really realised the importance of what he was doing, his connoisseur-quality music was the last piece in a jigsaw. The Lyceum was the first place in which all the recognisable elements of a modern club – lights, up-front dance records, disc jockey and dancefloor – came together. Dave Godin, later the man to coin the term 'northern soul', believes it deserves a place in history: 'The Lyceum was very important, I can't stress that enough, because in some ways it was the first place that could merit the name discothèque.'

'It changed my life in about three minutes,' says Jeff Dexter, the renegade Lyceum twister, recalling his first trip to the club. Walking in through the foyer, past the life-size cut-out of Ian Samwell which read 'LONDON'S NUMBER ONE DJ', and up to the balcony and the gigantic cloakrooms, the sheer spectacle of it all impressed him: 'The sound in such a big place just blew me away. It was great.'

Maximum R&B – mod about town Jeff Dexter plays the platters that matter at his Record and Light Show in 1966.

The mods and swinging London

The French, yet again, played a key part in bringing the concept of the discothèque to London. Spreading out like a virus from the south of France and Paris, the discothèque arrived in London via French students and the many au pairs working in the capital. Several of the early clubs were opened by the French – Madame Cordet at the Saddle Room, for example – and aimed specifically to attract the patronage of this young constituency. But what helped establish discothèques in England had nothing to do with France and everything to do with one of the many sub-cultures that post-war Britain had thrown up; the mods.

'Mods go to dance halls, Hammersmith Palais, the Marquee, and various "discothèques",' wrote Charles Hamblett and Jane Deverson in 1964's *Generation X*, 'clubs where they play gramophone records.' Throughout the sixties, British club culture – particularly in London and Manchester – was driven by this uniquely British sub-culture. 'Mod was the gap between full employment and unfulfilled aspirations, the missing link between bomb sites and Bacardi ads,' wrote Julie Burchill in *Damaged Gods*.

The mods had grown out of a split in the late fifties between trad jazz fans (who were mainly middle class) and the modernists, who favoured the modern jazz of Charles Mingus and the existentialist philosophy of Jean-Paul Sartre. Their initial constituency was Jewish, East End and working class. As the cult spread from its arty origins, the mods became noted for an obsessive attention to fashion and a predilection for necking amphetamines. They also loved dancing to Jamaican and black American records.

The Lyceum was an important precursor, but if you were a mod and loved black music in 1963 your first port of call would have been the Scene, owned by an irrepressible Irishman called Ronan O'Rahilly. Located in Ham Yard, Soho, it had formerly been Cy Laurie's Jazz Club. As the Piccadilly, it had also been where an unknown group called the Rolling Stones performed a disastrous early gig.

As the Scene it was a dank basement room, so small that there was no option but to dance. A young Jewish boy called Marc Feld was one of the club's 'faces'. (With the name Marc Bolan, he later became a pop star.) Although it was technically alcohol free, it wasn't too hard to get a hit of whisky added to your bottle of Coke, and you could certainly get amphetamines. The main reason most people went to the Scene, however, was to hear the DJ, Guy Stevens. If Ian Samwell at the Lyceum was the accidental revolutionary of British club culture, then Stevens was its Lenin, a confirmed believer in the revolutionary power of the disc jockey. He was a frizzy-haired obsessive, permanently bursting with enthusiasm, and his sets of maximum rhythm and blues were legendary. Though Guy didn't take drugs until much later in his life, most of the kids at the R&B Disc Night With Guy Stevens were speeding their way through a three-day weekend. 'It was on a Monday night,' explains his wife Di. 'You stayed out, went to the Flamingo and if you were still going on a Monday you went to the Scene.'

'Guy would play all these great rhythm and blues records and we'd groove all night,' sixties face Johnny Moke told the *Evening Standard*. 'Of course, nearly all of us were doing pills – you had to if you were dancing all night. Same way they take ecstasy now.'

'Everybody would come to hear Guy,' reflects Ronan O'Rahilly, 'the Stones, The Beatles, Eric Clapton – all the major stars. People would come from all over the country on Monday nights, and from France and Holland too; it was that good.' Stevens's sets at the Scene were prime source material for both the Who and the Small Faces, who reworked many of the records he played. The Who's manager brought the young band there to infuse them with the energy and authenticity of Stevens's night.

'He used to carry his records around in a huge trunk,' remembers O'Rahilly, 'and he was so protective of them that he used to sit on top of it while he DJed. I've seen him sleep on it. It was like religion to him.' Stevens would often spend days wandering around record stores looking for coveted rarities. Each Friday morning he would head for the basement of a shop in Chinatown's Lisle Street, where a rhythm and blues enthusiast sold freshly imported 45s from a tiny box on a table. By lunchtime, the records would be sold and the vendor melted into the Soho crowds.

There was a growing network of soul fans around the country and he corresponded and exchanged records with such people as Roger Eagle, resident DJ at Manchester's Twisted Wheel. Stevens's day job was A&R (artiste and repertoire) for Island Records' sister label Sue, where he signed songs by Ike & Tina Turner, Betty Everett and Rufus Thomas. He played a key role in the careers of Free, Traffic, Bad Company, Mott The Hoople and Spooky Tooth, and had a profound influence on the British record business overall. He was also a huge rock'n'roll fan, crazy about Jerry Lee Lewis, and the founder of the Chuck Berry fan club.

But his full-throttle approach to life had its consequences. He died on 29 August 1981 from an overdose of prescription drugs he was taking to help with his alcohol dependency. Tragically, it came shortly after he had produced perhaps his finest record: the LP *London Calling* by the Clash.

The Scene was not alone. There was the Flamingo, the Purley Orchid, La Discothèque, the Roaring Twenties and the Crazy Elephant (where black jock, Al Needles, plied his trade), as well as trendy bolt holes filled with London's rapidly growing pop aristocracy: the Cromwellian, the Scotch of St James and, epicentre of Swinging London, the Ad Lib – where there was always at least one Beatle.

Jeff Dexter joined Ian Samwell as a disc jockey and the duo spun at many of these places, including playing guest spots at the Scene's hip rival, the Flamingo. This was yet another unlicensed Soho dive, located underneath the (licensed) Whiskey-A-Go-Go (later the WAG) on Wardour Street, which featured all-nighters on Fridays and Saturdays.

The Flamingo drew an eclectic mix, including patrons from the American military bases in Hillingdon and Ruislip, as well as newly settled blacks from west and south London. 'That was the best gig because the audience were either very hip or West Indian,' recalls Ian Samwell. 'I played nothing but rhythm and blues or bluebeat.' Veteran jazz DJ Bob Jones remembers the Whiskey as the more accessible of the two clubs: 'The Flamingo was very black, dark, full of dodgy-looking people – but very smart, because everybody dressed up in those days.'

It was at the Flamingo that Count Suckle first brought the Jamaican sound of Ladbroke Grove into the West End. After booking him to play on Sunday nights the club's owner Rik Gunnell watched as the charismatic DJ drew a vast crowd from all over London. Gunnell's pleasure was short-lived however, when the Roaring Twenties on Carnaby Street poached Suckle to play every night.

Another club was Tiles, a Disneyland for pillheads. Once inside it was as if you'd wandered into a covered side street – the club contained a sort of mini-mall of shops including a Ravel shoe store, a soft-drink stand and a beauty parlour called Face Place. Completing the illusion that you were in some unknown London alley was a sign reading 'Tiles Street'. Each lunchtime, Tiles would fill with office girls in pale lipstick, skiving clerks, young merchant seamen on shore leave and mods who, somehow, never seemed to work – all there to dance in the middle of the day to soul and bluebeat. Tom Wolfe termed this strange mod sub-culture the Noonday Underground.

One of the backers of Tiles was Jim Marshall, owner of the Marshall PA company. Tiles, therefore, had a decent sound system (something that couldn't be said for any other club in London). By the mid sixties several DJs had worked there, including a cocky scouser called Kenny Everett, Mike Quinn, Clem Dalton, Ian Samwell and Jeff Dexter, who hosted his own night, the Record And Light Show.

It became so notorious as a pill palace, the police visited almost as often as the mods. It was finally closed and turned into an aquarium. John Peel, recently returned from a seven-year stint as a radio DJ in America, played the last night there. He was not popular. 'There were waves of irate customers coming up over the footlights to try and persuade me to play whatever it was they wanted me to play. Which certainly wasn't the Grateful Dead, Jefferson Airplane and Country Joe & the Fish. They didn't like me at all.'

London's culture of all-night dance parties quickly took off elsewhere, proving especially popular in the Midlands and north of England. While the dance clubs in the south succumbed to the prevailing winds of flower power, the working-class north continued to pursue doggedly its love of black American music. This quirky sub-culture would, in a few years, transform itself into northern soul.

Gay London

The gay scene was slowly coming out, too. 'How bona to vada your dolly old eek. Troll in and put your lallies up ducky!' By 1965 the secret gay language of polari, a wonderful mix of Romany, Latin, Cockney and backslang, and once a necessary subterfuge, was now heard by eight million people weekly as radio stars Kenneth Williams and Hugh Paddick camped it up on 'Round The Horne'.

Undercover cops were no longer likely to be wanking in public toilets to entrap men to arrest and beat up, as they had a decade before, but sixties gay nightlife was still fairly shadowy – largely restricted to East End sailors' pubs and sordid all-night 'grope hole' coffee bars. The Coleherne and Boltons in Earls Court had been gay pubs since the mid fifties. There was Le Deuce in D'Arblay Street, Stud in Poland Street (which later became punk hang-out Louise's), The Hustler and Gigolo in Chelsea, Spartan in Victoria and many more secret speakeasies, but few of these places even had a jukebox. It wasn't hard for men to meet men for sex, but the idea of enjoying yourself by dancing beforehand was a bit ambitious.

Tallulah (Martyn Allam), a hotel manager and DJ on the early London gay scene, recalls his trips to a pub in Woolwich. 'It was run by this queen called Selena The Horse. And she also owned the house next door. You'd pay one and sixpence to go in after the pub had closed and she'd pull an ironing board down in front of the entrance to the kitchen. In the lounge there'd be just a red light and a jukebox, and you'd buy the drink from her, from behind the ironing board. It was a mix of sailors, lesbians, drag queens. Really rough.'

These older places gradually gave way to a more visible nightlife, especially after the law against gay sex was repealed in 1967. Marianne Faithfull said of sixties London, 'There was a great honouring of the homosexual side of life. It was just in the air everywhere.' In fashion and the arts, gayness was increasingly acknowledged, even if it wasn't admitted, and a legion of gay managers were busy running the pop world – Brian Epstein with The Beatles, Andrew Loog Oldham with the Stones, Simon Napier-Bell with The Yardbirds, to name but three. The influence of a few flamboyant young moguls ensured that decent music started mattering in gay clubs.

The first such place was The Catacombs in Brompton Road, a cavern bar where a credible soundtrack of pop and soul was played by Gordon Fruin, who A&R'd for Berry Gordy and so went by the splendid DJ name of Pamela Motown. Then, at the end of the decade Yours and Mine (universally known as The Sombrero) opened in Kensington. Liberace was there on opening night, Bowie made it his court, and the pink pounds of the music industry filled the tills. The idea that gay Londoners might want their own discothèques wasn't going to go away.

Terry Noel at Arthur

Now that British club culture was booming, the New Worlders wanted a piece of the action. Energised by the twist, New York's society darlings championed a series of fantastical, theatrical clubs, each more chic than the last. One in particular became the talk of America. It was called, simply, Arthur and was the Studio 54 of the sixties jet set. Its disc jockey was a flamboyant cherub called Terry Noel.

He was the first DJ to mix records.

When actor Richard Burton dumped his first wife Sybil for Elizabeth Taylor, she took the divorce money and ran off to New York for some fun. In May 1965, with a great deal of society support and eighty donations of $1,000 each from her friends, Sybil Burton opened a club, Arthur, named after a line about George Harrison's haircut in the film *A Hard Day's Night*. It was an instant sensation. The day after it opened, a photograph of Sybil Burton and Rudolf Nureyev dancing together was splashed across several newspapers and the Arthurian legend was born.

Terry Noel, an art student originally from Syracuse, had danced himself into a job as a professional twister at the Peppermint Lounge. When Sybil Burton came down searching for talent for her new club, she passed Noel over in favour of his flat-mate's band, The Wild Ones. Green with envy, Noel gatecrashed Arthur's opening night and informed Sybil in no uncertain terms that the club was great but the music sucked. He must have convinced her because from the next night, Terry Noel was Arthur's resident DJ.

Burton had taken the idea of Soho's Ad Lib club and transplanted it 3,500 miles to 154 East 54th Street. The influence of Swinging London was immediately evident as Burton implored clubbers: 'Please dress up daft.' They obliged. To an appropriately Mondrianesque Pop Art back-drop, dancers whirled manically in a gala of man-made finery: plastic jackets, nylon shirts, chain mail dresses, vinyl suits and fake-fur hot pants. 'WILD NEW FLASHY BEDLAM OF THE DISCOTHÈQUE' trumpeted *Life* magazine. Amid this controlled pandemonium stood Noel, part showman, part shaman. The slim controller.

Sybil Burton's celebrity may have drawn them to Arthur, but it was Noel who kept them on the dancefloor. He took control of everything. Within six months of Arthur's debut he had redesigned the speaker system and taken charge of the lights. The sound engineer, Chip Monk, was asked to create speakers which operated independently of each other, with separate frequency controls. That way, Noel could move the songs around the room like a churning mess of controlled sound. Noel gave them a *show*.

'I wanna thrill,' barks Noel, remembering his DJ days. 'I want them to feel like they've never felt in their life before. I'd see people's mouths on the dancefloor going "Wow! What was that?" It's like those movie theatres today where you hear the gunshot behind you. It was the same with me. Except I was doing it in the sixties.'

Noel mixed records, too. On a primitive set-up – he just had a volume dial for each deck – he would take elements from a track and tease and taunt the crowd with them: a Jimi Hendrix guitar lick here or a Chambers Brothers acappella there – allusive whispers, barely heard fragments. Then he would slam the whole song through the mincer. 'People would come up to me and say, "I was listening to the Mamas And Papas and now I'm listening to the Stones and I didn't even know." I used to try some of the wildest changes without losing a beat.' Noel's reputa-tion had risen to the point where producers would bring test pressings of their latest confections. He still has the metal test disc that Smokey Robinson and Berry Gordy brought down of Smokey's new production, the Marvelettes' 'Don't Mess With Bill'.

Celebrities assailed the club. Everyone wanted a piece of Arthur, so the new and symbolic velvet rope kept the undesirables at bay, with Mickey Deans as door-picker (Deans later married Judy Garland, twelve weeks before she died, after meeting her at Arthur). What Burton was looking for was that perfect mix, like a great cocktail, where all the ingredients meshed together perfectly. She singled out what she termed the PYPs (Pretty Young People), the not-yet-rich, 'good-looking working girls with lots of dates, models, sub editors on magazines.' Burton even had a phrase for those terminally unhip folk who *still* did the twist: mippys.

Noel didn't suffer fools gladly either. 'John Wayne asked me for "Yellow Rose Of Texas",' he recalls. 'I said, "Gee, I happen to have it." And

I go – snap! – "Oh, it's broken," and I threw it on the dancefloor. He goes, "You faggot!" His toupée was falling off his head. Sybil was sitting behind where he was; Judy Garland was sitting beside her and Lauren Bacall next to her. They go, "Teeerrrry!" They loved it, because they hated him.'

Soon this new haunt of celebrities was no longer unique. Shepheard's opened in the Drake Hotel with a decor that recalled imperial Egypt; there was L'Ondine where Terry Noel moved after Arthur (and where a young Jimi Hendrix was briefly a busboy); Geoffrey Leeds opened L'Interdit in the Gotham Hotel; Trude Heller's The Trik made waves downtown. Whiskey Disque in Los Angeles became the first to open up on the west coast, with socialite Mimi London's Le Disque Alexis following swiftly in San Francisco.

As for Terry Noel, he eventually gave up his music career for art and today is to be found painting in his downtown studio. However, he had a long run as a DJ, moving from Arthur to L'Ondine and hence to a new Greenwich Village haunt, Salvation, where he continued his experiments, even to the point of mixing with three record decks.

'Salvation was very about the records,' he says. 'That was when I went into three turntables. I was really into it. Soul. Absolutely. The Chambers Brothers' "Time" was like the theme song to Salvation. I'd build up to that and everybody would know it was coming. I'd turn off all the lights and you'd hear – thud, thud, thud.'

He aimed to control as much as he could. 'We had this ball that had a light inside it and it shot out little rays of light and it actually had a string on it and I would pull it to make it rock across the dancefloor. The song's going "Time has come today", I'm doing lights, I'm pulling strings. I was like the Wizard of Oz.

'This is a play. You're directing a play. It's very dramatic. It has to be dramatic, and no automatic programming is ever going to be any use, because it's different every night and every time you play the record.'

For the DJs who came after him, Terry Noel was the man who wrote the instruction manual. Those in his wake would add considerable layers of artistry and intensity, but Noel was the prototype of the modern DJ. Unlike those later who would dig deep to find the most primal dance tracks, his tastes were resolutely pop; and his love of celebrity and celebrities prevented him from sacrificing everything for the dancefloor, but in technical respects, and in terms of putting on a show, Terry Noel was a founding force.

The DJ owes him a great debt for his obsessive control of the musical experience and for his cunning manipulation of the crowd. And we can never ignore the fact that this was the first DJ to ever mix records. His mixes may have been primitive by today's standards, but it was Terry Noel who first hit on the idea that two records could be somehow sewn together.

San Francisco and the Acid Tests

As we know, at some point in history nightclubs became places of grand spectacle – great throbbing systems of sound and light, otherworldly places that can shake reality right out of your bones; and clubbers were transformed from members of an audience into active, reciprocating participants, vital components of the transcendent musical ritual. This change happened gradually for a while, as the club experience trundled on behind technology, musical experiments and social customs. But then, all of a sudden . . . there was acid!

'Who needs jazz, or even beer, when you can sit down on a public kerbstone, drop a pill in your mouth, and hear fantastic music for hours at a time in your head?' queried Hunter S Thompson in the *New York Times*. 'A cap of good acid costs $5, and for that you can hear the Universal Symphony, with God singing solo and the Holy Ghost on drums.'

LSD arrived on the club scene in the early sixties. Club drugs before had been largely about increasing your energy, but instead of the paranoid frenzy of cocaine or the menacing endurance of amphetamines, LSD went straight to work on your very senses. One acid trip turned most into instant LSD evangelists. Or certifiable basket-cases. Or both.

The drug radically changed the complexion of nightclubs. In London, psychedelic vessels UFO and Middle Earth replaced the clenched-jaw dregs of mod's soul dream. In New York, the brain-frying experiences of Electric Circus took the elitism of Arthur and drenched it in blotter. But it was in San Francisco – at least initially – where the effects would be felt first.

Although the scene in San Francisco was by no means DJ-led (in fact, their role was insignificant), much of what happened was about dancing. It was also very much concerned with heightening visual and aural stimulation, and in line with the effects of this amazing new chemical compound, it spurred the creation of incredible light shows and daunting sound equipment.

When acid house and rave culture blossomed in the late eighties, it would find in itself all manner of evocative echoes from the psychedelic sixties – from the feelings of community and the scale of its events to the belief that this combination of drugs and music could really, no honestly . . . if only you'd try it . . . change the world.

Novelist Ken Kesey introduced San Francisco to LSD. Kesey had discovered lysergic acid after volunteering for government-sponsored tests at Menlo Park Veterans Hospital in Palo Alto, thirty miles south of San Francisco. In 1965, Kesey and his cabal of Merry Pranksters (a loose aggregation of freaks, drop-outs and former beatniks) began throwing parties under the title 'The Acid Test'. The acid was supplied by a wild-eyed and very gifted chemist called Augustus Owsley Stanley III, whose product was so coveted that Jimi Hendrix ordered a run of 100,000 tabs for his own personal use. Owsley was later described by a government official as having done for LSD what Ford did for the motor car. His first batch of acid was available for consumption on 5 March 1965.

The Acid Tests were a series of freeform 'events' at which the participants drank Kool-Aid laced with Owsley's finest. Music blared out, lights and slides were projected onto walls and people danced until their legs – or minds – gave out. The first Acid Test took place following a Rolling Stones concert at the San Jose Civic Center on 4 December 1965. Prankster lieutenant Ken Babbs handed concert-goers flyers asking, 'Can YOU Pass The Acid Test?' Around 300 turned up, tuned in and dropped out to a freakshow bombardment of the senses.

The band that day was the Warlocks, playing a wild amalgam of bluegrass, country and rhythm and blues. They changed their name specially for the event. After considering various options, among them Mythical Ethical, Icicle Tricicle and Nonreality Sandwich, they decided to call themselves the Grateful Dead.

The Dead did to rock music what the disco DJs would later do to dance music: they contorted it to within an inch of its life. As Tom Wolfe related in *The Electric Kool-Aid Acid Test*, 'They were not to be psychedelic dabblers, painting pretty pictures, but true explorers.' Their 'songs' became rubberised workouts that were tailored there and then, specifically for the needs of dancers, whose bodies – and, often, clothing – had been loosened from their moorings and set adrift on memory bliss. 'At the Avalon or the Fillmore,' wrote Joel Selvin in *Summer Of Love*, 'the Dead would play songs as long as they felt good, as long as they made people dance, and when most of the audience is high on something, that can be a long time.'

There may not have been a disc jockey or a turntable at work, but this was a radical new approach to music, one which today's DJs will recognise immediately.

In the centre of the room at one Acid Test, a tangle of scaffolding towered up into the eerie darkness. Kesey, sitting atop it, surrounded by projectors, lights and sound equipment, scribbled messages in gels on the projector. He then poured water onto his creation and watched the words dissolve into puddles of nonsense at the bottom. A troupe of conga drummers hammered hypnotic polyrhythms into the heads of the dancers below. Amid this chaotic muddle, there were people with their shoes off counting their toes, or talking to the scaffolding.

Owsley took the Dead under his wing, and began experimenting with electronic equipment for them to incorporate into their shows: tape loops, recording devices, even primitive video equipment. The Acid Tests became increasingly weird. 'Allen Ginsberg could be seen wandering around in this white hospital-orderly suit, staring around with a look of amazement,' wrote Charles Perry in *Rolling Stone*. 'There were *all* these . . . crazy . . . people . . . wearing antique gowns, paisley prints, spacesuits, with paint on their faces and feathers in their hair, dancing, dancing.'

The Acid Tests took place all over the Bay Area of San Francisco and, latterly, in Los Angeles. The last one was on 2 October 1966. The San Francisco scene that spawned peace and love slowly began to sink in a pit of heroin. A few days later, on 6 October, LSD was finally made illegal in the state of California.

UFO and psychedelic London

The links between London and the growing scene of Pranksters in the US were close, and acid fairly quickly started making inroads into the tight mod scene. (In fact, London's main supplier, Michael Hollingshead, had been the one to turn Timothy Leary on to LSD.) London clubs would soon dissolve in a haze of dope smoke and a rainbow of psychedelics.

A Ladbroke Grove-based group called the London Free School launched a club on 23 December 1966. The LFS was an informal brood of Notting Hill hippies, local working-class people and black activists like Michael X. One of their number was a talented young record producer called Joe Boyd, who went on to work with Pink Floyd, Fairport Convention and Toots & the Maytals. The club was called UFO (pronounced '*Yoofo*').

Housed in a ramshackle Irish ballroom at 31 Tottenham Court Road called the Blarney Club, UFO was not a dance club in any understanding of the word. There was no DJ, only an American electronics wizard called Jack Henry Moore who would play tapes, records by the Grateful Dead or reel-to-reels of electronic music. Pink Floyd and Soft Machine became the club's twin totems. Other bands would perform there; one was called the Purple Gang, whose Joe Boyd–produced 'Granny Takes A Trip' was an underground anthem. After performing there, their leader Peter 'Lucifer' Walker disbanded the group to become a witch. It was that kind of a club.

'The Acid Tests were coming over,' recalls Jeff Dexter. 'All the underground poets were arriving. UFO reflected this. It was totally unstructured. It was a free-for-all. There was no presentation as such, it just happened. For me, coming out of the straight world of ballroom showbiz, this was a brave new world.'

Dexter, by now resident at Tiles where his Record & Light Show straddled both worlds, would bring records for Moore to play. Moore reciprocated by introducing Dexter to records that he characterised as 'really weird American stuff'. Inside this psychedelic cocoon, people would trip out, read books, dance or simply stare at the refracting patterns of lights on the wall. John Peel was a regular visitor. 'The only time I took acid deliberately was at UFO because I felt I was kind of safe,' he recalled. 'It wasn't like clubbing is these days. Rather than dancing around – obviously some people danced about in a fairly idiotic manner – mostly you just lay on the floor and passed out, really.' He laughed energetically at this thought. 'It sounds like fun, doesn't it?'

UFO fell in Tottenham Court Road police station's patch. The cops there would draw straws from broken plastic spoons to decide whose turn it was to visit. 'The principal danger was from acid-crazed Hell's Angels,' wrote Miles in *NME*. 'Anxious to practise love'n'peace in order to pull hippie nookie, they would insist on French kissing every policeman they saw.'

The UFO found an echo in Middle Earth in Covent Garden. Middle Earth took the UFO template and exposed it to a more suburban crowd. Both John Peel and Jeff Dexter DJed there. Dexter may have been entranced by this brave new world, but he was still acutely aware of the purpose of a disc jockey in a nightclub: to make people dance.

'John hated ska and bluebeat and most of those records that I'd lived on,' remembers Dexter. 'He thought they were awful. I was totally into what he was doing, but he didn't understand what I was doing. The thing is, people still loved to dance and you really couldn't dance to a lot of the new psychedelic records that were around. They were horrible to dance to. So to keep people moving I had to mix it up a bit.'

The Electric Circus and Cheetah

New York's jet set was not immune. It, too, would soon succumb to the pretty category mistakes of LSD.

In 1966 Brooklyn-born Jerry Brandt purchased a beaten-down Polish meeting hall on St Mark's Place in the East Village. A talent-booker by trade, Brandt was no hippie but he could see an opportunity when it presented itself. He called his new venue the Electric Circus.

Just prior to its sale, another creative opportunist had noticed its potential. Andy Warhol booked it for the whole of April 1966, called it Exploding Plastic Inevitable and installed his latest protégés, the Velvet

Underground. He projected lights through gauze and onto a wall. Nico sang 'I'll Be Your Mirror', while Warhol showed movies behind her. As she performed, a silver ball sent shards of light scurrying through the room, like glass shattering.

'You trudged upstairs to this place that smelled of urine,' wrote John Cale in *What's Welsh For Zen*. 'It was filthy and had no lights in it, but Andy took it over and turned it into something totally different. Nobody had seen or heard anything like this before. We transformed this dump into an exciting, jumping place.'

Jerry Brandt maintained Warhol's approach when he made it the Electric Circus. After financing the club with an audacious scheme in which the Coffee Growers' Association contributed $250,000, provided coffee was the main drink served in the club, he brought in Ivan Chermayeff who had designed the America Pavilion at the World's Fair. The designer transformed Electric Circus into a gigantic psychedelic Bedouin tent comprised of white stretch yarn. Projections of home movies, liquid lights and morphing glutinous blobs glowed on the fabric. A gigantic sound system blasted rock freakouts to the Saint Vitus dancers.

The Electric Circus trumpeted itself as 'the ultimate legal experience' yet it was far from it. Drugs were rife. The *Village Voice* compared it with Rome shortly before the fall. 'There was no alcohol served,' Brandt told Anthony Haden-Guest. 'I was afraid, because everyone was doing LSD.' The Electric Circus was immortalised in *Coogan's Bluff* as the Pigeon-Toed Orange Peel Club, where Clint Eastwood chases an errant hippie prisoner into this den of iniquity. He soon collapses in a stoned stupor as the lights pulse and throb around him.

Electric Circus had a rival in the psychedelic stakes called Cheetah. Ironically, this had been opened by Le Club's staid Frenchman, Oliver Coquelin. On the site of the Arcadia Ballroom near Broadway's theatre district, it threw its doors open on 28 May 1966. The cavernous space had a dancefloor with silver circular podiums scattered randomly like outsized polka dots. Each supported a girl frugging. Above, a cavalcade of 3,000 coloured lights palpitated gently, while a boutique at the back sold the latest Carnaby Street fashions. And there was smooth and soft black velvet everywhere – except the bar, which was covered in fake fur.

In the basement there was a TV room and on the upper floor a cinema showed the latest, strangest, underground movies. *Variety* got rather excited about this new boîte: 'GOTHAM'S NEW CHEETAH A KINGSIZED WATUSERY WITH A FORT KNOX POTENTIAL' it declared.

A striking Puerto Rican teenager, Yvon Leybold, clad in hot pants and fishnets, ventured down from Spanish Harlem. 'Cheetah was the first real disco club I went to,' she recalls. 'That was a lot of fun. It was a very mixed atmosphere. It was the first time I went into a place and you see lights and you see atmosphere, instead of the rinky-dink places I was used to.'

The end of the beginning

The psychedelic era, though initially based on dancing, would eventually take the rhythm out of rhythm and blues. Rock, after a trip too many, would soon drift well away from the dancefloor and become *serious* music, sounds for the head rather than the body.

When the hippie dream spluttered to a halt, the same fate seemingly awaited the discothèque. The Electric Circus filed for bankruptcy, and Arthur spun its final disc on 21 June 1969. Under the headline 'DISCOTHÈQUES GO-GO INTO OBLIVION AS JUVES TURN TO NEW KICKS AND SOUNDS', *Variety* predicted the end for the nightclub boom. 'The closing of Arthur indicates that the day of the discothèque is virtually over,' it claimed.

In fact, it was only just beginning.

The whole hippie trip had opened up the doors of perception for club promoters, showing them just how much it was possible to do within the club experience. This brief era also acted as a powerful inspiration in the lives of future visionaries like disco pioneer David Mancuso – indeed disco's early years would be full of the brotherly love which sixties acid seemed to foment. Its styles, its artwork, its decor, and its *psychedelia* would be echoed in the shock waves of acid house twenty years later. And its events added a lot to the DJ's armoury, even if he hadn't played much of a part.

Once the disc jockey had come out from the radio and entered the dancing arena, his job changed radically. He was now no longer a simple record selector and tastemaker, he had the essential fact of audience response to deal with. Now that the relation between music and audience was interactive, the audience had become part of the event – in some sense, the audience was the event, and the DJ a responsive controller of their pleasure.

By the end of the sixties, the notion of the discothèque had come a long way. It was now supported by some relatively sophisticated hardware, some very creative disc jockeys and a complex series of interwoven cultures devoted to dance and music. In less than a quarter of a century, the idea of dancing to someone playing records had evolved from a bizarre experiment in a Yorkshire function room to an intricate world of nightclubs, DJs, drugs and music.

This world had matured more rapidly in the UK than the US – maybe because Britain seems to invest far more energy in its youth culture, which is somehow more accepting of outside novelties and is usually energetically downmarket in its social make-up. While the café society were twisting in New York's Peppermint Lounge, the kids doing the same dance in the Lyceum were clerks, apprentices and shop girls. Perhaps it's because Britain is a nation built on duty, a country of subjects not citizens, that its young people expend so much effort in trying to escape; but it was in Britain that club culture was founded, even if the records which filled it were from across the Atlantic.

The connections between the two countries have always been strong, and one theme has a particular resonance – the passionate romance between white working-class kids in the UK and black music made in America. Perhaps the connection is work, perhaps it's the refusal to defer pleasure. If you were black and American you sang about pay day, you waited for the eagle on your dollar to fly. If you were British and working class, you just said Ready Steady Go, the weekend starts here.

FOUR
NORTHERN
SOUL

After Tonight Is All Over

'Northern soul exists as a fascinating example of a predominantly working-class, drug-fuelled youth culture which (unlike house) was never controlled by the music industry, because the music industry never understood it. Northern soul was a true and near-perfect underground scene.'

– John McCready, *The Face*

'When the whole rave thing went ballistic it felt like northern soul twenty years on. Lots of people getting off their heads, dancing to fast music and this love attitude.'

– DJ Ian Dewhirst, aka 'Frank'

You live in a nondescript town somewhere in the north of England. Row upon row of factories fill the horizon with chimneys, scarring the sky with belches of dark grey smoke. During the week, in one of those factories, you work the nine-to-five drudge: manning the production line, sweeping the yard, shovelling shit. The job is unrewarding, but it pays enough for you to live. More importantly, it pays enough for you to go out and dance.

The factory may be your job, it is certainly not your life. Every weekend, you travel to other nondescript northern towns, you dress up, you pop pills and you dance to pacey, obscure soul records, all the time dreaming of singers from impossibly glamorous places like Detroit, Chicago and Philadelphia.

Your uniform is unfashionable but highly practical. From your white Fred Perry polo shirt down to your leather-soled Ravel shoes, everything you wear is built for comfort *and* for speed. The drugs you take are practical too: an array of amphetamines, swallowed with the express purpose of keeping you on the dancefloor till morning.

You dance to records by unknown artists, on labels no one knows about, singing songs that few have ever heard. Yet these records are the ones you treasure; the ones you spend dozens of pounds – sometimes even hundreds – from your meagre salary to acquire.

Your friends, still stuck on progressive rock or perhaps discovering the glittery modes of glam rock and Bowie, laugh at you. They don't understand the secret world you inhabit. They don't understand the clothes, the music, the rituals of your underground existence. For you are a member of a closed order, you belong to one of the most pure and untainted musical movements ever. You are a northern soul boy.

The first rave culture

A full fifteen years before rave culture would whistle into existence, northern soul provided it with an almost complete blueprint. Here was a scene where working-class kids came together in large numbers, across great distances, to obscure places, to take drugs and dance to music that no one else cared about. It was a scene in which togetherness and belonging were all important. It was long ignored or treated with contempt by the sophisticates of music journalism and London clubland, allowing it to develop largely undisturbed and unobserved. And, just like the rave movement (in which 'hardcore' diverged from the more mainstream side of the scene in an effort to preserve the music's original spirit), northern soul ended with a dramatic split, as the progressive DJs found their more open-minded musical policies fiercely opposed by the traditionalists.

Northern soul has largely been written off as a musical cul-de-sac, but in fact it was a vitally important step in the creation of today's club culture and in the evolution of the DJ. Many of the first records to dent the UK pop charts as a result of club play came from northern soul. Its DJs introduced an unprecedented sophistication to the craft, and it wasn't a coincidence that the first DJs forward-thinking enough to play house music in the UK came from a northern soul background. In fact, until disco emerged in New York, thanks to northern soul and clubs like the Catacombs and the Twisted Wheel, British DJ culture was far more advanced than its American counterpart.

What northern soul brought to the DJ was *obsession*. Because it placed an incredible premium on musical rarity, it made him into an obsessed and compulsive collector of vinyl. It taught him the value of playing records no one else owned, of spending months, years and hundreds of pounds in search of that one unheard song which would bring an audience to its knees. It sent the DJ across the oceans to hunt in dusty warehouses and tiny rural outhouses for unknown classics which his competitors didn't have and couldn't play. Northern soul showed the DJ how to turn vinyl into gold dust.

A genre built from failures

Roughly speaking, northern soul was the music made by the hundreds of singers and bands who were copying the Detroit sound of sixties Motown pop. Most of this was a complete failure in its own time and place – it was the music of unsuccessful artists, tiny labels and small towns, all lost within the vast expanses of the US entertainment machine. But in northern England from the end of the sixties through to its heyday in the middle seventies, it was exhumed and exalted.

It is named because of where it was enjoyed, not where it was made (though this would make sense, too). The word 'northern' in northern soul refers not to Detroit but to Wigan; not to Chicago, but to Manchester, Blackpool and Cleethorpes.

Basing a genre around a love of music that the rest of the world had forgotten was a bit like inviting a bunch of friends round to speak Latin, but in clubs dotted across the British industrial north, this was exactly what happened. It might have been because their drug-taking habits demanded a certain kind of music, or because this fast, escapist style – originating as it did in Detroit, the *Motor* City – somehow resonated with their mechanised existence. Maybe they were simply reluctant to see their favourite music die now that the rest of the world had tired of it. Whatever the reason, working-class youngsters (almost all white) in the north of England started to lionise a series of records which had been complete flops in their original context. The worship of such tunes became a thriving underground club scene.

For many years, because it was so independent, this scene was also very pure. Northern soul was entirely club-based, so it needed no chart approval, no crossover hits. And because it was a retro movement, it needed no new bands or bright young stars. In fact, since all its records had been made years ago, it needed absolutely nothing from the music industry. What it did require, however, was an army of dedicated and driven collectors determined to unearth enough good records to keep the scene going. Without 'new' records being discovered and played, it would have quickly degenerated into nothing more dynamic than an oldies appreciation society. Luckily, there was plenty of incentive for voyages of discovery.

Northern soul had a particular appeal for collectors since it was built almost entirely from rarities. A record couldn't just be good, it also had to be rare as hell. If a track sounded like it had been recorded in a garden shed in Detroit, then so much the better. (It probably had been recorded in a garden shed in Detroit.) On top of this, there was the enticing fact that a collection of northern soul was – in theory, at least – *completable*: because only songs made in a certain style during a certain period in a

Baggy trousers – northern soul not only pioneered breakdancing but also invented trousers big enough to accommodate a family of four.

certain place were acceptable, there was a strictly finite number of good records to discover and possess. Work obsessively enough and you could one day own the full set. Given this vinyl fetishism, the prestige which went with finding new records was enormous. In this closed world, the man who discovered a song like R Dean Taylor's 'There's A Ghost In My House' or 'Tainted Love' by Gloria Jones could expect showers of admiration. A DJ with an exclusive tune would watch his crowd swell rapidly and his status increase. The value of records rocketed accordingly.

'When you find an unknown record, it's like seeing a baby suddenly mature,' reflects Ian Dewhirst, a key northern DJ. 'You listen to it at home and wonder whether it will work. And then you see your vision confirmed. Suddenly it's a hot one. Seeing an unknown record go from zero value to being valuable. It was almost like the Stock Market.'

In the clubs, dancers drove themselves into ecstasies of excitement over the latest treasure from America. Posters for dances advertised not only the DJs who'd be there but also the rare records they would play. Given this unprecedented discophilia, the hunt for the rarest sounds went to comically tortuous lengths. Though the financial rewards were usually scant in comparison, there was no shortage of intrepid explorers scraping together a passage to the new world, confident that they would return not with a box of dusty and forgotten 7-inch singles, but with a casket of priceless pearls.

The Twisted Wheel

When Eddie Holland, Lamont Dozier and Brian Holland penned the follow up to the Four Tops' Motown smash 'Ask The Lonely' in 1965, little did they realise that it would be so influential for a strange sect of soul-obsessed DJs in the north of England. The song was called 'I Can't Help Myself (Sugar Pie Honey Bunch)'. From its opening salvo of drums, bass and piano to the dizzy whorls of strings, double snare hits and rhythmic vibraphone licks that perch underneath Levi Stubbs's spiralling vocal delivery, it provided a blueprint for northern soul.

'I Can't Help Myself' had *exactly* the kind of sound they liked at the Twisted Wheel. In this spartan basement club near Manchester city centre, around 600 kids would squeeze in cheek-by-jowl every Saturday night and dance to some of the rarest sounds in the country. And do so until 7.30 every Sunday morning.

The Twisted Wheel began business in November 1963 at 26 Brazenose Street as an all-nighter, playing a mix of blues, early soul, bluebeat and jazz (on 18 September 1965 it moved to a second location at 6 Whitworth Street). The fad for all-night dance parties had been around for some time and it was by no means the first to hold them. But within a couple of years, as the contours of clubland changed significantly around it, the Wheel would become a rare oasis for such music.

In London and the south, the rock underground began to dominate. In northern clubs, this trend caused not a ripple as the staunchly working-class north clung on to the escapism of all-night soul sessions. Maybe it was simply that pop culture moved far more slowly than it does now. Communications between London and the rest of the country were certainly more limited and the only significant music publications specialised in rock and pop. So the Wheelites, blissfully unaware that they were becoming an anachronism, continued to dance to the uptempo soul records that they loved.

There was a good reason for the fast nature of the songs played at the Wheel. Its clientele was wired on speed. They consumed the full range, from black bombers and purple hearts, to prellies and dexys (drinamyl, preludine and dexedrine) either bought from dealers in the club or stolen from pharmacies. It wasn't unusual for dancers travelling to a soul club to stop on the way to break in to a chemist's shop for the evening's sustenance.

'The bad lads must've reconnoitred all the different ways into Wigan,' remembers Ian Dewhirst, 'and looked at the chemist shops that didn't have the greatest security. And whichever way they came in, you could almost bet your life that a chemist would be broken into.' Later there would be regular drug deaths, as people's pill-popping habits grew more extreme. 'The Wigan court was full every week with prosecutions for possession of amphetamines,' remembers northern DJ Guy Hennigan, detailing the roadblocks, busts and mass police searches which became almost routine. Fellow DJ Keb Darge, then a champion dancer on the scene, would travel down from his native Scotland and if the drug squad stopped their coach, would squash a sandwich onto his pills: 'My mother would always pack some sandwiches. Howk it on the floor, step on the sandwiches, the drugs underneath them. Worked a treat.'

Fuelled by their prescription amphetamines, the Wheelites danced in a highly gymnastic manner to songs of a very specific type. Tempo was all. To make it at the Wheel, a record had to be energetic enough to keep up with the speed-freak dancers – propelled by an urgent, stomping, Motown beat, liberally sprinkled with horns and strings, and finished off with a melodramatic black vocal. This music wasn't funky, but it sure was fast. The lyrics told not of sex, but of love; sentimental tunes that provided a soundtrack of escape from the factory treadmill.

'The Twisted Wheel was an unusual little place with five rooms and stone floors,' remembers Dave Evison, who later DJed at Wigan Casino. 'Bike wheels everywhere you looked. It took me four weeks to work out where the disc jockey was: he was hiding behind a pile of scrap metal! As part of the dancing, the kids used to run up the walls to see how high they could get. It was young, eager. There was a respect for the disc jockey; there was a respect for what he played. It was a good scene.'

What was remarkable was the mobility of the clubbers who started going there. Soul aficionados travelled miles to reach the Twisted Wheel. If you thought no one went further than their home town to dance until the days of raves, think again: these kids were doing this not in 1989 but in 1969.

'Part of the enjoyment was actually travelling there,' remembers Carl Woodroffe, who as Farmer Carl Dene would become one of the scene's pioneer DJs. 'And the motorways didn't really exist then as they do now. The M6, for example, didn't start until you went north of Cannock to go to Manchester.'

Clad in casual clothes, Wheelites like Dene would journey up to Manchester before changing into their pristine, freshly pressed mohair suits, crisp white shirts and skinny ties. This style, ubiquitous in the Wheel, was handed down to its clubbers from the mods of the early sixties. And, irrespective of the heat in the club, that's the way they would remain until the drive home. 'You'd be wringing wet with sweat but still wearing your suit when you came out of the club,' laughs Dene. 'But a suit was always a good way of endearing yourself to the women. It went down well, that.'

The first Wheel, on Brazenose Street, was where the northern soul sound originated. Its resident DJ Roger Eagle had broad tastes in black music, playing the gritty blues of Little Walter, Art Blakey's rhythm-heavy modern jazz, and mixing in Solomon Burke and early Motown. Although imports were scarce in early sixties Britain, he had been making money importing Chess and Checker records from America, and played such records there right from the Wheel's opening night.

However, Eagle watched as the speeding dancers increasingly dictated the nature of his music. He would eventually leave in frustration at the Wheel's pill scene, as it forced his quite eclectic playlist towards a single, stomping tempo.

'I started northern soul, but I actually find the music very limiting,' he recounted, 'because in the early days I'd play a Charlie Mingus record, then I'd play a bluebeat disc followed by a Booker T tune, then a Muddy Waters or Bo Diddley record. Gradually, there was this blanding out to one sort of sound. When I started DJing, I could play what I wanted. But after three years I had to keep to the same tempo, which is what northern soul is.'

Sure enough, by the time the Wheel moved venues to Whitworth Street, its music had narrowed considerably. The club's later residents –

Phil Saxe, Les Cokell, Rob Bellars, Brian Phillips and Paul Davies – concentrated on more uptempo sounds. By then, the Wheel was the place to play. 'Oh, it was a bit of a cult thing at the Wheel, if you got to DJ there,' laughs Bellars. 'There were people begging to do it!'

Though there was a considerable variety of styles and tempos, these later DJs played strictly soul. Bellars and his cohorts hunted down records from all manner of places: from London's influential Record Corner, from a raft of sources in the Midlands and from Stateside stores like Randy's Records in Tennessee. 'We were playing more what you'd have called rhythm and blues, but then we were playing new releases like the Incredibles, Sandy Sheldon and all the good Stateside stuff. We were playing imports like "Agent Double-O Soul" by Edwin Starr. We were playing things on Revilot and Ric-Tic. Everything on OKeh came out of the Wheel. They weren't necessarily frantically fast, but these were the forerunners of what became known as northern soul.'

Hunting for treasure

The reason northern soul jocks were forced to look for rarities was quite simple: by the early seventies, the US had largely stopped producing the right records. Black America had moved on from the snappy pop-soul of Motown, and its producers – alongside the hugely influential James Brown and Sly & the Family Stone – had started experimenting with other rhythms and sounds. Soul begat funk, and the accent transferred to languorous fatback rhythms rather than yearning melody. For Manchester, this wouldn't do at all. It was still great black music, but it was too funky and slow for a crowd hyped on a head full of pills. They needed something with a bit more urgency than 'Say It Loud, I'm Black And I'm Proud'. So the DJs started to dig deeper and look for older records that had the requisite beat and the by-now *de rigueur* helping of strings.

Ian Levine, later to become northern soul's most influential DJ, first visited the Wheel in the final period of its eight-year run. He recalls the change as the search for obscure oldies began.

'People were fed up with the same old songs – like Frankie Valli's "You're Ready Now" and Earl Van Dyke's "Six By Six" – that had been played at the Wheel for years. There was a hungry crowd at the all-nighters, pilled out of their heads on amphetamines, who wanted to dance to fast Motown-style records,' says Levine. 'Rob Bellars discovered that by finding these hard-to-get records, the scene thrived.'

It was this hunt that would uncover a vast well of previously unknown black soul records (and, eventually, some pretty execrable ones, too). Fast enough for jaw-crunching youths to get off on, and sometimes even great enough to cross over and become pop hits.

And just as they went to great lengths to find the right records for their dancefloor, these DJs were also learning how to work a crowd. Although most of them talked in between records, they were also learning how to sequence tracks to keep the bug-eyed dancers happy. 'A lot of the DJs would play records in a certain order, because of the way the people danced,' remembers Bellars, describing how he'd play three of Bobby Freeman's discs, 'The Duck', 'C'mon And Swim' and 'The Swim' in that order, because they built up in tempo. 'You'd build it up gradually, and then you'd play about five fast records on the run. Then you'd slow it down because it was getting so manic.'

Visitors to the Wheel were astonished. 'The dancing is without doubt the finest I have ever seen outside the USA,' wrote Dave Godin, a black music columnist in *Blues & Soul* and the man who started Tamla Motown's UK operation. 'Everybody there was an expert in soul clapping; in the right places, and with a clipped, sharp quality that adds an extra something in the appreciation of soul music. There was no undercurrent of tension or aggression that one sometimes finds in London clubs, but rather a benevolent atmosphere of friendship and camaraderie.'

Noting the strength of the soul scene in the north, Godin, a Londoner, gave it its name. Inspired by his first pilgrimage to the Twisted Wheel, he coined the term 'northern soul' in a *Blues & Soul* column in 1970. Godin co-owned a record store in Soho's Monmouth Street called Soul City. He first remarked upon the difference in tastes between the north and south when northerners, down on football trips from the north-west, asked for a specific sound. 'What I noticed was that people who came from the north were not buying what was subsequently called funk,' says Godin. 'So I started using the term "northern soul", meaning that when we've got a shop full of people from the north, we should only play northern soul to them. That's how the term took off.'

Manchester's Twisted Wheel provided much of the groundwork for what was to follow. As well as helping to inspire the scene's name, it had started the DJ on his obsessive hunt for undiscovered oldies, it had given him a network full of devoted (and musically knowledgeable) clubbers, and it had sparked the start of an intense love affair between white northern working-class youth and soulful black American music.

It had also consolidated the UK's lead in club culture. In the same period, New York had the plushest nightclubs, the most beautiful clientele, and sound systems that put those in Britain to shame. It didn't matter. In terms of musical sophistication and devoted club culture, what was going on in the north of England was streets ahead of everywhere else.

Inspired by the Wheel, numerous soul clubs sprang up to serve the growing network of DJs, fans and collectors. Leicester had the Oodly Boodly (later the Night Owl). There was the Mojo in Sheffield (where the DJ was a young Peter Stringfellow), the Dungeon in Nottingham, the Lantern in Market Harborough and the Blue Orchid in Derby. In Birmingham there were all-nighters at the Whiskey-A-Go-Go, a club informally known as the Laura Dixon Dance Studios. However, none of these approached the influence of the Twisted Wheel. It was here, in a dank basement in Manchester, that a generation of collectors, clubbers and DJs fell in love with soul music.

Unfortunately, the Wheel's reputation as a drug haven meant it was finally closed down by Manchester City Council sometime in early 1971. In its final incarnation, the only way they had been able to open at all was with the cooperation of the local police drugs squad, who insisted on having a presence in the club during the all-nighters.

There were emotional scenes on its final night. 'We knew it was going to close,' says Rob Bellars, 'but people were still crying.' Reflecting on the club's legacy, in June 1974 one soul-boy told *Black Music*, 'Something changed when the Wheel closed. You know, there was never quite the same everything-for-the-good-of-the-music scene.'

Farmer Carl at The Catacombs

One club inextricably linked to the Twisted Wheel was the Catacombs in Temple Street, Wolverhampton. Although its early closing (it shut at midnight) restricted this Midlands club's direct influence, it was here that much of northern soul's early musical menu was drafted. Its DJ, Farmer Carl Dene, did more than perhaps any other to build firm foundations for the genre. He was probably the first DJ on the scene to actually make an effort to unearth rare records, and one of the earliest to realise that having more rarities than your competitors could actually be a creative part of DJing. And by introducing and lending records to the DJs at the new Wheel, he was responsible for breaking many of northern soul's early anthems.

Farmer Carl Dene ('farmer' came from a hat he wore; Dene he felt was a suitably popstarish name) had started life as Carl Woodroffe. He discovered soul as a clubber first in his native Birmingham at the Whiskey-A-Go-Go, then at the Mojo in Sheffield and at the Twisted Wheel itself.

'I think it was because you couldn't hear it anywhere else,' he says. 'It was so unique. You wouldn't hear it on the radio. You wouldn't hear it in a regular nightclub. You'd have to go to a chosen place; and there were only a handful of those.' A fervent collector, he started DJing at Le Metro in Birmingham, then at Chateau Impney in Droitwich and then, most famously, at the Catacombs.

Farmer Carl had records no one else seemed to have. Rather than playing the famous version of a song, he would seek out the rawer, more unfamiliar covers and champion those. An example is the wondrously named 'I'm Not Going To Work Today' by Boot Hog Pefferley And The Loafers. This had been a minor hit for Clyde McPhatter, but Carl preferred the obscure version. He bought his copy from Roger Eagle. 'It really hit me, that one,' he remembers. 'So I bought it for £1 10s, which was a lot of money then!'

'He was the one that discovered the records that were taken up to the Wheel,' says Ian Levine, just one of the DJs who see Farmer Carl as the scene's mentor. 'He found this record by Richard Temple called "That Beating Rhythm" on Mirwood Records. Nobody even believed it existed. You had to go to the Catacombs to hear it.' Dene also introduced the Sharpees' 'Tired Of Being Lonely', Gene Chandler and Barbara Acklin's 'From The Teacher To The Preacher' and Doris Troy's northern classic 'I'll Do Anything' (Troy later provided the background vocals for Pink Floyd's *Dark Side Of The Moon*). 'Farmer Carl was the one they all thought of as a god,' declares Levine.

There were others influencing the DJs' playlists, including a renowned collector from Gloucester known as Docker. He caused merriment among soul fans at the Wheel by carrying a lockable record box. One of the gems in this high-security safe was the only copy in the country of Leon Haywood's 'Baby Reconsider', now regarded as a Wheel classic.

Although the scene was still in its formative years, it was already having an influence on the wider music industry – it was the nascent northern movement which spawned the first chart hits to have broken through the clubs rather than the radio. When a Contours' 45, 'Just A Little Misunderstanding' (originally recorded in 1965 and co-written by Stevie Wonder), slithered into the charts in January 1970, it heralded a new era in dance music in the UK. Tami Lynn's 'I'm Gonna Run From You' on John Abbey's Polydor-distributed Mojo Records, which reached no.4 (UK) in May 1971, soon followed. Abbey, as founder/owner of *Blues & Soul*, was in a privileged position to see the possibilities of this music. Confirmation of this new phenomenon came when the Tams' 'Hey Girl Don't Bother Me', a record Farmer Carl Dene had been instrumental in breaking, reached no.1 (UK) in July 1971.

'Everybody, particularly the girls, went absolutely wild about it,' he says. 'The company reissued it and Peter Powell, who was from Stourbridge, near to the Chateau in Droitwich, heard it and brought it on to the radio. He'd heard about the clamour for the record.'

The Torch

If the Twisted Wheel was the foundry in which the northern sound was smelted down, and the Catacombs was where it was hammered into shape, then the Torch in sleepy Tunstall, on the outskirts of Stoke-on-Trent, was where it was polished into gleaming stainless steel. The Wheel and Catacombs created a fad; the Torch turned it into a fetish. Although the club only lasted for a year (most of 1972 until its closure in March 1973), it exerts a powerful hold over everyone who remembers it.

The Torch's precursor, the Golden Torch, had during the sixties been a regular haunt of mods looking for a fix of rhythm and blues (acts including the Graham Bond Organisation and Johnny Johnson & the Bandwagon performed there). To get to it required orienteering skills that would have deterred all but the keenest – the nearest branch railway, Longport, was at least a mile away. From the outside it looked like a social club in the middle of a humdrum row of terraced houses (it was actually a converted cinema). Inside it looked like a ranch, and when full of dancers it steamed like a sauna.

'There was an air of expectation going in there,' says Ian Dewhirst, recalling his first all-nighter. Dewhirst would later be a key northern DJ, under the name 'Frank' (after Huddersfield footballer Frank Worthington). 'It was like a dream. Like suddenly knowing you're home. And this wonderful feeling of togetherness . . .' – a subtly ironic smile – 'All these other enthusiasts, misfits and nutters that had travelled from all over the place. It just felt like a really little, elite, very tight scene.'

The Torch's soundtrack was almost entirely American soul imports, many of which were culled from the Wheel's playlists. Its residents – Alan Day, Colin Curtis, Keith Minshull, Tony Jebb, Martyn Ellis and, latterly, Ian Levine – were all from the north-west. Kev Roberts, later a resident at Wigan Casino, recalls his first visit there. 'I absolutely loved it,' he enthuses. 'I lived for that particular club. I'd never come across so many unknown records in my life. And every one of them was a stonker. The song element was very important at the Torch, and the record had to have some substance to it. But they were all fast, furious great vocals. Girl groups. Odd labels. Obscurities on the OKeh label. They were great.'

Colin Curtis (who changed his name from Colin Dimond because it sounded too much like a DJ) recalls the way the Torch all-nighters galvanised the scene. 'What made it so buzzy and so effective – almost every hour there was a different set of people arriving from somewhere else. All these people who previously had been dotted about in small clubs, were all coming together. It made an atmosphere that, at the time, was unparalleled.'

One particular night at the Torch will be long remembered by those in attendance, when a packed house gathered to hear a performance by Major Lance, a Chicago vocalist well past his peak. Immortalised on a later recording, *Major Lance Live At The Torch*, it was one of the northern scene's most legendary appearances. With the scene resurrecting forgotten American soul records, it was inevitable someone would want to dig up the singers themselves. Imagine: you're Major Lance – fallen far from stardom in your own country – and out of the blue you get a phone call from some nutty Englishman with a funny accent, gushing about records even you have forgotten about. That's pretty much how it went. Singers like Jackie Wilson, Brenda Holloway and Edwin Starr found their careers enjoying a bizarre rebirth as a result.

'It's an opportunity I never got in the States,' Brenda Holloway said on Granada TV's *25 Years Of The Wigan Casino*. 'It's like a second chance. When I come over here I'm a star.'

Major Lance had sung on a series of fantastic tunes on OKeh (mostly written by Curtis Mayfield) that had been resounding flops everywhere in the UK apart from on the floors of clubs like the Wheel. He had only ever had one minor hit in the UK, 'Um Um Um Um Um Um', and that was back in 1964 (he had enjoyed six Top 40 hits in the US). The Torch's promoter, Chris Burton, had pulled off the not inconsiderable feat of locating Lance in Chicago and bringing him over for a performance. In spite of his lacklustre accompaniment, Lance brought the house down.

'He sang with the worst band you've ever heard! It was some British band who had no concept of what northern soul was,' recalls Ian Levine. 'But that night was the first night I DJed there and it was the most electrifying night of my whole career.' His voice rising, he adds, 'You could not have squeezed one more person in that club. They were hanging off the rafters. It must've been a hundred-and-twenty degrees. It was so hot and packed, the sweat was rising off people's bodies as condensation and dripping back on to them from the ceiling.'

Wigan Casino vs Blackpool Mecca

Northern soul was too esoteric to ever become a mainstream movement. Its defining feature was rarity. You couldn't walk into Woolies and buy any of its records, you had to prove your love for them – either by paying a week's wages for a single dusty disc or by somehow visiting the States and scouring junk shops and cut-out warehouses. Even before you could do this, there would be an extended apprenticeship as you studied the names of the most prized tunes, and learned each record's evocative history: who made it, why it was passed over, how it was discovered, who played it first . . .

The scene did cross over to some extent. There were chart hits when certain records were reissued by major labels and there were new bands attempting to recreate that northern soul sound. On the whole, though, as a retro movement, it had an inbuilt protection against commercialisation, since it revolved around collectors not consumers. The converse of this was that it contained the seeds of its own destruction. By definition, a scene based on discovering 'new' oldies would eventually run out of fresh music.

The soul scene's golden era was centred around two clubs. In Wigan, a Lancashire cotton town, there was the Casino. An hour's drive away in Blackpool, at the mercy of the Irish Sea, there was the Mecca (more exactly, the Mecca's Highland Rooms). These two cathedrals of soul vied with each other to play the rarest, hottest records. Thousands of kids crisscrossed the country to hear their resident DJs throw down the latest unbelievable discoveries amid a barrage of scorching favourites. Clubbers to this day have fierce arguments over which was the best of the two places, their memories gloriously misted from the music, the people, the emotions and the drugs.

Eventually, these same two clubs would preside over the death of the scene. After sharing northern soul's glory years the rivalry between Wigan Casino and the Blackpool Mecca would accelerate into warfare as they fought over the soul of soul, enduring the scene's bitter identity crisis, disputing the direction to be taken when the world's supply of great lost tunes was finally exhausted. However, for many years before that, they were both amazing places. Both the Mecca and the Casino still conjure memories for a whole generation of northern clubbers – memories of walking in, their hearts in their mouths, ready to dance themselves into pools of sweat; memories of dancehalls steamy with gurning soul boys and girls leaping and spinning to stomping drums and pleading voices.

In 1978 *Billboard* declared the Wigan Casino the world's best discothèque, only a year before it awarded New York's Paradise Garage the same accolade. For many, Wigan Casino is synonymous with northern soul. Open between 1973 and 1981, in its heyday it was the biggest, most successful nationally known expression of a solidly regional scene. It had a huge membership (100,000 at its peak) and pulled in a vast number of punters week in, week out. It was undoubtedly popular. However, claims that it was actually the *best* of the northern soul clubs need to be taken with a pinch of salt. It wasn't the most influential, it certainly wasn't the most adventurous and, towards its final years, as it purveyed a procession of sometimes laughable records whose only merit was a snappy northern beat, it somewhat undermined its claims to the northern crown. Writer John McCready has compared it to today's Ministry of Sound, urging that historians shouldn't overemphasise its importance simply because it crammed in the most people. Nevertheless, the name Wigan Casino holds a special place in the memories of thousands, and even today for many it represents the true northern soul club: the Heart of Soul.

If the Casino was the punters' choice, then the Blackpool Mecca was the connoisseurs'. It was here that the most devoted dancers, collectors and disc jockeys gathered every week to check out the latest unearthed tunes. Mecca's resident DJ, Ian Levine, had a big advantage over other soul collectors and disc jockeys of the time. He had wealthy parents (they owned the Lemon Tree entertainment complex on the town's Golden Mile, which included a casino, disco and nightclub), and from 1970 onwards he had been making trips over to the US (his parents also owned an apartment in Miami) and unearthing rare records. Levine's first major discoveries were JJ Barnes's 'Our Love Is In The Pocket' and a bunch of other Ric-Tic rarities. 'I found them in a joke shop in a hundred-and-ten-degree heat in New Orleans,' he laughs. Levine is a large, loud, forceful character who now writes for and produces pop acts like boy bands Take That and Bad Boys Inc.

Levine had started DJing at the Mecca in 1971, then played at the Torch towards the end of its brief tenure in 1973, before returning to his residency at Blackpool. Here, he and Colin Curtis reigned for the rest of the decade. Blackpool had other notable DJs including Tony Jebb and Keith Minshull, and another soul club, Blackpool Casino (no relation), but it was Levine and Curtis who wowed the crowds with the most soul discoveries, courtesy of Levine's bottomless pockets and erudite taste.

The Mecca became a weekly must. 'If you were a serious collector, the only place you could conceive of going was Blackpool Mecca,' says Ian Dewhirst. 'Levine was there, and Levine was the arbiter of taste. He always had the most breathtaking array of records. You might not know them all, but you'd know they'd all be good. And he would take *chances*. You'd never have heard "Seven Day Lover" by James Fountain at Wigan. I have to give him respect, even though he's pretty irritating to be around a lot of the time.'

Construction had begun on the Wigan Casino in 1912. It was then known as the Empress Ballroom. As a result of the war effort, it wasn't completed until 1 November 1916, when local mayor JT Anson officially opened the vast arena. The Emp, as it was known locally, served various functions over the years, including a period as a billiard hall, but when Russ Winstanley placed the Sherrys' 'Put Your Lovin' Arms Around Me' on the platter on 22 September 1973, at the first Wigan Casino all-nighter, the building took on a new life. This was the first chapter in a club story that has passed into mythology.

In truth, few connoisseurs were impressed with what they found on that first evening. Russ Winstanley had some decent records, but few of them were particularly rare, while his cohort, Ian Fishwick, was nothing more than a local pop DJ struck lucky. Kev Roberts stopped off on the way back from the Mecca that first night. 'I distinctly remember it,' he says. 'There weren't many DJs on, and the music wasn't crap exactly, but the records were easily available. There wasn't much I didn't know.' After the Mecca, where he could be sure of hearing rare records he didn't yet own, it was an anticlimax to hear such familiar music.

Roberts's friends were so incensed that they harangued Winstanley to give their friend a DJing spot, arguing that his collection was far superior. He got his chance that same night.

'I played an hour's worth of my top tunes and they went down a storm,' chuckles Roberts. 'They loved them. I was up there absolutely petrified. It was a massive room. And Russ came up to me and said, "Great. Do you wanna work here every week? Ten pounds."'

The recruitment of another DJ, Richard Searling from Va Va's in Bolton, helped seal Wigan's place as the spot of the moment, especially since when the Mecca was closing at 2am, Wigan was just opening. Many soulies went to both clubs regularly, not caring about any distinction between their playlists. When the Mecca closed, they would often head for Wigan to dance out what was left of the night.

'By Christmas of 1973, no disrespect to Blackpool Mecca but they were running second,' claims Kev Roberts. 'There were two thousand people at the Casino every week. Even though Ian Levine at the Mecca was the most creative, he was the most innovative, he had the best records, it didn't make any difference. With Russ, myself and, by January 1974, Richard Searling, whatever we played, we had an even bigger dancefloor.' Even Levine himself is reflective about their rivalry, freely conceding that 'it was Kev, Russ and Richard who took Wigan to great heights.'

There's no questioning the atmosphere at the (alcohol-free) Casino. It was electric. The huge maplewood dancefloor would bounce as though it had independent life, while a monochrome blur of dervishes performed ever more complex rituals of drops, backflips, handclaps and spins. The dancers were dressed from head to foot in soul garb: high-waisted pleated trousers with wide flapping legs known as 'Brummie Bags', bowling shirts, singlets or Ben Shermans, white socks, flat leather-soled shoes and an Adidas or Gola sports bag stuffed full of the night's essentials. These would include talcum powder to dust the dancefloor, a change of clothes, a few 45s to sell or trade and, of course, gear.

The room took on an opaque sheen from the condensation steaming off the dancers. It was like looking through net curtain. And while the grandeur might have long since deserted the Emp (it didn't bear to inspect the carpets, fittings or toilets for too long), there was no doubt about the ambience. They might not have had the best music. But they had the most fun.

Reissues and commercialisation

A few sharp movers were soon realising there was money to be made from reissuing some of the biggest songs. On visiting the Casino, an old soul DJ called Dave McAleer, who was also an A&R man for the British label Pye, realised northern soul's sales potential was growing. The success of the Tams and Tami Lynn had hinted as much, and by this stage the Mecca and the Torch had broken two other records: Archie Bell & the Drells' 'Here I Go Again' and the stone-cold northern monster, 'Love On A Mountain Top' by Robert Knight. McAleer set up the Disco Demand label to specifically deal with northern soul. Others followed his lead.

By the mid seventies, commercial successes would happen almost weekly: Betty Wright's 'Where Is The Love?', Esther Phillips's 'What A Difference A Day Makes', George Benson's 'Supership' and Al Wilson's 'The Snake' all crashed the charts. But it was pastiches rather than reissues which crossed over with more force. Despite Pye having the UK licensing rights to some sought-after labels like Scepter and Roulette, the first pop hit was 'Footsee' by Wigan's Chosen Few, a faintly risible concoction that had originally begun life as the B-side to a surf record. (The 'Wigan' was added to avoid court action from Island Records, who had a Chosen Few on their roster.)

'Footsee', although mitigated by having the credible 'Seven Days Is Too Long' by soul-howler Chuck Wood on the flip side, was miles away from true northern soul. However, for the *Top Of The Pops* TV appearance in February 1975, they recruited some of the best young dancers from the floor of the Casino. Kids around the country must have wondered what this bizarre dancing was all about: part jazz dance, part freestyle, with even a foretaste of breakdancing in there, too. As Russ Winstanley said, they made Pan's People look like clog dancers.

Then there was Wigan's Ovation. If anything, even worse than Wigan's Chosen Few, the Ovation were a white pop act previously called Sparkle whose cover version of the Invitations' 'Skiing In The Snow' (the original record is as rare as hen's teeth) made the top 20 two months later. The connoisseurs and true soul fans were disgusted. 'They had these horrible pop novelty hits that were masquerading as northern soul,' fumes Levine. 'Thousands of new people would see these dancers on *Top Of The Pops* and a new crowd descended on Wigan, who were really like sightseers and tourists who'd got into northern soul through the TV exposure it got.'

To be fair to the Casino, it was breaking other records, too: Frankie Valli & the Four Seasons' 'The Night' and Rodger Collins's 'Sexy Sugar Plum' were two of the more credible additions to the canon which came from Wigan. And what was undeniable was that it captured the imagination of many thousands of clubbers. In that sense Wigan Casino was probably the first truly national club, drawing dancers from all corners of the British Isles.

Fighting for the soul of soul

'There was only one golden era of northern soul,' says Kev Roberts. 'There was only one definitive playlist. Now, you can argue about how many records were on that playlist – the absolutely stonking mega dancefloor fillers, I'm talking "Landslide", "There's A Ghost In My House", "Tainted Love" – but really it's no more than about two hundred.'

Dave Godin agrees. 'When the northern soul scene was at its most vigorous,' he says, 'there was this tremendous search for obscurities, and a lot of great records surfaced as a result. But after a while, the chances of discovering some old masterpiece diminish. All the masterpieces have surfaced.'

This was the issue that started to face northern soul around the mid seventies. Where could it go when there were no more old records to discover?

At Wigan, the DJs stuck doggedly to what they knew, maintaining the traditional sound by championing oldies of rapidly decreasing quality. Preserving the styles their dancers loved so much led to an unrelenting diet of stompers (the term for the frenetic Detroit-style soul oldies), songs which fitted the northern soul blueprint however crass they were.

Levine's answer, far more controversial, was to look to the present for fresh sounds, adding modern soul tunes, disco 12-inches and jazz–funk to the menu. In the eyes of many, this was a travesty. This was a scene that fetishised the old, the dusty and the anonymous. A northern soul DJ was breaking the rules of his trade if he dared tamper with its stomping sound and play genuinely new (and easily available) records. As Levine exercised his broad tastes, he found himself cleaving a deep split in the scene.

He may have been determined to break with the constraints of the music, but Levine had not entirely forsaken the northern sound. On one of his Stateside forays – he claims it was as early as 1971 – he returned with yet another rarity. Incredibly, it was on Motown, a label so successful – and available – that its records normally had little cachet on the northern circuit.

'Levine comes back from the States and, of course, I'm on the phone on the Saturday afternoon,' recalls Ian Dewhirst. 'And he says, "I've got the greatest northern soul record ever" – but he used to say this all the time – "It's 'There's A Ghost In My House' by R Dean Taylor." That night he played it about six times and by the third play everybody realised that, yes, it is the greatest record ever.' Overnight this became the most wanted record in the country. The buzz spread. Levine had done it again. When Tamla Motown reissued it, it shot to no.3 (UK). Nowadays, because Taylor was white, Levine has less affinity for the record.

'R Dean Taylor, really, is a nasty white pop record on Motown,' he says, surprisingly. 'I suppose I should be ashamed of it.'

Despite extracting such gems, Levine continued to innovate. He and Curtis brought in records that, although still relatively rare, were new releases. Over the years, certain new releases had been accepted, but only when their sound fitted the soul mould (jazz drummer Paul Humphrey's fluke northern hit 'Cochise', being one example). However, at the Mecca, the mould was being defiantly broken.

The division got deeper and more unpleasant as time went on. The diehards saw their traditions being shattered; the modernisers felt Levine was breathing new life into the scene. Like the 1965 furore over Bob Dylan going electric, it showed just how important this music was to people.

Ian Levine remembers a time when the Blackpool and Wigan crowds were brought together in Manchester's Ritz for an all-dayer put on by Midlands promoter Neil Rushton. The Mecca clubbers were there to hear Levine and Curtis, the Casino dancers to hear Richard Searling. The Wiganites made it clear what they thought of Levine.

'It was like two football crowds: Manchester City and Manchester United. It didn't work,' he recalls. 'At that time we were playing all this modern disco stuff: Doctor Buzzard's Original Savannah Band, Tavares, "Car Wash", "Jaws" by Lalo Schifrin. And they were playing anything with a stomping beat. All of these Wiganites with their singlets and baggy pants were shouting, "Fuck off! Get off! Play some stompers!" ' A campaign was started to get rid of Levine. Casino fans sported buttons with the bald legend 'LEVINE MUST GO'. One Saturday, two fans even walked through the Mecca with a huge banner bearing the same slogan.

Today, even Levine has his regrets. 'I'll go on record here and say: We went too far,' he states firmly. 'The northern soul scene was very special. We started with the Carstairs and Marvin Holmes, which were equally rare but more modern. Then we're playing Tavares and Crown Heights Affair, Kool & the Gang even. And suddenly, you weren't hearing anything that you couldn't hear anywhere else. It had no uniqueness about it. We should've stopped it before it went too far. Because what we did was split that scene into two with an axe.'

Levine was gaining much of his inspiration from his frequent trips to the clubs of New York's underground gay scene. Visiting places like Infinity and 12 West, he saw how the early disco records could generate as much energy on the dancefloor as any northern stomper. As well as Levine's distinct sensibilities (he would later enjoy a second career as the pioneer of hi-energy, a fast disco variant with obvious northern soul features), there were other factors encouraging a split. Since the Casino was an all-nighter, it's safe to assume that its dancers were more intoxicated than the Mecca's. There was also the fact that the Wigan dancefloor was much bigger. Kev Roberts agrees that the size of the venue made a big difference. 'On that massive dancefloor, unless the tempo was really kicking immediately the record was a no-no,' he explains. As has often happened in dance music, at Wigan the needs of the dancers and their drugs were in the driving seat.

As the music changed, the Mecca's clubbers became noticeably more urban in appearance, wearing more current styles than their Wigan comrades. As clubber and DJ Norman Jay noted on a late-seventies visit there, the fashions wouldn't have looked out of place in London.

Incidentally, the Casino/Mecca split conjures interesting parallels with the evolution of jungle many years later. In the early nineties, as the masses moved in to the clubs and adjusted their tastes to a less frenetic music, the diehards of the rave scene partied on in their own, largely ignored world, and in an echo of the Wigan love for stompers, hardcore rave music became a faster, rougher, ever more absurd parody of itself (undeniably an acceleration driven by changing drug habits). The irony is that out of this fierce preservationist attitude and its much-reviled music came the radical new genre of jungle.

In northern soul's case, it was the progressives rather than the traditionalists who came up with the goods. It's hard to imagine such deeply held opinions now, but many considered Curtis and Levine heretics and pariahs for what they were doing. However, they took northern soul out of its fossilised past and gave it a future. The new sound emerging at Blackpool Mecca was led initially by records like the Carstairs' 'It Really Hurts Me Girl' which, as Levine says, still had 'a northern soul feel but with a slightly shuffly beat'. But the changes were really crystallised when another record made it to the turntables.

'The O'Jays' "I Love Music" really opened the doors, I think, to new singles,' says Kev Roberts. 'It paved the way for things like "Heaven Must Be Missing An Angel", which was a northern soul monster, and "Young Hearts Run Free", another one perfect for a northern crowd.' Levine was given the O'Jays' record to play by Roberts, who had by now quit Wigan in a dispute with Russ Winstanley and was making judicious use of Freddie Laker's £59 each way flights to New York for record-hunting trips. Somehow he managed to prize a test-pressing out of the hands of New York jock Tony Gioe, who had got it straight from Kenny Gamble, its producer.

The success of this Philly disco stormer on the Mecca's dancefloor encouraged Levine to break completely with any lingering traditions.

'From the moment "I Love Music" had been accepted, Ian made a pact with himself to say northern is unofficially dead,' affirms Roberts. 'He went completely into the disco thing. In some quarters it worked a treat, and he captured a different audience. But some of the hustle type records he was playing were not well received in northern soul terms.'

As Mecca moved determinedly on, throwing anything from Philly International to Funkadelic into the melting pot, Wigan reacted violently with an increasing horrorshow of pop stompers. Ron Grainer Orchestra's 'Theme From Joe 90' got played. As did 'Hawaii 5-0' by the Ventures. One DJ, Richard Searling, did his best to preserve some dignity in the music selections, his thumb stuck in the dam, but it wasn't enough. It looked like northern soul was parodying itself.

Cleethorpes

In 1976 a third player entered the fray as the Lincolnshire seaside town of Cleethorpes hosted some golden-era soul. A husband and wife team, Colin and Mary Chapman from Scunthorpe, found a venue on the faded east-coast resort, which had staged everything from Leo Sayer concerts to Nolan Sisters' summer shows. When the wind blew, the Pier audibly creaked. Stuffed full of several hundred northern soul dancers, it creaked some more. They recruited the roster of disc jockeys mainly from local unknowns like Poke and Chris Scott, and after adding veteran residents like Ian Dewhirst, forged a sound that was essentially an amalgam of the Casino and Mecca.

'That has to be one of the greatest venues ever, as far as mystique goes,' claims Dewhirst. 'I used to get to the Pier about four in the morning and by that point all you'd hear was this stomp, stomp, stomp from about a mile-and-a-half away. It would be the dancing. It was surreal. There's this place jutting out into the sea. It's four in the morning. And all you can hear is STOMP! Multiplied times a thousand.'

Dave Godin championed Cleethorpes. Ian Levine got mad. 'Cleethorpes's success grew out of Dave Godin's attention to them,' he asserts. 'But it was better music than Wigan.'

Jonathan Woodliffe recalls a trip there back in its soul days. It was a freezing winter's night. The snow was being blown in almost horizontally from the North Sea. 'All I can remember is this door opening in the distance,' he says, 'a mountain of steam coming out and the smell of Brut talcum powder, and entering the room and hearing World Column's "So Is The Sun". Whenever I hear that record, it always takes me back to that smell and that time.' Perhaps tellingly, these days the Pier plays host to occasional wild hardcore raves.

Stafford

Another latterday contender arrived in the early 1980s with the Stafford all-nighters at the Top of the World. Its two rooms incorporated the many strands of northern, with DJs like the Casino's Richard Searling playing an increasingly modern sound (to increasingly disgruntled traditionalists), but with Dave Thorley striking a conciliatory tone with sixties and seventies sounds, while Pat Brady, Butch and Dave Withers looked to the past for the future.

Stafford's two militants were Guy Hennigan and Keb Darge who brought an ascetic rigour to their sets and set about breaking a bewildering series of new 45s. They were aided considerably by contacts at reissue outfits Charly and Kent (where northern soul fan Ady Croasdell worked) giving them access to unreleased material on the Scepter, Wand, Brunswick and Sound Stage 7 labels, yielding songs like Roscoe Shelton's 'You Are The Dream' and Chuck Carter's 'I'm A Lover'.

'When Guy and me came in we were, "Right, we're going to play sixties newies," ' recalls Keb Darge, 'and it was four or five years of constant sixties newies. There were so many new good records to be played. And our sets were so much more soulful than the sets they played at Wigan. They could have done the same fuckin' thing. They just didn't want to do the work to find the stuff.'

The birth of the trainspotter

Northern soul's most significant contribution to the DJ's trade was to introduce the idea of connoisseurship. Previously, this had been the exclusive province of the collector of classical music, with a few jazz and blues addicts following behind. But until soul, dance music had been largely about playing the hits of the day. Since the northern scene thrived on rarities, it made the DJ's profession as much archaeology as record playing. The DJ had a new avenue of creativity to explore: he was a musical researcher, an evangelist of obscurities – a 'trainspotter'.

Back in the Catacombs and the Twisted Wheel, the DJ started to realise that the rarity of his records was another tool with which to build a distinctive performance. Today's notion of rarity is less about old gems and more about anoraked techno nerds championing unheard-of test-pressings by twelve-year-old geniuses on tiny labels based in garages in Canada, but the prestige of rarity introduced by northern soul has never left dance music. Clubbers would journey hundreds of miles at the thought of hearing that one elusive disc. Posters included lists of the rare records you would hear at a particular event, and a DJ's standing on the circuit could rocket overnight by the simple expedient of acquiring one desirable 45.

'The more the DJs had got a record that was on a tiny little Los Angeles or Detroit or Chicago label,' says Levine, 'the more people would travel from Gloucester, Scotland and Yorkshire to hear them, because they couldn't hear them anywhere else.'

Ian Dewhirst's big break came when he chanced upon a copy of the Carstairs' 'It Really Hurts Me Girl' lying ignored at the back of a London soul dealer's box at the Heavy Steam Machine in Hanley. Although it was a new record, it was incredibly rare since its label, Red Coach, had lost their distribution deal with Chess in Chicago and it had never been released; the only copies being ultra-rare radio promos.

'I'm flicking all the way through and the last two records are the Carstairs' "It Really Hurts Me Girl" and Dena Barnes's "If You Ever Walk Out Of My Life",' recalls Dewhirst. 'The two biggest records in the country and he's got them at the back of his box in paper sleeves.' Dewhirst handed over the £15 for the Carstairs (he didn't have enough for the pair).

'Jesus Christ, man, if you want everything on one record, then this record's got it,' he gushes. 'The most passionate vocal on it, scintillating beat, brilliant strings, and produced by Gene Redd, the fucking archdeacon of northern soul. Everything compressed into this one record. I spent almost a week looking at the label.' He also found his gig rate rocketed overnight.

Kev Roberts tells a similar excited tale. On trading some British releases for a grab bag of US records, he found to his astonishment two incredible and super-rare records: Patti Austin's 'Pain Stain' and Sandra Phillips' 'World Without Sunshine'. 'I was the first person ever,' he beams. 'I mean, Ian Levine didn't even have them. So I started to play them and my reputation went like *WOW!* Suddenly I was getting gigs from all over the place. Really, my reputation grew over the course of four weeks.'

The northern grapevine was such that if a hot record was played at the Mecca or the Casino one evening, by lunchtime the next day everyone would know about it. The legend of Levine discovering 'There's A Ghost In My House' is a case in point. As soon as the record was heard, dealers were sent scurrying to the US. Calls were made. Shops were scoured.

Nothing. 'Then the weirdest thing happened,' says Ian Dewhirst. 'Someone was coming back from Wigan Casino and went into a motorway service station. They bent down to get a Sunday paper and there was a rack of those old Music For Pleasure budget LPs, and in among them was an R Dean Taylor compilation called *Indiana Wants Me*. Track three, side two, there it was: "There's A Ghost In My House". So it's in every record shop in the country and we all fucking missed it!'

The world's rarest record

The undisputed champion of champions in the northern soul premier league of rare records is Frank Wilson's 'Do I Love You?'. For a long time there was only one known copy in existence in the whole world. Wilson worked for Motown, and had already had some success as producer of the Checkerboard Squares' 'Double Cookin', already a big hit on the soul scene.

'Do I Love You?' had all the ingredients for a dancefloor smash, including soaring production, a zippy vocal delivery and an instantly familiar hook (since this book first came out British readers have heard it in a KFC ad). However, after Wilson had recorded it, and even after the records had been pressed up ready for distribution, Motown boss Berry Gordy somehow convinced him not to put it out. 'You don't want all the pressures of being an artist, stick with production,' Gordy is said to have told him. Consequently, all but one or two copies of the record were destroyed.

The record came to light courtesy of Simon Soussan, a Burton's tailor who had fallen for soul at the Twisted Wheel in 1969, and who had been the first person to trek to America and sell commercially, via collectors' lists, the rare records he found there. (Some of the great records he introduced were Connie Clark's 'My Sugar Baby', Louise Lewis's 'With You I'll Let It Be You Babe' and 'Dirty Hearts' by Benny Curtis.) On a trip to LA, Soussan got his hands on 'Do I Love You?'. Stories vary as to how. Some say he *acquired* it from the Motown vaults in Los Angeles. Others claim he was loaned it by Tom dePierro, a Motown employee and former DJ.

Soussan knew immediately the record was a monster and had an acetate copy made and sent to Russ Winstanley at Wigan Casino, who protected its identity by telling people it was by someone called Eddie Foster (Winstanley's claims to ownership of the actual record, as documented in his book, *Soul Survivors*, are entirely false). It was an immediate hit.

The original eventually came to the UK when dance music retailer Les McCutcheon (who later discovered Shakatak) bought Soussan's collection. Jonathan Woodliffe bought it from McCutcheon in a deal worth £500, which was then so much money that he paid in instalments. 'At that time – I suppose it's like the transfer market with footballers – £500 was the highest anyone had paid for a record,' says Woodliffe. The record became nothing less than legendary. People wanted to see it, touch it. 'I used to go to gigs and people used to ask me to get this record out of my box so they could take a photograph of it,' laughs Woodliffe.

Woodliffe sold it to Kev Roberts, who held on to it for the next ten years, until Tim Brown, one of Roberts's partners in the Goldmine reissue label, paid him £5,000 for it in 1991. However, the plot thickened when another collector, Martin Koppel, somehow unearthed another copy in 1993. This one sold to a collector in Scotland in the summer of 1998 for an amazing £15,000. The track was reissued by Tamla Motown UK in 1980, and even copies of the reissue now fetch upwards of £40.

Cover-ups

Inevitably, competition grew between DJs, and to protect new discoveries they would cover the label and give them false names. 'Covering up' can be seen as the forerunner to modern DJs' white label exclusives, or the hip hop DJs' habit of soaking off the labels from their most treasured breaks. The practice actually originated in the early sixties. Mick Eve, a musician active on the all-nighter scene, recalls Count Suckle covering up records like Nina Simone's 'My Baby Just Cares For Me', a practice the DJ had imported from Jamaica. However, it was soul jocks who popularised it, both to preserve their exclusives and also as a way of throwing bootleggers off the scent.

'It's only really the same as people playing acetates today, but these days instead of covering old records they've gone right to the source,' argues Jonathan Woodliffe.

Dave Godin, however, hated the practice. 'If I went somewhere and a DJ had some exclusive cover-up I knew, I would immediately blow the whistle and review it. Fuck it. They were putting their own ego above the singer, the composer and everyone else, and I couldn't abide that.'

Farmer Carl Dene, the first northern DJ to cover up, would cut out the centre of an unused record and place it on top of the record spinning, something he did for Jackie Lee's 'Darkest Days', Donald Height's 'She Blew A Good Thing' and others. Rob Bellars at the Wheel was the first person to cover up *and* rename the song. Thus Bobby Paterson's 'What A Wonderful Night For Love' became Benny Harper's 'What A Wonderful Night'. This trend spread like a virus: the Checkerboard Squares' 'Double Cookin' became the faintly ludicrous 'Strings-A-Go-Go' by Bob Wilson

Sound, while the Coasters' 'Crazy Baby' was transformed into Freddie Jones' 'My Heart's Wide Open'.

Ady Croasdell, a regular at the Casino (and later the man behind both the 100 Club all-nighters and Kent Records), took a Tony Blackburn version of Doris Troy's 'I'll Do Anything' and handed it to DJ Keith Minshull, claiming it was Lenny Gamble. Incredibly, Minshull played it. 'It was just supposed to be a joke,' Croasdell said in *Soul Survivors*. 'When he played it and everyone danced to it, I thought that maybe the punters weren't too discerning.'

Rip-offs and bootlegs

The new obsession with rarities provided fertile ground for rip-offs and bootlegs. Simon Soussan, who had discovered the Frank Wilson record, would bolster his sales lists with fictitious titles, asking customers always to include second choices with their requests. One such imaginary record was 'Reaching For The Best' by Bob Relf (Relf was a genuine artist who'd had some success with a song called 'Blowing My Mind To Pieces'). With the status of his list enhanced by such a 'rare' record, Soussan garnered several offers. None, of course, received the new Bob Relf, though Soussan cleared his stockroom by selling everyone their second choice records. In a hilarious turnabout to the tale, Ian Levine stole the title from Soussan and wrote a real song for it. It was his first production, 'Reaching For The Best' by The Exciters, and it reached no.31 in the UK pop charts in October 1975.

It was common practice for DJs to have acetate copies made of their rarest records. Such 7-inch one-off bootlegs were known as Emidiscs and were used by many jocks desperate for the next best thing to the genuine article. However, this was only the tip of the bootleggers' iceberg.

Selectadisc in Nottingham (a crucial store in the development of the northern scene) was supplied with an endless supply of 'pressings' by Simon Soussan, based in the US. Pressings were, supposedly, legally licensed limited runs of certain sought-after records. Their legality was debated, although in an interview with *Black Music* in February 1976, Soussan denied bootlegging. 'You can go to jail for two years and pay a fine of $10,000 for bootlegging. I haven't paid any fine because I haven't bootlegged any records.'

There were several other bogus labels, one of which was Out Of The Past. Many original soul records sounded like they'd been recorded in a barn. By the time they emerged on Out Of The Past, they sounded like they'd been recorded in a bucket.

Beach music

There is a strange echo of northern soul in America called beach music, a thriving sub-culture based around a series of resort towns in North and South Carolina, where kids gather to dance the shag to obscure rhythm and blues records. Its initial constituency was mainly working-class whites whose clandestine trips to resorts like Myrtle and Virginia Beaches provided an opportunity in a deeply racist society to dance to forbidden black records. (Beach music was even immortalised in the utterly dreadful 1990 movie *Shag*.)

Although beach music only gained its tag in 1965, it has been around since 1945 thanks to influential radio jocks like John Richbourg, Hoss Allen and Gene Nobles. And because beach music exists apart from the mainstream recording industry, it has retained much of the original integrity of northern soul. Both scenes have several classics in common: Guy Darrell's 'I've Been Hurt', The Tams' 'Be Young Be Foolish Be Happy' and 'What A Difference A Day Makes' by Esther Phillips. Incredibly, there were even a couple of clubs in the Virginia Beach district called the Mecca and the Casino.

Nowadays it's organised around the Association of Beach and Shag Club DJs and thanks to the efforts of DJ John Hook and a specialist record store called the Wax Museum in Charlotte, North Carolina, the sound of beach music lives on. In a small corner of the American southeast, the search for rare vinyl and great dance records continues.

From northern soul to nu-energy

Northern soul was the revenge of the small town. Although it was cradled in metropolitan Manchester, its fabled clubs formed a map of deep geographical unfashionability: Tunstall, Wigan, Blackpool, Cleethorpes. Despite its near-complete isolation from London and from the established music industry, its influence was impressive.

Many DJs schooled in the dance halls, bingo halls, and discos of the northern circuit ended up playing a role in the early UK development of house: Mike Pickering, Colin Curtis, Jonathan Woodliffe, Ian Dewhirst, Ian Levine, Pete Waterman. Musically, its effect has been greater subsequently than it ever was at the time. In tracks like Soft Cell's 'Tainted Love' and 'What' (originally by Gloria Jones and Judy Street respectively), and M People's 'One Night In Heaven' and 'How Can I Love You More?' (which owe a debt to Linda Carr's 'Highwire' and the Trammps' 'Where Do We Go From Here'), the northern songs have lived on. Artists including Paul Weller, Ocean Colour Scene, St Etienne and Belle & Sebastian openly acknowledge their love for the genre, and Fatboy Slim's huge 1999 no.1 (UK) hit 'Rockafeller Skank' sampled the northern instrumental 'Sliced Tomatoes' by the Just Brothers to great effect. As we'll see there is a direct lineage from northern soul to Ian Levine's hi-energy and hence to the 'nu-energy' of popular DJs like Blu Peter, Tall Paul and the late Tony De Vit.

As a scene built entirely from flops, it has also bequeathed an impressive vault of classic Motown-influenced soul records that would have otherwise remained undiscovered. It also gave careers – albeit brief ones – to singers who'd long since returned to the car plant assembly lines of Detroit. And all thanks to the thousands of dancers from nondescript northern towns who held the torch and kept the faith.

Perhaps the greatest legacy of northern soul was a cultural one. It is impossible to ignore its uncanny resemblance to the house/rave movement of a decade-and-a-half later, and given the number of DJs with a hand in both scenes it would be hard to claim that this was simply coincidence. Praising its spirit of togetherness, Jonathan Woodliffe compares northern soul to the post-Ibiza house network. 'It's the only scene I've come across in twenty-three years' DJing and clubbing where there was such a close-knit community,' he says. 'Everybody knew everybody.'

Northern soul created a nationwide network connecting clubs, record collectors and DJs. Although it provided the charts with their first club-born records, for every tune that crossed over there were another fifty that never made it beyond the walls of an all-nighter. Northern soul was as pure an underground movement as is ever likely to exist. It encouraged a fierce, tribal loyalty and it provided nights of sweaty drug-ridden escapism for thousands of devoted dancers. For those who think that the rave movement started club culture: think again.

Nowadays, most northern all-nighters are populated by originals returning after their kids have grown up, looking to rediscover the music of their youth (if not their hair or figure). Even with the rise of the weekender events and their popularity with a younger crowd, the northern scene can never have the same vibrancy it once had. But that shouldn't detract from the great records and special clubs of twenty-five years ago.

'Everybody thought I was crazy,' laughs clubber Andy Wynne, recalling when he told friends he intended to buy the sign from the Wigan Casino. 'I told the people at work I was taking Thursday and Friday off. They asked if I was going away. I said, "No, I'm going to Wigan." You couldn't begin to explain to them. They wouldn't understand. It signified a particularly happy time in my life when I discovered the greatest music, the greatest atmosphere, the greatest scene . . .' Wynne fondles the sign. 'It's great. It's a piece of art to me.'

And the records speak for themselves: 7-inch slithers of raw emotion. Collectors today are regularly paying four-figure sums for rarities and, while you may question the sanity of someone offering fifteen grand for a 7-inch single with a coffee stain on the B-side, ultimately it's the music that compels them to do this. 'I'll die of shock if, in twenty years' time, you get out of bed and travel two hundred miles to listen to some old Prodigy B-sides,' wrote John McCready in *The Face*. 'Or pay five thousand pounds for an Aphex Twin record.'

FIVE
REGGAE

Wreck Up A Version

'No matter what the people say . . .
These sounds lead the way . . .
It's the order of the day from your boss deejay.'

– King Stitt, 'Fire Corner'

'Dub – verb, to make space.'

– *Coldcut A–Z*

When it was untouched by Europe, the Arawaks called their fertile island Xaymaca, meaning 'Land of Springs'. When it was the pirate capital of the seven seas, its main city Port Royal was the wickedest in the world. When it was a colonial sugar plantation powered by stolen African muscle, a slave owner could be fined if one of his chattels was caught banging a drum. When it was reborn independent of Britain's imperial rule, in Jamaica the DJ was king.

This tropical volcanic rock only 200 miles long was where many of dance music's key innovations were first made flesh. To many, reggae is just a quirky local flavour, bouncy beach-party music. In fact it is one of the most forward-thinking genres in history. Reggae was the first style to value recorded music more than live performances. It was always driven by producers and DJs far more than by musicians – the majority of its artists were mere sessioneers hired and fired by the producer. And the things it brought us – the dub mix, toasting, the version, the sound system and the sound clash – have proved to be momentous. Quite apart from its many technical advances, reggae is proud father to today's dominant form. Jeff Chang makes it clear in his history *Can't Stop, Won't Stop*: 'The blues had Mississippi, jazz had New Orleans, hip hop has Jamaica.'

'Within that small place there is this huge thing,' marvels Steve Barrow of Blood And Fire sound system, a world authority on Jamaican music. 'You look at Jamaica, and you think it can't be, 'cos the place is too small, it couldn't have that influence. Then you say, what about the remix? What about drum and bass foregrounded in the mix? What about personality

DJs playing exclusive dub-plates? And no one can deny it. The arsenal of techniques at the disposal of someone operating the decks – most of these things were developed in Jamaica.'

Unique Jamaica

In Jamaica the DJ stripped the voices off his records and grabbed the microphone. Then he stripped his records apart even further, separating out each strand of sound. And from each dissected record he built a hundred more, each made with a different weave of noise. He built a towering skyline of loudspeakers and filled them with quaking bass and piercing treble, and as he used music as a weapon to fight his rivals, he built a whole new culture of dancing, a dance hall with no instruments – just a voice, some dub-plates and a system of sound.

Jamaica's music was propelled almost wholly by the needs of the DJ, creating a unique musical culture. Importantly, it was the first place a recording was no longer seen as a finished thing. Instead, in the studio, it became the parent to a whole series of similar but different versions, the raw material for endless 'dubs'. Thus, the concept of the remix was born, several years before the same idea would dawn on the disco and hip hop DJs.

The other Jamaican innovation was to start using recorded music as a tool, as part of a performance rather than the whole thing – to use a record not like a complete piece of music but as if it were an instrument in a band. When a record was played by a sound system, a deejay might sing or toast over the top, the selector might spin it back (audibly) and play the same part twice (a 'rewind'). He might put it through an echo chamber to distort it into rumbling thunder, use volume changes to add drama, or play just the highs or just the lows for a few bars to make the dancers go crazy. The person playing the records was no longer sitting passively while a song played to the end; he was distorting it creatively, responding to the audience in front of him and doing everything at his disposal to make the music more 'live'. Hear a record played like this and you're no longer just listening to the artist or the song; you're also listening to the DJ's performance as he brings a piece of recorded music to life. This was an exciting new approach, and again something which wouldn't occur outside Jamaica until disco and hip hop.

Given these ideas, it was also in Jamaica that the recording studio was first pushed to its limits as an instrument in itself. Here, in the service of the sound system, the producer realised he could create music long after the musicians had gone home – his work lay as much in giving shape to sound as in simply recording it.

A quick matter of terminology: in Jamaica, the 'deejay' is now a vocalist, akin to a rapper, and the person who plays records is called the 'selector'. Throughout this chapter we will distinguish between the 'DJ', who is the subject of this book, and the 'deejay' who in Jamaica can be found holding the microphone.

Sound system roots

As the meeting place of African, European, North American and native influences, the Caribbean has an astonishing range of musical cultures. Jamaica added something more which would make its music radically different – the sound system: huge mobile sets of amplifiers and loudspeakers designed to play records in the open air with as much impact as possible. Run by flamboyant neighbourhood heroes, a sound system (often just called a 'sound') enjoys the same kind of popular support as a local football team. There are regular dances in Kingston itself and out in the smaller towns people await each one with real excitement. First the colourfully lettered posters go up, then a few days later the sound arrives, its endless speaker boxes filling the back of a truck. The equipment is set up, usually in a specially built courtyard (a 'dance hall' is rarely indoors), tickets are sold and the party begins.

The sound system resulted from a combination of social factors peculiar to Jamaica. In a country with generally low incomes, people were unlikely to spend much money on records to play at home, yet, like everyone, they wanted to get together and dance. On other Caribbean islands people met this need by partying to music rooted in the 19th century – salsa, soca, samba, calypso – but in Jamaica the local folk music, mento, enjoyed nowhere near the same dominance. And when Jamaica began its rapid post-war urbanisation, its people looked for a more assertive soundtrack for their new city lives. They found this largely in American and American-influenced music. There were plenty of emigrants living in the States who would send back records, and Jamaica is close enough to the US mainland to receive radio transmissions from WINZ in Miami, WLAC in Nashville and WNOE in New Orleans, among others.

On clear nights the sound of artists like Fats Domino, Amos Milburn, Roy Brown and Professor Longhair would drift into the AM transistors of thousands of Jamaicans, placing the music of Memphis and New Orleans – with its syncopated shuffle beat – at the heart of the island's musical tastes. (Later favourites who had an important influence were Otis Redding, Sam Cooke, Solomon Burke, Ben E King, Lee Dorsey and especially Curtis Mayfield.) Much of Jamaica's musical output can be seen as a response to such imported American sounds: ska, rocksteady and, later, reggae grew largely from local interpretations of this music.

The most popular post-war music was big band swing. Although there were 'orchestra dances' through the forties, only a few Jamaican bands could recreate this style, and many musicians had been lost because of emigration. In any case, live musicians were an expensive way to fill a dance hall. Since a DJ could play all the best American music – and didn't need umpteen helpings of beer and curry goat – it was hard for live musicians to compete.

Radio, too, helped the sound system's cause. Jamaican radio was extremely conservative; both RJR (a cable radio service) and the BBC-modelled JBC had rather elitist broadcasting policies. For a long time they refused to play reggae, the people's music. Their stuffiness left a wide gap and the sounds filled it.

Sound systems were integral to Jamaican political life, too. With the journey to independence, granted in August 1962, and amid the tumultuous politics which followed, there was a strong revolutionary spirit on the island. Reggae and its associated forms emerged as rebel music, the voice of opposition, and the sounds grew to be an important part of this. Deejays often satirised current affairs and local events, taking on the old singing newspaper role of the mento minstrel. Free of any broadcasting restrictions, and often allied to particular political groupings (or at least to local gangs in the pocket of a particular party), they had a powerful influence as they chatted over the music to hundreds of people. Politicians would gauge their popularity by the mood in the dance.

In the 1972 election this connection between music and politics was intensified when Michael Manley won victory after allying his far-left People's National Party with the Rastafarian cause. He chose reggae for his campaign song ('Better Must Come' by Delroy Wilson) and took to holding out the 'rod of correction' he'd been given by Ethiopia's emperor Haile Selassie, the Rastas' living god.

Rastafarianism is a religion based on the 1930s teachings of Marcus Garvey, who led a back-to-Africa movement and prophesied that the 'God of Ethiopia' would deliver the black man from his suffering. Haile Selassie (whose name at birth was Duke, or 'Ras', Tafari) was deemed to fit the bill. With its 'Dread inna Babylon' attitude, Rastafarianism might be seen as Jamaica's hippie movement; a back-to-nature creed that opposed established power, stopped cutting its hair and saw marijuana as a holy sacrament. Jamaica's fairly straight-laced society saw Rastas as little more than scruffy drop-outs, until the late sixties when they became the island's counter-cultural heroes – a role epitomised by Bob Marley, the Jamaican John Lennon. By 1976 music and politics were so intertwined that Marley was the victim of an assassination attempt.

The sound system's important role in public life had grown from far more humble beginnings – the habit of using public music as a method of sales promotion. Liquor stores and shops selling records and electronic equipment would set up loudspeakers on the street and play music to entertain and attract passers-by. Gradually the retailers hit on the idea of enlarging on this and taking the music to the people (and selling them booze at the same time). Sound systems have kept this close connection with the alcohol trade, and the fact that the most popular sound stands to make the heftiest profit from drinks' sales has always encouraged fierce competition. It was well worth investing money in the best records, the loudest speakers and the most entertaining deejays.

Vantastic! – the rolling thunder of a Jamaican mobile record store. Vehicles like these helped provide the inspiration for the first sound systems.

The first sounds

At the beginning of the fifties, in an area of the capital which became known as 'Beat Street', on a series of outdoor dance spaces called 'lawns', the early sound systems plied their trade, attracting crowds of snappily dressed Kingstonians. The women wore spiralling petticoats and the men put on their best suits and wide-brimmed hats, and carried a hand towel to wipe their sweat. The dancing itself was lively jitterbugging and there would be several notoriously flash hoofers on hand showing off their latest steps.

Like the great bandleaders, the sound system pioneers awarded themselves aristocratic titles, 'Duke', 'Count', 'King', and so on. Also like the big bands, they all had theme tunes; exclusive records which were ferociously protected for fear another sound should get hold of a copy. They played on just one deck (in reggae circles the use of a single turntable has persisted even to this day, with the gap between songs covered by a deejay or some echo). The first sounds were Waldron, Goodies, Count Nick the Champ, Count Jones and, the most successful of the first generation, Tom Wong, the part-Chinese proprietor of a hardware store who called his sound Tom the Great Sebastian after a famous circus performer. Tom had started playing as early as the 1940s, on a system built for him by an RAF-trained technician called Headley Jones. He played a variety of music: the US rhythm and blues favoured by the poorer folk, as well as more genteel selections – including merengue and calypso – for the middle classes.

Immigrants in Britain kept pace with their homeland and there were soon Jamaican sound systems there as well. Duke Vin, who built the first London sound shortly after arriving in 1954, had been an apprentice of Tom's.

Tom the Great Sebastian reigned supreme until the rise in the middle fifties of the so-called 'Big Three' – Sir Coxsone Dodd's Downbeat, Duke Reid's Trojan, and King Edwards's Giant. As the sound systems injected the latest American songs into the island's blood, Jamaican rhythm and blues was born in answer – then ska, then rocksteady, then reggae.

Born in 1932, Clement Seymour Dodd started DJing on a 30watt Morphy Richards gramophone for the customers of his parents' liquor store, obtaining records from visiting sailors via his father who was a dock foreman. Billy Eckstein, Sarah Vaughan, Lionel Hampton and Louis Jordan were favourites. He went on to build speaker boxes for some of the early sounds, and by the mid fifties was running his own – Coxsone Downbeat (named after a Yorkshire cricketer) – and had started travelling to New York to buy records. In addition to a wealth of jazz, he would bring back the rocking blues of artists like T-Bone Walker and BB King. By 1957 Dodd, now known as Sir Coxsone, had three separate sound systems touring the island.

Sir Coxsone's rivals were Arthur 'Duke' Reid and Vincent 'King' Edwards. Duke Reid was a bombastic ex-policeman who owned Treasure Isle, a combined liquor business, dry cleaner and restaurant. He wore an ermine robe and a gold crown to his dances and had the crowd carry him aloft to the stage when it was time to change a record. He carried a couple of handguns, a rifle and a belt of cartridges at all times, and was said to fire off a few shots over the heads of the dancers if any trouble broke out. His signature tune was 'My Mother's Eyes' by alto player Tab Smith; his Trojan sound system was named after the Bedford Trojan truck which carried it, a name which would later be used for the famous record label.

King Edwards had started in 1955, bringing records and a sound system back with him when he returned from a brief spell living in the US. He was known for having the best records and was the first to really emphasise volume. By 1959 he had the island's most powerful system, Giant, and that year, with selector Red Hopeton, he was declared the number one sound in Kingston, overtaking Reid and Coxsone.

The sounds' rivalries soon led to more formalised head-to-head competitions, with sound systems setting up deliberately within earshot of each other, or even playing at the same dance. The first 'sound clash', as they would be known, was between Count Nick the Champ and Tom the Great Sebastian in 1952. These events further dramatised the ongoing battle for supremacy and similar rituals would be adopted by later forms of music, most notably hip hop.

Competition was fierce and almost any tactic – fair or foul – was used to 'flop' your rival and woo the crowd to your side of the dancefloor. Building up the power of your system was one approach; having the best tunes was another, and record-buying trips to the States became essential. King Edwards recounts how he 'started to ride the plane like a bus' in his search for 'specials' – exclusive tunes to wow the crowds. In addition, Coxsone Dodd started scratching off record titles and renaming songs to throw off the competition. Thus 'Later For Gator' by Willis Jackson became 'Coxsone Hop', his sound system's theme song. This is the first recorded instance of this time-honoured DJ practice and it can be traced directly from Jamaica to the northern soul scene in the UK and to the world of hip hop in New York.

Others used simple intimidation to get ahead. Duke Reid's gang were renowned for using strong-arm methods; one tale tells how they shot to pieces the sound system of a rival simply because they had a better selection of music. Sabotaging rival dances by starting fights or throwing rocks into the crowd was quite common.

Another gangster was Prince Buster, an ex-boxer originally named Cecil Bustamente Campbell. Buster would later become one of the island's best known vocalists and producers, but he started out running security for Coxsone's dances. His tough posse and hard-man reputation came in very useful in warding off the destructive efforts of Duke Reid, especially when Buster himself was quite prepared to resort to sabotage; on his first night for Coxsone Buster trashed the Duke's needle. Later, Buster was instrumental in the rise of ska music, and when he set up his own Voice Of The People sound it quickly rose with that style to become the most powerful of the early sixties; by which time the sounds dominated Jamaican entertainment. As he recalled in Stephen Davis's book *Reggae Bloodlines*: 'There was no radio in those days and sound system was everything. To hear a new record, thousands would go to the dances.'

The deejay grabs the mic

As the sound systems put all their creative resources into beating their rivals, they began to really expand the DJ's range of possibilities. In transforming recorded music into a unique live show, the DJ has always strived to add excitement wherever he can. Already the engineers who built the systems had been heavily upping the bass power of their speakers to boost the oomph of the music. Already the DJs were travelling far and wide to seek out exclusive records. The next steps would have to be big ones.

The first great change was the addition of a live vocal element, in the shape of the rhyming personality deejay. Inspired by the verbal creativity of US radio DJs, the Jamaican DJ divided his role and added a dedicated announcer. Now, instead of a single figure playing and announcing records, there were two – the selector and the deejay, also called a toaster or an MC (master of ceremonies). Nowadays, these performers are the greatest stars of Jamaican music, with deejays like Yellowman, Shabba Ranks, Buju Banton and Beenie Man enjoying the same worldwide fame and adoration as rock stars or rappers.

The vocalist deejay took his first steps around 1956. Winston 'Count' Machuki, who had been playing records since 1950, first for Tom the Great Sebastian and then for Coxsone's Downbeat, decided to do more than just introduce the songs.

'I said to Mr Dodd, "Give me the microphone," ' Machuki recalled in Steve Barrow's *The Rough Guide To Reggae*. 'And he handed me the mic, I started dropping my wisecracks, and Mr Dodd was all for it. And I started trying my phrases on Coxsone, and he gave me one or two wisecracks too. I was repeating them all the night through that Saturday at Jubilee Tile Gardens. Everybody fell for it. I got more liquor than I could drink that night.'

Machuki was far from satisfied and thought he could add more to his performance. Chancing on an issue of Harlem's *Jive* magazine, he started absorbing the slang of black America, the cool rhyming style that the US radio DJs were using to introduce their records. Pretty soon he tried out his own compositions. He remembers his first one: 'If you dig my jive/ you're cool and very much alive/ Everybody all round town/ Machuki's the reason why I shake it down/ When it comes to jive/ you can't whip him with no stick.'

Machuki also started the practice of adding little vocal clicks and beats – anticipating rap's 'human beatboxes' by about twenty years – which became known as 'peps' because they pepped up the record. 'There would be times when the records playing would, in my estimation, sound weak, so I'd put in some peps, "*chicka-a-took, chicka-a-took, chicka-a-took*",' says Machuki. 'That created a sensation.' He proudly recalls that people often bought particular records they'd heard at a dance thinking that his live contributions would be included, only to return their purchases once they realised that he wasn't actually on the record. 'They didn't realise that was Machuki's injection in the dance hall,' he laughs.

The second big deejay was King Stitt, whose energetic dancing led him, in 1957, to become Machuki's stand-in, and whose congenitally twisted features led him to subtitle himself 'the ugly one'. At this stage the deejay was still selecting the records as well as working the mic, and although Stitt was the first to show that the deejay could transfer his verbal skills to vinyl – he made a few successful records with producer Clancy Eccles in the late sixties, such as 'Fire Corner' and 'Lee Van Cleef' – it was only as the seventies dawned that the deejay era began in earnest.

As U-Roy, Ewart Beckford took the deejay's role to new levels. U-Roy was so magnetic a performer he could hold a crowd's attention even without backing music, a fact proved when rain forced him to turn off the amplifiers at a dance he was deejaying and he kept the dancers enthralled with just his voice. He made a series of records, produced by Duke Reid, that proved how popular the deejay had become. Using the instrumental tracks from existing rocksteady recordings, with his rhymed lyrics recorded over the top, 'Wake The Town', 'Rule The Nation' and 'Wear You To The Ball' were so successful that in one week in 1970 they held the top three places in Jamaica's pop chart.

U-Roy was bemused by such success. 'At the time it was a joke,' he told David Katz. 'A deejay is just a person who comes to a dance, he talks over the mic and puts records on and reads the invitation where the next dance is going to keep. Who could ever tell that this thing would ever reach like this, people having number one on the chart!'

Carl Gayle, editor of Kingston's *Jahugliman* magazine, tried to explain it: 'What separates U-Roy from the rest is the fact that he gave reggae this live jivin' dimension which is so electrifying. With his will-of-the-wisp Kingston jive talkin' he turn the tables on a Jamaican recording scene full of singing talent, paving the way for a dance hall full of imitators.' And sure enough, after U-Roy's success came Big Youth, I-Roy, Dillinger, and a hundred more deejays, stealing the limelight from the singers.

Into the studio

The other great innovation which came from the sound systems' fierce competition was the practice of making exclusive, custom-made records. These were 'versions' – new instrumental versions of a song made from a recycled backing track – and later 'dubs' – where a song underwent a more radical reconstruction; the very first incarnation of the dance remix. They both came about simply because the DJ, in the shape of the sound system operator, wanted a constant flow of exclusive records to play to his dancers.

At the end of the fifties, just as the sounds were coming into their own, there started to be a noticeable lack of the kind of American records which the dance halls loved best, as the US began to move to a smoother sound. To fill this gap the sound system men started making their own exclusive tracks. From 1957 onwards Coxsone and Reid, closely followed by Buster, began recording instrumental copies of the southern soul tunes of Memphis and New Orleans. It was here that the distinctly Jamaican sound crept in, as the local musicians who played on these tracks started to over-emphasise the slightly crooked shuffle beat of New Orleans rhythm and blues and the producers began to turn up the bass.

'We realised that we were not getting enough stuff from America, so we had to make our local sound,' explained Coxsone Dodd in *Reggae International*. 'I had a couple of sessions, basically tango and calypso and some rhythm and blues-inclined sounds. After a couple of times in the studio, I found a sound that was popular with the dance crowd in Jamaica, and we worked from there.'

These first studio efforts of the DJs-turned-producers were never intended for sale to the public. As Dodd himself confessed, 'I didn't realise that this could be a business. I just did it for enjoyment.' Indeed, these recordings existed only in the form of one-off soft wax pressings, made at considerable expense, as crowd-pulling exclusives for the producer's own sound system. Such discs can only be played about ten or fifteen times before the grooves wear out. Today's DJs and producers in almost all genres carry out exactly the same process (although these days you're more likely to burn yourself a CD). The soft wax discs are now known as 'acetates', 'dub-plates' or most recently 'slates', and they remain things which DJs get very excited about.

Since these were instrumentals, the deejays were able to really come into their own. Previously they could only thread their toasting into the spaces left by the record's singer; now they could cut loose and chat over the whole track.

In 1959 the first 7-inch Jamaican 45s were released commercially, and as they continued their forays into production, the sound system bosses started setting up their own studios and record labels. After several others, Coxsone Dodd started his famous Studio One – on which Bob Marley & the Wailers' first efforts were released – and Duke Reid launched Trojan. Soon there was a steady flow of singers and musicians trying their luck as recording stars and Jamaica's indigenous music was gathering a real momentum.

Since they were making music primarily for their dances rather than for home or radio play, the soundmen producers emphasised the sonics which made records work better in the open air (where sound carries less) – ear-thwacking drums and great gutteral bass. These biases were the main evolutionary forces at work as Jamaica forged its lineage of unique music. Ska, rocksteady, reggae and, later, ragga all evolved this way – in the service of the sound systems and the DJ.

Version

A version is a record with the vocals removed, an alternative cut of a song made to let a deejay toast over the top. By recording such instrumentals and pressing them up as soft wax discs, the producers had plenty of hot exclusives with which to wow their crowds. When a sound system played these one-off tracks, with a live deejay 'riding the riddim', the audience was hearing something absolutely unique, with much the same immediacy as a traditional live performance. In terms of showmanship, the DJ – represented now by the trinity of producer, selector and deejay – was really delivering the goods.

The *style* known as version is simply music made from existing backing tracks. These are used as the basis of a new song by re-recording them with new elements, perhaps a deejay's vocals, or an organ melody line instead of a guitar, and so on.

All forms of reggae thrive on the idea of recycling or quoting favourite 'riddims' (rhythms), as the familiar patterns of bass and drums on these recycled backing tracks are known. Such patterns may be copied (or versioned) on hundreds of different records. Many are so well-known they have names of their own (usually onomatopoeic): 'Death In The Arena', 'Waterpumping' and 'Shank-I-Sheck' are three of the best known. Many rhythms have their origins, as might be expected, in America. One striking example, 'Death In The Arena', can be heard on literally hundreds of records – including, for example, King Tubby's 'The Champion Version' – and can be traced back to a bassline used by drummer Bernard Purdey on his 1968 track 'Funky Donkey'. When a new rhythm appears, the dance halls will ring with it for a month or two, until the next seductive bassline gets introduced. Their thriving, multiplying existence is proof, as Jamaican producer Dermott Hussey pointed out, that 'you can copyright a song, but you can't copyright a rhythm.'

Although it represents the kind of organic transmission and copying common in African-derived musics, version owes its emergence largely to technology. The earliest Jamaican records were captured on simple one-track recorders. This meant that all the instruments and any vocals had to be recorded live, simultaneously. However, when Coxsone Dodd returned from England loaded with new equipment for his studio, he carried with him a *two-track* recorder. With this, the instrumental part of a song could be recorded completely separately from the vocal, so any track made in Dodd's Studio One could be recorded free of lyrics.

Once you could isolate the rhythm track, you could use it as many times as you liked and add whatever you wanted to it. Producers eventually realised that they were able to release endless reworkings of the same rhythm, each made fresh by a new melody or new lyrics from that month's hottest deejay. The practice dates back to at least as early as 1965 when a rhythm from 'Hold Down' by Lee Perry & the Dynamites had the vocal track removed and replaced by Roland Alphonso's sax playing. The new track was renamed 'Rinky Dink'. In the seventies one producer in particular, Bunny Lee, showed how a single rhythm could be creatively recycled into many different forms. For Lee this was a matter of economic necessity; he didn't own his own studio and wanted to maximise the results he could get from each expensive hour of studio time.

Version fever took hold in 1967 when Ruddy Redwood, the wealthy operator of a sound called Supreme Ruler of Sound, took away an acetate copy of an established hit 'On The Beach' by the Paragons, which was missing the vocals; at Duke Reid's Treasure Isle studio the engineer Byron Smith had cut the dub-plate with the vocals accidentally turned down. After rocking the crowd with the original vocal pressing of the song, Redwood played them this new voiceless version. The crowd went crazy, singing along, and he played the song so many times that night that by morning the acetate was worn out.

Popular demand soon led the style away from purely sound system use. Joe Gibb's engineer, Errol Thompson, started using rhythm versions as B-sides to commercially released singles in 1971. Eventually there were even whole albums of a single rhythm; ten or more cuts of the same backing track, each with a different vocal.

Dub

Dub is a new universe of sound. It is the first full flowering of the dance remix. Dub opened up such dramatic possibilities that it is considered a whole new genre. Dub techniques are so powerful they are now used across the entire spectrum of popular music. And as music made expressedly for sound system use, dub owes its existence largely to the DJ.

Dub has been described as 'X-ray music'. A dub mix is essentially the bare bones of a track with the bass turned up. Dub separates a song into its stark component parts, and adds and subtracts each strand of sound until a new composition is made. By adding space to a track, what is left has far more impact. By boosting a bassline until it's a monstrous shaking presence, dropping out the whole of the song except the drums, sending a snatch of singing into a reverberating echo, stretching out a rhythm with an interminable delay, dub can make a flat piece of music into a mountainous 3-D landscape.

The word 'dub' comes from 'double', as in making a copy. It was essentially just an extension of version – because once the producer had a multi-track recorder he wasn't going to stop at simply removing the vocals (dub styles really came into their own with four-track recording). Dub's most obvious technique involves isolating the rhythm track, the 'drum and bass', and emphasising it beyond all nature, adding layers of disorienting echo and a barrage of other sound-processing effects.

The story of dub centres on King Tubby. Born Osbourne Ruddock in 1941, Tubby had an almost supernatural understanding of electronics, garnered from years of building sound equipment and fixing radios and TVs. In his later years, it is said that if he was dissatisfied with how something sounded, he would dive into his mixing desk armed with a soldering iron and rebuild a circuit or two on the spot until he had adjusted it exactly as he wanted. A shy and obsessive perfectionist, Tubby insisted on bizarre levels of neatness in his studio (which for years was in his bedroom). He even went to the bank to exchange crumpled banknotes for new crisp ones. However, he was very generous, sharing his knowledge with the producers who rose up beneath him. In fact, it is also said that, even when he was considered a superstar producer he still took in toasters and hairdryers for repair.

Tubby (he was very slim) started operating a sound system, Tubby's Home Town Hi-Fi, in 1964. His was one of a new breed that by virtue of their innovations were starting to overtake the older sounds. He put together a very special rig, with a built-in echo, the first reverb unit of any sound system on the island, and exceptional power. It didn't hurt, also, that his main deejay was the imminently legendary U-Roy. By 1968 Tubby was crowned 'number one sound'.

Tubby also worked as an engineer and disc-cutter for Duke Reid and it was here in 1972, inspired by the way the sound systems were using

Cool ruler – King Tubby turns it up to eleven.

version records, that he discovered ways to bring out the amazing contours hidden in a piece of music.

'I had a little dub machine and I used to borrow tapes from the producers and mix them down in a different fashion,' Tubby related. 'I used to work on the cutter for Duke Reid and once, a tape was running on the machine and I just drop off some of the voice, y'know. It was a test cut.' When this test record was played for an audience, the response was phenomenal. 'The Saturday we was playing out and I said, "Alright, I going test them, 'cos it sounds so exciting the way the records start with the voice, the voice drop out and the rhythm still going." We carry them to the dance, man, and I tell you, 'bout four or five of the tune, them keep the dance, 'cos is just over and over we 'ave fe keep playing them.'

Tubby's first experiments, as he described, involved dropping out the backing to leave the singers acappella, and then reversing the process to let the band have centre stage. The success of this style encouraged him to delve further and add exaggerated echo and reverb. Other producers, notably the musically insane Lee Perry, one of Coxsone Dodd's apprentices, quickly jumped aboard the dub express train and a whole barrage of remix techniques was developed and refined. (Perry was also the first to use sound effects on records, adding such 'sampled' noises as pistol shots and breaking glass.)

Soon, producers were lining up for a dash of the Tubby magic. Augustus Pablo, Lee Perry, Winston Riley and, especially, Bunny Lee among them. A producer would take him a tape of their latest track and Tubs would remix it into a staggering number of different takes for different sound systems, each take in a style that best suited that sound or the deejay that would toast over it.

By 1975 King Tubby was given full label credits for the tracks he reconfigured, and not just as an engineer or remixer. Those who really know Jamaican music recognise him as one of its true founding fathers. Tragically, he was shot dead in 1989, only four years after opening his own state-of-the-art studio. And amazingly, despite his huge contributions to his national music, King Tubby's death didn't even make the papers.

Echoes and reverberations

Reggae set a great many precedents. It laid down the principles of remixing, it made an artist and a star of the producer, it transformed playing records into live performance, and it showed how music could be propelled into whole new genres by the needs of the dancefloor. Although many of these ideas would emerge independently elsewhere, they happened in Jamaica first.

Hip hop owes reggae an enormous debt. Kool Herc, hip hop's founder, was Jamaican and what he did in the Bronx was based largely on wanting to build a New York version of the Kingston sound systems of his youth, toasting deejays included. The first disco remixers developed their techniques – which were initially more about lengthening and restructuring than about sonic dismemberment – without being aware of what was happening in Jamaica. However, the lessons of dub quickly washed through New York. François Kevorkian admits it was a major influence on him, and in the weird post-disco styles of producers like Arthur Russell and Larry Levan, a distinct dub sensibility is obvious. Today's remixers still use principles first developed by Jamaica's visionaries, and almost every dance track has some sort of 'dub' mix to fuel the dancefloor. Dub forms are at work in some of today's most popular bands, most notably Massive Attack, Underworld and Leftfield.

Reggae's biggest impact outside the Caribbean has undoubtedly been in the UK, which became Jamaican music's second home. As we'll see in later chapters, the Jamaican influence was what made British music distinct, and it was sound system traditions that led to Britain finally developing dance music styles it could call its own. Without a strong undercurrent of reggae and dub running through the UK's soundtrack, it is inconceivable that such forms as jungle, drum and bass and UK garage would have been born.

In return, reggae has kept its keen ears open and absorbed all manner of new possibilities from the wider world of music. In recent years it has closed the circle with hip hop and taken much from the US. Ragga, the hard electronic style of reggae, is analogous with house or techno: an older musical form reconstructed on synthesisers and drum machines. The producers, selectors and deejays are still plundering everything they can use to 'nice up the dance', and their dancefloor-driven efforts continue to exert a major influence on the world's music.

'The fact is reggae has nourished dance culture to an extraordinary degree,' insists Steve Barrow. 'I'm not saying anything so banal as "everything sounds like reggae" – it's in the conceptualisation of what you're supposed to be doing when you make dance music. It's in the practice, it's in techniques, and it's in the forms that have arisen out of Jamaican music. In all of this, this little island has had a profound influence.'

SIX
DISCO
ROOTS

Love Is The Message

'O body swayed to music, O brightening glance,
How can we know the dancer from the dance?'

– WB Yeats, *Among School Children*

'Disco was a whole movement – people really felt that. They felt
disappointed later on that the idealistic quality of it was being
trampled in favour of money and celebrity. As much as disco was
glitzy and certainly loved celebrity culture, there was never a sense
of it being driven by that. It was much more driven by an
underground idea of unity. The manifesto was the music. Love Is
The Message.'

– Vince Aletti

'We are the Stonewall girls. We wear our hair in curls. We wear
no underwear. We show our pubic hair. We wear our
dungarees. Above our nelly knees!'

It's the night of 21 June 1969 and you are out in front of the Stonewall
Inn in Manhattan's Greenwich Village. It's a hot New York summer's
night and the air is thick with humidity and the tension of unfolding
drama. Around you there are men that look like women, women that
dress like men, a few spaced-out hippies, bar staff from the Stonewall and
quizzical Villagers coming to find out what the rumpus is here on
Christopher Street. Behind you is the Women's Correction Center,
whose inmates have joined the party by dropping lighted tissue papers
onto the sidewalk below. In the bar are several police officers, originally
there on a routine raid, but now barricaded in, terrified of the sudden and
unexpected reaction from the freaks and the queers. A black gay man
walks past yelling, 'Let my people go!' Pennies and dimes hurtle through
the air, along with loaded insults: 'Faggot cops!' A rock shatters a window
above the bar.

This was the Stonewall rebellion, the night when gay New York took
to the streets and threw itself a revolution. But this was a rebellion of a
different kind – more vivid street theatre than armed revolt. It was the

culmination of decades of oppression and humiliation. Spurred by black Americans' fight for civil rights, and inspired by the women's liberation movement, Stonewall was the landmark event which initiated the birth of gay pride.

Twelve hours before the disturbance, Judy Garland had been buried, after killing herself with an overdose of barbiturates. Garland was an icon in the tight-knit gay community, and the Stonewall Inn was one of several gay haunts in the Village mourning her passing that night. Being without a liquor licence meant that it was run as a private club, a 'bottle bar', where you had to be signed in to get a drink and where warning lights were in operation to alert clients of impending raids. The Stonewall's mafia owners could usually ensure it remained relatively free from cop interference. Not tonight.

No one knows exactly why the Stonewall Inn was raided that evening, but there's no doubt that the police would come to regret it. New York cop Seymour Pine later commented: 'There was never any time that I felt more scared than then.' The *New York Daily News* reported: 'HOME NEST RAIDED, QUEEN BEES ARE STINGING MAD'. Because this was the night that rocks replaced diamanté; anger replaced camp. A cross-dressing lesbian called Stormé DeLarverie (who many believe kick-started the action) said, 'The police got the shock of their lives when those queens came out of that bar and pulled off their wigs and went after them.' This was a revolution in a sequined shift dress.

On that same night, a few yards away from the Stonewall Inn, something else is happening. If you turn and walk down to Sheridan Square, on the site of legendary jazz club Café Society – where Billie Holiday once performed – you'll reach the Haven on Christopher Street, a small, illegal, after-hours club. You go through the cramped entrance, dip down to the bar and join a phalanx of hucksters and hustlers, drag queens and nightbirds. You grab a drink and survey the compact, dimly lit place. Barflys chatter, dancers dance, ice clatters on glass.

All this action is played out to a soundtrack of intense rhythm and blues and funky rock music, powering through the largest speakers you've ever seen. Ensconced at the back, positioned behind a rudimentary set of turntables, is a young Brooklyn-born Italian-American. He's wiry, muscular and handsome, and the sweat drips off the end of his nose as he lines up the next record: Chicago Transit Authority's 'I'm A Man'. Layer after layer of percussion is added to the rocksteady drum-beat, until a steely guitar motif signals the song's start. The dancefloor's tempo is visibly raised. The dancers grind that little bit more, their hips moving in circular motions.

While Christopher Street is raging with the fight for gay

emancipation, this DJ is busy rewriting the rules on the way we hear records in nightclubs.

Underground origins

Disco was the revolution. Disco was freedom, togetherness, love. Disco was dirty, spiritual, thrilling, powerful. Disco was secret, underground, dangerous. It was non-blond, queer, hungry. It was emancipation.

Before commercial success twisted the music into a polyester perversion of itself, and wrenched the scene out of New York's gay underground and into the funkless lap of mainstream America, disco was the hottest, sexiest, most redeeming and most deeply loving dance music there has been. It relied on phenomenal musicianship, it was often poetic and highly lyrical, it could be as experimental and as profound as it wanted, and it was always funky beyond the call of duty. These days the name 'disco' is stuck to *Saturday Night Fever*, to the Bee Gees, Abba and the Village People, to plastic compilation CDs and tacky retro club nights. In its own time, however, for its original family, it was the word of salvation.

In fact, many of the people involved with its early days blanch at using 'disco' to describe the music and clubs they knew and loved. They don't really have an alternative, but they have a strong need to distinguish their music – funky and soulful – and their scene – small, gritty and underground – from what disco eventually became and from how disco is seen by most people today. The last days of disco might have recalled the decadent fall of Rome, but the first days were filled with hope.

Disco presided over an era of dramatic social change. As war raged in Vietnam and an oil crisis and deep economic recession brought further misery, it provided a soundtrack of escapism. Conversely, it was also the music for celebrating new freedoms. After the Stonewall rebellion, gay Americans felt able to turn up the volume on their existence, and despite the rioting and let-downs of the post-civil rights period, black people were also enjoying the benefits of greater equality. Inspired by these minority freedoms, the majority, too, felt a release. Legal abortion, antibiotics and the Pill meant attitudes to sex had changed; it was for enjoyment, not procreation (this notion definitely helped soften the straight view of gay sex). The 'Make Love Not War' ideals of the late sixties were still reverberating; Vietnam and LSD had greatly broadened young people's world view. It was clear that your experience of life would be very different from that of your parents.

Emerging in New York in the first half of the seventies, disco could still vividly recall the Summer of Love a few years before. Its music grew as much out of the psychedelic experiments of Sly & the Family Stone and Motown producer Norman Whitfield as from Gamble & Huff's Philadelphia orchestrations. Its original spirit – an emphasis on equality, freedom, togetherness and love – was just sixties idealism matured by the experience of Vietnam and refuelled by the promise of black/gay liberation. And disco not only reflected these changes, in creating a new and vital sub-culture – one which was eventually coopted by the mainstream – disco also, in a very real sense, helped to further them.

Musically, disco was revolutionary to an astonishing degree. It was at the heart of some of the most radical innovations to date in the way music is envisaged, created and consumed. It changed clubs almost beyond recognition, it affected radio dramatically, and it had an important effect on the balance of power in the music industry between the independent labels and the majors. By the end of its reign had been born the 12-inch single, the remix and a host of new studio techniques. And with songs being constructed specially for the dancefloor (longer, more beat-oriented, more *functional*) and records being treated as DJs' tools rather than just representations of a live performance, there arrived a new conception of what popular music could be.

As for the club DJ, the disco era was when he came of age. This was when he became a star, even a god to his dancefloor. This was when he learned his vocabulary of mixing techniques, and this was when the industry recognised him as the person best placed to create dance music rather than just play it.

The death of rock

However, before any of this could take place, there had to be a shift. As the sixties ended, club culture was based on the ideals of celebrity, international travel and playboy status, epitomised by places like Arthur in New York and Scotch of St James in London, or on the inner voyages of psychedelic places like Electric Circus or UFO. While it was thriving, having introduced a new kind of jet-set classlessness, this nightworld of beautiful people was hardly likely to inspire any novel musical movement. Before disco could happen, the night had to fall back into the hands of the energetic underclasses, a prerequisite of almost all clubland innovation.

And with the end of the sixties, this was what happened. In the closing month of the decade, the Rolling Stones' free performance in Altamont was bittered by the Hell's Angel murder of a black concert-goer. Four months later, state troopers opened fire on student anti-Vietnam protesters at Ohio's Kent State University, killing four. These two events splashed blood in the flower children's faces and provided chilling symbols for the end of the hippie odyssey. Then The Beatles broke up and Hendrix and Joplin died. Sensing that the party was over, the jet set turned their backs on the psychedelic scene.

Around the same time, organised crime had seen the money-laundering potential of clubs and moved in, further repelling the classier elements and encouraging an atmosphere of violence and seediness. In addition, the authorities moved against many clubs' blatant disregard for drugs and alcohol laws, and a series of busts for liquor licence violations took place. This inadvertently encouraged the opening of juice bars, unlicensed all-night hang-outs which were subject to far less scrutiny and which could stay open much later. 'Juice joint' became a by-word for depravity.

As the jet set and their followers moved on and clubs needed to fill the space they left, new faces found their way in. Black, Hispanic and working-class white kids found it far easier to get through the door, and since gay New Yorkers – a sizeable clubland constituency – no longer had to hide in illegal speakeasies, they were a valuable new market. In fact, several clubs 'went gay' at this time, largely for financial reasons.

Moreover, the dominant music – rock – was changing. Before the seventies were very old, rock had abandoned its early danceable psychedelic forms for the bloated self-aggrandisement of its 'progressive' era. It was the age of the concept album, the rock opera, the tortuous guitar solo. Set on giving proof of its artistic nature, rock no longer provided much in the way of a dance beat. In its place, clubs reverted to rhythm and blues and more Latin styles, a process encouraged by the greater black and Hispanic presence.

Francis Grasso – the first modern DJ

If it took many factors to prepare the social fabric of New York for the arrival of disco, to make ready the dancefloor it took but one disc jockey. He is the ancestor of all modern DJs, the godfather of the craft, the first DJ that we would recognise as doing the same thing as DJs do today. On the night the Stonewall Rebellion started the social revolution that would nurture disco, he was a stone's throw away, playing at the Haven, staging the musical revolution that would give it roots. His name was Francis Grasso.

DJ Francis didn't just bend the rules; he changed the game. Before him, the DJ had been a musical waiter, serving the songs required by the crowd and periodically directing them to the bar with a few slowies, much as a good waiter can craftily recommend the most profitable dishes. In the UK, northern soul DJs had started to change this, as had some US DJs, like Terry Noel, whose flamboyance raised him to the status of charismatic maître d', but they were essentially still part of the serving staff.

Grasso stormed the profession out of servitude and made the DJ the musical head chef. DJ Francis didn't follow the pop chart menu, and he didn't meekly bring the customer what he'd asked for. Instead, he cooked up a nightly banquet of new and exotic musical dishes which the diners, though they devoured them eagerly and came back for more, might never have known to order.

As a result, he completely changed the relationship between the DJ and his audience. Dance at a club where Francis was playing and though it was a reciprocal thing – with him responding to the enthusiasms of the dancers – you had to submit to his taste, to his choice of music and, most importantly, to the mood journey he took you on.

Francis Grasso was the first DJ to present a true creative performance. He was the first to show that a nightful of records could be a single thing: a voyage, a narrative, a set. Before Grasso, the DJ might have known that certain records had the power to affect the mood and energy of the crowd; only after Grasso did the DJ recognise that this power belonged to him, not to the records. It lay in the DJ's skilful manipulation of the dancers, in the way he sequenced or programmed the records, and to a far lesser degree in the individual songs themselves.

Other DJs still thought of themselves as the stand-in for a band; they still thought of a record as an imitation of a live performance. Francis, on the other hand, saw that records were the vital components of *his* performance.

DJ Francis played music, the disc jockeys before him had just put records on.

You can see that Francis Grasso was a wild one. As he flicks and strokes a long mane of dark grey hair, a sparkle in his eyes, he has stories that only stars can tell. There was a time when strangers would scream out his name as he walked his dogs on the streets of Manhattan. He would take eight or nine of his friends out and they would be whisked into clubs and drink free all night. He dated Liza Minnelli. He was a good friend to Jimi Hendrix (not to mention to Hendrix's 'main old lady', who moved into Grasso's bed after the guitarist's death). He used to spend more than his rent on drugs. Though never married, he has been engaged to at least three women – one of them a Playboy Bunny – and during his time as a DJ he screwed hundreds more.

Sitting in a bar in his native Brooklyn, the scars of a life lived to the full are only too apparent. The speed-sped metabolism of his youth has left him skeletally trim, and there are several signs – the gaunt curves of his face, the misarrangement of his nose and teeth which leaves his voice both nasal and slurred – that he has also been visited by violence along the way.

His love for his dogs, he reckons, is the only reason he is still alive: if it wasn't for the duties of caring for them – having to head home each night to walk and feed them – the druggy hedonism of his glory years would have claimed him completely. He has always kept dogs, mostly Great Danes. This week he has a new litter of puppies.

Like Terry Noel before him, Francis entered clubland as a dancer. Injuries from a series of motorcycle accidents had left him with poor coordination in his feet, and his doctor suggested that he take up dancing as therapy. This led to a job at Trude Heller's Trik, a couples-oriented Greenwich Village nightspot owned by socialite Trudy 'Trude' Heller, where he performed perched precariously on a ledge at one side of the club.

'Yep, I was one of the original Trudy Heller go-go boys,' he grins. 'You had twenty minutes on and twenty minutes off, and you could only move your ass side to side because if you went back and forth you'd bang off the wall and fall right onto the table you were dancing over. You'd have a partner, and the band would play "Cloud Nine" by the Temptations for about thirty-eight minutes. Going home, my muscles were killing me. It was the hardest twenty dollars I ever made in my life.'

His debut as a DJ came one Friday in 1968, when he found himself in Salvation Too on the night that (as he recalls) Terry Noel had decided to drop acid before setting off for work. Noel didn't show up until 1.30am. By that time Francis was the new house DJ, having displayed an instinctive command of the equipment – two Rekocut broadcast-quality turntables and a single fader switch – and having watched Noel get fired on arrival.

Francis can't recall the first record he played there, but he knows he had 'a hell of a good time'. They paid him handsomely and he went home hardly believing what had happened. 'I would have paid *them*. I had that much fun.'

There couldn't be a clearer example of a DJ snatching the torch from his predecessor. Judging by this first night, DJ Francis must have been immediately and noticeably different. What had distinguished him so clearly from those who came before? Shrugging his shoulders in a cheeky display of false modesty, he says simply, 'There *wasn't* really guys before me.

'Nobody had really just kept the beat going,' he adds. 'They'd get them to dance, then change records, so you had to catch the beat again. It never flowed. And they didn't know how to bring the crowd to a height, and then level them back down, and bring them back up again. It was like an experience, I think that was how someone put it. And the more fun the crowd had, the more fun I had.'

In contrast, he remembers that Terry Noel, though he was able to mix records, would often trip up the continuity of the night with an incongruous choice. 'He used to do really weird things. Like he'd have the whole dancefloor going and then put on Elvis Presley.' Francis would never sacrifice a busy dancefloor. 'I kept 'em juiced,' he growls.

Before him, people had played records as if they were discrete little performances, Francis treated them like movements in a symphony; continuous elements in a grand whole. By conceiving of his music in this way, he was no longer just providing a soundtrack to sixties social razzmatazz, he was envisaging the far more dance-centred clubs of the future. And with this ideal of an unbroken flow of music, the recent notion of mixing records gained new importance.

Perhaps his effortless success was due to his musicality. Having started with the accordion when he was young, he admits to also playing guitar, drums and saxophone, at least in high school and during college (he studied English Literature at Long Island University). He prefers, however, to attribute the source of his talent elsewhere. 'I was a dancer!' he declares, as if it's all the explanation necessary. 'I was a dancer, so it was rhythmically . . . not hard.'

Ironically, he says he wouldn't have enjoyed being down on the dancefloor – he hates crowds – but, as he puts it, he loved to be in control and to absorb the feeling in the room.

Francis Grasso's choice of music was quite different to his predecessor, too. Seduced by the tastes of the jet set, Noel had played rock and pop with a soul accent: The Beatles, a lot of Motown, the Chambers Bros. But DJ Francis, though he played a lot of the same music (remember there were far, far fewer releases in those days), accented a harder, funkier sound than Noel's soulful pop, picking up on a lot of British imports and the grittier end of black music. In his hands the funkier side of rock such as the Rolling Stones or Led Zeppelin met heavy black rhythms like Dyke & the Blazers or Kool & the Gang, and he introduced his audience to the drum-heavy African sound of bands like Osibisa, making a personal signature tune of Michael Olatunji's (much-sampled) 'Drums Of Passion' (aka 'Jin-Go-La-Bah'). He felt that a Latin beat made most people dance, so Santana was a staple. And Mitch Ryder & the Detroit Wheels, early Earth Wind And Fire, the Staple Singers, Ike & Tina Turner, all found their way into his set.

Previously, a DJ's records belonged to the club, but Francis owned the music he played and put considerable effort into buying it, badgering the staff at Colony Records in Times Square to find him exclusives. Like all

DJs, he fetishised imports, Brian Auger's English jazz-rock LP *Befour* being one example. He played James Brown and of course Motown – the Four Tops, the Supremes and especially the longer, weirder tracks being produced for the Temptations by Norman Whitfield – as well as the Stax Memphis sound including Sam & Dave and Booker T & the MGs. Sly & the Family Stone were a particular favourite, and he unearthed the various records Sly made as a producer. He would close his performance with the sound of the Doors' 'The End'.

Soul survivor – outside his Brooklyn local, Francis Grasso shows the wear and tear which comes with having invented the modern DJ.

The Sanctuary

When Salvation Too closed, Grasso had a brief spell installing air conditioners, rescuing himself with a successful audition at a club called Tarot. From here he was poached by a nightspot in the Hell's Kitchen district. This club, the place where Francis would fully hone his pioneering DJing skills, was the Sanctuary.

Sanctuary was splashed in controversy right from its inception. Initially named the Church, since it occupied the shell of an old German Baptist church at 407 West 43rd Street, its decor – chosen by its founder Arnie Lord – stretched the credulity of even the most secular. Across from the altar a vast mural of the devil looked on menacingly, its demon eyes seemingly alive and mobile. Around him were clusters of angels with exposed genitalia, all engaged in some sexual act, each more depraved than the last. 'The mural was unbelievably pornographic,' recalls Francis. 'And no matter where you stood in the club, the devil was looking at you.' Drinks were served from chalices, the banquettes were pews and the building's stained glass windows were illuminated from outside. On the altar itself sat the record decks, where the disc jockeys served a new kind of sacrament.

When it first opened, the protests against this blasphemous night spot were so vociferous that it was quickly forced to close (thanks largely to an injunction gained by the Catholic church). When it reopened, the angels had bunches of plastic grapes gingerly placed over their offending gonads, and the club was renamed the Sanctuary.

Then, after building up a good business as a couply straight club, the day manager ran off with the night manager and $175,000 of the club's money. A rescue plan put it into gay ownership, all the women were fired and, with Stonewall a recent memory, the place proudly became the first public flowering of all the scene's seedy juice bar energy, the above-ground representative of places with names like Thrush, Fabulous, Forbidden Fruit, Together and Superstar. As Albert Goldman described it, Sanctuary was 'the first totally uninhibited gay discothèque in America'.

DJ Francis found himself the only straight man left. This had its advantages. He'd always had difficulties making toilet runs without letting a record finish (quite a problem since most of the tracks he played were 45s lasting about three minutes). Now this was solved. 'I just started going to the ladies' room 'cos there were no ladies,' he grins. 'One night a reporter came down to do a story on the club. He asked the doorman, "Do you get any straight people here?" and he just pointed at me and said, "Yeah, there he goes." '

As a gay club, Sanctuary grew steadily wilder. Francis developed his skills to the point where he could keep the dancefloor packed far beyond capacity all night, seven nights a week. 'It was so crowded, and they were passing poppers around. Even if anybody wanted to pass out, there was no room. They were literally holding each other up, it was so packed.' Sanctuary had a legal maximum occupancy of 346 people; Francis remembers nights when the doorman stopped counting at more than a thousand. Eventually it lost its alcohol licence and became a juice bar, slashing profitability but allowing it to stay open all night. On Fridays and Saturdays this meant noon the following day.

When a nightclub is poured full of newly liberated gay men, then shaken (and stirred) by a weighty concoction of dance music and a pharmacopoeia of pills and potions, the result is a festival of carnality. This was the Sanctuary. A 1965 law against 'deviant sexual intercourse' ensured gay sex was still illegal in New York State (this law, which applies to all instances of oral and anal sex, is on the statute books to this day), and the American Psychiatric Association still classed homosexuality as an illness (until 15 December 1973). But Stonewall had loosened the lid on an entire oppressed culture, and gay New York ran at life like greyhounds out of the trap. Tom Burke, writing in *Esquire* magazine, described this new breed of homo: 'An unfettered, guiltless male child of the new morality in a Zapata moustache and an outlaw hat, who couldn't care less for Establishment approval, would as soon sleep with boys as girls, and thinks that "Over The Rainbow" is a place to fly on 200 micrograms of Lysergic Acid Diethylamide.'

The Sanctuary was patrolled by Puerto Rican dealers dressed like fifties wiseguys who doled out downers like tuies (Tuinal), reds (Seconal) and Quaaludes (and their methaqualone mates, Paris 400s and Rorer 714s), as well as amphetamines and a lexicon of psychedelics from LSD to DMT. The downers were so strong they were nicknamed 'wall-bangers' (or 'gorilla biscuits') because they effected an almost total shutdown of the motor neurone system. Francis bought sealed bottles of 400mg Quaaludes (an aphrodisiac tranquilliser) from a pharmacist friend. Normally $5 each, he'd give them to all his friends for a dollar apiece. The *Daily News* called Sanctuary a 'drugs supermarket'.

As for sex, though fucking was banned on the dancefloor, the club's dark corners hid many a writhing body and its toilets hosted scenes of all-out orgies. Francis remembers the problems caused in the summer when the club's neighbours would complain about guys using their hallways for sex (this was what would eventually bring the club's closure). On his insistence, women were grudgingly allowed in the club and he began to share in the sexual abandon. 'I was caught so many times getting oral sex in the booth it was disgusting,' he says. 'I would tell the girls, "Bet you can't make me miss a beat." '

When Alan J Pakula wanted to depict a place of sin in his 1971 movie *Klute* (for which Jane Fonda won an Oscar), he chose Sanctuary. Francis is in there for about three seconds, playing a DJ. During filming, the place's genuinely sinful nature invested the proceedings. 'To get the feel of real hookers, they had real hookers. Then the cops arrived because there was a lot of drug dealing going on in between takes. It was a lively crowd!'

Francis started playing at another club, the Haven, in 1969 (he would move between Haven and Sanctuary several times). The Haven is remembered as the last place which the cops smashed up with impunity simply because it was a gay bar. Here, Francis continued his sonic experiments, redeploying records culled from the freeform rock shows on the burgeoning FM wavelength for his dancefloor. Iron Butterfly's progressive rock epic 'In-A-Gadda-Da-Vida' (the album version was seventeen minutes long) and Rare Earth's drum heavy 'Get Ready' were, because of their length, accidentally perfect. Using two Thorens turntables, a pair of piggyback Dynaco amps and behemoth speakers 'acquired' from the rock band Mountain, DJ Francis grew to the peak of his powers.

Revolutionary techniques

Francis claims he was able to beat-mix – that is to overlap the ending of one record with the beginning of a second so that their drum beats are synchronised – almost as soon as he started. Even with today's superior equipment, to beat-mix records containing the tempo fluctuations of a live drummer is an impressive feat indeed.

Whether he really did have this ability straight away, Francis was certainly the DJ who made beat-mixing a required skill. He was not the very first to mix, but he certainly took it to a whole new level, and could hold a blend – two songs playing simultaneously with the beats synchronised – for two minutes or more.

'Nobody mixed like me,' he boasts. 'Nobody was willing to hang on that long. Because if you hang on that long, the chances of mistakes are that much greater. But to me it was second nature. I did it like I walk my dog.'

Beat-mixing gave a DJ unprecedented scope for creativity and would be essential to disco's development. Nowadays, it is fairly easy since most dance songs, thanks to drum machines, have an unwavering tempo, and modern turntables have sophisticated pitch control allowing the DJ to bring one record's speed up or down to match the other. Francis, however, had neither of these advantages.

'Back then, you couldn't adjust the speeds,' he remembers. 'You had to catch it at the right moment. There was no room for error. And you couldn't play catch up. You couldn't touch the turntables. I had Thorens at the Haven, and you couldn't do that on Thorens. All you had to do was start at the right moment.'

He also perfected the slip-cue. This now basic technique requires a felt disc (a 'slipmat') between the record and the turntable platter. The record about to be played (the one which is being 'cued up') can thus be held stationary while the turntable spins underneath. This allows the DJ to start it instantly, exactly at the point of its first beat. The technique was already used in radio and Francis had been introduced to it by the engineer on his friend Bob Lewis's CBS radio show.

Grasso would use this technique to bring a fresh record in right on the beat of the one that was already playing, as if the musicians had changed tune without stopping. At other times, he says, he trusted his instincts to effect the same move, recognising the record's desired passage by eye, placing the needle into the correct groove and deftly manoeuvring the slide fader to make the switch from one disc to another. 'I got so good I would just catch it on the run.' Such mixing was essential, considering that the songs of the time were so short, but what he was doing was prefiguring the remixing techniques which would be a vital part of all subsequent dance music.

He would often use two copies of the same record to extend it, a technique he describes with 'You're The One' by Little Sister (a Sly Stone side project): 'Part one ended musically, part two on the other side would begin with a scream, so you could blend right into the scream side, and then go back to "You're The One". Or play the scream side twice, part two, then flip it over and play part one, twice. They didn't know I was playing two 45s.'

He would play 'Soul Sacrifice' by Santana and put the live Woodstock version of the same song on the other turntable. By moving back and forth, alternating between the two records, he could extend the song and keep the dancers locked in its groove. But then by blending the two songs – overlaying one completely over the other – he could achieve a dramatic echo effect. It sounded, he says proudly, 'phenomenal'. Skilful DJs today do something very similar called 'phasing', where, by playing two copies of the same record very slightly out of synch, they produce a climactic whooshing sensation in the sound.

Another of his signature mixes was a blend of Led Zeppelin's 'Whole Lotta Love' with the drum break of Chicago Transit Authority's 'I'm A Man'. He sent Robert Plant's primal moans surging over the top of a sea of Latin percussion. The dancefloor mirrored the music's ecstatic rite and reciprocated with cacophonous wails. 'I just basically tried everything there was to try,' he shrugs.

DJ Francis's disciples

In 1970 Steve D'Acquisto was a recently qualified funeral director, driving cabs on the graveyard shift while his embalming licence came through. He dropped off a passenger at 1 Sheridan Square, the Haven.

'I decided I'd try and get into this place. I had long hair right down my back at this point so they let me in, figuring I was some kind of freak.'

D'Acquisto was astonished at the music he heard there. It wasn't just the funky and unfamiliar records being danced to; it was the way they were played – they were being mixed. 'On radio, basically the fade would arrive and the new one would come in, and here was this guy, playing records, mixing records, doing all these great things that had never happened before.'

D'Acquisto, entranced by Francis Grasso's music, would quickly become his partner in crime. He was an immediate regular at Haven, joining the DJ in his drug-fuelled nights of wild rhythm and blues. 'Francis and I got friendly. By now I'd be going every night and we'd speed together. He was a speedfreak as well; loved speed. I always had good drugs; he always had good drugs.' Grasso even got his friend hired to work the lights, a job D'Acquisto held for about six months. 'Then one night I was at Francis's house and he'd been playing for two weeks straight and his alternate hadn't showed. They called Francis and told him he had to come in; it was a Monday night, one of the off nights.' But Grasso was feeling pretty burnt out, and at the Haven there was rarely an early end to the night. 'It would depend on how high people were as to how late the club stayed open. So Francis says, "I can't do this." And he looked at me and said, "Do you wanna go play some records? Just make believe you're me." So I did and I liked it.'

Soon afterwards, the Haven added a third disc jockey to its rota, a head-turning Brooklyn Italian called Michael Cappello, another clubber sparked by Francis's DJing. Younger than both D'Acquisto and Grasso, yet extremely streetwise, Cappello completed a troika: three music-crazy youngsters who'd been turned on by flower power and seduced by rhythm and blues. With Grasso as their mentor, the two new apprentices eagerly learned his techniques.

'I had to teach somebody,' says Francis. 'I was teaching in secret because it was really hard to do what I do. I needed somebody reliable who knew what they were basically doing, at least had an idea. I may teach you the basic moves, but it's your interpretation that makes or breaks you.'

The trio became tight friends, often spending day after day together, hunting for records, getting tips from the radio, often not sleeping for days. All fuelled by a prodigious intake of amphetamine. 'Sometimes Michael, Francis and I wouldn't sleep for three or four days at a time,' recalls D'Acquisto. 'We'd go on and on, snorting speed and crystal meth. We were very serious about our speed! We had to be, though– we were playing twelve or fifteen hours in a night, every single night.'

When reminded of this, Grasso just laughs. 'Was it only *four* days at a time?'

Despite being only sixteen years old when he began DJing, Cappello quickly forged a reputation as a consummate spinner – first at the Haven, then joining D'Acquisto and Grasso when they moved back to the Sanctuary. 'As far as I'm concerned, Michael Cappello was the best DJ who ever did his thing,' asserts D'Acquisto. 'I could listen to Michael hour after hour, night after night, and he never bored me. Always inventive, always genius; extremely clever.'

Cappello would later be one of the key spinners of the disco period, playing at the original Limelight, where his smooth, climactic style was much admired. 'Michael would peak the crowd,' remembers Nicky Siano, another rising DJ star of the time. 'He would take it up and it would stay up, and it would go up and up and up and up, beyond where you'd feel you could go. It was great.' Siano, like many others, also remembers him for his looks. 'Michael was so easy to look at, and he was not a very talkative kind of person. But he was just really good at playing records.' Today, Cappello is believed to own a Brooklyn construction business.

With their revolutionary mixing techniques, not to mention their stalwart drug consumption and adventurous sexual antics, Grasso, Cappello and D'Acquisto were to have a powerful influence on the scene, providing much in the way of inspiration for what would become disco. Their technical skills, their attitude to their performance, and their abilities to manipulate a dancefloor were what gave the nascent club scene much of its momentum. And to hear them play was to realise that DJing would never be the same again. People recall that the impact was as dramatic as first hearing hip hop years later.

Steve D'Acquisto went on to help launch the first record pool and recorded with Arthur Russell as Loose Joints. After a long career working in audio manufacturing, he died in May 2000. He honoured us shortly before his death by playing his last gig at the American launch party for the first edition of this book. It was a miracle he turned up, since his mother had died that day, but he wanted to pay tribute to her in the only way he knew how: with music. His last record was a suitable memoriam, Curtis Mayfield's 'Love Me, Love Me Now'.

Francis Grasso is also no longer with us. He was found dead at his Brooklyn home on 18 March 2001, apparently from suicide; recent years had not been kind to him. He had carried on DJing until 1981, although his career was almost stopped at the height of his fame when he was beaten mercilessly by mafia goons for daring to leave a club residency in order to set up Club Francis, a rather ill-advised project bankrolled on the strength of his name. Ignoring the command to merely scare him, the hoods crushed his face in to the point where he was in hospital for three months undergoing reconstructive surgery. 'I was beaten to a bloody pulp,' he says. 'I was in the emergency room of St Vincent's hospital in Manhattan, I remember these two doctors, they said, "Shame, must have been a good-looking guy." ' To add insult to injury, while he was in hospital his neighbour moved house and took all his records.

If this was his worst moment, his best, he says, came after he had just left the Sanctuary for the Haven. Returning to help fix some equipment, he was mobbed by the dancers, who thought he was going to play for them. 'I walked in and the customers saw me behind in the booth, they all applauded, there was this big cheer. They loved me. I got immediately humbled. *Immediately*. People didn't want to see me leave.'

Ironically, despite laying its groundwork, Francis never much cared for disco, although he carried on playing right through its heyday. He has little time for DJs nowadays, arguing that these days the records do all the work, not like when he was playing for ten hours and changing the record every two minutes.

If you are a club DJ today, Francis Grasso is your forefather; he changed the whole idea of DJing. The disc jockey before him had been a slave to the records. After him the DJ would be a slave only to the rhythm.

Sound system evangelist

As well as the existence of such pioneering stars, crucial to the rapid rise of the club DJ were the innovations in sound processing that were also made at this time. Luckily for Grasso and his colleagues, the sound systems at both the Haven and the Sanctuary had been built by a true loudspeaker evangelist.

As a child Alex Rosner had been spared the horrors of the Holocaust by his love of music. Having been sent to Auschwitz he accompanied his violin-playing father on the accordian at a concert for the guards. The commandant was touched by his performance enough to single him out for survival, giving his father a wink as he marched all the other children to their deaths. By the early sixties, he was in America working as an engineer in the defence industry. As a hobby, he liked to experiment with stereophonic audio systems, indulging his passionate belief in the superiority of recorded sound.

'To this day, I like the concept of the discothèque,' he explains. 'I like the concept of reproduced music as opposed to live music. And I thought that the technology was available to make things sound good and sound realistic. I experimented a lot.'

Rosner constructed his first sound system for the Canada-A-Go-Go and Carnival-A-Go-Go stands at the 1964-5 World's Fair. This was where he built the world's first stereophonic disco system. 'Up until then it had all been mono. There was no equipment available at the time. There were no mixers; no stereo mixers; no cueing devices. Nothing.' He swiftly moved into clubs, first with a little place called the Ginza and then with the Haven, where he made the first ever stereo mixer – used to devastating effect by Francis Grasso. 'The cueing system was one of my old-fashioned adventures,' Rosner says. 'They called it the Rosie because it was painted red. It was really primitive and not very good. But it did the job. And nobody could complain, because there was nothing else around.'

Rosner was also instrumental in building the world's first commercially available mixer, the 1971 Bozak, advising its inventor, Louis Bozak, on the more practical side of nightclub requirements. 'I had to invent the wheel until the Bozak mixer came along,' he remembers. 'But I helped Bozak design his mixer; I gave him suggestions so he could make it better. He already had a ten-channel input mixer. I suggested to him that he only needed to make minor modifications to this unit to make it into a stereophonic disco mixer. And right off the bat, he did it the right way.' Bozak's prototype mixer became industry standard for the next fifteen years and is now a collector's item.

David Mancuso at the Loft

If disco has an angel, it is the raggedy figure of David Mancuso; if it has a birthplace, it is his club, the Loft. More influential than any nightclub before or since, it was the place where the music you dance to today, and the places you go to do it, were first envisaged.

Mancuso discovered and championed more classic dance records than anyone can remember; he inspired a whole generation of DJs, record collectors, club founders and label owners; he set the standards for club sound reproduction and, in the Loft, he created a place where the equality and love of a thousand corny dance lyrics was a reality. Fortified by the cosmic perspectives of the hippie generation, turned on by a profound love of music and finding himself alive in a time of exciting possibilities, David Mancuso laid the cornerstone of modern clubbing.

While Grasso and his compadres had started to release the creative potential of a DJ and a pile of records, Mancuso would draw up the blueprints for the transcendent dancefloor experience, ideas which have been copied consciously and unconsciously by clubs and clubbers ever since. And the Loft lives on. Regular parties in London and New York mean Mancuso's club has enjoyed a more or less unbroken thirty-five-year existence.

Mancuso himself, a shy man who speaks in mumbles from behind wild eyes and a bushy beard, is viewed by many as a crazy musical mystic. He demands perfect sound reproduction, he refuses to mix records, insisting that they be heard entire and unchanged, and when he talks about music his words are usually a universe away from how your average DJ would put things. However, most people who have ever felt the emotional

Disco daddio – David Mancuso provided the blueprint for nightclubbing and inspired a generation of DJs with names ending in 'O'.

charge of a dancefloor instinctively understand the elusive feelings that he's trying to express.

Mancuso has lived with a lifelong obsession about the relationship between recorded music, the person who plays that music and the bodies and souls of the people listening and dancing. As a DJ he would never lay claim to anything so egotistical as 'playing a great set'; for him, a wonderful night is made as much by the dancers as the music, guided as much by the spirit of joy in the room as by the hand which chooses the next record.

David Mancuso, born in Utica, New York, on 20 October 1944, tells of being raised by a kindly nun in an orphanage of twenty kids. To this day, he can recall how she would treat the children with juice to drink and put a stack of records on a big boxy radiogram for them to sing and dance to. He is convinced she had a profound impact on how he conceived the parties he would later create. 'I have a feeling part of my influence – why it's communal, why I do it the way I wanna do it – it has to be to do with back then. Sister Alicia would find any excuse to have a party.'

By the age of fifteen, Mancuso was working as a shoeshine boy. After moving to New York during the Cuban missile crisis in 1962, he worked at various jobs – including designing towels and as a personnel manager – before he got bored, as he says, 'of the nine to five thing'. He drifted through life in the city, making friends, struggling to make money, struggling harder to have a good time, until in 1970 he began throwing after-hours parties starting around midnight in the loft where he lived – at 647 Broadway, just north of Houston Street. Though it was never formally titled, this balloon-filled party space soon became known by all who attended simply as the Loft.

The Loft wasn't much to look at and it wasn't very big. But it was homely, it had a great domestic hi-fi system, and in Mancuso it had a musical director with an acute ear for the dramatic, the atmospheric and the heavily rhythmic. Mancuso, as much a product of the psychedelic era as he was a black music aficionado, conceived the Loft as a series of rent parties, with invites bestowed only on close friends.

'I was in a commercial loft,' he remembers. 'There were sprinklers and everything. I sent out thirty-six invitations; but it took a while to get going. After six months, it opened up every week.' He was very strict about the status of his guests, guided by clear aims and well thought-out principles. 'When you came in, everything was included in the contribution. You were not a member. It was not a club. I didn't want to be in that category. It meant different things to me. I wanted to keep it as close to a party as possible. It was $2.50 and for that you'd get your coat checked, food, and the music. In those days the bars were only open till 3am and if anything was open after three, you could be pretty sure it was gambling or liquor and I wasn't into any of that. I didn't want to be into any of that. I wanted it to be private. And you have to remember that the Loft was also where I slept, where I dreamt. Everything.'

As well as carefully controlling who came to the parties, Mancuso paid exquisite attention to the music. He understood that the dynamics of sound he projected were as important as the records he was playing. 'I wanna hear the music. Once you hear the sound system, that means you're getting ear damage; ear fatigue. So you wanna hear the music, not the system.'

Sometime during 1971, he was introduced to Alex Rosner. 'A mutual friend said I should stop by and look at David's club, because I could be of some service to him. Which I was. I rebuilt his club for him and made his sound much better. He had what was basically a home system. When I got through with it, it was a disco system.'

The precision of the sound system which Rosner and Mancuso created between them has subsequently become the accepted standard for every nightclub in the world. 'It's just a matter of quality,' says Rosner. 'See, I was an audiophile. I applied audiophile techniques – hi-fidelity – to commercial sound, which until then had never been done. Most commercial sound systems sounded lousy. I made it sound good by putting in good components. There were no secrets; it was just a matter of persuading the owner that he had to spend the money to up the ante and put in the proper components. I knew where to put the loudspeakers. I knew how many to use and how to make it sound good.'

The two made a formidable alliance, with Mancuso supplying the visionary ideas for Rosner's practical expertise. One day he asked Rosner to create two tweeter-array clusters (tweeters are the small speakers which deliver the high-end, or treble, of a recording). 'He told me to build them and I said I didn't think it was a good idea,' recalls Rosner. 'He said, "I don't care what you think, just make it anyway." I didn't think it was a *bad* idea, I just thought it was too much. Normally in a sound system, there's one tweeter per channel. He wanted eight. I thought it would be too much high frequency.'

But on this occasion, the visionary was right and the expert was wrong, as Rosner admits. 'It was so high up, that's not where the pain level is. That's not where the hardness is. The more you have up there the better. So it was actually a terrific idea.'

Once completed, the resulting system was peerless. As Mancuso says, 'The one thing the Loft did do was set a standard: getting your money's worth, providing a decent sound system.' Klippschorn speakers (developed by Paul Klippsch in the 1920s and renowned for their simplicity and purity), JBL bullet tweeter arrays and, later, Koetsu hand-crafted cartridges and Mitchell Cotter turntable bases. 'He put the Klippschorns in such a way,' recalls Nicky Siano, 'that they put out the sound and they reflected it too, so they covered the whole area and exaggerated the sound.' And the Loft was a great place for sonic experiments. 'His room was perfect to do this with. He used to be on the dancefloor, the lights would go out and there would be these little table lamps in the corner and the tweeters would come on and the lamps would go out. It was freaky deaky.'

A clientele selected by genuine friendship, music and sound that was out of this world, and a uniquely welcoming environment: no one had ever been anywhere quite like this before. The Loft was a revelation. Only a couple of miles separated it from glamorous clubs like Arthur, Le Club and Cheetah, but it was worlds apart in concept and execution. Since his many friends were drawn from the full spectrum of the counter-culture, Mancuso's club became a refuge from the outside world; a secret cabal of the disaffected and disenfranchised. 'We used to squeeze fresh orange juice and organic nuts and raisins,' he remembers. 'We did the place up. Everything was quality. Everyone used to come there: Patti Labelle, Divine, all of them. As people, too, because everybody that came there was able to relax. And, of course, you would not get into this space unless you had an invitation.'

Loft babies – a precious invite to the Loft in New York.

Inevitably, Mancuso encountered the West Village triumvirate of Grasso, Cappello and D'Acquisto. 'I went to see Steve D'Acquisto at his club,' he recalls, 'and I liked the way he was doing things. So I walked over to him and said, "You know, I really like the music. Look, I have this place; it's downtown. It's my place, it's a private party. Do you wanna bring a friend?" And he did. That's how I met Michael Cappello and Francis.'

When Steve D'Acquisto discovered the Loft, he felt he was finally home.

'I went there on my own one night and I walked into a world of unbelievable sound and tremendous beauty. Just special as can be. There was nothing like the Loft. The Loft was a small little place. But it was just unbelievable.'

In return for his hospitality, Grasso and his pals introduced Mancuso to their new mixing techniques – the segué, slip-cueing and beat-mixing

– showing him how they created the suites of interlocking sound with which they energised the Haven and Sanctuary. Mancuso had been experimenting with ideas of his own, and already owned an extensive collection of sound effects albums which he would play over the ends and beginnings of songs (an idea he had copied from New York radio station WNAW). Gradually he learned the skills needed to mix records although later, as he formulated his ideas about the purity of the song, Mancuso would refrain from mixing altogether.

'He wasn't mixing when I met him,' recalls D'Acquisto. 'He had two turntables, but when one was stopping the other was starting. He did mix eventually, for a lot of years. The most popular years of the Loft were when he mixed. I said to him, "You should never let the music stop." '

The late Larry Levan, Mancuso's most revered protegé, paid tribute to him in 1983, speaking to journalist Steven Harvey. 'David Mancuso was always very influential with his music and the mixes. He didn't play records unless they were serious. When I listen to DJs today, they don't mean anything to me. Technically, some of them are excellent – emotionally, they can't do anything for me. I used to watch people cry in the Loft for a slow song, because it was so pretty.'

The message is love

Hear Mancuso spin today and you will probably find it unusual to hear a DJ play records with so much reverence. He leaves space between each track, plays them complete from beginning to end and with no change in pitch or adjustment in EQ. However strange this seems, it will gradually start to make sense as you realise that his skill lies not in tricks and mixes but in using records to tell a story, to generate and reflect a changing mood. Each song follows the last in a profound musical narrative.

'I spent a lot of time in the country, listening to birds, lying next to a spring and listening to water go across the rocks,' Mancuso told the *Village Voice*'s Vince Aletti in 1975. 'And suddenly one day I realised, what perfect music. Like with sunrise and sunset, how things would build up into midday. There were times when it would be intense and times it would be very soft, and at sunset it would get quiet and then the crickets would come in. I took this sense of rhythm, this sense of feeling . . .'

Aletti, a young journalist who had immediately recognised the Loft's cultural importance, was himself a true devotee of the club.

'Dancing at the Loft was like riding waves of music, being carried along as one song after another built relentlessly to a brilliant crest and broke, bringing almost involuntary shouts of approval from the crowd, then smoothed out, softened, and slowly began welling up to another peak,' he wrote in 1975.

Indeed, he was so struck by the magically evolving atmosphere of Mancuso's musical wonderland that he would purposely arrive before anyone else.

'I would go early and hang out with David in the booth, because I loved hearing the music that started out the night,' he remembers. 'Some of my favourite music was David's early records. He would make this whole atmosphere when people were coming in. Before people started dancing. Oddball things that he would discover, mostly jazz-fusion records or world music. Things that didn't have any lyrics for the most part, but were just cool-out or warm-up records. And I loved that kind of stuff. It was great to see the mood getting set. Little by little, they would get more rhythmic and more and more danceable and people would start dancing. I loved seeing the whole theatre get underway. It was like being at a play before the actors had started.'

Aletti had been one of the very first journalists to take dance music seriously. Born in Philadelphia in 1945, he had caught the Motown bug while studying literature at college in Ohio. He got his writing break with one of the many counter-culture rags that sprang up in late sixties New York, *Rat*. He was soon writing for *Fusion, Rolling Stone, Creem* and *Crawdaddy*, usually as a black music specialist. He figured himself an expert in his field; and when a magazine needed a review of the Jackson 5 or Mary Wells, it was to Aletti they increasingly turned. As disco began to surface from its underground beginnings, he was quickly its most vocal cheerleader, championing the scene and its music whenever he could.

'I heard about the Loft through this group of friends, some of whom were would-be disc jockeys. But I wasn't used to staying up until twelve in order to go out to some place, so they had to really get me into it. But once they did . . . it was like nothing I'd ever done before. And it was exciting to go to a place where almost every record I heard was completely new and great. So all I wanted to do was write down all the titles. "What is this?" '

Aletti was struck not only by the music but also by the mix of people. Even today, he remembers disco very passionately as a unifying force, a loving rejection of long-accepted social barriers. For him, the Loft epitomised this. 'It was like going to a party, completely mixed, racially and sexually, where there wasn't any sense of someone being more important than anyone else. It really felt like a lot of friends hanging out. David had a lot to do with creating that atmosphere. Everybody who worked there was very friendly. There were people putting up buffets, and fruit and juice and popcorn and all kinds of stuff.'

Alex Rosner, too, was struck by the Loft's vividly unifying atmosphere (it was probably about sixty per cent black and seventy per cent gay). 'When I first went to his club and saw the excitement and energy there, it was very inspirational to me. At that point I thought discos were a wonderful idea. There was a mix of sexual orientation, there was a mix of races, mix of economic groups. A real mix, where the common denominator was music. I remember ripping off my shirt and dancing. I loved the music. It was the real stuff. It was terrific.'

The club's pan-sexual attitude was revolutionary in a country where up until recently it had been illegal for two men to dance together unless there was a woman present; where women were legally obliged to wear at least one recognisable item of female clothing in public; and where men visiting gay bars usually carried bail money with them. All were disarmed and united by Mancuso's hypnotic mysticism and quasi-religious karma, all of which permeated his music.

Taking influences from the hippie era, he would play the blue-eyed soul of Rare Earth, white soul singer Bonnie Bramlett (whose 'Crazy 'Bout My Baby' was an unlikely Loft anthem), 'Glad' by Traffic and the West Coast sound of the Doobie Brothers. Added to the mix would be the Temptations' 'Papa Was A Rolling Stone', War's City 'Country City' or the heavy Afro-funk of Manu Dibango. Andwela's 'Hold On To Your Mind', a bizarre piece of Irish psychedelic rock, was a Loft exclusive, as was 'Wind' by Circus Maximus, alongside hundreds of other beautiful oddities. A kind of theme tune was Fred Wesley's 'House Party', which summed up the spirit of the place. Mancuso would play a lot of instrumentals and lots of more percussive Latinesque tracks. And he would always be drawn to a song whose lyrics carried positive meaning. The rules were simple: it had to be soulful, rhythmic and impart words of hope, redemption or pride. Love was the message.

Because his impact on the nascent disco scene was so great, it's hard to say whether David Mancuso's strong ideals were merely a timely reflection of a common feeling, or whether to some extent he gave dance music its obsession with freedom and inclusivity. Even if this gentle man is not its definitive source, his spirit was certainly a catalyst for disco's optimistic faith in equality. Certainly, his message of love rarely went unnoticed.

'He's picking a record that's not just a hit record, but he's picking a record that's timely for these particular people; and he's also talking a message,' relates Danny Krivit, another Loft regular and a DJ himself since childhood. 'There's a story being woven. With, say, Nicky Siano at the Gallery, it would be a vocal story. With David it was a mood story. David in general was always about love, and he'd always try to stay with that.'

Krivit had been raised in the nightclub business and was perfectly placed to observe the developing scene. His stepfather Bobby owned the Ninth Circle, a downtown landmark, and the young Danny had served John Lennon, Janis Joplin and Jimi Hendrix before he was ten, and was making tapes for the place – which, significantly, had 'gone gay' in 1971 – since the age of fourteen. Krivit was also at that time another aspirant DJ mesmerised by the Loft.

'I just remember it was unique,' he recalls. 'Before that, my idea of a club was more dressy, the Saturday night out feeling. The Loft was the opposite of that – it was a professional house party. These were eccentric club people who were really into dancing. They knew music, not just the top ten hit parade, but they knew music you'd never heard before. That impressed me. The type of music that was being played, it just had a lot more substance to it.'

Breaking records

Mancuso was paving the way for a new kind of club DJ; not necessarily as technically adept as Francis Grasso, but a figure who is librarian, antiquarian, archaeologist. With his zeal as a musical missionary, Mancuso was far from the human jukebox of old. He was driven by a desire to discover great music, to track down records and then share his secrets with other DJs. In truth, he was rarely one to scrabble for them himself; Loft regulars would often bring them to him. But if Mancuso found a record he loved, he wanted everyone to hear it and know its name.

Barrabas' debut LP is a case in point. Barrabas were a Spanish rock-funk outfit signed to RCA in Spain, with members of the band hailing from Cuba, Portugal and the Philippines, a fact reflected in their oddly Afro-Latin sound. 'I was in Amsterdam looking for some records,' recalls Mancuso. 'I'd never heard of them, I just liked the information that was on the sleeve; it looked interesting. I brought it back, checked it out and there were a couple of good things on it.' Both 'Woman' and 'Wild Safari', white-voiced Latino rock work-outs, became Loft staples. Mancuso called the record company in Spain and imported several boxes of the album. He would sell them, at cost price, to Loft regulars.

Another record which came to prominence via the Loft was Babe Ruth's 'The Mexican', now regarded by hip hop connoisseurs as a defining b-boy hymn. Like Barrabas, Babe Ruth's track record did not suggest greatness. Formed in Hatfield, in suburban England, they had instant success with their first album in, of all places, Canada. This LP, *First Base*, a mainly rock-by-numbers workout, was spared only by the inclusion of 'The Mexican'. Coincidentally, after some run-ins with club owners in New York, Steve D'Acquisto was in Montreal when the record broke there. He quickly brought it to Mancuso's attention. 'I worked with Rob Ouimet in a place called Love. I was his alternate. And Rob gave "The Mexican" by Babe Ruth to me; then I brought it back here.' Once the record had been popularised in the Loft, DJs across New York started searching it out; news of this obscure gem even reached the closed world of the Bronx, where the DJs formulating hip hop would make it an anthem.

'The New York grapevine was so intense,' says Aletti. 'A record could break in a club one night and next day everybody who cared about it would know about that record and would be running around town trying to find it. At this point, everybody was friendly and it didn't feel like a scene full of rivals. They really wanted to share the music.' An infectious camaraderie became the norm, with DJs swapping notes and tipping each other off about records. The loose tangle of jocks would either meet in West Village omelette house David's Pot Belly or, more often, could be found hanging out for hours on end at Downstairs Records in Times Square or Colony on Broadway.

'There was a period, at the beginning, where all the disc jockeys felt like proselytisers. Not just to their audience but to each other,' says Aletti. 'It was a real community. They were happy to share and make connections with other people. It seemed like a small scene and they were real buddies. They lived and breathed music and didn't talk about anything else. It wasn't like they had a big life outside of the clubs anyway.

'Before clubs became very successful and made a lot of money, a lot of DJs played several nights a week at several different clubs and they lived for nothing else. That was their currency: the newest record. There was a constant trawling of record stores and places where they knew they could find things. It was an active, and great, network, and it was all about sharing.'

Another key Loft record was Manu Dibango's 'Soul Makossa'. The success of this obscure gem showed how powerful the Loft's influence (bolstered by the growing number of underground clubs at that time) had become. Mancuso had picked up the record, then on a tiny French independent label, Fiesta, from a Jamaican store in Brooklyn sometime late in 1972. With its distinctive Afro-jazz rhythms it was an immediate success with jocks throughout the city, breaking out of the clubs thanks to radio DJ Frankie Crocker at WBLS. Eventually, after Atlantic picked up the rights to the track, it punctured the *Billboard* pop chart. Something was becoming rapidly apparent: these new clubs not only had power to break songs to the clubbers on their dancefloors, they also were capable of making hit records.

'The best discothèque DJs are underground stars, discovering previously ignored albums, foreign imports, album cuts and obscure singles with the power to make the crowd scream and playing them overlapped, non-stop, so you dance until you drop,' wrote Vince Aletti. 'Because these DJs are much closer to the minute-to-minute changes in people's listening taste, they are the first to reflect these changes in the music they play, months ahead of trade magazine charts and all but a few radio stations.' This piece, from *Rolling Stone*, 13 September 1973, was the first ever story about what would become known as disco.

And so disco was born. Grasso's mixing and mood manipulation, Alex Rosner's sound systems and Mancuso's musical investigations and ideals of togetherness all came together against the background of New York clubland's new black/gay democracy and the wider liberating forces of social change.

Music was evolving, too. Funk's 'on the one' danceability was meeting crossover soul's prettiness, and a new sound had emerged. Sly & the Family Stone and the Temptations' more psychedelic moments were key points in this, but the thrust of the new music came from song-writer/producers Kenny Gamble and Leon Huff and their Sigma Sound studios in Philadelphia. In the first half of the seventies – with groups like the O'Jays, Harold Melvin & the Bluenotes, MFSB and many more – they produced songs which retained the driving funk beat but which ameliorated its harshness with more complex melodies and rhythm patterns, by adding the soaring sounds of a whole orchestra. As JB's trombonist Fred Wesley put it, 'They put a bow tie on the funk.' This lush music was both commercially successful and also exactly what the new clubs wanted to hear. All the elements were now in place.

Nicky Siano at the Gallery

Arguably, the first commercial club to bring everything together was the Gallery. Nicky Siano, an energetic, bisexual Brooklyn tearaway, had moved into Manhattan at the tender age of sixteen with his girlfriend Robin. It was 1971 and he had already been exploring the post-Stonewall New York nightworld for nearly a year. By the time he was seventeen, he owned his own club.

He had begun DJing at a club called Round Table after Robin charmed the owner into letting Nicky play records there. Then, with help from his older brother, $10,000 from a friend who had received an insurance payout, and another borrowed $5,000, the Gallery was opened in a loft on 22nd Street (it would be later forced to move, for a lack of fire exits, to 172 Mercer Street, after a Fire Department swoop which closed seven similar nightspots). Siano had been transfixed on his visits to the Loft and aimed to create a place as close as possible to David Mancuso's famous house parties.

'I always feel like I took what David did on to a more commercial level,' he says. 'Ours was like a club version of David's. That feeling, that atmosphere, was there. The caring about people and stuff like that. The only thing was, we didn't live there. So it was a little different.' At 3,600 square feet it was bigger, too. With an Alex Rosner sound system (including copies of Mancuso's tweeter arrays) and with Siano's canny move of opening while Mancuso was on vacation and the Loft was on temporary hiatus, it was an immediate success.

'The wildness is exquisitely wholesome,' wrote Sheila Weller about a trip to the Gallery in the *New York Sunday News*. 'Furious dancing. Gentle laughter. Crêpe paper and tinsel. Body energy shakes the room, yet sex is the last thing it calls to mind – except, perhaps, hostility. In darkness pierced by perfectly timed bursts of light, Labelle's rousing "What Can I Do For You?" takes on a frenetic holiness. The floor is a drum to the dancers – many of them gay, most of them black – whose upsprung fists and tambourines lob the balloons and streamers above at what seem to be collectively-chosen intervals.'

Weller's host for the night is another DJ, Richie Kaczor. Noting the direction of the music, he whispers to her, 'Get ready for a rush.'

'And the song smoothly melts into "Love Is The Message" over which DJ Nicky Siano – one of the city's best – blares jet-plane sound effects. On every other bar, the lights vanish and the dancers send up a jubilant uniform chant. "Nicky knows these people like the back of his hand," Richie says, admiring the rite.'

Bob Casey, founder in the mid seventies of the National Association of Discothèque Disc Jockeys (NADD), remembers the Gallery fondly. He recalls watching, as Siano did, his little 'Nicky twist' behind the decks while his friend Robert DaSilva, another 'young white chicken cherub', as Casey describes him, worked the lights.

'And these two little guys are doing the hottest black club in the world. To me, little conservative me, it was the hottest disco I was ever at *in my life*.'

Larry Levan called the Gallery his 'Saturday Mass'. Casey has similar enthusiasm.

'Why? Because they began with the basic colour BLACK! and they worked it up from there. There was no neon. There was no automated anything, there was a few light switches, a couple of light pedals, that's all it was. They'd grab the mirror ball and give it a spin. And you see the reflections – *sshwwwoo* – all over the place. That's where the whistles began. That's where everything like that began. But the thing is, they began with black.'

Casey, who was a nightclub sound engineer throughout the period, explains that by 'black' he's referring as much to the nature of the sound as anything else, detailing how Siano's love for sub-bass drove the atmosphere (and the construction of the system); another early example of a DJ pushing technology forward for his own ends. (Siano also claims to have been the first DJ to use three turntables, inspired by a dream in which he was mixing two records together and wanted to bring in a third.)

'Nicky Siano took his sub-bass . . . *beyond*,' says Casey. 'Because of this black . . . He wanted this heavy sound.' Siano had the crossover points (the circuits which divide the sound's treble, midrange, bass and sub-bass) engineered so he could wow the audience with just the sizzling highs of a record, then just the earth-quaking lows. Casey remembers how the young DJ would use this and have his dancers in the palm of his hand.

'Every once in a while, everybody would be so *together* with it, so together – and they'd be singing along – and Nicky would bring it up and then all of a sudden BOOM! out would drop the centre and everybody would be stunned – "Awwwww!" – and then BLAMM!!, in would come this incredible bass. And by that time – and there's essence of amyl nitrate all over the place – it was flawless.

'And the lighting was with it perfectly. When the music went to black, the room would be black. And you couldn't see your hand in front of your face. And yet there'd be a couple of hundred people in there dancing. It'd be so intense. It would be so intense.'

While Mancuso's influence had worked by way of an underground grapevine, Nicky Siano's was more direct. 'When I played a record it was played everywhere,' he boasts. DJ Kenny Carpenter, a regular at the Gallery, agrees.

'Nicky was the one everybody would go study at the Gallery,' he affirms. 'Nicky knew how to talk with music. He used lyrics to send a message to you. I love you, I hate you, I miss you. You remember Freddie Prinze, he was an actor in a famous sitcom here. He died and that night Nicky played "Freddie's Dead" from the *Superfly* soundtrack. Those kind of things.' And while Mancuso had used music as a mask for his shyness, Siano was a shameless exhibitionist.

'Everyone basically played the same records back then,' Siano recalls. 'It was just how people put them together. My style was to link the fillers and let them build and then go into the good ones and just go off, on an hour of good ones, until people were screaming so loud they couldn't stand it any more.'

With songs like Diana Ross's 'Love Hangover', Harold Melvin's 'The Love I Lost', the Trammps' 'Love Epidemic', 'Where Is The Love?' by Betty Wright, and of course his theme tune, MFSB's 'Love Is The Message' (many DJs claimed this as their own; Siano and Mancuso probably have the most rights to it), all mixed through Thorens TD125 turntables and a Bozak mixer, Siano would encourage his dancefloor to completely lose it, creating more abandon than any DJ before.

'People got really out of control,' he says. 'I remember someone having an epileptic fit one night because they were just driving themself so hard. There were points when the music was taking people so far out and getting so peaked out that people would be chanting, "TURN THIS MOTHERFUCKER OUT." That started at the Gallery – they're blowing whistles, and screaming, "Yeah! Yeah! Yeah! Yeah!" And then I'd turn up the bass horns and the lights would flash and go out, and everyone would *screeeam* so loud you couldn't hear the music for a second.'

Tony Smith, who made a name for himself at Barefoot Boy, a small but influential midtown club, was one of the many young DJs who partied at the Gallery. 'Nicky was just crazy!' laughs Smith 'He got famous even younger than I did. He'd play the most insane things; he would take any chance. The other DJs, I didn't know whether they were taking drugs, but I knew Nicky was – because he was so crazy. There was just no way he couldn't have been.'

'He would be like: I'm in the DJ booth. This couldn't be a tape. This couldn't be just a record you like. *I'm* playing this record. He had a presence,' remembers Danny Krivit. 'He was also very much about drugs, especially towards the end of the Gallery. High, but not too high to play the music. There'd always be a point where it seemed like he'd collapse in a very dramatic manner: fall on the turntables and stop the music. Everyone knew what was going on, and they'd be patient and know that somehow, somebody would help him get it together and an even better record would come on. And usually it did.'

'The first year that the new Gallery was open,' Siano told writer Tim Lawrence, 'we had this huge party on the Fourth of July. We rewrote the Declaration of Independence. Wherever it said, "We the people of the United States" it was "We the people of the Gallery" and "We want to dance all night". I came out as the Statue of Liberty. I had these draping robes and this big crown, and when they turned out the lights to sing the national anthem, my crown lit up. People went bananas. And my friend Monica, she was so stoned on acid, she starts screaming, "They're electrocuting him! They're electrocuting him!" We had to drag her off the dancefloor because she was ruining my act – and my hat.'

The Gallery messed with people's heads until 1978. On its closure, Siano left for a club called Buttermilk Bottom (he also spun for three months at Studio 54), playing there until a serious drug problem got the better of him. He returned to New York a few years ago, having beaten his demons, has published a successful book *No Time To Wait* about alternative HIV treatments, and has resumed a successful DJing career.

To this day he maintains a belief in the vast power of music to unite and heal.

'There is a force that connects us,' he insists. 'And if I connect with that force, which I think is love, if I connect with that force and I'm playing from that centre, we're all gonna get it, we're all gonna get off on it.'

The discothèque boom

By the mid seventies, there were an estimated 150–200 clubs in New York. Several were inspired by the Loft (which had by now moved to a larger space at 99 Prince Street): the Gallery, the Soho Place, Reade Street, Tenth Floor and the Flamingo. Many others were updates on the chic niteries that had formed the backbone of midtown nightlife since Le Directoire and Arthur in the sixties. Others still, opening in the city's outer boroughs, were clones of the hottest Manhattan hangouts.

The growth in nightlife was so explosive it was hard to quantify accurately. As Bob Casey told *New York Sunday News*: 'It's hard to give a firm number on how many discothèques there are in New York because every Joe's Pizzeria in town is now hooking up a couple of turntables and calling itself a "discothèque". I've heard reports that there are as many as a hundred and seventy-five in the five boroughs now, but I'd say there are only twenty good, genuine ones.'

Like the twist craze before it, disco was forged amid a terrible recession and the deep scars of war, this time in Vietnam. 'People have always lost themselves in dancing when the economy's been bad,' Casey told the same paper. 'The discos now are doing exactly the same thing that the big dance halls with the crystal chandeliers did during the Depression. Everyone's out to spend their unemployment cheque, their welfare: to lose themselves.' This was the 'Bad Luck' that Harold Melvin & the Bluenotes had so potently sung about.

Recession or no, David Mancuso and Francis Grasso between them had created a blossoming DJ culture. 'The typical New York discothèque DJ is young, Italian and gay,' wrote Vince Aletti, referring to the scores of pretty boys with names ending in 'O' who were taking over the city's nightlife.

While some resented the newer clubs and upstart spinners, Mancuso welcomed them. 'I wasn't really bothered that those places opened. I was glad they were doing it.' Ever the evangelist, he was happy to see more people enjoying this music. 'There are eight million people in New York. A lot of people want to party. And the more people partying, the better it is. Why not? It was like the civil rights movement: the more people you had marching the better it was.'

The Loft had unleashed the greatest period of creativity in the history of nightlife. Early disco inspired great leaps in club sound reproduction, in the equipment available to the DJ, and, of course, in the music and the styles which he played. The waves even rippled out as far as Brooklyn, the Bronx and Harlem, where mobile disco DJs like Grandmaster Flowers and Pete DJ Jones would put their own spin on the music and help give birth to hip hop.

As disco spread throughout New York and beyond, the DJ's art was gradually and constantly refined. Several key disc jockeys in particular contributed to the refinement of the art; each one adding to the growing accumulation of wisdom.

Larry Levan and Frankie Knuckles at the Continental Baths

Though they are remembered more for their post-disco experiments, both Larry Levan and Frankie Knuckles began their trade during the underground days of disco. The two had been best friends since their teenage years – so inseparable that people confused their names – and as they danced across the city together, they were soon known in Manhattan's clubs as energetic party catalysts. Their adventures started in a tiny gay bar called the Planetarium, but soon they were regulars at the Loft, where Levan was mesmerised by David Mancuso's musical mastery. When Nicky Siano opened the Gallery, he recruited the two club bunnies to put up the decorations, set out the buffet and pop acid blotters into the mouths of arriving guests.

'Part of our job description was spiking the punch,' explained Knuckles in an interview in *Muzik*. 'We'd be given tabs of acid and we'd spike the punch with them. We'd always have lots of people coming up to us and saying, "When's the punch going to be ready, when are you going to bring out the punch?"'

By 1971 they were DJs, Knuckles having landed a six-month job at Better Days and Levan having talked his way into a job at the Continental Baths, working the lights for DJ Joseph Bonfiglio – a permanent fixture on the early disco scene – and playing the warm-up slot twice a week. At first Knuckles refused to visit his friend in the Bacchanalian 'Tubs', as it was known, even though Levan was now living in an apartment there. When he finally set foot in it, he didn't leave for three weeks.

Christmas baubles – Frankie Knuckles (*left*) and Larry Levan (*right*) pose outside the steam room of the Continental Baths to send their 1974 seasonal message to readers of *Melting Pot* magazine.

The Baths was no ordinary club. Situated below the Ansonia Hotel on 73rd and Broadway, it was an opulent gay bath-house with steam rooms, swimming pool, private apartments, restaurant and disco. Its owner Steve Ostrow was instrumental in helping to liberalise the city's laws on sex clubs. 'We kept thrashing it out with the authorities, the police, the Department of Consumer Affairs, and eventually we got action,' he told the *New York Sunday News*. 'We've done such a good job liberating the city, we've almost hurt our own business. We used to be the only ball game in town.'

The Tubs had originally gained fame as the place where Bette Midler had cut her formidable teeth in cabaret (with a young Barry Manilow accompanying her on piano). It would later become the swingers' paradise Plato's Retreat, with a DJ called Bacho Mangual and one of the era's few women jocks, Sharon White. For several years in between, it was also a successful disco, capitalising on its revered homo decadence by allowing straight folk in to dance at the weekends. It was kitted out by Bob Casey, who gave it sixteen Bose speakers and 3,500 watts of power. 'A lot for that small space,' he recalls.

'It was very upscale,' remembers Nicky Siano. 'It was like, "We're so chi-chi in our towels, cruising each other and slapping each other's dicks." It was like a kind of orgy, kind of Roman. And then people came out in their towels and everyone would dance.'

In 1973 Levan became the club's main DJ, with Frankie playing warm-up and on the quieter nights. Levan left in 1974 to start his own club along with his partner, sound engineer Richard Long. This acted as the prototype for the legendary Paradise Garage. Though it was the Garage that made him a star, Levan never forgot that his roots lay in disco's first heady years.

After Levan left, Knuckles became the Baths' resident, playing there until its closure, when he, famously, moved to Chicago and, as we'll see, forged house music. He never forgot the Continental Baths, however, telling Sheryl Garratt, 'Playing there every night, listening to music over and over. That's how I got most of my education.'

Walter Gibbons at Galaxy 21

Galaxy 21 was a spectacular concern on 23rd Street, near the Chelsea Hotel, open from approximately 1972 to 1976. The dancefloor ran the length of the building – two brownstone town houses knocked together – with the DJ, Walter Gibbons, in a cramped booth at the back. It was like a glamour tunnel. Upstairs there was a restaurant, a chill-out area, a movie theatre showing X-rated flicks, and on the top floor, a cabaret. It was a saturnalian assault of the senses, with Gibbons conducting the ritual at its centre.

Tony Smith recalls the first time he heard him. 'He blew me away. More than Nicky, Richie Kaczor, all of them. Walter was just way ahead.'

'Walter played in a black club and he was as white as can be,' remembers Tom Moulton, the pioneer of remixing. 'But when it came to black music, he'd give you a run for your money. He was Mister Soul when it came to deep, deep black. He knew his stuff.'

What was remarkable about Gibbons' style was his use of portentous drum patterns: tribal percussive symphonies played out with religious fervour. Prefiguring the amazing cut and paste skills later developed by the hip hop DJs, Gibbons would take two copies of a track, for example 'Erucu', a Jermaine Jackson production from the *Mahogany* soundtrack, or 'Two Pigs And A Hog' from the *Cooley High* soundtrack, and mix and splice the drum breaks so adroitly it was impossible to tell that the music you were hearing hadn't been originally recorded that way. DJs of the time described his style as 'jungle music'.

'I thought I was the best DJ in the world until I heard Walter Gibbons play,' Jellybean Benitez, a young Bronx-born DJ destined for stardom, told Steven Harvey. 'Everything people are doing now, he was doing back then. He was phasing records – playing two records at the same time to give a flange effect – and doubling up records so that there would be a little repeat. He would do tremendous quick cuts on records, sort of like b-boys do. He would slam it in so quick that you couldn't hear the turntable slowing down or catching up. He would do little edits on tape and people would freak out.'

'Everyone knew how to mix,' explains Tony Smith, 'but Walter, he could remix a record live and you don't know he's remixing it. I heard him playing "Girl You Need A Change Of Mind". There's a famous bootleg that loops the bongoes – Walter used to do that live. He would loop the break in Rare Earth's "Happy Song" and that's just twelve seconds long! He did it live, in front of a thousand people, without a crossfader – *on acid* – and never made mistakes!'

Alongside Gibbons, the club also hired a drummer, François Kevorkian, who would set up his kit on the dancefloor and play along to the heavy-duty black rhythms pulsing through the club. François had only recently arrived in New York from his native France in the hope of receiving tuition from Tony Williams, Miles Davis's drummer, and putting a band together. His gig at Galaxy brought him right into the heart of the early disco scene and would provide the basis for a prodigious career in dance music. 'It was very underground at the time,' he recalls. 'Very downtown, very black, Latino, and quite a bit gay, too. Those worlds weren't ones I was very familiar with. But it was a very friendly and very sweet scene overall.'

Quite often, Gibbons – who was initially annoyed at the idea of a drummer playing in the club over his records – would really put François through his paces, the DJ giving the drummer an accelerating bombardment of different rhythms to try and match. But Kevorkian prided himself on knowing all the drum breaks, and Gibbons was rarely able to trip him up. 'The whole thing: his selection, his mixing technique, his pace, sense of drama, sense of excitement. And he was featuring all these big drum breaks that nobody else was really using. He was really into drums.'

Gibbons's following grew so large that he was eventually powerful enough to influence the running of the club, a rarity for a DJ, even today. Alex Rosner recalls what happened when Galaxy's owner, George Freeman, brought him in to install a separate control to limit the sound system's overall volume.

'I tried to talk the owner out of putting this volume control in. I said you should talk to Walter and agree on sound levels. George says, "No, I'm the boss, I own this club and I pay you to fix this sound system, so you do as I say." So I put it in. There was a hidden volume control in his office.' The repercussions were dramatic. 'When Walter found out, he quit.' However, laughs Rosner, 'all the people went with him. George had no business, so he had to get Walter back and get rid of the volume control.'

Gibbons retained this kind of independence until the end, even, eventually, at the expense of his audience. After a period at the end of the seventies living and DJing in Seattle (in another George Freeman-owned club, Sanctuary), he returned to New York a born-again Christian. As his religious beliefs influenced his music, the size of his dancefloor dwindled.

'By the time Walter had turned into that whole religion thing,' says François, 'he had stopped playing a whole section of music and only concentrated on songs with a message. There's nothing wrong with that, but it really limited the audience that would listen to his music. Unfortunately, it mainly fell on deaf ears. In fact, it didn't fall on very many ears at all, because there weren't many people going to his parties. At the same time, there's nothing you could say about Walter that was bad, because he followed his vision. It's just his vision was more difficult.'

Gibbons, who died in September 1994, outlined his feelings in an interview he gave to Steven Harvey. 'You really have to think that every time you change the record, the title or something about the record is going into people's heads,' said Gibbons. 'For me, I have to let God play the records. I'm just an instrument.'

Tee Scott at Better Days

Another club with a reputation for playing the most recherché rhythm and blues was Better Days, opened in 1972 at 316 West 49th Street. By day this was just a bar but by night it transformed magically into a darkened nightclub. The first resident, a lesbian DJ named Bert, was fired soon after the club's opening and replaced by Tee Scott.

Danny Tenaglia, fated to become one of the DJ stars of the nineties, was then a young tentative clubgoer. He remembers Better Days as the first place he encountered people vogueing, and recalls being impressed by Scott's advanced mixing techniques, which included long overlays, or 'blends': playing two records simultaneously for an extended period. 'Tee Scott was obviously different from other DJs,' says Tenaglia. 'He would try things like these long overlays. Back then it was so much harder – people really don't realise how hard it was to mix those records with live drummers. And he would do them much longer than other DJs. The fact that the next time you went you'd hear the same mix meant it was something he obviously worked at. But also that it was worth repeating.'

Better Days was also one of the clubs where François Kevorkian began DJing after he had made the transition from drumming.

'The crowd there was incredibly intense,' he says. 'It was very black, very gay. Sometimes I think Better Days was almost better than the others because it was closer and small and more intimate, but the energy level when people were dancing was just so amazing.

'Tee was more focused on the real soulful grooves that would work the dancefloor to an absolute frenzy,' adds François. 'And very beautiful music, too. He was more into squeezing the last drop out of a record and making it into a hit. It might not be a very strong record to begin with but just the way he would work it, cut it, and make his crowd like it, it would become a hit.'

Scott, who died on 12 December 1995, confessed that he felt his priorities were centred on his audience.

'If you come to the club on a crowded night, your hair could stand on end from the static electricity,' he told *Billboard*'s Brian Chin. 'It rises off the bodies and the hum is in the air. People are going through a particular experience, especially if they go on a regular basis. The music, the people and everything fits together.'

In later years, Better Days was known as a more intimate rival to the Paradise Garage. Bruce Forest, who replaced Tee Scott, was a crucial figure in the city's transition from disco to house. He had to work hard to gain the respect of his crowd, however.

'These people loved Tee Scott, they idolised him,' Forest explained in 1989. 'This was a hardcore black gay club, and the last thing they wanted was a white heterosexual replacement. I busted my balls trying to please them. I had three tables working, cutting records to death.' But the crowd remained outraged at his presence. 'I needed a bodyguard. I had death threats. People would throw bottles at me while I was working. On the big Friday night, I would have fifteen hundred people standing in a semi-circle on the dancefloor with arms folded.' Eventually, revered black DJ Timmy Regisford took over most of the nights, but he was ill one evening and Forest vowed to finally win over the crowd. Pulling a tarpaulin over the booth so no one could see who was DJing, he spun for all he was worth. They danced with abandon.

At 4am the tarpaulin was taken down: 'You just saw fifteen hundred jaws drop and they just started to applaud.'

David Rodriguez at the Ginza

Among the period's most expressive disc jockeys was David Rodriguez.

'Some DJs don't look like they're having a good time. David *always* looked like he was having a *great* time,' remembers Tony Smith. 'I connected with him because he looked like he was having a ball up there. Always smiling, always in a good mood, and his music showed that. One thing I learnt from David is that every night is a different night and you don't know what you're gonna do. He was totally spontaneous.'

'He is the person who influenced me most,' says Nicky Siano. 'He was just a wonderful friend and he really helped me launch my career.'

Siano recalls how Rodriguez would discover so many great new records that he rarely devoted enough time to break any one of them. 'Of the five records that he discovered every week, two were really good. Michael Cappello and I would look at each other and we'd both pick the same two that were good, and then we'd play the same two over and over and really get the crowd going. Now David, he would play all five, and so he never really left an impression on you. But really, he took more risks in playing new music than anyone else back then. He was a real innovator.'

Having started out DJing at the Ginza, Rodriguez moved on to the Limelight on Sixth Avenue and 10th Street, where he drew a predominantly, though not exclusively, gay Puerto Rican crowd. He later made appearances at several clubs, where his combative style resulted in a tendency to blow up sound systems. Nicky Siano remembers him blowing up all of Le Jardin's speakers on his first (and last) night there; DJ trade magazine *Melting Pot* reported that he achieved a similar feat at the Continental Baths.

His propensity for drug consumption was as impressive as his DJing. A favourite confection amongst clubgoers was ethyl chloride, an anaesthetic used to numb the flesh before receiving shots. When sprayed on a handkerchief and inhaled through the mouth, it gave an effect not unlike that of poppers. Nicky Siano recalled a night DJing at the Gallery when a narcoticised Rodriguez destroyed his set. 'He's standing there with a rag in his mouth and he's got the bottle in front of the rag and he's just spraying and spraying the rag, and inhaling. All of a sudden – BOOM! Fell right on the turntables. I got six hundred people all turning around looking at me and I just looked at him: "You fat fucking bastard!" And I pulled him by the hair, threw him on the floor and started kicking him. I was like, "You did this on purpose, you fat fuck!" He cut his head on one of the milk crates in the booth and he had to get three stitches.'

Tom Moulton remembers Rodriguez as probably the most aggressive DJ he has ever known. 'David played what he wanted to play when he wanted to play it. At that time there was a song that everybody liked called "A Date With The Rain" by Eddie Kendricks,' recalls Moulton. 'Everybody kept saying, "Play 'Rain', play 'Rain'." So he played "Make Yours A Happy Home" by Gladys Knight & the Pips, which was a kind of uptempo ballad. Nobody would dance. "You're gonna hear it all night, then." The owners are banging on the glass. He plays it over and over again. Finally, he takes the microphone. "I'm serious. Unless you get up here and dance, this is all you're gonna hear, so you better leave." So they get up and dance. And he says, "Okay, one more time with a little more enthusiasm." Then he played fifteen minutes of these crashing sound effects and all of a sudden you could hear "The rain, the rain" through the noise. It was Eddie Kendricks. They started screaming and yelling. It was unbelievable.'

Sadly, David Rodriguez was one of the first people to die of AIDS, a tragic loss which shocked and touched many on the scene. Siano remembers his extreme bravery in the face of this then little-known disease.

'I view the whole scene as a spiritual congregation,' Rodriguez declared in an interview in the mid seventies, exploring a theme that has become recurrent for many DJs. 'You've got hundreds of people in a room, and their bond is the music. There isn't any tension between gays and straights; the common denominator is the music. I can get high – literally high – just on the music alone. Sometimes I weave the records together to tell a whole love story in one night. Do you know what it's like to hear the whole room sigh when a record starts? It's like applause to me!'

The birth of modern DJing

In many ways, the club DJ of thirty years ago was as fully accomplished as he is today. He had become far removed from his original role – a musical waiter serving whatever the diners requested – and was now almost as exalted as some of our current well-marketed DJ stars. Some, at least to their regular crowd, in their own clubs, had god-like powers.

As he explored the creative possibilities of mixing, programming and sound adjustment (and as his audience explored the creative possibilities of all manner of misappropriated chemicals), the DJ was learning more and more about manipulation. Central to his art was an understanding of his audience and the dynamics of a dancefloor, as well as of the records he was playing. Many DJs, of course, were dancers; some, like François Kevorkian and Francis Grasso, were musicians, too. All had a deep understanding, whether learned or instinctive, of what made people want to dance, and what made people want to dance harder, longer, with more abandon. Without a doubt, disco heralded the arrival of a new figure: the DJ as high priest.

There had been hints of this before, in clubs with names like Salvation and in the blasphemous imagery of a place like Sanctuary. Several earlier DJs, such as Grasso, had been able to whip up their crowds into a devotional frenzy and had been compared with witch doctors, priests or other religious figures. During the rise of disco, the relatively recent line which the western world had drawn between dance and religion was questioned and blurred.

By the mid seventies, clubs, especially the gay ones, had truly become places of worship. For many, this was where you went to receive your weekly sacrament. 'There is a lot to it,' agrees Alex Rosner (who, after having built many of the disco era's more revered sound systems, now spends his time designing custom amplification for churches and synagogues). 'George Freeman at Galaxy 21 often talked about that. He said he was providing a venue for a spiritual experience.'

Interviewed for the *New York Post* in 1975, Steve D'Acquisto asserted, 'Disco music is a mantra, a prayer – nobody goes to church anymore, and if you listen to those songs, like "Fight The Power", "Ease On Down The Road" and "Bad Luck", you're getting religious and political instruction.'

In his insightful book *Disco!* Albert Goldman shared the sentiment: 'The disco scene is a classic case of spilled religion, of seeking to obtain the spiritual exaltation of the sacred world by intensifying the pleasures of the secular.'

SEVEN
DISCO

She Works Hard For The Money

'Disco is a four-billion-dollar-a-year industry, with its own franchises, publications, top-forty charts, three-day sales conventions, catalogues of special equipment, and keenly competitive marketing agents – who are aiming to make every finished basement and rumpus room in America into a mini-disco.'

– Albert Goldman, *Disco!*

'They narrowed it down to one beat, to try to corner the market on a particular music, and when you do that with rhythm, talk about something that would get on your *nerve*! Try to make love with just one stroke.'

– George Clinton

The disco that drives West End musicals, the disco that compels drunken students to don afro wigs and platform shoes, the disco that gets everyone on the dancefloor after a million weddings, has very little to do with disco's roots, or indeed with the larger body of work which comprises disco. It is instead the legacy of a short (roughly 1976–79) period when some of the music crossed over into super-profitable commerciality.

After the disco sound proved to be so irresistible, so universal and so *effective*, disco swept through the wider world like a new kind of fast food. It enjoyed a brief but near-total dominance of the global music machine, it made billions and it brought nightclubbing resolutely into the mainstream. In the process, it also changed much about the music business and the profession of the DJ.

Disco profitability

The big-budget music industry as we know it came into being with rock. The Beatles, the Stones and their ilk brought the music moguls a new class of wealth, and for the first time their business was compared to Hollywood. However, by the mid seventies, rock appeared to have died and profits were dropping dramatically. Disco seemed to come to the rescue. It was completely alien to the music biz moneymen – who'd only just started feeling comfortable in the company of hairy musicians with guitars, and were unlikely to want to rip off their shirts in a dark loft full of black homos – but they could still see its potential to become a big fat cash cow.

The reason being: it appealed instinctively to nearly everyone. To this day, no music has bettered disco for its ability to entice the broadest cross-section of people – both young and old, whether nimble or uncoordinated – onto a dancefloor. This was a sales opportunity of golden goose proportions. To see disco's mass market possibilities, you didn't need to know about its loving, sharing spirit, or its special social significance. You just had to see how it got everyone's feet tapping.

Watching the independents who had cultivated the music, larger record labels hurriedly created disco departments or sub-labels, and found them immediately profitable. Has-been rock artists knocked out a disco tune or two and found fresh success. Radio stations which abandoned rock for disco saw their ratings skyrocket. Clubs, bars and restaurants found that adding a DJ and a dancefloor drove up their takings significantly. Disco was big business, it was everywhere, and it started wearing a suit.

Though few made any effort to understand the origins or culture of this underground music, everyone loved the associations it seemed to have with decadence, cocaine and sex. Plenty of marketing men would figure it out just enough to rip out its heart and suck out every last drop of its blood. By the end of 1977, when Hollywood got in on the act with *Saturday Night Fever*, it seemed as if the whole world had 'gone disco'.

In these latter days of disco there was an astonishing number of really bad records produced, mostly exploitative cash-ins by artists who knew nothing about the music (other than the restorative power it might exert on their careers). Greed and cynicism were rampant as the major label late-comers hurried to rake in some disco dollars. It was inevitable, from the weight the industry expected it to bear, that disco would crash.

By 1979 there was simply *too much disco* and people started to hate it. Many who had banked on it were left high and dry and the backlash was swift and enduring. Suddenly everyone remembered that it was faggot music, that it 'sucked'. This is one reason why today's dance-based pop has had so much trouble getting established in America – it is still tarred with the same brush as disco. For the rock-headed straight masses it still has too many gay associations, and for the US music business too many bad memories of extreme over-investment.

But of course, it was the post-disco backlash which left the DJ alone to develop dance music further. And even while disco was riding its overground peak, it was building structures which would be invaluable to future DJs. Disco's commercial era resulted in the 12-inch single, the remix, club-based record promotion, and a completely new approach to making records. And though there is a clear theme of the music industry acting to limit the disc jockey's growing power, it was also when the DJ was acknowledged as the expert on what makes people dance, and thus when he was handed the keys to the recording studio.

Society disco at Le Jardin

On 13 June 1973 a club opened in Manhattan which showed the direction in which disco was headed. Much the same music was played here as in the black lofts of the Village, but in style and ambition it was another world entirely, with the ambience not of a dark cave but of an upscale restaurant. Now that the good ship disco had been shown to be a sturdy vessel, it was time to polish the fittings so the society folk felt comfortable jumping aboard.

Le Jardin opened in the basement of a shabby hotel called the Diplomat at 110 West 43rd Street. It was heavily influenced by Tenth Floor, a private gay club with a similarly sleek appearance, and run by an eccentric South African called John Addison. With his deadpan face, affected English accent and lounge lizard demeanour, Addison, an ex-waiter and juice bar proprietor, was hardly the typical club owner of the time. But then Le Jardin was hardly the typical club.

In its look, it echoed the Parisian-style nightclubs of the sixties. There were potted palms and nice furniture and the staff wore neat uniforms. The resident DJ was Bobby Guttadaro; in later years Steve D'Acquisto held a residency. Guttadaro had been recruited specially from the Ice Palace on Fire Island, an almost exclusively gay resort where the cream of homosexual New York had summer homes and partied accordingly. The clientele was the flotsam and jet set of gay Manhattan society. Costumed muscle boys in aviator goggles with clothes pegs on their nipples danced next to famous fashion designers and wealthy hairdressers with just one name. There was a smallish quota of beautiful women and fashionable straights. It was a scene right out of Fire Island: the city's gay upper echelons at play.

In an interview with Johnny Carson, renowned club hag Truman Capote described the scene, emphasizing both the club's elegant surroundings and its highly mobile dancefloor: 'It has these art deco couches all along the room, these palm fronds dropping down everywhere, and out on the dancefloor, this terrible churning, the whole place churning, like a buttermilk machine.'

There had been an element of face-spotting and chatty socializing at all but the sweatiest of disco's early clubs – indeed even the dance-till-you-drop Gallery enjoyed its coterie of gay celebrities – but Le Jardin, in its more refined pretensions, made itself a place where 'Look who's here!' and 'Darling you must meet . . .' might push 'Let's go dance' lower down the agenda.

Bob Casey pinpoints the opening of Le Jardin as the moment that disco left the underground. 'Diana Ross was at the premiere. That hit the papers, and all of a sudden "discothèque" became in and popular at that point, and came above ground.'

The DJ's promotional power

As well as helping disco to do a little social climbing, Le Jardin also brought the scene's commercial clout to the attention of the record companies. It was here, thanks largely to the clued-up Guttadaro, that the industry woke up fully to the promotional power of the club DJ.

Gloria Gaynor's 1973 'Never Can Say Goodbye' had been the first disco record to chart as a result of club play, closely followed by 'Do It 'Till You're Satisfied' by BT Express. (Both also highlighted the new phenomenon of the remix, on which more later.) Added to the much-noted success of Manu Dibango's 'Soul Makossa' the same year, it had become clear that club DJs could exert impressive influence on the record-buying public. The next club crossover hit would be so big it would change forever the way the recording industry promoted its music.

When 20th Century Records promotions man Billy Smith handed Bobby DJ a copy of 'Love's Theme' by Love Unlimited Orchestra, led by LA producer-turned-singer Barry White, he played it till the groove wore smooth. The city's other jocks spun it just as ardently and the song ended up at no.1 on the pop charts. Its success was clearly due to club play, since the LP it was on, *Love Unlimited*, sold 50,000 copies before the song was ever heard on the radio. In recognition of his work on the record, Bobby Guttadaro was the first club DJ to be presented with a gold disc – handed over in person at Le Jardin by Barry White.

'Billy Smith broke Love Unlimited Orchestra and Barry White when they were totally dead,' says Nicky Siano. 'He literally went down to the basement and pulled out an album they considered a dead record. He had given us these albums and they had black people on the cover, so we thought maybe we can do something with this. And we made them huge hits. Billy Smith became the hottest promotion man in the business.'

'GOD BLESS BILLY SMITH' read the headline in the first issue of Bob Casey's disco DJ trade magazine *Melting Pot* in August 1974. The article underneath read: 'Billy has not only opened the door for the disco deejay to the record companies, he has knocked it off its hinges.'

There were still no radio stations emphasising disco, yet it was selling in its thousands. The primary sales focus of music changed overnight. For rock it had been radio; now, for disco it was clubs.

Barry White was not alone, either (was he ever?). Hues Corporation's 'Rock The Boat', Carl Douglas's 'Kung Fu Fighting', George McCrae's 'Rock Your Baby' and the Average White Band's 'Pick Up The Pieces' were all propelled into the *Billboard* chart on the strength of club play. Even obscure cuts like Consumer Rapport's 'Ease On Down The Road' on tiny independent Wing And A Prayer were shifting 100,000 copies before ever getting a sniff of radio.

Exciting though this new avenue of marketing records was, it presented something of a dilemma for record companies, since their promotions people were not the kind to frequent discothèques (or, indeed, to even *know* what a discothèque was like). They were largely middle-aged family folk with houses in the suburbs.

'They realized that they had to deal with these clubs, and they had to deal with the disc jockeys,' says Vince Aletti. 'Little by little, they realized that they would have to bring someone in, and often they would hire somebody who was an ex-disc jockey, or someone who was working in a club. They were almost exclusively gay.'

Aletti noted the change which this recruitment brought to many record companies. 'It was really interesting to watch this happen, because they were having to deal with some fairly flamboyant characters who they still didn't know how to handle.' This new breed of promotions men would form a crucial line of communication between the DJs and the record industry. They called themselves the 'Homo Promos'.

DJ mix tapes

Le Jardin figures in another small chapter of dance music's rise. Noticing the increased interest in the disc jockeys' performances, John Addison began to make nightly recordings of their sets on reel-to-reel. Through a telephone information line, he sold these to anyone interested for $75 per programme – one whole night's set.

In its 12 October 1974 issue, *Billboard* alerted the industry to this illegal practice, pointing out that these tapes were bypassing payment to copyright holders, record labels and artists. 'Tapes were originally dubbed by jockeys to serve as standbys for times when they were not in personal use of disco turntables,' read the article. 'They represent each jockey's concept of programming, placing and segueing of record sides. The music is heard without interruption. One- to three-hour programs bring anywhere from $30 to $75 per tape, mostly reel-to-reel, but increasingly on cartridge and cassette.' These were not confined to home use. Walk into any downtown bar, café or hip clothes store and the sound of syncopated disco music could be heard blasting out of the speakers.

Billboard claimed that some DJs were making more than $1,000 per month from these sales. In fact, as in Le Jardin's case, it was often the club proprietors who profited. Steve D'Acquisto, who had replaced Bobby DJ at Le Jardin when he moved to play at Infinity, was aware of what was happening: 'John Addison used to *sell* our tapes. He'd tape it every night and sell them. We never got a penny from it.'

No doubt many of the DJs did boost their income this way. Certainly few were paid well enough to ignore it, and many were turning to more desperate means. 'We used to supplement our income by selling drugs,' one DJ says. 'You had to. We weren't making enough money.'

Bob Casey, who set up NADD in 1974, tried early on to legitimise the practice of selling mix tapes, contacting ASCAP to inquire what kind of royalty payments would be required.

'I said, "OK, I'd like to reproduce disc jockeys playing," and this guy had no idea what I was talking about. I explained that the disc jockeys in the clubs mix the records together. I said, "Look, I want to send you money for this . . . how much?" He said, "You can't send it because we're not gonna allow it." '

Though the copyright organisations wouldn't allow DJs to sell mixed tapes, they were quite prepared to let record companies use the same idea. In the same month that the *Billboard* piece on DJ tapes appeared, Spring Records released *Disco Par-r-r-ty* as the first non-stop dancing LP record. This featured tracks segued together, including James Brown, Mandrill and Barry White. The label said their main concern was creating a 'classic' disco album. There was no DJ credit on the record.

Nowadays, DJ-mix albums represent a sizeable portion of the music market. Although they had little idea of how profitable this format would be, the record industry and its copyright organisations acted (largely unwittingly) early on to make sure that the DJ was shut out. Only in recent years, when they had clearly become marketable stars, were disc jockeys allowed a piece of the action.

The birth of the remix

Remixing is a vital part of today's dance industry, both as a marketing tool and as a creative outlet for DJs. Its roots lie firmly in the disco era, when DJs learned to transfer the kind of live mixing they had introduced – the extending of intros and breaks – onto tape and eventually vinyl.

The early club DJs learned their phenomenal mixing skills by necessity. Records were short and if they wanted to make them more effective for the dancefloor, disc jockeys were forced to work quite hard. The three-minute pop tune was designed to be perfect for radio. Here the songwriter has to concentrate his mind and deliver a simple message without repeating himself. However, a dancer's needs aren't the same as those of pop listeners – the body makes different demands from the ears. The dancer 'wants to get in a groove and stay there until he has exhausted his invention or his body,' wrote Albert Goldman in *Disco!*. 'The time scale and the momentum of any physical activity is vastly different from the attention span of listening.' Increasingly, club DJs were searching for longer tracks, songs that gave them the freedom to work the crowd into the required pitch of excitement.

Coincidentally, inspired by the lengthy improvisations of jazz and the lavish epics of prog rock, pop producers had started experimenting with longer tracks, often seen as the sign of greater musical seriousness. Norman Whitfield at Motown was one such producer: his later work with the Temptations and Undisputed Youth was clearly infused with the trippiness of psychedelic rock. Whitfield's notions were taken a step further by another member of Berry Gordy's assembly line, Frank Wilson. Working with former Temptations' vocalist Eddie Kendricks, he produced 'Girl You Need A Change Of Mind', released in early 1973 and arguably the very first disco record.

In *Rolling Stone*, Vince Aletti had written a prescription for great dance music: 'The best disco music is full of changes and breaks, which allow for several shifts of mood or pace and usually open up long instrumental passages. If the break works, it becomes the pivot and anticipated peak of the song.' 'Girl You Need A Change Of Mind' fitted this perfectly. It was seven minutes and thirty seconds of sizzling, understated bliss, with a lengthened rhythm passage, vamping keyboard parts and doubled-up snare hits.

The effect was perfect for a dancefloor, but this was not intentional. Wilson himself says the record's distinct structure came from his gospel roots and from his intentions to make the song sound more 'live'. In the sleevenotes to a recent Kendricks compilation, he explained: 'People always ask me about the breakdown. Well, my background is the church. It's not unusual in a church song to have a breakdown like that. Here, the idea was spontaneous. I stood in the studio with the musicians, giving instructions as we were cutting for them to break it down to nothing, then gradually come in one by one and rebuild the fervour of the song.'

The rhythm was a departure, too: 'At the time we did think, instead of four on top – which is what Holland Dozier Holland had been famous for – let's start with four on the floor and build it from there. Still, when

I began hearing reports about what was happening with the record in the New York disco clubs, I was shocked. That was not what we were going for. We were after radio.'

As well as searching out such serendipitously lengthy tracks – and of course, mixing his records live to produce a similar effect – the DJ would quickly take advantage of the opportunity to reconstruct songs, on tape, ahead of time. Reel-to-reel recording offered the chance to splice and edit favourite tracks to make them longer and more danceable.

One of the first people to gain attention from this practice was, surprisingly, not a disc jockey but a model by the name of Tom Moulton. The craggy Moulton, who wouldn't have looked out of place in an ad for macho shaving products, had previously worked in record retail and promotion (he worked at Syd Nathan's label King in the fifties, where James Brown cut his most urgent material). Though never a disc jockey, he developed a strong DJ-like affinity with the dancefloor.

His introduction to clubs had been on Fire Island. As a black music freak, he had been impressed by the fact that the largely white crowd were dancing to rhythm and blues, yet appalled at the standard of the disc jockey. It had given him the idea of producing a tape specifically made for dancing. 'The reason I wanted to make this tape was that I was watching people dance and, at that time, it was mostly 45s that were three minutes long. They'd really start to get off on it and all of a sudden another song would come in on top of it. I just thought it was a shame that the records weren't longer, so people could really start getting off.' Moulton watched what parts of songs made people leave a dancefloor and – just like a good DJ – constructed his music to minimise the dancers' opportunities of escape. 'So that way, if they go to leave, they're already dancing to the next record. That was the hardest. I made one side of forty-five minutes. It took me eighty hours.'

Strictly speaking, these tapes were re-edits and not remixes. A re-edit is a new version made by cutting up and splicing together chunks of the original song in a different order, usually using a tape recorder, a razor blade and some sticky tape. A remix is a more involved process where the original multi-track recording of the song is used to build a new version from its component parts. If you think of re-editing as making a patchwork version, then remixing is where you actually separate the individual sonic fibres of a song – separate the bass track from the drum track from the vocal track – and weave them back into a new piece of musical fabric.

Moulton's forays into editing soon led him to studio-based remixing. The first of his studio projects was BT Express (the BT stands for Brooklyn Trucking) with 'Do It 'Till You're Satisfied' in mid 1974. His remix nearly doubled the track in length, from 3:09 to 5:52, but even so, many radio stations programmed the long version, and it provided the band with their first *Billboard* crossover hit. Despite their success, the group gave Moulton little or no credit. 'The band absolutely hated it,' he says. 'But it reached number one and they were on *Soul Train*. Don Cornelius interviewed the band and asked them about the length: "Oh yeah, that's the way we recorded it," they said. I was so fucking mad!' The record eventually went from no.1 on the rhythm and blues chart to no.2 on the Hot 100.

Such successes further encouraged the labels in their efforts to promote their records through the clubs, and with this in mind they started commissioning more and more remixes with which to entice DJs. And thanks to his growing track record, Moulton quickly cornered the market. When he remixed a previously released song called 'Dream World' by Don Downing, his version sold some 10,000 copies without airplay.

By the end of 1974, *Billboard* could report that several labels had started releasing DJ-only vinyl pressings of such remixes as part of their new emphasis on club promotion. A piece in its 2 November issue read: 'Specially mixed versions of commercial singles are being offered to discothèques here by a number of labels looking to capitalize on the clubs' growing reputation as record "breakout" points. At such labels as Scepter, Chess/Janus and Roulette, executives say that the clubs are a definite influence in breaking records and that they consider it well worth the time and effort to reach the disco audience. When airplay on radio stations is missing, the clubs themselves have the power to move sales.'

Moulton's reputation grew. His work for Don Downing and BT Express led to an encounter with producers Meco Menardo and Tony Bongiovi, who were working on a Gloria Gaynor project.

'I had this idea to make a medley, and the disc jockeys would play it because then they could go to the bathroom,' says Moulton. 'It would be eighteen minutes long; one song straight into another. It would be perfect.' When the *Never Can Say Goodbye* album came out, a whole side of it was a single suite made from three two-and-a-half-minute songs – 'Never Can Say Goodbye', 'Honey Bee' and 'Reach Out' – extended and segued together. When released as a single, one of them, 'Never Can Say Goodbye', became the first *identifiably* disco record to chart. Like BT Express, at first Gaynor didn't appreciate Tom's version too much. 'I remember sitting in the office and Gloria hearing it,' recalls Moulton. 'The first thing out of her mouth – I'll never forget it: "I don't sing much." I felt so hurt over that.'

The evolution of the remix quickly opened up a whole new career path for the DJ. Since disc jockeys had an unparalleled expertise in what makes people dance, it was only logical for more of them to make the leap from booth to studio. DJs like Walter Gibbons, Richie Rivera, Larry Levan, Shep Pettibone, Tee Scott and Jim Burgess would soon join Tom Moulton in refashioning dance music to their own end.

Another jock to move quickly into the studio was François Kevorkian, destined to become one of the world's most respected (and prodigious) remixers. Kevorkian, a talented drummer, started by creating re-edits like 'Erucu', an instrumental from the *Mahogany* soundtrack, and 'Happy Song' by Rare Earth, which he admits were based largely on Walter Gibbons' own live mixes. In June 1978 he was offered an A&R gig at Prelude. His first job was to remix a record that had been doing good business for the label, Musique's 'In The Bush'. Despite his inexperience, his deep understanding of the dancefloor made this a huge hit.

'It was really my first experience in a studio,' remembers François. 'And the record just blew out. I mean, it exploded. Anywhere you would go in the summer, they were playing that fucking record. So my first record becomes a huge hit.' As a result, his golden touch was in constant demand. 'They put me in the studio night and day. It would not end. I got to pick whatever I wanted. I ended up doing a lot of records for Prelude. Two or three records a week on average. It became like an assembly line.'

Though many musicians felt it was sacrilegious for remixers to tamper with their work – a denial of their artistic integrity – the commercial success of many remixes convinced most people that the practice had a place in music. Norman Harris, who produced Loleatta Holloway's 'Hit And Run', was one. Although he felt strongly that the album version he produced was 'artistically correct', when Walter Gibbons' remixed version was released it sold more than 100,000 copies. Harris was forced to agree that 'those figures were an indication that Gibbons' mix had a better feel for what's needed at today's marketplace'.

The birth of the 12-inch single

Tom Moulton's mixes became famous throughout New York clubland and beyond. However, as they became longer and more complex – more modulating suites than mere songs – it was clear that 7-inch vinyl was not of a sufficiently high quality to do justice to them. The closer a record's grooves are packed together, the lower their volume and sound quality become. When you're talking grooves, bigger is better. A larger record has the added advantage of being easier for a DJ to manipulate.

But the 12-inch single happened quite by accident. Moulton went to have a mix pressed onto vinyl but his mastering engineer, José Rodriguez, had run out of the usual 7-inch metal blanks needed to cut the master disc. 'José told me he was out of 7-inch blanks and would have to give me a 12-inch. I said, "*Eeugh*, that's ridiculous." So he said, "I know what we'll do: we'll spread the grooves and make it louder." And of course, when I heard it I almost died.' This record, the very first 12-inch single, was 'So Much For Love' by Moment Of Truth. It was something which Moulton made for a very select group of his DJ friends and although Roulette later released it on 7-inch, the larger format was never commercially available.

For a while, the only 12-inch singles were these handfuls of test pressings which Moulton made of his mixes (the songs were still only actually released in the 7-inch format, usually with the song split into two parts, one each side). Eventually, though, the record companies got wise to the benefits of the 12-inch and started using the format for DJ-only promotion. No one is exactly sure when these label-sanctioned promotional 12-inches arrived on the streets, though the general view is that the first was 'Dance Dance Dance' by Calhoun, in spring 1975.

Surprisingly, despite its advantages, the 12-inch was initially greeted with much scepticism; it was seen as little more than a marketing gimmick. 'People weren't impressed to start with, because they really weren't putting the best stuff on them,' says Danny Krivit. 'Everyone was saying, "well, there are a lot of hits out there, why are they putting *these* songs on them?" It was almost like 12-inches were going to be laughed at.'

This derision ended in June 1976 when Salsoul, a small independent label, released a 12-inch that was far too good to ever be a gimmick – 'Ten Percent' by Double Exposure. Producer Arthur Baker recalls hearing Gibbons play 'Ten Percent' at Galaxy 21: 'He had this record which just seemed endless, with all of these cuts in it. I was like, "How is he doing this? He must be so quick." It was amazing. I went up to the booth and it was one record. It was called "Ten Percent".' Salsoul boss Ken Cayre recalls the extended jam at the orchestra session. 'We did the regular song but they kept playing, they laid down a track of maybe eight or nine minutes.' After Walter Gibbons laid his hands on the mix the result was a ten-minute epic of sparse conga-led rhythm patterns and strident orchestral sweeps.

When they'd heard this version in the clubs, no one wanted the puny three-minute 7-inch. Cayre recalls: 'It had been out maybe a month. We immediately started getting bad feedback. So I said, "Let's give them what they want, let's sell the 12-inch".'

Where Tom Moulton had pioneered the remix, it was Gibbons, a DJ, who really showed its full potential. Moulton's early mixes didn't radically change the sonic nature of the songs, they were mostly about extending the better parts and eliminating the weaker ones. Gibbons was much more radical in his approach, stripping songs right down to their most primal elements and reconstructing them into complex interlocking layers of sound. Like his wild, tribalistic DJing, his remixes emphasised the rhythmic essence of a track. Walter Gibbons loved his drums.

With his masterful mix of 'Ten Percent', the new 12-inch format finally took off. DJs quickly appreciated its advantages and their enthusiasm drove record companies into adopting it for all their promotional dance releases. And when this single was released to the public, it wasn't split in two and squeezed onto a 7-inch. Instead, it was the very first commercially available 12-inch single.

However, the prognosis for the 12-inch was by no means certain. Two years after its initial introduction, *Billboard* was still questioning whether the infant format had a future at all. In a 1978 piece by Radcliffe Joe announcing that Salsoul, TK and Vanguard had ceased commercially releasing 12-inches, he wrote: 'Several key labels specializing in disco product have begun cutting back on commercial 12-inch disco discs on the ground that they are slicing into album and 7-inch sales, cost too much to manufacture, and exact a high royalty price by music publishers.' Record stores like Downstairs and Record Haven saw it somewhat differently. As Scott Dockswell of Record Haven told *Billboard*, 'People who want the 12-inches buy them regardless of price, and we have found that many, especially disco DJs, buy both the 12-inch single and the album by the same artist.' Only through the sales demand of DJs was the health of the 12-inch single ensured. A fact still true today.

Until the music industry belatedly embraced the digital MP3 format, the 12-inch was the only format of recorded music introduced as a result of consumer demand rather than record company marketing guile.

The Philly sound

To most music historians, disco begins in Philadelphia. And if one song sums up classic disco it is, with little doubt, 'Love Is The Message' by MFSB on the Philadelphia International label. Originally a B-side to the hit 'TSOP' (which also became the theme for TV's *Soul Train*), 'Love Is The Message' became the era's keynote record, the one which all disc jockeys claimed as their own.

Vince Aletti, in common with many, regards it as a Paradise Garage track; others cite the Loft as its true home. Nicky Siano claims it as his baby, too, maintaining he was championing it at the Gallery while others were only playing the A-side.

MFSB was an acronym for Mother Father Sister Brother (though some claimed it actually stood for Mother Fuckin' Sonova Bitch). They became the Philadelphia house band and, although Gamble and Huff usually take the credit for the Philly sound, this aggregation of musicians, as their track record shows, were clearly a vital force behind it. Bassist Ronnie Baker, guitarist Norman Harris and drummer Earl Young had already been playing together from the mid sixties in a group called the Volcanoes. As MFSB (or parts thereof) they played for artists on several labels, going on to provide musical backing for everyone from the Trammps to First Choice, Double Exposure, Salsoul Orchestra, the Three Degrees, Jean Carn, the O'Jays, Harold Melvin & the Bluenotes, and Teddy Pendergrass.

Tom Moulton recalls working with MFSB in the studio. 'When you watched them record a track, they'd be like running it down, and all of a sudden this movement would just *click*. It would lock. "All right. Let's take it. One, two, one, two, you know what to do!" It was like watching magic; it was scary. You had no idea what the song was or what the melody or the words were going to be, but you knew that that track was *there*.' He thinks their influence was profound. 'If you took all this stuff, by the same musicians, and put it all under one label, you'd have said "Motown who?"'

The Philadelphia International sound was a complex epiphany of rhythm and blues rhythms, classily charted guitar and horn parts, and deftly arranged strings. Its home, Sigma Studios in Philadelphia (there was later a Sigma in New York, also), with its sound honed by owner/engineer Joe Tarsia, became the Mecca for dance producers and singers alike – the Village People, the Ritchie Family and David Bowie all used Sigma.

In 1976 Tom Moulton got the chance to remix 'Love Is The Message'. Moulton's mix – one of several he did for the *Philadelphia* Classics album – took the song to another level, recasting it as eleven minutes and twenty-seven seconds of constantly shifting soul-fugue. Progressing from its dramatic minute-long opening, Moulton extended the main part of the song to over five minutes, before gliding the dancer back to the floor with fading strings and then off into the stratosphere for the final saxophone and keyboard vamps. It was and still is a masterpiece of penthouse soul. 'That was probably the greatest thing I ever did,' he says. 'I would have done anything to mix "Love Is The Message". And it's still one of my favourite songs. When I got to certain parts of it, it was like being pushed off a cliff and not falling. *Suspended*. Because that's what that song does to you. It's one of the most brilliant songs I've ever heard, for beauty.'

Since Moulton recast it so brilliantly, there have been numerous other remixes of the song. Danny Krivit reworked it by taking parts of Salsoul Orchestra's 'Love Break', a Gil Scott Heron sample and the second half of

'Love Is The Message'. This appeared as a bootleg on TD Records and for many is now the definitive version of the song.

The *Philadelphia Classics* remix album confirmed the City of Brotherly Love's place at the heart of disco. Kenny Gamble's socially conscious lyrics resonated with many of the DJs, his meditations on corruption (Harold Melvin's 'Bad Luck') and spiritual awareness (Melvin's 'Wake Up Everybody') summing up the democratic aspirations and upwardly mobile ambitions of the gays, blacks and Latinos who danced to these records.

Independent labels

Like many successful businesses, the disco empire started with a handful of grass roots entrepreneurs whose profitability was then noted by larger corporations. Double Exposure's 'Ten Percent' record had been released by a Hispanic mom and pop concern called Salsoul Records, which had formerly been a ladies' lingerie manufacturer. They went from the bustle to the hustle and, in the process, sealed the incipient 12-inch market for the independents.

As with subsequent new dance genres, at first disco was something which only the indies could really profit from. Many of their employees, like Carol Chapman at Salsoul, were regulars at places like the Loft in any case, and understood both what was happening and how best to capitalise on it. Right under the majors' noses, a locomotive force was gathering speed. As John Brody, Casablanca Records' promotion man, commented at the time: 'Before disco there was one pie. Warners, Columbia and RCA had it, and no other record company could get a piece of it.'

The smaller labels were quickly carving themselves a slice. Along with Salsoul, there were companies like TK in Miami (helmed by industry veteran Henry Stone), Neil Bogart's Casablanca in Los Angeles and, on the east coast, Roulette (owned by the well-connected Morris Levy), Spring, Wand and Scepter, whose boss Marv Schlachter went on to start another important label, Prelude. Philadelphia International was only nominally an independent – it was actually bankrolled by Clive Davis's CBS.

While these indies started enjoying some disco cashflow, the majors were looking the other way completely. Having attempted to push reggae and, later, punk rock as the Next Big Thing, they settled for Peter Frampton. The press were fairly slow as well. As music critic Andrew Kopkind pointed out in the *Village Voice*, 'John Rockwell was still writing Hegelian analyses of the Sex Pistols in the Sunday Times when two-thirds of the city was listening to Donna Summer.'

He always got in – Larry Levan's membership card for Studio 54.

Record pools

One of the biggest barriers preventing the majors from cashing in was the DJ. It wasn't that they were against disc jockeys, it was simply that they didn't know what to do with them. Although the new breed of club promotions' men and women were making inroads, the current system of distributing promotional records to DJs wasn't working. It was haphazard, the labels often had ludicrous regulations for collecting records, and there was little prioritisation of exactly who should get them.

Vince Aletti sums up the problems many DJs experienced. Aletti, by this time, was working at trade weekly *Record World* and was friendly with many of the DJs. 'A lot of what I heard was how difficult it was to get records,' he remembers. 'And at this point, it was clear that disc jockeys were really breaking records; they were really selling records. Especially selling records that the companies thought they would never sell. Here were all these people coming knocking on their door, saying we want a record, and the labels didn't know how to verify where they were working; didn't know who they were. So it was obvious that there had to be some kind of organisation to give the disc jockeys credibility and power in the business. And also to verify who they were.'

It all came to a head in 1975 over a record by Esther Phillips called 'What A Difference A Day Makes' (as one of the first 'modern' records on the northern soul scene, this also had an impact in the UK for entirely different reasons). Kudu Records, Phillips' label, had refused a copy of the disc to Steve D'Acquisto, then playing at Le Jardin. His friends were outraged and a gathering was convened in club Hollywood.

'The record companies and disc jockeys got together for the first time.

It was a total disaster,' remembers David Mancuso. Steve D'Acquisto was also at the meeting. 'It degenerated into this big screaming match. In the middle of it, David turned round and said: "Why don't we start a record pool?" We chatted amongst ourselves and I stood up and invited all the DJs down to the Loft. I said it was pointless arguing here. We needed to get our act together. Suddenly we were standing up for ourselves. So we had this DJ meeting and we wrote this declaration of intent.'

The idea behind the pool was simple. It would be an organisation that provided legitimacy for the disc jockey as well as providing easy access for corporate labels (many of the indies were instrumental in helping to set it up). The disc jockey would enrol into the pool, pay a subscription fee, and in exchange for free promotional records, offer written feedback on the discs supplied by the labels. The DJ got his records; the labels got a line of communication to the clubs.

Mancuso, D'Acquisto and another DJ, Eddie Rivera, set up the first pool, known simply as the Record Pool, in the summer of 1975. It worked well and Mancuso believes it's no coincidence that many great records rose to prominence in this period. 'The music that came out when we had the Record Pool in existence was the best. Most of the classics are right there.'

Vince Aletti introduced Mancuso to his friend Judy Weinstein, and she ran the pool from Mancuso's loft. (Weinstein's present pool, For The Record, grew from the ashes of this admirable bout of idealism; she now also heads Def Mix, Frankie Knuckles' and David Morales' production company.) The Record Pool worked well for a while but, eventually, began to fall apart amid recriminations, confusion and arguments among its members. Soon it splintered, first with Eddie Rivera leaving and forming his own pool for the outer boroughs. 'What was sad about that, sad about Eddie Rivera, sad about Judy having to pull away,' says Aletti, 'was that it had started out as a very idealistic thing pulling everybody together. And, more and more, it became a big business and became more ego-driven and complicated. The more money was involved, the less people got along.'

One person vehemently opposed to the pools was Bob Casey. He felt that while the record companies acknowledged the importance of the pool, nothing had been gained for the actual DJs.

'It wasn't the way that disc jockeys were gonna be recognised by the record companies. Your pool is recognised, period. So there was somebody else playing lord and master.'

Casey proposed what he saw as a radically different solution: setting up a clearing house which would distribute the labels' product to any DJ accredited by his National Association of Discothèque Disc Jockeys. He had formed this in July 1974 and for the next two years published a highly regarded DJ magazine, *Melting Pot*, named after David's Pot Belly, the Village café where the scene's first DJs would meet and swap tips. *Melting Pot*, with its extensive club charts, industry news and a sprinkling of camp scene gossip, illustrated Casey's ambitions of gaining proper respect for the DJ.

'I was trying to formalise the disc jockeys,' he says. 'I had put together an entire situation; a way a disc jockey is verified, legitimised. To a record company, it would have been the same as being a legitimate radio station. To help them get the product to the right people.' Casey insists that under his plan (never put into operation), the balance of power would have been weighted more in the DJs' favour.

It is hard to see what real difference there was between his proposal and the notion of a pool, except that the DJs would have been mailed their records and they would have paid less for the privilege. However, Casey's idea was only a small part of a noble plan to elevate the overall status of the disc jockey profession, rather than just a way of providing record distribution. For example, he laboured hard to win pension plans and group medical insurance rates for his members. It seems most likely that his vehement dislike of the Record Pool stemmed largely from friction with the prickly Steve D'Acquisto.

In Chicago in 1979, Rocky Jones (who would later run DJ International, one of the first house music labels) attempted to set up a disc jockeys' trades association. Jones never got this off the ground, claiming the pools sabotaged his plans by preventing their members from joining.

In the end, probably because it was the easiest structure for the record companies to deal with, the pool won out. Despite all the disagreements, the Record Pool was a success and within a few years of its inception, the concept had been copied in every major city in America. By 1978, a National Association of Record Pools was founded, with approximately 150 member pools. Such organisations still thrive throughout the US, although the concept never caught on elsewhere (British DJ Paul Oakenfold attempted unsuccessfully to introduce the idea to the UK in the early eighties).

Studio 54

A ruthless scene of life and death at the door, where the ignominy of not getting in is worse than getting knifed, and where on his wedding night a man will leave his new wife outside if it means he can gain entrance: Grace Jones arriving completely naked so many times it became tiresome; Margaret Trudeau, wife of the Canadian prime minister, caught

Some nice birds in a club – at her infamous 1977 Studio 54 birthday party Bianca Jagger (*left*) took some doves with Liza Minnelli (*right*).

on camera with her muff getting some air; a famous fashion designer buying sex from a busboy; Bianca Jagger riding in on a white stallion led by a man wearing nothing more than a coat of paint; Liz Taylor photographed having something placed on her tongue; Liza Minnelli chewing the fat (and her inner cheeks) on a banquette. Someone dying in an air vent trying to get inside; Sly Stallone ordering drinks at the bar next to John Travolta while a child-like Michael Jackson sits on a sofa in between Woody Allen and Truman Capote, with Andy Warhol over to the side, Jerry Hall next to him deep-throating a bottle of Moet & Chandon . . .

And all the time the man in the moon watches over, a coke spoon scooping up to fill his nose and a spray of shooting stars erupting as it does. The most expensive light show, the best sound system money could buy. Half a million tax-evading dollars stuffed into trash bags in the ceiling. Cocaine, sex, money, sex and cocaine. Ladies and gentlemen . . . Studio 54.

On 26 April 1977, this is where disco had arrived. Le Jardin had pointed the way and now, upon Studio's opening, disco's social ambitions had brought it right to the top. By cultivating the highest level of glamour, mystique and expectancy of any club before or since, Studio 54 made the most famous people in the world feel completely comfortable about getting fucked up in public. It might not have been the birth of the velvet rope and the elitism it represented (that honour goes to Arthur), but it certainly legitimised it. Those inside felt they had passed some kind of entrance exam, so a bizarre sense of equality and safety was generated. All the club's inhabitants, however recognisable, felt they were part of a great conspiracy of decadence. But the debauched democracy inside depended on fascism at the door. In this, Studio 54 was consciously the antithesis of the original disco clubs. It was not about the mass dancing *en masse*. It was about money, celebrity and *individual* fabulousness.

'The way it was put together was a total atmosphere, like the Loft,' says Nicky Siano. 'But the thing is, they added this other dimension. It was about the body; it was about the look; it was about the drugs; it was about sex. That hadn't been the *raison d'être* of clubs before that. And it fucked the whole thing up. It was so self-centred.'

Control of the door was not only tight, it was whimsical. Nile Rogers and Bernard Edwards of Chic were turned back, even as their records were riding high on the club's playlist. In protest they went home and wrote a song called 'Fuck Off'. Later, when they substituted the words 'Freak Out', 'Le Freak' was born, one of the biggest selling dance records ever.

The sexual antics were legion, for this was the last throw of the seventies dice. Blowjobs in the balcony; adultery in the ante-rooms below; buggery in the bathroom. Movie star Alec Baldwin was a waiter. He compares himself to the Humphrey Bogart character in the movie *Casablanca*: 'I was the Rick Blaine of well-heeled homosexual balcony dwellers at Studio 54.'

The club was opened by Steve Rubell and Ian Schrager – one gay, the other straight, both relative newcomers to the world of clubs. Most of its story has been told far too often to require further detailing here: *Amazing theatrically opulent nightclub full of celebrities misbehaving gets its owners slammed up for tax evasion.* However, in among all the spangles, the photo books and the bad movies, little has ever been told of its music.

The principal DJ there was Richie Kaczor, who had made his name at Hollywood, a gay haunt on West 45th Street on the site of the old Peppermint Lounge.

'All these things on Studio 54 recently, and not one of them has talked about the DJs,' fumes Nicky Siano. 'Never mentioned Richie Kaczor. Richie was a fabulous DJ. "I Will Survive"? He *discovered* that record. He made a hit out of it. He was incredible. One of the reasons Studio happened was because he was so incredible, and they never even mention him.'

'When I heard about the Studio 54 movie I said, "Oh well, at least they'll have 'I Will Survive' on there," ' says Tom Moulton. 'When I was told they weren't going to put it on the soundtrack, I thought, "Well, it can't be about Studio 54 then." I remember when Richie first played that record. It's the B-side of "Substitute". Everyone walked off the floor. He kept right on playing and finally turned it around. Became his biggest record.'

Kaczor, who died in the eighties, was remembered as a rare glint of down-to-earth humanity amid the supercharged glitz of Studio.

'Richie was a sweetheart and we all knew him from Hollywood, which was a little more edgy and more underground,' remembers Danny Krivit. 'So he had a lot of respect from all the underground DJs. When he did Studio 54, instead of thinking, "Oh, you're just playing that commercial stuff," we thought of him as someone who does this, but is playing the commercial stuff *there*.'

Nicky Siano also enjoyed a brief residency, playing from the club's second night (and presiding over Bianca Jagger's infamous birthday party). However, he only lasted a mere three months, his drug consumption, by his own admission, out of control. Nicky Siano managed the impossible: to be sacked from a club where drug-taking was almost compulsory. 'I was so strung out on heroin,' he recalls.

Siano had DJed at Schrager and Rubell's earlier club, a place called Enchanted Garden in Queens, just at the distance from Manhattan where a yellow cab could legally charge you double the fare. Siano laughs as he tells the story of his recruitment.

'Steve Rubell comes to the table and introduces himself and says, "And this is my fiancée, Heather." And I'm like, "*fiancée*! *You have a fiancée?*" I was very confused at that point.' They asked him if he would DJ there, and because he didn't want to stop playing at his own club, Gallery, Siano only agreed to play for twice the going rate – $150 a night. 'Anyway, after the evening was over, Steve gave me a lift back home; I invited him in and fucked the shit out of him. After that he was at the Gallery every Saturday night.'

Siano played at Enchanted Garden for a year but eventually gave it up on account of the trek out to Queens every week. 'They were offering me coke and stuff, but by that stage I wanted heroin. I tell you though, honey, Steve Rubell was no longer straight when I got done with him. That fiancée? Fell to the kerb shortly after.'

Kenny Carpenter, who had started in clubland doing the lights at Galaxy 21, was another DJ who played at Studio 54, spinning there from 1979-81 when Rubell was in jail. He says that under Rubell's stand-in, Mike Stone, he was able to move towards a slightly more underground sound. When Rubell was released and returned, he showed Carpenter just how little he cared about the DJ.

'Steve Rubell comes down with Calvin Klein, Bianca Jagger and Andy

Warhol to the booth. And he says, "Can you play 'Your Love' by Lime?" '
Carpenter didn't have this, a proto high energy record. 'I said, "It's not my
kind of record." I hated it. He says, "Well, listen, I own this club and I've
got Bianca and Calvin and Andy and they wanna hear that record." I said,
"Listen, Steve. Sorry I don't have that record, but even if I did have it, I
wouldn't play that record because it's not my style." He got mad. Stormed
out of the booth. The following weekend, he hired Lime to perform live.
And through the whole show he stood there looking up at the booth.'

Danny Tenaglia concurs. 'Studio 54 was like going to see a movie, you
know? It wasn't about the music. When you went there, it was gimmicky.
It was the first club where you had people painting their whole body
silver. "*Oh, there was somebody in there on a horse!*" People would talk about
that instead of the music. So it was all about *who* was there: Liza Minnelli,
Diana Ross.'

Le Jardin's John Addison set up a rival at 33 West 52nd Street – New
York New York – where François Kevorkian was resident. Another nearby
competitor was Xenon off Times Square at 124 West 43rd Street, where
Jellybean was resident along with Barefoot Boy's Tony Smith. These two
midtown spots attempted to share in the excitement, not to mention the
steady stream of customers who had been turned away from Studio itself.
Although its success was largely the result of outrageous self-fulfilling
hype, François admits that, as a club, Studio 54 provided the goods.

'You cannot say anything other than that Studio had the biggest
venue, the best lights, the best sound,' he says. 'It was quite superior in
some respects to New York New York, just because it was so vast, and so
spectacular and theatrical. Studio 54 was *nice*, but it was really for the
uptown, glitzy crowd.'

To the preachers of the downtown underground, for whom music was
far more important, there was no doubt Studio 54 was a BAD THING.
Many viewed it as the anti-Christ. 'I certainly did,' says Vince Aletti. 'It was
not what we thought this was all about. David Mancuso's idealism was
very widespread in terms of the way people felt. I think disco was, to some
extent, a movement, and a lot of people felt that very strongly. Studio
totally got rid of the democracy of the party. It was the beginning of disco
becoming a business of a whole other sort. And, I thought, really
unattractive.'

Like many from the earlier scene, Aletti felt the emphasis on
appearance and social standing was simply wrong. 'I would never go to a
place where I had to worry about whether they would let me in or not.
A lot of other clubs aspired to this and were jealous when it happened for
Studio. But I think it was destructive to have a velvet rope. It was
completely against the idealism of disco and the community of disco.'

Marketing jeanius – in recent years, the superclubs have all launched branded clothing collections, but Studio 54 had its own line of designer jeans way back in 1980.

Saturday Night Fever

With Studio 54 generating headlines, it took but one further event to complete disco's coming out. When *Saturday Night Fever* premiered on 16 December 1977, its success took everyone by surprise. It was based on a short story by a Dublin-born writer called Nik Cohn and published in *New York* magazine under the title 'Tribal Rites Of The New Saturday Night'. It told the story of an aspirant, working-class Italian-American from Brooklyn with his sights set on Manhattan and his dancing shoes set on stun. With its partnered dancing rituals, the movie was essentially a clever update of the fifties musical and owed little to the scene which spawned it. Especially since the sexual ambivalence of Cohn's original anti-hero had changed: John Travolta's Tony Manero was definitely heterosexual.

The success of the movie, its soundtrack and the singles culled from it were the spark that finally ignited major label interest in disco. Much of its triumph can be attributed to three brothers from Australia, via Manchester. The Bee Gees had been one of the better vocal groups of the late sixties, but their transformation to great white hopes in the mid seventies was nothing short of remarkable. When they moved labels to RSO from Atco, impresario Robert Stigwood suggested a more American and rhythm and blues-oriented direction. The ensuing pair of albums, *Main Course* and *Children Of The World*, generated three hits: 'Jive Talkin', 'Nights On Broadway' and 'You Should Be Dancing'. Stigwood had discovered the white Temptations.

The *Saturday Night Fever* soundtrack dislodged Fleetwood Mac's *Rumours* from its eight-month residency at no.1 in the Billboard Hot 100. The week it reached no.1, five other tracks from the soundtrack were dotted about the singles chart: 'How Deep Is Your Love', 'Night Fever', the Tavares' 'More Than A Woman' and KC & the Sunshine Band's 'Boogie Shoes'. 'Stayin' Alive' was no.1. To keep it company, Andy Gibb and Samantha Sang also had Bee Gees' productions on rotating airplay. *Saturday Night Fever* went on to sell over thirty million copies, the world record for an album until Michael Jackson's *Thriller*.

The Bee Gees did for disco what Elvis Presley did for rhythm and blues, what Diana Ross did for soul, what Dave Brubeck did for jazz; they made it safe for white, straight, middle-class people, hauling it out of its sub-cultural ghetto and into the headlight glare of the mainstream. Here was something middle America could move its uptight ass to.

This is not to say that the *Saturday Night Fever* soundtrack was an implacable enemy of the underground, since the Trammps' 'Disco Inferno' was already regarded as a club classic and the Bee Gees, too, enjoyed downtown club play. Hardly surprising, either, since their taut, muscular productions – aided by some of the best sessioneers in Miami – captured the disco moment far better than the film ever did.

'I remember hearing the Bee Gees' "More Than A Woman" at the Loft where, I think, it had a special meaning,' says François. 'You played "More Than A Woman", but it was being played alongside things like Barrabas' "Woman". It was not the same record that was being played on dancefloors uptown.'

Overloading the disco bandwagon

Pretty soon the world and his wife (and, on a few alarming occasions, his grandmother) had gone disco. It was a musical panacea and the instant revivifier of any ham entertainer's career: Andy Williams, Dolly Parton, Frank Sinatra, Frankie Valli, the Rolling Stones, Rod Stewart and, bizarrely, Ethel Merman all recorded disco tracks. Percy Faith even recorded a disco version of the Jewish folksong 'Hava Nagilah'. Anything that could be conceivably recast as disco was, with TV and film themes providing particularly fertile grounds. Even James Brown was guilty of cashing in − far from 'inventing' disco, as he's often claimed, he made some of his worst records during this period. Ironically, it took a disco producer, Dan Hartman, to relaunch Brown's career with 'Living In America' in 1984.

Disco saturation began in earnest when radio realised its potential. In July 1978, a largely unlistened-to mellow rock radio station, WKTU, 'went disco'. Within two weeks, Disco 92, as it was informally known, had increased its listenership five-fold. By the end of November, WKTU had overtaken the behemoth of New York broadcasting (and the home of Rick Sklar's Top 40 format), WABC. WKTU's Arbitron book rating − the measure of US radio listenership − had gone from 0.9 to 7.8, whilst WABC's had dropped from 8.7 to 7.5. Radio stations all over the country would adopt a disco format in their attempts to emulate this success.

It was the broadcasting story of the decade, and WKTU's methods were, initially at least, rooted in the discothèques. Staff would trawl record stores like Downstairs, Disco Disc, Record Shack and Disc-O-Mat looking for hot 12-inches. Programme director Matthew Clenott told *Billboard*: 'We use our ears and judgment. We let the music happen from the bottom up. It's street-level research. We've got to get on the records when they are happening at the clubs.' By the end of the year, its 6-10pm weeknight disc jockey, Paco Navarro, had achieved a personal rating of 15.8, the highest ever recorded. Alan Freed, at the height of his popularity, never exceeded 15.

Disco was now impossible to avoid, and it spread as a 'craze' or a 'fad' world-wide. By the late seventies there were over 20,000 nightclubs in the USA alone. Some 200,000 people frequented New York clubs every weekend. At the end of the decade, disco accounted for anywhere up to forty per cent of the singles chart. The disco industry's worth was estimated at $4 billion, greater than movies, TV or professional sport.

Eurodisco

As disco became a financial force, the music changed considerably. It had begun not as a genre, but as an amalgam of whatever danceable records the DJs could lay their hands on. Rock, soul, funk, Latin: there was no single style or tempo which characterised the music played in disco's underground years. In its commercial period, the opposite became true. Few major label A&R executives had any great understanding of the club scene from which this music had emerged, so they could only see it in terms of its most basic generalities. They looked at the records which had crossed over, noted a few common denominators, and concluded that there was a simple formula for making disco. There soon was. And much of this formula came from Europe. If the Philly Sound became a blueprint for disco's initial propulsion into the mainstream, then Eurodisco heralded a second wave and a departure from the genre's original black idioms.

France in particular had become a vibrant exporter of dance music during the disco era, thanks to producers like Jean-Marc Cerrone, the duo of Henri Belolo and Jacques Morali (Ritchie Family, Village People) and groups like Space and Voyage. Daniel Vangarde, father of Daft Punk's Thomas Bangalter, wrote and produced material for the Gibson Brothers and Ottowan, including the cheesy holiday hit 'D.I.S.C.O.'. Belolo, who grew up in Morocco and produced his hits in America, puts his success down to the way he energised Morali's flowery French melodies by welding them to the insistent rhythms of disco.

The most famous expression of this idea came from Giorgio Moroder and Pete Bellotte, two transplanted foreigners set down in Munich; one Italian, the other English. Their first hit together was the faintly ridiculous 'Son Of My Father' by synth-pop act Chicory Tip. They then produced Donna Summer's 'Love To Love You Baby', a breathy Philly pastiche. Moroder – inspired by, of all things, Iron Butterfly's prog-rock epic 'In-A-Gadda-Da-Vida' – lengthened what had originally started out as a four-minute song to fill one whole side of an album, nearly seventeen minutes in all. It became one of disco's first worldwide hits.

The follow-up, 'I Feel Love', with its electronic pulse-beat, sequenced throb and thrum and Summer's auto-erotic delivery, was a deliberately futuristic record, a Fritz Lang vision for the dancefloor. Black music purists accused Moroder of chlorinating the black sound. American writer Nelson George said it was 'perfect for folks with no sense of rhythm'. Yet somehow, submerged underneath its nervous electronic sequences, like Kraftwerk, it was still funky. Moroder and Bellotte became Europe's most sought-after producers. They sparked an avalanche of records, many of which really *were* perfect for folks with no sense of rhythm. If this was disco's commercial apogee, it was also its musical nadir. The musical experimentalism that had characterised the indie releases of the early seventies was jettisoned in favour of tried and tested formulas as the major labels sought to wring disco dry. Within a few years, it had crashed and burned.

Disco crashes

That disco started to suck can be blamed squarely on the majors. They were slow to follow the success of the smaller independents, but once they had developed an efficient line of communication with the DJs (through the pools and the new idea of club promotion), they were soon able to join the party.

However, to make disco work for them, they squeezed it into the star-based marketing structures which had worked so well with rock. They hated the fact that disco was made by anonymous producers bossing a bunch of session musicians around, and that the real star of the show, as everyone kept telling them, was the DJ. (Ritchie Family was named after its *engineer*, ferchrissakes!) Most major labels, used to marketing famous people whose poster you could buy and whose career you could follow, only felt comfortable with this club music if they could dress it up with all sorts of artists and group-based fronts. Naturally, when the wider public saw so much fakery and lip-synching, it reinforced the idea that the music was artificial and inhuman.

There were no bands in disco. No tours. No souvenir T-shirts. Its champions were no more than a bunch of feckless disc jockeys. Critically, outside of the likes of Vince Aletti and Tom Moulton at *Billboard*, disco had little press, and most of what it did have was negative. In the UK, the rock inkies, overwhelmingly middle-class and white, were singularly unable to bring their critical faculties to bear on a music that was made for the body not the mind. As Danny Baker – one of the few rock journalists to have a handle on what disco was – wrote in the *NME* at the time, 'how can you critique this music *sitting down*?'

But perhaps most destructively, the major labels never got over the belief that disco was only a brief fad to be exploited as quickly and thoroughly as possible. This proved to be self-fulfilling, as the disco bandwagon collapsed from all the expectations which had been piled into it.

In 1980 Marvin Schlachter of Prelude told *Billboard*: 'The problem started with the companies which were late getting into the disco scene.

When they woke up, they cut lots of disco records and flooded the market.'

The story of the shortlived Warner Brothers-backed RFC Records illustrates how quickly the majors pulled out. The launch of the label was a lavish affair at Studio 54, but the hangover was not long coming. 'It seemed like everything was happening, then suddenly it was all over,' recalls Vince Aletti, who in 1979 joined the label which was headed by veteran promotions man Ray Caviano. 'Halfway through our tenure there, disco was over and they changed the department's name to "dance music".'

Aletti puts the problem down to the industry's love of instant gratification. 'When something becomes so big and so successful, the business thinks it's got to move on. It milks it for all its worth. And then it's over.' He also blames the lack of real support from radio. 'Radio was still very traditional, very straight, very rock'n'roll, and most of the people there were just not interested. They didn't care about the music, they only played it because it was a hit. And they were only too glad to see it go.'

In the wake of disco the nightlife dialectic revolved a few more notches, mainstream interest faded and there was space for fresh energy to emerge. As had happened before and would happen again, the clubland motor went back underground and another period of intense creativity was set in motion. Despite its demise, disco would live on in numerous other dance forms. As we'll see, hi-energy, house, garage, techno and hip hop are all reconstructions, deconstructions or selective evolutions of disco – the primal parent of the modern dancefloor.

It would take a decade, but disco would have its revenge.

EIGHT
HI-ENERGY

So Many Men, So Little Time

'We met, we organised, we sang, we danced, we fucked, and it was all part of a project, a comprehensible and totalising project. We were the soldiers of ecstasy.'

– Aaron Shurin

'Strange how potent cheap music is.'

– Noël Coward

It's the perky sound of the world's pop. The sweet smell of synthetic chords and overcooked strings set to a pulsing uptempo stomp. It's the soundtrack to Greek beach getaways, the background score for shopping at Bluewater, the staple diet of MTV Germany. It's where trance got its melodies; it's where Kylie met Jason. From Polish divas caked in make-up, to sexually ambiguous Israelis on Eurovision, from Take That, Steps and the Pet Shop Boys, to DJ Sammy, Tiësto and Paul Van Dyk, our planet moves to the sugar-plum pump of hi-energy.

If the funky black and Latin facets of disco evolved, as we'll see, into house music, the whiter Eurodisco sound of Moroder, Bellotte and Jean-Marc Cerrone lived on in a genre that would eventually be known as 'hi-energy' (or 'hi-NRG'). This valued melodies over basslines and velocity over funkiness, it professed a love of Donna Summer over Chaka Khan and Amii Stewart over D-Train. Hi-energy was epitomised in the high camp of artists like Sylvester, Divine and Miquel Brown.

And its influence was huge. Hi-energy became the *lingua franca* of white gay dancefloors worldwide, and then crossed over into the mainstream without any hesitation. This is the music which was appropriated by UK producers Stock, Aitken and Waterman, who sold this unashamedly gay sound as teen-pop with bubblegum acts like Bananarama, Kylie Minogue, Dead Or Alive and Mel & Kim, among many others. Though R&B has pulled the rug from under it in some countries, it remains the predominant pop-dance style in all the rest.

When combined with the force of nineties European techno, in shirts-off homo-hedonistic clubs like London's Trade, hi-energy evolved into various forms of hard dance – nu-energy, trancecore, hard house (and whatever happened to hardbag?) – becoming the staple of such hugely successful DJs as Blu Peter and the influential but departed Tony De Vit. Australians everywhere can be glad that DJs like Andy Farley and Ian M both learnt their trade in hi-energy clubs. Even the current house underground displays some overt hi-energy elements – 'electro-house' is a style almost entirely built on the mechanised basslines of Giorgio Moroder and the vroom-vroom of Divine's producer, Bobby O.

But hi-energy is still disco; its original DJs were disco DJs. Hi-energy is what happened after commercial disco collapsed and the Village People checked out of the YMCA. It is the music which evolved in the upscale white gay clubs in New York, and grew to fruition in London, New York and San Francisco. Although its story is doused in tragedy, its roots lie in liberation, as it parallels the rise of out-and-proud gay culture.

Fire Island

'We would not stop dancing. We moved with the regularity of the Pope from the city to Fire Island in the summer, where we danced till the fall, and then, with the geese flying south, the butterflies dying in the dunes, we found some new place in Manhattan and danced all winter there.' So relates the narrator of Andrew Holleran's gay love story, *Dancer From The Dance*.

If you head out on a train from New York's Penn Station to Sayville on Long Island, and catch the passenger ferry across the thin strip of water on its South Shore, you will arrive at Fire Island, a thirty-two-mile-long isthmus of designated National Seashore. Most of it is out of reach of the automobile, mapped with walks rather than streets. Its remote wildness is a stark and welcome contrast to New York's rattle and hum about sixty miles away.

Here, an endearingly ramshackle cluster of clapboard beach houses and hotels and winding boardwalks was the world's first significant gay community. In Ocean Beach during the 1940s (where Sis Norris's was the favoured haunt) and then subsequently at Cherry Grove and the Pines, gays and lesbians were able to forge a secret suburb intimately connected with but quite apart from the shimmering lights of Manhattan. The geographically isolated Fire Island was where affluent homosexual New Yorkers bought or rented summer homes and escaped to a world where the sun shone, the air was clean, and everyone was gay. In areas like the Meat Rack (the charming name for an area of land between the Cherry Grove and the Pines), it also represented the far reaches of gay sexuality. Here, queens would parade themselves among the gently undulating dunes – often completely naked – in search of action.

By the mid sixties, Fire Island had a fully fledged community of largely middle-class or rich, mainly white, gays. Each summer weekend they would flock to the Pines and the Grove to wind down from the stresses of a successful city life, pick up beautiful men and fuck them. Since residents here were wealthy enough to afford a summer home, a rather narrow social spectrum evolved. The scene's lack of a significant black presence meant it also served a slightly different sound from the mainland clubs, with smoother, more sophisticated songs. And as the seventies dawned, at private parties and at clubs like the Sandpiper (now the Pavillion) and Ice Palace – and later the Boatel and the Monster – the beautiful and the rich would gather and dance the night away, their perfectly toned torsos glistening under the cascades of stars that shivered in the Atlantic air.

For many, disco had its genesis on Fire Island. 'I've yet to hear of another spot in the world where disco came to its formality,' claims Bob Casey, 'where you had two turntables, so the disc jockey could go from one record to the other and make it a perfect mix.' Casey, newly returned from a tour of duty in Vietnam, fell in love with Fire Island right away, and later built a sound system for its most famous nightspot, the Ice Palace.

And Fire Island was not merely a gathering of the beautiful and gilded. Through the disco boom it also served as a crucial testing ground for new records. Like Ibiza and the summer resorts in Europe today, the island attracted many of the leading promo men of the day, most of whom had summer houses there. Getting a tune played and broken in the clubs on Cherry Grove and the Pines guaranteed it would get an instant hearing back in the humid basements of New York nightlife.

Bobby DJ at the Ice Palace

The DJ at the Ice Palace was Bobby Guttadaro, born in Bay Ridge, Brooklyn, and known, for simplicity's sake, as 'Bobby DJ'. By 1971, when he began playing at the Ice Palace, replacing Don Finley, the former pharmacy student had amassed an awesome record collection, and here he put it to propitious use. This street-smart kid had all the savvy that accompanied growing up in Brooklyn. His neighbourhood was later the setting for *Saturday Night Fever*, and if John Travolta's Tony Manero had been a disc jockey rather than a dancer, he might well have been modelled on Bobby Guttadaro. His business sense ensured he went on to work at other important spots, too, like Continental Baths and Infinity, and would eventually sequence the music for disco cash-in movies like *Thank God It's Friday*. Bobby loved the crowds out on the Island: 'They were there for one reason: to party,' he told Albert Goldman in an interview in *Penthouse*. 'They put themselves completely in the hands of the DJ. They said, "Do it to us!" '

Broadway dancer Michael Fesco opened the Ice Palace in May 1970 after an inspirational visit to Francis Grasso's Sanctuary. It was a cavernous, tacky confection, with slanted beams and a 'blender bar' where many a famous cocktail has been shaken into life. Huge groups of men socialised, danced together and celebrated their good fortune: not only were most of them well-heeled, they also had all the sex they could want, the best drugs, and some of the finest music in the world.

'The Ice Palace in the Grove was the most fabulous disco I'd ever been to in my life,' claimed Fire Island habitué Philip Gefter, 'because there were two thousand writhing, drugged, beautiful bodies dancing on this dancefloor. By 6am we were outside around the pool, and we were dancing under the stars as the sun was coming up. And I believed at that moment in time that we were having more fun than anybody in the *history* of civilization had ever had. Because there was the combination of that sexual tension among all of these men, in concert with the drugs they were taking and the electronics of the music – and the sun coming up. It created a kind of *thrill* and excitement and sensation that I believe no culture had ever experienced before.'

The Ice Palace's main competitors were the Boatel and the Sandpiper, which opened in the summer of 1970. There was intense rivalry between the three spaces, as the capricious weekenders were pulled by seasonal ebbs and flows, or by the sudden draw of a DJ of the minute.

The Sandpiper holds a particular place in dance music history because it was here in 1972 that Tom Moulton's legendary mix tapes were first heard. Moulton, the godfather of remixing, began his career painstakingly editing reel-to-reel tapes, splicing and stretching his favourite soul and funk songs to suit the new-born desire for an endless beat. He spent eighty hours making the first tape, originally intended for the Boatel, only to have the owner hand it back, saying, 'Don't give up the day job.' Two weeks later, after the tape had been passed to the Sandpiper, and Moulton had all but forgotten about it, he was woken at 3am by a flurry of jubilantly coked-up phone calls congratulating him; he could hear the crowd screaming in the background.

After Moulton's tapes set the standard, a succession of DJs forged reputations at the Sandpiper, among them Howard Merritt, Jimmy Stuard (tragically killed in the 1977 Everard Baths fire in New York) and Robbie Leslie, one of the founding fathers of the 'circuit party' scene of the US gay social calendar. Leslie got his break while working as a waiter there, perfect grounding for a wannabe DJ. 'At Sandpiper I'd hear the beginning from the first song right through the close of the night. I wasn't getting there at peak time like a club kid, I was hearing the entire package.'

By 1975 Fire Island life had its own set rhythms. During the week you'd while away the afternoons at Boatel, famous for its tea dances. When evening came, although Boatel tried hard to keep hold of the crowd, the majority would make a move to Sandpiper. It was a better place to have dinner, and, in the more upscale Pines, it was a better place to be *seen* having dinner. When Saturday night arrived though, there was no question: you'd hit the Ice palace, dance to the subtle disco rhythms and delicate strings played by Roy Thode – another legend of the emerging scene – and see what fresh meat had dragged itself in from the city. 'Everybody went to Cherry Grove for the Ice Palace on Saturday nights,' remembers Leslie. 'The Sandpiper and the Pines would be deserted.'

It was inevitable that what was happening on Fire Island would impact on New York, whence this sheltered isle drew most of its clientele. When summer ended, the alliances made here were continued in the city and there were certain clubs – Tenth Floor, the Flamingo, 12 West, Le Jardin and, latterly, the Saint and a second Ice Palace (on 57th Street) – where you might see much the same faces.

Many of these clubs had been inspired by the Loft, particularly its membership-only ethos (though not its hippie egalitarianism). The first to open was Tenth Floor, in December 1972, on the site of an old sewing machine factory at 151 West 25th Street. Opened by a trio of designers famed for their lavish Fire Island house parties, its monochrome decor left the guests and the flower arrangements to provide the visual splendour. DJ Ray Yeates, a very rare black face there, played to a strictly A-list gay crowd.

The Flamingo, at 599 Broadway, was opened by the Ice Palace's owner Michael Fesco in December 1974, and was bigger and more impressively professional, but just as exclusive as Tenth Floor – membership was $600 and even Calvin Klein had a hard time getting one. The DJs, who alternated, were Howard Merritt playing calorie-rich disco and Richie Rivera, whose music was far more druggy, moody and tribal.

It was in these places that the 'clone' look emerged – moustaches, lumberjack shirts, jeans and web belts – as a newly liberated culture created a super-masculine visual code that was defiantly obvious to those in the know. They also furthered the Fire Island tradition – now standard on the gay circuit – of throwing black or white themed parties, where guests could indulge either the black leather or the snowy white side of their personalities.

When 12 West opened at 491 West Street a few months later the sniffy said it was merely an overspill for Flamingo, though its easy racial mix suggests otherwise. With its vast floorspace, state-of-the-art Graebar sound system and ambitious marketing plans, 12 West was nothing less than the first superclub. 'Within the year, 12 West expects to add a restaurant, to present cabaret, sponsor charter flights, market T-shirts and, in December, it's said, Bloomingdale's is planning to open a Disco Shop wherein will be sold, among other items, bathrobes and toothbrushes bearing the 12 West logo,' confided a spokesman to the *New York Post*.

Despite these grandiose intentions, 12 West was much more democratic than its rivals. 'Flamingo was elitist. Flamingo was all about your appearance and your bank account and your title at work during the week. Flamingo was about hooking up and who you were going to sleep with that weekend,' insists Robbie Leslie, 12 West's resident DJ, 'whereas 12 West was more mixed; it was just a wonderful melting pot of gay culture. People were there strictly for the music. 12 West was really about dancing all night so the focus was purely on the dancefloor. The ambience of that club was great. The music was fantastic. The backlash hadn't happened. Disco was still king.'

Smooth operator – the well-pressed Robbie Leslie.

Dancer From The Dance includes several scenes in 'the Twelfth Floor'. Holleran makes great play of the after-dark equality to be found there.

'The boy passed out on the sofa from an overdose of Tuinols was a Puerto Rican who washed dishes in the employee's cafeteria at CBS, but the doctor bending over him had treated presidents.' After some insights into the sexual politics of the time, and a lovingly detailed dancefloor scene, the author goes on to describe the night's drug-binge climax. 'There was a moment when their faces blossomed into the sweetest happiness, however – when everyone came together in a single lovely communion that was the reason they did all they did; and that occurred around six-thirty in the morning, when they took off their sweat-soaked T-shirts and screamed because Patty Joe had begun to sing: "Make me believe in you, show me that love can be true." By then the air was half-nauseating with the stale stench of poppers, broken and dropped on the floor after their fumes had been sucked into the heart, and the odour of sweat, and ethyl chloride from the rags they clamped between their teeth, holding their friends' arms to keep from falling.'

Though hi-energy as a genre wouldn't be formally codified until 1984, New York's white gay scene was already starting to distinguish itself musically. Another predominantly white club was Barefoot Boy where (black) Tony Smith was resident. He recalls how in the mid seventies, despite a generally broad playlist, the funkiest tracks were off-limits. 'The only thing I couldn't really play there was black urban music. I got away with "Doin' It To Death" by the JB's but I couldn't get away with "Give It Up Turnit Loose" or "Sex Machine".' Smith also noted another feature of his crowd's taste that would become key to the hi-energy sound. 'What they *really* liked was female vocals.' As the eighties turned, this particular strand of disco would become even more strongly defined.

The Saint

On 20 September 1980, a new place opened which was to drive the competition into the Hudson River. The Saint, on Second Avenue and 6th Street, was for many the city's most eloquent symbol of gay emancipation. 'It was the headiest experience I've ever had in my life,' said one clubber. 'And it is unrivalled still. It was liberating, spiritually uplifting. That's where I learned to love my brothers.' $4.2 million was spent in transforming what had been the revered rock venue the Fillmore East into a huge club, purpose built for its newly liberated gay constituency. Within three weeks of its opening, 3,000 men had paid $250 to become members. In a matter of months, both Flamingo and 12 West closed down.

'The Saint just blew all the competing clubs out of the water and everyone wanted to work there,' says Leslie. Flamingo's entire membership – the A–Z of New York's gay aristocracy – migrated over to the Saint. 'Flamingo was gone by February I think. It was that extreme.' 12 West died even more unceremoniously. 'People were coming to go dancing and they got there and found the doors padlocked.'

'There never was a club like the Saint,' gushes Ian Levine, formerly a leading northern soul DJ and then the founding resident at London's Heaven. 'The Saint was unique in the history of disco music,' he sighs. 'The best ever. At Heaven, all we could even vaguely hope to do was aspire to be a tenth of what the Saint achieved. It was the *ultimate*.'

The Saint was quite the most spectacular club anyone in New York had seen. The entrance was unmarked. You walked through a pair of gleaming stainless steel doors into a massive area with bars, banquettes and cushioned chairs. Upstairs was the vast 5,000-square-foot dancefloor, and above this the club's famous dome. Imagine a hemisphere seventy-six feet across made of aluminium and theatrical scrim. Lit from inside it appeared solid, but when illuminated from above it became formless clouds of psychedelic light. In the centre of the dancefloor was a planetarium projector, and when the moment was right this would cast the image of the night sky onto the darkened dome. Greg James, the American DJ who brought mixing to the UK, remembers how disorienting this effect could be. 'At two in the morning the projector would come out of the floor, the music would come to a grinding halt and there was Bette Davis from *Now, Voyager* saying, "And we have the stars!" and suddenly the whole place would light up with stars. Then the music would start again with a slow beat and the projection would start moving so it felt like the whole room was turning. If you were stoned your feet would come from underneath you. It was brilliant!'

The Saint's dancefloor would be a mass of bodies, each sculpted to perfection, moving in tribal unison. To the strains of the club's ornate music, these beautiful men would proceed to get utterly trashed – on angel dust, Quaaludes, ecstasy, cocaine, amphetamines. They were Greek gods with drug habits. The lights would go down, the projector would come on, and as New York went about its Sunday morning chores, a few thousand men would take a snort of their poppers and continue dancing near-naked under the electric stars.

'It was the apotheosis of the underground dance experience,' says Michael Fierman, one of the Saint's DJs. 'The main point of what we did was to create a commonality of experience for everyone there, unifying several thousand people.'

'Inside it was like some sort of religious gathering,' adds Levine. 'It was crammed to the rafters and they were all blowing whistles and screaming.'

With a night at the Paradise Garage – the Saint's mostly black gay contemporary – you could never be sure what you might hear. But at the Saint you could almost bank on the playlist. The roster of DJs there – Roy Thode, Sharon White, Terry Sherman, Shaun Buchanan, Robbie Leslie and Michael Fierman – favoured a very particular sound, playing melody-soaked songs with a heavy kick–drum, richly orchestrated strings and sentimental lyrics that told of love lost and spurned. The Weather Girls were favourites, as was the classic diva soul of Thelma Houston, Phyllis Nelson and Linda Clifford, alongside Eurodisco, especially French acts like Voyage and Cerrone, whose 'Call Me Tonight' was a particular favourite.

These weren't all new records. With disco wearing a tag on its toe, the DJs went back to their crates and dug deep, searching for tunes that had been overlooked during the years of abundance. 'Just as northern soul discovered the records of the sixties and played them in the seventies, so the Saint discovered the records of the seventies and played them in the eighties,' explains Ian Levine. 'They made gods out of the cult disco records of the seventies.'

Ian Levine at Heaven

'In the beginning, God created Earth, and God said it was good.

'Then God created Man.

'And then Man created Heaven.'

On 6 Dec 1979, 2,000 men were crammed into a vast half-lit dancefloor listening to the bizarre twenties-style disco of Dr Buzzards Original Savanna Band played at a whisper. At the stroke of midnight, the club was pitched into darkness and American actor Doug Lambert biblically intoned the words quoted above. Lights flashed the place into action and the crowd gasped as the sweeping pump of Dan Hartman's 'Relight My Fire' launched a mass of jumping male bodies. From then on, Heaven was on Earth.

After giving London its first taste of a modern purpose-built disco in the Embassy, publisher of Burke's Peerage, Jeremy Norman had decided the time was right for something much bigger and much gayer. An expensive refit later and Global Village, a jazz-funk club under Charing Cross station, became Heaven, his explicitly gay discothèque. Greg James, resident at the Embassy, then recommended Ian Levine as a DJ who could drive this new vehicle with the momentum it required. At Blackpool Mecca, Levine had helped establish the northern soul scene and then coerced his clubbers into disco, as his stateside soul-buying trips evolved into gay escapades in New York's new clubland. He was also one of the only DJs in the UK who could mix records. Levine determined to bring a slice of the Saint's homo paradise to Britain. By doing so he would distil the club's musical tastes into a lasting genre.

'We created a new scene at Heaven by playing purely American disco music, but it was at about the same time that the disco market slumped,' he explains. 'Suddenly there was a shortage of new records. I explained to

Howard and Geoff from Record Shack that I didn't want all the funk records they were selling to the straight DJs. I wanted much faster music and they would have to get it.'

As well as seeking out speedier tunes, Levine made his own. Already an experienced producer, in the mid eighties he started to make records tailored specifically for the dancefloors of Heaven and the Saint. These were largely extensions of the Eurodisco sound, but Levine exaggerated the style, bringing to it the aesthetic he'd developed in his northern soul career. The result was fast, stompy music filled with swirling melodies and featuring a series of female vocalists – Eartha Kitt, Hazell Dean, Evelyn Thomas – singing lyrics with which every gay man could identify. One song, 'High Energy' by Evelyn Thomas, would clarify the style's name (it was also known as 'boystown' or simply 'gay disco').

Hi-energy was Levine's way of keeping his beloved northern soul alive. 'Gays like melodic, straightforward dance music that's not too funky,' he explained to Dave Hill in *The Face*. 'Like Motown, it's zingy and pretty, but powerful.'

In his disco history *Turn The Beat Around*, Peter Shapiro connects the sound of hi-energy to wider changes. Now freed from the shadows, gay culture, especially in Manhattan's fiercely competitive social circles, was imposing increasingly ruthless standards of physical beauty, forcing men to spend hours at the gym in fear of 'no pecs, no sex'. And if the men on the dancefloor were ever more sculpted and polished, so was the music they moved to. Shapiro argues that hi-energy 'would blanch disco, not so much by bleaching its black roots but by striving for superhuman perfection, by pushing the clone aesthetic to its furthest limits'. Like the fantasy men in Tom of Finland's erotic illustrations, hi-energy was shiny, perfect and pumped – with all grit and blemishes removed.

The UK became a major production centre, as former northern soul DJs capitalised on their expertise – Levine, Kev Roberts, Les McCutcheon (who was also responsible for the cocktail funk of Shakatak). Many of the songs they used were either steals from the northern canon or simple cover versions; the tempo and emotion of northern soul fitted perfectly. Thus the Ad Libs' 'Nothing's Worse Than Being Alone' was covered by the Velvettes, Mary Love's 'You Turned My Bitter Into Sweet' was sung by Linda Lewis, and Joy Lovejoy's 'In Orbit' was reworked by Yvonne Gidden.

What's more, by studiously avoiding the word 'girl' in his lyrics, Levine cannily made music that appealed to his core audience of gay men, and still managed to cross over to the teenage pop consumer, who remained blissfully unaware of its leather-and-poppers origins.

These records formed the core of Levine's DJ sets at Heaven, founding the tastes of a generation of gay British clubbers, and forming an important addition to the Saint's musical canon. In fact, such was his impact on the New York scene that Levine would fly over to debut many of his tracks there. He recalls just such a trip in Easter 1983, for the first airing of 'So Many Men, So Little Time' by Miquel Brown. The song had only been finished on the Monday, but Levine rushed it to the factory for pressing and then flew it to New York for DJ Robbie Leslie's Thursday night at the Saint. He remembers the excitement the record caused: 'Three o'clock in the morning, at the peak of the night, he stopped the last record dead, plunged the room into blackness, and then there was boo-boo-boo-BOO-BOO-BOOM! By the Monday, it was the talk of New York.'

By the mid eighties the hi-energy sound was the principal soundtrack in most British gay clubs, like La Chic in Nottingham, Heroes in Manchester (where yet another northern soul veteran Les Cokell presided) and Nightingale in Birmingham. In Scotland it was enormously popular in straight clubs, founding a taste for speedy tempos that can be seen today in the Scottish affection for gabber.

Nu-energy and hard dance

Today hi-energy and Eurobeat, hi-energy's slower offspring (massive in Japan and Germany), have been replaced by their frisky offspring hard house, trance and nu-energy – the latter term coined by Blu Peter, who connected Goa's spatial trance with laughably fast German techno on labels like No Respect and Superstition. By the mid nineties nu-energy was a serious force in gay clubs worldwide. In London it soundtracked the gay weekend, from Heaven and Trade's churning dancefloors to the Monday morning casualties at the delightfully named FF (fist fuck).

'It's best described as an uplifting, melodic techno,' React Records' Thomas Foley told *Mixmag*. 'Techno with a tune, the nearest to a song that techno gets. For want of a better phrase, it's hi-energy for the nineties.'

After the nu-energy craze, 'hard house' became the umbrella term, encapsulating the broad palette of tougher sounds like trance and European techno being played at Trade by DJs Steve Thomas, Malcolm Duffy, Tony De Vit and Alan Thompson. Labels like Tinrib, Tripoli Trax, Nukleuz and Tidy Trax (from the same people who gave us Jive Bunny) sprung up to replenish the DJs' record bags.

Andy Farley, one of today's leading hard dance DJs (he got his start playing with Tony De Vit back in the eighties) explains the evolution. 'In the mid nineties they'd play what they called techno at Trade, but if you listened to it now you'd call it trance. When the trance sound exploded big in 1997 and '98 I played some of it, too. If you listen to it now, you'd class it as hi-energy.'

Curiously, this is one of the few areas of house that has had a significant input from women, with Anne Savage, the Lisas Pin-Up and Lashes, Mrs Wood, Rachel Auburn and Madam Friction playing key roles.

Stock, Aitken and Waterman

In 1984 Evelyn Thomas's 'High Energy', produced by Ian Levine, crossed over and reached no. 5 (UK). The same year former Midlands club DJ Pete Waterman, together with session musicians Mike Stock and Matt Aitken formed a songwriting partnership that would take the hi-energy sound to stratospheric commerciality. In the next six years Stock Aitken and Waterman would put more than a hundred songs in the UK Top 40, garner thirteen UK number ones and sell thirty-five million records worldwide.

Waterman had learnt the industry ropes at Magnet Records and as assistant to John Travolta. As hi-energy boomed he was sharing a flat with gay club promoter Barry Evangeli, whose tiny Proto label had just signed Hazell Dean. When Evangeli exposed him to the sound, Waterman, with typical arrogance, felt he could up the ante. He later boasted to *Record Mirror*, 'The records they were playing were cheap and nasty. I knew I could give them exactly what they wanted, with quality.'

During their writing years Waterman would visit gay clubs with a Dictaphone, record the latest sounds and feed them back to Mike Stock. Their first acts were as gay as pyjamas. There was Divine, star of John Waters' outrage-inducing movies, a 300-pound drag queen with McDonalds arches for eyebrows. Divine's growling challenge, 'So You Think You're A Man' reached no.16 (UK) in 1984. 'I knew it was going to be a hit because it was so camp,' admitted Waterman in his autobiography, *I Wish I Was Me*. 'If it had started off 90 per cent camp it was 120 per cent camp by the time we'd finished with it.' SAW followed this up by extracting a global number one from Dead Or Alive – a goth-lite Liverpool band fronted by sharp-tongued he-she Pete Burns – 'You Spin Me Round (Like A Record)'.

Waterman declared his love for shiny synthetic sounds. 'I don't want any traditional instruments . . . I had a vision of Motown-type songs with more modern chords and techno, gay disco rhythms. I wanted to make technologically brilliant records.'

Musicologist Daniel P Hyde offers a complex dissection of the SAW method in his dissertation *The Search For The Magic Formula*. Much is fairly technical, but the main thrust is that their song structures give 'a degree of predictability that's reassuring and comfortable', and their melodies are, 'full of musical clichés, all of which are in place for ease of remembrance'.

Another point is telling. Hyde notes all the songs are in 'uplifting' major keys 'more likely to appeal to younger age groups'. Their most successful act, former soap star Kylie Minogue, proved a milestone in that, while aimed firmly at gay dancefloors, she was also the first major act to be marketed energetically at pre-teens. This double-headed market, where records (and the acts themselves) are shaped to draw in both pocket money and pink pounds, has defined the pop world ever since.

San Francisco

San Francisco has been a magnet for the disaffected and the dissolute for more than a century. When the 1906 earthquake razed the city, fire-and-brimstone preachers regarded it as retribution for 'Sodom by the sea'. A thriving port and naval base allowed gay bars, though covert, to thrive. And in the Second World War those men and women issued with dishonourable discharges for their homosexuality were shipped back through San Francisco. Rather than face the shame of returning home – the discharge papers' blue colour denoted their 'deviance' – many settled in the more liberated atmosphere that prevailed. By the late forties, bars like Finocchio's (a female impersonator club founded in the roaring twenties), Mona's and Black Cat were already well established. Despite McCarthyism and persecution, gay culture grew and prospered. In 1964, *Time* magazine declared San Francisco the 'gay capital' of America.

Businesses catering to a specifically gay clientele appeared on Polk Street (the precursor to Castro Street) in 1965, with a gay community centre opening the following year. The hippie explosion nurtured growing feelings of liberation. 'At the Capri you stood outside in the street together, on your home turf, talking, making liaisons, having friendships outside in the open, in the air,' poet Aaron Shurin said of San Francisco's first hippie gay bar. 'For me it was deep because it wasn't governed by pain, it wasn't governed by loneliness. It didn't live under the sign of loneliness. It lived under the sign of something new, a new light and a new order that was just being named.' In fact, by the end of the sixties, in San Francisco the gay community was already enough of a political force to have seen off the kind of police harassment which so inflamed New York. 'There was no Stonewall in this city because we were so far ahead,' says Nan Alamilla Boyd, gender studies professor at Sonoma State University.

Music is embedded in the fabric of gay San Francisco. Its very signature tune, 'I Left My Heart In San Francisco', was written by two gay men, George Cory and Douglas Cross. In the late 1960s, bars with dancing sprang up all over the North Beach area and Polk Street. The magnificently named Big Basket was among the first, along with the Rendezvous on Sutter Street and Toad Hall and the Cabaret on Montgomery, which became City Disco, the city's first major club. These were swiftly followed by Oil Can Harry's, Busby's, In Touch, the End Up, and I-Beam, where DJ Tim Rivers was an early star. Down the road in Los Angeles was Studio One where Paul Dougan and Mike Lewis, one of Disconet's star remixers, were residents.

City Disco was a huge entertainment complex that included a restaurant, disco and several stores. Its first DJ star was the flamboyant John Hedges from Ohio, who began spinning at the Mineshaft under the name Johnny Disco, wearing a trademark cowboy hat. Hedges made his name using two copies of the same 45 to create his own extended mixes (he later started the San Francisco pool Bay Area Disco DJ Association). Another key jock was Frank Loverde, *Billboard*'s DJ of the Year 1976. When Hedges moved to Oil Can Harry's, his place at City Disco was taken by Marty Blecman (DJ of the Year 1978). Blecman was not only a gifted DJ but an accomplished musician who'd worked at Fantasy Records, before forming leading San Francisco label Megatone Records with Patrick Cowley (Marty died from AIDS in September 1991).

Bobby Viteritti at Trocadero Transfer

In July 1979, around the time rock DJs were announcing the death of disco, San Francisco was in tumult over weightier matters. The previous November Dan White had gunned down Mayor George Moscone and city supervisor Harvey Milk – the world's first openly gay public official. Part of White's defence included the fact that he was depressed from eating too much junk food. When the jury convicted him of 'involuntary manslaughter' with a laughably light sentence, the city's gay community erupted and rampaged down Castro Street causing thousands of dollars of damage. Twenty-four hours later Castro was again full of gay men, this time partying all night. Randy Shilts marveled at 'the unique homosexual ability to stage a stormy riot one night and then disco peacefully on the streets the next'.

Although the crash of disco wiped it from San Francisco's radio, the gay community danced on. The leading clubs, eager to play catch-up with New York, began luring its foremost spinners into West Coast residencies. Howard Merritt was hired to play Dreamland, while Long Island jock Bobby Viteritti was brought over for a residency at Trocadero Transfer. Merritt came from the original wave of New York disco DJs, having learned his craft at the Cock Ring, played at the Sandpiper and been resident at the Flamingo for five years (he was also a promotions director at Casablanca Records).

But the city's real star was the arrogant and supremely talented Bobby Viteritti. Viteritti demanded respect in a job that rarely enjoyed it. He'd originally made his name in Florida at the Marlin Beach Hotel, one of the first gay hotels on the East Coast. 'He was definitely very full of himself, but he was very masterful,' says Robbie Leslie, who had done the lights for him there. 'At that point DJs really didn't regard themselves as any big deal, it was just a guy who played records. But Bobby had the self-opinion that he was an artist and he behaved accordingly. This was the time in the industry when you could hire a DJ for $35–40 a night, but he was a pioneer and he raised the level of playing music to artistry.'

He arrived with a secret weapon – boxes of the soul tunes that were staples in New York but unheard in San Francisco. 'I had a lot of music that the West Coast didn't have,' he says. 'They were playing "Disco Duck", can you believe it?! They'd never heard "I'll Bake Me A Man", or "Dirty Old Man". They'd never heard Creative Source's "Who Is He", "Atmosphere Strutt" by Cloud One or "One Monkey Don't Stop No Show" by Honey Cone. They never heard songs like that.' The Trocadero was quickly the city's most popular club.

Viteritti had a great advantage in that the Troc was then the only after-hours in San Francisco, so the meticulous DJing experiments he planned with his light man Billy Langenheim had a captive – and druggy – audience. 'Billy and Bobby would get together at the beginning of the night and plan where they would take the crowd and with what songs,' explained a clubber in David Diebold's book *Tribal Rites*. 'They believed that if they could totally control the audio and visual environments, then they could actually control the group consciousness and influence people's trips, which they unquestionably did. It was like nothing I've ever seen.'

One trick was to get the dancers to fever pitch with three-minute snippets of all the current big tunes, and then lock them into a greatly extended and hypnotically repetitive edit he'd made. 'Bobby would play a long version of something he'd re-edited the heck out of,' explains Troc diehard Chris Njirich. 'He'd pick out this little sound in the song and accent it and he'd re-edit it over and over and really work it. It made the audience go crazy. For instance Viola Wills' "If You Could Read My Mind" was a really big song at Troc. When he played that, the crowd would just go *insane*.'

When Robbie Leslie played his regular Trocadero Transfer guest spots, he brought a very contrasting style. 'Robbie would take them on a smooth trip with a lot of soul,' says Njirich, who describes Leslie as the gentleman of disco. 'He'd still work them up in peaks of energy, but keeping them on an even keel. The way he mixed was the way he dressed. He always looked like he'd just stepped out of the shower and was just about to have a very nice dinner. Whereas Bobby Viteritti would come in a T-shirt and jeans, all cranked up, rarin' to go. Robbie Leslie came in with his records so neat you would expect them to be tied up in a nice bow.'

Viteritti and his club inspired incredible devotion from their clubbers. The 'Trocadites', as they styled themselves, still get together for commemorative Remember The Party events. But after a wage dispute Viteritti left and moved to rival nightspot Dreamland. Modeled on New York's swank Flamingo in every way, Dreamland was chi-chi and cool, dazzling and bright. 'It was not unreasonable to ask a man if he was a Trocadero guy or a Dreamland guy, though chances were you could guess within the first few minutes,' wrote Joshua Gamson in *The Fabulous Sylvester*.

It was a question of atmosphere. 'Dreamland was white, Trocadero was black,' elucidates Njirich, talking of mood (both clubs were very white, racially). 'Dreamland was pretty boys in white tank tops and shorts; the muscle A-crowd. Trocadero was the people who wanted to go and dance all night and basically do drugs. Dreamland was a great place but it was definitely the cocaine and attitude club.'

As mainstream disco collapsed, local indie labels like Megatone and Moby Dick sprang up to fill the chasm left by the majors' withdrawal from the marketplace. Slashed budgets precluded the epic orchestral productions disco had grown used to, and instead DJs and producers began crafting synthesised disco records specifically for the clubs. The most talented among them was the light man at City Disco. Patrick Cowley was an intractable, fully liberated white man who lived, as his songs suggest, for sex and music. Cowley grew to fame for his alliance with Sylvester, a well-established black jazz singer turned disco-drag-diva with a piercing falsetto, who he met at City Disco. Cowley became the driving force behind Sylvester's sequenced soul, producing such classics as 'You Make Me Feel (Mighty Real)' and 'Do You Wanna Funk?'.

Cowley's music was decidedly homoerotic and where it lacked subtlety (as on the fantastically indiscreet 'Make It Come Hard') it made up for in thrust. Even his instrumentals managed to be full of suggestion, as on the brilliant 'Sea Hunt', named after a TV series in which Lloyd Bridges played a hunky frogman on whom Cowley had a crush.

He was not alone in making records for the scene. Linda Imperial was a local star, as was producer Paul Parker. The Boystown Gang were huge (and even scored a hit in the UK with their horrible cover of Andy Williams' 'Can't Take My Eyes Off You'), but beyond Sylvester there was little made in San Francisco of enduring importance. Notable exceptions include the Weather Girls (Martha Wash and Izora Armstead), who started as Sylvester's backing singers and had a huge hi-energy hit with 'It's Raining Men', as well as making the amazing 'Just Us' in their original guise as Two Tons O' Fun.

Morning music

Hi-energy has often been characterised as workout music for moustachioed steroid-bashers. However, the scene was also instrumental in promoting music of depth and texture, namely the 'morning music' or 'sleaze' that followed at daybreak. Born in the after-hours clubs of New York, this was the relief after the bpm onslaught of the rest of the night. As the light rose, the tempo dropped, and while the earlier programme would be characterised by raw expressions of sex, morning music concentrated on romance, love and heartbreak. It was the beauty that followed the beat.

'From eight onwards was what we'd call sleaze,' beams Ian Levine. 'It wasn't sleazy sounding, it was very pretty, because the Saint was about beautiful music.'

The real musical devotees, bored of the rigid programming early in the night, would often arrive around 6am specifically to hear the DJs' morning sets. Most of the early hi-energy DJs had come from the same era as Francis Grasso and David Mancuso, and sleaze can be seen as their attempt to wrest control of the dancefloor from the diktat of drugs. In any case, as the evening progressed and limbs gradually tired – aided by a barbiturate or Quaalude, perhaps – so the dancefloor mellowed out. Robbie Leslie neatly described this as, 'the bell curve for a night of dancing'.

These songs were the measure of a great hi-energy DJ. 'A lot more heart went into it than in the middle of the night,' claims Leslie. 'For a lot of my contemporaries, that was their time to shine and really stand out and make a statement. In the middle of the night you could almost blindfold someone because the DJs were a lot closer in format but with "morning music" you had more variety.'

Recordings that exist today of DJs like Bobby Viteritti, Robbie Leslie and Roy Thode show not only breathtaking dexterity moving from one track to the next, but also programming eclectic enough to make any Balearic DJ proud. On one, Viteritti glides from Ozo's leftfield instrumental 'Anambra', into 'Rotation' by Herb Alpert, followed by two Love Unlimited Orchestra tracks – 'Love's Theme' and 'Under The Influence Of Love' – then the heartbreaking (and heartbreakingly rare) 'Changin'' by Sharon Ridley, finally arriving at Bee Gees' 'Night Fever', somehow sounding completely different in such context. On another recording he manages to segue the kooky 'Anambra' into Abba's 'Dancing Queen', as likely a juxtaposition as Jordan lapdancing for the Queen.

In New York, morning music was soul and rhythm and blues-oriented, reflecting the rich heritage of the city's early discos. Many of disco's early classics were resurrected: 'Pull Yourself Together' by Buddy Miles, Lamont Dozier's 'Take Off Your Make Up' and the Van McCoy-produced 'Walk Away From Love' by David Ruffin.

The big sleaze records at the Saint were things like 'Take Me Down' by Johnny Bristol or 'Somebody's Eyes' by Viola Wills. 'It was beautiful, lilting music at around 105bpm, as opposed to 130,' explains Levine. 'Anything with that Barry White mid-tempo feel, but it had to have those sweet chords and rich orchestration. That's what they really got off on.' Levine studied the morning music each time he visited and crafted a song specifically made for the session, Miquel Brown's 'Close To Perfection', which became another Saint classic.

The sound in San Francisco was more electronic, demonstrating Patrick Cowley's considerable influence. The DJs would often deploy the same record twice, playing the vocal at 45 at peak hour and then in the morning flipping it and playing the instrumental at 33. Magnifique's 'Magnifique', a huge German hi-energy tune at the Troc – thanks to an energetic re-edit by Bobby Viteritti – was used in this manner, turning it from strident disco into a dislocated and druggy groove. 'Souvenirs' by Voyage and Salsoul Orchestra's 'Magic Bird Of Fire' received the same treatment with similar results. They were not averse to leftfield selections either, Gil Scott Heron's 'In The Bottle' and 'Pass The Dutchie' by Musical Youth being two examples.

This trajectory, of fast music about sex, followed by the slower devotional sound of loves lost and gained, was a gay man's life encapsulated – coquettish flirt, lustful warrior, tender lover and, finally, heartbroken vamp. Each evening told a new story, narrated by the DJ. Viteritti explained his modus operandi to David Diebold: 'We'd suddenly go into a wild, frenzied set and we'd beat the crowd with strobes and wild music. We'd whip them up with one rough song after another.' But then, when morning came, 'throw them into a whirlpool, smoothing out . . . and bring everybody back together into the same head space'.

Tragedy

The stories of disco and gay liberation run in close parallel. For the core of its devotees, the discothèque boom and the hi-energy that followed was more than pure hedonism. It was a movement through which gay people made substantial social gains. Not only was it the soundtrack to their emancipation from years of invisibility, a rallying call for togetherness and tolerance, it was also a Trojan horse by which important aspects of gay culture were pushed into mainstream acceptance. Because of this, when disco collapsed, it seemed like an attack on the freedoms that had been won – especially since the disco backlash was usually voiced with unmistakable homophobia. This effrontery was compounded by all-out tragedy as another force emerged that would have an unprecedented impact on the gay community.

If the disco movement was beaten down by rampant commerciality, it was laid to rest by AIDS. A story that began with the liberation symbolised at Stonewall ended with a disease which seemed at first to discriminate along exactly the same bigoted lines as society at large. In its early years, the as yet undiagnosed 'gay cancer' AIDS was first known as GRIDS: Gay Related Immune Deficiency Syndrome. Novelist David Leavitt described this period as 'a time when the streets were filled with an almost palpable sense of mourning and panic'.

The abandon with which many disc jockeys approached life saw to it that AIDS ravaged the dance community hard. Many DJs – hedonistic pioneers all – succumbed to the disease. Others lost their lives through drug overdoses. As writer Brian Chin commented, 'I wasn't constantly hanging around DJs because the drug-taking *scared the fuck* out of me.' In many New York clubs, like the Anvil, Mineshaft and Crisco Disco, dancing took second place to sex. AIDS was initially nicknamed 'the Saint's Disease', since so many of the club's members were among the first to die.

An important part of gay recreation in urban America (especially for the hi-energy community) was the baths' scene with its charged sexual atmosphere. The bath-houses (or just 'baths') were essentially gay sex centres. Based around steam baths, swimming pools and saunas, they were places where men would go to fuck and be fucked by as many men as they desired. Some had music and restaurants, all had endless orgies. The arrival of the HIV virus meant the hedonism of these places would ultimately result in mass tragedy. By the time AIDS had become a manageable disaster rather than unmitigated catastrophe, it had claimed fifty per cent of all gay Manhattanites.

Over in San Francisco, Patrick Cowley was one of the first well-known people to succumb. 'He was very driven by music,' recalled his room-mate DJ Frank Loverde. 'He really didn't have much of a social life. It was just music and the baths, music and the baths. That's probably how he got sick.' So little was known about the disease at the time, that when Cowley fell ill on a tour of South Africa everyone thought he had an acute bout of food poisoning. In the final stages of his life, and after what people thought would be a terminal stay in hospital, Cowley dragged himself into the studio to record 'Do You Wanna Funk?' with Sylvester. 'He'd be in the studio laying on the couch,' recalled a friend, 'directing the engineer, really out of it, yet determined to finish that record.'

Patrick Cowley died on 12 November 1982. Sylvester was performing at Heaven in London. In an emotional scene, he announced the death of his friend and collaborator before performing 'Do You Wanna Funk?' Sadly, Sylvester also died from AIDS six years later, on 18 September 1988. Almost everyone from Megatone and Moby Dick died, too. 'It killed our customers, it killed our artists, it killed our founders,' recalled John Hedges. 'It was kind of a three or four year blur, and then everybody was gone.'

Despite the first wave of AIDS deaths, and long after it was accepted that it was a transmittable disease, the bath-houses refused to close. Only after July 1983, when the Hothouse in San Francisco shut its doors in recognition of the crisis, did the baths accept their role in the disease's transmission. 'Before AIDS, going to the baths had an aura almost like smoking,' commented one AIDS campaigner. 'People knew it wasn't too good for them, but it was socially acceptable. Now it has the aura of shooting heroin.' One by one the San Francisco baths admitted defeat. New York moved to shut down its remaining baths in late 1985. Finally, on 5 May 1987, the last one in San Francisco, 21st Street Baths, locked its doors.

'You'd read a different obituary every week,' comments Njirich. 'You became afraid to open the paper. But what is weird is the shock you would get every time. "I just saw him yesterday and he's gone." It really felt like the end of everything. Nothing ever recovered from it and the parties were never quite what they had been before.'

Its clientele decimated, the Saint closed in April 1988 to the music of Jimmy Ruffin's 'Hold Onto My Love' and the final movement of Beethoven's Ninth Symphony (the club reopened briefly without its dome at the end of 1989). The Saint lives on today in massive quarterly parties complete with sex shows and a good deal of bad behaviour. When the building was sold, gay campaigners felt very strongly that there should be a memorial erected in memory of the club and its clubbers – for here was a place where gay freedom was shouted to the world, and here was a place where that freedom was crushed by terrible tragedy. Rodger McFarlane, executive director of New York AIDS charity Gay Men's Health Crisis, reflected on the bittersweet memories the Saint conjures. 'We didn't know we were dancing to the edge of our graves.'

There was no memorial. Today, the building is a bank.

NINE
HIP HOP
ROOTS

Adventures On The Wheels Of Steel

'Betwixt decks there can hardlie a man catch his breath by reason there ariseth such a funke in the night . . .'

– W Capps, 1623

'Think rap is a fad, you must be mad.'

– Stetsasonic, 'Talkin' All That Jazz'

't was violent, but the whole neighbourhood was violent, you know,' recalls Sal Abbatiello, the owner of the Bronx club Disco Fever, open between 1977 and 1985. 'I mean, I had three murders in the club in ten years, but if you compare that to the neighbourhood . . . I had three in ten years, they had one every week! I thought my percentage was better than theirs. I had one of my bouncers died in my arms, over telling a guy "don't sniff blow at the bar".

'But we were open seven nights a week. Monday was like a Saturday. We've got Grandmaster Flash on Monday, Lovebug Starski on Tuesday, I go get this other kid for Sundays called Eddie Cheeba, and now I give Kool Herc a night, Kool Herc has a night with Clark Kent. And I always wanted to get DJ Hollywood, but Hollywood wouldn't come to the Fever, he just wouldn't come. Finally I convince Hollywood, and he does a Wednesday. And there's Jun-Bug. So now I got everybody. The club is mobbed every night.

'It was two dollars to get in. Never advertised, never went on radio, just word of mouth and the music and the party. Everybody knew all the customers, and it was pretty wild that a white guy owned the club, and the main DJ was Latin, you know, Jun-Bug.

'I'd have a doctor sitting here, I'd have a pimp sitting here, I'd have a hooker here, I'd have a lawyer here, I'd have a frigging correction officer here, a girl worked on Wall Street here, but in there it was just . . .

[Acts sniffing coke]
' "Throw your hands in the air!!"

' "Somebody got a gun."

[Ducks]

' "He's gone."

' "OK."

' "Ho-ooo!!"

'I'd have a shooting and the whole place would leave. They'd stand outside and then, "Can we come back in now?" Like, "Did you drag out the fucking body?"

'The rappers would come in and have contests. Jun–Bug would DJ in the booth, and Furious Five, Melle Mel would be lined up, and Kool Moe D, Kurtis Blow, and Sugar Hill Gang, and Sequence, and all these groups would be lining up, they'd all be waiting their turn to get on the mic. And try to outdo each other.

'If Flash was in London, he would call up and we had a phone in the DJ booth, we'd put the phone near the microphone and he would rap. They would be rapping on the mic to the people from London.

'This music just had you involved with it from beginning to end. Fever was the biggest neighbourhood club in the world. Copacabana was in Manhattan, Studio 54 was in Manhattan, they had all the glamour and the press; we just had that music. That sound. And it was ours.'

Fever in the Bronx

The Bronx has not been a fashionable address for sixty years. Carved into unliveable shadows by the great highways of city planner Robert Moses, burnt by riots and insurance arson, and finally rinsed in floods of heroin, by the mid seventies it had been left by all those who could leave. In places it looked blitzed, in statistics it was the third world. But for half a decade, unknown to the fearful outside, it hid some of the planet's most exciting and revolutionary music.

Hip hop, or (loosely speaking) rap music, is defined in a hundred proudly self-referential songs as music made with just two turntables and a microphone. As such, like reggae, hip hop is DJs' music first and foremost. It grew from the innovations in turntable techniques of a few young Bronx disc jockeys, who taught themselves phenomenal record manipulation skills in order to adapt the music available to them – the disco hits of the day and funk tracks from a few years before – to better meet the distinct needs of their dancefloors.

These DJs saw that certain dancers exploded with their wildest moves not only to certain records but also to certain *parts* of records. Following DJ rule one – that such energy should be encouraged – they looked for ways to play only these particular sections, and to repeat them over and over. In the process, they were creating a completely new kind of live music; and not a guitar in sight.

Eventually there were hip hop recordings, but these were records made to sound just like a DJ playing other records. Even now, with a twenty-five-year body of work behind it and an ever more sophisticated approach to production, hip hop is still about recreating in the studio the kind of music that a DJ would make in a basketball park in the shadow of a Bronx tower block.

As music made from other music, with chunks snatched and sampled from existing records, hip hop dramatically affected concepts of musicianship and originality as well as radically changing recording techniques and copyright practice. Of course, sampling, copying, making a version or a cover, has always happened in music, and has been especially important in black music. But hip hop's blatant approach – to steal whatever you like from whatever source and throw it all together (with some rapping over the top) – caused plenty of fuss, especially when digital sampling made such theft as easy as pressing a button.

Hip hop is now a whole culture (indeed, 'hip hop' is not now strictly synonymous with 'rap music'; instead the term refers specifically to the cultural trinity of rap music, graffiti and breakdancing) and seems to have ten sociologists for each recording artist. Despite this, its history is often submerged by its mythology. In place of facts there are a few endlessly repeated fables, some respectful nods to its legendary creators and a deal of misty-eyed clichés about 'back in the day'.

The Bronx DJs who released the creative possibilities hidden in a pair of record turntables were real people in a very real world. All they wanted to do was throw a better party than their rival up the block. In fact, they were creating an entirely new genre of music and sowing the seeds for several more.

Breakdancing

Face your partner, holding hands. Tap one foot behind the other and bring your feet together again. Repeat with your other foot. (Your partner does the same in mirror image.) Then take two half steps back and one step forward. Smile.

You are now doing a basic version of the hustle, a dance crystallised in the mid to late seventies by millions of disco-dancing partygoers worldwide. The hustle's undemanding nature lay at the heart of disco's democratic aspirations, and the dance's regular, uncomplicated moves perfectly matched the music's constant pulse-rate tempo and four-on-the-floor beat. It's simple to pick up, requires very little in the way of coordination or concentration, and can be safely practised by even the most noncommittal dancer, without risk of embarrassment or serious injury, while wearing a suit, tie and sensible shoes.

But you're a teenage boy. Everything in your chemistry says you should be burning energy parading your sexual promise. And you sure as hell aren't wearing a suit. The floor is filled with hustle-busy couples, and while you might love some of the music that's being played, you want to look cool and be noticed. When you venture out to dance you feel uncomfortably unpartnered and inconspicuous. In your mind, the only place you want to be is right in the middle of the dancefloor with a circle of astonished onlookers. You want the hustlers to pause their toe-tapping steps and watch you do something incredible.

Before there was anything called hip hop, there was breakdancing. It evolved, as an expression of peacocking male prowess, from the 'Good Foot' steps of James Brown, from the robotic 'locking' and 'popping' moves of West Coast funk dancers, and from the extrovert dancing of the podium stars on TV's *Soul Train*. It took influences from such acrobatic styles as tap dancing and Lindy-hopping, even from kung fu. Part of an unbroken black dance heritage, breakdancing was far from unprecedented (the flying, confrontational moves of capoeira, a kind of choreographed martial art with roots in Brazil, are strikingly similar). It is named after the 'break', a jazz term for the part of a dance record where the melody takes a rest and the drummer cuts loose, this being the explosive, rhythmic section of a song which most appealed to the teenage show-offs.

Back in the early seventies, breaking consisted mostly of moves which today's dancers would call 'up-rocking' – the rapid circling steps and floorwork which precede their more gymnastic exertions. The 'power moves' – such as the headspins and backspins which would capture the world's attention and sweep breakdancing into TV commercials and Hollywood movies like *Flashdance* – were yet to develop, but at clubs and parties in the Bronx, a generation of kids, many of whom would become rap's first stars, were starting the custom of dancing with wild abandon to the breaks; their chance to compete for attention.

'I used to love the roar of the crowd when I would do my moves,' remembers Kurtis Blow, an early breakdancer and later the first major label rapper. 'And then I used to go downtown to the disco where there was no competition, no b-boy competition, so I used to reign supreme.'

Many dancers would completely forgo the rest of the music, standing against the wall until a song's break came in. They were eventually known as b-boys, the 'b' almost certainly for 'break' (some say it was also for 'Bronx'). The stern 'b-boy stance', beloved of rappers even today – with shoulders curved inwards and arms folded tightly under the chin – was not so much a signal of aggression as a b-boy's way of looking cool while he waited for a break.

The dancefloor was soon split between the meandering moves of the hustlers and the youthful explosion of the breakers. When a record reached its break, the entire room's energy level shot up. The same thing was happening when certain oldies, notably James Brown tracks, got an airing. It couldn't be long before the DJ would take notice.

Kool Herc

The DJ was a six-and-a-half-foot Jamaican giant, Clive Campbell, known since school as Hercules: DJ Kool Herc. A suitably mythological name.

One west Bronx night in late 1973, Herc tried an experiment.

'I would give people what I know they wanted to hear. And I'm watching the crowd and I was seeing everybody on the sidelines waiting for particular breaks in the records,' he recalls.

That night he tried playing a series of breaks one straight after the other, missing out the other parts of the songs.

'I said, let me put a couple of these records together, that got breaks in them. I did it. *Boom! bom bom bom.* I try to make it sound like a record. Place went berserk. Loved it.'

Herc recalls the records he used that night. 'There was the "clap your hands, stomp your feet" part of James Brown's "Give It Up Or Turnit A Loose", "Funky Music Is The Thing" by the Dynamic Corvettes, "If You Want To Get Into Something" by the Isley Brothers and "Bra" by Cymande.' All this was topped off with the percussion frenzy of the Incredible Bongo Band's 'Apache', a record destined to become Herc's signature tune, a Bronx anthem, and one of the most sampled records in hip hop.

'Took off!' he smiles.

Herc's mixing technique was extremely basic. There was no attempt to cut each record into the next or to preserve the beat. Instead he just faded from one to another, often talking over the transition, saying perhaps, 'Right about now, I'm rocking with the rockers, I'm jammin' with the jammers', or 'Party with the partyers, boogie with the boogiers'. Sometimes it was just a single word, sustained with the echo chamber he liked to use, or 'Rock on my mellow' or 'This is the joint'. Most of the time, he was actually seated, a boom mic in front of him like a radio jock. The response was incredible. Herc played the older, funkier tracks they loved, and he repeated and repeated the parts they loved most. The b-boys had found their DJ.

Right away, Herc began to always include a sequence of breaks in the music he played over the course of a night, and he started to buy two copies of each record so that he could repeat the same break back to back. He would still play records in full, including a lot of James Brown, and the latest disco numbers. But there would always be a set of records he aimed squarely at the ears of the b-boys. He even had a name for this part of the night: ' "The Merry Go Round": See, once you hear it, you got to hop on. You're not comin' back, you're goin' forward.' His style was very different from today's hip hop DJs, in that he mostly played the full thirty seconds or so of a break rather than chopping it up any smaller, but he had invented what we now know as the 'breakbeat': the use of a record's percussive break in place of playing the whole song.

DJ Grandmixer D.ST, best known for his scratching on Herbie Hancock's 'Rockit', remembers being taken by a friend to a club called the Executive Playhouse in 1974 and discovering Herc.

'I stood there, and at the time I was a b-boy, so I was ready to break-dance at the drop of a dime. I'm listening, checking out people doing the hustle, and I'm waiting for "Apache" to come on, so I could b-boy.

'There was a bunch of guys waiting around for Kool Herc to play the beats. And he was playing the disco for the disco crowd. Then all of a sudden he would play the beats and it's b-boy time. And some of the best hustlers were some of the best breakdancers too. And back then it was still into, you know, asking a woman to dance. With some class. But now you could impress her by doing a spin on the floor.

'Herc didn't cut on time or nothing like that, he just . . . his variety of music, the songs that he had, it was very clever. It was a combination of the old and new. And it moved the crowd.'

Like many other b-boys, D.ST had found a DJ who would give him just the kind of music he wanted to hear.

'Now there's a place, there's a guy, I can go to his party and practise my skills. Herc gave me the opportunity to just go there and work on my moves. So that became it. I became a fan, instantly, of Kool Herc.'

To the ears that heard it, Herc's style was revolutionary. He was playing music which you couldn't hear on the radio, reviving the hard funk sound that elsewhere was being displaced by soul and disco. And with his new technique he could extend the excitement found in a piece of music, focus attention on a record's most danceable part, and work the b-boys to boiling point.

'I had the attitude of the dancefloor *behind* the turntables,' he says. 'I'm a dance person. I like to party.

'I'd come home from dancing and my whole clothes was soaking wet. My mother would be, "Where you going with my towel?" And I be, "Ma, it gets like that up in there!" A sweat box.'

Indeed, Herc's ambition to try DJing came from frustration as a dancer hearing too many DJs cut records in the wrong places.

'I'm dancing with this girl, trying to get my shit off, and the DJ used to fuck up. And the whole party'd be like, "Yahhh, what the fuck is that . . . ? Why you took it off there? The shit was about to explode. I was about to bust a nut." You know. And the girl be like, "Damn, what the fuck is wrong?" And I'm hearing this and I'm griping, too. Cos the DJ's fucking my groove up.'

His other great inspiration was Caribbean sound system culture. Herc is a Jamaican, brought to New York as he entered his teens, who even has a wisp of the islands left in his accent. He has clear memories of living near a Trenchtown dance hall and watching the huge speakers of a sound system run by King George being wheeled in.

'We used to be playing at marbles and riding our skateboards, used to see the guys bringing the big boxes inside of the handcarts. They used to make watercolour signs and put them on lightposts, let people know there's going to be a dance coming.'

Too young to get inside, Herc and his friends would listen to the music, watch the partygoers enter and discuss in whispers the guests' reputations for violence.

'We on our skateboards, skating round, you know, and you saw the little gangster kids, and they knew who was from the gangs, or the bad bwoys. *[He whispers]* "Yeah, that's such and such, man." "Awww!" And you see all the big reputation people come through. We're little kids, and we sit on the side and watch.'

The parties Herc was around as a child in Jamaica were at the front of his mind when he was building his equipment and his DJing style. Especially important were his memories of the sound systems themselves.

'Little did I know at the time, that would be a big influence on me,' he admits.

The two other leading players in hip hop's creation also have Caribbean roots, but both deny that Jamaican dub culture influenced them directly. Only Herc represents a direct link. New York, specifically Brooklyn, enjoyed large Jamaican-style mobile sound systems before Herc started his parties, but he definitely brought several Jamaican elements to bear. For one, the highly influential rhyming style he and his MCs (Masters of Ceremony) used was clearly based on Jamaican toasting rather than on the elaborate couplets of the rapping disco DJs. He used an echo chamber, another Jamaican staple. Also, he was ready, in a way reminiscent of dub selectors, to treat records not as separate songs but as tools for composition. And of course, he prized bass and volume.

In his early parties Herc even played reggae and dub, although, he says, 'I never had the audience for it. People wasn't feelin' reggae at the time. I played a few but it wasn't catching.' New York's West Indians have remained surprisingly separate from the city's main currents of black culture (possibly because they can distinguish themselves as voluntary immigrants). Certainly, as hip hop was being formed in the Bronx, reggae there was either disliked or seldom heard. So instead, Herc moved to the funk and Latin music his Bronx audiences were used to: 'I'm in Rome, I got to do what the Romans do. I'm here. I got to get with the groove that's here.' However, in choosing records and in tailoring the sound, he emphasised the same factors prized in Jamaican music, the 'boonce', as he says his musically minded father would pronounce it, and the bass. 'A lot of my music is about bass,' he says.

Herc's DJ career began with a few local house parties on borrowed gear. His father, Keith Campbell, supplied the sound for a local band but kept his equipment strictly off limits to his son. However, when Herc showed him how to get the most out of his powerful speakers, his father relented and, as well as getting him to play records between the band's sets, let him borrow the big Shure columns for his own events. Herc started throwing parties for his high-school friends in the Sedgwick Avenue Community Center, the public hall attached to the housing project where they lived. The first one was his sister Cindy's idea – she wanted to raise some back-to-school clothes money. It was so successful they were soon doing them almost monthly. With Campbell senior on hand to prevent any trouble, the parents knew their kids were safe from any gang influence; equally the kids knew they wouldn't have their fun ended abruptly by their parents, as happened too often at house parties. And they had music far beefier than any home hi-fi. With all its growing energy, Herc's teenage party scene was soon set to make a wider impact.

Around this time, as well as dancing regularly at local clubs the Puzzle and the Tunnel, Herc was an early graffiti writer (he'd write 'CLYDE AS KOOL', with a smiley in one of the O's). He was also making a name for himself running track and playing basketball. But gradually everything paled against his success as a DJ. By the end of 1974 he had progressed from 25-cent recreation room jams to all-night block parties to playing in a series of Bronx clubs now considered the sacred sites of hip hop: Twilight Zone, the Executive Playhouse, the Hevalo and Disco Fever.

It's 1998, and Herc stands on Jerome Avenue, where these clubs were all within a few blocks of each other. They are now car parks and shoe stores; Twilight Zone is a mattress factory. 'This is Herc Avenue, really,' he says wistfully, as a subway train rumbles overhead. Then a pronouncement:

'After I who have entered through this door and certain places such as the Executive Playhouse should be known as a car park . . . So it is, baby! After I who have entered through this door, DJ Kool Herc, no one else shall enter, certain places like the Hevalo, should remain a car lot . . . So it is, baby!'

Herc became a legend. His parties were soon famous throughout 'Uptown' – the Bronx and Harlem – and here he enjoyed superstar status. Because he played a radically different kind of music, tailor-made for the teenage b-boying masses, his local crowd-pulling power was nothing short of heroic. On seeing him play, D.ST realised that Herc had the same kind of marquee value as the local bands. 'People go see him just to see *him*. I just stood there and watched him DJ and I was amazed.'

As well as trusting his dancer's instincts, Herc added MCs to the mix to whoop up the crowd even more and to allow him to concentrate on the turntables. Many people credit Herc and his main MCs, Coke La Rock and Clark Kent, as being the first hip hop rappers, because they didn't emulate the style of jive-rhyming practised by mobile disco DJs like Hollywood or Eddie Cheeba – a style in turn copied from the personality radio DJs. Theirs was far more like the 'toasting' of Jamaican reggae deejays – hyping up the crowd with short phrases like 'To the beat, y'all' or 'Ya rock and ya *don't* stop', all with the added drama of Herc's echo chamber.

Herc's other secret weapon was his system. In a time and place when the DJ provided his own sound equipment – just like the club bands he was steadily replacing – Herc had the biggest and the best. Even though the DJs he inspired would eclipse him on technique, no one ever beat Herc on volume. At the heart of his Herculoids system (which many mistook for the name of his crew), amassed piece by piece from a lesser DJ who played at the Twilight Zone, were two McIntosh 2300 amps – 'The big Macs, top of the line' – and those huge Shure column speakers.

Grand Wizard Theodore, one of the many DJs inspired by Herc, remembers the first time he heard the Herculoids's power.

'It made you listen to a record and made you appreciate the record even more. He would play a record that you listened to every day and you would be like, "Wow, that record has *bells* in it?" It's like you heard instruments in the record that you never thought the record even had. And the bass was like WHUMM! Incredible!'

Herc's later system was so powerful he named it 'Not Responsible'.

'Every time you play that set somewhere, some shit always jump off, some dispute, some shit, so I call it Not Responsible.'

Herc would be a massive, looming influence. Suddenly every b-boy dreamt of enjoying the same kind of local adoration; everyone wanted to get their hands on some turntables and throw parties just as wild. It all seemed so possible. After all, he was just digging out old records and playing their best bits. As Jazzy Jay, another DJ inspired by Herc's legend, would put it, 'All of them was sitting in your house – they were all your mom's old and pop's old records. Soon as Kool Herc started playing, every motherfucker started robbing his mother and father for records.'

'I went to the Hevalo when I was thirteen,' recalled the Cisco Kid – an early hip hop MC – in Bill Adler's book *Rap*. 'It was very dark inside, but there was an excitement in the air, like anything could jump off. Then Herc came on the mic and he was so tough. You'd get transfixed by this shit. You thought, "This is cool, I want to be like this." '

Like so many originators, Herc has reaped much respect and little remuneration. By the time those he had inspired were signing record contracts and touring Europe, he had retreated from the game and turned to drugs, demoralised by the tragic drowning of his father and discouraged completely in 1977 after being stabbed through the hand at one of his own parties, when he 'walked into a discrepancy'. Twenty years later, the Chemical Brothers invited him to London to open one of their shows, paying homage to the man who created the breakbeat, the core of their music. However, at that time most hip hop stars, while knowing his name, would have been hard pressed to say whether Herc was even still alive, his absence from a billion-dollar industry only serving to heighten the mythic status of this classically named giant.

Grandmaster Flash

Flash is fast, Flash is cool. If Herc was the DJ who discovered the electricity of the breakbeat, it was Grandmaster Flash who wired it up and put a plug on it. As Kidd Creole of the Furious Five put it, 'It's a known fact – the Herculoids might cause a disaster, but there only could be *one* Grandmaster.'

Flash, aka Joseph Saddler, born in Barbados, was an intense, scientifically minded kid majoring in electronics at Samuel Gompers vocational high school. He would take Herc's raw ideas and subject them to laboratory-style development, emerging with a style of playing that had all of Herc's frenzied b-boy appeal, but that was also polished and continuous. In the process, Flash transformed hip hop from a quirk of Bronx partying to a genuinely new form of music.

While Herc had given the world the breakbeat, his technique, by all accounts, was pretty slapdash. The excitement of his Merry Go Round sequences came from the records he chose and the parts of those records he played – he had no concern for making clean mixes. But Flash, methodical and obsessed, set himself the goal of playing breakbeats *with precision*. He wanted to take the phenomenal power of Herc's style and deliver it to the dancefloor with a constant, unbroken beat. At first, he had no idea whether it was possible, just that it would be amazing – and that if he could get it right, he would make history.

Flash was blown away when he first saw Herc. 'I saw people gathered from miles around just for one individual, playing music. When I saw Kool Herc sitting up on his podium, heavily guarded, and all these people in the park enjoying themselves, that was it: I was gonna be a DJ.' Crucially, though, he was just as mesmerised by a disco DJ, Pete DJ Jones. Like Herc, Pete Jones was a giant among men, a six-foot-eight stud famed for his harem of female assistants who set up his equipment for him (including his capable stand-in spinner Ms Becky Jones). 'Here is one dude that doesn't have to wear any flashy clothes to stand out in a crowd,' wrote New York DJ fanzine *Melting Pot* in 1975. 'When he lights a match, he looks like the *Towering Inferno*.'

Originally from Raleigh, North Carolina, Pete Jones was the leading DJ in early disco's straight black overground, a close-knit scene of mobile DJs who would set up their rigs in parks, hotel ballrooms and, following the 1971 beef shortage, in otherwise under-populated restaurants in New York and New Jersey. Besides Jones, the other main players were: the Smith Brothers; Cameron 'Grandmaster' Flowers, the scene's founding big-shot who started playing in 1967 and sadly ended his days panhand-ling outside Tower Records (he was also an early graffiti writer); Maboya, a Panamanian who pioneered outdoor parties at Riis Beach before returning to Central America, and Ron Plummer, a chemistry graduate who shot to fame as the scene's Deejay Of The Year 1975 before heading off to medical school in Boston. 'Flowers was the best,' remembers DJ Tony Smith. 'But he was the most egotistical too. Flowers had the best music and a really great sound system but Maboya and the Smith Brothers were definitely more friendly.'

While the music they played was hardly ground-breaking – the length and breadth of the *Billboard* R&B chart sprinkled through with funky oldies and a smattering of more obscure southern soul – Jones and his peers were key in spreading mixing techniques beyond downtown's underground clubs. On the gay scene Francis Grasso had made beat-matching and blends (or 'running' records, as Pete calls it) required skills. Flowers and Pete Jones deserve credit for developing the same techniques at the same time and, crucially, for showing them off to wider New York, including the Bronx.

Jones explains how in those early days DJs were considered either 'mixers' or 'choppers' depending on their style. He regularly used two copies of a record to extend it. 'Best part of the record is usually that groove part,' he says with a Deputy Dawg chuckle, dusting off a stack of what he calls 'gutbucket' 45s – the JB's 'Monorail', Leon Haywood's 'Believe Half Of What You See' and 'Mister Magic' by Grover Washington – to play through his GLI mixer the size of a television. 'I'd play a record

⦿WANTED⦿

KEN WEBB

DESCRIPTION
HEIGHT: 6'0" WEIGHT: 165 lbs.
BE ON GUARD FOR: Unusual loud mouth and has tendencies of talking a lot and incessantly — You'll hate him in the mornings.
LAST HEARD: On radio station WBLS this morning.
LAST SEEN: M.C. at Bohannon Concert
IDENTIFYING MARKS: Small ½ inch scar on left check — Also likes to see people having a good boogie down time! Likes to mingle with the crowd — he's a very shifty dude — we extreme caution upon approach him.

PETE D.J. JONES

DESCRIPTION
HEIGHT: 6'8" WEIGHT: 230 lbs.
BE ON GUARD: For very heavy stereo equipment he lugs around. Armed with over 2,000 watts of disco power, and should be considered dangerous — dance on site of him.
LAST HEARD: At Adrians disco, The Club, Jimmys, Pippins, Riis Beach.
LAST SEEN: With female accomplice known only as "Becky".
IDENTIFYING MARKS: Mole on left theigh and extreme height. Also likes to play non-stop boogie music

ALIVE & PLAYING   SAT. OCT. 5

THE FACTORY

94-21 Merrick Blvd.
Jamaica, Queens
On Merrick Blvd. between Archer & Liberty

FREE GRUB
(Chicken & Rice)

EXTRA
A Special Presentation will be made
to the "Women of Distinction of Queens"

$4.00
10-4 A.M.

SHOWDOWN DISCO FUN

KEN "SPIDER" WEBB & PETE D.J. JONES WILL BE TOGETHER
WITH 3,000 WATTS
OF DISCO SOUND POWER

Alias Webb and Jones – rounding up a posse for their disco showdown.

over and over again, because you didn't have many hits in those days, and you had to keep playing until four or five in the morning. So you'd play it over again and you'd shine a light on that groove and play it awhile.'

Pete was Flash's greatest inspiration. Why? Because, unlike Herc, he kept a seamless beat. Having seen Jones play at local block parties, Flash imagined a music which combined the two DJs' styles.

'Herc was playing the break parts of records, but his timing was not a factor. He would play a record that was maybe ninety beats a minute, and then he would play another one that was a hundred and ten. He would play records and it would never be on time.

'But timing was a factor, because a lot of these dancers were really good. They did their moves *on time*. So I said to myself, I got to be able to go to just the particular section of the record, just the break, and extend that, but *on time*.

'I had to figure out how to take these records and take these sections and manually edit them so that the person in front of me wouldn't even know that I had taken a section that was maybe fifteen seconds and made it five minutes. So that these people that really danced, they could just dance as long as they wanted. I got to find a way to do this.'

As Flash tells it, this involved a long period of experimentation and research. He apprenticed himself to Jones as a warm-up DJ, and studied the technical mysteries of turntable torque, cartridge construction, needle configuration and the like, examining every aspect of the machinery which he aimed to master. For months, during high school and then while a messenger for a fabric company, this 'scientist of the mix' spent as much time as possible shut in a room relentlessly pursuing his goal.

'Friends of mine used to come to my house and say, "C'mon, let's go to the park, let's go hang with girls." I'm like, "Naw, man, I can't do that. I'm working on something."

'I didn't know what I was working on, didn't have a clue. All I know is that with each obstacle there came an excitement on how to figure it out. How to get past it… How to get past it, how to get past it.'

One particularly thorny problem was cueing – listening to the next record to find the desired passage without the audience hearing it too. At this time, mixers with the necessary extra pre-amplifiers and headphone sockets were the preserve of custom-built club systems, and Flash was only vaguely aware that such technology even existed. Using Pete Jones' system showed him the immense value of cueing and, using his electronics' knowledge, he was able to create the device for himself.

'I called it the peek-a-boo system. How do you hear it before the people hear it? The mixer I was using at the time was a Sony MX8. It was a microphone mixer. So I had to go out and buy two external pre-amps from Radio Shack, and these would take the voltage of the cartridge and boost it to one millivolt, so now it has line output voltage and I could put it inside the mixer and hear it. I had to put two bridges in between the left and right turntable so that I could hear the music before it goes out, so I had a single-pole, double-throw switch, and I had to Krazy Glue it to the top of the mixer.' (Flash notes that Herc, though he had an impressive GLI 3800 mixer, didn't use its cueing system until much later.)

His doggedly clinical approach paid off and by the summer of 1975

Flash could put into practice a series of 'theories' enabling him to cut and mix records exactly as he had envisaged.

'I called my style "Quick Mix Theory", which is taking a section of music and cutting it on time, back to back, in thirty seconds or less. It was basically to take a particular passage of music and rearrange the arrangement by way of rubbing the record back and forth or cutting the record, or back-spinning the record.' His supporting 'Clock Theory' involved marking the record with a line on the label like a hand on a clock face to show where a chosen passage began. This let him speedily rewind the part of the song he wanted to repeat.

'I had to figure out how to recapture the beginning of the break without picking up the needle, because I tried doing it that way and I wasn't very good at it. And that's how I came up with the Clock Theory: you mark a section of the record, and then you gotta just count how many revolutions go by.' (To this day, a hip hop DJ's records will be plastered in little stick-on paper lines.)

'I would use what I call the Dog Paddle, which is spinning it back [*fingers on the edge of the disc*], or what I call the Phone Dial Theory, where you would get it from the inner [*fingers on the middle of the disc*].'

By teaching himself to flit between his two turntables at breakneck speed, find the first beat of the chosen part of a record in a matter of seconds, and to play, repeat and recombine a few selected bars, Flash became able to completely restructure a song at will. This manual sampling and looping of a record, done without losing the beat, is the fundamental basis of hip hop (as well as all other breakbeat musics, ie drum and bass, breaks, big beat, trip hop). It prefigures the cut and paste techniques of constructing music which would become ubiquitous as soon as digital sampling technology was developed.

He had long been called Flash (named by his friend Gordon after a comic book character). Now, to mark his achievements he was awarded the martial arts title of Grandmaster.

'That came from a fellow by the name of Joe Kidd. Said to me, "You need to call yourself a Grandmaster, by the way you do things on the turntables that nobody else could do." ' (It's almost certain that Kidd's inspiration was Grandmaster Flowers, then well-known across New York.) 'It sounded good. It connected with Bruce Lee, which was the leading box office draw for movies at the time, and it connected to this guy that played chess. And these guys were very good at their craft. I felt I was very good at my craft. I found it fitting.'

Surprisingly, though, when Flash showcased his new cut-up music, his first audiences were far from thrilled.

'When I first created the style, I played in a few parks in the area but nobody really quite understood what it was that I was doing. A lot of people ridiculed it. They didn't like the idea of it.

'I was so excited, but just nobody would get it. Nobody would get it for quite some time.'

Despite his unique skills, Flash found it impossible to make a crowd appreciate the quick mix. While his techniques were revolutionary, he had yet to figure out how they could be best used to drive a dancefloor.

'What I said to myself is, if I take the most climactic part of these records and just string 'em together and play 'em on time, back to back to back, I'm going to have them totally excited. But when I went outside, it was totally quiet. Almost like a speaking engagement. I was quite disenchanted. I was quite sad. I cried for a couple of days.'

But Flash would soon be vindicated. The initial confused reaction to his music was in fact an indication of its power. Less than two years later, on 2 September 1976, after residencies in two small clubs – the Black Door and the Dixie Room – and innumerable parties in parks, basketball courts and school gyms, Grandmaster Flash was so famous throughout uptown New York that he could fill the massive Audubon Ballroom in Harlem, the theatre where Malcolm X had lectured (and been shot). With his MCs the Furious Five to back him, he was introduced by his lead rapper Melle Mel. With screams and cheers, two or three thousand people welcomed 'the greatest DJ in the world'.

'When we took the crowd to a climax, the floor was shaking,' he remembers. 'The floor was fucking shaking, it was really something. And next day, man, Grandmaster Flash and the Furious Five was heroes. It was like, after that there was nothing else we couldn't do. After that there was no hurdles we couldn't climb. Anything after that, it was a piece of cake.'

Afrika Bambaataa

'Zulu Nation is no gang. It is an organisation of individuals in search of success, peace, knowledge, wisdom, understanding and the righteous way of life. Zulu members must search for ways to survive positively in this society. Negative activities are actions belonging to the unrighteous. The animal nature is the negative nature. Zulus must be civilised.' So reads the Principles of the Universal Zulu Nation, parts one and two.

In 1975, a high school student from the Bronx River housing project won a trip to Africa in a UNICEF essay competition. He had entered the contest the previous year, for a visit to India, but had missed the judging in favour of giving out invitations to one of the parties he used to throw. The second time around, after making a special effort to convince the judges that he needed to visit the land of his ancestors, he found himself spending two weeks in the Ivory Coast, Nigeria and Guinea-Bissau. His

Breakers' yard – hip hop's holy trinity, Grandmaster Flash, Kool Herc and Afrika Bambaataa (left to right) together in 1993.

(Newsday, Inc. © 1993)

reasons for wanting to see Africa were no doubt passionate indeed. As the founder of a music and breakdancing collective he called the Zulu Nation, and as the proud owner of a colourful self-given African name Afrika Bambaataa Aasim, he possessed a powerful identification with the people of the dark continent. (His real name is unknown – Afrika Bambaataa, 'Affectionate Chieftain', was the name of a twentieth-century Zulu king.)

It is on his leadership of Zulu Nation, an organisation aimed at giving hip hop culture a unified (and international) foundation, that Bam is most eloquent. He has told the story many times of receiving divine inspiration to form Zulu Nation when he saw Michael Caine and his scarlet-uniformed British soldiers defending themselves against an onslaught of the proud tribesmen in the 1963 movie *Zulu*. Today there are Zulu Nation outposts in such unlikely places as Switzerland and the Canary Islands. It is now the *Universal* Zulu Nation and Bam has said he is ready to offer the hand of hip hop friendship even to extra-terrestrial Zulus, should they present themselves.

Alongside his sociological importance – in offering an alternative, post-gang model of comradeship based on music and dance rather than violence in settling disputes or 'beefs' between hip hop crews, and in creating a global network of hip hop fans – this courteous, impassive bear of a man is equally important because he is a DJ: Afrika Bambaataa's other self-given name is 'Master of Records'.

In common with Herc and Flash, Bambaataa can claim Caribbean forebears (his grandparents were from Jamaica and Barbados). However, any link to Jamaica in terms of its DJ culture was not a factor. The sound systems he knew were those of Kool Herc and the mobile disco DJs; he knew nothing of reggae, except its records, until much later.

From as young as eleven or twelve, he was throwing parties with his friends in the Bronx River Community Center. Without access to anything more complex than a pair of their home hi-fis, the kids used flashlights to signal across the darkened room to keep the music continuous.

'I would bring my house system down and we would bring out flashlights and we would give parties in the centre. You have the lights off and you signal to the other side for them to play the next record. When the flashlight goes on, the guy knows to start his record off. So you put on one record – say, "Dance To The Music" by Sly and the Family Stone – then when you know that it's ending, somebody might put on James Brown's "It's A New Day" on the other side.'

Bambaataa's early years were a whirl of creative mischief. His friends remember him as the catalyst for no end of inspired activities. Whether it was convincing them to buy bows and arrows to hunt rabbits along the banks of the Bronx River, or pouring and lighting gasoline on the sidewalk during a war game siege, Bam could be relied on to fill a day with something memorable. Since his mother, a nurse, regularly worked long and late and owned an expansive record collection, the basis for his own growing music library, Bam's house was often the place for impromptu partying.

In the context of the Bronx at that time, it was almost inevitable that such a charismatic youngster would be swept into a gang. From 1968, tribalistic groupings had emerged to replace the original fifties gangs wiped out by the late sixties flood wave of heroin. The largest was the Black Spades, who dressed in jeans, Levi jackets, military belts and black engineer boots. They existed to fight white north Bronx gangs such as the Ministers, but were also fairly civic-minded in cleansing their neighbourhoods of drug dealing. You joined them because you liked their style, because wearing their colours offered you protection, and, simply, because you were a teenager.

During a ninety-two-day confrontation between the Black Spades and another black gang, the Seven Crowns, Bronx River project was filled with enough gunfire to be christened 'Little Vietnam'. Bambaataa has admitted that he 'was into street gang violence', and remains otherwise silent on his 'negative' past. However, he is remembered by his compadres as a mediator rather than a warmonger, as a Black Spade who could happily walk on Nomad or Javelin turf, and as someone who was, in any case, usually off scouring New York for records.

After a peak around 1973, gangs faded fast. The rise of graffiti and breakdancing offered less dangerous ways to express your male competitiveness, and besides, the girls had decided to stand for no more belligerent nonsense from their men. 'Get peaceful or get none' seemed to be their message. Bam declared his party-minded friends to be Zulu kings and queens, and following on from an earlier collective he'd founded with similar aims – the Organization – formed the Zulu Nation, a group of b-boys and b-girls.

'I'd probably be dead if it wasn't for getting straight into hip hop, and making a culture out of it, and bringing a lot of my people from that type of way of life,' he admits.

He washed his hands of the gangs completely in January 1975 when his best friend Soulski was killed by the police. On his graduation from high school later that same year, his mother bought him a sound system. On 12 November 1976, he played his first official party as a DJ, at the Bronx River Community Center. 'I never had a problem in pooling a large army or crowd. So when we shifted right into the DJ thing, I already had a packed house,' he grins.

Herc had the head start and the volume, Flash had the techniques, but

Afrika Bambaataa had the records. And with no regard for any criteria other than 'Will it add to the party?' he was a fearsome hunter of vinyl. While others in the Bronx were wedded to funk, disco and soul, Bam was ready to play anything that would make people dance, ready to buy any record that had just a few seconds of funky rhythm: an intro, a break, a stab of brass.

'His record collection was just *incredible*,' recalls Theodore. 'He would play the B52s and everybody in the party would be going crazy. He would play Rolling Stones' records, Aerosmith, Dizzy Gillespie. Jazz records, rock records.

'I remember I went to an Afrika Bambaataa party and he played "Honky Tonk Woman" and I thought, "Wow, what's that?" And after I went home and thought about it, I was like, "That's Mick Jagger and them." It didn't matter if you were listening to a white artist or a black artist, it was any record he could find that had a beat on it.'

'We just was comin' out with crazy breaks,' enthuses Bam. 'Like other DJs would play they great records for fifteen, twenty minutes or more, we was changing ours every few seconds, or every minute or two. I couldn't have no breakbeat go longer than a minute or two. Unless it's real crazy funky that we just want the crowd to get off on – then we would extend it for two minutes, three minutes, four minutes . . . I just was finding music from all over the place.'

The audiences which gathered around Bambaataa were as open-minded as he was, and if anyone dared to get snobbish about music, he delighted in tricking them; whipping in some obscure track and then gleefully informing them they'd just danced to The Beatles or the Monkees. (For the spotters: Bam would play the drum part from 'Sergeant Pepper's Lonely Hearts Club Band' and the 'Mary, Mary, where are you going' part from the Monkees' 'Mary Mary'.) Taped TV themes and commercials, Hare Krishna chants, Siouxsie & the Banshees, the Flying Lizards, even Gary Numan, all made their way onto his system.

Grandmaster Flash remembers Bam's music and shakes his head – he was rarely able to identify the obscure records he heard.

'I couldn't get too much from Bam because Bam's shit was so deep and so powerful I just didn't know where he got it.'

'He broke so many records,' adds Theodore. 'I can't begin to name the records he broke into hip hop.' Billy Squier's 'Big Beat', Foghat's 'Slow Ride' and Grand Funk Railroad's 'Inside Looking Out' were just three of the obscure, forgotten or just plain unlikely records which Bambaataa broke to the hip hop consciousness of the Bronx.

Information about records with hot breaks went around like nuclear blueprints and the records themselves were soon plutonium in value. By summer 1978, *Billboard* had noticed this peculiarly localised commerce and ran a story on how Downstairs Records, New York's 'leading disco retailer', was doing a roaring trade in 'obscure r&b cut outs', mentioning Dennis Coffey's 'Son of Scorpio', Jeannie Reynolds' 'Fruit Song' and the Incredible Bongo Band's 'Bongo Rock'. Profiling Kool Herc as the instigator of this phenomenon, the paper noted '. . . young black disco DJs from the Bronx . . . are buying the records just to play the thirty seconds or so of rhythm breaks that each disc contains.'

The bigger jocks had learned from the disco DJs to press up one-off acetate discs, putting album tracks (and occasionally even primitive mixes and edits) on more manageable 10-inch dub-plates. It was an obvious commercial move for someone to start making bootleg copies of the most hard-to-find tunes.

Harlem entrepreneur Paul Winley launched his *Super Disco Brakes* series of breakbeat compilations (ie albums of songs which contained an exciting break). These were notoriously poor quality recordings mastered straight from records in his collection; others, such as ex-chauffeur 'Bootleg' Lenny Roberts, offered a better quality product. At the Music Factory record store in Times Square, Stanley Platzer (known as Fat Stanley, King of the Beats) kept a notebook in the store, recording for Lenny all the songs that customers requested. On Lenny's Street Beat Records, the *Ultimate Breaks And Beats* series of albums eventually ran to over twenty volumes. Many others followed suit, meeting the demand for tracks which by now ranged from expensive to unobtainable.

Each DJ worked to keep their exclusives exclusive, and so took up, probably from Herc, the practice of soaking off or obscuring labels to evade tune detection. Charlie Chase, DJ for the Cold Crush Brothers – perhaps the biggest rap group of hip hop's pre-commercial days – has many a tale of such happy competition.

'One time I did a party and Flash turned up, and I played this beat that he never heard. So what I did, on one record I wrote, "For the name of this record, go to turntable two", and you see this on the label and it's spinning. So Flash went over to the other turntable to look and the other record said, "Get off my dick!" He was laughing, man. Those were the days.'

Charlie also remembers acts of surprising generosity.

'Yeah, we always looked out for each other in the past. Sometimes the DJs wouldn't want to give the names of records up, but at the same time we would always cover them, so it was OK to lend somebody a record because they didn't know what the fuck it was. We just pointed to where the break was, and that was it, that was your cue.'

He recalls a time playing on the same bill as Bambaataa. Both had received a promo pressing of Trouble Funk's 'Pump Me Up', but each had but one copy.

'So I'm cutting it in with something else because I only had one copy, and all of a sudden Bam says, "Yo, I got a copy of that. I have one copy of that." He gave it to me and I went berserk. I had two for the night. I was just cutting it and like, "Oh god!", that was the first. Then Bam took his copy back, 'cos Bam was the king of records.'

Bambaataa's key move, as well as his out-of-state vinyl searches in New Jersey and Connecticut, was to join all the record pools, the disco-born DJ cooperatives through which the labels promoted their dance product. Few in the Bronx knew about these at first, but Bam was in there early. Especially rich pickings came from Rock Pool, where he picked up on such crucial oddities as Kraftwerk and the Yellow Magic Orchestra.

European synth pop, via acid rock, all the way to cartoon theme tunes: even from its very beginnings, hip hop was hungry and eclectic. The DJ had no concern for the genre of the records he played, his only thought was for their effectiveness as sonic components and their effect on a dancefloor.

'This was the only time, this was the only kind of music where you could hear James Brown playing with . . . Aerosmith! You can just fuckin' mix two bands *together*,' beams Charlie. 'We were there to listen to all eras' music, you could just mix it together. It was really something. It was weird, but it sounded good.'

Skills to pay the bills

The Bronx is the only part of New York City on the American mainland. Its western half is rippled with steep hills, while the land east of the Bronx River slopes gently down towards the sea. In its forty-two square miles it has a man-made beach, about 1.3 million inhabitants and the busiest highways anywhere in the US. In 1976 it was ruled by three people.

'Flash was in the south Bronx, we was the south-east Bronx, and you have Herc in the west Bronx,' explains Bambaataa. 'Flash was always in the Black Door, or in 23 Park in the summertime. Herc was in the Hevalo, and Sedgwick Avenue Park. I was always in the Bronx River Center, or in high schools or junior high school gyms in the south east Bronx. But we respect each other.'

By this time there were other crews making their way. The mobile disco DJs started adding hip hop spinners to their line-ups. DJ Breakout (and the Funky Four) came to hold the north Bronx. Charlie Chase was starting to bring Cold Crush together. And Harlem and Queens were developing their own DJ and MC talent. Crowds at shows were getting bigger as word spread about this new music. Things were quickly more competitive.

'It was basically for who had the most showmanship between Bam, Herc and myself,' says Flash. 'Bam had the records, Herc had the sound system. My sound system was pretty cheesy, so I knew I had to constantly keep adding things and innovating just to please my audience. Because once they'd go to hear a Herc sound, then heard my sound . . . eurggh.'

Flash tried rapping. He was horrible at it. Then, like any good side-show circus, he discovered a child star: his DJing partner 'Mean' Gene Livingstone had a little thirteen-year-old brother, Theodore. Theodore could do something amazing: he could find the beginning of a break by eye and drop the needle right on it, with no need to spin the record back.

Sure enough, this cute short-stuff standing on a milk crate at a block party in 63 Park quick mixing by needle dropping was a big draw, but he was to develop as a DJ in his own right a whole lot faster than Flash had planned. Calling himself Grand Wizard Theodore, the kid acquired more than just a name. He acquired 'scratching' – twisting the record back and forth while manipulating the mixer's cross-fader to produce a dramatic new percussion noise.

A decade later, as we'll see, this surprising sound would form the basis of an entire style of DJ music, now known as 'turntablism'. Its origins were far less dramatic.

'I used to come home from school and try to practise and try to get new ideas,' Theodore recalls. 'This particular day I was playing music a little bit too loud. And my mom's came and like [*banging on the door*] boom, boom, boom, boom, boom. "If you don't cut that music down . . ." So she had the door open and she was talking to me and I was still holding the record, and my earphones were still on. And while she was cursing me out in the doorway, I was still holding the record – "Jam On The Groove" by Ralph McDonald – and my hand was still going like this [*back and forth*] with the record. And when she left I was like, "What is this?" So I studied it and studied it for a couple of months until I actually figured out what I wanted to do with it. Then that's when it became a scratch.'

So your mum invented scratching?

'Yeah, God bless my mama.'

Scratching is often attributed to Flash, but most people will tell you it was Theodore's invention. The truth, Theodore admits, is that Flash *conceived* of it first but that the Grand Wizard beat the Grandmaster to the decks: 'He had a vision of scratching records, but he couldn't really present it to the people.'

Scratching, as well as being a huge conceptual leap towards making turntables true instruments, was a massive crowd draw. When people heard familiar songs restructured by the quick mix they might be surprised, but when this was accompanied by a DJ's futuristic *zigga-zigga* scratch percussion, they were really stunned.

'If you knew a record, and you hear that record but you hear a part going *bam, bam, bam*, you walk over to the turntables and go, "What the hell is that?" So everybody was very astonished about what I was doing.

'People were dancing, and then when I started scratching, everybody would eventually stop dancing and walk up to the front of the stage and try to see what the hell is this guy doing: the arm movement and the cross-fader going back and forth, and everybody was like, "Wow".

'They'd be screaming out. Imagine: listening to your favourite record and I'm going *ba-bam, ba-bam, ba-bam, ba-bam, ba-ba bam bam*, and they'd be like . . . "WOW!" Our crowd really increased, because everybody was talking about this little short guy Grand Wizard Theodore. Every time we gave a party it was a humungous crowd.'

But these crowds were now for himself, not for Flash. Shortly before the scratch emerged, Flash had fallen out with Gene, who formed the L Brothers with Theodore.

The relentlessly innovative Flash was undeterred. He is credited with the important idea of punch phasing, where a stab of horns or a lick of vocals is 'punched in' from one record over the top of the other, and he was the first to do 'body tricks' like turning his back to the decks or spinning records with his feet. And . . . Flash was on the beatbox – the first to introduce a drum machine to the mix.

'There was this drummer who lived on 149th Street and Jackson, I think his name was Dennis. He had this manually operated drum machine and whenever he didn't feel like hooking up his drums in his room, he would practise on this machine. You couldn't just press a button and it played, you had to know how to play it. It had a bass key, a snare key, a hi-hat key, a castanets key, a timbale key. And I would always ask him if he ever wanted to get rid of it I would buy it off him. A day came that he wanted to sell it and I gave it a title: beatbox. My flyer person at the time put this on the flyer: "Grandmaster Flash introduces the beatbox. Music with no turntables." '

He didn't play the machine, a Vox percussion box, over the top of records.

'No, what I would do is play it, play it, play it, *doomm ah da-da uh-hah*. Stop. Zoom. Play in a record. And then, while the MC was MCing, where you would fade the beat out for a minute, I might switch back to the turntables. It was a real high part of our performance. A real high point.

'I stayed in my room for a month. And once I learned how to play it, myself and my MCs made up routines, "Flash is on the beatbox." So the first time we did it, we didn't get screams and yells and whatever. It was,

"Oh shit! Flash got this new toy." It probably got back to Bam, it probably got back to Herc, "Flash is making music – drum beats – with no turntable." '

Rapping

The other great area of competition was rapping, or MCing as it was then known. As the DJs plundered each other's hot tunes, their playlists (except perhaps Bambaataa's) got ever more similar. Having the most impressive rappers became a new way for a DJ to distinguish himself.

To audiences raised on performers like James Brown, Isaac Hayes, Millie Jackson, Barry White, the Last Poets and Gil Scott Heron, on comedians like Pigmeat Markham, Nipsey Russel and Moms Mabley, on radio DJs like Jocko Henderson and Eddie O'Jay, on local disco DJs like DJ Hollywood and Eddie Cheeba – and let's not forget Muhammad Ali – rapping was absolutely nothing new. In 1991, in William Perkins' book *Droppin' Science*, legendary bandleader Cab Calloway reminded us, 'I was rapping fifty years ago. My rap lyrics were a lot more dirty than those in my songs.' He added, for good measure, 'I did the moonwalk fifty years ago, too.' The Afrocentrists among us will trace rap from griot poetry, through the dozens and storefront preaching right to the door of the latest gangster group. Black American culture has never been short of oral dexterity.

Hip hop, however, made it def, dope and fresh. When Herc, drawing on memories of dub toasting, used his MCs (who sat with him behind the decks) not strictly as performers but as party energisers, he set off the new era of the MC. In this way, hip hop took an established form – rapping – and let it evolve from a new year zero. The greatest impetus for this was the fact that the DJ, using the breakbeat, could now provide an MC with an unshakeable beat over which to rhyme. To someone who could rap, the minimal, repetitive, funky-ass drum patterns that emerged from the quick mix were an irresistible invitation. From the initial couplets and 'Throw your hands in the air', 'Rock it, don't stop it' crowd-raisers and clichés, the form quickly gathered steam.

The rappers drew constant inspiration from rhyming radio DJs like Gary Byrd and Frankie Crocker. Byrd insists that the radio DJ was their main model. 'Now I've got a mic, what do I say on it that's gonna make me fly? I'm gonna say what I heard the DJ say. That's my starting point. So the DJ is the seminal influence on the whole piece. You're coming into the seventies, where we've just seen some of the greatest spoken word of the twentieth century: Malcolm X, Martin Luther King, Stokely Carmichael. This is a rhythm that's in the air. So when you get someone who makes a record, Sugar Hill Gang or Fatback, what are they doing?

They're actually doing what they heard DJs do! Because if an MC is on a mic, what is he going to imitate? He is going to imitate the DJ.'

The Bronx party MCs were soon introducing new elements and styles apace. Cowboy, the late Keith Wiggins, was Flash's first permanent MC. He is remembered as the first to rhyme about his DJ, and the first to step out in front and act as an actual showman-like Master of Ceremonies. Flash credits him with adding the humanising element which finally made his quick mix style palatable to an audience. 'If it wasn't for Cowboy, I don't know . . . Cowboy found a way to complement what I was doing.' Another of Flash's cohorts, Melle Mel (Melvin Glover), is the MCs' MC: his name comes up more than any other when rappers are discussing their heroes.

Astonishingly, the first person in hip hop to actually sit down and *write* a rhyme was possibly Flash himself. Theodore recalls how, early on, sick of hearing the same old clichés, Flash took it on himself to progress things.

'He said, "Yo, the only thing you guys say on the mic is 'Clap your hands and throw your hands in the air, this person over here, that person over there, this person's in the house, that person's in the house.' " So he wrote a rhyme and tried to get everybody to say the rhyme, but nobody wanted to say it. He actually sat down in a corner, wrote a rhyme and tried to get his MCs to say it. "Dip dive, socialise, try to make you realise, that we are qualified to rectify and hypnotise that burning desire to

3D b-boys – breakdancers at the Wheels of Steel night at the Roxy, NYC, in 1983.

boogie, y'all," that's exactly what he wrote. Couldn't get anybody to say it, so he got on the microphone and he said it himself.'

Eventually, as happened in Jamaica, the person playing the records would be eclipsed by the person out front saying the rhymes. But for now, largely because he owned the sound equipment and because rapping was still fairly primitive, the DJ was in control. Herc had Coke La Rock and Clark Kent; Flash collected his Furious Five. Bambaataa garnered several rap crews including the Soulsonic Force, the Jazzy Five and Planet Patrol. DJ Breakout had the Funky Four (Plus One More), Cold Crush came together around Charlie Chase, Theodore would become DJ for the Fantastic Five. But already there were performers for whom the DJ was secondary: Treacherous Three (including Kool Moe Dee), the Nigger Twins from Queens, Kurtis Blow . . .

From the rappers, this music and these parties – which had previously been referred to as 'break' or 'wildstyle' music – gained a name: 'hip hop'.

'The reason that became the name of the culture,' explains scenester and impresario Fab 5 Freddy (Freddy Braithwaite), 'was because that was the one thing that almost everybody said at a party: "To the hip, the hop, the hibby-hibby, dibby-dibby, hip-hip-hop, and you don't stop." And when you would be describing to somebody what kind of party you were at, you would say, "Yo, it was one of them hibbedy hop . . . you know, that hibbedy hop shit." So that became the one defining term within the culture that everybody related to.'

Although its use was so universal as to defy exact accreditation, popular consensus holds that it was Lovebug Starski, one of the early rhyming DJs, who coined the phrase. Other main contenders include DJ Hollywood, whose regular shows at Harlem's Apollo Theater and Club 371 were the first places many were exposed to hip hop, and Phase II, an early graffiti writer and one of the very first b-boys. Grandmixer D.ST, however, holds that Cowboy was the first to use the term, and that it was a reference to military parade drill.

'The story goes that a friend of his was getting ready to go into the service. And he was saying, "When you get in there, you're gonna be going, 'Hip hop the hip hop, hi hip hi, and you don't stop'," and that's how the story stuck. Cowboy started it. Lovebug Starski just took it and made it the thing of the day.'

Whatever the term's derivation, there was now a name for what was going on in the Bronx and by the last few years of the seventies, hip hop had a well-defined identity. The scene was all about intense partying, and whether this was in the parks, the high schools or in the few clubs – like T-Connection, Disco Fever, Club 371 and Harlem World that risked the boisterous crowds it attracted – the driving force was fun. DJs, MCs and the partygoers themselves competed to add as many exciting elements as they could, and hip hop grew to be about improvisation, showmanship, enjoyment and that greatest of party feelings, living for the moment.

Then in the summer of 1979, out of nowhere, riding on the pump of Chic's 'Good Times' bassline, came the sinuous rhyme that would change it all.

I said a hip hop

The hippie the hippie

To the hip hip hop and you don't stop the rock it

To the bang bang boogie, say up jumped the boogie

To the rhythm of the boogie, the beat

Sal Abbatiello of Disco Fever remembers the first time he heard 'Rappers' Delight'.

'I was in my office, I heard the record and I'm like, "Who's out there rapping?" They said, "No that's a record." I said, "About time somebody was smart enough to put this shit on record. Now they won't be breaking all my microphones." '

TEN
HIP HOP

Planet Rock

'The Bronx is so named because it once belonged to the family of Dutchman Jonas Bronck, who built his farm here in 1636. It is, therefore, The Broncks'.'

– Time Out Guide To New York

'A neighborhood is where, when you go out of it, you get beat up.'

– Murray Kempton

Hip hop today thrives on a sense of its own past. It is obsessed with 'keepin' it real' – grabbing its nuts and proclaiming its thug life, its loyalty to 'da ghetto' from whence it came, and to the 'old school' pioneers who created it. Ironically, this concern for staying true to its roots (seen by most of today's young guns as a need to appear blacker and angrier and more acquisitive than thou) has obscured a few facts about its history.

In practice, hip hop rarely has any time for its first generation of performers. Its definition of 'old school' rarely goes further back than 1982, and while figures like Herc and Flash may be venerated ancestors, they are irrelevant beside next week's young street-corner discovery. For similar reasons there have been radical revisions in the story of the genre's musical origins. Hip hop is usually portrayed as some mythical disco-hating force which came out of nowhere; in fact, it was inextricably connected to disco, it has an important debt to Jamaican reggae, and, perhaps most surprisingly, it owes part of its practical success to punk rock.

Most regrettably, perhaps, hip hop has largely forgotten that it was originally all about having *fun*. After years of 'ghetto reality' subject matter, with rappers dwelling relentlessly on crime and politics, the culture has lost sight of its original party purpose, its sense of celebration. You might think it's strange when a grumpy, gun-toting gangster asks a concert audience to put their hands in the air ('and wave them like you just don't care'), but all he's doing is displaying a relic from the days when hip hop wore a smile.

Rockin' it in the park

Born in 1974, it took more than half a decade before hip hop was heard beyond the Bronx. That it remained a secret to white New York for so long was not entirely down to fear and racism; it was also a result of the DJs' narrow horizons. Recording contracts, professionally managed careers, even the simple notion of playing outside your own neighbourhood: these things weren't considered. Eventually, the record companies and the cool downtown clubs would catch on and the music would begin its mutation into the worldwide business it is today, but hip hop's first five years were centred on nothing more complicated than throwing the best party.

To poor New Yorkers, block parties were nothing new. Local festivities in closed off streets and in the city's many parks have a long tradition (a New York park can be as small as a single asphalt basketball court). The entertainment might come from a local band playing funk and soul or, in Hispanic areas, salsa and merengue. As well as live music, there were mobile DJs who would bring their own sound systems and play a blend of Latin, funk, soul or disco, depending on the crowd.

As hip hop grew in popularity, the new generation of uptown DJs followed these traditions and threw their own events, giving free parties in the parks through the summertime as promotion for paying events in schools, clubs and community centres. In the parks the music would last from the afternoon well into the early hours, with the police usually turning a blind eye, reasoning that it was keeping teenage troublemakers out of harm's way. If they were out of reach of any other power supply, DJs and their crews would break open the base of a street lamp and risk electrocution to hotwire the sound system. 'Playing music was more important than our lives,' jokes Charlie Chase, confirming that this dangerous practice happened fairly often. 'We didn't give a fuck, we wanted to play music.'

Basements and abandoned buildings were other favoured settings, especially for an older crowd, and here the atmosphere could get much heavier. The scene was far more druggy than today's rap stars prefer to remember, and along with pot, plenty of less innocent pleasures were enjoyed. In between sixties heroin and eighties crack, the Bronx whizzed along on cocaine, which was then held to be non-addictive. Hence names like Kurtis *Blow* and *Coke* La *Rock*, and the fact that Melle Mel's record 'White Lines' actually started life as an ironic *celebration* of cocaine, with the 'Don't do it' message tacked on for commercial reasons. As well as coke there was angel dust, aka PCP, a manic-making animal tranquilliser which stank like stale sweat when it was smoked.

'It used to be so ill: the energy and the vibe,' recalls Fab 5 Freddy, who would travel to Bronx parties from his native Brooklyn. 'Back then in the hip hop scene it was very weird. It'd be really dark, the DJ would have a couple of light bulbs rigged up on a board. A lot of DJs had one strobe light and they'd have it on a table, and that was the lighting.

'Motherfuckers used to smoke angel dust on the scene. At least up in the Bronx, that was a popular drug at the time. And it makes a really sickly ill smell, when guys are smoking that in a hot funky room. There used to be a lot of heavy dust-heads. That might have inspired a lot of the sound, I don't know. I'm not saying any DJs were smoking that shit – I never got into it – but the scene was weird.

'That's why you wanted to go. You wanted to be a part of that world, hear that sound, just be in a cloud of angel dust smoke, all that energy, just funky perspiration odour, some stick-up kids that could rob you. I mean, all that shit was a part of the party. It was a whole world. That's what hip hop was at the time.'

Battles

In this closed world, competition grew intense and DJs duelled for local glory in what became known as 'battles', setting up their sound systems on opposite sides of a basketball court or a school gymnasium, just like their counterparts in Jamaica's dance halls. They then fought it out with records, technique and volume, to see who could win the largest crowd. Their MCs sparred verbally in support, and rapping evolved into complex rhymed boasts about the indefatigable MC and his spellbinding DJ. Likewise, the b-boys who breakdanced to their music fought each other with an escalating vocabulary of impossible moves.

Battles are one of hip hop's great romantic notions. They did happen – frequently – but they had no elaborate tribal customs, just agreements about who played when and for how long. Battles were never for settling disputes more serious than performers' rivalry; on the whole they were just a way of making an event more exciting for all concerned. The loser did not automatically forfeit his equipment (although foolish was the DJ who set up in a Bronx park without a tough crew to protect his system); the winner simply gathered more respect – and more of the audience for his next show.

'It was territorial,' urges Charlie Chase. 'It was like a cat where it sprays its territory, just to let people know, this area's been taken. Basically, all this shit stems from us wanting to impress the girls.'

At first, DJs would simply try to drown each other out. 'You play your system, I play my system, a bunch of noise going at the same time,' recalls Bambaataa. 'You out-louded the next person.' But this led to frayed tempers and the possibility of sabotage. 'Someone might get mad and go and knock the turntable or something, and it leads into a rumble. So then we started having it where we play an hour, you play an hour, and this way the audience decides, and it got more peaceful.'

If the contest was for volume, it was a brave man who battled Herc. As he would rap, 'Kool Herc is not a stepping stone. He's a horse that can't be rode, a bull that can't be stopped. Ain't a disco I can't rock.'

'Kool Herc used to just destroy people,' remembers Jazzy Jay, the Zulu Nation's champion DJ. 'Herc was the ultimate 'cos he had the records, *and* his system was unmatched.'

Flash recalls being shamed by Herc's system without even battling. He had popped in to check out the Hevalo one night.

'He'd say, "Grandmaster Flash in the house," over the mic, and then he'd cut off the highs and lows on his system and just play the mid-range. "Flash," he'd say, "in order to be a qualified disc jockey, there is one thing you must have . . . highs!" Then Herc would crank up his highs and the hi-hat would be sizzling. "And most of all, Flash," he'd say, "you must have . . . bass!" Well, when Herc's bass came in, the whole place would be shaking. I'd get so embarrassed that I'd have to leave. My system couldn't compare.'

Many people talk of the time, at the Webster Avenue PAL (Police Athletic League), when Herc's Herculoids washed Bambaataa out completely. Herc strolled around casually, taking ages to set things up, so Bam and his DJs carried on playing past their allotted time and were really getting into it. 'We was throwing the records on and we was *killing* it,' recalls Jazzy Jay. When Herc was finally ready, he warmed up his speakers with a series of polite but booming requests, delivered with the ominous vibration of his echo chamber. With a smile, Jay relates what came next:

'He said, "Ah, Bambaataa, could you please turn your system down?"'

'So Bam's getting all gassed by the Zulus – "Yo, fuck that nigga, Bam! We got his ass! Throw on them funky beats!" So Bam passed me some shit, I slice that shit up.

'Herc said [*louder*], "Yo, Bambaataa-baataa-baataa, turn your system down-down-down."'

'"Fuck you!" Niggas getting on the mic, cursing.

'Now Kool Herc, he said [*louder still*], "BAMBAATAA-Baataa-baataa, TURN YOUR SYSTEM DOWN!"'

'Couldn't even hear our shit. Whoa! We started reaching for knobs, turning shit up, speakers started coughing. And he comes on with "The Mexican". You ever hear "The Mexican" by Babe Ruth? It starts out real low – ba-doom-doom. By about sixteen bars into the song, we just gave up, turned off all the fucking amps. Turned everything off. And the drums didn't even come in yet. When the drums came in, all the walls... just like VROOM! That was it.'

Bambaataa, however, insists that the Zulus remained unbowed.

'He had a louder system, but when it came to the music they couldn't fuck around. At the battle, we funked them up with our music so much that when we left, the whole crowd left with us too.'

Battles weren't always a simple head-to-head. Fab 5 Freddy remembers a battle between seven separate systems in an armoury building in Brooklyn. Bambaataa recalls a time at James Monroe high school when a Bronxdale DJ called Disco King Mario put out a call for help in order to battle Flash. Mario ended up fighting the Grandmaster with his own system, plus amps and speakers from Bambaataa's, plus another system belonging to a DJ Tex. 'We put our stuff all together. It looked like the wall of Jericho,' says Bam biblically.

Charlie Chase, a former musician, had more stage experience than most and with the weighty lyrical skills of Grandmaster Caz, the Cold Crush Brothers used showmanship and theatricality as their trump cards.

'When you saw us perform, it was unforgettable,' boasts Charlie. 'Nobody else had the stage presence we had. We couldn't just get on the stage and just rap, we've got to give them a show.' For the group's entrance, Charlie would use a classical record for a single note: the strike of an entire orchestra.

'When you hear a symphony strike, that shit is intense, so we have to match that visually onstage. So I would take a record and take a strike, and the guys would pose, BAMM! Then you'd see the guys spin round one at a time. I would play "Catch the Beat" by T-Ski Valley, they would do more dance steps. Once the whole group was on the stage, I would play instrumental breaks that they could do their dance steps to. Then the whole group would do a song together, and then two members of the group would do a chant, and the other three members of the group would do the rap. And then the chant comes in, and then the rap, and the chant . . .

'That shit was not done in hip hop. We dressed the part. We played the part. We had a show called the Gangster Chronicles. We came onstage with pinstripe suits, the hats, and Uzis, plastic toy Uzis.'

Cold Crush's mobster outfits made their debut at one of the most famous battles ever: Cold Crush Brothers vs Theodore & the Fantastic Romantic Five, winter 1981, in Harlem World. It was a grudge match, stemming from the fact that two of the Fantastics' MCs had been protégés of Cold Crush MC, Grandmaster Caz.

'I remember, we made scenes in the street,' laughs Charlie. 'We were this close to fighting in the street, fist fights, with them. It was like

Muhammad Ali facing Joe Frazier at the time, where he would meet him in public just to humiliate him. Some shit. And the promoters at Harlem World got wind of it and they said, we'll put up a thousand dollar prize if you guys come here and battle. And the buzz was growing in the hip hop community, like, "Fantastic is better," "Hell no, Cold Crush will bust they ass," "No, Fantastic is better," and little tiffs and arguments in clubs and in public.'

In the end, despite the polished Cold Crush show, the Fantastic Five won the affections of some wild girls at the front of the crowd and were screamed to a dubious victory.

Hip hop on record

The idea of capturing these low-rent street thrills on records just seemed contradictory. While the music industry was entranced by disco's glitzy aspirational sound, what would they find of interest in these ghetto parties? The DJs and MCs might be stars in the neighbourhood, but they could hardly conceive of any greater level of fame; none of them thought of making records. The closest these kids – few were even out of their teens – had come to the music business was a brief negotiation with a local nightclub owner. Partying in the projects was worlds away from the record labels and their midtown mirror glass.

In late 1978, mere months before the Sugar Hill Gang would hit the charts with 'Rappers' Delight', Fab 5 Freddy first saw Grandmaster Flash and the Furious Five perform. He remembers, after the show, in the community centre of the Lower East Side's Smith Projects, talking to Melle Mel.

F5F: 'Yo man, wassup. Are you aware of how big this is? You guys should make a record.'

MM: 'Yo, who would buy it?'

F5F: 'Well, at least all the people coming to these parties.'

MM [*unconvinced*]: 'Yeah?'

Flash himself claims to have turned down some very early offers of record deals, thinking that music made from other people's records was simply not commercial enough. 'I was asked before anybody. And I was like, "Who would want to hear a record which I was spinning re-recorded with MCing over it?" '

In any case, the scene already had an established communication network as DJ-mix tapes were copied and circulated throughout black New York, and played, of course, on 'ghetto blasters', the era's suitcase-sized portable radio cassettes (a similar trade had developed downtown in tapes of the disco DJs' performances). The hip hop sound was heard even further away as people sent tapes to relatives outside the city and servicemen took them overseas. In the Bronx, echoing the Pullman railroad conductors who had distributed blues records decades ago, car services helped to market tapes.

'Those were our biggest promotional vehicles,' puns Charlie Chase. 'You had the OJ cab service and then you had Community Cab service, they were the first cabs that used to drive luxury cars.' (The OJ cars were immortalised in several songs, including 'Rappers' Delight'.) 'If they knew you were a DJ, they would come by and buy tapes off you. And then they'd play them in the cars. People would go, "Yo, whose tape is that?" and the cabdriver would say, "This is Charlie Chase," or they'd give them your number.' Charlie would sell his tapes from his ground floor apartment. 'My window was always being knocked on. They would knock on my window and I would sell 'em tapes. My neighbours thought I was a fuckin' drug dealer for a while.'

Cassette technology was also a way for would-be DJs to practice their skills at cutting up songs without the need for expensive equipment. Many of the DJs inspired by Herc, Flash and Bambaataa would begin their careers on a home hi-fi with their fingers hovering over a hot pause button. Grandmixer D.ST was one of them.

'I had pause button tapes all over the place. Everyone had one of my pause button tapes. I was one of the biggest pause button guys.' All this despite the fact that his tape recorder didn't actually have a pause button. 'I would just cut with the tape on play and the record button halfway down. And then when the part on the tape would get to the cut part, I would just push the record button all the way down.' He laughs at the thought of such primitive techniques. 'Then when I got a pause button, I was off the hook!'

It would take a handful of independent (and often predatory) entrepreneurs to see the commercial possibilities of committing hip hop to record. All had experience of bringing money and music together since the fifties; most had a dislike for disco, which kept them away from what was then the most lucrative genre for independent labels; and several saw in the hip hop scene a parallel to earlier forms, especially the street corner harmonising of doo wop.

'Rappers' Delight'

In 1979, an ailing Brooklyn funk band, Fatback, slipped an unknown rapping DJ, King Tim III, onto the B-side of their single 'You're My Candy Sweet', and laid claim to the first modern rap record. When New York's powerful disco station WKTU played this track, 'King Tim III (Personality Jock)', over the A-side, it became a surprise hit.

Hip hop's breakthrough song, however, was the fatally infectious

'Rappers' Delight' on Sugar Hill Records, the latest label from experienced soul and funk mini-moguls Sylvia and Joe Robinson (the husband and wife team behind such imprints as All Platinum, Turbo, Stang and Vibration; Sylvia had also enjoyed a long singing career). 'Rappers' Delight' stole the bassline of that summer's disco hit 'Good Times' to full effect – recreated in the studio by session musicians mimicking the music of a quick-mixing Bronx DJ – and this fourteen-minute groove stormed the clubs and the radio like a police raid.

But the Sugar Hill Gang? Who were they? Their record was selling thousands a day, but the Bronx had never seen them pick up a microphone.

'Never heard of them. They didn't pay no dues at all,' is how Flash remembers it. 'We all thought, "If they're not from any of the five boroughs, where are they from?" '

Far from veterans of the scene, they were a manufactured group, put together by the wily Sylvia Robinson. She originally claimed she signed them after seeing them perform at her niece's birthday party at Harlem World. Others remember band members Wonder Mike as a friend of her son, and Big Bank Hank as a bouncer at the Sparkle, one of Kool Herc's clubs – the rest of the time he worked in a pizza shop in Englewood, New Jersey, where Robinson was based.

Although the group was unknown in the Bronx, the rhymes in 'Rappers' Delight' were all too familiar – an amalgam lifted, it's said, from the MCs which club doorman Hank had heard onstage. Grandmaster Caz (short for Casanova) of the Cold Crush Brothers has always claimed authorship of most of the lyrics, even to the extent of saying he lent Hank (who had offered to manage him) his rhymes notebook. Since one of the song's lines is, 'Check it out, I'm the C-A-S-AN-the-O-V-A . . .', this seems pretty likely.

Whatever its provenance, the record went to no.4 on *Billboard*'s R&B charts and no.36 in the Hot 100, proving beyond any doubt that this music had a market.

After the Bronx had heard 'Rappers' Delight', everyone realised the rules had changed. Bambaataa says he was immediately fearful that hip hop on record would kill the party. 'I was one who stood away longer. Flash and all them jumped on the scene. I stood more watching.'

Flash, always chasing firsts, was incensed.

'I was like, "Damn, I could'a been there first." I didn't know the gun was loaded like that. Blew up. It was a huge record for them.' He vowed to turn his anger into action. 'It was OK, though. 'Cos we were gonna come later . . . We had the talent, and they didn't.'

'Adventures Of Grandmaster Flash On The Wheels Of Steel'

Soon after 'Rappers' Delight', Flash & the Furious Five leapt into the fray with 'Superrappin' on Enjoy, a Harlem label started by another veteran record retailer and producer, Bobby Robinson. Years ago, Enjoy had been home to saxophone legend King Curtis, just one of the artists Robinson had nurtured for success with larger companies. (Robinson can also claim the discovery of Gladys Knight & the Pips, who he signed to his Fury label.) After 'Superrappin', a funky rip-off of 'Seven Minutes Of Funk' by Tyrone Thomas & the Whole Darn Family, Flash would follow this tradition when he moved his deal to Sugar Hill, complaining that Robinson had failed to get any radio play for his debut single.

DJ Breakout's group, the Funky Four (Plus One More), had been the first to record hip hop for Enjoy, with 1979's 'Rappin' And Rockin' The House', a take on Cheryl Lynn's 'Got To Be Real', but they, too, would move their business from Enjoy to Sugar Hill, as did Spoonie Gee (even though he was Bobby Robinson's nephew) and the Treacherous Three. Once signed to Sugar Hill, Flash and the Furious Five quickly made up for lost time and emerged as recorded rap's first superstars.

Their most famous song is undoubtedly 1982's 'The Message', which made no.4 in the R&B chart (no.8 in the UK), as hip hop's first socio-politically charged rap. A hugely inspiring record, its conscious lyrics were an innovation of Sylvia Robinson's which the band, armed with a power-ful lack of political consciousness, strongly resisted. But Sylvia's uncanny commercial acumen triumphed and rap's enduring sociological agenda was born. With the song's success, a whole series of 'message raps' followed.

' "The Message" was the announcement that hip hop was gonna be culturally significant,' considers Richard Grabel, one of the first journalists to cover the scene. 'White rock fans, and certainly white rock critics, have always been content oriented. Up to that point rap hadn't given them much to write about lyric-wise. But now it was doing it. And that's when all the writers started covering it.'

From a DJ's perspective, however, 1981's 'Adventures Of Grandmaster Flash On The Wheels Of Steel' remains a far more important record. Seven minutes of quick-mix excitement starring a host of the period's hit tunes, this was the first track made successfully with records and turntables, not session musicians.

'It took three turntables, two mixers and between ten and fifteen takes to get it right,' recalls Flash. 'It took me three hours. I had to do it live. And whenever I'd mess up I would just refuse to punch. I would just go back to the beginning.'

And how did he react when he heard the playback?

'I was scared. I didn't think anyone was gonna get it. I thought, "they might understand this. DJs'll probably love it." '

'Adventures . . .' didn't enjoy huge success in America, only managing no.55 in the R&B chart, but in clubs, both at home and in Europe, the record was huge.

To those who heard it at that time it was a revolutionary moment in the history of music: a record made from nothing more than other records, a record made by a DJ, a postmodern collage of existing texts, the scratch-filled proof that turntables could be real instruments. Theorists heard the creaking of concepts like authorship, copyright, originality, musicianship – 'Adventures Of Grandmaster Flash On The Wheels Of Steel' was the first time hip hop had been captured on record rather than translated; music's possibilities had been expanded dramatically.

'Vicious Rap'

Another key figure early on was experienced entrepreneur Paul Winley. Having recorded doo wop groups in the fifties, some of whom he describes as 'real hoodlums', Winley saw hip hop as familiar territory. 'The doo wop era and the hip hop era, in the beginning it was the same thing. It was kids. Young kids.'

The affable Winley, who can greet anyone over forty by name as he ambles down Harlem's 125th Street, had been a Tin Pan Alley songwriter with a number of hits to his credit, had worked for the young Atlantic Records, and had run a successful independent label, Winley Records, since 1956. (He recalls being cursed out by Billie Holiday when he suggested she record for him: 'She was a rough woman.')

Winley already knew the hip hop scene from producing compilation albums of breakbeat songs. When his daughter Tanya started coming home from school reciting the raps going through her playground, he decided to put her on record and squeezed her into the studio at the end of one of her mother's vocal sessions. Against a live funk backing and some police sirens, she became Sweet Tee and recorded 1980's 'Vicious Rap', a great, if rather lo-fidelity record.

Winley didn't necessarily see hip hop as an enduring art form, but he thought it was more than a mere novelty. His view was typical. 'It was grass roots people, grass roots kids. Just like the blues, just like gospel. It came from the soul, and it was natural writing, and it wasn't no great productions.

'I saw it as rhyming. Rhyming, with a beat, with music. I just saw it as entertaining. I didn't say that it was music or that it was gonna be a big thing. I saw it as something the kids enjoyed doing, and anything that the masses can participate in could be big.'

He would later record Afrika Bambaataa's first records, 'Zulu Nation Throwdown' (1980), a rap backed with some minimal guitar and Hammond organ vamps, and 'Death Mix' (1981), an exciting but inaudible live show. Bambaataa claims this was mastered from a second or third generation cassette tape – such haphazard quality control meant Winley's early entry into recording hip hop was followed by an equally early exit.

'Planet Rock'

Of hip hop's founding trio, only Kool Herc never got the chance to transfer his skills to vinyl. Afrika Bambaataa, after a couple of false starts on Winley Records and a minor club hit with 'Jazzy Sensation' (based on Gwen McCrae's 'Funky Sensation'), was to emerge with one of history's most influential records. His renowned eclecticism would pay off as 1982's 'Planet Rock' lit the fuse on not one but several genres of dance music. It's the source of electro, the root of Miami bass music, it was an acknowledged inspiration for the genesis of house and techno and was a massive influence on the way future hip hop records would be made.

Arthur Baker, the record's producer, recognised the significance of 'Planet Rock' immediately. 'Oh, I knew,' he insists. 'I knew before we even mixed it. I knew before there was even a rap on it. I went home the night we cut the track and brought the tape home, and I said to my wife at the time, "We've just made musical history." '

Baker, now one of dance music's most successful producers, had started making records a couple of years earlier, entering production after admitting to himself that he lacked the obsessive nature that makes a good disc jockey. Despite this, he has a DJ's acute instincts for the dancefloor and says he always made records with a particular club in mind, tailoring them to reflect the DJ's style and the feel and energy of the scene.

'Planet Rock', a sci-fi vision of crashing electronic drums and eerie keyboard melodies, was a reflection of Bambaataa's eclectic live performances – it was constructed by recreating elements from a stack of records high on his playlist, notably 'Trans Europe Express' and 'Numbers' by German synth futurists Kraftwerk. Bambaataa used to overlay Malcolm X speeches over 'Trans Europe Express's thirteen minutes (Grandmaster Flash put it on when he needed a toilet break). Other elements added included the beat from 'Super Sperm' by Captain Sky and a part of 'The Mexican' by Babe Ruth.

'I'd been into Kraftwerk and Bam was into Kraftwerk, and we just had the idea of merging the two songs together,' says Baker. 'I used to hear "Trans Europe Express" *all over* the place. In playgrounds, clubs, everywhere. At that time, I'd just moved to New York. When I had lunch,

I'd sit in the park and there'd be guys with a big beatbox breakdancing to it. I used to hear it all over.'

Though Bam had hardly any studio experience, he had very clear intentions for the project.

'I wanted it to be the first black electronic group,' he says. 'Some funky mechanical crazy shit with no band, just electronic instruments. When I made it, I was trying to grab the black market and the punk rock market. I wanted to grab them two together. I always was into "Trans Europe Express" and after Kraftwerk put "Numbers" out, I said, "I wonder if I can combine them two to make something real funky with a hard bass and beat?" '

It was probably the first hip hop record to use a drum machine (a Roland TR808), a fact which marks it as the starting point of the spin-off genre known as electro, and makes it a clear inspiration for Run DMC's beatbox work-outs – a style which made them the undisputed leaders of hip hop's second wave. Baker, who had no experience with drum machines, recalls hiring a programmer out of the paper. 'There was an ad in the *Village Voice*: "Man with drum machine, $20 a session." I don't even remember the guy's name or anything. So I got him for twenty dollars and said, "Programme this." ' With its unshakeable beat, making mixing easier, 'Planet Rock' couldn't fail to appeal to DJs.

The record's orchestra strikes and explosions were conjured out of a Fairlight synthesiser, 'a hundred thousand dollar waste of space,' as Baker puts it. The Fairlight, an Australian monster machine beloved of prog rockers like Peter Gabriel, was the sampler's hulking prototype, but since its sampling ability was minimal, Kraftwerk's melody lines were masterfully replayed by programmer/keyboardist John Robie.

Though it doesn't use sampling in the digital push-button sense that today's hip hop producers would understand, in conception 'Planet Rock', like 'Rappers' Delight' and Flash's 'Adventures . . .', is a sampled record. In fact, all three songs show a considerable leap from the kind of organic sampling which has always existed in music – the slow transmission of melodies and rhythms – to a more unmediated form of musical thievery. Here are songs made from very little more than snippets and snatches of others, not *versions* of other songs, not *improvisations* of other songs, but *copies*, either re-recorded from existing records or replayed note for note as exactly as possible.

And what set 'Planet Rock' apart from its hip hop predecessors was that it was more than just a medley of pop hits. Baker and Bambaataa showed that sampled elements didn't necessarily have to be preserved intact: instead they could be collided into each other and woven into an intricate new sound tapestry. Today, this idea is regularly pushed to its limits, as producers make records from a multitude of tiny samples, often distorting and disguising them as much as possible. This process can be seen to have started with 'Planet Rock', a record in which the DJ's pioneering ability to create new music from old was on clear display.

Another key aspect of sampling was also highlighted: its ability to generate litigation. When 'Rappers' Delight' had used 'Good Times' so overtly, Chic's Nile Rogers and Bernard Edwards had been able to successfully claim full writing credit. On hearing 'Planet Rock', Kraftwerk launched a lawsuit claiming royalties, which continued unresolved for many years. (Baker had in fact anticipated legal problems and had recorded an alternative melody line for the song. When Tommy Boy's Tom Silverman decided to release the record intact, Baker used this as the basis for Bambaataa's next record, 'Play At Your Own Risk'.)

As for the song itself, Bambaataa recalls the incredible reaction it generated.

'It was faster than any other rap record before, but the crowd was just dancing crazy and couldn't get enough of it, especially when I turned it over to the B-side with the instrumental – it just was a whole different thing to people. They'd heard the techno-pop records, but this was the first thing that had bottom, rhythm, the hard bass and all that.' He first played it in the Boys' Club, in the Soundview Section of the Bronx, 'A straight-up hardcore party. We had to play it four or five times. Because the crowd just went crazy.'

Sampling

There were many other key records, of course. Kurtis Blow's 'Christmas Rappin'' (late 1979) would become the first major label release (on Mercury); Blondie would show their insight into the scene by releasing 'Rapture' (1981), a US no.1 and important for the fact that it was by an established (and white) group. There was the post-'Planet Rock' boom of electro records, including the influential sound collages of Mantronix and Double Dee & Steinski, not to mention shedloads of records about breakdancing and Pacman. In the UK charts, the rap phenomenon started as little more than a joke and a series of novelty hits, including Kenny Everett's 'Snot Rap' and Roland Rat's 'Rat Rapping' (both 1983), were the first rap records to hit the mainstream. Luckily it was a different story in the clubs.

The explosion of recorded hip hop brought the DJ's cut and paste aesthetic to bear on studio production and furthered his inexorable move into the producer's chair. As early rap producer Marley Marl said in 1988, 'There's not much of a difference between making a record and being a DJ, cutting up beats and stuff.' Sampling would become especially important – used these days by everyone from bedroom dance producers to major rock bands. Making records this way is nothing more than using clever studio electronics to exaggerate what a good DJ can do on his turntables.

Indeed, the story of sampling is a tale of technology catching up with the DJ, of equipment being created that could do faster, more accurately and more easily what a DJ had long been able to. After the Fairlight Computer Musical Instrument, which allowed a tiny burst of sampled sound to be played, there was the EMU Emulator, first used in hip hop in 1982 by Marley Marl, who sampled the beat of a snare drum by accident during a remix he was doing. As he told writer Harry Allen, he realised the potential of this immediately: 'I could take any drum sound from any old record, put it in here and get that old drummer sound.' Old drummer Max Roach realised sampling's promise too, when he declared that, 'Hip hop lives in the world of sound, not the world of music, and that's why it's so revolutionary.' In contrast, the inventor of the Emulator, Dave Rossum, had little idea how important his machine would be. When asked in the early eighties whether sampling was the 'future of the sound industry?', he just laughed.

Sampling is now an accepted part of music, and record labels have entire departments selling sampling permissions. For many years, however, it generated considerable confusion, as everyone tried to avoid setting a standard practice. This was partly settled by a landmark decision in 1992 against comedy rapper Biz Markie for sampling part of Gilbert O'Sullivan's 'Alone Again Naturally' on his *I Need A Haircut* album. A federal judge, declaring 'Thou shalt not steal,' set the precedent by ruling against Biz and, instead of having his record label (Cold Chillin', owned by Warner Bros) pay O'Sullivan a royalty, demanded the offending sample be removed and the records containing it recalled.

The validity of sampling has long been debated, with irate musicians decrying it as non-creative. Hip hop fights back by claiming archivist status, referring to the interest it generates in older and forgotten artists. As Brooklyn rappers Stetsasonic rhymed in 'Talking All That Jazz' (1988): 'Tell the truth/James Brown was old/'Til Eric and Rak came out with "I Got Soul"/Rap brings back old R&B/And if we would not/People could have forgot.'

In hip hop, reliance on sampling reached its peak in the late eighties in the wall-of-sound productions of Public Enemy and in the kooky grab-anything styles of De La Soul, before it became too expensive and/or risky to base records on large numbers of lengthy and recognisable samples. Commentator Nelson George makes the interesting point that it was only when hip hop started sampling white music –

specifically in the Biz Markie case, and also in lawsuits relating to De La Soul's *Three Feet High And Rising* LP and Public Enemy's *It Take A Nation Of Millions To Hold Us Back* – that the industry perceived a problem.

Hip hop goes downtown

Obviously, hip hop's graduation to vinyl was what allowed it to develop into an accepted musical genre, but in some people's view, the records were all that saved it from extinction. In the Bronx around 1979, after a peak of interest three years before, there was what Jazzy Jay refers to as 'the drought', a time when grass roots interest in the music seemed to be dying. Party attendances were waning so fast that even the DJs themselves were convinced hip hop had already had its day. This before most of the world had even heard of it. 'If you wasn't in hip hop, you wouldn't know about the drought,' says Jay. 'But around 1979 it was dying down. Everybody thought it was a dying art form.' With the domination of crossover disco, audiences were turning their backs on hip hop in favour of more glamorous sounds. 'Everybody was starting to swing back towards R&B and the club disco-type scene. Everybody was getting *sophisticated*. They were through with hip hop: "Oh, that's childish shit, we don't want to deal with it no more." '

As well as saving the uptown scene, hip hop's first records had a phenomenal impact around the world; people remember hearing them and feeling they were listening to a completely new musical language. Naturally, there was an intense curiosity about where this music had started. Few were prepared to venture to a derelict Bronx basement to see it in its natural habitat, so hip hop gradually headed downtown. In doing this it became a vibrant part of post-disco clubland, meeting other established scenes and infecting other forms of music with its impressive DJ techniques and its innovative cut-and-paste creativity.

One style of music which is rarely connected with hip hop outside of cultural analysis is punk. And yet punk and hip hop shared a great deal more than a do-it-yourself ethos and a rebellious attitude. In fact, in cahoots with Manhattan's posey artworld, punk was what brought hip hop to the world's attention. Former art student Johnny Dynell, then starting his DJ career at the arty punk disco that was Manhattan's Mudd Club, remembers seeing Flash for the first time. It changed his view of DJing completely.

'I was a DJ but I always thought of myself more as a visual artist,' he says. 'I never saw DJing as artistic or creative. But then in 1979, I went with this friend to this church basement and I saw this battle, with Grandmaster Flash, Hollywood, all those early guys. And Flash was DJing with his toes. He was scratching, which I'd never heard before. He just rocked my world.'

With his art school background, Dynell was thrilled by the conceptual implications of what he'd seen. 'They were playing the same records I was playing, like James Brown, but what they were doing was taking two copies and going back and forth and making this new thing out of them. To me, coming from the art world, I thought it was brilliant. I thought, I'm going to have to tell Andy [*Warhol*] about this. This is incredible. It's like Marcel Duchamps.'

Dynell was so excited that he tried to bring Flash together with Alan Vega of punk band Suicide, reasoning that Vega's music, like Flash's, was all about repetition. This ambitious attempt at cross-pollination raised little enthusiasm from either side. The collision of punk and hip hop would have to wait a couple of years.

Punks from the Bronx

In 1982 Malcolm McLaren declared, 'I think punk rock is more alive in Harlem, in some respects, than it is in Bracknell.'

Speaking in *Time Out* to Jon Savage, punk's master hypester spun an unlikely but intriguing yarn: 'I was in the Bronx and I saw a boy and a girl, hand in hand, two black kids from the south Bronx, and they were walking down the street and they were both wearing "Never Mind The Bollocks" T-shirts. Now they may not even have known of the Sex Pistols. They liked the look of it. They homed in on it. They saw something. They liked the words.'

In August 1981 McLaren had been introduced to Afrika Bambaataa by Michael Holman, a black video artist who had taken him up to the Bronx to witness this amazing new music scene. The Sex Pistols' ex-manager was then steering the fortunes of pop band Bow Wow Wow, and formulating an ambitious album project based on smelting together the world's folk-dance music (this would become his *Duck Rock* LP). Despite a harrowing night during which he was, by most accounts, completely petrified, McLaren was mesmerised.

'It was like *Heart Of Darkness*,' laughs Holman. 'I go to the hotel and I'm about to take them up to the Bronx on a summer evening – McLaren and Rory Johnston from RCA – and they're dressed like fucking pirates, in all that Vivienne Westwood gear. I thought we were gonna get stuck up or shot at any second. We finally get there and we go from a place that's completely deserted to masses and masses of kids, nothing but teenagers running from one corner to another, watching fights break out in the crowd. It's insane. Bottles flying everywhere. Malcolm's dressed like a pirate – and nobody noticed us. And now he starts to see the special effects DJs and the b-boys throwing down, and he's starting to see it all. So he says, "Let's get out of here. But I've got an idea." '

McLaren gave Holman $1,500 to put together a hip hop revue to open for Bow Wow Wow. Holman booked Bam and his cohorts, including the Rocksteady Crew (destined to become the world's most famous breakdancers), to open the band's New York show.

Ruza Blue, an English girl just into her twenties, was fresh off a plane from London for a two-week stay in New York. With her hair dyed in a black and white skunk cut, and with good contacts from her time on the London club scene, she would end up staying stateside. Employed for her dress sense more than anything, she started working for McLaren and his ex-wife Vivienne Westwood. At the Ritz to see the Bow Wow Wow show, Blue, like most of the audience, found herself transfixed by the support act. A DJ, a stocky black guy with long lashes, was playing some kind of crazy chopped up disco-funk music, and a gaggle of hyperactive Puerto Rican teens were cutting up the dancefloor like demented spinning tops.

'I was like, "What the fuck is this?" I was completely blown away,' says Blue. 'I just knew that whatever it was, I wanted to get involved in it.' She introduced herself to the Bronx kids after the show and in the coming weeks this punky British girl started venturing uptown to a club called Disco Fever. 'That was *the* hip hop club. No one downtown knew what the hell was going on up there, and that was wild. Flash was the DJ, Melle Mel was the MC and there were all these other MCs there. All the Sugar Hill Gang were hanging out. I'd go up there and I'd be the only white face in the club, and that was wild, and I thought, "Oh my god, I've got to bring all of this downtown." '

Blue asked Holman to put on a similar night for her at Negril, an East Village reggae joint run by Kosmo Vinyl, manager of the Clash (it had once been Bob Marley's Manhattan hangout). Holman brought down Bambaataa, Jazzy Jay and other Zulu Nation DJs, as well as Theodore and the Rocksteady Crew (who are Zulu-affiliates), and he and Blue began promoting the club to the punky downtowners.

'To get people to come down and check it out, I'd put people like the Clash on DJing,' she recalls. 'Combining the hip hop scene with the dregs of the punk scene brought the general public down. They were all like, "The Clash are gonna be there, we'd better be there." Once they arrived, they'd find what was really going on: the hip hop.'

Holman insists that what drew the crowds was in fact the breakdancing. Punk was old news to his trendy Mudd Club friends, but breakdancing had them completely enraptured. 'The first gig at Negril was a white guy, Nick Taylor, the High Priest on the turntables, Bambaataa, Fab 5 Freddy. Ramelzee is there putting up giant graf pieces, like armoured letters. I had TV monitors showing this breakdancing footage I'd filmed. And Rocksteady Crew came down.'

Holman eventually fell out with Blue (now Kool Lady Blue), who then took the concept to the next level. When Negril was closed by the fire department for overcrowding, she moved it to Danceteria, the trendy post-disco new wave club, and then – despite advice that she was mad to book such a huge space – to a 3,000-capacity roller-skating rink: the Roxy.

Everyone remembers the Roxy years as very special.

'The Roxy embodied a certain vision of what New York could be – a multi-racial centre of world culture, running on a current of flaming, uncompromised youth. The night had a thousand styles, a hundred dialects,' recalled club queen Chi Chi Valenti.

Every Friday from 18 June 1982 to the end of 1983, Kool Lady Blue's Wheels Of Steel nights brought teenage Bronx b-boys together with spiky-haired punks, new wave musicians like Blondie and Talking Heads, and the gentry of the downtown art world, Andy Warhol included. It was

Zulus take Manhattan – the opening night flyer for the legendary Wheels of Steel at the Roxy, taken from Kool Lady Blue's forthcoming book.

one of those rare clubs where a true cross-pollination was happening; the opposite of the selective decadence of Studio 54.

Richard Grabel declared in the *NME*, 'The feeling hits you when you walk into the Roxy on a Friday night the way it doesn't hit you in any other New York club. Everywhere else it's hesitation and uncertainty; at the Roxy, you know you're in the right place.'

'It was fabulous. It was such a great feeling,' says Johnny Dynell, one of the downtown DJs who played there at the time, recalling how the Roxy mixed up cultures and races. 'That was the great thing about it. For me it was great; it was like both of my worlds. I would actually see both groups of my friends in the same place. That was really unusual.' Dynell is sure that Blue was able to pull this off precisely because she didn't share the usual American assumptions about race. 'An American couldn't do that. It took an English person.'

Graffiti hung on great canvas sheets. Kurtis Blow, Sequence, Indeep performed. Fab 5 Freddy MCed. Run DMC had their first gig there, as did New Edition. Madonna sang there, starting her climb to stardom. The young Russell Simmons was running around networking. Every week a photographer would take pictures of the partygoers and a huge projector would show the portraits from the week before. With solid residences from the Zulu DJs Bambaataa, Afrika Islam, Jazzy Jay, D.ST and Theodore, and a constant breakdancing presence from the Rocksteady Crew, it drew an astonishing mixture of people, all riding the energy wave of this thrilling new music.

'I didn't have too many MCs. It was very focused on the DJ. I just kept it strictly DJs and dancing,' says Blue. 'I used to mix it all up. One night I had a whole troupe of American Indians doing sundances on the floor with the breakers. And that was like a really weird thing, but it worked. Or the Double Dutch girls, that was a complete fluke. I just saw them on TV one night in a McDonald's commercial and thought, they'd be good. Double Dutch girls have nothing to do with hip hop whatsoever. But all of a sudden, because it was showcased at the club one night, it was suddenly, "Oh, that's hip hop." '

Fab 5 Freddy, who was steering Blue around the uptown pantheon of DJs and MCs, remembers the pivotal party as the night they screened *The Great Rock And Roll Swindle*, never released in the US, for the downtown glitterati.

'Right after the screening was around the time when the uptown heads from the Bronx, the hip hoppers, would start coming in, and these two scenes had never been mixed on this level. When you went to clubs, the downtown scene was pretty much predominantly white, and the uptown scene was black and Hispanic. And I couldn't imagine it was gonna work. I just anticipated kids from the Bronx beating the shit out of weird-looking punk rockers.'

Instead, uptown and downtown were brought wholeheartedly together, a near-impossible achievement, even today. 'The fashionable, on-the-edge punk rock people: when the movie ended, they stayed. And sure enough, here come all the little b-boys and b-girls, the fly guys and fly girls coming in. Kids was coming in just dancing, the energy was right. And it seemed to me, from that point on, you had this great mix. You had punk rock kids with mohawks, standing next to b-boys. It was the first time each other was seeing each other.'

And the two scenes weren't just cautiously observing each other. A lot of real mixing was taking place. 'A lot of fucking going on,' laughs Freddy. 'In short, a lot of fucking going on, because the hot dance at the time was the Webo, or the Freak. It came out of the Latin scene, where you would dance and you would get all up on a girl and really rub your two pelvic areas together, furiously. Like really wind and grind on each other.' Since the white girls didn't know that it wasn't really cool to let just anybody do this, the uptown guys took advantage.

'You would see three or four Puerto Rican dudes all around one chick, and the chick would be like [*dizzy abandon*] "Aahhh, this is great!" And them guys would be like, "Yeeeahhhh!" There'd be a lot of energy like that, just people rubbin' on each other and shit. I used to be like, "Yo! This is kinda hot!" '

Bambaataa has similar recollections.

'At first, people was buggin' when they first seen the punk rockers. Blacks and Latinos looked at them like they crazy. They had the spikes and the hair, and the colours and all the different clothing, but then when that music hit, you just see *everybody* tearing they ass up dancing.'

Cold Crush were so taken by punk that they recorded 'Punk Rock Rap', one of several records which failed to convert their legendary live shows into a recording career of any note. Cold Crush DJ Charlie Chase remembers the fun of the Roxy, including a night when Bianca Jagger was crowding the DJ booth.

'She was starry eyed, looking at me doing my thing on the turntable. She was fine. She was gorgeous. So I said to Bam, "Who's that chick down there looking at me?" He says, "Yo, that's Bianca Jagger." I says, "Bianca Jagger, you mean Mick Jagger's wife?" He says, "Yeah." I was like, "Shit, we movin' on up now on the pussy scale! We movin' on up now, kid, this is big time!" '

Fab 5 Freddy was another important link between uptown and down. His motivation for bringing the two together was to gain art world respect for graffiti – which had evolved alongside rap music and breakdancing – and thereby further his own career as a graffiti artist. By the early eighties, Bronx spray-can Picassos were painting startling subway-train-sized masterpieces, and with the patronage of Andy Warhol, serious critical respect was being accorded to Jean-Michel Basquiat and Keith Haring, who had both started as graffiti artists. The galleries were jumping on this 'street art' fairly quickly, and as he ventured deeper into the art world, meeting people like Glenn O'Brien, editor of Warhol's *Interview*, and Blondie's Chris Stein and Debbie Harry, Freddy soon found himself the Bronx's unofficial cultural ambassador.

This role led him to put together *Wildstyle* with novice director Charlie Ahearn, a film aimed at documenting the nascent world of hip hop. 'I was serious about trying to be a painter, and I wanted this graffiti movement to be seen as a serious movement like Futurism or Dada. I didn't want us to be looked on as folk artists.

'I wanted to let people know that this was a complete culture, which I had read somewhere included dance, painting and music. So I wanted this film to be made to demonstrate that this graffiti thing, which was the focus, was a complete culture: that it was related to a form of music and related to a form of dance. Prior to that, nobody had seen these things as being connected.'

He also arranged for DJs to spin at gallery events. Thanks to Freddy, Bambaataa had actually been playing for the downtown art trendies since 1980, considerably before Holman and Blue's Negril and Roxy nights. Of the Bronx DJs, Bam had the closest connections to the downtown club world (as well as being in many of the record pools, his playlist was published in several dance music newsletters) and Freddy brought him down to play in Club 57 on St Mark's Place, the Fun Gallery and the Mudd Club, the after-dark home of post-punk weirdness. Since he was as flamboyant as anyone on this new wave scene in both his outlandish dress sense (P-Funk goes witch doctor) and his musical tastes, Bam couldn't wait to play for them. In fact, he soon started dying his hair green and orange and wearing a mohawk (later, he would team up with Sex Pistol John Lydon for a single, 'World Destruction'). Make no mistake, Afrika Bambaataa was as punk rock as anyone in New York.

Hip hop and disco

Then there is disco. Musically, hip hop likes to set itself up in opposition to disco. The accepted wisdom is that hip hop was the ghetto's reaction to disco's gayness, its polish and its monotonous beat (all faults which today's hip hop folk are equally happy to ascribe to house). Actually, hip hop's debt to disco as a whole is high (just ask Def Jam mogul Russell Simmons, who was a regular at the Loft and Paradise Garage).

Boxing match – Tina Weymouth of Talking Heads and Tom Tom Club matches her boombox against Flash's, 1981.

In addition to funk, disco was the music the hip hop DJs played in the many years before the scene produced its own tunes. Compare playlists between the Roxy and the Paradise Garage and you'd find a huge number of the same records. You can't get much more disco than Chic's 'Good Times', a record deeply embedded in early hip hop, especially in Flash's career. Bambaataa's first hero was Kool DJ D, who played disco. Flash's earliest inspiration was Pete DJ Jones. Another influential mobile disco jock was Grandmaster Flowers, for whom Fab 5 Freddy has a particular affection. And that's not to mention the DJs like DJ Hollywood and Lovebug Starski, who were important to the development of rap but who were playing largely disco.

A striking parallel underlines the connection. The disco scene had actually developed a prototype version of the quick-mixing style before Flash even owned a pair of decks. Walter Gibbons was renowned for using quick cuts and two copies of the same record to extend favourite passages, and for favouring funky percussion-based tracks. Gibbons' style has often been compared to that of a hip hop DJ. He was doing all this around the same time as Flash, and in all likelihood he was even using some of the same records. Before Gibbons, Michael Cappello, too, had a reputation for working fast cuts and extending the lightning short intros of that era's songs. Even Francis Grasso, the granddaddy of them all, can claim that as early as 1969 he was picking out drum breaks to excite his dancefloor.

Finally, without disco it is unlikely that the hip hop scene would have discovered so many of its important vinyl oddities. 'The Mexican', a big Loft record long before it was a hip hop anthem, is a case in point, and there are many more. Bambaataa admits that many of his finds (including the all-important Kraftwerk) came about as a result of tips from the disco-based record pools he eagerly joined.

So, far from rejecting disco as some have suggested, the Bronx DJs simply reformulated it. Think of hip hop as an offshoot of early disco which then grew in parallel – a version of disco's dance revolution tailored to the tastes of the Bronx. The formula 'hip hop = disco + ghetto' isn't too far from the truth.

The end of the old school

Hip hop's first commercial flowerings came at the beginning of the eighties; by the middle of that decade, the music – and its culture – was developing into a very different thing. Though its horizon expanded and records streamed out, much of the original party spirit was fading. Blue and Freddy had taken hip hop on tour to Europe in 1982 and the music was beginning to make its presence felt, exerting influence on other genres. Breakdancing and graffiti were (over)exposed to the world in magazines and TV commercials. Round the corner, the next generation of rappers were honing their lyrics, ready to bring in the complexities of social commentary, hard-knocks reportage and character-filled fictions. Rap's first magnate Russell Simmons would soon spring Run DMC, Def Jam and his ruthless commercial instincts on the scene. KRS 1, Eric B and Rakim, Public Enemy, the Beastie Boys and LL Cool J weren't far behind, not to mention the west coast's gang-obsessed entry into hip hop.

But while the music was establishing itself, its backdrop changed. Many of the new stars had middle class suburban backgrounds, so the focus moved away from the inner city. Clubs like the Roxy closed or changed promoters and were soon violent ghetto outposts rather than happy melting pots. Reaganomics started biting hard, and crack made Bronx neighbourhoods into war zones. Things weren't as much fun as before. It was the end of the old school.

Through these changes, the DJs carried on doing what they knew. And of all the people involved in creating hip hop, it was the DJs who came off worst when the music became commercial. Once there were records to be produced and stars to be created, the spotlight was firmly on the visible and charismatic MC onstage, not on the guy behind the decks. MCs didn't need a DJ to make records, just a studio and a producer. Most of the first wave of rap records were made using session musicians rather than turntables, and fairly soon there was easy-to-use sampling technology which meant anyone could loop up a sample and recreate the effects of a quick-mixing DJ.

After the old school, the DJs who made names for themselves were mostly famous as producers rather than for playing records, even though this was the source of their skill. From Eric B and Marley Marl, through Pete Rock, Large Professor and Premier, to Dr Dre, the RZA and Prince Paul, to name just a few: these are all artists known for their studio work first and foremost. Hip hop moved decisively into the concert arena and became a performance spectacle more than a dancefloor genre. It maintained a thriving underground club scene, but there are very few hip hop DJs who have risen to fame through playing in clubs (with Funkmaster Flex and perhaps Stretch Armstrong as notable exceptions). Playing in concerts raised the DJ to the status of live musician, but reduced his input to a forty-minute showcase. And eventually there was the dreaded DAT to contend with – mistake-proof digital tapes which all but replaced DJs in live hip hop gigs.

But somehow, the DJ survived.

Turntablism

Hands whipping from one record to the other, stopping lightning fast on the crossfader in between, shoulders dipping slightly in time to the beat, but running no risk of unplanned movement, fingers moving in millimetre-precise formation, each flick or slide or rub controlled to a hair's breadth, and from the speakers a pounding beat with a barrage of 'skribbles and skratches' running in and out of it, the bare bones of a song repeated and repeated and repeated, then let go, dropping into the climax of another.

The hip hop DJ's skills were showy enough to be pursued as an end in themselves, and as the rapper and the DAT stole the attention from the DJ, this is exactly what happened. The essential elements of hip hop DJing were distilled until it became an art form almost completely detached from its original dancefloor function.

It all starts with the scratch. With this technique, instead of playing records, or even recognisable *parts* of records, the DJ was able to chop previously recorded music up so finely that he was manipulating *sounds* – discrete notes or beats or noises – to make compositions, just like any other musician. In the hands of a skilled 'turntablist', as these DJs eventually became known, the record deck became a genuine musical instrument. Indeed, with a recent surge of interest in this form of DJing, there are now several ensembles who play multiple turntables as bands – each DJ/musician laying down component basslines, rhythms and lines of melody until a whole song is constructed. Some have even created systems of turntablist musical notation.

'Manipulating sound with just your hand is like a miracle,' urges DJ Q-Bert of San Francisco's Invisibl Skratch Piklz crew, one of today's best-known scratch DJs. 'The basic root of scratching is that the turntable is a musical instrument: you're figuring out all these time signatures and rhythms and patterns and notes.'

Rob Swift of the X-Men (now, for superhero legal reasons, the X-ecutioners), another leading turntablist, agrees: 'With the turntable you can create your own rhythms and sounds. In other words, the turntable can adapt or mimic the violin, the drum, the guitar, the bass. The turntable can morph into almost any instrument. Out of the turntable you can coax high pitches, you can coax low pitches, there are notes involved. If you move the speed a certain way you can create slow noises and fast noises. There are so many things you can do with the turntable, it's definitely an instrument.'

At times, though, these scratch DJs seemed in danger of becoming obsessed hobbyists, vying with each other in increasingly esoteric competitions. What saved them from becoming completely isolated was that they were in a very real sense keeping alive the traditions of the 'old school' of hip hop pioneers. While hip hop culture was moving fast into the mainstream, the turntablist DJ was preserving the music's roots.

By showing off his tricks, the hip hop DJ retained his status as a star performer and preserved an important aspect of the old school: the battle. Back in the Bronx, the most skilled DJs had been like feudal champions, and even when hip hop left the park for the concert hall, a rap group would find time in their show for the DJ to flex his muscles. In later years, the competition between DJs was formalised in showcase events. DMC (Disco Mix Club), a British-based DJ organisation and the founders of dance magazine *Mixmag*, has been staging global competitions since 1987. The New Music Seminar (NMS), a New York music industry forum, ran a well-respected contest for many years. The International Turntablist Federation (ITF) is a more recent grass-roots collective with aims to gain 'industry awareness in the future and development of the turntable as a musical instrument'; its contest has been rapidly gaining ground since starting in 1996. These competitions, filled with fast-scratching demons showing off the latest techniques, have kept much of the music's original DJ-based spirit alive. And following a recent resurgence of instrumental hip hop, interest in scratch DJing is greater and more global than ever.

Turntablism (the name was actually coined as late as 1995) had been envisaged many years before hip hop's DJs made it a reality. The idea of playing recorded sound like an instrument has existed almost as long as sound recording itself.

French composer Pierre Schaeffer was the founding member of the avant-garde *musique concrète* school, which aimed to create music from natural sounds rather than with musical instruments. Through the forties and fifties, Schaeffer and his friends searched for new ways to record, play back and combine everyday sounds. Schaeffer experimented mainly with the new technology of magnetic tape, but he also messed around with turntables (he, of course, knew them as 'gramophones'). Using a group of record players and a series of specially cut discs containing various captured sounds (some of which had been looped), he would produce a musical performance by changing the discs and adjusting the speed and volume controls.

American avant-garde composer John Cage had envisioned turntablism even before Schaeffer. Cage, who wrote that 'Percussion music is revolution', had once performed a piece called 'Cartridge Music' that involved rubbing a gramophone cartridge against various unlikely things. And in 1937, in a speech to a Seattle arts society, he praised the wonders of record-playing technology in highly prescient terms,

'With a phonograph, it is now possible to control any one of these sounds and give to it rhythms within or beyond the reach of imagination. Given four phonographs, we can compose and perform a quartet for explosive motor, wind, heartbeat and landslide.'

Grand Wizard Theodore

Though they acknowledge these conceptual antecedents, turntablists trace their practical roots to hip hop's pioneer DJs, notably Grand Wizard Theodore, who, as we've seen, discovered the basic scratch noise – or at least figured that it could be used creatively – and Grandmaster Flash, who as well as exploring the possibilities of scratching started the craze for doing body tricks such as scratching with his elbow or using his belly to move the crossfader. There were in fact other, lesser-known DJs who came upon the idea of scratching, including a young spinner called DJ Tyrone who played the breaks for a mobile disco set-up of Cool DJ D. Tyrone, now all but forgotten, would do the simplest of scratching, just rocking the first beat of 'Apache' back and forth before starting the song, or catching a break on the beat and doing a few *zik-zak* scratches before letting it go again.

'That's all he would do,' recalls Zulu DJ Grandmixer D.ST. 'But it was so dope, because nobody ever did it before. That's all he did, but it was enough to go, "Ohhh, shit!" '

It is Grand Wizard Theodore, however, who most turntablists regard as their forefather. Theodore, surprisingly modest about his contributions, feels it was his adventurousness which set him apart.

'All the other DJs played music the same old way – "Bongo Rock" or "Dance To The Drummer's Beat", they played it the same way. I was like, "You gotta be different." That's why I started scratching and trying to do tricks with the records. It was so that people can look and say, "Wow! This guy's really into it; he's not just putting one record after another – he's actually giving us a show." '

D.ST is less reserved about Theodore's talents.

'He was phenomenal, and he was a prodigy. He was so skilled so young, it was ridiculous. It was effortless, his cutting ability. And remember he was a student of Flash, and Flash was a definite technician, but there was something about Theodore that made him different.'

He puts this down to Theodore's highly expressive style.

'Without opening his mouth, he was articulate. He was physically articulate, in his gestures, and in his ability to be so precise, and synchronise. The way he would physically move – it was an expression. It may be esoteric to most, but I understood what he was saying. I'm a DJ and it was a language that I understood.'

D.ST and 'Rockit'

D.ST would himself have an important role to play, showing that scratching could have a melodic as well as a purely rhythmic impact. Beginning his musical career as a drummer in local Bronx party bands, Derek Showard (named D.ST, or D.St. for the fact that he hung out on Manhattan's Delancey Street) had been a regular DJ at the Roxy.

'By that time I was off the hook,' he recalls. 'I was doing all kinds of crazy tricks and stunts. I did everything but blow up the turntable. I was running around the place, coming back and cutting on beat with no headphones on. Breakdancing, kicking the mixer, everything.'

Jean Karakos of electro label Celluloid hired him for a series of DJ gigs in Paris, and here D.ST's turntable dexterity brought him to the attention of jazz keyboardist Herbie Hancock and earned him pride of place in the grooves of Hancock's 1983 single, 'Rockit'.

This, more than any other track, was what propelled scratching into the world's consciousness. Aided by a great Godley & Creme video of sexy, robotic legs, it helped break MTV's de facto 'No black music' policy and was a very visible video hit, even if it only reached no.71 (it was no.8 in the UK).

And D.ST's contribution was central to the song. He was providing more than just a few flourishes: his scratches were proper rhythmic, melodic elements – *notes*. Based on ideas he had recorded previously on his own single 'Grand Mixer Cuts It Up', his scratching on 'Rockit' was a series of climactic manipulations of part of Fab 5 Freddy's record 'Une Sale Histoire (Change The Beat)'. As it wove expertly between the bassline and melody, D.ST's urgent, insistent vinyl percussion was the essence of the record. Judged as 1983's Best R&B Instrumental Performance, 'Rockit' also gave D.ST the honour of being the first DJ to win a Grammy.

Following 'Rockit', he was given a place in Hancock's band, both on tour and in the studio, but it took a long time for the other musicians to treat him as an equal. The penny didn't drop until during a rehearsal when they were badgering Hancock about a particular passage that actually D.ST had created.

'There was some trouble with the song, and they were asking Herbie – I think Herbie was just a little annoyed that day anyway – but they were saying, "Hey, Herbie, this part?" And he said, "Yo, man, don't ask me, ask *him*, he did the damn song." '

However, D.ST didn't feel fully accepted as an artist until veteran producer Quincy Jones paid him a visit. 'He took a chair, spun it around backwards and sat in front of me and said, "Go ahead, play." Just like that. And when I finished, he picked me up and gave me a bear hug, then it was official for me. He said, "That's some dope shit you doin', that shit is so bad, it's incredible." He said, "You playin' triplets. You playin' a lot of triplets." He was talking music. I was like, "Yeah, I play triplets." '

'Buffalo Gals'

Though 'Rockit', by virtue of its MTV visibility, was most people's introduction to scratching, two important scratch-based records had preceded it. Flash's 'Adventures On The Wheels Of Steel' was crucial, as we've noted earlier, but another record was more widely heard, at least in Britain, than even the Grandmaster's finest hour. Malcolm McLaren's 'Buffalo Gals', produced by Trevor Horn, reached no.9 in the UK chart in late 1982.

The infectious single was the first release from McLaren's album *Duck Rock*. A plundered collage based on a western square dance song by one Peyote Pete, McLaren's version showcased the hip hop sound he had heard in the Bronx, notably the scratching talents of the World's Famous Supreme Team.

By day the Supreme Team – Just Allah The Superstar and C Divine The Mastermind – were a pair of Times Square rogues; by night they became rapping black nationalist DJs on obscure uptown radio station WHBI. Without really knowing what their contribution would be, McLaren brought the duo over to London where, despite some expensive studio shenanigans, they proved to be the essential cement that brought together his sprawling project. When the album was released, McLaren included on the sleevenotes some brief instructions on how to breakdance, as well as this helpful introduction to scratching:

'The performance by the Supreme Team may require some explaining but suffice to say, they are DJs from New York City who have developed a technique using record players like instruments, replacing the power chord of the guitar by the needle of a gramophone, moving it manually backwards and forwards across the surface of a record. We call it "scratching".'

By the mid eighties, hip hop DJ techniques, and scratching in particular, had had a dramatic effect on record production and a rash of scratch-like techniques were being used, made extremely easy by the emergence of the sampler. In the US, Steinski, aka advertising copywriter Steve Stein, used the concept of scratching to produce a series of records built around arresting collages of sound. In the UK the scene was greatly energised by these new ideas and many followed suit. And although the over-use of stuttering, cut-up vocals served to date many a pop dance remix of the time, important new possibilities were becoming clear.

Scratching as a concept was so influential that its impact spread even beyond music. It is possible to see it in the graphic design of the period, and given the new affordability of video equipment at the time, we were even treated to the new 'art form' of video scratching, a precursor to TV's now ubiquitous fast-edits.

Transforming and beat-juggling

Turntablism's next big step came when a pair of Philadelphia DJs found that by cleverly manipulating the mixer's crossfader switch, a basic scratch could be chopped up in all sorts of new ways. 'Transforming', as this was called, made the scratch far more flexible and percussive, and gave the DJ more precise control over the sound. From here a whole vocabulary of techniques evolved.

Said to have been first practised by DJ Spinbad, also from Philly, transforming was perfected through heated competition between DJs Cash Money and Jazzy Jeff. Cash Money showcased the transform to great effect in 1988, winning the DMC world DJ championships in the process. Jazzy Jeff (DJ for the Fresh Prince, aka Hollywood golden boy Will Smith) was the first to put it on record, in 'The Magnificent Jazzy Jeff'.

'They brought out all these weird styles and ways of scratching that had never been done before,' explains Q-Bert. 'When transforming came out it just flipped the whole scratching world around.'

Today there is rarely anything like a simple scratch. A dedicated turntablist would be able to tell you the difference between the chirp, the tweak, the scribble, the tear, and the stab (or chop), not to mention the more advanced techniques of the transform – the hydroplane, the flare (a reverse transform), the orbit or the twiddle. The crab, a tricky technique which Q-Bert introduced in 1996, is worth describing to give an idea of the complexity involved in all this. To do a crab, your thumb pushes the crossfader to one side while your four fingers (of the same hand) each push it back momentarily to the other. And this is done in just a fraction of a second, while your other hand is doing something equally difficult with the actual record.

Now, if all this talk of scratching is making you itch, you might want to sit down . . . because in 1990 a whole new – *and even more complicated* – arena was opened up when 'beat juggling' was invented.

Beat juggling goes a step further than scratching. Instead of using a relatively long noise (a scratch) for your rhythm and cutting it up with the crossfader to make a percussion sound, you use a record's individual drum beats more or less intact, juggling them, as the name suggests, to construct new and untold percussion patterns.

Roc Raida, another of the X-Men/X-ecutioners, explains with deceptive simplicity: 'Beat juggling is taking two records, and just rearranging the beat.' He clicks on his gold-plated Technics (his prize as 1995 DMC world champion) and demonstrates. With a flurry of little jet-fast moves, he flicks around with two breakbeat records. The result is an impossibly complex pattern of improvised drumming; he seems to be able to put each beat exactly where he wants it. As if that isn't enough, he then speeds up the pattern in a ballistic sequence of funky syncopation and double beats. It sounds, of course, nothing like the original records. Without a doubt, this is an act of musical creativity.

Beat juggling was pioneered by 'The Cut Technician' Steve D, who introduced it at the NMS Superman battle for world supremacy in 1990, and his mentor 'The Cut Producer' Barry B from Doug E Fresh's Get Fresh crew. Roc remembers the astonishment it caused at the NMS competition. 'People were just fucked up, like all the judges that were on the panel. Like Ritchie Rich, DJ Scratch, all the popular DJs at that time were just fucked up. "Oaawww, what the *hell* is he doing?" ' Steve D won a hands-down victory and used his sudden notoriety to found the X-Men, for many years the pre-eminent scratch crew.

Beat juggling is really no more than a superfast version of the basic spinback techniques developed by Grandmaster Flash. The key move is the loop, in which a short drum pattern is repeated and repeated. The other important moves are the breakdown, a manual slowing down of a drum pattern whereby the DJ halts the record in between each beat; and the fill, where beats from a second record are added to the first to give double or triple beats or an echo effect. It's all reminiscent of the early days when one measure of a DJ's skill was how fast he could cut between two copies of Chic's 'Good Times'. D.ST remembers one of Herc's DJs, a guy named Imperial JC, who could catch it faster than anyone.

'JC was also the fastest out of everybody. Out of *everybody*. JC was the first person to go "Good . . . good . . . good . . . good . . ." with "Good Times". I got this fast: "Good times . . . good times . . . good times . . . good times . . ." I remember the first night I seen him do that and I went [*sharp intake of breath*] "I gotta go home and practise." '

Today's beat jugglers – who practise and practise and practise – can do even better. D.ST recalls judging a DJing competition alongside Flash, and the two being blown away by the phenomenal skills on show.

'I love to go to these new DJ battles and see these guys, 'cos now it's off the hook!' he enthuses. 'To actually know that you have inspired a genre, a whole movement... I look at these guys and I think, "We started that shit." It's incredible what these guys took from us, and there's no end to it.'

Turntablism seems to be finally shedding its image as a cryptic cult. All-turntable crews such as the Invisibl Skratch Piklz, the X-ecutioners and the UK's Scratch Perverts are performing as bands and the emphasis seems finally to be on what the finished product sounds like, rather than how many zillion flicks of the wrist a DJ can manage.

As Q-Bert puts it: 'Before, when it was just a baby, it couldn't express itself in too many ways. You couldn't have a whole album of just the same baby talk. But now it's maturing. It's twenty years old, I guess it's becoming of legal age, so there's a lot more intelligence put into it, it's got much more of an intellectual life to it now, it can express itself in many more ways.'

Digging

Another arena of DJ competition taken to new heights is crate digging, the DJ's endless search for funky breaks that no one else knows about. DJ Shadow (Josh Davis) led the way for a new breed of DJ by building a whole recording career entirely from existing records. Shadow will happily spend days in cellars below the Mason-Dixon line searching for rare and unusual vinyl.

As a kid, he collected comic books. 'I have a collector gene in my blood. I suppose in some ways, it's obsessive compulsive,' he admits. 'But I have this fear that one day I won't be able to bring records in through the door any more. You know used record stores *are* closing down. So I want to make sure I'm not caught playing the last record and I don't have *any* more new records to play.'

It was natural that once every Meters' album had been wrung dry and James Brown had been sampled to within an inch of his pompadour, DJs and producers would turn their attention to the rest of the world. These days anything is fair game, from Turkish pop records, Indian disco and, of course, funk 45s, the basic tool of the hip hop producer. For the DJ the motivation is clear – to look for records no one else has. For the DJ/producer there's also money to be made. Hip hop is now a billion-dollar industry and the best breaks and rarest records come at a premium. In the summer of 2005 (in what may or may not have been a publicity stunt), it was widely reported that rapper Nas had paid production duo the Neptunes $2 million for a beat.

Even without these motivations, there's something aggressively addictive about the search for rare vinyl. 'You're constantly looking for the best record ever, that you've never heard before,' says northern soul collector Guy Hennigan. 'But you don't want to find it, because once you've got it you haven't got the best record in the world,' he laughs. 'I have a backing track I'm looking for which is my main aim, ever, and I hope I never find it. But I hope nobody else does. If anybody else gets it I'll just fuckin' spit.'

The most obsessed diggers will go to any length to find elusive tunes. Convinced there was rare US vinyl to find, Hennigan rushed to Vietnam straight after the war, the first week that travel restrictions were lifted. 'I was rooting about in snakes in this fuckin' cellar. You'd chuck a chicken down for the snake occasionally.' He didn't find anything.

Collector Keb Darge deliberately brought the maniacal acquisitiveness of his first passion, northern soul, to the funk scene. 'If you didn't bring it in you'd be playing the same old shite and it would become a revival scene,' he argues. 'It's exactly the same as northern. They need new records, new discoveries.' The market in funk 45s has rocketed thanks to the digging exploits of DJ/collectors like Shadow and Darge. In 2004 a collector in Essex paid a staggering $4,293 for Arthur Monday's 'What Goes Around Comes Around', an excruciatingly rare (but rather average) funk 45.

Digging goes back to the noble role of the DJ as a record promoter and musical evangelist, rescuing forgotten songs by never-heard artists or long-forgotten producers, maybe putting them in a mix or on a compilation so this lost music can live again. Digging can even help resurrect an artist's career, as happened for David Axelrod, or shine a light on forgotten albums, as the Finders Keepers label did with Jean-Claude Vannier's *L'Enfant Assassin Des Mouches* or Motel did with their reissue of Gary Wilson's privately pressed (and fantastic) *You Think You Really Know Me*.

DJ Shadow considers it urban archaeology. 'Sometimes, looking through records in a unique place in the country or in the world, there is an electrical charge that I get. You feel like you're doing something noble.' Who knows what amazing music lies utterly forgotten to the world? Who else but an obsessed DJ would try to rescue it? 'There've been basements where there are rats running around, water seeping in from the Michigan River and you're knee deep in it and you're just sitting there thinking, "shit, this is my one shot to get in here and rescue stuff."'

Thirty years of hip hop

When it first came to mainstream attention, most people wrote hip hop off as nothing more than a novelty. Hardly anyone, even those on the scene, thought it would grow into an enduring influence on the world's music. Richard Grabel was one of the few believers. When he started writing about hip hop in 1979, he saw in it a formidable depth of commitment and musical understanding.

'Part of it was being able to see the dedication that these kids had,' he recalls. 'You'd see them coming to the Negril to breakdance and they had really practised. You'd see Bambaataa or Flash come and do a DJ set and it was obvious that it wasn't something they'd just thrown together. The crates of records that they were lugging down to these clubs spoke of a real collector's and connoisseur's knowledge of music that was deep, and wide. Hearing those DJs made me think, "Wow, it's not just throw your hands in the air and let's throw a party". These guys really had a deep knowledge of musical history.'

In 2006, hip hop is the dominant force in music. It overtook America's next biggest-selling genre – country – seven years ago, with sales of eighty-one million CDs, tapes and albums. It's a thoroughly international form today, and rapping can be heard in just about any language. Nigeria is producing some great tunes; in New Zealand, Maori rap is a potent force. Once it left the US hip hop found its greatest echo in France, where the curling lyrical panache of French made this offshoot altogether distinct. Bred in the ghettoes of *les banlieus* around Paris, French kids of African descent like MC Solaar and the charmingly named Nique Ta Mère (Fuck Your Mother) showed what could be done with a bag full of beats and a head full of rage.

Beyond music, hip hop's vast cultural influence can be seen

throughout the world in the fashions it has spawned, and the way it made black American English a global vernacular. In the mid eighties, Cornell West, one of many sociologists intrigued by hip hop's rise, asked himself, 'Where will rap end up?' His answer was telling: 'Where most post-modern American products end up: highly packaged, regulated, distributed, circulated and consumed.'

Such is hip hop's mastery of marketing that its current kingpin, Sean 'P-Diddy' Combs of Bad Boy Records, seems able to have hits in his sleep; most of them cynical karaoke-style remakes of tried and trusted pop hits with the latest ghetto sensation rapping over the top. Amazingly, despite having no studio experience, Puffy became the world's highest paid remixer overnight, simply because of the selling power of his name and his unapologetically commercial ear. He personifies the crass materialism that has infused hip hop (a result, no doubt, of thirty years of escalating bragging), but he has an undeniable insight into the business of music.

Giving his impression of hip hop's cultural power, he told *Time* magazine, 'In five years, if Master P and I were to endorse a presidential candidate, we could turn an election. Hip hop is that deep.' Will Smith, whose star rose as pop-rapper the Fresh Prince, might take hip hop even further – William Hill are currently offering odds of 100-1 on him as the first black US president.

All this from just two turntables and a crate of your mom and pop's old records.

ELEVEN
US GARAGE

I'll Take You To Paradise

'I'm not a fan of disco. I find it mindbending . . . It's a contributing factor to epilepsy. It's the biggest destructor in history in education. It's a jungle cult. It's what the Watusis do to whip up a war. What I've seen in the discos with people jogging away is just what I've seen in the bush.'

— Harvey Ward, director general of the
Rhodesian Broadcasting Company

'I know that it is not one record that makes a night, it's the combination of all things together that leaves the person satisfied.'

— Larry Levan

Homer Simpson once confessed that few songs had moved him as much as Lipps Inc's 'Funkytown'. However, when the eighties dawned, he happily applied a 'DISCO SUCKS' bumper sticker to his car. Homer sums up the mainstream's engagement with disco. Its brief crossover pop phase gave people songs they would hum forever, but as a style of music, few saw it as more than a glittery craze that had outstayed its welcome.

In Chicago, radio DJ Steve Dahl hated disco so much he raised a 'disco destruction army' and mobilised it to attack disco wherever possible. His followers rallied around the overtly homophobic 'Disco Sucks' slogan and fought the evil faggot music by haranguing club DJs whenever it was played. 'Disco music is a disease. I call it disco dystrophy,' Dahl ranted over the airwaves. 'The people victimised by this killer disease walk around like zombies. We must do everything possible to stop the spread of this plague.'

One stunt saw Dahl – who had quit radio station WDAI in disgust when it switched to an all-disco format – giving away a hundred tickets to a Village People concert provided the recipients took marshmallows bearing the words 'Disco Sucks' to throw at the band. Dahl's greatest moment came on 12 July 1979 when he whipped up thousands of baseball fans into a full-scale anti-disco riot resulting in injuries and arrests. A joint promotion between Dahl's all-rock station WLUP and the Chicago White Sox, his 'disco demolition' rally at the team's Comiskey Park was centred around giving fans reduced admission to a double-header against the Detroit Tigers in exchange for depositing a disco record at the turnstile. More than 10,000 discs were collected and then at half-time blown up inside a container in the centre of the field. Middle America's anti-disco feeling couldn't have been made clearer as a violent crowd invasion ensued, with chanting protesters fighting, starting fires and digging up turf. Police failed to restore order in time for the second game and the White Sox forfeited it.

Dahl's campaigning was far from unique. Dislike for disco was everywhere. The rock generation saw it as the antithesis of all that was holy: no visible musicians, no 'real' stars, no 'live' performances. It was music based wholly on consumption, music with no aesthetic purpose, indeed with no purpose at all other than making your body twitch involuntarily. Dehumanising, expressionless, content-less – the judgements were damning.

'Kill Disco' became a popular piece of graffiti. New York's WXLO held 'No Disco Weekend'. Pasadena DJ Darryl Wayne made his show's motto 'Abolish disco in our lifetime,' and took calls from listeners suggesting how this could be done. 'Cut off the Bee Gees' oestrogen supply' was one idea. All over the world, the disco menace was confronted; right-wing Americans denounced it as morally degraded and probably a form of communist mind control; communist countries banned it as decadent and capitalist. Perhaps the most bizarre expression of anti-disco sentiment came from Turkey, where scientists at the University of Ankara proved that listening to disco turned pigs deaf and made mice homosexual.

Given the depth of this backlash, it's hardly surprising that the story of popular music has been largely revised to disavow its debt to disco. This often has to do with lamentable homophobia, but usually it is because those writing the history, like their readers, equate the genre with the overexposure of a few whitewashed and commercialised acts, and are ignorant of many of the artists and much of the music which either came before or lay beneath such acts. If you wanted to sum up the spiritually powerful (and highly influential) dance music which rocked clubs like the Loft or the Gallery, you might talk about MFSB, Chaka Khan or Eddie Kendricks, or a host of lesser-known names who created raw, earthy and uplifting disco; you certainly wouldn't leap to mention Donna Summer, KC & the Sunshine Band, the Village People or (of all people) Abba. The poppy, flat-footed rhythms of disco's most formulaic moments might be what most people remember, but they should hardly be seen as exemplary.

Indeed, reports of disco's death were always greatly exaggerated. Its brief commercial era may have ended in dramatic collapse, but the music that originally drove the scene remained alive and reasonably well and has been with us ever since. Such global forms as house and techno are really nothing more than disco continued by other means. Disco simply underwent some cosmetic enhancements, changed its name a couple of times, and had its mail forwarded to a less glitzy neighbourhood.

From disco's ashes

In the early eighties – in keeping with the well-worn dialectics of nightlife – as the wealthy and celebrated left the clubs, the young and unsung flooded into their place. In New York, the gay dancefloors which had produced disco began to project a new underground vitality, as did the straight black and 'ethnic' (the city's racial code for Italian and Hispanic) places where the city's Latin music flourished alongside the newer forms of hip hop and electro. The DJs in these clubs were suddenly producers and remixers; they now had the power not just to tailor their music live for their dancefloor, but to record original material and have it released commercially. With the support of a growing network of independent dance labels and with the inevitable attention of key radio DJs, they could even use their clubs to push records (including their own) into the mainstream charts. The DJ had proved he knew more than anyone about making dance music. Now, thanks to the structures set up during disco, he could increasingly put this expertise into practice.

The other crucial developments were technological. As the silicon revolution brought studio equipment crashing down in both size and price, the leap from DJing to producing was narrowed even further. And in the first half of the eighties, eager to nourish their dancefloors with something new, a generation of young jocks jumped this line. Several proved to be so innovative, both behind the decks and in the studio, they would later be credited with kick-starting entirely new genres of music. A focus on disco's fastest, campest elements created hi-energy; Chicago's attempts to preserve disco would give us house; in Detroit the eager adoption of electronic instruments would forge techno, with a similar futurism in Chicago giving rise to acid house. Though each took a dramatically different set of chromosomes from its mother, all were born from disco's broad hips. As the age of the DJ/producer began in earnest, dance music entered one of its most fertile periods.

After Bambaataa and the Zulus' Roxy years, the raucous sounds of hip hop and electro were incubated, together with the city's Latin dance sounds, in a vast New York club called the Funhouse. Here a cult of personality emerged around a young Hispanic DJ, John 'Jellybean'

Benitez, who would become a star remixer and the first DJ to sign a major label album deal as an artist in his own right. Meanwhile, over at Danceteria, Mark Kamins, Johnny Dynell and Anita Sarko exerted a considerable influence on the city's music as they exposed it to the freaky sounds of European post-punk funk and American new wave (Kamins also steered the young Madonna into a record contract).

And in New Jersey, Tony Humphries was championing the more soul- and gospel-influenced side of disco's remnants and planting the roots of what would become known as the Jersey sound, or – courtesy of a slight misnomer by British journalists – as garage.

Larry Levan and the Paradise Garage

One club more than any other paved the way for disco's many offspring to take their first steps: New York's Paradise Garage. Open from 1977 to 1987, the Garage was the crucial link between disco and the musical forms which evolved from it.

Here a young DJ, Larry Levan, exemplified his profession's new possibilities – consolidating the club DJ's new role as producer, remixer and commercially powerful tastemaker. Levan showed just how much creative control a DJ could exercise, and with one of the most devoted and energetic groups of clubbers ever, used the Garage to preserve and amplify much of disco's original underground spirit. In doing this he carved out an oasis of shared pleasure in a city that was becoming increasingly ruthless, and grew to enjoy such a passionate relationship with the people on his dancefloor that they worshipped him more or less as a god. The Garage sound system is reckoned by many to have been the greatest of them all. Elements of the club have been carefully copied by many which came after it. It even has a genre of music named after it. Today, Larry Levan is regularly hailed as the world's greatest ever DJ and his club elevated to mythic status whenever it is mentioned.

'This is the Paradise Garage in a nutshell,' says New York DJ Johnny Dynell. 'One night, Chi Chi, my wife, was bartending at the Garage. And, having worked at Danceteria doing the same, she couldn't believe it when she saw these boys making everything so clean. They would take the garbage out and then wash and scrub the garbage can, then dry it, and put a new garbage bag in. She was in awe at the *love* these kids showed that garbage can. Because to these kids, it's the temple. It's sacred. This isn't just a garbage can, this is a garbage can *at the Garage*. It's very Old Testament. And for everyone there, it really was the temple. It was sacred ground.'

The Paradise Garage inspired an unparalleled reverence. It dominated gay New York's dance vista for a full decade, with only the Saint – which catered for a very different crowd – as a serious rival. For its members, the

Garage was a sanctuary from an increasingly cruel and voracious city, a role made more poignantly necessary as AIDS's viral vapour trail drifted over New York. Dance there and you were treated as an honoured guest, with a level of courtesy and respect that is virtually unheard of in clubs today. 'You felt special,' says Danny Tenaglia, one of many DJs inspired by early visits to the Garage. 'You felt like you were an elite group, with people who were on the same level of understanding about music as you.' Here was a private world based on disco's original ethos of loving equality. In stark contrast to the harsh city lights outside, the Garage represented freedom, compassion and brotherhood. It was as much community centre as discothèque.

Dave Piccioni, owner of London's Black Market records, then living and DJing in New York, was a regular at the Garage in the late eighties. 'It was New York cut-throat money time,' he remembers. 'Everybody was sticking knives in each other's backs. It was dog eat dog. Aggressive. Dealing, sixty thousand people living on the street. It was a dog of a place to live in. And then you'd go to this little oasis, where people were really well-mannered and friendly to each other. You just felt completely comfortable. People who shared something, and that was an open mind. America is a very narrow-minded place. The thing they had in common wasn't just getting high, like it is here – it was much more than that.'

Whether the club's central figure, Larry Levan, was really the greatest DJ ever is irrelevant. What's more important is that he acted as the central inspiration for almost every DJ above the age of thirty in New York, many of whom are now titans of dance music. David Morales, Danny Tenaglia, Cevin Fisher, Junior Vasquez, Danny Krivit, Kenny Carpenter, François Kevorkian, Joe Clausell – they all readily acknowledge their debt to Larry Levan.

Junior Vasquez built his whole career on following the lead he set.

'I idolised Larry,' he says. 'I still do to this day, he was the greatest. And I do live in the past when it comes to that, and I keep striving, wanting to create that feeling, that lounge, that booth.' Junior's Sound Factory was a conscious copy of the Garage and at its best came close to the same feelings of community. When the Factory first opened, the Garage's illuminated sign was hung over the entrance (a rather presumptuous move which was quickly stamped on by irate Garage-heads). The Shelter, later Vinyl, home of the well-known Body & Soul nights, was another club founded more or less wholly on preserving memories of the Paradise Garage.

Garage lore has been made more enduring by the fact that Levan died at the tragically young age of thirty-eight, after suffering heart failure (he had a life-long heart condition, though his legend-affirming drug habit can't have helped). Music mythology loves nothing more than a good-looking corpse, which lends Danny Tenaglia's description of Levan as the 'Jimi Hendrix of dance music' yet more aching resonance.

Reade Street

Larry Levan was born Lawrence Philpot on 21 July 1954 in Brooklyn. By his teens he had started to make the magical trek across the East River to Manhattan with his boyhood friend from the Bronx, Frankie Knuckles. The pair, both black and gay, were a perfect yin and yang – Levan excitable, childlike, eccentric, Knuckles laid-back, personable, *nice*. After they'd worked together at the Gallery and then, as DJs, at the Continental Baths, Knuckles moved on to Chicago, where he catalysed house music. Levan moved first to the Soho Place then to the Garage prototype, Reade Street.

The two-floor warehouse space at 143 Reade Street was one of many clubs that had sprung from the idealism of David Mancuso's Loft. Levan was invited to spin there by its owner Michael Brody. This is where the seeds of the Paradise Garage were sown. It was also, according to those who went, even better than the Garage.

Like the Garage, Reade Street was a predominantly black club, with a clientele that comprised everyone from telephone operators, to dancers from local ballet company Alvin Ailey's, to singers on downtime like Teddy Pendergrass, Rick James and Chaka Khan. It was almost exclusively gay. The top floor was a cavernous loft space, with balloons, gently pulsing lights and a gigantic silk parachute draped above the dancefloor. At the end of each Saturday, balloons would be released from above and cascade on the dancers below. It was post-gay rights but pre-AIDS; it followed the Loft and anticipated the Garage. Everything came together perfectly and for a brief disco moment, Reade Street was the place to be.

'The punch was always spiked,' chuckles clubber Yvon Leybold. 'Someone was always passing a joint around. Somebody's passing around the opium pipe. Somebody's handing out the blotter. It was very free and open. I remember going there dancing *topless*. It was hot in there, but it was so much fun that *you wanted* to take your clothes off. I even remember having sex there a couple of times!'

Reade Street finally closed in the early summer of 1976, after the fire department had made one too many visits. Michael Brody and Larry Levan's next venture, in tandem with sound man Richard Long and aided by Brody's lover, West End Records' Mel Cheren, would be a much more professional affair.

The Garage

Walking up the darkened ramp, with tiny flickering egg-strobes running down each side, was like heading along a darkened runway – with the lift-off chemically, rather than mechanically, provided. Inside there was an alcohol-free bar decorated with murals of Greek and Trojan warriors locked in battle, from where you could catch a tantalising glimpse into the huge DJ booth, plus changing rooms, a cinema – through which you could ascend to a roof garden – and a giant, relatively spartan dancefloor. The Paradise Garage was in an old parking garage at 84 King Street in west SoHo. It opened in January 1977 with a series of 'construction parties'. Members were invited to dress as workmen and dance in what was nothing more than a raw space with an amazing sound system. Slowly the club began to take shape – and as it grew, so did Levan's reputation.

Larry Levan's greatness is proof that technical prowess is but a tiny part of DJing. Technically speaking, he was no match for the likes of Walter Gibbons or, indeed, most of the early disco DJs. His mixing was slapdash, and he'd often prefer to slam something in awkwardly rather than seamlessly blend. What made him great was his obsessive control of all aspects of his clubbers' experience and his heightened ability to transmit his personality and his mood through the very grooves of his records.

Unquestionably, Siano and Mancuso were his main inspiration (he'd had brief affairs with each) and in the early years it was possible to trace each of Levan's records back to either the Loft or Gallery. But he never hid his obvious debt to his forebears. 'Nicky Siano, David Mancuso, Steve D'Acquisto and Michael Cappello, David Rodriguez,' Levan told Steven Harvey. 'This is the school of DJs I come from.'

He had a fierce controlling instinct, as well as a self-destructive streak that manifested itself in tireless drug abuse. This lent the Paradise Garage an aura of intense drama. And thanks to his different club jobs – from spiking the punch at the Gallery to doing the lights at the Continental Baths – he understood how to make a visit to his nightclub a total experience. He was also a dazzling sound man, and the crystalline system, although constructed by Richard Long, was honed, manipulated, tweaked and *loved* by Levan.

Each week was a lesson in improvisation, an unscripted performance on the emotional level of high opera. What would be served up on a particular night depended on any number of variants. He could shock you. He could thrill you. He could amaze you. He could even appal you. The only certainty was that he would surprise you.

David Morales, who was lucky enough to play at the Garage as a young DJ, says Levan's mood swings were dramatic. 'He could be *shit* for seven hours and he could take fifteen minutes and kick the shit out of you, and that made your night! That's what it was about. There was nobody that was able to do that.'

Levan could drive dancers wild with desire or work them into a fury of frustration, often on the same night. Sometimes he would simply disappear from the booth. Occasionally, he would play an hour of dub reggae, or the same record three times in succession. Once (while sitting on a rocking horse), he had the whole club dancing to nothing more than a few of his live keyboard doodles, unaware that the record he was accompanying had finished minutes ago. Occasionally he would collapse in a stupor; somehow always managing to keep the party – if not himself – going. François Kevorkian, a regular guest DJ there, remembers him once putting on a movie instead of music. 'What are you gonna do? There's two-and-a-half-thousand people there and you suddenly play *Altered States*. That's the kind of freedom that I think people need to know exists.'

'He had *attitude*,' remembers Cevin Fisher, another DJ/producer whose formative years were spent on the floor at King Street. 'He would leave the DJ booth and the record would end and just spin around. Who knows what he was off doing . . . Actually, we all know what he was doing! And he would come back into the DJ booth totally trashed, lift the needle off the record and start it again. People got off on that.'

Although the Garage had a very talented light man in Robert DaSilva – who had also worked the lights at the Gallery and Studio 54 – Levan had a second set of controls fitted on a rail along the top of the booth. When the mood took him – when he was ready to take people for a *ride* – he would draw the console towards him and decant the booth of its occupants. It was like clearing the flight deck for take-off.

'They used to do these blackouts and they would switch *all* of the lights out,' recalls Johnny Dynell. 'Exit lights and everything. Totally illegal, you can't turn exit lights out! You couldn't see a hand in front of your face.' He would build the intensity to a peak and then let fly with an acappella or sound effect – one time Dynell recalls him playing 'The Wizard Of Oz' – before the system would crank up and . . . BAM! . . . he'd hit the crowd with another favourite. 'Oh, man, it was fabulous. He would just take control,' sighs Dynell.

This was a club poured full of love and devotion. 'I feel like I'm part of something important when I come to the Garage, a nightly musical happening,' comments Robert, a Garage regular, in the book *Nightlife*. 'The songs Larry plays are so new, so different from what's going on in other clubs. I know when I come to dance here that I'm hearing songs that very few people outside the Garage, even in New York City, have heard yet.'

Happy as Larry – inside the booth at the Paradise Garage with its loving driver Larry Levan, 1986.   (© Tina Paul)

Levan's life revolved around the Garage. When it first opened he even lived there, a fact which drove Michael Brody to distraction. During the day, Levan's coterie would assemble at King Street and hang out, do drugs, play on that pristine system and roller-skate around the dancefloor. Johnny Dynell recalls receiving DJing lessons from him during these languid afternoons; Levan, conscious of the lineage from which he'd sprung, was keen to pass on disco's traditions. 'You don't realise how much power you've got up there,' he would tell Dynell, pointing up at the DJ booth.

On Friday and Saturday evenings, this took on the role of private party zone. 'The Garage had a very social DJ booth,' recalls Krivit. 'It was huge; like another club in itself. There was a real scene going on there. You were right above the dancefloor and you'd get the whole feeling of the crowd. The light show, everything.' Boy George wrote about the scene in his autobiography *Take It Like A Man*. 'We made friends with DJ Larry Levan and hung out with him in the booth overlooking the dancefloor. That's where all the drugs were. I took my first line of coke in that dark disco cocoon.'

George also recalls how democratic it was. 'I remember being in there one night and seeing Diana Ross saunter in wearing a fur coat, drop it to the floor, dance around and then leave. It was just like . . . it was all about the music.'

Record promoter Bobby Shaw tells of a time when he brought Prince to the club. '1999' was coming out and the purple one sat in silence waiting to hear his new record on the Garage's monster system. Levan left him sweating for over an hour without playing the track. 'So I said to Larry, "We're leaving" and he played an hour's worth of Prince stuff.'

The power behind the myth

'The Larry legend is beyond any reason; it feeds on itself to some extent,' suggests critic Vince Aletti. Dave Piccioni is equally sceptical. 'I hate this shit that just because someone dies, they have this mythology that grows around them. If he was alive now, he'd probably be playing the same stuff that Tony Humphries plays.'

Many have criticised Levan's technique – or at least his consistency. 'Larry was awful, he was too loud, he'd leave big gaps and let records jump, he'd play ballads in the middle of the night,' said DJ Bruce Forest, one of Levan's contemporaries. 'But that was only five per cent of it. On the other hand, he had an atmosphere nobody will achieve ever again. He made it seem like he was playing records to you in his living room. His rapport with the crowd was immense. If you went to the club one week and a light bulb was red and the next week when you returned it was blue, people would say, "Larry changed the bulb this week." '

Nicky Siano, never a DJ to restrain the energy of his dancers, feels that Levan could be a little *too* controlling at times. 'If I saw it getting out of hand on the dancefloor, I would think, "Oh, this is cool, show me how I can go further than this." That would scare Larry. He would try to bring it back. My thing was [*Siano laughs uproariously*] – *out of control!*'

And clubbers Yvon Leybold and Terry Hayden insist that Levan's previous club was far superior. Things were never really the same once AIDS cast its dark shadow. The abandon and freedom they'd experienced at Reade Street would never be recaptured.

'Don't misunderstand me,' says Leybold, 'the Garage was a nice place – for the lack of having anywhere else to go – but it was certainly no Reade Street.'

'The Garage was more focused on making money,' adds Hayden.

In truth, Larry Levan's prominence derived from several sources besides his DJing. Doubtless, much came from the greatness of his club – the fact that it recreated the generosity and intimacy of Mancuso's Loft, but on such a vast scale. In both 1979 and 1980, the *Billboard* Disco Convention voted the Paradise Garage best club and best sound system. 'There's nothing else that will remotely compare to what the Garage was,' says François Kevorkian. 'He understood everything about what the Loft did, but very quickly took it beyond all that into his own domain. I think what Larry did was nothing short of absolutely astounding.'

And his friendship with radio DJ Frankie Crocker at WBLS gave him influence unprecedented for a club DJ. 'At that point it was *the* radio station and he was *the* big disc jockey. So Larry became incredibly important,' explains Vince Aletti. 'Beyond the fact that he was a good disc jockey and he had a great club, he had the ear of the most important radio disc jockey in the city.' Both were mavericks, kindred spirits. 'Larry was the only really successful black DJ, so they became friends, I think, because of the race issue,' says Nicky Siano. In stark contrast to the notoriously ponderous pace of American radio programming, Crocker was swift in bringing records to the airwaves.

'He used to just steal the record right off Larry's plates,' laughs record promoter Bobby Shaw. 'If you got a record played at the Garage on Friday or Saturday night, there was a very good chance that Monday at four o'clock it was gonna be on the air on WBLS.'

Frankie Crocker was no ordinary radio hack. Born in Buffalo in upstate New York (a city that produced many great black radio DJs, including Eddie O'Jay and Gary Byrd), he got his first break on Pittsburgh's WZUM and moved swiftly to WWRL in New York. Here, with his racy patter and throaty velvet delivery, he built up a considerable female following. Oozing out of the speakers like golden syrup, he was the airwaves' equivalent of Barry White, and known variously as 'Lover Man', 'Fast Frankie', 'Chief Rocker' and 'Hollywood'. Crocker became one of the first DJs to cross radio's colour line when he joined the all-white 'Good Guys' team on WMCA in 1969. But it was at WBLS in the seventies where he had his most successful reign, championing the jazz-fusion of Grover Washington Jr and Miles Davis, and the socially conscious soul of Donny Hathaway and Marvin Gaye, as well as incorporating white groups like the Bee Gees and Queen into his playlists.

Levan naturally shot to the top of the list of DJs when it came to receiving new product. One record promoter pointed out, 'He's someone to whom top record industry people hand-deliver new albums. When a record goes here, we know we've got a hit.'

The Garage's power was equally apparent in its effect on the local record trade. In late 1978 a husband-and-wife team, Charlie and Debbie Grappone, opened a compact little rock music store called Vinylmania on Carmine Street in Greenwich Village. It happened to be just around the corner from the Paradise Garage and Grappone soon noticed the bedraggled hordes streaming towards the subway each Saturday morning. People started asking for strange records that Grappone – who prided himself on his knowledge of music – had never heard of, the stuff 'that Larry played'.

As soon as they could, the Grappones opened a dance music shop next door to their rock store. They were the first retailers to capitalise on the desirability of 12-inch singles, especially the new promo-only releases aimed at club DJs. They recruited two Garage devotees, Judy Russell and Manny Lehman, and once the store began to orientate its stock towards the Garage, sales went through the roof.

'You should've seen Saturday morning,' says Grappone in his Brooklyn drawl. 'Thirty-five, forty, fifty people *waitin'* for me to get there. I'd open up the door and Manny would put somethin' on, because Manny had been *there* the night before. "Shit! That's what he played last night." We'd sell sixty copies of a record between ten and eleven in the morning. *Sixty copies!'* The crowds were unbelievable. 'You would look in the store and think there was something wrong. There was guys crushed. *Crushed!'* The store would sell hundreds of copies of Garage favourites. 'Larry was the king,' grins Grappone. 'If Larry played the record, it was going to sell at Vinylmania.'

One such record was 'Heartbeat' by Taana Gardner. Originally produced by Kenton Nix for West End Records, it was remixed by Levan and broken at the Garage. 'Heartbeat' was an oddball song, with a slow, capricious tempo, dizzy vocal delivery and off-key accompaniment. The first time Levan played it, the reaction was not favourable. 'When "Heartbeat" came out there wasn't hip hop on the radio like there is today,' recalls Danny Krivit. 'There wasn't any downtempo music like that. And when he put that record on, a full club of people left the room to get food. There was not one person left on the floor.' But Levan persisted, often playing it several times in an evening. Soon people would run to the floor when it was aired. 'By the end of the month, there was no one left *off* the floor when they played that record,' says Krivit. 'And now, of course, they had to go to Vinylmania and bug Charlie for it.' Vinylmania went on to sell over 5,000 copies of 'Heartbeat'. It's still their biggest-selling record.

The music of the Paradise Garage

The Garage opened in 1977, just before *Saturday Night Fever* consigned disco to mainstream boom and bust. After its crash, DJs had to search that little bit harder to find records to feed their ever hungry dancefloors. No one did this more resourcefully than Larry Levan, who played all styles and tempos and showed that in the wake of disco there was a whole world of possibilities. The Garage was Rough Trade obscurities as much as Salsoul classics; weird electronic oddities as much as soul, rap and funk; Yazoo as much as Loleatta Holloway; Jah Wobble, Talking Heads, Marianne Faithfull and Ian Dury as much as MFSB and Gwen Guthrie. That all of this converged so effectively is testament to Levan's forceful personality. 'Garage music was kind of breaking the rules,' says DJ Danny Krivit. 'It was what he felt like playing. It was really about having no boundaries.'

Levan took this to extremes and, as a determined manipulator of his clubbers' tastes foisted on them unusual, sometimes bizarre records, making them work through his immense force of will. One such record was Yoko Ono's sonic sonnet, 'Walking On Thin Ice'. A rock mantra in which Yoko's dissonant far-eastern wail weaves around a wall of heavy percussion, it was the song John Lennon had been working on the night he was murdered. Levan loved it.

When Johnny Dynell DJed at Sean Lennon's tenth birthday party, he told Ono about her new-found popularity among the dancers of downtown Manhattan. He even took her down to the Garage one night. 'It was a big thing for Yoko to see all these black kids dancing to her record,' he says. 'But she loved it. I think she went back a few times, too.'

Levan's willingness to go against the grain meant he would just as easily champion a commercial record as he would the most obscure underground cut. Dave Piccioni remembers him playing 'Fascinated' by Company B, a real electro-pop commercial record. 'It was tacky in the extreme. But, fuck me, he played that for twenty or twenty-five minutes and you could not help but get into it. He thought, "I like this record and it's gonna sound great in the club, and I don't really care if you like it or not." And he got away with it because he had talent and creativity.'

Another example was Pat Benatar's 'Love Is A Battlefield', one of several extremely unlikely Garage anthems. 'Someone said he could never play that there,' chuckles Danny Krivit. 'That was reason enough for him to play it – and make it happen, too.'

Freaky disco

As the eighties dawned there were hectic collisions of music genres. Hip hop and electro were blossoming onto record, new wave was rising from punk's corpse, quirky electronic disco was bubbling around, and around the time of Bob Marley's passing in 1981, reggae was about as popular as it would ever get in Gotham City. When Larry Levan began to express his renowned eclecticism in remixes and productions, this culture clash sensibility was set in vinyl.

'If you could see my collection, you'd know I like all music – you'd think it belonged to four different DJs,' he explained. 'And because of this, I found myself taking things from here, from there – reggae, pop, disco, jazz, blues – and using lots of things as a base.'

Levan's late seventies remixes – such as Cognac's 'How High' and Dee Dee Bridgewater's 'Bad For Me' – sound much like the regular disco mixes of his peers. But by the start of the eighties, he was experimenting with drum machines and synthesisers and, like François Kevorkian around the same time, forging a new electronic, post-disco sound. This was epitomised by his group Peech Boys – Levan, keyboard player Michael de Benedictus (who had worked on 'Heartbeat') and vocalist Bernard Fowler – and their digital-funk excursion 'Don't Make Me Wait'.

' "Don't Make Me Wait" is about sex, and *everyone* can relate to that,' Levan told *NME* journalist Paolo Hewitt. 'It was very, very passionate, very rough, then it was tender, then it was cold and then it was sparse. It touched on all bases.'

The song was a significant breakthrough for Levan, one that gave him world-wide acclaim in the dance community (it was even a minor pop hit in the UK).

Card sharp – Danny Krivit's treasured membership to the Paradise Garage.

'*Everyone* was influenced by the Peech Boys record,' says Arthur Baker. 'When those handclaps started whipping around the place . . . oh, man.' Fired by this new sound, Baker produced 'Walking On Sunshine' by Rocker's Revenge. 'That was specifically *made* for the Paradise Garage,' he says emphatically.

Although the Peech Boys' eventual album was a disappointment, they furthered their stripped-bare soul with the much-sampled '(Life Is) Something Special'. This record, while not garnering the same plaudits as its predecessor, actually pushed their razored, bass-heavy sound deeper still, offering a tantalising glimpse of the future.

With reggae making its presence felt, New York started to absorb

Jamaican dub as an influence. Dub's warping basslines and luxuriant wide open spaces suggest much by saying little, and demand supreme self confidence in your ability as a producer. It's all nuance, a nudge and a wink. The rest is left to the dancer.

Levan's interest in dub came, no doubt, from the people he encountered at Island Records, for whom he did many remixes. Jamaican producers Sly Dunbar and Robbie Shakespeare, and in particular the engineer Steven Stanley, were to exercise an important influence on his tastes. Levan started airing many of the tracks coming out of Nassau's Compass Point studios – records like Will Powers's 'Adventures In Success', Ian Dury's 'Spasticus Autisticus', and a succession of Grace Jones singles.

Levan would use echo and reverb to dramatise records in much the same way that Jamaican sound system DJs had done. The flitting handclaps on 'Don't Make Me Wait' were an approximation of a reverb trick he would often do live. And on the Garage's superb system, certain dub-inflected records sounded simply awesome. One such was Funk Masters' 'Love Money', which François Kevorkian introduced to the Garage. Played there, the record's reverb, echo and spatial decay were nothing short of thrilling. Greatly inspired, Kevorkian incorporated these ideas into a series of remixes that sound classic even today: D Train's 'You're The One For Me (Reprise)', Sharon Redd's 'Can You Handle It?', Yazoo's 'Situation' and, most spectacularly, on the Arthur Russell-produced 'Go Bang' by Dinosaur L.

Russell was a crazy-eyed mystic who worked with everyone from Allen Ginsberg (whom he taught to play guitar), to Laurie Anderson and Philip Glass (and also CBS A&R legend John Hammond). His interviews were as abstract as his music, often filled with comments that made Phil Spector sound normal. 'In outer space you can't take your drums – you take your mind,' he told David Toop in 1987. An avant-garde cellist with an obsession for echo, he is oft-cited as a pioneer of dub-style disco, yet his music was often undanceable. 'I will not deny that Arthur was an absolute visionary,' says François, who honed Russell's genius into more palatable form, 'but I don't think he really knew how to sort out what he had created. When I remixed "Go Bang", I really focused that record. I stripped it down. I spent hours and hours going over it.'

Russell had discovered disco music on a visit to Nicky Siano's Gallery in the early seventies and collaborated with several of the scene's pioneers, first with Siano himself on Dinosaur's 'Kiss Me Again', then later with Steve D'Acquisto on Loose Joints' 'Is It All Over My Face?'. 'He had this energy and the beauty of his music; such strength and tenderness,' raves D'Acquisto. 'He was an abstract painter, really.' Although his work was

largely overlooked at the time, it has been recently exhumed by such fans
as DJ Gilles Peterson.

Time waits for no one

Larry Levan treated the recording studio in much the same way as he
treated the booth and everywhere else. It was another good place to have
a party. 'He was a record company's nightmare,' laughs Danny Krivit.
'Basically, he'd show up really late and while he was there it was about
socialising and drugs. Eventually he would get to the mix, but he would
be distracted very easily. And the mix, instead of taking a day or whatever,
it would go on for weeks.'

Just such a session was the one which resulted in Gwen Guthrie's
'Padlock' EP, a mini-album of six songs which spiralled out of a simple
project to remix 'It Should Have Been You'. As Levan's druggery took
hold, this became a sprawling marathon. 'Island were so pissed off at the
price and how long "It Should Have Been You" took that they just
shelved it,' recalls Danny Krivit. 'For a year or two he was just playing it
at the Garage and kicking it there.'

The one constant in the kinetic chaos of Levan's daily life was Judy
Weinstein. She acted as manager, record tipster, guide and mother figure.
'She was totally enamoured of him,' says Nicky Siano. 'She really did a lot
for him.' Weinstein's position in charge of For The Record, the most
important record pool in the country, meant she heard about tracks
before anyone else. 'She would hear about things before they were even
made,' claims Vince Aletti.

'When she used to walk into the Garage, all of a sudden Larry would
start really playing,' recalls Johnny Dynell 'She was a goddess.'

Towards the end of the Garage's life, Levan had entered into a steep
decline in which his DJing was running a distant second to his drug use.
The club had developed a significant inner clique of heroin users, of
which Levan was one. 'He was definitely into drugs,' says Krivit. 'But it
didn't seem like it was running his life. Towards the end it was probably
clear to him that the Garage was closing. I think at that point the drugs
seemed to be more obvious and he was there less.' In the final year, he was
relying increasingly on the club's alternate DJs, David DePino, Joey
Llanos and Victor Rosado. The club finally closed, a victim of Manhattan
real-estate speculation, on 26 September 1987, after a momentous two-
day party in which an estimated 14,000 passed through the club's doors
to bid it a tearful goodbye. Although its closure was long anticipated, it
nevertheless had a deadening effect on New York clubland. 'It was like
somebody had died in my family,' says Charlie Grappone.

People recall Levan selling his records – unthinkable for a DJ who loved music so much – in order to finance his escalating habit. After the closure of the Garage, whenever he was booked to DJ, his friends had to trawl the rummage sales to buy back his collection, just so he could fulfil the date. Danny Krivit remembers finding Levan's unique acetate remix of Syreeta's 'Can't Shake Your Love' on a record stall and realising that most of the other records there were his also.

Justin Berkman, an English wine dealer and DJ who had lived in New York, opened a club in London directly inspired by the Garage, called Ministry of Sound. He booked Levan to come over and play.

'We brought him over for three days,' recounts Berkman. 'He arrived eight days late with no records and ended up staying for three months. I was like, "Larry, where are your records?" He said, "I haven't got any. I've sold them all." ' But records were scraped together, and even in the depths of addiction Levan pulled off a great set.

His final trip abroad was on a tour of Japan with François Kevorkian in August 1992. They played together at a club called Endmax. 'Larry went in to a set of Philadelphia classics,' recalls Kevorkian, 'which was just so poignant, so emotional, because the message of all the songs said he was really hurting. We all felt it at the time – I think he pretty much knew he was dying – and all the songs he played were so deeply related to how

Party starter – an invitation to Larry Levan's birthday bash on 18, 19 July 1986, drawn by his good friend Keith Haring.

fast life goes, how temporary it is. He played a song by Jean Carn called "Time Waits For No One" and the Trammps' "Where Do We Go From Here?" and all these other things. I was just standing there in the booth looking at Larry playing these records, and then I realised that this was one of the best moments of greatness that I had ever witnessed in my life. It was so obvious, so grand. There was such drama to it, that you just knew.' Three months later, on 8 November 1992, Levan died.

With his epic club and his grandiose personality, Larry Levan epitomised what it is to be a DJ – to play music you love to people you love. His success included an element of being at the right place at the right time, but no one can deny the profound effect he had on the New York dance scene. He dramatically bridged the uncharted territory between disco and house. He inspired more world-class DJs than anyone before or since, and he showed that with the right effort and attention to detail, a club could express the ideals of togetherness and love, no matter how large it was.

'Larry could take two thousand people and make them feel like they were at a house party,' says Mel Cheren, co-owner of the Garage. 'That was his magic.'

Nicky Siano points to Levan's many classic remixes as proof of his genius. '"Can't Play Around", "Ain't Nothin' Going On But The Rent", "Is It All Over My Face?", "Heartbeat" – incredible work,' he says. 'There are certain things he did that will live forever.'

Johnny Dynell believes that Levan showed him what DJing was really all about: 'When you're creating that magic on the floor. When they've thrown their hands up in the air, and they're totally lost and abandoned into this other world. And *you've* taken them to that other world. *That's* what DJing is. Before that I was just playing records, which is not DJing at all.'

Tony Humphries and 'garage' music

'Garage is the main thing in the States, and I'm the granddaddy of it,' claimed Levan in 1985. However, if you name a genre of music after a club which was open for ten whole years and which was known for its wild eclecticism, you're going to run into problems of definition pretty quickly.

The word 'garage' is by far the most mangled term in the whole history of music. What we now call garage – most likely pronounced British-style as '*garridge*', and more helpfully called 'UK garage' (or previously 'speed garage'), is a style that emerged when soulful house music was sped up a little and attached to skippy drum and bass-style rhythms and cavernous half-tempo basslines. You can read all about that in a later chapter.

What 'garage' meant to Levan was, more or less, 'New York house music'. He was probably thinking about the kind of dubby electronic records he produced and championed at the Paradise Garage, just a small part of its broad playlist. In the UK the term was seized on as a way of marketing compilations of New York dance music, a way of separating the city's output from Chicago house and Detroit techno. This was solidified by titles like *Garage Trax* and *The Garage Sound Of Deepest New York*. Eventually the name came to refer to the more soulful, more jazz- and gospel-inspired side of house: vocal tracks with lush, melodic production, or jazzy instrumentals with a good deal of sizzling hi-hat cymbals. We'll call it 'US garage'. [to make it easy for you. Keeping up?]

Now, just in case you thought it was simple, the US garage sound doesn't strictly come from New York. It was crystallised in the nearby city of Newark, New Jersey. So it is more accurately called 'the Jersey sound' and owes its emergence to the taste-making of DJ Tony Humphries.

Newark is the third oldest city in the United States, the largest and blackest in New Jersey, just eight miles away from New York across the Hudson River. Sadly its greatest fame came with its 1967 race riots. But more recently, in dance music circles, it was best known for a nightclub, Zanzibar.

In the mid seventies a businessman Miles Berger bought a Holiday Inn in a rundown district of Newark at 430 Broad Street and renamed it the Lincoln Motel. The area was an unofficial red-light quarter and the motel was the kind of place where you could hire rooms by the hour. Berger opened Abe's Disco on the ground floor and installed a DJ named Gerald T. In 1978 he was joined in the booth by a young Jersey Latino named Hippie Torrales, later the producer of such classics as Turntable Orchestra's 'You're Gonna Miss Me'.

Early the following year Berger paid a visit to the Paradise Garage and was blown away. 'He fell in love with it,' recalls Torrales, 'and he wanted to bring it to Jersey.' Immediately the hotel's second-floor ballroom was gutted and transformed into the best appointed nightclub the city had ever seen, complete with a Richard Long sound system. Opening night was 29 August 1979, attended by jugglers, magicians and Vegas-style showgirls. Berger even had lions and tigers prowling in cages outside. The music was broadcast live on WNJR radio and the cream of New Jersey musical royalty turned out, with Kool & the Gang, Tasha Thomas and the All Platinum records' stable hanging in the booth. All Platinum boss Joe Robinson had just set up another label, Sugarhill, and brought along a promo for Torrales to play. 'He came up to me saying, "Nobody else has played this in the New York area. I want you to play it." It was "Rappers' Delight".'

Hippie Torrales played with the same eclecticism as Larry Levan and, in New York, Zanzibar grew to be seen as an outpost with the same musical mission. Levan himself even had a midweek residency there for a while, turning Wednesday nights into a teaser for his epic weekends at the Garage. When Hippie left, replaced by Larry Patterson, the music began to focus more on a certain style, not least because the club's new favourite was regular guest Tee Scott. The Newark crowd, almost all black or Latin, loved soulful vocals and deep, slow grooves and Scott had an abundance of them.

'Tee picked really good songs,' says François Kevorkian. 'He was into playing a very solid, steady, no-nonsense set, but also very beautiful. He was more focused on the real soulful grooves that would work the dancefloor to an absolute frenzy.'

Tony Humphries was a Brooklyn DJ just starting his career. He'd had gigs at chi-chi Manhattan joint El Morocco and Club Tribeca, then through various strokes of good fortune had landed one of New York radio's most coveted jobs – the mastermix show at KISS FM, from which Shep Pettibone had just stepped down. In the following years this would bring him international fame, as tapes of his stateside shows became prized possessions in the UK. But a decent club residency still eluded him. Then in early 1982, thanks to his radio exposure, Larry Patterson invited the rookie Humphries over to Newark. It was the start of an eight-year tenure.

Initially at least, some of the patrons were underwhelmed. 'At first we wasn't impressed, but we really wasn't really listenin' to him, you know?' reflects DJ Quincy Vaughan, a keen Zanzibar clubber. 'Tee Scott was slammin' so hard that we didn't pay *anybody* any mind. When people used to say Tony Humphries, we used to say, "Tony *Who*? Tee Scott's the Man!"'

But Humphries was determined to win them over. Vaughan remembers the particular night when he finally got everyone's attention. 'He *turned it out*. From this point he started ripping this place out. He had this mix of "Somehow Someway" by Visual and "Release The Tension" by Colonel Abrams that was off the hook. He had a mix of Giorgio Moroder's "Evolution" and "Nobody's Got Time" by Eddy Grant which was amazing. Even to this day when I get a DJing brainfreeze, I'll revert back to some of those old mixes just to get the crowd movin'. He was really throwin' down there.'

Richard Long's sound was on proud display, with the amplifiers visible behind glass. It was so powerful that clubbers waiting to get in recall watching the entire building shake. They called it the 'earthquake system'. For Doug Smith of the 95 North production team it was the first time he'd heard a proper sound system. 'It wasn't loud all over, it was just focused on the dancefloor. If you stepped off it you could have a conversation with people in a normal tone of voice. As soon as you crossed the threshold onto the dancefloor, though, it was just amazing, it hit you right in the chest.'

With the loyal tight-knit crowd at the 'Zanz', Humphries was able to build a scene as energised and musically sophisticated as that of his idol Levan, and when the Garage closed Zanzibar carried the standard. In the process, he nurtured a stable of local acts – including Adeva, Phase II and Turntable Orchestra – and championed local producers such as Paul Simpson, Smack Productions and Blaze as well as Jersey labels Ace Beat and Movin'.

'The whole purpose of my two hours on KISS is to break new people,' he told *Muzik* in 1997. 'If you can't break them you shouldn't have the job. Anybody can play to a crowd and play last week's hits and have people screaming. What does that accomplish? They pay you a couple of hundred dollars and you go home. People won't remember you; they'll remember the records. You have to make them think, "That's the record I heard Tony play at Zanzibar." If they don't do that, who are you?'

In the late eighties and early nineties, though his club playlist remained wilfully eclectic, this 'Jersey sound' became Humphries' signature style, and was what he highlighted on his radio shows, and in his growing list of remixes and productions. As the different house styles evolved he selected records for their musicianship, their use of real voices and instruments and for their respect for pre-electronic ways of making music – their soulfulness.

'I would focus on more of the gospel part, or more of the jazzy part or melodic part,' he explained. 'The closer it sounds to a real band or something from the past, then the more I'm going to lean towards that.' This was what became known in Britain as 'US garage'.

Of course this wasn't a sound unique to New Jersey. Chicago's Terry Hunter and Steve Silk Hurley, New York's Victor Simonelli and Tommy Musto and the Strictly Rhythm and Emotive labels, as well as Brit Joey Negro (Dave Lee), all shared this aesthetic, but in the US it remained known as the 'Jersey sound'.

In the UK, as we'll see, this became the music of choice for glamorous nineties club culture, and later evolved a distinctly British offshoot. Reflecting Tony Humphries' role as the godfather of this sound, in January 1993, the Ministry of Sound hired him as their weekly resident; the icing on the cake for their homage to the Paradise Garage.

TWELVE
HOUSE

Can You Feel It?

'House is the first black American sound that relies on European pop for its inspiration, and he who steals from the thief is blessed.'

– Stuart Cosgrove

'I view house as disco's revenge'

– Frankie Knuckles

Many DJs speak of their work in religious terms, few with as much clarity as Frankie Knuckles. 'For me, it's definitely like church,' he explained on Chicago's WMAQ TV. 'Because, when you've got three thousand people in front of you, that's three thousand different personalities. And when those three thousand personalities become one personality, it's the most amazing thing. It's like that in church. By the time the preacher gets everything going, or that choir gets everything going, at one particular point, when things start peaking, that whole room becomes one, and that's the most amazing thing about it.'

In Chicago, as the seventies became eighties, if you were black and gay your church may well have been Frankie Knuckles' Warehouse; a three-storey factory building in the city's desolate west side industrial zone. Offering hope and salvation to those who had few other places to go, here you could forget your earthly troubles and escape to a better place. Like church, it promised freedom, and not even in the next life. In this club Frankie Knuckles took his congregation on journeys of redemption and discovery.

'In the early days between '77 and '81, the parties were very intense,' he remembers. 'They were always intense – but the feeling that was going on then, I think, was very pure. The energy, the feeling, the feedback that you got from the room, from the people in the room, was very, very spiritual.'

One day a week, from Saturday night to Sunday afternoon, a faithful crowd gathered at 206 North Jefferson, waiting on the stairway to enter on the top floor of the building and pay the democratically low $4 admission. The club held around 600, but as many as 2,000 people – mostly gay, nearly all black – would pass through its doors during a good night. They dressed with elegance, but in clothes that declared a readiness to sweat. Many would sleep beforehand to maximise their energy. Once in the club, some stayed in the seating area upstairs. Others walked down to the basement for the free juice, water and munchies. Most people, however, headed straight to the dark, sweaty dancefloor in between. For them there was no need for distraction: they came here for Frankie Knuckles's music. They came to the Warehouse to dance.

'It was amazing because you had those down-to-earth, corn-fed mid-western folk,' recalls Frankie, 'and yet the parties were very soulful, very spiritual.' He smiles his gentlemanly smile as he remembers the feeling of communion, the intense focus his club created.

'For most of the people that went to the Warehouse, it was church.'

DJ/producer Chez Damier (Anthony Pearson) was one of the people mesmerised by the club.

'It was something you couldn't recreate,' he remembers. 'It was like no other sensation: being in a club full of kids that you didn't know but you knew. To try and understand it, all I can say is you have to imagine all the fabulous feelings you've had over your own partying years.'

To reach the dancefloor at the Warehouse you had to enter through a stairwell from the white, plant-filled lounge above. Heat and steam drifted up to meet you, generated in the murk of the underlit room by the glistening black bodies that were down there 'jacking' away. And as you descended into the shadowy cavern, you were hit by the power of the sound system; sparked by the energy of the dancers, many of whom were energised further by acid and MDA powder (a precursor to ecstasy). Frenzied bodies were packed in wall-to-wall throughout the space, their clothes reduced to a minimum of athletic gear, their bare skin dripping with sweat and condensation.

'That room was dark,' Frankie told writer Sheryl Garratt. 'People would say it was like climbing down into the pit of hell. People would be afraid when they heard the sound thumping through and saw the number of bodies in there, just completely locked into the music.'

And Frankie's music was something completely new to most of these people. He would work the crowd into a frenzy by twisting songs into frantic new shapes with mixes and edits: New York DJing skills of which Chicago clubs had little experience. And at a certain stage in the evening he'd black out the room and throw on a sound-effect record of a speeding steam locomotive, panning the stereo sound from one set of speakers to another so it felt like a real express train was thundering through the club.

Chez recalls the effect of a night at the Warehouse: 'Kids would totally lose their minds.'

Frankie Knuckles (originally Nichols) had learned his craft playing alternate for his great friend Larry Levan in New York's Continental Baths, becoming the club's main DJ when Levan left in 1974 and playing there until the Baths closed, bankrupt, in 1976. Around this time, Levan was contacted by the owners of the Warehouse in Chicago, a warehouse party which had built itself a permanent home, and offered a residency (the Warehouse was a nickname; officially it was 'US Studio'). Since he was committed to the idea of the Paradise Garage – and was busy cultivating its forerunner, Reade Street – he declined. In his place he recommended Frankie, and told his friend that it would be a great opportunity.

In March 1977, Knuckles went out to play for the opening night and also a night the following week. Both nights went well and he decided he liked Chicago. He was offered a permanent job; the terms included a financial interest in the club.

'At that point I realised I had to think about what I wanted to do. If I really wanted to uproot from New York City and move there. Then actually when I looked at it, I didn't have anything holding me here. I figured, what the hell. I gave myself five years and if I couldn't make it in five years, then I could always come back home.'

Before those five years had passed, Frankie Knuckles had become famous in Chicago. As well as popularising the funky, the soulful – the dangerous – side of disco, which the city had rarely heard, he also imported its spirit, fostering among these polite, God-fearing mid-westerners the communal, emancipating hedonism of disco's gay underground. In doing this he was the catalyst for an unprecedented explosion of musical creativity.

His club would give its name to a new genre of music; he would become known as its godfather. The music was house.

The meaning of house

'In the beginning there was Jack, and Jack had a groove, and from this groove came the groove of all grooves, and while one day viciously throwing down on his box, Jack boldly declared, "Let there be house."' So booms 'My House' by Rhythm Control.

For a long time the word 'house' referred not to a particular style of music so much as to an attitude. If a song was 'house' it was music from a cool club, it was underground, it was something you'd never hear on the radio. In Chicago, the right club would be 'house', and if you went there, you'd be 'house' and so would your friends. Walking down Michigan Avenue, you would be able to tell who was 'house' and who wasn't by what they were wearing. If their tape player was rocking the Gap Band, they were definitely not 'house', but if it was playing Loleatta Holloway or the Eurythmics, they were, and you'd probably go over and talk to them.

One day soon, Chicago kids would invent a stark new kind of dance music, and because of where this came from, and because of where it was played, it would steal the name for itself. But for several years, 'house' was a feeling, a rebellious musical taste, a way of declaring yourself in the know. Certainly, the word 'house' was used long before people started making what we would now call 'house music'.

Chip E, an early house producer, claims that the name came about from his methods of labelling records at the Importes Etc record store, where he worked from late 1982.

'Kids were coming in looking for the older disco music. They'd say, "I want some of that music played at the Warehouse", and this was referring to disco music. And so we found that if we put up signs that said, "As Heard At The Warehouse", the records would fly out the racks. Eventually that got cut down to just "The 'House". That became the vernacular.'

Frankie Knuckles says that the first time he knew of the term was in 1981. Driving south through the outskirts of his adopted city to visit his goddaughter, he noticed a sign in the window of a bar: 'WE PLAY HOUSE MUSIC'. Bemused, he turned to his friend and asked, 'Now what is *that* all about?' She looked at the sign and told him, 'It means music like you play at the Warehouse.'

The name fitted for all sorts of reasons. A 'house record' could be one belonging to a particular club, one which was exclusive to that DJ. It could be a song which simply 'rocked the house'. A 'house party' was more intimate and friendly than a club, and of course 'house' conjured the idea of family, of belonging to something special. If you were part of it, house was your home. Later, as an army of young kids started producing electronic dance music in their bedrooms, it enjoyed another resonance: it was simply music you made in your house.

These meanings made it appropriate, but they were not where the word originated (some will try and tell you otherwise). The word 'house' came from the Warehouse, referring to the music played there, the DJing manipulations which Frankie introduced, and the underground vibe the club engendered.

Frankie Knuckles at the Warehouse

If house music was named at the Warehouse, it started as disco, pure and simple. Frankie Knuckles began spinning in Chicago around the time that disco was reaching its commercial peak, and he would have been playing the same records as his peers in New York: songs from labels like Salsoul,

West End and Prelude. His audience took to this music immediately, but he soon faced a drought of good material as the major labels felt disco burning their fingers. In New York, this problem was solved for many DJs by the blossoming of new styles, notably hip hop and electro, but in Chicago Frankie looked for ways to keep his beloved disco alive. This encouraged him to look backwards and emphasise older music in his sets.

'Songs lived in people's consciousness a lot longer than they do now,' he says. 'So a lot of the stuff that came out in the early seventies on Salsoul and Philly International, I was playing a lot of stuff like that; that was still working pretty strong in '77 when I moved to Chicago. And a lot of the popular disco R&B club stuff and dance stuff that was coming out then.'

As the eighties began, Frankie played the weirder dubbed-up post-disco sounds emerging from his hometown – the Peech Boys and D Train – and added obscure imports, especially from Italy, where disco – albeit a more mechanical version of the genre – was refusing to die. He also started working on re-edits of songs in an effort to rejuvenate old favourites, experimenting with the remixing ideas he had seen DJs do back home. He started playing these publicly around 1980.

'A lot of the stuff I was doing early on I didn't even bother playing in the club, because I was busy trying to get my feet wet and just learn the craft. But by '81 when they had declared that disco is dead, all the record labels were getting rid of their dance departments, or their disco departments, so there was no more uptempo dance records, everything was downtempo. That's when I realised I had to start changing certain things in order to keep feeding my dancefloor. Or else we would have had to end up closing the club.'

Using a reel-to-reel tape recorder, and assisted by his friend Erasmo Riviera, who was studying sound engineering, Frankie would take weird tunes like 'Walk The Night' by the Skatt Brothers (which sounds like the Glitter Band on angel dust) or jazzy disco records like 'A Little Bit Of Jazz' by Nick Straker, or 'Double Journey' by Powerline and re-edit them – extending intros and breaks, adding new beats and sounds – to make them work better for his dancers.

'Even stuff like "I'm Every Woman" and "Ain't Nobody" by Chaka Khan, just things like that, completely re-edit them, to give my dancefloor an extra boost. I'd rearrange them, extend them and rearrange them.'

Chez Damier remembers how Frankie would rework the ballsy disco song 'Can't Fake The Feeling' by Geraldine Hunt:

'Frankie would do something like, "You can't fake it . . . *voom*, you can't fake it . . . *voom*, you can't fake it . . . *voom*," and it would go three times, and the stop was really hard, VOOM!! And then it would go "L.O.V.I.N." and it goes into "You can't fake it . . ." eight times, and then it would hit, and it would break into something else, "L-O-V-I-N." which is Teena Marie.'

Another record Chez remembers is 'So Fine' by Howard Johnson, an uptempo disco tune. 'It goes, "So fine, blow my mind", and then, "Throw your head back, move it to the side", and Frankie would change it to "Throw your head backbackbackback . . . *Dum! Dum! Dum!* move it to the side DUMM!!" Little tricks like that were such sensations. We were like followers.'

The receptive audience loved all this DJ alchemy and Frankie revelled in the chance to work with a blank canvas. 'Those type of parties we were having at the Warehouse, I know they were something completely new to them, and they didn't know exactly what to expect,' he says. 'But once they latched on to it, it spread like wildfire through the city.'

Eventually, his tape projects with Riviera would become complex remixes, as he ran completely new rhythms, basslines and drum tracks underneath familiar songs. This kind of DJ creativity was at least half a decade old in New York, and was certainly being done in other American cities, but in Chicago it was very new. 'I'm sure there were other people that were doing it, but to my audience it was revolutionary,' he says.

It is these experiments which constitute the roots of house music. As these ideas and techniques were copied, often in much-simplified ways by far less skilled DJs using far more basic equipment, the house aesthetic was born.

At first, the Warehouse was seen by the wider Chicago club world as marginal – it was a club for black gay people (of both sexes) with a black gay DJ – and Frankie's music was written off as 'fag music'. The disco backlash was building steam and the straight dancefloors in the city were moving to new wave rock and European synth pop. Eventually, though, by virtue of it being the only after-hours club in the city, some adventurous straight kids started going. Many were swept away by the power of the music they heard.

One such visitor was Wayne Williams, a young DJ from the city's south side, who was so stunned by the energy he saw that he became a regular.

'For two years or so I would go and stand by the DJ booth and ask the guy next to Frankie to give me the name of the record he was playing so I could write it down and go back to the record store and get them,' he recounted. 'Being in a gay club, I was a bit scared to ask Frankie.' Williams, shopping at Sounds Good, bought as many of Frankie's tunes as he could find and introduced them to his south side audiences. Used to more current sounds, his crowd at first completely cleared the floor. However, he persevered and, by playing music that none of his peers would touch, quickly became one of the city's most successful DJs. 'I was the only one who had balls enough to go there and bring back this music to the south side and play it to the straight kids.' His success at the Loft (no relation to the New York Loft) had a considerable influence, and in the early years of the eighties the older, funkier sound known back then as 'house' started to spread out beyond the gay clubs.

Ron Hardy at the Music Box

By late 1982, the Warehouse had become a victim of its own success, its gay clientele increasingly diluted. Frankie remembers 'a lot more hard-edged straight kids trying to infiltrate what was going on'. The owners got greedy and doubled the entry fee. In the second half of 1983 Knuckles left and opened the Power Plant, a former electrical substation at 1015 North Halsted. His crowd followed him loyally, but the owners of the Warehouse had an ace up their sleeve: moving the Warehouse to 1632 South Indiana and renaming it the Music Box, they hired another young DJ, black and gay like Knuckles and with similar tastes, but with a distinctly different approach.

Sharing a house – Ron Hardy (*left*) and Frankie Knuckles (*right*), the two founders of Chicago house music, in 1986.

Because in fact, the Warehouse wasn't the first place Chicago had heard underground disco. At a gay club called Den One, a young DJ had played nights of hard black disco at least two years before Frankie arrived. Around 1977 he had left town to work in California, leaving the clubland gap which Knuckles would later fill. But at the end of 1982 he returned to play at the Music Box and retake the Windy City by storm. His name was Ron Hardy, and to many in Chicago he was quite simply the world's greatest DJ.

'Ron Hardy? Everybody hated him, he was mean and nasty, a drug addict. He had a huge ego, that's how he was. But, oh man, he was GREAT!' Veteran house producer Marshall Jefferson remembers Hardy. 'He was the greatest DJ that ever lived.'

If Frankie Knuckles is the godfather of house, his child was raised by Ron Hardy. Knuckles's arrival had started a period of intense experimentation. He had created an excitement and a thirst for underground music, and he had shown that a DJ could be a truly creative force. Returning to Chicago to find this energetic laboratory, Ron Hardy was to become its mad scientist. While Frankie's efforts were based around trying to keep disco alive, Hardy created a forum that looked to the future. And while Frankie's dancefloor experiments were conducted with characteristic level-headed momentum, Hardy was fuelled by a far more demonic appetite – for both music and narcotics. Knuckles was stimulating change, but Hardy was ready to tamper with nature, eager to release musical forces beyond his control.

Seasoned clubber Cedric Neal recalls the effect Hardy had on an audience.

'He was like an idol. The first time I saw him spin, it was his birthday, and just to see people literally crying because this man had them so hyper, seeing people pass out, I was like, "Hey, this is my type of party!" I'd never been to a place where the DJ had a control over the people where they would dance and scream, and at some points cry. Depending on how high they were, they were passing out from pure excitement. It was the energy that was there.'

The two DJs' sharply distinct personalities soon attracted their own distinct crowds. The older, smartly turned-out partygoers followed Frankie to the Power Plant, bringing with them a certain musical snobbery and a degree of conservatism. The younger kids and most of the straight presence left for the craziness of the Music Box, which Chez Damier describes as 'more the ghetto version of the party'. Here the more radical sounds of house would find their home. For Hardy to change the scene like he did was no mean achievement. Knuckles had enjoyed a five-year supremacy in Chicago's underground.

'Frankie was ruling the roost,' recalls Marshall. 'They were calling it house music now, and that was because of Frankie. And for Ron Hardy to come in there and steal Frankie's thunder, it was really something.' Power Plant gave up Saturdays and only opened on Fridays, and eventually the week was divided between the two clubs, with Wednesdays and Fridays being Power Plant nights, and Tuesdays, Thursdays and Saturdays belonging to the Music Box. 'They were competitive,' laughs Marshall. 'Like two gunslingers.'

'People thought they were rivals, but they were actually good friends,' clarifies Chip E. 'On Friday you might find Ronnie hanging out at the Power Plant and on Saturday Frankie at the Music Box.'

Both DJs were able to generate incredible energy levels on their dancefloors. They would both extend everything for ages, stretching out their dancers on an endless beat, teasing them in a highly sexual way with a repetitive rhythm until the final release of the actual song. Both used a reel-to-reel to play edits and rhythm tracks, and for many this was the best part of the evening. 'I used to love it when they went to the reel,' says Earl 'Spanky' Smith of acid house group Phuture. ''Cos that's when you knew they were gonna play something exciting.'

Chip E maintains that neither DJ did his own editing: 'Erasmo did editing for both of them, but there were a lot of people who gave both of them edits.' Despite this, recordings show their edits to be quite distinct: the ones Hardy played were more repetitive, closer to what we'd now call house music.

Frankie's style was more orderly and he kept his tempo much lower. He paid greater attention to the quality of his sound and his sets were more technically precise and structured, with the pace rising and falling in waves throughout the night. In keeping with his 'star' status in the city, his booth rendered him relatively inaccessible. Ron Hardy, on the other hand, played with a raw, lo-fi energy that left you in no doubt which moment he was living in. He played at floor-level and all he cared about was energy, about pushing his dancers to their limits. He had little time to plan anything. As Marshall puts it: 'He didn't give a fuck about programming or none of that. Hardy did every single drug known to man. How the fuck you gonna programme *that*?'

Their playlists were quite similar: favourite songs like 'Let No Man Put Asunder' by First Choice, 'I Can't Turn Around' by Isaac Hayes, 'There But For The Grace Of God' by Machine, 'The Love I Lost' and 'Bad Luck' by Harold Melvin & the Bluenotes and 'I'm Here Again' by Thelma Houston, plus a good deal of Loleatta Holloway, all found their way into both clubs; as did dubby mutant disco – ESG's 'Moody', Dinosaur L's 'Go Bang', Atmosfear's 'Dancing In Outer Space' – and European synth tracks

like 'Frequency 7' by Visage, 'Dirty Talk' by Klein & MBO, and 'Optimo' and 'Cavern', both by Liquid Liquid.

However, Hardy played his music much faster, stripped it down more, and welcomed more European weirdness. He would even add overtly commercial tracks like 'It's My Life' by Talk Talk, 'Sweet Dreams' by the Eurythmics, and songs by neo-glamsters ABC. Hardy's music was about bombshells and surprises, an onslaught of sound reaching climax after funky climax. He upped the energy levels using anything at his disposal, playing the EQ avidly – dropping out and slamming up the bass or the treble for extra effect (this would become a Chicago trademark, though Knuckles was far less blatant with his EQing) – or speeding everything up as fast as he could, pitching records to plus six or plus seven per cent. Detroit techno pioneer Derrick May remembers a visit when he heard Stevie Wonder's 'As' played at plus eight. Some clubbers even recall him playing reel-to-reel tracks backwards.

'Ronnie was kind of skinny and Frankie was kind of fat,' laughs Chip E, referring to their styles more than their waistlines. Ronnie would take more chances. I could take a tape to Frankie and he might wait for two or three hours and listen to it in headphones and say, "I think I can fit it in here." Whereas Ronnie – I could take him a tape and within ten to fifteen minutes he had it on and banging it and then playing it several times a night. He was much more courageous.'

Marshall Jefferson had been led to the Music Box by a wild girl he worked with at the Post Office. She was a stripper as well as a mailman and Marshall says he wanted to see her body in action on the dancefloor, so he told her, 'I want to see the wild clubs you go to.' Previously a die-hard rock fan with Thin Lizzy records in his collection and a tendency to believe that disco sucked, he was converted to dance music immediately, such was Hardy's power. 'She took me to this place called the Music Box. I was touched by God! The volume, man, just BOOM!!! It penetrated through my chest and took hold of my heart.'

Above all, Hardy loved to crank it up. 'The *volume*, man!' Marshall exclaims. 'It was really amazing. I have never heard music at that volume since. In fifteen years I have not heard a single club that even came close to that volume, and the reason, I would suspect, is there would be loads of lawsuits from damaging your hearing. The Music Box was so loud that anywhere in the club, the bass would physically move you – not just on the dancefloor, but *anywhere* in the club!'

Cedric Neal and his friends would always arrive early so they could sit outside drinking and getting high before they went in.

'The front opened up at a quarter to one. And Ron would always start with "Welcome To The Pleasure Dome". This was '84, it just came out, and he would play that for twenty minutes. And you'd just sit around and wait till the crowd just built. Come five o'clock in the morning you gain the momentum, and come six you'd pick up speed. People would come in there and just dance all night.'

After its first incarnation in the old Warehouse, the club moved into a second venue at 16th and Indiana, then to an industrial cave beneath an elevated city highway at 326 Lower Michigan Avenue. With a capacity of around 750, it was at least half gay, and in the years immediately preceding awareness of AIDS, a culture of sexual abandon prevailed for gay and straight clubbers alike. Cedric grins as he describes 'the big speaker'; ten feet tall, all the way at the back of the club, where couples would get under the stage. 'We'd take girls in there: get a blowjob, a quickie. It was still the end of the sexual revolution.' He remembers how there were pillows in the girls' bathroom. 'There'd be guys in there, getting high, having sex together. Maybe you'd see two lesbians in there.'

This sexual openness would work dramatic transformations on the rougher straight kids who ventured in. There was little or no sense of homophobia. 'If you couldn't stand to be around gays, you didn't party in the city of Chicago,' Cedric recalls. 'They would ask, "Are you a child or a stepchild?" Meaning, are you gay or not? If you were a stepchild it meant you were straight but we accept you.' It became fashionable for a time to act gay even if you weren't. Cedric recalls people who would experiment with bisexuality in an attempt to get closer to the true meaning of house.

Music was undoubtedly the central focus, but club drugs like pot, poppers (known as 'rush') and LSD were present (with a smattering of MDA, and the pricier intoxicants like cocaine and ecstasy). Music Box had more of everything in its veins than Power Plant, notably a lot of acid and also PCP. Popular highs were 'happy sticks' (joints with a sprinkling of PCP), or 'sherm sticks' (joints dipped in formaldehyde). With the resulting manic energy, the Music Box could be an intimidating place indeed. Chicago DJ Derrick Carter remembers being truly scared after sneaking in aged seventeen.

'It weirded me out. There were speakers hanging from the ceiling, Mars lights spinning. For some reason the place made me think of junkies. I didn't know anything about the drugs, but Ronnie would play something like Eddie Kendrick's "Going Up In Smoke" and everybody would be . . . going up in smoke! It would just lift everybody off the ground, people would be crying, and just freaking out, they got so charged.'

'The way Ron Hardy spinned, you could tell how he was feeling,' says Cedric. 'The way he played records, the sequence he played them, how long he played them. You could tell if he was depressed, because him and his loverman had had a fight. You could know if he was up and happy or you could know if he was just high, out of his mind because of the drugs.'

The emotional intensity of the city's dancefloors, combined with the twin genius of Hardy and Knuckles, gave Chicago a nightlife whose energy and focus were unrivalled. With no Studio 54 celebrity scene to fuck things up, and without New York's overbearing industry presence, music in Chicago stayed dirtier, funkier, more about dancing till you dropped. And without any competing scene, the house underground managed to spread beyond its gay origins without losing direction or momentum.

A recognisable house style soon developed. The early days saw designer labels to the fore, with Armani tank tops and Gucci belts a must. Upscale retailers suffered a wave of theft as Music Box kids got the look (one famously managed to 'boost' a fully dressed mannequin).

Later, baggy Girbaud or leather-detailed Guess jeans and sports' sweatshirts were popular (a look later taken up by the world of hip hop, which at this stage was dressed in tracksuits and Kangols). And since house kids were outsiders, the punk look was appropriated, so bleach-splashed jeans and spiky hair could also mean you were house. Punk styles of dancing came in, too: it was quite normal to see the younger kids slamdancing to house. Another crucial look was the 'pump': a tall, flat-topped haircut. You'd get extra credibility for the height of your pump, and the sharpness of its corners. DJ Pierre was known for his: 'People'd be like, "Damn! Look how high his pump is," ' he laughs.

The most distinctive fashion, however (and this would seem to have parallels with London's New Romantics), was a sort of Ralph Lauren preppie meets English country gentleman style, with cardigans, woollen jodhpurs and riding boots being an indisputable sign of house-ness. Some people even remember carrying a horse whip.

The Hot Mix 5

Those who were too young to go to the Music Box or Power Plant were switched on by another vital impetus: radio. Veteran Chicago radio DJ Herb Kent had switched his black audience on to new wave with his 'Punk Out' show. Then from 1981-86 on station WBMX (and later on WGCI), a racially diverse quintet of DJs introduced mixing records to Chicago's airwaves. Captained by Kenny 'Jammin'' Jason, the Hot Mix 5, as they were called, included at first Ralphi Rosario, Steve 'Silk' Hurley, Mickey 'Mixin'' Oliver and Farley Keith Williams, aka 'Farley Jackmaster Funk'. They played mostly new wave European pop, including British groups like Depeche Mode, Human League and Gary Numan, the German technopop of Falco, and even the hi-energy of Divine.

This musical diet had profound influence on the tastes of the city, forming the backbone of the more commercial clubs' playlists. More sophisticated DJs searched out obscure imports along similar lines, like Wire, Yello and DAF. DJ Pierre, later to pioneer acid house, recalls Italian tunes like 'You Must Feel The Drive' by Doctor's Cat, Capricorn's 'I Need Love' and Trilogy's 'Not Love', as well as 'Brainwash' by Belgian group Telex. European records were key to the development of house, but their popularity was hardly a Chicago anomaly. In 1983 nearly a third of all US chart positions were taken up by British acts.

Italy's attempts to continue disco were huge in Chicago. Chip E argues this was because the style helped DJs emulate the flashy skills of the Hot Mix 5. 'The Italo-disco records, because they were so synthesised, were really easy to mix. It was almost like a system; you'd put them on the decks and they just *worked*.'

With a name coined by Bernhard Milkulski of German label ZYX, 'Italo-disco' was unashamedly drawn from hi-energy's simple genes, frequently with a four-on-the-floor kick-drum. A mutinous use of English and a fanciful group name was the norm; Den Harrow, for example, was a play on *dinaro*, the Italian slang for money.

Italo-disco was enormously popular in Europe as well as Chicago, even causing Italian rock groups like N.O.I.A. and Gaznevada to convert to the cause (scoring big hits in Chicago with, respectively 'The Rule To Survive' and 'I.C. Love Affair'). The more advanced tracks were clear precursors to house, such as 'A Love Supreme' and 'Problèmes D'Amour' by Alexander Robotnick (Maurizio Dami), and a series of club smashes by Klein & MBO (Tony Carrasco and Mario Boncaldo). Several early house records took directly from Italo tracks. 'MB Dance' by Chip E sampled Klein & MBO's 'MBO Theme' while Jamie Principle's 'Your Love' plucked the bassline from Electra's 'Feels Good'. Such was the style's influence that Chicagoans might use Italo-disco to mean any synthesised music from the early eighties; it isn't unusual to hear Gino Soccio (Canadian), Robert Görl (German) or Shock (British) described as Italo.

One record that had a particular influence was a Dutch compilation of rhythm tracks called Mix Your Own Stars. 'These were nothing more than drum tracks,' explains Chip E. 'The most popular track was one called "119" because it was 119bpm. It went "do-do-doo-chak-chak-chak, do-do-doo-chak-chak-chak." It was just a bass drum, a little snare, some toms and a clap. You could pack a dancefloor just by playing this. It was one of the early inspirations for house music.'

Such was the dominance of this European synth-driven sound that there was at first a real prejudice against the blacker songs which Knuckles and Hardy had been championing. Pierre remembers his friend Spanky introducing him to Isaac Hayes' *Chocolate Chip* LP, and feeling there was no way he could ever play it. 'I was like, "I ain't playin' this old song. Do people even dance to this?" '

The Hot Mix 5, as well as being important taste-makers, mixed like maniacs – far better, it is said, than either Knuckles or Hardy.

'All of the Hot Mix 5 were amazing, technique-wise,' agrees Marshall. 'They would have two records of everything, everything was phased, then they'd do backspinning and things on every song. Perfect, no mistakes, slamming shit, man.' For many, the 'Hot Mix' shows were the first time they'd ever heard records mixed. DJ Pierre was one of them.

'I used to have a tape player and make edits of stuff by using the pause button, but when I used to listen to the Hot Mix 5 and I heard two songs playing at once, I had no idea how they were doing it.' Like many others, hearing these radio jocks show off their skills was what pulled him into DJing. And the power they enjoyed was phenomenal. WBMX claimed audience figures of up to half a million – a sixth of the city's population. Maurice Joshua, then a suburban DJ, remembers the excitement whenever the 'Hot Mixes' were on.

'Everybody used to listen, especially when they brought it to lunchtime. Twelve o'clock you'd be glued to the radio. People would even skip school to tape the mixes.' At Importes Etc, then the city's leading specialist dance music store, there was a notice board describing the songs that had been played in each mix, to save the staff from a barrage of 'Hot Mix' questions.

The membership of the five was fluid and many of the city's DJs took a turn. Frankie Knuckles was even included for a while, but there was constant in-fighting and people recall the backbiting politics which surfaced whenever it was time to choose a new Hot Mixer.

As the only long-term black member of the ethnically mixed five, Farley enjoyed the most influence among the house kids of the south side. He also had a residency in a club called the Playground, where he capitalised on his radio success. Here he tried playing an 808 drum machine under old Philly records like 'Love Is The Message', something he also did on the radio. The boosted beat was known as 'Farley's Foot'.

'I brought my drum machine to the club and learned to play records that used the same machine, like "Dirty Talk" by Klein & MBO,' he says. 'Frankie Knuckles and I used to play many of the same records, but whereas he would make a re-edited version at home, I played my drum machine along with the records, so that the crowd could really feel that heavy, heavy foot. To play a record like Shannon's "Let The Music Play" that didn't have a really driving foot was to get tomatoes thrown at you. You had to drive them with your beat. Call me the foot doctor.'

In fact, though Farley reaped the most acclaim for the idea, Frankie Knuckles was also trying it using a Roland 909 he bought from Detroit's Derrick May. The 909 drum machine, with its distinctive kick-drum sound, would become a standard component of house records. However, rather than playing an actual drum machine in his club, Knuckles says he preferred to play rhythm tracks *made with* drum machines. These tracks were what became house music.

Jamie Principle, Jesse Saunders and the first house tracks

House was disco made by amateurs. It was disco's essence – its rhythms, its basslines, its spirit – recreated on machines that were as close to toys as they were to musical instruments, by kids who were more clubbers than they were musicians. The DJ, aiming to preserve a music which had been declared dead, had created another from its ashes. And in Chicago this new music even shared the name of its forebear, because remember, the disco that Ron and Frankie played was called 'house' even before house was.

As house culture boomed its arrival in this lakeside city, the DJ's aim was to drive dancers into states of drum-hypnotised fury, using endless thundering rhythm tracks to work the dancefloor towards the orgasm of a great vocal song. This style demanded a steady supply of simple, repetitive drum tracks. People had seen how basic a track could be. Studio equipment had just become small and affordable. Suddenly, everybody in

Chicago became a producer, eagerly pushing tapes under DJs' noses.

It was inevitable that these would eventually be committed to vinyl, and in 1984 there were two defining moments:

1. Byron Walton was shy and religious, could play the drums and had a thorough college grounding in sound engineering. His favourite musicians were Prince, Bowie, Depeche Mode and the Human League. Calling himself Jamie Principle, he created 'Your Love', an achingly beautiful musical poem so good that every DJ in the city wanted a cassette copy of it to play, so good that few people believed it had been made by anyone in Chicago.

2. Jesse Saunders was a chancer, wanted to gain recognition in order to get girls, was a big Chicago DJ, and had a friend, Vince Lawrence, whose father owned a local record label and who egged him into making a record. Under his own name, Jesse created 'On And On', a rhythm track so basic that everyone knew it had been made by someone in Chicago; so basic that everyone with a drum machine and a four-track recorder felt sure they could do better.

These were the first significant home-grown Chicago house artists.

Jamie Principle's music was heard first – his songs played from tape for more than a year before being put on record – but his work was too accomplished to spark an avalanche of copyists; most people thought 'Your Love' and 'Waiting On My Angel' were songs from Europe. It took Jesse Saunders' success with 'On And On', a far inferior track, to open the floodgates.

'That's what inspired everybody. It gave us hope, man,' says Marshall Jefferson. 'When Jamie was doing it, nobody thought of making a record. His shit was too good. It was like seeing John Holmes in a porno movie. You know you can't do better.'

Continuing his penile analogy, Marshall compares Jesse's track, on the other hand, to a rather less endowed figure. 'But if you saw a guy in a porno movie with a three-inch peter, and all the women are swooning all over him and he's a fucking millionaire, you would seriously consider having a go yourself, wouldn't you!' Marshall booms with laughter at his comparison. 'That's what inspired everybody about Jesse. They saw somebody make it big . . . *But not be that great.* When Jesse did his stuff, everybody said, "*Fuck! I could do better than that!*" '

After more howls of laughter, he says, simply, 'Jesse changed music, man.'

Jesse Saunders was one of the city's most successful DJs, having learned to play in the late seventies alongside his half-brother Wayne Williams at the Loft, which he describes as the straight version of the Warehouse. By 1983, as well as guesting in other clubs and doing a radio mix show on

WGCI, he was spinning at the 2,000-capacity Playground, favouring a Hot Mix 5-type style heavy on turntable tricks, and playing commercial new-wavey pop like the B-52s alongside a few more underground sounds. A night there could last twelve hours, and to stretch out his material he would use a drum machine (a Roland 808).

'A lot of the time I would take the drum machine to the club and just leave it playing the same beat the whole time and just mix things in and out,' he says. There was one track in particular that he liked to use for this, the B-side of a 1980 bootleg (the A-side was a megamix of popular tunes) credited to Mach, called 'On And On'. This consisted of a funky bassline and a loop of the 'hey, beep beep' part of Donna Summer's 'Bad Girls'. 'Whenever I played, my first record would be this bootleg "On And On" because that was like my signature tune,' recalls Saunders. 'So I had a drum machine going, "On And On" going on one turntable, and I'd be bringing in another record like "Planet Rock" on the other.'

When he couldn't play this any more (depending on who you believe it was either stolen from his DJ box, or it belonged to Wayne Williams who'd vetoed him playing it) Saunders vowed to recreate it. As he told Jonathan Fleming, 'I was so pissed off 'cos now I didn't have my signature record and I couldn't make the crowd go wild the way I used to when I came on. So I was like, "Well, I'm gonna make one myself." '

Despite having had music lessons all his life – his mother was a music teacher and he'd learned piano, trumpet, flute, guitar and drums – he had never before thought he had the skill to create the kind of music he was playing as a DJ. 'I hadn't really associated the fact that someone actually writes a song, goes in the studio, records it and then presses it on a record – that never really occurred to me at that time. But by the time I got a drum machine I was thinking, "maybe I can do a record".'

In 1983, with his 808, a Korg Poly 61 keyboard that his mother bought, a TB 303 bassline machine and a four-track cassette recorder, he started making tracks. 'I just kinda used the feel from a lot of the songs and records that I played that were hits, to kinda concoct them and embrace them into this one thing.' The first he called 'Fantasy' and another he called 'On And On', in tribute to his stolen signature tune.

Jesse negotiated the task of releasing records with help from his friend Vince Lawrence. As Vince tells it, the alliance was forged with one thing in mind. 'I was just trying to get pussy,' he declares. 'You know – trying to get laid!' As one of the city's biggest DJs, Jesse had an instant promotions' network. As for Vince, he knew about getting a record made since his father Mitch owned Mitchbal, a tiny independent blues label, and a year or so earlier, as Z Factor, he and some school friends had recorded a pop-rocky electronic single, '(I Like To Do It In) Fast Cars'.

Though it enjoyed a few airings on Chicago radio, 'Fast Cars' – a distant approximation of the lush style of Vince's idol Trevor Horn – had little to do with what was happening in the clubs. However, some – especially Vince – like to think of it as the first house record.

In January 1984 'On And On' came out on vinyl on Jesse's Jes Say label. A month or so later, 'Fantasy' came out on Mitchbal (Fantasy should have been first – it was due for release at the tail end of 1983, but Vince's dad was a great procrastinator). Vince then hooked up with a jazz pianist Duane Buford and both Vince and Jesse watched the cash roll in as they released a stream of local hits.

'Jesse was first,' remembers Farley. 'He put out records before anyone conceived of doing it, got all the girls, and all the fame. Jesse wanted to be the next Motown.'

'What we did was gather all the right ingredients,' says Jesse, 'and luckily, I was able to take all of that and make it into the sound we know today as house.'

'Jesse got all this shit played on the radio,' recalls Marshall. 'And next to songs like Prince it would sound like bullshit. It would sound like tin cans, man! *But* . . . everybody knew Jesse, so it was popular shit. By the time he finally did "Real Love", which was *one fifth* the quality normally necessary to make the radio – everything else was about one twentieth! – when that shit came out, it was huge! In Chicago, man, Jesse was bigger than Prince.'

The rush to record

Almost overnight there was a frenzy of releases as everyone realised that with a few pieces of home studio equipment they could make a track, and with a few hundred dollars and a bit of leg-work they could even have it released on vinyl. Whereas only a few months before, DJs were racking their brains to fill a whole night with the uptempo music their crowds demanded, now they had an army of young clubbers-turned-producers thrusting tapes under their noses – and a growing stream of actual vinyl releases as the more successful of those tracks made it onto record.

DJ's rushed to recreate rare exclusives. As Chip E explains: 'There were lots of records and edits you couldn't get anywhere so we would emulate them. And people were already familiar with the bassline so by emulating the bassline you were almost assured to have a hit.' Chip knew that records like this would be easy to sell. 'Myself, Farley, Steve Hurley and Jesse Saunders, we thought, "You know what, all we gotta do is make a record and put "house" on it and it's gonna fly off the shelves." So why don't we make some new music and call it house. And that's essentially what we did.'

The secret lay in these tracks' simplicity. 'Our sound is so different because we can make just a bassline and a rhythm track and we can sell ten thousand copies of that just in the city,' Farley told *The Face*'s Sheryl Garratt in 1986. 'All you need is a feel for music. There are people who've been to college to study music and they can't make a simple rhythm track, let alone a hit record. It's weird. And it seems like a waste of time to learn that, because now a little kid can pick up a computer, get lucky with it, and write a hit.'

The first wave of house tracks broke in late 1984 and early '85. Farley put out early efforts like 'Aw Shucks', which was basically a drum machine and some dogs barking, and his 'Funkin' With The Drums' EP – a drum machine and some MFSB basslines. Chip E's 'Jack Tracks' EP and 'Like This' were similar concoctions, put together with the Power Plant's 909 and a $200 Boss sampling pedal. Adonis was one of many who were unimpressed and therefore, inspired by Jesse Saunders' 'On And On', he jumped into the fray with 'No Way Back'.

Musician Larry Heard brought his more sophisticated jazz influences to bear on the music and began his Fingers Inc project with vocal star Robert Owens. Recorded in 1984 but released in '85, Heard's 'Can You Feel It' and 'Mystery Of Love' added jazzy, soulful flavourings, while his track 'Washing Machine' was an early Chicago example of the more chilly, angular style of house which would eventually be called techno. Amazingly, he claims to have recorded all three of these tracks on the same day.

With Heard as a rare exception, most of these youngsters had no musical training, and until a few months before had never even dreamed of making records. Marshall Jefferson's story is typical. After being 'baptised into house' at the Music Box, he maxed out his credit and simply bought everything he would need to make a track. He says he spent about nine grand getting kitted up, leaving the store with: a Roland JX8P keyboard; a Korg EX8000 module; Roland 707, 909 and 808 drum machines; a TB 303 and a Tascam four-track recorder. After unpacking them, he couldn't play a note. His colleagues at the Post Office laughed long and hard.

But in two days, impelled by the ridicule showered on him, he had made a track. He realised quickly that the technology he was using opened up all kinds of possibilities. For example, though he couldn't play keyboards, it was simple to make his efforts sound like a virtuoso: he just recorded the melodies at a third of their final speed.

' "Move Your Body" was one hundred and twenty-two beats per minute. I must've recorded those keyboards at forty, forty-five beats per minute. *[He mimes playing the stretched-out keyboard line.]* "Dum dum DER

DER DUM bombombom." Then I speeded it up.' The effect was impressive. He recalls the reactions: ' "Oh Marshall's jamming! Oh man!!!" You know.'

Marshall's debut release was the 'Virgo Go Wild Rhythm Tracks' EP, made with the help of Vince Lawrence. This was mostly just 808 drum machine lines, but it contained elements that would later become Jefferson's 1986 classic 'Move Your Body', the first house record to include a piano melody. One of the first tracks he produced, 1985's 'I've Lost Control' by Sleezy D, was huge at the Music Box, becoming an anthem for the wild abandon of the club. Marshall recalls the first night that Ron Hardy played his tracks from tape. 'He played seven of my tracks in a row. Seven! And by the time the fifth one got on, it was "I've Lost Control" and that was the biggest reaction. They *ran* onto the dancefloor. It was like a stampede. Everybody going *aaaarghhh*, and I was thinking, "Oh, man. Yes!" '

A system of patronage had evolved whereby a producer would construct tracks for a particular DJ, with the big guns, Knuckles and Hardy, getting the cream of the crop. Frankie favoured the more polished material and, with his greater emphasis on sound quality, was unlikely to play the really rough cassette mixes which were the most common currency. Ron Hardy, on the other hand, would play anything that he thought would get his crowd moving, regardless of what format it arrived in. 'I used to take my tapes down to Frankie,' recalled Steve Hurley. 'That's how you got your score, that's how you found out if that song was gonna make it or not; by giving it to Knuckles, and if the people screamed, if you got that crowd going, it gave you a feeling like there was no stopping you.'

House hits

House quickly grew from its underground beginnings into a thriving local scene. 'Us Chicago kids thought we were listening to a different music from anyone else on the planet,' says Derrick Carter. Carter was part of the music's second wave, rising to success as a DJ by playing in the warehouse parties which continued in Chicago into the nineties. He, like many of his peers, was from the city's sprawling suburbs, and joined the party as it got into full swing.

Perhaps the most memorable events of that time were the 'marathons', explosive two-day dances put on at the Warehouse and Music Box. Also notable were the huge parties which Lil Louis (later to gain fame as the producer of seminal house track 'French Kiss') organised in the ballroom of the Bismarck Hotel. Louis had in fact been DJing in the city since the late seventies, and drew as many as 8,000 kids here to rock the night away, sweating and slamdancing to this music that few others in the world knew about.

By the time his example had started to bear fruit, Jesse Saunders had signed a major-label deal with Geffen and moved to Los Angeles. But the founders of the music, Knuckles and Hardy, sustained the energy which had propelled the scene, and with a whole generation of kids trying their hand at DJing and producing, house looked set to accelerate. New clubs opened to capture the growing house constituency. Record shops like Importes Etc, Loop Records and (later) Gramophone thrived, and Farley and the Hot Mix 5 drove around in fancy cars as their mix shows drew enormous ratings. House in Chicago would never be truly mainstream, but now it was no longer underground.

In JM Silk (Steve 'Silk' Hurley and vocalist Keith Nunally), house found its first hitmakers. Hurley, who had risen to prominence as a DJ at the Playground alongside his erstwhile friend Farley Keith, put out 'Music Is The Key' in August 1985. This was pumped so much in the clubs and on Farley's radio mix show that on the day it was released it reputedly sold 2,000 copies in Chicago alone.

It was another of Hurley's tracks, a reworking of Isaac Hayes's 'I Can't Turn Around', which propelled the music even further. Hurley's own version, although he had long played it in the clubs, was pipped onto vinyl by his friend Farley, now calling himself Farley Jackmaster Funk. (Hurley claims the name 'Jackmaster' was originally his, too, hence the 'JM' in JM Silk.) Farley renamed the song 'Love Can't Turn Around', and with a vocal sung across the mountainous Darryl Pandy's six-and-a-half-octave vocal range, the track made house international. It was accepted as a pop record in the UK, reaching no.10 in September 1986. Hurley had his revenge, however, as in January 1987 'Jack Your Body' became the UK's first house no.1.

Chicago's hip hop

Intriguingly, house took on exactly the same cultural role as hip hop had done in New York. Its original constituency was poor and black. Its energy came from DJs competing on a local level. Its aesthetic was a result of DJs, dissatisfied with the prevailing sound, rediscovering older music and recasting it in new ways.

Just like hip hop, house stole basslines and drum patterns from old songs (both musics were initially about creating a very minimal and repetitive version of disco). Its creative progression was a result of DJs constantly introducing new elements to their performance in order to outdo the other guy. And house, like hip hop, depended on a fierce 'do it yourself' spirit. Even the clothes which characterised house in Chicago –

baggy and functional – were what would later be identified as hip hop styles throughout the world. The only fundamental differences were the tempo of the music, and that house accepted rather than rejected disco's gayness and its four-to-the-floor beat.

Some Chicago DJs, like Pierre, can even recall battles, just like those between rival hip hop crews in New York, where a series of house DJs would perform for the honour of having impressed the largest number of dancers – complete with MCs.

'A DJ had to bring his own sound system, his own MC, and bring a big sign with his name on it. And it'd be in a big school gymnasium,' he recalls. 'Then another DJ, he'd bring his sound system, and a third DJ'd bring his sound system. And you had to do your thing for like thirty minutes or an hour, and whoever's sound system and DJing skills sounded the best won the competition.' Pierre even remembers losing a battle because he didn't have 'Time To Jack'.

Given the nature of the house subculture, it's no wonder, then, that for many years hip hop was virtually unheard in Chicago. Only in the middle nineties, after house as a local phenomenon had gone resolutely back underground, could hip hop claim any kind of listenership there. Today, the musical spectrum on Chicago radio still has a high ratio of uptempo dance music compared to other American cities, but increasingly it is succumbing to the R&B and hip hop which now chokes the US music business.

Exploitation

As Chicago's home-made music started making money, the rip-offs began. In the furious competition of the time, copying and bootlegging were the norm, ownership of tracks was shaky, and few people profited financially from their talents. The music business – dance music especially – is one of the most corrupt there is. In Chicago, things were worse.

Two men came to dominate virtually the whole output of house: Rocky Jones of DJ International and Larry Sherman of Trax. Jones was a veteran DJ who ran the local record pool, Audio Talent. His label's first release was JM Silk's 'Music Is The Key'. Larry Sherman was a Vietnam veteran and local businessman with a taste for acid rock. He started his label, Trax, with advice about the local scene from Vince Lawrence, who designed the Trax label. Sherman was so confident that house would never sell, he bet his Corvette on the failure of Jesse Saunders's 'On And On'. With the record's success he handed over the car (which Lawrence later managed to wrap round a lamp post).

The key to Sherman's success was the fact that he not only owned the city's most profitable house label, he also owned the only record-pressing plant in Chicago. Even if you ran your own label, you still had to pay Larry Sherman to make your records. And as people found out, there was nothing stopping him from making some more copies that you didn't know about and selling them himself.

Marshall Jefferson recalls how his song 'Move Your Body' miraculously changed labels at the pressing stage, appearing on Sherman's Trax imprint instead of his own Other Records (he still has the original, unused printed labels). Jesse Saunders recalls that although Sherman was very helpful at times, often financing tracks by pressing records for free in exchange for a cut of the wholesale price, he would forget who had the rights to the masters.

'If he happened to get an order from somebody who asked if he had any "On And On" records, he'd go, "Oh, no, but I'll press some up and get them over to you." '

Chicago pressings were also renowned for their poor quality, a result of Sherman's habit of recycling old vinyl. 'They used to put all sorts of things in there. People say you'd even get bits of old sneakers in the record,' says one Chicago producer.

In early reports about the developing Chicago house scene, Jones and Sherman come over as enthusiastic supporters of the local music. And certainly, they invested a lot of time and money turning the city's musical hobby into something resembling a business. Hundreds of artists were signed, records flooded out and many of the young producers saw their work translate into success and hard cash. However, when it became clear that this music was capable of global impact, their rather casual business practices started to look less than helpful.

It was common practice to buy tracks outright with a minimal contract and no mention of royalties or publishing. The label bosses would encourage the producers to get some advice and would recommend a lawyer: they didn't explain that this was *their* lawyer. Ask any of the house pioneers whether they ever received a royalty cheque and they'll probably laugh. The kids were too naive to protest, indeed they were only too happy to take a one-off payment of a few hundred to a couple of thousand dollars for a track, never imagining that once the income from licensing started rolling in it might prove to be worth fifty times that. To be fair, even after they got wise to the way it was supposed to work, many continued selling music to Trax and DJ International, happy to get some quick cash for a quick track. 'We were young and these guys had cheque books,' sighs Chip E.

Perhaps more damagingly, though, Trax and DJ International seemed to do little to invest for future success, concentrating instead on quick foreign licensing deals, the proceeds of which were kept secret from most of the producers. It's often claimed they frightened away almost all the major label interest in Chicago. 'They took the money and ran with it,' insists Farley, 'instead of developing any artists.'

In a city with a long history of organised crime, there are plenty of stories flying around about mafia connections and hidden agendas, and the house scene is no exception. One conspiracy theorist claims that some figures wanted house to remain merely a local success because they had such murky pasts they needed to avoid unwanted attention. One is alleged to have operated under a false name for years because he was on parole – something which should have prevented him from leaving Illinois, let alone flying all over the world. Another is whispered to have been under the FBI witness protection scheme after involvement in some dramatic mob saga – a fine reason for not wanting too much publicity. There are even myths of arson and murder. Ask someone in Chicago to tell you about the record business there and you'll hear no end of entertaining rumours.

Acid house

No one in Chicago had expected their music to have an impact outside the city, let alone over in London, but it was in the UK that this music would rise to its greatest heights. 'Love Can't Turn Around' and 'Jack Your Body' led the way, but the export market was secured when Nathaniel Pierre Jones discovered the super-synthetic sci-fi squelch noises hidden deep within an otherwise redundant music machine. Jones is better known as DJ Pierre, his group was Phuture, and the music they pioneered would become known as 'acid house'.

The invention of acid house is a perfect example of an available technology being creatively perverted in the name of dance music. The Roland TB 303 bassline machine was designed to provide an automatic bass accompaniment for solo guitarists. At this task it was fairly useless. When Pierre and his friends Herb Jackson and Earl 'Spanky' Smith started messing with the controls, however, they managed to find some remarkable new noises which were perfect for the druggy dancefloor at Ron Hardy's Music Box.

'I wanted to make something that sounded like things I'd hear in the Music Box, or I heard Farley play on the radio,' says Pierre. 'But when we made "Acid Tracks", that was an accident. It was just ignorance, basically. Not knowing how to work the damn 303.'

In late 1985, by turning up all its controls past the point at which any pub guitarist would dare to venture, Herb and Spanky made the 303 produce a sort of tortured alien bleep. Pierre then leapt on the machine and turned things up even more. 'I started turning the knobs up and tweaking it, and they were like, "Yeah, I like it, keep doing what you're doing." We just did that, made a beat to it, and the rest is history.' The resulting record would be called 'Acid Tracks'. Its name and its sound would be the basis of an entire sub-genre of music.

The first thing the young producers did with their revolutionary track was to take a cassette tape of it over to the Music Box for Ron Hardy to play. They waited for two freezing hours outside the club for his arrival. 'Because he was the man. If he said he loved something, that was it. But if Ron Hardy had said he didn't like it, that would have been the end of acid.'

When Hardy played it, the results were astonishing. 'The fuckin' floor cleared,' recalls Pierre with a laugh. 'We just sat there thinking, "OK, I guess he won't be playin' that ever again." ' But Hardy waited for the dancefloor to fill up and then forced the song on his clubbers again, gaining a slightly better reaction. He waited a while and then played it a third time. By the fourth time he played it, at 4am when everybody's drugs had kicked in, the crowd went ballistic. 'People were dancing upside down. This guy was on his back, kicking his legs in the air. It was like, "Wow!" People were going crazy, they started slamdancing, knocking people over and just going nuts.'

Spanky, Herb and Pierre had originally titled the track 'In Your Mind', but the clubbers at the Music Box, tripping on the club's spiked punch, had other ideas. It fitted so well with their LSD-infused frenzy, they called it 'Ron Hardy's Acid Track'. It caused a storm.

And it was only a tape. Pierre and his friends had no idea how to have it released properly. 'We was running around trying to ask people, "How do you make a record? How does a record come out? Who do you go see?" ' In the end, he scribbled a note to Marshall Jefferson, by then a recognised force on the scene. It read: 'My name is DJ Pierre. I'm in a group called Phuture, and we did a track called "Acid Tracks", and Ron Hardy has been playing this track off a reel. Could you help us make a record?' Marshall helped them mix it and told them to slow it down considerably – the original track was pitched around 130bpm. For New York to get into it, he advised, it should be slowed down to around 120.

If the main stream of house was originally about reheating disco, acid house pointed in a much more radical direction. The acid records – mutant, synthetic and unworldly – came from nowhere; they were inheritors of no tradition, inspired more by new technology than by existing musical ideas. In his sleevenotes to *Acid*, Tim Lawrence argues that this experimental side of house should be analysed quite separately from the more traditional sounds. 'While some of Chicago's house producers gazed longingly in the direction of disco central (New York) and its key satellite states (Philadelphia, Los Angeles, Miami), others gazed into space, hoping to break with the past and gamble with the future.'

Indeed, Chicago's avant-garde output perhaps had more in common with the Detroit sound that would be known as techno. As techno pioneer Juan Atkins told Lawrence, 'Chicago came out with its own version of techno a couple of years down the road, but they didn't call it techno because we already had the term, so they called it acid house.'

With the success of 'Acid Tracks', the 303 became a coveted piece of hardware, and its aggressive bubblings quickly drenched the house scene. Part of its attraction was that its circuits will quite literally write the music for you, courtesy of the machine's randomising function. Turn it on and there are a series of mutant basslines all ready to go. If you want a new pattern, you simply remove and replace the batteries and there'll be a whole new composition ready and waiting. 'Spookily,' Pierre says, 'the line used in "Acid Tracks" is preserved forever in the bowels of that particular machine.'

Moving house

Chicago is known for its pool of church-trained vocalists. These angelic voices are kept in steady work because the city is also the advertising jingle capital of the world. A similar happy mix of the sacred and the profane is exactly what powered house. It was a genre inspired as much by the classic spiritual dance songs of the seventies as by basic consumer computer technology. Thanks to this combination, in a process that owed virtually nothing to the musician and almost everything to the DJ, Chicago was the clearest example of disco being lovingly continued under another name.

But by 1987 the Chicago scene was faltering. Rap's belated arrival in the city caused some tension as the two rival cultures clashed, not least over the presence of gay clubbers. Many blame the rise of hip-house, a hybrid of the two genres popularised by artists like Tyree and Fast Eddie, for a weakening of the club scene. Marshall pins similar blame on the success of acid house, suggesting that because it was so easy to make an acid track, there was a flooding of the market and a massive fall in the number of records you could expect to sell locally. Acid's manic qualities also served to edge out the less frenetic styles of house.

The mafia, too, had a role in house's downfall, exerting their influence on the city's revitalised venues and accelerating clubland's cycle of openings and closures. After Power Plant closed in 1985, Frankie Knuckles went to CODs, a smaller, short-lived club. From there he opened a place called the Power House, but in 1987 the city authorities moved against after-hours clubs and he returned to New York. The Music Box closed in 1987.

Hardy got caught in a downward spiral of drug abuse. He started injecting, and would sell his mix tapes for a fix, his ravenous appetite for excitement degenerating with the years into a sickness that drove him to sell the rarest of records for a few dollars apiece. He died in 1992.

House, driven by its success overseas, became an export business. Because back at the end of the eighties, just as the music seemed to wither in its birthplace, across the ocean it was being championed to unforeseen heights.

THIRTEEN
TECHNO

The Sound

'The race which first learns to balance equally the intellectual and the emotional – to use the machines and couple them with a life of true intuition and feeling such as the Easterns know – will produce the supermen.'

– Paul Robeson, 1935

'There are millions of people in Detroit. I'd say about thirty of them have heard of techno.'

– Marc Kinchen, 1990

Chicago is only 300 miles from Detroit; you can make it in four hours. Summer 1987: Derrick May and Kevin Saunderson are driving west on I-94 and traffic's not too bad. Derrick scans the radio; they should be close enough to pick up WBMX. Last trip they caught Farley playing 'Triangle of Love' and screamed like madmen, with Kevin going nuts at the wheel hearing his first track on the radio. It makes it all worthwhile to know people outside the little Detroit cliques are getting their music. Soon they'll have more proof: the trunk is full of their latest 12-inches – on Transmat and KMS, plus some from Metroplex, their friend Juan's label – pressed up for the Chicago stores. When they drop the boxes off they'll pick up the cash from last time and stock up on some house tracks.

Back home in Detroit, these producers have a new blueprint for dance music. Pure, modernist, synthesised soul. But only in Chicago can they see the full power of their compositions. Their trips to the Music Box are where they find inspiration. They take tracks to see them tried out on Ron Hardy's maniac dancefloor.

Detroit is worlds apart from the bustle of Chicago. Coming back you always feel a little torn: you realise how empty it is here, you wish Detroit had those big, fired-up clubs, all those kids frantically making records, hanging out, biting ideas off each other, talking about who made a track, or who got theirs played. And just sometimes you wish you could throw tunes together as carelessly as they do: just see what works and rip it off

– an old Philly bassline, drums – press it up fast, hear it out and forget it.

But then you'd make music that's only *effective*: throwaway. In Detroit's quiet suburbs you have space to expand your ideas, the chance to analyse your music and take it to another level. To take it *seriously*. Why bother otherwise? Especially now there's people in *Europe* interested. Asking us the ideas behind our music! Fuck it, Chicago's fun, but do you want to be just a kid feeding the dancefloor, or do you want to be a musician, a composer, an artist?

Since starting their labels they've moved into Eastern Market, the last gasp of downtown, to bring some business back to the city. Hard to stay optimistic when you drive through Detroit though: it's burnt out, boarded up, surrounded by rusting railheads, dead car plants. 'Like *Titanic* rotting above the water,' Derrick likes to say. But it suits the melancholy mood of the music. Plus, rent is cheap.

Techno is an ambitious sonovabitch. It wants to free itself from the baggage of all the world's previous music and take a few brave steps into the future. Where other forms are copying, emulating, recycling – returning to favourite themes and trusted basslines – techno hopes for the clarity of pure creation. It rejects representation in favour of abstraction, and tries to achieve something newer and bolder. High ideals indeed. In a city wiped out by the loss of faith in progress, techno tried to construct a new belief in the future. Its basic notion is this: if house is just disco played by microchips, what kind of noise would these machines make on their own?

The Electrifyin' Mojo

Detroit – the motor city. Here Henry Ford had pioneered mass production, seeding the world's most concentrated centre of automobile manufacture. Here Berry Gordy had powered up another conveyor belt, the pop factory of Motown, from which came the optimistic soul of sixties America. Motown was the music of full employment, the integrated sound of blacks and whites working side by side for fat auto company pay cheques. A little later the same Detroit affluence allowed George Clinton to connect raw soul to some Marshall amps, add a heavy dose of acid and create the sci-fi funk rock of Parliament-Funkadelic. The city also has a good claim as the birthplace of punk: both the MC5 and Iggy Pop hail from Detroit. And here, in the eighties, as the factories were downsizing and the city beginning to die, a trio of techno renegades would develop yet another new form of music.

Juan Atkins, Derrick May and Kevin Saunderson met at junior high school in Belleville, a leafy community between west Detroit and university town Ann Arbor. They were black living in a very white suburb, so this brought them together. Derrick and Kevin both had dreams of playing pro football, another link. What really cemented their friendship, however, was music.

The three teenagers would listen to a nightly show 'The Midnight Funk Association' and find themselves transfixed by the hypnotic voice and compelling music of DJ Charles Johnson – 'the Electrifyin' Mojo'. With a philosophy of 'counter-clockwiseology' that put 'mood-mats' over formats, Mojo ignored the racial separatism of the city's airwaves to dispense a variety of futuristic sounds – he linked the galactic funk of hometown heroes Parliament-Funkadelic with an eclectic stew of soundtracks, classical music and the latest European synth pop. Mojo gave Detroit a strong taste for Prince, and crucially, in 1981, when he got his hands on Kraftwerk's *Computer World*, he regularly played the entire album.

Originally from Little Rock, Arkansas, with a career starting in the Philippines, Mojo came to Detroit radio in 1977. His refusal to bow to convention meant his show regularly moved stations. Mojo's voracious appetite for new and unusual music was an important starting point for 'the Belleville three'. He fed them music and fuelled their taste for musical exploration. Eventually he would be among the first to play their records. Equally important perhaps, to a future techno sensibility, was the mysterious and disembodied persona he cultivated. His publicity photo was simply a darkened silhouette, and there is no doubting the seductive, spaced-out authority of his shows. At a certain point every night, he would make arrangements, P-Funk-style, for the mothership to land, instructing his listeners to flash their lights on and off to guide the cosmic Afronauts home.

This music fell into the posh homes of Belleville, where the money of Detroit's past had settled in lakefront properties and tree-lined streets. Here lawn parties and high school sports propelled the social calendar, a musical hobby was well fed with pricey equipment, and the days stretched out in comfortable teenage self-absorption. 'This is important,' stresses Derrick. 'Juan myself and Kevin, we come from middle-class, upper-middle-class families, so most of the people we associated with were upper middle class to very rich. There was no abject poverty around us.' Also, until their families relocated, all three had enjoyed city childhoods. So finding themselves trapped in safe, unsophisticated Belleville gave a real sense of dislocation.

Belleville's narrowness was a shock. 'I remember being called "nigger" for the first time and I didn't know what it meant,' says Kevin. 'There were only three or four black families there. When we moved in someone threw our garbage over our lawn, things like that.' Derrick recalls a racial awakening of a different kind. First day in school, he sat down to eat with Troy, a white kid he'd hung with over the summer. Behind a sea of well-behaved white faces, two rows of rowdy black kids from across the tracks in West Willow were throwing obscenities and French fries at each other. 'Hey man, why you sitting with the honkies?' Derrick cringed as he realised he'd crossed an unspoken line, declared himself a misfit. 'It was a culture shock for me,' he says. 'It blew me away. I had never experienced voluntary segregation before. It made me feel outside who I thought I was.'

After Kevin made the same lunchroom faux pas, for the rest of the year he and Derrick reluctantly dined in the animal house of the black section. 'I sat back there with them with pure disgust,' recalls May, 'I found myself entertained by my own people.' Forced to watch these kids selling themselves short, he vowed to transcend any self-limiting 'black' perspective. 'I sat there feeling this is fucked up. I pitied these people. And I made a promise to myself that I was going to be better than that.'

Kraftwerk

Kraftwerk were producing techno back when Detroit still made cars. Four Germans dressed as robot librarians didn't look like they had a dancefloor explosion hidden in their party-pants, but they would be more influential on dance music than any other single group. Classical musicians Ralf Hütter and Florian Schneider met in 1968 at Düsseldorf's Academy of Arts. As early electronic instruments emerged they conceived a music that would give life to Germany's wiped-clean post-war culture.

'When we started it was like shock, silence. Where do we stand?' Ralf Hütter told Jon Savage in the *Village Voice*. 'We had no father figures, no continuous tradition of entertainment. Through the 1950s and 1960s, everything was Americanised. We were part of this 1968 movement, where suddenly there were possibilities, then we started to establish some form of German sound.'

They also developed a calculated techno image to challenge the whole rock aesthetic. What greater satire on pop stardom than to replace yourselves onstage with showroom dummies? Kraftwerk's appearance was an austere contrast to their long-haired contemporaries like Can, Faust and Tangerine Dream, the 'Krautrock' groups that were adding electronics and repetitive minimalism to guitar, bass and drums; as well as to the 'Kosmische Rock' ('Cosmic Rock') movement which fused electronics with jazz and psychedelia. All these German experimentalists took their lead from radical classical composer Karlheinz Stockhausen and his vastly influential electronic music studio in Cologne. Stockhausen was in turn a pupil of former French TV engineer Pierre Schaeffer and his *musique concrète* school.

In 1970, after recording an album of seriously avant-garde college musings under the name Organisation, Hütter and Schneider built an electronic playpen, their Kling Klang studio, and teamed up with Klaus Dinger, Thomas Homann and visionary producer Conny Plank, the 'Phil Spector of Krautrock'. Their first release as Kraftwerk (which means 'Power Plant') was more in the trippy vein of Tangerine Dream, but after Dinger and Homann quit to form Neu!, they turned to the drum machine and never looked back.

'We are playing the machines; the machines play us,' Hütter said to Danny Eccleston in Q magazine. 'It is really the exchange and the friendship we have with the musical machines which makes us build new music.'

In 1974 'Autobahn', a twenty-two-minute hymn to the monotony of driving, gave them a world-wide hit, and showed the early disco scene that computers could be funky as well as add up your taxes. After this, Kraftwerk increasingly pushed their rhythms towards the dancefloor. Electronic percussionist Karl Bartos, who joined them for their best-known albums, *Trans Europe Express* and *Man Machine*, admitted, 'We always tried to make an American rhythm feel, with a European approach to harmony and melody.' Such was their ability to create dance pressure from stark, rigid beats that when Leonard Jackson, one of Norman Whitfield's sound engineers, came to Düsseldorf to mix *Man Machine*, he confidently expected Kraftwerk would be black. As techno producer Carl Craig later said, 'They were so stiff they were funky.'

Though electronic instruments were still very expensive, a handful of producers emerged determined to base a career on them. Kraftwerk's contemporaries included Jean-Michel Jarre, Giorgio Moroder and Vangelis Papathanaious. By the late seventies, synthesisers were boxes rather than rooms, and electronic groups were seeping into the pond of pop. Human League, Gary Numan, Ultravox, Devo, Yello: in the wake of punk's revolution there was a steady flow of synth groups. If you were a black teenager looking to get as far away from the culture America expected you to enjoy, this was it – Morse code from Mars.

Cybotron

Padding around his house, plucking at the bass guitar he wore like a T-shirt, charting music that would be known world-wide, scribbling down sci-fi names for future song titles: each day Juan Atkins moved a little closer to his destiny. He knew all along he would be a famous musician.

Juan was raised in a tough part of Detroit, the son of a successful concert promoter who had moved to the suburbs after he and his wife split. Juan had made music throughout his childhood, playing bass and drums in garage funk bands. His tastes were wide, but after hearing 'Flashlight' he found himself entranced by the synthesised keyboard bass Bernie Worrell had introduced to Parliament-Funkadelic. When one night on Mojo's show he heard this aesthetic taken to its limits by Kraftwerk, he was stunned. 'I just froze in my tracks,' he said. 'Everything was so clean and precise, so robotic.'

On graduating from high school in 1980, Juan bought himself a Korg MS10 keyboard and spent the summer putting tracks together. After playing these to his new classmates at his college music course, he hooked up with Rick Davis; a rather shell-shocked Vietnam veteran, eleven years older, who went by the name 3070 and had an Aladdin's cave of sound equipment. Davis had already made an avant-garde electronic album *The Methane Sea*, which Mojo played. He and Atkins immediately formed a band, Cybotron.

Juan neglected his bass as the synthesiser pulled him in. Its eerie noises spoke to his teenage alienation, and gave his melodies an appealing gravitas. He admits the technology was firmly in the driving seat. 'The synthesiser was the main catalyst. You play with a synthesiser, there are certain things you hear in the machine: it's gonna prompt you to do certain things. Especially if you make all your beats and rhythms from that same machine.'

Cybotron's first release, 'Alleys Of Your Mind', came out in 1981 on their own Deep Space label, pressed as a 7-inch. (Juan laughs as he recalls how one DJ glued it to a spare 12-inch in order to play it.) A sparse, pulsing electro track with a paranoid robotic voice, it was a local hit, selling more than 10,000 copies in Chicago and Detroit, aided by regular airings courtesy of the Electrifyin' Mojo. Most who heard it were convinced it was made by someone white someplace in Europe (it owes a clear debt of inspiration to 'Mr. X' a track on Ultravox's *Vienna* LP). But when people realised Juan was a Detroit teenager they knew the bar had been raised. 'It was incredible,' recalls Detroit DJ and producer Jeff Mills. 'Juan was so far ahead. The only thing we had to compare it with was Kraftwerk. If you really think about how young he was and his technique of putting the music together. It was mind-blowing, incredible.'

Davis had a distinct personal philosophy based on science fiction and the mystic numerology of Kabbalah (hence his name, 3070). Juan and he also shared an interest in Alvin Toffler, whose popular book *The Third Wave* niftily predicted a post-industrial future that would belong to society's techno renegades – rebels able to turn technology to their own ends. Such thoughts resonated powerfully with Atkins's dreams of

Mirror Man – Derrick May reflects on the true nature of techno.

futuristic music made with mass-produced electronic instruments. He and Davis spent hours discussing all this, applying these ideas to the grim post-industrial cityscape which was Detroit.

Though 'Alleys Of Your Mind' had beaten it by months, the electro crown was seized by Afrika Bambaataa's vastly more successful 'Planet Rock', which pursued an almost identical vision of electronic funk. Cybotron put out two more singles, 'Cosmic Cars' and their classic 'Clear', which peaked at no.52 in *Billboard*'s Black Singles chart. They landed an album deal with Fantasy in California and made an album, *Enter*, but when the Hendrix-loving Davis made it plain he wanted to pursue a more rock-oriented direction, in 1984 the band split. Free to follow where his synthesiser was leading him, Juan already knew what was next. Though the final Cybotron release was a poor choice to follow 'Clear', its name was destined to resonate. It was called 'Techno City'.

The Belleville three

It was the streetwise Aaron Atkins whom Derrick May befriended at first. Aaron told Derrick some tall tales about owning a car. As he was barely a teenager, Derrick thought this unlikely. 'Then one day he shows up, thirteen years old, with a Fleetwood Cadillac. Big red crushed velvet interior, Funkadelic pumpin' through the sound system. He let the windows down, it was like a Cheech & Chong movie. Out comes this big cloud of weed smoke.' The impressionable May was blown away.

Aaron's older brother Juan took an instant dislike to this naive kid. And Derrick was certainly intimidated by Juan as he prowled the house with his hair permed back, always playing music, rarely speaking to anyone. 'I'm a complete square to these guys,' laughs Derrick. 'I'm just a kid who likes to play baseball, watch cartoons. I believe everything my mother tells me.' The ice broke after they played chess. But it was music that sealed their friendship. Juan had recorded some Gary Numan, Kraftwerk and Tangerine Dream onto a tape that Derrick had left at his house. 'Juan said, "To be honest with you there's some shit on the tape you're not gonna like." But I said, "No, give it back to me." ' Derrick came back bugging Juan to educate him in the wonders of this stark European sound.

'Music became our common denominator. We would sit in Juan's bedroom and talk until both of us fell asleep. Analyse records, put on a piece of music and try to figure out what that person was thinking when they made it.' Hearing music in this isolated way, they loaded it with philosophical weight. A track like Manuel Göttsching's epic 'E2-E4' had them transfixed. 'It was always instrumentals.' Derrick recalls. 'When we heard things like that we just listened to it for hours man: days, weeks.' Not hearing songs in a club context, they developed a contempt for anything less than serious. 'We just thought vocals were stupid. Talking about love and getting some pussy and you broke my heart. Nothing political, nothing conscious.'

There was also a pair of turntables, and Juan's mentoring soon evolved into the two of them learning DJing skills and making pause-button tapes. 'These few records that we had, we'd just mix them over and over again,' Juan was already releasing music as Cybotron, and Derrick's attitude was more or less hero worship. In return for the musical education, he gladly became Juan's keenest promoter and greatest fan.

Completing the trio and bringing a different outlook was Kevin Saunderson – his father a real-estate agent, his mother a college lecturer – who'd grown up in Brooklyn until the age of thirteen. Kevin got to know Derrick on the football field where the loudmouthed May regularly showered him with verbal abuse. One day Derrick ran his mouth too far, Kevin punched him in the face and knocked him out.

All through high school, Kevin would make summer trips back to Brooklyn. One of his brothers, Ronnie, was a sound engineer and road manager for Brass Construction (he even wrote a song for them), and so, armed with precocious facial hair, Kevin sampled the excitement of New York's clubs, including the Loft and the Paradise Garage. 'I had a beard at a young age, so I could get in to all these clubs. I don't wear it now 'cos I'd look about eighty-five,' he jokes. The Garage, especially, made a big impression. 'It was amazing, blew me away. I never knew something like that could exist. My brothers, my cousins, we all used to go together, and just dance.'

As his friend Derrick started making music with Juan, Kevin remained focused on sport. 'They were making tracks for at least four years before I even considered DJing.' Eventually, though, he would join them in setting up a studio and making records, and with his more club-based aesthetic would enjoy the greatest commercial success of the three.

The high school parties

By the eighties central Detroit had been convincingly wiped out. The oil crisis had sent the US auto industry, with its two-ton chrome dinosaurs, into shock; swift lay-offs and factory closures followed. Even Motown had upped sticks for LA. While Detroit still had America's most affluent black population, anyone with money had scattered to the suburbs, leaving a dead inner city whose grand boulevards and civic buildings were now 'demolished by neglect', as a famous art project once labelled them. Detroit's people, too, were demolished, crushed by mass unemployment, waiting in vain for something to 'trickle down' – the cruel lie of Reagan's voodoo economics. In the wake of such desperation Detroit was now 'Murder Capital'; battle surgeons went there to learn about bullet wounds.

There were clubs in the city, but few you'd convincingly call under-ground; certainly nothing like the well-equipped after-hours venues that drove the scenes in Chicago and New York. Nevertheless, if you were at high school, you'd find yourself at the heart of a surprisingly progressive nightlife. From opulent house parties to raucous one-offs in bars and clubs, the city's most enthusiastic clubbers and most competitive DJs were to be found on the teenage 'prep-party' circuit.

'The high school scene was amazing,' says Derrick. 'They were highfalutin' – teenage black kids with money. You had guys wearing Polo and Versace, and all this ridiculous stuff, in high school. It was crazy how much money these parties were making. People were charging $25 to get in.' The promoters, high school students themselves, trumpeted their sophistication by identifying with Italian high fashion and the British New Romantic movement, and adopted names that reflected these rarefied aspirations: Plush, Funtime Society, Universal, GQ Productions and, later, Ciabattino, Courtier, Cacharel, Schiaparelli, Gables. They ran their parties like private clubs, focused around particular high schools, and the dress was as important as the music: Sidewinder side-lacing leather boots, double-breasted shirts, technicolour Fiorucci gear. One of the most successful party crews was Charivari – the name appropriated from a chain of New York clothing stores. In 1981 this would provide the title of another of Detroit's early forays into electronic music, the Italo-disco style 'Sharevari' by A Number Of Names (the title's spelling altered to avoid conflict).

In parallel to the preppy scene, the city's rougher east side hosted 'jit' or 'jitterbug' parties where electro and Funkadelic held more sway – the ancestor of Detroit's current 'booty bass' scene. There was never any real confrontation, although prep party flyers would often include coded messages; 'no hats and canes' was one popular invocation, a reference to gang members' penchant for carrying walking canes. The two scenes merged briefly in 1983, but after that the more hip hop oriented crowds made the running.

The music was vitally important. 'Although they were very young, they were very sophisticated,' remembers Jeff Mills. 'The DJs were very carefully picked and the music was exceptional.' Detroit had been washed with a whiter strand of disco than either New York or Chicago, with its uptempo sister sound Eurodisco having taken hold. As in Chicago, a flurry of Italo-disco came to the fore; in Detroit it was known as 'progressive'. Producers like Jacques Fred Petrus (Peter Jacques Band/Change), acts like Alexander Robotnik, Capricorn, Klein & MBO and Telex, danceable new wave groups such as the B-52s, and British synth groups like Human League, ABC and Ultravox also enjoyed success on dancefloors. Listen to Visage's 'Frequency 7' today, with its pulsing rhythm and harsh analogue sounds, and it could quite comfortably pass for an early Detroit techno record.

In *Music Technology*, Derrick May said he considered his music a direct continuation of the European synthesiser tradition, continuing the agenda laid down by artists like Depeche Mode, and suggesting that British bands of the early eighties 'left us waiting. Somebody like Gary Numan started something he never concluded.'

'The real inspiration of European music was simply that you could make music with electronic equipment,' argues Kevin Saunderson. 'I was more infatuated with the idea that I can do this all by myself.'

Jeff Mills thinks Detroit's international outlook came from its earlier affluence and its proximity to Canada. 'We grew up wanting to go beyond the barriers of Detroit. A lot of us searched out certain things, unique things, to define ourselves. Music was one, fashion was another.' One way to understand teenage Detroit's obsession with European music is to think of it as rebellion against the rhythm and blues tradition, the music of their parents. And simple snobbery: what better way to distance yourself from the scruffians of the ghetto than to listen to cool, detached, European pop?

Along with 'Sharevari' and Cybotron's various releases, other locally made records found their way on to the party circuit's turntables. Don Was (Donald Fagenson) and David Was (David Weiss), released a series of inventive and playful tracks under the name Was (Not Was), gaining broader success with 1988's 'Walk the Dinosaur'. During studio downtime, Don Was produced a disc under the name Orbit called 'The Beat Goes On', a popular local hit. He would also occasionally get together with the city's leading disc jockey, Ken Collier, and remix his own tunes under the name Wasmopolitan Mixing Squad (Collier and Was are credited as remixers on 'Tell Me That I'm Dreaming' by Was (Not Was)).

As a DJ Collier was a uniting force. Having learned his craft during the disco era, he was a fixture on both the high school scene and in the city's gay clubs. He would also be among the first DJs in Detroit to play techno records like 'No UFOs' and 'Strings Of Life'. Prep party promoter Hassan Nurullah recalled Collier in Dan Sicko's excellent history, *Techno Rebels*: 'He was awesome. He'd get that big booty going, have a little glass of cognac . . . and he didn't do anything fancy, he just had a sense of what worked. He kept that party booming the whole time.' Tragically Collier died in 1996 from a late-diagnosed ailment related to his diabetes.

It was into this scene that 'Magic' Juan and Derrick 'Mayday' launched themselves in 1981 when they set themselves up as DJs with Keith 'Mixin' Martin, Art 'Pumpin' Payne and Eddie 'Flashin' Fowlkes. They called themselves Deep Space Soundworks, and despite their dynamic new middle names their first gig was far from auspicious. After some begging, these amateurs opened up for Ken Collier at a Pink Poodle party in the Downstairs Pub. 'We're playing 7-inch singles on decks with the rubber mats still on them,' recalls Derrick. 'Not one person is dancing. Ken Collier arrives, puts a real slipmat on, cues up a record, pulls back and boom. In ten seconds the floor was full.' Deep Space would be the underdogs on this fiercely competitive scene for most of their existence. 'There was another company called Direct Drive, and we hated those motherfuckers,' laughs Derrick. 'They played this prissy disco music, and we hated that. They were the establishment and we were fighting against them.'

Kevin joined Deep Space in 1984 (as 'Master Reese' – his middle name is Maurice), when his sporting career began to falter. At first he found mixing impossible, but after spotting an ad for a DJ course in Ohio, he secretly left town, paid to learn how to DJ, and joined the crew. 'Once I could mix, I got a real feeling for making music,' he says. 'It suddenly seemed easy.' He also joined a college fraternity, a move that ensured bookings.

Ever the hustler, Derrick swung the collective a prestigious radio gig when he convinced WJLB to let them put together a Detroit version of Chicago's 'Hot Mix 5' show. 'Street Beat' premiered in 1985, with Juan, Derrick and Kevin joined by Mike Grant (later a house DJ) for a show heavy in prepared re-edits, immersing them all in the craft of production.

They were eclipsed, however, by the prodigious mixing talents of another young radio DJ, a voiceless vinyl whirlwind known as the Wizard, later to become second generation techno producer Jeff Mills. On his slots on WDRQ from early 1984 he threw together a breathtaking array of records, stitched together with ultra-fast dexterity, a style he later brought to bear on his incendiary club DJ performances. Mills soon ruled Detroit radio with a blaze of hip hop and other fresh sounds, thrown down in the style of his heroes D.ST, Jazzy Jeff and Cash Money. 'I stayed at the station all day,' says Mills, 'and when the programme director decided it would be interesting to do something mix-wise I was called into the studio.' Following these brief flurries, where he'd cut up, say, two copies of Chaka Khan, he was given a fat record budget for a wide-ranging three-hour nightly show which broke many artists to Detroit. 'I created each show with a theme based around sound effects,' he says. 'I would go into the sound library, and grab all the things I could use. That's how I got into conceptual music.' And, as competition for ratings heated up, the Wizard would re-edit tracks; he'd even make his own new music for the show.

With its radio getting creative, and with mobs of high schoolers pushing each other to new heights, Detroit became an inspiring place for would-be electronic musicians. Despite the lack of a forceful club scene there was plenty happening. 'The scene in Detroit wasn't anywhere near as developed as Chicago's,' asserts Dan Sicko. 'But it was that much more idiosyncratic. Detroit was very small cliques and very quirky, and that's why Detroit ended up sounding so different.'

'If there had been a party scene in Detroit, we wouldn't make the music we do,' Eddie Fowlkes told *Muzik*. 'It's what separates us from New York and Chicago. They're all too busy going out.'

Techno recorded

As young as seventeen Juan Atkins told his friends that one day he'd start a label called Metroplex. In 1985, with Cybotron finished, he was free to do it, and as Model 500 – which he thought was a suitably 'non-ethnic' name (also perhaps a nod to Rick Davis's numerology) – he laid down techno's founding record. 'No UFOs' was a dark challenge to the dancefloor built from growing layers of robotic bass, dissonant melody lines and barks of disembodied voices. It was music he'd originally intended for Cybotron, and in its theme of government control it continued Cybotron's doomy social commentary, but was noticeably faster-paced, with the electro breakbeat replaced by an industrial four-to-the-floor rhythm. This was the sound of Detroit's future.

Juan's next releases 'Night Drive (Thru Babylon)' and 'Technicolor' returned to a tight electro pulse, but by his fifth, 'Play It Cool', the house-style kick-drum was here to stay. Juan continued tutoring his friends, helping them arrange and mix their musical sketches into finished tracks. In 1986 Eddie Fowlkes became the second Metroplex artist with 'Goodbye Kiss', and Derrick May launched his own label.

May's imprint, Transmat, had (and still has) matrix numbers prefixed 'MS' for 'Metroplex Subsidiary', as a tribute to Juan. Its debut release was 'Let's Go', a mess of computerised Latin percussion that Juan produced from Derrick's half-baked ideas. After his shaky start, however, Derrick would soar. With no musical training, and none of Kevin's 'traditional' disco inspiration, he was least encumbered by musical preconceptions, and best placed to let the machines have their day. This became apparent in 1987 when, as Rhythim Is Rhythim, he released timeless classics such as 'Nude Photo' and 'Strings Of Life' in quick succession. These abstract compositions of bittersweet synthesised sound evaded most established rules of dance music – 'Strings Of Life', built from piano riffs and orchestra samples, had no bassline – but cleverly managed to drive clubbers wild.

At the same time, with Juan's help, Kevin Saunderson embarked on an ambitious journey, his sights set high from the start. His very first record, as Kreem, was a vocal track 'Triangle of Love', with Paris Grey lending the tonsils. He started a label, KMS (Kevin Maurice Saunderson), and showed his more dance-driven credentials with his Reese & Santonio underground classics: 'The Sound', 'Rock To The Beat', and 'Just Another Chance', with its much-emulated thunderous rolling bass – all made specifically with the Paradise Garage in mind. By 1988, as Inner City, Kevin was making fully-fledged pop hits with Grey. 'My inspiration was a little different, definitely,' he admits. 'I was into vocals, I was into Evelyn Champage King, McFadden & Whitehead, Chaka Khan. Those were anthems to me, so when I create my music I'm thinking about melody, about song, about uplifting tunes.' In fact, he'd argue that he had been following a very different path to Juan and Derrick all along: 'I was really doing my own thing. I had my own vision. We were just using the same tools.'

As Detroit's musical output gathered steam, it found a vital market in Chicago. Derrick May's mother had lived there since his last year in high school and through the first years of the eighties. Derrick – while living at Kevin's house to avoid breaking up his schooling in Detroit – had visited her regularly and had soaked up the underground club energy that was lacking in his home town. He remembers on his first visit hearing 'Feel The Drive' by Doctor's Cat on the radio. It was a revelation to realise that obscure music like this had a market. In his role as Juan's champion, helping to promote Cybotron, it was great news. 'There was a period when Juan thought he was in this vast ocean in a rowboat with no oars. But when I heard this it was like a beacon, a lifeboat.'

Chicago clubs, too, were a revelation: When he first visited Frankie Knuckles's Power Plant, Derrick was blown away. No high school party could have prepared him for the intensity of the crowd, the music, the euphoria: 'It lifted me off my feet. I was elevated.' But then he witnessed the phenomenal abandon of Ron Hardy at the Music Box. 'I kept hearing his name. Finally I went to hear Ronnie. And this time I wasn't just elevated, I was flat-out busted down. I was beat up by it. It was kids from the south side, younger kids, more physical, more athletic. Young girls who let you put your hands on them when you danced. It was straight up ghetto house. And I was right there with those kids, screaming, dancing every week. Shirt off, going nuts.'

Juan didn't care for the gayness of the scene, 'He was like, "Oh man, fuck that fag shit." ' But Derrick made Chicago the centre of his efforts. 'I remember making "Nude Photo" and "Strings of Life". My first ambition was to get Ron Hardy and Frankie to play them. I thought if those guys play my record, I've made it.' It was Knuckles who named 'Strings Of Life', after May gave him an early demo. He brought several friends to see Hardy play, including Kevin who was so impressed he later wrote 'Bounce Your Body To The Box' in tribute. Derrick even played a small part in the avalanche of tracks which had started to flow out of Chicago, since he provided the Power Plant with a 909 drum machine. Initially, Knuckles used this to boost the kick-drum sounds in older records, but the machine found itself in constant use as a series of would-be producers borrowed it to record tracks, with Chip E and Steve Hurley among them. Pretty soon the Detroit producers were regularly driving carloads of records over to the Windy City. 'Chicago gave us hope, gave us inspiration,' says Kevin, 'so even though there wasn't much at home, there was plenty right next door.'

Despite its initial dependency on Chicago, it soon became clear that techno was strikingly different to house. It was inevitable with all that post-urban introspection, sci-fi imagery and affection for stark European synthesiser music that Detroit's music would end up someplace different to that made by the party kids of Chicago. In common with many, Dan Sicko believes that techno as a genre began with 'Nude Photo'.

'The first "x" number of records, you can definitely argue that Detroit was an adjunct of Chicago,' he says. 'Until "Nude Photo", where it was like, "OK, this isn't house music anymore." ' Sicko argues that it was its radical construction, its unwillingness to simply throw pre-existing elements together, that made it such a turning point.

Jeff Mills, then hungrily devouring music from everywhere for his radio show, claims he heard the uniqueness of Detroit even earlier: 'It was the programming of the drum machines, the melodic sequences, the basslines were very different,' he argues. 'The music was more progressive than Chicago house. It was more difficult to listen to because it was more complex. Kevin Saunderson agrees: 'We had more energy, we took more chances. I think Chicago was pretty safe. They were vocal-oriented. And our energy level was definitely faster, bpm-wise.'

While house was happy to reheat old tunes, techno rejected tradition. Whereas house rejoiced in funky, soulful disco, techno was transfixed by Giorgio Moroder's uptempo computerised version. Where house stole melodies and basslines wholesale, techno composed new ones note by note. Techno was about going back to first principles, to sounds and composition, to musicianship. The two styles were very different emotionally too, in keeping with the cities that bred them: while house was about lustful churchy energy, techno dealt in lament and anxiety. Even today, in discussing what defines the style, Derrick casually relies on the word 'melancholy'.

Techno defined

'Techno' was first used as the name for a completely separate genre as late as 1988. Before that, its creators were happy to be labelled 'house' and thrown in with the Chicago scene. In the *NME* in August 1987, Simon Witter described Derrick May as 'one third of a team of Detroit house obsessives'. May himself nonchalantly referred to his own music as house and didn't once mention anything about machines, computers or science fiction: 'House represents basement music, club music, and if they forget that and go soft, kids will think that's what house is about,' he said. 'We're diehards.'

Indeed, initially the 'techno' tag was largely a marketing ploy. Neil Rushton, a Birmingham northern soul DJ who set up Kool Kat and later Network Records, started licensing tracks from the Detroit producers in 1987. 'The Chicago thing was already sewn up,' he explains. 'People like Damon D'Cruz at Jack Trax and the majors like Pete Tong, they'd already got Steve Hurley and Farley and all those guys.' But Detroit was as yet untouched, and thanks to his connections as a northern soul collector (His label Kool Kat was named after a Detroit soul record by Joe Matthews), Rushton was immediately drawn to records bearing a 313 area code. 'When the imports started coming in on Transmat, KMS and Metroplex I was probably more interested than the average person. So I rang up the number of one of the Transmat releases – "Nude Photo" I think, just before "Strings Of Life" came through. I rang up Derrick and asked about releasing records.'

Rushton started licensing tracks for UK release, and quickly realised there was enough material for an album. He convinced Virgin subsidiary Ten to let him put together a compilation showcasing the Motor City: plenty of Atkins, May & Saunderson, plus a couple of tracks by Blake Baxter, who Derrick decided would give techno some pin-up potential. Its working title was *The House Sound Of Detroit.* This only changed at a very late stage when Virgin realised the advantage of hyping the music as the Next Big Thing.

Now managing Derrick and Juan, Rushton took journalists Stuart Cosgrove and John McCready to Detroit to write articles for *The Face* and *NME* around the album. When asked for the name of their music Juan Atkins said, 'We call it techno.' May preferred 'hi-tech soul' and begged Juan to reconsider. 'To me techno was the stuff coming from Miami. I thought it was ugly, some ghetto bullshit. Juan said, "Naw man, this is techno".' When the album came out, its title screamed *Techno! The New Dance Sound Of Detroit.*

As he prodded them to explain their music, Cosgrove elicited some fine prose from the Belleville three. Derrick May came up with the much-repeated line: 'The music is just like Detroit, a complete mistake. It's like George Clinton and Kraftwerk stuck in an elevator.' Kevin Saunderson explained he'd once been sacked from a radio station for being 'too ahead of his time', and Juan Atkins told Cosgrove, 'Berry Gordy built the Motown sound on the same principles as the conveyor belt system at Ford's. Today their plants don't work that way – they use robots and computers to make the cars. I'm probably more interested in Ford's robots than in Berry Gordy's music.'

This was gold-dust. The new name made techno a distinct musical form, and with all its science fiction influences and the producers' socio-political concerns, it had an enticing philosophy behind it, neatly connecting the city to its sound. 'Detroit's electronic music community don't fear the robot,' wrote McCready. 'They are the Techno Rebels – musical agents of the Third Wave who see the fusion of man and machine as the only future.' The post-industrial imagery was laid on thick and the producers saw that intellectualising their music would help them promote it. McCready even had Derrick declaring that 'Strings Of Life' was about the death of Martin Luther King.

'I wasn't used to being interviewed, people talking about the music,' says Kevin. 'I'm thinking, "why you want to know that? Why is this important to you?" And then you start getting the picture, you see the magazine come out and talk about the "Sound of Detroit".'

'It changed the way we saw the music, and what we saw the music was worth,' agrees Derrick.

The fact that these pioneers were treated like rock poets and asked for the ideas behind their music would have an enduring significance. It's impossible to say how much this scrutiny affected techno's evolution, or how much the producers post-rationalised their philosophies, but certainly it encouraged ever deeper introspection, leading Detroit's producers to continually analyse their intentions and consider the 'meanings' of their tracks in a way alien to all previous forms of dance music.

'We intellectualised it,' agrees John McCready, 'with Cosgrove gleaning those fantastic quotes. They weren't ready for us to come over and do that to their music. They were making dance records for themselves, and suddenly they found their music described as "a listening experience". Derrick, Kevin and Juan were all clever blokes and they switched on like light bulbs when they realised this was the way to play it.

'They realised, "Oh, that's what you want then," and hence all these mixes started appearing with no drums on them, and Derrick was encouraged into ridiculous tuneless noodling over the beginnings of his records.'

Techno quickly gained an image as an auteur producers' medium, as something detached and experimental. Because, like composers or jazz-men, they assembled their music from notes rather than samples, techno's creators were raised to genius status. Because Detroit's decay is striking and there's no club scene to write about, the music was relentlessly characterised as a soundtrack to post-urban desolation, rather than music to make people sweat on a dancefloor. Finally, the fact that techno is made with computers somehow became a mysterious truth about mankind's cybernetic future.

These ideas have certainly fuelled many interesting developments, but never forget that, initially at least, techno was propelled by the same simple DJ-led dynamic as house and garage: bedroom producers creating home-made versions of the music they loved in order to feed the DJ and his hungry dancefloor. While it's easy to be carried away by its intellectual baggage, bear in mind that techno's poetic search for the soul of the machine is just a brainy way of saying, 'We wanted to make funky dance music on cheap synthesisers.' The producers in Chicago didn't feel the need to explain why they used machines – they simply couldn't play regular instruments.

Journalists loved the idea of degree-level dance music, and techno producers responded well to their flattering cerebral approach. Eventually, however, the music had been so comprehensively analysed that techno's inspirations and early working methods started being mistaken for immutable principles. Producers began thinking there was a blueprint for making 'proper' Detroit techno. A purist attitude crept in that served in some ways to fossilise the sound: those orchestral strings, those frosty hi-hats. At times Detroit's vision of the future seems stuck in 1987.

Ironically, despite techno's futuristic aspirations, the three Brits who initially championed it were drawn by the music's historical links. 'One of the things I always thought was the techno stuff had a jazz feel to it – as Carl Craig proved later,' says Rushton. 'We kept making comparisons to the past. They were pressing records at Archer's Pressing Plant – which was a tiny little company – and the guy there was the son of the guy who used to do all the independent northern soul classics.' Once, while Derrick was finishing a mix of his white-hot new music, the Brits were upstairs annoying him by cranking the volume on a load of ancient soul singles they'd bought.

'The other thing people got completely wrong is this image of techno being a new wave of dance music made in super studios. In fact, it was all

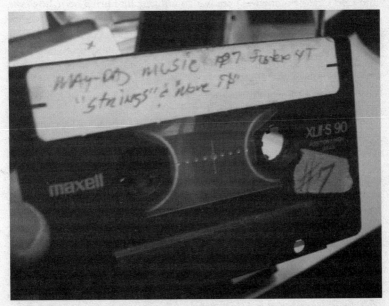

Strings attached – the original cassette from which 'Strings Of Life' was mastered.

made on old equipment,' adds McCready, pointing out that 'Strings Of Life' was mastered from a cassette. 'There were a lot of paradoxes going on there.'

An export market

'Wake Up America, You're Dead' was the subtle title for a panel discussion at 1989's New Music Seminar. Launching the attack, Factory Records' boss Tony Wilson argued that house and techno wouldn't have happened without Britain. The Happy Mondays backed him up with thuggish jeers, as did pop barnacle Keith Allen. Incensed, Marshall Jefferson walked out and Derrick May called Allen an asshole. Today, however, May admits he largely agrees. 'The diving board was Detroit; the pool that it dived into would be England: the home of pop culture, the cesspool of that shit.'

'In America it was hard for people to accept what we were doing as a new form of music that they could understand,' explains Kevin Saunderson. 'You didn't hear it on any format of radio; you didn't see it, obviously, on any TV.'

In the UK, Detroit's music was swept up in the wave of music feeding the acid house movement, and tracks like 'Strings Of Life' and 'Just Another Chance' became rave anthems. Despite this the *Techno!* album actually did quite badly (it's 1990 follow-up, with tracks by Octave One and Carl Craig, bombed). There was an unlikely hit buried on it, however, which would make Kevin Saunderson techno's first pop star. 'Big Fun' by Inner City, added at the last minute, sold six million copies world-wide and entered the UK top 10 in September 1988. A follow up, 'Good Life', showed that it had been no fluke. Immediately, DJ trips to the UK were filling the Detroiters' diaries, first to promote the compilation, then to play at raves. As European interest grew, May even moved to Amsterdam for a couple of years.

Having sold thousands of records on their own labels, and being hailed as DJ stars in Europe, it was a crushing disappointment that the US majors still wouldn't take them seriously. Detroit techno remained almost unrecognised in its own country, rarely heard even in Detroit itself. The first black musical form in America that broke decisively with black music tradition, techno seemed destined to confuse – at least until it developed a whiter face. 'It's not black, as far as the music business is concerned,' argues Derrick. 'Their attitude was, let's monitor it and watch what happens. When they realised it wasn't going away they picked it up on the second wave. They got Moby.'

Detroit enjoyed a brief flush in the summer of 1988 when Alton Miller and George Baker opened a small club called the Music Institute (or more correctly, the Detroit Musical Institution) at 1315 Broadway, where May, Darrell 'D' Wynn, Miller and Chez Damier (Anthony Pearson) played. Although the MI only remained open for just over a year, it served to catalyse more of an actual techno scene in the city. Very dark, with a huge mural of an eye behind the booth, it belatedly gave Detroit a venue in which to hear its own music. DJ/producer Alan Oldham posted his recollections recently: 'The MI brought a European vibe to our city. Before we were just a bunch of middle-class black kids who read *The Face* and *GQ* and *Melody Maker* and dreamt about what London or New York would be like.' He gushingly recalls the British artists who visited the Institute. 'Now ABC and Depeche Mode came to the MI to witness the relentless Mayday at work, and to hang out with us. Real Brits! Real accents! In our club.'

May's reworking of 'We Call It Acieed' by D-Mob was the Institute's anthem, played amid local releases and other hot tunes of the British acid house explosion. Carl Craig remembers May's powerful sets there. 'He played the craziest edits of the wildest music. When Derrick DJed, you didn't know whether he was playing records or manipulating equipment. People would go crazy. He would play "Big Fun" three or four times and every time it blew my mind, as well as everybody else's.' Sadly, central Detroit wasn't ready to support an after-hours club that played great dance music but didn't serve alcohol. And since its main DJs were often away earning big money in Europe, the club's momentum was soon lost. The Music Institute closed on 24 November 1989. Partygoers recall Derrick May mixing recorded clock bells over the top of 'Strings Of Life' and closing with 808 State's 'Pacific State'.

Detroit techno, radical in style and made on readily accessible equipment, was internationally inspiring, and in Europe it started to recombine with the industrial genres which had partly inspired it. Meanwhile, Derrick and Juan had a fallow period, Inner City were being led by A&R men into R&B, and Detroit's second wave of producers were signing to European labels in any case. Techno quickly came to mean the music emerging from Belgium and Germany, with techno evolving fast into a global stew of scenes and styles. The Euro sound began to dominate and the spotlight was stolen from techno's American pioneers. It made more sense to industry ears to hear this music coming from white Europeans.

Germany

Berlin, 9 November 1989, East German authorities, admitting economic exhaustion, allow their citizens to flood into the once-forbidden West. Guards who used to shoot at escapees wave people through, smiling. Collapsing Trabant cars splutter fumes from their two-stroke engines as whole families cross the crumbling iron curtain. The westerners offer flowers and drinks and handshakes and hugs and, as the partying continues, open up their homes. Jackhammers punch holes in the wall and a girl passes a red carnation through to people standing in what used to be no-man's land. GERMANY IS REUNITED IN THE STREETS, declare tomorrow's headlines. A group of East German lads buy water pistols and fill them with beer, dizzy with their new future. As the frosty night goes on, thousands dance on the defeated wall, lending each other hammers to chip away at history. From a rooftop, Beethoven's music soars over Berlin. It's the 'Ode To Joy' from his Ninth Symphony, chosen for its stirring words: 'We enter your sanctuary intoxicated with fire. Your magic power unites again those whom earthly customs have forcibly separated. All men will be brothers again under your gentle wing.'

As you'd expect of a dislocated city floating inside another country, West Berlin was rich with artists, musicians, squatters and draft dodgers. Sound systems were not hard to come by. The fall of the wall and the chaos in the East had opened up scores of empty industrial spaces. The next day was a Friday and everyone wanted to keep celebrating. An amazing weekend was inevitable, and you can bet the soundtrack wasn't Beethoven.

For three days and longer the new Berlin partied hard amid the rubble, to house and techno. 'After the wall came down it was like, *everybody scream!*' DJ Westbam (Maximilian Lenz) told Matthew Collin in *i-D*. 'It's to do with people in East Germany wanting to freak, after all this control. We call it the liberation dance.'

'It was like a gold rush. The fascination of a city grown back together,' recalled techno promoter Disko to Dom Phillips.

Germany already had a tradition of hard music to draw on, Frankfurt had championed the 'electronic body music' movement of the mid eighties, a techno precursor which dressed itself in fascistic black fatigues and danced to the hard industrial sound of Front 242, Skinny Puppy and Nitzer Ebb. Another key reference point was the recent Neue Deutsche Welle electro-punk scene, starring Düsseldorf's DAF – a sort of black leather S&M Kraftwerk – and Einsturzende Neubauten (collapsing new buildings), who took 'industrial' literally and built rhythms with pneumatic drills. Frankfurt's dance scene was centred on the Dorian Gray, a luxurious four-floored carpet-and-chrome club at the airport, which boasted the only Richard Long sound system in Europe. Here Luca Anzilotti and Michael Munzing (who would later form Snap) were DJing a rich mix of electronic music. Their group Off, which included a young Sven Väth, had a massive hit with 'Electrica Salsa', a single that was influential in Chicago, and which gave the swank, moneyed city a claim to its own dance sound.

House had come to Germany early courtesy of DJ Klaus Stockhausen at the Front in Hamburg, who had long championed electronic music. Photographer Wolfgang Tillmans was a regular: 'Front is the cradle of German house culture. Klaus's mixing was special because of his incredible use of the EQ. Switching from piercing highs only to a full bass kicking in was so modern at the time, before it was a clichéd rave technique.'

'I loved the crowd,' recalls Stockhausen, now fashion director at German *GQ*. 'The booth was completely enclosed, so I really had to work hard to hear them scream!' Another Front regular was aspiring DJ Boris Dlugosh, who replaced Stockhausen there and became one of Germany's leading house producers. Hamburg house also lived at the Shag, a converted sex club, and at the Opera House in the red light district; Celal Kurum played at both. By 1988 US records were flooding in, and both Kurum and Berlin DJ Westbam had started making German acid tracks.

After the wall fell, however, Berlin stole the show. And it was clear the Easterners wanted things hard, as if to blast away decades of sensory deprivation.

'This is how the future was always supposed to sound,' wrote Dave Rimmer in *Mojo*. 'Techno is the first wave of music that young East Germans have been able to access, enjoy, feed into and make their own.'

'For the people from East Germany, it's a social revolution,' declared Juergen Laarman in *i-D*. 'Before, the highlight of their year would be their brother bringing over an old Bob Dylan record from the west. Techno was the music of their liberation.'

To keep the party going, clubs were established amid the concrete of East Berlin. Planet, in an old chalk factory, was one (it later became Paul Van Dyke's E-Werk). Tresor, opened early in 1991, led the way, five metres underground in the strongroom of a bombed-out department store, minutes away from Hitler's bunker. While some clubs served to exaggerate the lingering social and economic divide, Tresor, with its cheap admission and cheaper drinks, was among the places that brought kids from East and West together. Techno's military look, cheap to achieve, was another unifier. No one knew what the law was so these clubs operated as they chose, staying open as long as people were dancing, playing a diet of hard house and techno that seemed to grow harder every week.

'Berlin was always hardcore,' DJ Tanith told Matthew Collin. 'Hardcore hippie, hardcore punk, and now we have a very hardcore house sound. At the moment the tracks I play are an average one hundred and thirty-five beats per minute and every few months we add fifteen more.'

Annie Lloyd, a promoter at Tresor, explained to Dave Rimmer, 'When techno first started in Berlin, it was really apocalyptic. Deafening noise, concrete bunkers that sunlight never reached, toxic air, people wearing gas masks and utilitarian clothes, camouflage and so on – the kind of stuff you might wear to clamber through barbed wire. It was like preparing for a really horrible future.'

Westbam, a former hip hop fanatic who would become one of Germany's most famous DJs, had his own cheeky explanation for his country's love of hard techno: 'The only rhythm Germans understand is the beat of marching feet.'

Belgium

Antwerp's Christian Bolland claims he was thrown out of school for repeatedly smuggling a Roland 303 acid machine into class and programming it on headphones under his desk. After getting some tracks on a pirate station he found himself with a record deal with Ghent label R&S, and practically living in the home studio of its owners, husband and wife Renaat Vandepapeliere and Sabine Maes. In 1987, aged seventeen, by making a track of unassailable hardness CJ Bolland ignited hardcore techno.

'Do That Dance' by the Project was a nightmarish assault weapon made specifically for the Boccaccio club in Destelbergen near Ghent – where Bolland went nuts to DJ Olivier Pieters – a place where the weekend lasted virtually unbroken from Friday to Tuesday and clubbers would often crawl into the speakers. Having gone insane for the indigenous sound of new beat, with its slo-mo bass attack, the Boccaccio crowd had readily accepted acid house and was hungry for whatever excitement the DJs could throw at them. The club would rapidly become a test bed for a series of producers aiming to give electronic dance music the anger and velocity of hard rock.

'If you've got this huge sound coming at you, especially if you've dropped an "E", it just blows your mind completely,' Bolland told Tony Marcus in *Mixmag*. 'If you've got a Chicago tune with just a little piano on it and then this hard tune came on, it's like: "Whooooah, what's happening to my head?" So then everyone started doing hard tunes. Hard tunes was all they wanted because it blew their minds.'

'Belgium is very, very advanced. They're in a world of their own,' declared US techno producer Joey Beltram in *i-D* in 1991. 'I would tell everybody in New York that they're doing some really kicking music in Belgium and they would go, "*Belgium*?".' The country's new confidence was best expressed by R&S, which in 1991 sold more 12-inches in Belgium than all other labels combined. Listening globally, Renaat and

Sabine created a formidable international roster, releasing tracks by Derrick May, Aphex Twin, Frankfurt's Jam & Spoon, Belgium's Frank De Wulf, Japan's Ken Ishii and many more. Joey Beltram, a young producer from Queens, NYC, headed the pack. With 'Energy Flash', a pulsing emergency of a record, he threw down the gauntlet. Then with 'Ment-asm' Beltram created another monstrous new waveform: the 'Belgian hoover' sound, a rushing drone like a neutron bomb running for a bus. A few weeks later this fearful noise could be found on scores of white labels.

Renaat was very much an evangelist and saw techno as heralding a new internationalism. 'Because there are no words, it leaves your imagination free,' he told Simon Reynolds in *Details*. 'You can escape from anything.' This electronic heavy metal would prove irresistible to clubbers world-wide, and equally irresistible for bedroom producers, all of them keen to squirt the next unimaginable new noise into the sonic gene pool. We were entering a spiralling vortex of hardcore.

United Kingdom

In Britain, techno would prove incredibly fertile, not least for its message of 'you can do this'. Elegant tracks from Guy Called Gerald, 808 State, Orbital, and LFO and the other Warp acts led the way, then quickly the hardcore breakbeat virus started spreading, forming the bedrock of a distinctly British sound. As we'll see in later chapters, techno seeded several forms of music which Britain could claim as her own, not least jungle, drum and bass and UK garage.

An equally fruitful second phase gathered pace in the early nineties. Largely a reaction to the spiralling velocities of the hardcore scene, this was defined by ambient exploration, 'ambient' having been coined in 1978 by pioneering producer Brian Eno to describe such music 'as ignorable as it is interesting'. 'I think therefore I ambient,' pronounced silver-suited DJ Mixmaster Morris (Morris Gould), implying the intellectual superiority of the introspective and largely non-dance-oriented music evolving in chill-out rooms at clubs and raves. In case of any doubt he spelt it out: 'intelligent techno' was the opposite of 'stupid hardcore'. Warp sent a similar message with a compilation titled *Artificial Intelligence* on which acts like Black Dog and Autechre declared their fidelity to the more cerebral techno of the original Detroiters. Supporting this notion, techno DJs Dave Clarke, Colin Dale, Dave Angel and Carl Cox set themselves apart from the hardcore scene.

Here was music to be listened to away from the booming distractions of the dancefloor, where you could appreciate its subtle nuances and its superior aesthetic standards. Blending the ambient approach with myriad other dance influences were the Orb, (Alex Paterson and the KLF's

Jimmy Cauty) who had hosted the VIP room at Oakenfold's Land Of Oz; and stridently ploughing his own furrow was the Aphex Twin (Richard James), whose relentless creativity set him outside classification. Tom Middleton's album *76:14* as Global Communication was another key moment. Later, Leftfield and Underworld showed how effective techno could be in a live 'band' format.

Producers reconnected with the missions of classical music experimentalists Steve Reich, Karlheinz Stockhausen, Philip Glass and John Cage. They also plundered the natural world, picking up the 'new age' tradition with recordings of whales, wind chimes and birdsong, as well as using ethnic samples – non-western music scales, gamalans and didgeridoos. A flower power revival scene grew up around ambient music as Fraser Clark pushed the idea of zippies – high-tech hippies – with his *Encyclopaedia Psychedelica* magazine and his massively popular club Megatripolis, which filled Heaven with a more or less complete hippie festival.

Techno became the staple sound of the crusties, or 'new age travellers' as anarcho-punks took to dance music and adopted the rave ideal as a way of furthering the free festival tradition. Travelling techno sound systems became as much a crusty signifier as a dog on string, with Club Dog and Whirl-Y-Gig giving London static versions. These sonic outlaws would be at the forefront of the government's battle against dance culture.

Detroit's second wave

'If Belgian techno gives us the riffs, German techno the noise, British techno the breakbeats, then Detroit techno supplies the sheer cerebral depth,' wrote Matthew Collin in 1991. 'Europe may have the scene and the energy, but it's America which supplies the ideological direction.' And sure enough, Detroit was regrouping for a second assault – harder, faster, with no prisoners. Where Juan and Derrick had been inspired by Kraftwerk, many in the second wave were motivated by more aggressive industrial bands – Skinny Puppy, Cabaret Voltaire, Front 242. And where the Belleville three had tried hard to build something in their own city, the younger guys were aiming beyond from the start.

They ignored the mainstream US record industry, instead starting their own labels or releasing tracks on Transmat, KMS and Metroplex. Or on European labels like Tresor, Djax and R&S. The defiant anti-industry ethos was taken to extremes when Jeff Mills and former funk keyboardist 'Mad' Mike Banks (later joined by Robert Hood) set up Underground Resistance and started releasing hard industrial techno, packaged and promoted with militant self-assurance. Banks told Collin what they were about: 'We're fighting for the cause – underground music against the Top

40 jingle bells shit. What we stand for is resistance. We'll always be fighting against that shit. Revolution for change.' Kevin Saunderson for one was surprised by how hard their initial sound was. 'They're so heavy they kinda shocked me,' he admitted. 'I never knew anyone would get that hard in Detroit, especially two black guys.'

Another key label, +8 (named for the maximum acceleration on a turntable), was set up just across the Detroit River in Windsor Ontario by two young DJ/producers Richie Hawtin and John Acquaviva. The label's slogan 'the future sound of Detroit' brought initial accusations of cashing-in, since it was actually Canadian and they were the first white producers on the scene, but Hawtin's DJing at Shelter had preserved a Detroit club base for techno (as did Blake Baxter's nights at the Majestic) and they quickly proved themselves worthy. As well as releasing their own material as FUSE, Plastikman and States Of Mind, they signed Europeans like Dutchman Speedy J (Jochem Paap), and launched Detroiter Kenny Larkin.

Detroit's brief local scene had lasted just long enough to energise new producers. Stacey Pullen and Alan Oldham were both inspired to make music by their nights at the Music Institute. Another was Carl Craig, the second wave's leading light, a gifted producer destined to justify all those comparisons between techno and jazz. He made his first record, 'Elements' by Psyche in May's apartment. 'When I first met Derrick all I wanted to do was put a record out. I thought my material was ready and he told me it wasn't. I would experiment more and do whatever it took to get good enough for his label. Then one day, when he left his apartment for a couple of hours I made "Elements". He came back and was like, "Oh my god".' Collin saw producers like Craig as proof Detroit was reasserting itself. 'They outline how far most Detroit music is removed from the beeps and bangs rotating around every techno club in Europe. Techno as art rather than techno as functional sound. Sweet noise not vicious noise. Mindfood, not mindfuck.'

Netherlands

Of the techno tracks that made global shockwaves in the early nineties, two of the biggest were from the Netherlands. Human Resource gave us the monstrous 'Dominator' and, as LA Style, classically trained pianist Denzil Slemming made 'James Brown Is Dead', its eponymous sample implying techno had murdered funk. In clubs as far apart as New York's Limelight and London's Labrynth these became anthems of new-born hardcore scenes. In their home city of Rotterdam, an industrial port with a strong working-class tradition, the scene they fostered evolved rapidly into 'gabber', techno's most extreme incarnation.

The modern Dutch dance scene dates from the underground disco nights thrown by Eddy de Clercq at Club De Koer and De Brakke Grond, and the harder, more electronic sound of clubs like Cartouche in Utrecht and Down-Town in Maassluis near Rotterdam. De Clercq, who arrived in Amsterdam from his native Belgium in 1977, later engaged on a distinctly uphill struggle to bring house to the Netherlands, pushing it on his Amsterdam crowds at Pep Club in Paradiso and then at his new venture the Roxy, from 1986.

'People hated it. Even our own staff were anti-house,' he recalls. After a mere fifty people turned out to see Fingers Inc and just one hundred to see Derrick May, he took a coach-load of clubbers on a field trip to the Boccaccio, hoping the crazy scenes there might baptise them into the new music. After two years of arduous promotion, house finally clicked in Amsterdam in 1989, throwing up new champions like the much-adored DJ Dimitri. In Rotterdam Ted Langenbach was throwing glamorous MTC (Musik Takes Control) parties, and in Eindhoven Miss Djax (Saskia Slegers) started putting on events at Effenaar. Her Djax label and its many offshoots were instrumental in promoting house and techno, quickly becoming a world player and signing many second-wave Chicago producers. The Netherlands went on to be enormously influential in dance circles, spawning dance festivals Dance Valley and Mystery Land, the excellent Fresh Fruit and Touché labels, and an array of trance monsters from Ferry Corsten to Tiësto. It is also culpable for the Teletubby techno of Vengaboys and 2 Unlimited.

But the country's most distinctive contribution is 'gabber', Rotterdam dockyard slang for 'mate', which has all the musical charm of a steam-hammer. It is impossibly fast, with bpms regularly reaching well beyond the 200 mark. A record of 160bpm is considered downtempo. A spin-off, 'speedcore', takes tempos right up to 300bpm. Tracks are filled with satanic samples, football chants (usually a verbal shit-kicking of Amsterdam's Ajax), occasional anti-semitism and morbid gloominess. One record, Euromasters' 'Alles Naar De Klote' translates as 'Everything Is Bollocks' and spends most of its time dissing Amsterdam's DJ Dmitri. Another has a cartoon sleeve showing Rotterdam's Euromast tower leaning over and pissing on Amsterdam.

1992's 'Poing' by Rotterdam Termination Source set the course. Along with its B-side 'Feyenoord Reactivate' the track was an anthem world-wide, selling over 70,000 copies, and superfast techno became a way for Rotterdam to distinguish itself. In her book *This Is Our House*, Dutch club culture academic Hillegonda Rietveld offers some insight into the rabid escalation that created gabber. She believes the relatively affluent kids in Rotterdam didn't need uplifting music or messages of hope. Like

Scandinavian death metallers they just wanted aggression and oblivion. But it was territorial, it had to be *their* oblivion. A kind of sonic football hooliganism. 'In the process of trying to outdo each other in being harder, faster and more outrageous the Dutch have defined their own aesthetic.' By taking the music to extremes, she argues, gabber became 'as Dutch as tulips'.

Trance

If gabber aims at brutal unacceptability, trance is perhaps the most acceptable form of techno yet devised, the staple of twenty-first century dancefloors from Singapore to Seattle. Bombastic and uplifting, it fuses hard fast rhythms to extreme tunefulness. Trance makes sure it has plenty of notes per square inch and epic soundscape melodies you can swoon along to – whether classical, poppy or psychedelic. A defining feature is an emphasis on drug-friendly arrangements and Pavlovian tricks, such as impending snare-drum rolls and floaty atmospheric breakdowns, where those soaring melodies are given space to work their magic. These moments of pure melody leave the dancers positively begging for a beat, making the pumping percussion even more exhilarating when, after nipping out to the shops, changing a light bulb and feeding the cat, it finally kicks back in. Because trance is so damn melodious, many DJs will actually mark what key each record is in. Mixing two songs in different keys would make your teeth itch, but cutting from one track to another in a higher key gives a dramatic feeling of new energy (modulation, or changing key, is the musical equivalent of changing gear in a car). By moving up the scales with his records, a trance DJ can create the impression that the music's energy level is constantly rising. If you asked a psychologist to study the effects of music on ecstasy-fuelled humans and then design a music style that would press all their buttons, it would be trance. No wonder those kids love it so.

'It's powerful music,' agrees Sasha, whose progressive house sound was one of the many strands of influence that fed into trance in the early nineties. 'Whenever I go to one of those festivals and you see a tent with fifteen thousand people in, you see how powerful that trance music thing is. You see all those kids going nutty to one of those classical pieces of music with 145bpm trance beat behind it. It just works in that environment, but it's a million miles away from where the scene came from.'

In 1992 New York's DJ Moneypenny, who had moved to Belgium the previous year, reported back on how European techno was evolving. 'Those who play in the bigger clubs in Antwerp, Frankfurt and Amsterdam are witnessing the whole sound of hardcore techno crumble before their ears,' she wrote. 'The sound that is rising from its ashes is trance. Ambient trance, acid trance, pure trance, a de-evolution of that techno sound which seems to have gotten completely out of control.'

Sven Väth was at the forefront of this change. With his monstrous party appetite, his billowing personality, and his can't-stop-now approach to music, Väth was the embodiment of German dance music's evolution through the eighties and nineties. He's DJed since childhood – his parents met near Frankfurt after escaping from the East, and built themselves an English pub, where little Sven stood behind the decks introducing Hot Chocolate singles. The teenage Väth was a New Romantic, powdered and painted and robot-dancing to Kraftwerk, and in 1983, aged eighteen he started his DJ career playing soul oldies and hi-energy, and later electronic bodymusic, at the Dorian Gray. Aged twenty-one, he toured Europe in Michael Münzing and Luca Anzilotti's chart-topping synth band Off.

In October 1988 Sven built himself a club on his boy-band proceeds. The Omen was on the site of Vogue, another place he'd held a residency before pop stardom had beckoned. At the Omen his DJing led Frankfurt through new beat to acid house and then techno. Before the wall fell and ignited Berlin, Frankfurt was Germany's techno capital, with Sven as its unchallenged star. His marathon sets (fifteen hours was not unknown) were its focus, getting harder all the time. Then, after two years of techno, Sven and fellow Frankfurt producers, DJ Dag, Pascal FEOS and Resistance D, planted the roots of trance.

'We had all listened to industrial music since the early eighties and had been living and working in the same, relatively small city for years,' he told *Muzik*. 'By 1991 everything was in place for something big to happen. Frankfurt went boom and the Omen was at the centre of the explosion.'

Berlin was led away from hard techno by Paul Van Dyk. An apprentice carpenter in East Berlin, Van Dyk would listen to West German radio, falling in love with the Smiths and New Order and imagining in frustration the forbidden club scene just a couple of miles away. 'I practised on these old communist turntables with little wheels to adjust the speed,' he told Dave Fowler in *Muzik*. 'Nobody had Technics and I couldn't afford 12-inches.' After the wall came down he joined the exploding Berlin scene, but felt its music was lacking in feeling. As he told *DJ Times*, 'The music I'd heard on the radio was this sort of deep electronic music – early Warp records and things like this. But when I went to all the clubs in Berlin it was really hard, Detroit-oriented techno, which I'm not too much into.'

Van Dyk's DJ career started after tapes he'd made for friends, mixed together from compilations, caught the attention of promoters. Since his apprentice's wages wouldn't afford him more than two records a month, he asked for half the fee for his first gig upfront so he could go and buy some records. His tastes hit a nerve and from these Cinderella beginnings he soon enjoyed residencies at Tresor and E-Werk, playing what he preferred to call 'emotional techno'. As this grew into today's trance, Van Dyk became one of the world's biggest DJs.

The term 'trance dancing' had caught on during acid house and 'trance' had previously been used in American circles to refer to minimal repetitive house music – hypnotic tracks like DJ Pierre's Wildpitch mixes – so when these DJs shifted to a less aggressive, more mesmerising techno sound this was the name that fitted. Their early style was more what we'd now call progressive house, epitomised by a burning groove like 1990's 'We Came In Peace' by Dance 2 Trance (DJ Dag and Rolf Ellmar). Another keynote track was Age Of Love's 'Age Of Love', sometimes cited as the first trance record; here a hypnotic rhythm loop is drenched in super-emotive choir-of-angels synths, giving a clear indication of where trance would head. At the forefront of German trance were Sven Väth's label Harthouse, and MFS – a Berlin label set up by Brit Mark Reeder from the ashes of the East German state record company – alongside producers Jam & Spoon (Rolf Ellmar and Mark Spoon), Cosmic Baby (Harald Blüchel) and Oliver Lieb.

It was almost inevitable that trance would be fattened up with ever more melodies. Crossover pop success lured producers into adding soaring strings, operatic vocals, heart-tugging arpeggios, hi-energy refrains and Wagnerian melodies. Gradually the hypnotic rhythms of the first trance records gave way to epic stop-and-start concertos. Meanwhile, Van Dyk's long run at Gatecrasher, together with Paul Oakenfold's adoption of the sound, ensured its dominance in the UK, the springboard to global success.

Goa trance

Another, entirely separate scene had nurtured trance in parallel. Centred on Anjuna and Vagator beaches in Goa, a former Portuguese colony in south-west India, psychedelic or Goa trance evolved directly from progressive house. Exemplified by tracks like Moby's 'Go' or the Future Sound Of London's 'Papua New Guinea', and the work of William Orbit, progressive house was house made like techno, with melodies built from layers of precisely orchestrated synthetic sounds; its name was a *Mixmag* piss-take referring to the self-important progressive rock of the early seventies. Trippy psychedelic mandalas and ethereal ethnic samples soon crept in, like the gamelans and noseflutes of ethno-techno bands Loop Guru and Banco De Gaia. The results were perfect for the shoeless sunrise-gazers on Goa's beaches, led by acts Juno Reactor and Man With No Name. London's Dragonfly label run by ex-Killing Joke bassist Youth was a vital force, with the party scene itself led by a DJ named Goa Gil, a tripped-out hippie from San Francisco.

Goa had cheap hash, a ton of psychedelic drugs and a thriving eighties open-air dance scene built on much the same industrial, new beat and hi-energy music that Germany had enjoyed before techno. There was a strong affinity with the UK's crusty lifestyle and Goa was seen as a place to further the rave movement's spiritual journey in the wake of the restrictions imposed by Britain's Criminal Justice Act. In the years following acid house the Goa vibe was spread globally in fluorescent yogic waves by the great backpackers' diaspora, and the resort gained an image as a *Lonely Planet* version of Ibiza. When restrictions preventing their travel to India were lifted in 1988, thousands of Israeli kids made it their own, and the Goa trance and psy-trance styles were adopted wholesale by the clubs and producers of Tel Aviv, who now dominate.

After a decade, trance in all its forms has truly conquered the world, forming the backbone of the rave scene in America as well as the expanding international club circuit around which the unholy trinity of Oakenfold, Van Dyk and the all-conquering Tiësto continue to orbit.

Love Parade

Powerful testament to techno's supremacy was the rapid rise of Berlin's Love Parade, which at its peak in 1999 saw one-and-a-half-million people techno-partying through Berlin, with neon hair, silver hotpants, bare chests and water pistols. There are now Love Parades in San Francisco, Acapulco, Tel Aviv and Santiago, Chile. From its first year in August 1989 when its founder DJ Dr Motte (Matthias Roeingh) gathered 150 friends behind a VW van for a spontaneous sound system take-over of the plush shopping district of the Ku'damm, numbers at the street carnival grew exponentially. Motte had cannily registered it as a political event, a 'House Music Demonstration' fostering unification, which meant the city paid for security and clean-up. But in 2001 they argued that Sven Väth wearing a pair of angel wings and thousands of half-naked techno-Mädchen didn't actually demonstrate very much, and withdrew funding. Falling numbers and the difficulty of finding sponsors in Germany's unhappy economy led to the event being cancelled in 2004 and 2005, a year that ominously also saw E-Werk and Tresor closing their doors.

If techno seems to be slipping in its adopted capital, back in Detroit, the city of its birth, things are finally looking up. Here, too, the festival has had its share of financial difficulties and organisational wrangling (and three different names), but for the last few years Detroit has hosted a free techno festival to welcome the start of the summer: FUSE-in, formerly Movement, formerly the Detroit Electronic Music Festival. And in November 2004 the state of Michigan recognised Atkins, May & Saunderson's contributions with an international achievement award. They join previous recipients including Smokey Robinson, Aretha Franklin and Arthur Miller. The Detroit Historical Museum even ran an exhibition 'Techno: Detroit's Gift to the World', which included Juan Atkins' synthesiser and Derrick May's bulging globetrotting passport.

In an age where marketing dominates, it has been suggested that what Detroit needs, now the car plants are closed, is not investment, not jobs nor a functioning urban centre. No, it merely needs re-branding. Flailing around for a name to replace the 'Motor City', and belatedly aware of the musical revolution which started here, some city burghers have come up with something. Why not, they suggest, call it 'Techno City'?

FOURTEEN
BALEARIC

Bryllyant

'If in the next ten years we haven't managed to give a soul to
Europe, to give it spirituality and meaning, the game will be up.'

– Jacques Delors, 1993

Yes a bang, a boom-a-boomerang
Dum-be-dum-dum be-dum-be-dum-dum
Oh bang, a boom-a-boomerang

– Abba

'**W**ho do I call if I want to call Europe?' demanded a frustrated
Henry Kissinger, incensed that the Old World still refused to
speak with one voice. Whatever your views on the
Maastricht Treaty, when it comes to DJ culture the glory of Europe has
been its lack of homogeneity, its pockets of quirky musical isolationism.
Many countries' dance scenes were founded on imported US soul, funk
and disco, but when the supply of American music began to dry up DJs
showed incredible ingenuity in finding alternatives. Forced to use
whatever resources lay closer to home, their music evolved into curious
little dance species, unknown anywhere else. This gave a huge boost of
confidence to indigenous movements, as they shook off the chains of
English-language dominance.

While these scenes all highlighted the DJ's scope for creativity, some
were never more than curious anomalies. Others, however, would prove
massively influential. For years, the UK accorded the music of its
neighbours little respect, but when the sunshine eclecticism of Ibiza
helped wash away rare groove and usher in the acid house revolution,
British DJs would finally find time for records that weren't made by black
Americans. And more recently, when it became clear that the very
foundations of house and techno were built with records from
continental Europe, snobby British musos started reappraising Italian,
German, Spanish, Dutch, even Belgian club history, re-evaluating the
music these scenes prized and produced, and plundering them for
unheard tracks. As well as inspiring such historical revision, by making

lyrics largely irrelevant, house and techno further eroded the English-speaking world's great pop-cultural advantage.

The Balearic spirit is a willingness to try anything in the service of your dancefloor. Forget music snobbery, an artist's credibility is irrelevant. Forget the division of different genres, and the obsession with newness, you can even sometimes ignore the correct speed of a record. The established rules of DJing need not apply. All that matters is the power and beauty of each song in the context you place it. Named after the Mediterranean archipelago which contains Ibiza, and originally referring to the music of Ibiza's DJ Alfredo, 'Balearic' implies a musical openness, an anything-is-possible attitude. It was often born of necessity – the need to stretch a limited number of records to fill long summer nights – but it taught an important lesson to any DJ who treated music with too much reverence.

Balearic is 'Flesh' by A Split Second played at the wrong speed to turn it from gothic industrial to deep proto-house; it's the indie guitar mash of The Woodentops energising glamorous queens in the open air at Amnesia; or trippy Klaus Schulze records washing over kids zonked out on heroin by the side of a gorgeous Italian lake. Balearic invokes the holiday defencelessness you get from warm sand between your toes and a horizon of sparkling waves. Importantly, Balearic is an attitude to music more than a specific style or location. Or, as dance music writer Frank Tope quipped: 'It's pop music that sounds good on pills.'

Ibiza

It wasn't always just about sex and drugs. Ibiza's famous hotelier Tony Pike recalled how quiet and reserved the island used to be back in the seventies. 'After dinner it was the done thing to ask for another plate, turn it upside down and chop out lines of charlie. Most of the guests did that. Then everybody fucked everybody else, if they hadn't already done it.'

Ibiza was first settled by the Phoenicians, who mined it for tin and named it after Bes, their god of safety, protection and dance (Phoenician gods were nothing if not versatile). After the Phoenicians came the Carthaginians, who worshipped Tanit, the goddess of sexuality, who you'll see on trinket stalls all over the island. Many are convinced that Ibiza has mystical properties, that these deities' influence still permeates, but the reasons for Ibiza's appeal may be as prosaic as lovely beaches and guaranteed sunshine. Add drugs and horny young people to the equation and it's a no-brainer.

One constant has been the Ibicencos' tolerance of new arrivals. For many centuries Ibiza has been a refuge from mainland Europe for everyone from Romans and Arabs to the Vandals and the Catalans. Jews escaping persecution, draft-dodging Americans, pop stars looking for a limelight-free party, as well as religions and cults from the banal to the barmy have all washed up here. Before its development as a tourist resort, Ibiza relied heavily for its income on the salt flats that made it the 'White Island'. Its allure for many settlers was precisely that it was so backward and isolated (the airport was only built in 1967). Beatniks followed the trail to enlightenment there, film stars like Errol Flynn, Terry Thomas and Ursula Andress were regular visitors, and during Franco's despotic rule on the mainland, news spread fast among the gay community that it was a place where men could hold hands without fear of assault. In 1960, the island's hotels reported just 30,000 visitors; by 1973 the numbers reached half-a-million.

Heard al fresco at a hilltop party or open-air discothèque, with the bass generous and the highs fizzing up into the night sky, Ibiza's music has always been loose and liberated. Although there had been other music on the island, like the jazz brought over by renegade GI Bad Jack Hand (who was so bad he ended up in a Barcelona jail for murder), Ibiza's club scene is steeped in hippie roots, its musical tastes based on psychedelic rock.

Twisting by the pool – freaky dancing at Amnesia, Ibiza, in 1989.

Both Ku (now Privilege) and Amnesia started out as hippie hang-outs, the former a restaurant called San Raphael, the latter a simple finca. After Pink Floyd recorded the soundtrack for Barbet Schroeder's 1969 film *More* on the island it brought a further influx of counter-culture pilgrims to San Juan and San Carlos.

In 1973 Pacha, a company with several nightclubs in mainland Spain, opened an Ibizan outpost, the first big club on the island. The musical menu typified Ibiza's brash and occasionally schizophrenic approach, with a mish-mash of rock, reggae, pop and soul. James Brown would mingle uncomfortably with Crosby, Stills, Nash & Young or the bubblegum pop of the Archies; you might hear Jethro Tull next to Bob Marley. Away from the clubs, hippies organised free open-air parties, always by word of mouth and often in inaccessible areas to deter outsiders. At their peak, party organisers like French hippie Anant commanded a following of thousands, until the powerful clubs pressured police to stage a clampdown.

By the 1980s, glamour had replaced Emerson Lake & Palmer, as Pacha and the vast open-air Ku dominated Ibiza's nightlife. The beautiful people – a rich fashion and music crowd with a strong gay presence – would arrive from Paris, Milan, Düsseldorf and Barcelona and congregate at luxurious boltholes like Pike's Hotel. This was where Wham! shot their 'Club Tropicana' video and where Freddy Mercury threw his legendary party peopled by dwarves carrying silver platters laden with cocaine. Ibiza was awash with drugs and money. 'I knew people who would to go to Ku and buy coke over the bar with a bent credit card,' laughs British DJ and veteran Ibiza-goer Trevor Fung. 'They knew it was bent, but they also knew the banks would pay it out.'

Don MacPherson, writing in *The Face* in 1985, described the dance-floor at Ku: 'A *Deutsche fraulein*, decked in leopardskin and thigh-length boots, valiantly roused her leathery mate to one more rock climax, while a balding man who looked very much like Charlie Drake – but with a G-string firmly pulled between his buttocks – boogied soulfully as his gut sagged in time to Tina Turner and the Eurythmics.'

The music was fairly orthodox at both clubs, although Pacha had forged a reputation for excellence by regularly flying DJ Cesar de Molero over to New York to buy records. (White Island veteran DJ Pippi later played there). Over at Ku, another Caesar, a black New Yorker who later died of a heroin overdose, is said to have been the island's first DJ to play more underground dance music.

Ecstasy began arriving on the island sometime in the early eighties courtesy of the Bhagwan Shree Rajneesh religious cult, famous for its free love and the ninety-three customised Rolls Royces of its leader. Rajneesh had discovered ecstasy via psychoanalysts near its US base in Oregon, who had been experimenting with the drug in therapy and marriage counselling. Not yet illegal, the cult employed it in 'Who I Am' sessions to aid emotional bonding.

However, the drug of choice, showing the hippie influence, remained mescaline, a trippy psychedelic, as well as LSD and cannabis. 'Ecstasy was for the rich people that used to go to the private parties,' explains DJ Alfredo (Fiorito), who now lives drug free. 'Everyone used to say, "Yeah, it's a drug to shag with; you give it to a woman and she opens her legs." But the hippies and post-hippie people, they used to take the drugs more seriously. They wanted an experience that was going to open their mind, and ecstasy wasn't that type of thing, it was a pleasure drug.'

Alfredo at Amnesia

Alfredo Fiorito is a legend, not only in Ibiza, but throughout the clubbing world. The acid house revolution that spawned today's dance culture was sparked by the music he played and the atmosphere he created on his dancefloor. His achievement was to unify a wild mix of sounds, blending Chicago house with a distinctly European pop sensibility. The British press swiftly dubbed this 'Balearic beats'. When mixed with the combustible effects of ecstasy it would prove unstoppable.

Guided by his deep love for the song, Alfredo's knack was to choose tracks which were individually unremarkable, but as part of a whole evening's entertainment sounded spectacular. And with his profound Latin sensibility he could find splinters of fiery Catholic passion in even the most Anglicised pop. On Alfredo's decks the Cure's 'The Blood', an Amnesia favourite, sounded gloriously Mediterranean despite Robert Smith's dour estuary delivery.

Another influential factor was the limited availability of music. With long sets to play and few sources of records, Ibizan disc jockeys had to squeeze out every playable track from their collections. This meant finding rare gems on mainstream albums, scouring unthinkable artists for anomalous masterpieces and repurposing tracks never intended for the dancefloor. In addition, they developed highly sensitive programming, which let them recontextualise records to highlight qualities in them that might otherwise remain hidden.

Jose Padilla, Ibiza's famous chill-out DJ, agrees that the Ibiza sound has as much to do with expediency as with Tanit's magic pixie dust: 'There was not much choice. It's not because in Ibiza we *like* to play like that. We *have* to play Talk Talk, we *have* to play Belgian new beat, we *have* to play rock, we *have* to play reggae, because we have to fill the space of so many hours.'

Alfredo arrived in Ibiza in 1976, fleeing the military dictatorship of his native Argentina. He began DJing in 1982, while looking after a friend's bar, spinning Ibiza favourites like Pink Floyd, mixed up with Chic Corea-style jazz-fusion. Right from this first gig his only ambition was to play at Amnesia, then the poor relation to the more glamorous Ku and Pacha.

Finally, in 1984 he was Amnesia's resident. But the season was a disaster. Alfredo claims that for four long months there were never more than three people in the club at any one time, and these brave few were usually his friends. It all changed late one August evening as they were closing. 'My work colleagues asked me to play for them while we waited to get paid.' Hearing Amnesia going later than usual, some people dropped in after Ku. 'Fifty to sixty people. The next day there was three hundred. The day after, five hundred, and four days later there was a thousand in the club. Just like that.' Amnesia took the hint and became Ibiza's first major after-hours club, opening at 3 am and often continuing up to lunchtime.

Alfredo comes from a line of Ibiza DJs that stretches back to the hippie days. He cites as his main influence Jean-Claude Maury, a DJ from Brussels who had played at Glory's and Ku. 'He was a very simple guy, without a massive ego. He had a real love for the music and he had great taste. He would take what was considered different music at the time, like Cargo and Indochine or Kid Creole.' Later on, as Trevor Fung recalls, it was DJ Carlos at Es Paradis, who carried the baton. 'Brilliant disc jockey. He used to play all the indie stuff. I used to think, "where did you get *this* from?" And then I looked at the labels and it was all English stuff, from Leeds and places like that. He was the first disc jockey who really changed my views on the way music was played.'

For his first few seasons, Alfredo's music followed similar patterns to his island forebears, mixing up pop and rock with obvious dance tracks. He threw in Italian and Spanish songs by the likes of Lucio Battisti and Radio Futura, and jumped on records with a flamenco feel. There was one small import store on the island, Flip Music, but Alfredo's restlessness led him on regular record-buying trips all over Spain, as well as to Germany, where his son was living, and to Italy's two main music stores Disco Più and Disco Inn.

In 1985, while in Madrid, an American dealer sold him his first house track: 'Donnie' by the It on DJ International. 'I went mad for this record,' he enthuses. 'This is fantastic music!' As more of these vinyl spaceships landed in Spain, he added them to his playlist, along with offbeat tunes, such as the live version of the Woodentops' 'Why Why Why' (found in Italy) and Thrashing Doves' 'Jesus On The Payroll' (bought from a store in Valencia) – both future Balearic classics.

Trevor Fung claims even though Alfredo often repeated himself, the *way* he strung his music together was so charismatic you could not help but be mesmerised. 'The music from Amnesia is imprinted in my head. It's like I know Alfredo's set from start to finish. I know it off by heart. I know what he's going to play after this song, I know what he's going to play after that one. But it *worked*. Even though you knew what he was playing, it was brilliant.'

By the time the 1987 season arrived, ecstasy was making its presence felt on Ibiza's dancefloors. Added to Alfredo's Balearic beats in the warm starlit night, it was irresistible. No wonder then, that when Fung shared the experience with three of his London DJ friends – Paul Oakenfold, Danny Rampling and Johnny Walker – they would throw all their energies into recreating this kind of carefree clubbing back home. Their nights at Amnesia would provide acid house with its creation myth. 'We went there every night for a week,' smiles Walker. 'We just couldn't get enough of it.'

José Padilla at Café Del Mar

With beach cafés soundtracking a hard day's sunbathing, and pre-club bars marking the gentle transition into another night of hedonism, Ibiza's other significant contribution has been its promotion of the chill-out ideal.

Midsummer at the Café Del Mar in San Antonio. Art Of Noise's 'Moments In Love' plays as the sun sinks gently into the horizon. The sky burns the sea a fierce orange and the gathered souls fall in silence at the perfection of it all. At the decks is former prog-rock fan José Maria Padilla, the godfather of chill-out. He's been playing in Ibiza since 1976, both as a dance DJ and with his fabled sunset sessions. His *Café Del Mar* CD series has sold nearly four million copies world-wide, a landmark in a booming chill-out economy that fosters groups like Air, Zero 7 and Bent, and has spawned entire music festivals in Big Chill and Bestival.

Padilla was inspired by Ibizan dancefloors' high tolerance for strange music, in particular the night he heard 'Music For A Found Harmonium' by Penguin Café Orchestra played in a disco. This almost beatless song sounds more like an asthmatic hornpipe than a dance tune. 'Paco, a DJ from Valencia, played it. It was the beginning of ecstasy, and it was the first time I saw people doing the acid house-style dancing with that track. I thought, "what is this?" '

His first bar venture, Museo at Cala Vadella beach, had ended tragically when his partner committed suicide. Padilla, burnt out and drinking heavily, quit regular DJing and began selling tapes on the hippie market. He was soon doing a roaring trade in his own chill-out sets and mixes he'd bought from the island's big DJs. This landed him the gig at Café Del

Mar, famous for its sunset views. Soon after, London-based label React started releasing his CD compilations. The first volume sold a modest 8,000 copies, but by the fifth sales passed half-a-million.

Ibiza uncovered

After acid house hit Britain, there was a keenness to take the new party vibe on holiday. Naturally Ibiza was high on the destination list. In June 1990 promoter Charlie Chester took 500 UK clubbers and DJs over (all captured in *A Short Film About Chilling*); others followed and the island's fate was sealed. Although it somehow held on to the core of its magic, as numbers expanded, clubbing in Ibiza would never be quite the same. As if to signal the end of an era, in 1989 the beautiful open-air venues Ku and Amnesia had been forced to add roofs.

Each summer the dance press would speculate over which resort – Rimini or Riccione or Ayia Napia – might replace the White Isle in clubbers' affections, but Ibiza's popularity rose unabated. By the mid nineties, the superclubs were in charge – Ministry of Sound, Cream and Renaissance – who all put on nights in the island's established venues. But in 1994 their supremacy was challenged by a cheeky Manchester upstart, Manumission, a club which proved how far from acid house everything had come. Manumission was about the spectacle rather than the DJ. They admitted they weren't particularly interested in house music. Instead they concentrated on pseudo-performance art – like a man on a toilet in the middle of the dancefloor – and rather tawdry amateur sex shows. Each night thousands of sunburnt pill-monsters stopped dancing to gawp at baldy promoter Mike McKay shagging his girlfriend onstage. 'Manumission is about freedom. What could be greater freedom than having sex in a club?' he declared, as everyone wondered how much he'd been bullied as a child.

In 1996, Radio One began decamping to Ibiza for the summer, transmitting live for whole weekends at a time. Club magazines *DJ*, *Muzik* and *Mixmag* started publishing separate weekly bulletins for the island. The annual drug trade there was now said to be worth £200 million. The vice-consul on the island, Michael Birkett, was so horrified by the behaviour of British tourists he resigned in 1998, and its image was further grubbied by Sky TV's *Ibiza Uncovered* in 2000, which concentrated on the tits'n'tatts of San Antonio's dreaded West End. By 2003, tourism had grown to a staggering 1.1 million visitors per annum. Ben Turner, then editor of *Muzik*, summed up its appeal in a *Guardian* newspaper report on lax Ibizan policing. 'We have tried other places, such as Portugal and Cyprus. But nowhere else gives you such freedom to misbehave.'

Despite a waning reputation there are still great nights in Ibiza, they just might not be in the main clubs. DC10, an open-air party held near the airport, enters its ninth season this year and is still one of the best in Europe. But all signs of Alfredo's original Balearic menu have long since been crushed by the four-on-the-floor kick-drum. 'It's been lost all over the world,' he laments. 'The pressure for money, and to live, it's much greater than it was thirty years ago, and the music is reflecting the life we live.'

Hearing Simply Red's 'The Right Thing' in the middle of a deep house set in the sweltering Mediterranean can be magical – completely different to hearing it on Magic FM in a cab in Peckham. As with all great DJing, it's about context. Played badly, Balearic can sound like a kitsch wedding DJ; done well, it can make you listen to songs with fresh ears. 'Alfredo used to play a couple of U2 tunes, "I Still Haven't Found What I'm Looking For" and "With Or Without You",' remembers Johnny Walker. 'And to hear those when it's seven o'clock in the morning, the sun's come up and you're in an open-air club absolutely off your tits – whoah! – they just sound so fabulous. I'm sure people could stick 'em on now and say "well, it's just a U2 record", but I can listen to them and still get a shiver.'

'I was in the right place, at the right time doing the right thing,' shrugs Alfredo modestly. But in 1987 his rapturously open-minded approach was just the tonic the self-conscious London club scene needed.

'I went out there in the first place because I thought it was too stuffy in Britain – the clubs, the people, the music,' confesses Trevor Fung, who, more than anyone, channelled Alfredo's ideas back to the UK. 'Ibiza has changed people's ideas of clubbing. It's changed the way you go out and the way you enjoy yourself.'

Belgium

We've got it all wrong about Belgium. Chocolate, Tin-Tin, Hercule Poirot, *moules marinières*, the clichés pile up. In fact, it's a country full of mischief. Having been occupied by just about everyone, and having had its own languages – Dutch and Walloon – banned in favour of French, Belgians have a profound suspicion of authority and a wonderfully subversive side. Charles De Gaulle called Belgium, 'a nation invented by the British to annoy the French'. Its name comes from a tribe of Celts called the Belgae, which means 'the boasters'. Their national sport is tax evasion.

'The Belgians are basically Northern English – the surreal sense of humour, the self-mockery – with a dash of Latin,' says Harry Pearson, who wrote a whole book on the country. 'It's kind of Mediterranean sensuality in a Yorkshire climate – sex in duffel coats.'

Belgium also has the most interesting club history in mainland Europe.

Regular visitors to that money-drain eBay may have noticed the word 'popcorn' frequently used as a selling tool for old soul, jazz and ska records. This plays on the collectors' fervour that still exists around popcorn music, Belgium's northern soul.

Popcorn is far from the disposable pop the name suggests. The music was a rich stew of soul, doo-wop, modern jazz, ska and Latin, with weird exotica thrown in. Like northern soul it was a retro scene running from the late sixties to the mid seventies, built on stateside visits and the search for obscure oldies. Also like northern, popcorn paved the way for future dancefloor innovation, bequeathing DJs, clubs and an obsessive music culture to later forms. Popcorn's legacy explains why this small, quirky country was the first on mainland Europe to have commercial success with house and techno.

Importantly, popcorn also gave Belgian DJs a lasting taste for down-tempo music. Popcorn's soul is much slower than northern. Imagine the early northern scene before it was clamped in a Dexedrine frenzy, the diverse music that Roger Eagle played at the Twisted Wheel rather than the stompers played in the closing days of Wigan. Edwin Starr, Jackie Mittoo, Prince Buster, the Temptations – this is popcorn. Driven by nothing more sinister than beer (bottled Tuborg being the tipple of choice), its fans would dance a slow partnered jive that eschewed acrobatics in favour of graceful angular lopings. With such balletic, decelerated dancefloors, DJs would often pitch records right down, lending a druggy weightless feel to the music. As we'll see, this would remain a distinctive Belgian technique.

Freddy Cousaert was one of the scene's founding DJs. A legendary figure in Belgium, it was Cousaert who resurrected Marvin Gaye's career in the early 1980s (Gaye lived in Ostend for eighteen months, as featured in the documentary *Transit Ostend*); he also brought Muhammad Ali over for a promotional tour after the champ had an unlikely popcorn hit with 'Stand By Me'. Cousaert was proprietor and resident DJ at the Groove in Ostend, where the menu was an exotic blend of his beloved rhythm and blues and jazz. 'The Groove was *the* club for that kind of music,' claims Frie Verhelst, who with husband José Pascual opened the USA Import record store in Antwerp to cater for the popcorn craze. 'They played Marvin Gaye and soul and jazz and danced this slow bop with a lot of fantasy. It was really beautiful to see those people dancing to this music.'

The music's name came from Club Popcorn, a country café between Ghent and Antwerp that since September 1969 played soul music on Sunday afternoons. Eddy de Clercq, who would later be instrumental in bringing house to the Netherlands, recalls arriving there around 3pm, the peak hour. 'The streets were filled with parked cars and well-dressed punters all heading to this farm in the middle of nowhere. It was so packed there was hardly any room to move. People were dancing on the bars, behind the bars and even on the cars parked outside. The atmosphere was so exciting that when a popular tune came on, people started cheering and throwing fountains of beer. Sometimes people stage-dived into the crowd or started stripping to the music. The sound was unique and, to me, very decadent.'

By the late seventies, popcorn had become a nation-wide pheno-menon, with major-label compilations, an endless slew of bootlegs and several entirely new songs. Belgian's answer to Jonathan King (minus the kiddy-fiddling), Lou Depryck – who also wrote Plastic Bertrand's 'Ça Plane Pour Moi' – had two 'popcorn' ska hits with 'Kingston Kingston' and 'Hong Kong Ska'. It now thrives as a nostalgia scene. You can still get lessons in popcorn jive. And while popcorn couldn't be more different, it made possible the gut-wrenching music that Belgium would make next.

New beat

'Entering the Boccaccio club in Ghent is like falling into a dislocated version of life in slow motion. Two-and-a-half-thousand dancers are standing, backs rigid, limbs swinging at robotic half speed to a soundtrack of deconstructed, underground Eurobeat. The tempo is cast down so low that the vibrations are close to heart-stopping. Bass drums explode in cascades of digital reverb, electronics undulate sensuously and any stray shreds of voice are ground to a growl. Bass, "how low can you go?" "Lower still" say the dancers. For the music they're calling New Beat, they'll go as low as you like.'

When Matthew Collin wrote his September 1988 *i-D* scene report, 'new beat' was seen by some as a hot contender for dancefloor supremacy. A sort of downtempo Belgian house sound, it took the dark electronic mood of Europe's industrial music and by dramatically lowering the tempo gave it a grand cinematic minimalism. Belgian clubbers considered 120bpm a breakneck speed for a record. As DJ Marc Grouls told Collin, 'In Belgium, if the beat is fast, they won't dance. They want to hear the beat, the smashing sound.'

'New beat is a reaction to disco. New beat is completely soulless – it's sterile music created to dance to and nothing else,' explained producer and new beat label boss Maurice Engelen to the *NME* in 1991. This was dance music stripped of its soul, its funk, indeed most of its contents – a musical burglary that left only rhythm and a vast, churning bass-throb. In other countries new beat was largely subsumed by the house music avalanche, but in Belgium it hit the charts and launched a fierce pride in the nation's music, sowing the seeds for global success with techno.

The genre's origins lie in the early to mid eighties in a club scene of extreme Balearic eclecticism. Fat Ronny (Ronny Harmsen) wasn't fat at all, but he was a hell of a DJ. Using a wealth of obscure, rare and often very odd floor fillers, he created a style so distinctive it was honoured with its own name: 'AB-music', named after his Antwerp club Ancienne Belgique. 'His eclectic sets were a true revelation for me; he had an incredible ear,' enthuses Paul Ward, who furthered Ronny's mission on his influential 'Liaisons Dangereuses' radio show. 'He defined what a good DJ should be: leading you along new paths without compromising too much.' Though he strung sets together from a vast variety of music, Ronny's genius lay in generating a quite singular mood; it was this which would inspire new beat. As Ward explains, the thread which ran through AB-music was a slightly menacing operatic drama: 'He created this kind of darkish movie atmosphere.'

As well as playing conventional dance records, like James Brown and ABC, Ronny would incorporate soundtracks, jazz and oddball pop tunes (he broke both 'Requiem Pour Un Con', Serge Gainsbourg's 1968 leftfield pop gem, and Max Berlin's superb Barry-White-goes-French 'Elle Et Moi'). He favoured selected rock tracks like 'I Wanna Be Your Dog' by The Stooges, a good deal of European electronica, as well as electro-African tracks like Unknown Cases' 'Masimbabele' and 'D'Yu Al Feza' by Zazou/Bikaye/CY1 – a demented argument between Belgian electronic musicians and Zairean singer Bony Bikaye. As AB-music was the scene from which new beat would arise, these are all now regarded as new beat classics even though they are not new beat – the same way an Eddy Grant record might be a 'garage classic' (ie played at the Paradise Garage) while clearly not garage of any kind. Thus 'Monkey, Monkey' by the Eurythmics is regarded as a new beat classic, as is Public Image Limited's 'Death Disco'.

At the USA Import store, AB-music took over from the popcorn craze, as its owners (Frie Verhelst and José Pascual) sold thousands of the records Ronny was playing. When he made Pierre Henry's funky exotica 'Psyche Rock' into an unlikely AB anthem, they scoured the country and found a cache of albums lying in EMI Belgium's stockroom. When these sold out, they persuaded EMI to press some more.

'It was never my intention to become the father of some music style,' Fat Ronny told Antwerp's *In & Out* magazine when asked about new beat. 'I *play* music, I don't make music. I select the music and try to create an atmosphere.' The mood he conjured was far from conventional. He confessed how he loved to throw in the occasional record so strange it was undanceable, just to clear the dancefloor and start again from zero. 'There were always weirdos who kept dancing while that undanceable record was playing. I loved the atmosphere in those days; it was dirty, decadent, strange and uneasy.'

Sadly, in the mid eighties, towards the end of his reign Ronny succumbed to a heroin habit and has shuffled in and out of prison ever since. But the music he collated has had a significant impact, coalescing into new beat. AB-music is Belgium's own Balearic, a more gothic version of the Ibizan adventure. It is musical liberation set under dark clouds and drizzle instead of optimistic sunshine, with flamenco guitars replaced by angular drum patterns and thundery synthesisers.

Fat Ronny's ideas can be traced back to a Frenchman based in Brussels, Jean-Claude Maury, resident at the Mirano there – said to be the Studio 54 of Belgium (not least because it was hard to get into). A former punk, Maury would drop the doom-laden sweep of the Human League's 'Being Boiled' next to the disciplinarian post-disco of Grace Jones and the hypnotic bassline chug of Bill Withers' 'You Got The Stuff' and Kowalski's 'The Arbeiter'. His style, while wide-ranging, seems to have revolved around a certain downtempo moodiness. Those deepest on the scene stress it was Jean-Claude Maury (now dead) who gave Belgium its taste for Balearic exploration: 'Everybody tried to copy him,' insists Boccaccio resident DJ Eric B (Eric Beysens).

And Maury's influence extends far beyond the roots of new beat – he also played in Ibiza, passing his style on to a young Alfredo Fiorito. It is Maury who Alfredo claims as his greatest inspiration. So the eclecticism most famously expressed in Ibiza actually has its origins in Belgium.

By the time the drugs had hold of Ronny his playlist had been stolen wholesale by the 'Liaisons Dangereuses' radio show on Antwerp's Radio SIS, presented by Paul Ward and Sven Van Hees, who recorded successfully together as Liaisons D (not to be confused with the German group Liaisons Dangereuses). Their show would be the link between AB-music and new beat proper. When it started in autumn 1984 it was little more than a Fat Ronny appreciation society. 'We copied him and tracked down all his records,' confesses Ward. 'I think it took us from '84 to '86 to catch up with him.' But the show then took on a distinct personality, aided considerably by a crafty seven-till-nine timeslot. 'Because the new imports arrived from the airport around 6pm we could play all the new stuff before anyone else.' They dropped a beguiling mixture of post-punk electronica mixed in with house, industrial and a crazy assortment of leftfield tunes. Some of these became templates for new beat – like former Associate Alan Rankine's 'Rumours Of War', or the Sisterhood's brilliant paean to the AK47's 'Finland Red, Egypt White', written and produced by Sister Of Mercy's Andrew Eldritch (goth-disco, anyone?).

'Liaisons Dangereuses' grew enormously popular. Their outside broadcasts were road-blocked; anything they played became sought after. 'People would drive to Antwerp from all over Belgium, park their car somewhere, tape the radio show on their portable radio-cassette and drive back home,' chuckles Ward. To throw rivals off the scent they would frequently make up bogus titles. A song might become 'Eat Shit & Die', with the artist name the generic 'Tatouage' (literally 'tattoo', but hinting at a Flemish expression for 'forget about it'). USA Import would advertise songs played on the show as 'Les Disques Decadantes', and they'd sell like hot cakes.

In 1986 a single tune turned new beat into a tangible genre. 'Flesh' was a danceable industrial track by Belgian group A Split Second, who were regarded as exponents of EBM (electronic body music). The record is a steely piece of machine aggression and ominous minor-key synths that clocks in at 135bpm. However, press 33 instead of 45, (with the pitch control at +8), and it turns into a 105bpm heroin groove, with the four-on-the-floor kick-drums hitting every second swinging beat. There are drawn-out rhythms and crashing subsonic explosions where before there was only speed.

Credit for making this inspired adjustment has often gone to Marc Grouls, an Antwerp DJ resident at relatively commercial club Prestige, who was on hand when journalists came knocking. He is said to have flipped the tempo on A Split Second's track while listening to new releases at USA import, wowing a group of fellow DJs with the result. But Eric Beysens insists that the man behind this new beat eureka was in fact Jean-Claude Maury, granddaddy of the scene: 'He was the person who changed the pitch on A Split Second to 33.' It's easy to see how Frenchman Maury might have been written out of this very Belgian story, especially since he was based in Brussels, rather than Antwerp where the scene grew strong, or Ghent where it exploded.

Regardless of who did it first, the move ignited new beat. Playing records at 33 rather than 45 made a whole wealth of new tracks fit the mood everyone was chasing. 'Records were played more for the feel than the beat – the effect,' explains Beysens. 'When you play it slower, the bass becomes bigger.' DJs plundered their collections with a finger on the speed button, finding all sorts of weird surprises. Essex industrialists Nitzer Ebb gave them 'Join In The Chant' and 'Let Your Body Learn', there was 'Bryllyant' by Boytronic, 'Dead Eyes Opened' by Severed Heads and 'The Great Divide' by Portion Control. Liaisons Dangereuses also slowed down early Chicago house tracks, including 'Dub Love' by Master C&J and Risque 3's 'Risque Madness'. Even Soft Cell became new beat, with the instrumental of 'Tainted Love' slowed to a magnificent crawl.

After the low-velocity version of 'Flesh' there was a rush to emulate its quaking bass on vinyl. Most new beat records were by experienced producers jumping ship from other genres to try their hand at the latest craze. Its foremost exponents were Jo Bogaert, who recorded as Nux Nemo (and later as pop-techno act Technotronic), and the trio of Roland Beelen, Jo Casters and Herman Gillis who called themselves Morton, Sherman & Bellucci, a piss-take of Stock, Aitken & Waterman (Casters and Gillis were also both members of Belgian electrowave group Poésie Noire). The main new beat label was Subway, a sub-division of the industrial label Antler, founded by Maurice Engelen (of Praga Khan and Lords Of Acid) and Roland Beelen. Key record stores USA Import in Antwerp and Music Man in Ghent also launched labels.

In 1986, the first new beat tunes appeared, Nux Nemo's 'Hiroshima', a cover version of Snowy Red's doomy AB classic 'Euroshima (Wardance)' and 'Not Afraid To Dance', a Morton, Sherman and Bellucci production under the name Fruit Of Life. Originally this was a much more complex track. Beelen recalls how the scene's DJs told them to strip away all the breaks and effects, leaving just the basic rhythm elements. 'It was just bashing for six-and-a-half minutes,' laughs Beelen. 'Alright, we thought, if they want it, they'll have it that way. In two or three weeks we sold five thousand copies.'

In June 1987 the new sound was given its temple. Boccaccio's opening was timed perfectly, just as new beat exploded and the Carrera, the rival club next door, mysteriously burnt down. Originally helmed by Olivier Peters (Eric B joined a year later), Boccaccio was an enormous amphitheatre on the outskirts of Ghent, gleaming with chrome while smears of lasers splattered overhead. Its gladiatorial aspect was exaggerated by the booth's high position, with the DJ peering down over the vast arena. In Antwerp Marc Grouls presided over the Prestige, and in Brussels Vertigo led the new beat cause. But Boccaccio swiftly became the most popular club in the country, attracting clubbers from all over Belgium, as well as Holland, Germany and France.

'First time I went to Boccaccio it was like, "holy shit! I'm in *Close Encounters Of The Third Kind*",' exclaims Geert Sermons, owner of the Doctor Vinyl record store in Brussels. 'You had lasers everywhere, and combined with the sounds that you heard, you felt like you were *in* the light and *in* the sound. Life was never the same afterwards.'

'I'll remember it for the rest of my life,' sighs DJ Eric B of his August 1988 debut at the club. 'There were over five thousand people there, thousands outside. It was really mad. There were so many people that the windows in the entrance smashed from the pressure. I put on D Mob and there were three thousand people with their arms in the air.'

Such was the excitement, this new music crossed over almost immediately, the first time Belgians had seen their own dance music in their national charts. Erotic Dissidents had a huge hit with 'Move Your Ass And Feel The Beat'; Nux Nemo's 'Euroshima' made number one. Quickly there was a commercial high and a creative low as *everyone* made new beat records. The doorman at Boccaccio, Luc Devrieze, became one half of L&O, with DJ Olivier Peters. Fashion designer Walter Van Beirendonck made a record. Crooner Rocco Granata had his 1959 Belgian hit 'Marina' remixed into a new beat pop hit (imagine Max Bygraves remixed by Paul Oakenfold). The waiter at Antwerp club Confetti's became the frontman for an act of the same name, whose 'The Sound Of C' was yet another hit.

Many early releases were cover versions or blatant rip-offs of previous club hits. DNM covered 'French Kiss', 101 did a version of Reese & Santonio's 'Rock To The Beat' (a top 10 pop hit in Belgium). L&O's 'Even Now' was based on the Residents' 'Diskomo'. Thanks to the local labels' power, these cover versions kept the imported originals off the shelves. 'It was hard to find US records in Belgium,' wrote journalist Joost DeLijser in *Surreal Sound* magazine. 'There were maybe three to five stores carrying what little got through.'

British A&R men rushed to Belgium desperate to find the next acid house. FFRR rush released *New Beat: Take 1*, a compilation of Antler/Subway acts. Interestingly, this was originally going to be called *Balearic Beats Vol 2*, and with Nitzer Ebb, and the Residents, on volume one it seems curiously apposite.

Though new beat sounded thrillingly new at the time, now most of the records sound exactly what they were: quick cash-ins. But new beat ensured house received a warm welcome in Belgium (most Belgian clubbers thought house was just fast new beat). More importantly, it laid the groundwork for the looming hardcore techno revolution. Even as it championed new beat, Boccaccio was becoming the foundry from which European techno would be hammered out.

Italian afro-cosmic

Perhaps the strangest Balearic scene of all was Italy's afro-cosmic movement. In the wake of disco, on a club circuit on the wealthy playground of Italy's Adriatic coast, two DJs responded to dancefloors awash with drugs with some of the most surreal dance music ever. We're using 'afro-cosmic', a term coined in 2001 by Louise Oldfield in *7* magazine, since no two Italians can agree on a name for the scene. Afro-cosmic took the Balearic notion of recontextualising music to its furthest extremes. Trippy Krautrock nestled next to tranquillised Brazilian batucadas, slowed-down afrobeat slid into OMD at 33; the whole of music history jumbled into an electric soup.

Gabicce Mare, near Rimini, a club called Baia Imperiale, a tacky structure overrun with porticoes and plaster centurions; it looks like a garden centre run by hairdressers. Legend has it this was the site of Baia degli Angeli – the Bay of Angels – a breathtaking nightclub overlooking the sea, designed to hold 3,000 of Italy's wealthiest, most beautiful people. As the cocktail hour descended, actresses, artists, playboys, designers and heiresses would gather, framed by the startling scenery around them, either indoors or under the darkening sky. The DJ booth was built in a glass elevator so the *discaires* could play for four different dancefloors at once, gliding from one to another as they selected their tunes. Everywhere was snowy white, including the dust that made the night sparkle. Valentino is said to have designed the interior. Armani, Fiorucci, Grace Jones would be there. Imagine Monte Carlo maybe, a Bond film. Very elite. Very exclusive.

It is said Baia was the dream of a wild tycoon who had married a Russian princess. Having seen the lights of New York, he returned to Rimini with a plan to build the most fabulous club in Europe – he also returned with two New York DJs to put in it. And what DJs they were. Handsome, gay and laden with the same magical records he'd heard in America. Not only that but they could slide one song smoothly into another in an unbroken cascade. A heart-stopping talent – no stops, no gaps. Soon it was the talk of all Italy. People came out of their way to visit the beautiful club and hear these marvellous disc jockeys. They felt proud that Italy had what America had. Yet they had no idea how unique they were – these were among the very first DJs to mix records in Europe.

And then all of a sudden, the New York DJs were gone.

But left in their place were two even more amazing DJs, two apprentices to whom the Americans had taught their secrets. These two young Italians were so talented, so completely immersed in music, it didn't matter that the Americans had left. Together they brought music into Baia that was even more spectacular than before. The club was now a legend. People came to be near Baia even though they couldn't afford to go in. Kids would stand on the hillsides, catching the music as it drifted on the night air. They'd gather in cars, smoking dope and shooting smack, blissing themselves out to this dance music that didn't exist anywhere else.

Baldelli, one DJ was called. The other was Mozart. They say kids would wait outside the club watching for their heroes, refusing to enter until the DJs arrived. They say a terrible rivalry erupted, that clubbers would only want Baldelli, or only want Mozart. They say the DJs stopped speaking to each other, would even refuse to acknowledge the other's existence. They'd play on different nights, leading their followers into the club behind them, before tearing up the dancefloor with music from outer space. Finally the club closed and they went their separate ways.

The almighty head-start the Americans had given them put their music way beyond anyone, and it evolved by reaching into the unknown. Mozart and Baldelli spent every waking hour listening to music, searching out fresh wonders. It is said one of them ordered a copy of every single album released. As both continued their experiments, the heroin and acid flooding the dancefloor let tempos creep downwards, and their selections grew stranger.

Their sound? Otherworldly. Dislocated. Unreal. Cosmic. It was as if their music had a different history to the one you knew, like they'd been shopping for records on a parallel planet. Dubby funk, jazzy electronics,

Slaves to the rhythm – Baldelli and Mozart play host to the ever afro-cosmic Grace Jones.

spacey rolling drums, nodding, warping weirdness, all pushed endlessly forward by lazy, overweight basslines. There was little sense of individual tracks; you lost any firm ground as elements shifted and merged, as you entered tunnels of EQ and phasing, as songs exchanged sides with each other and back. It was put together like film music, as if every tiny shift in sound and feeling was accounted for. Wildly eclectic, but not sunny like Ibiza, not gothic like Belgium, in Italy the music was channelled straight from the moons of Jupiter.

That's the legend. Most of it is true. The tycoon was called Giancarlo Tirotti. He was indeed married to a Russian princess. The New York DJs were Bob Day and Tom Sison. They played at Baia from 1974 to 1976. They used record sleeves as improvised slipmats. As the first 12-inch singles were released, they had them all. People assumed they were famous in New York. We checked. Nobody has ever heard of them.

Mozart came from a club called New Jimmy and Baldelli from Tabu. They played at Baia from September 1977 after new management brought in a younger, more democratic crowd. Mozart (Claudio Rispoli) was a classically trained musician and went on to become a well-known producer, the man behind acid-jazzers Jestofunk. Daniele Baldelli still DJs throughout Italy. Their rivalry wasn't that fierce, but kids really did hang out on the hillsides, too poor to go in.

What else do we know? The police closed Baia at the end of the 1978 season, saying, 'Its mere existence promotes drugs between young people'. We know it reopened for a final summer in 1979 with just Mozart at the decks, and that it was closed for good that same year when someone died there, presumably from an overdose. Mozart started playing other clubs nearby, Baldelli went to a residency at a club called Cosmic near lake Garda. We know heroin was a big problem throughout Italy at that time, and that the coolest car on the scene was the Citroën DS.

Baldelli was a scientist. His sets were based on obsessive research. Locked away at home, he might try out a hundred different records to see which one mixed most perfectly with a new track. Gianni Zufo, owner of the Disco Più record store in Rimini, did actually send him one of everything. 'If there was a record, whether it was jazz, rock or pop, I'd get him a copy.' Zufo soon learnt that what Baldelli wanted above all was the freakish and unloved. Mozart was just as obsessed, but far more impulsive. Zufo recalls him (on acid) playing tracks as soon as he was given them.

'Baldelli was more technical, and was playing harder stuff,' remembers clubber Giovanni Salti. 'Mozart was more funky – funky disco, jazzy disco. They began introducing electronic sounds and African sounds, experimenting with equalising of the music, adding strange effects. With the music, the drugs, the people, a combination of it all . . .'

Disco was drying up and neither DJ had any love for the Italo-disco records which tried to sustain it (these were huge in Chicago and Detroit). And so, at Baia, the experiments began. Baldelli recalls: 'At the end of the evening – at 5am – I started to play maybe something strange. Ravel's "Bolero", which lasted twelve minutes, I play Pink Floyd, Jean Luc Ponty, electronic effects or African chant acappellas over the top. Also, maybe I started to play something electronic in between, a thing like Eddy Grant "Time Warp".'

He denies there was any conscious effort to move into stranger territory. 'This change was not something that I think about. I just select the music I like. If something changed, it was natural.' His broadening playlist included Codek's 'Tim Toum', a sparse electronic instrumental that sounds like the Neptunes remixed by aborigines; Logic System's 'Unit' (also massive in Belgian clubs), prog-rock made by cyborgs; and 'Time Actor' by Richard Wahnfried (aka Klaus Schulze), deep house slowed to a pensioner's stroll – with Arthur Brown on vocals. The common thread is a love of electronica, but these tracks also share a certain claustrophobia, quite out of character for a Latin DJ.

Cosmic opened in April 1979. Here Baldelli started playing his weirder tracks earlier in the night. 'I stopped to play dance music – it was dying – and I came to play the music I told you about. And the beat was very slow, from 90 to 105bpm at the most.' While he denies that the druggy crowd influenced this change, he admits the narcotics helped its success. 'A lot of people smoke and a lot of people were doing heroin. So they had to dance slowly, you know,' he laughs.

From a booth shaped like a space helmet with two hands around it, he began playing certain records at the wrong speed, pitching up reggae tunes like Yellowman's 'Zungguzungguguzungguzeng' to 45, while slowing others, like OMD's 'Enola Gay', down to 33, turning electronic pop into heavy-legged drug funk. In Chicago's Music Box, Visage's 'Frequency 7' was played at +8 and it sounded like a techno record; at Cosmic – played at 33 – it floated, ominous and metallic, the soundtrack to a thriller. Peering at a list of artists he played at Cosmic, it looks like a musical catastrophe: the few easily recognised names include Mike Oldfield, Peter Gabriel, Tony Orlando, the Monks, XTC, Genesis keyboard-player Tony Banks and Plastic Bertrand. Yet, however dislocating it is to hear a song like Gabriel's 'Biko' on 45 – like twisted Inuit folk music – it somehow works. Baldelli even played vocal tracks at the wrong speed. 'With vocals, the voice became like Mickey Mouse. But we don't care. Italian people can't understand the words. So this sound – the sound of the voice – became music to me.'

Mozart didn't care for such radical speed changes. He preferred the purity of digging out wilfully unusual tracks, increasingly from Brazil or Africa. As other DJs took up the spaced-out style, many preferred this more organic, percussion-led sound, incorporating Manu Dibango and Fela Kuti, Jorge Ben and Airto Moreira, hence the name 'afro' (which fights many an argument against the term 'cosmic'). After things peaked creatively the music continued down this path, and these days the scene favours WOMAD-like world beat.

Many DJs sprang up in Mozart's and Baldelli's wake, all with a slightly different take on the sound, including Rubens, Meo, Ebreo, TBC (who was Baldelli's alternate at Cosmic) and Flavio Vecchi, one of the few DJs to forge a successful career once house music swept away all afro-cosmic traces. Baldelli played Cosmic until 1984, Mozart played all over northeast Italy. The scene never shook off its drug associations and local authorities would close clubs simply for having afro-cosmic DJs on the bill. In the end most of the DJs were as tripped-out as their music and the scene faded around 1984.

Afro-cosmic produced no records, and the only press attention concerned the drugs. That's not to say it wasn't influential. From Lake Garda, holidaymakers exported the music over the Alps to their own clubs in Switzerland, Austria and southern Germany. And when house arrived many of Italy's more reflective tracks were inspired by afro-cosmic classics. Sueno Latino's 'Sueno Latino', which samples Manuel Gottsching's 'E2E4', and the Heartists' Airto-sampling 'Belo Horizonte' are just two.

Of course, the earlier Italo-house records are the ones everyone remembers, great storming piano monsters with divas set to gas mark eleven and ivory-tickling that made Les Dawson sound like André Previn. Not only did they fill many a UK house night, but they also acted as a template for the UK's early forays into hardcore. Gianfranco Bortolotti's production house, Media – a veritable mini-Motown – released the first Italian house record with the M/A/R/R/S-inspired 'Bauhaus', followed by a wave of hits, including 49ers' 'Touch Me' and 'Helyom Halib' by Cappella. But it was the summer '89 smash, Black Box's 'Ride On Time', the year's biggest-selling UK single, that set Britain off on a piano frenzy. By the time Italy was making music like this, afro-cosmic was a fading memory.

Until recently the afro-cosmic scene was unknown outside Italy. It's intriguing to ponder what recordings this musical Galapagos might have generated had its DJs distilled its spirit onto vinyl. More fruitfully though, consider how the internet makes it possible to rediscover such gem-filled time capsules. With treasured DJ mixes traded digitally in minutes, and obscure records tracked down and bought from your armchair, twenty-first-century communication means a forgotten scene like this can emerge from the mists of history and powerfully energise DJs in the present. And the wonder of such Balearic styles is that the oddness of the music prevents much of it from dating. In *Faith Fanzine*, DJ/producer Daniel Wang recalled the first Cosmic Club mixes he got hold of: 'Frankly, these were some of the most unique and AMAZING DJ mixes I had ever heard.'

A Balearic attitude opens a DJ's ears – to other genres, to other eras, to other countries. For record dealer Mark Seven the Balearic spirit drove the very best in DJing. 'It meant DJs weren't limited to just going to the record shop and buying what was out that week. People were actually striving to add something new to the pot that was their own; a message from their heart.' Afro-cosmic epitomised this. Seven agrees: 'Through listening to those Cosmic mixes you think, "Rules? Well, there are no rules." Whatever you think can work for you, can work.'

FIFTEEN
ACID
HOUSE

I've Lost Control

'The sixties was a party had by someone else; acid house and the culture that came out of it was a party had by everyone you knew. The decade of looking good and feeling lonely was over.'

– Jane Bussmann, Once In A Lifetime

'Me. We.'

– Muhammad Ali

The night your mate danced like a tree.
The night the whole club thought they'd been up in a spaceship.
The night you met all the people who are now your best friends.
The night everyone's name was Doug.
The night you gave away your Gucci boots 'cos they were annoying.
The night it was all about being underwater.
The night you thought you'd lost everybody but it turned out they were just hiding.
The night you danced in a car park.
The night you gave up trying to get promoted.
The night you decided to make clothes instead.
The night we stroked people's hair for drinks.
The night you talked about losing your dad and cried and finally understood.
The night you twisted your ankle but didn't tell anyone in case they made you go home.
The night we ended up in Chester – with Scottish accents.
Fun.
Suddenly it was important.
Acid house was when Britain shook off the grey dust it had been wearing since the war. A nation built on acceptance and duty started asking a few questions. Though there weren't many answers, it started to be a very different place. There'd been plenty of sunny moments before, but none as weirdly, disruptively, creatively universal. In the sixties you could tune in, turn on, and drop out, but only if you were a hip

photographer or if daddy kept up the rent on the Kings Road flat. This time, a voyage of discovery was opened up to nearly everyone. Gas fitters became record producers, market traders launched fashion labels, cooks started magazines; and all over the country boys and girls stopped wanting to grow into cool, successful Armani-suited adults, and settled gleefully for being boys and girls. At the tail end of a decade which had been about greed and shoulder-pads and black marble office blocks, along came a youth culture of smiley faces and togetherness and talking bollocks. Like puppies tumbling around the garden, we found the best way to learn about our world was to *play*. It taught us a lot we might have missed otherwise – most importantly that while the things that make people different are pretty fucking obvious, the things we all have in common aren't that hard to find either.

If you're reading this in Britain you live in an acid house-shaped world. If you're under thirty you need to know how shit it was before. Pubs closed at eleven, bars didn't exist except for wine bars full of yuppies whining, clubs kicked out at two – if you were lucky. For the majority, recreational drugs didn't go much further than booze, speed and weed, and the latter two were usually tricky or scary to buy. We didn't even have Red Bull for god's sake. And clubbing was far from the accessible mainstream thing it is today – the dance cultures in previous chapters were largely the preserve of music-obsessed weirdos; ordinary people had Cinderella Rockerfella's. Finally, if you lived anywhere other than a major city, none of this applies, because the only entertainment going was eight pints of Watney's Red and a fight. Your world is the way it is because twenty years ago a generation made clubbing the centre of their lives.

Acid house was cultural revolution. You couldn't fully understand today's Britain without knowing the changes it brought. As Margaret Thatcher swept away the post-war community ideal and replaced it with the free market and its cult of selfish individualism, here was a youth movement that proposed the opposite. Here was music that meant little unless you shared it, and a drug that reminded its users that humanity's greatest achievements are social. A drug that took away the fear of others, that eased communication and made scared, lonely people step happily into each other's lives. A drug that was nearly called 'empathy'.

Strictly speaking, 'acid house' refers to a few records made using the distinctive mewlings of a distressed Roland 303 bassline machine; the productions of the Chicago kids who were looking to the future rather than merely reheating disco. After Phuture's 'Acid Tracks' set the mould, a bleeping flurry of similar records followed, both imported and UK-made. However, with most listeners ignorant of any distinctions, 'acid house' was soon shorthand for house, techno and even Balearic tunes as a whole. The acid records were the name-makers because they were the weirdest of the lot, the tunes most likely to upset your parents, and because they held that all-important drug reference (even though it was the wrong drug).

So while 'acid house' began as a specific musical sub-genre, in Britain it became a blanket name for this new electronic dance music, and then for the whole culture this ushered in when it joined forces with ecstasy.

For the majority who tried it, the ecstasy/house combination brought intense feelings of freedom and communion. After this powerful epiphany a generation began to redefine itself around the emotions and etiquette of the dancefloor. When this experience became mainstream, these new nightlife rules swept Britain clean and 'an Englishman's castle' became 'all back to mine'. For a country based on division (of class, of geography, of race, of accent, of football team), the acid house experience – dancing with thousands of smiling friends you'd never met before – was genuinely

Smiley culture – a sly northern stylist named Barnsley promoted the idea of grinning yellow faces, seen originally in Shoom and on the cover of *i-D* in late 1987.

revolutionary. Acid house was nothing less than a defining era of British social history.

Musical meteorites

The first explosion was loud, alien, devastating. It was the sound of hip hop announcing its British arrival: 'Rappers' Delight', Flash's 'Adventures On The Wheels Of Steel', Kurtis Blow, Tanya Winley, Funky Four, and most radical of all, the stark electro of 'Planet Rock'.

DJ Noel Watson was hit square in the chest by the blast: 'Blew me away. "What the fuck?!" ' On hearing Flash's 'Adventures . . .' his brother Maurice jumped on a plane to New York to buy records, unable to do anything else until he understood more about this music. Matt Black of Coldcut, also a DJ and later a UK house pioneer, was similarly stunned, 'It just blew apart conceptions of what a song should be like. It was so far out, so radical.'

'Everyone was completely like . . . "Oh my god, what *is* this?" ' recalls Dave Dorrell, DJ and another early UK house producer. 'Rap, hip hop, was way beyond anything that you were accustomed to, or able to comprehend. It was a foreign language. "What are these people doing? How do they do this?" And "what would it be like to see them doing it?" It had just arrived here, and it was causing mayhem. Devastation. All of a sudden it was like, "How can we get more of this drug?" '

The second impact, a few years later, came from house. Another alien musical language, equally explosive – 'Jack Your Body' and 'Love Can't Turn Around', 'Acid Tracks', 'I've Lost Control', 'Nude Photo', 'Your Love', 'Move Your Body' . . .

'House just had a phenomenal impact,' says Black. 'Even straight away you realised that here was a new kind of music. As soon as you heard it you realised that here was a new form of energy that had materialised.'

This wasn't just the latest batch of hot tunes from the States. This was a new dawn. This was music that belonged to the disc jockey as never before; envisaged, created and produced by the DJ, with little regard for musical traditions, and with the sole purpose of shaking up the dancefloor. As these new forms arrived in the UK they shocked club culture to its foundations.

Hip hop immediately drew a thick, inky line between the open-minded, who – even though they didn't understand it – still got excited by its slaughtered beats, and the diehards writing in *Blues & Soul* magazine who screamed 'This isn't music', who couldn't believe the chiselling sound of scratching was rhythm, or that rhyme could replace singing. They didn't get it; they just couldn't find its soul.

And house? House was even more divisive. House upset established taste so much that DJs were abused, threatened, even attacked, for introducing it to British dancefloors. The brave few who began playing it quickly realised they were handling something truly incendiary. Dave Dorrell remembers the first three acid house records he got his hands on – Phuture's 'Acid Tracks', and Armando's 'Frequency' and 'Land Of Confusion'. As soon as he played them, he knew how powerful this music would be.

'It was like a caveman with a spaceship. In the world of music, acid house was so far out there that it was beyond anything. There were no direction signs.' Not only did they clear the floor, but these records kept it empty for a full thirty minutes, even as the human pressure on the edges of the dancefloor grew to breaking point. Finally, he gave in and played them something they knew. 'I had to play, I think, "Across The Tracks", and they literally *ran* onto the dancefloor. I thought, "boy, this music is going to do something".'

The birth of UK mixing

The jolts of hip hop and house exposed just how different the American and British club scenes had become since the transatlantic sixties. The widest gulf was in mixing. In the early 1970s, connoisseurs not technocrats governed the UK club scene. The mixer was somewhere to rest your Capstan Full Strength fag as you introduced Len Jewell's 'Bettin' On Love'. While mainland Europe and America were awash with hi-tech gear, swish lighting systems and proper DJ booths, most British DJs were still using pub function rooms and decks held together with chewing gum. Their peers were not New York disco revolutionaries, but bingo callers, hospital radio presenters and the Masters of Ceremonies at the local working men's club. Mixing was for cakes.

Liam J Nabb, an English DJ raised in Italy, was surprised when he visited in the early eighties and realised no one could mix. 'Even when house started the mixes were still pretty dodgy. I couldn't understand it, because everyone in Italy could mix really well.'

'We knew about mixing,' clarifies Greg Wilson, a northern club DJ who would make his name with electro. 'We'd tried it, but we didn't have the proper equipment.' Also, with heavy duty jazz leading the tastes of many DJs, mixing was simply not a required skill. Densely layered instrumentation and challenging time signatures call for judicious segués rather than disco style beat-matching.

'You can't mix Chic Corea and Jeff Lorber,' points out northern soul pioneer Colin Curtis. 'Over here there was the individuality of different sounds and different records. It just didn't *need* to be mixed. We'd been used to contrast, spaces, voices . . .'

So instead of a continuous blend, the UK DJ would pick up the mic and lovingly credit each tune. Most came from a mobile DJ background in which talking was part of the job description, the best way to warm up a frosty wedding reception. And while the leading disco DJs in New York were already moving into production and remixing, in the UK the successful club DJ still had his sights set on radio. All this meant that basic mixing techniques, de rigueur in New York since the start of the seventies, didn't make it over to the UK until 1978.

Greg James at the Embassy

It was rich gay Britons, consciously copying what they had seen in New York, who brought mixing to the UK, when a consortium headed by Jeremy Norman, publisher of Burke's Peerage (he now owns the Soho Gyms company) opened the Embassy Club in April 1978.

'The Embassy was London's little Studio 54,' says veteran gay DJ Tallulah. 'The gay night, Sunday night, was the nearest to a chic club that London ever got. The music was great and Greg James was a great DJ.'

Greg James taught Britain how to mix.

A DJ from the Pocono Mountains in Pennsylvania, he learnt his trade in New York, having installed the sound in club Hollywood, and perfected his deck skills watching Richie Kaczor extend tunes by mixing two 7-inch copies of each track. 'I used to buy the same records he had and then go back to Pennsylvania and figure it out. He didn't actually sit me down and teach me, but I was always over his shoulder watching,' says James.

James was imported to London as the finishing touch to a peerless club. The Embassy was a beautifully restored ballroom on Old Bond Street, where exiled Russian royalty had danced to twenties bandleader Bert Ambrose. Given modern twists, like a state-of-the-art GLI sound system installed by James, and lighting by Tony Gottelier's company Illusion, no detail was left to chance. Even the trees that flanked the sunken dancefloor were designed (by sculptor Andrew Logan) rather than grown. Norman and his hostess Lady Edith Foxwell attracted a constituency filled with present-day royals, both the real kind and the rock variety, as Greg James, the only mixing DJ in the whole country, served up the latest 12-inch disco imports from America. The Embassy was light-years ahead of anything else in Britain – though in truth that wasn't particularly difficult.

Although James played for only the first six months at Embassy, he left a lasting impression. He installed several other sound systems – including one at the Warehouse in Leeds, where he was also founding resident – and he schooled a series of DJs in mixing techniques, among them Jazzy M,

Tony De Vit and former northern soul DJ Ian Levine, who became nothing less than an evangelist. 'Ian knew what I was doing was the right thing and he wanted to see the industry change.'

Mixing was long seen as a threat to good DJing. 'Growing controversy is developing over the introduction of American-style mixing techniques into Britain,' wrote Neil Rushton under the headline 'DOES THE TALKING HAVE TO STOP?' in the DJs' trade mag *Disco* in February 1979. 'Despite pressure from various fashion leaders in the UK industry many of the top jocks are firmly against what they see as "mixing-mania".'

'American bad habits are not going to catch on here,' said an indignant Robbie Vincent, then one of the country's best-known jazz-funk DJs. 'People in the UK don't want to hear three solid hours of identical music.'

But apparently, they did. First at the Embassy and then at Heaven, a huge gay club opened in 1979 by the same owners, who installed Ian Levine as resident on James's recommendation. 'The British disco scene is pathetic,' Levine told Rushton. 'The only true disco clubs are the gay clubs in London. Two or three years ago when disco was taking off in the States, Britain was on exactly the same level. But now all that's changed and a head-in-the-sand attitude towards exclusivity has developed and people have developed into jazz-funk freaks.'

Objections only softened with the arrival of new music. Hip hop, especially the electronic splutter of electro, demanded new techniques. Even the confirmed 'jazz-funk freaks' started to reconsider, not least when *Record Mirror* took some of them to see the Paradise Garage and hang out with its revered sound engineer Richard Long. Steve Howlett, better known as Froggy, one of the so-called 'Soul Mafia', returned with a head full of ideas about sound and mixing. 'It changed my life completely,' he says. 'I studied Larry Levan, Tee Scott, Shep Pettibone, went to KISS FM and watched them. And then adopted it at the Royalty on the Saturday night.' Within eight weeks, Chris Hill, godfather of the Soul Mafia, told Froggy he was definitely on a par with the Americans. Froggy also returned from New York with the first pair of Technics 1200s in the country.

In Manchester, Haçienda resident Mike Pickering, had a similar New York awakening. 'I came back to the Haçienda and I said, "This is what it's got to be like." So I removed the microphone, "This is the future!"' But Greg Wilson, one of the first DJs to discard the mic, admits the climate wasn't exactly conducive to change. 'There was no way you could have just started mixing because people would see it as being lazy: "why aren't you talking?" '

As late as 1983 – fully ten years since it had first taken root in Manhattan – Wilson demonstrated the 'new' phenomenon of mixing on TV's *The Tube*, hosted by Jools Holland. 'You get records and change them about don't you?' queried a puzzled Holland. 'Don't you think that might annoy the people who made them?' Using two copies of David Joseph's 'You Can't Hide Your Love', Wilson scratched, doubled beats and slammed in echo effects to an amazed TV audience, possibly annoying the people who made it.

Resistance meant that in the UK, it was house, not disco, that finally made mixing compulsory. Synthetic four-to-the-floor kickdrums, extended intros and simple eight-bar structures made it almost idiot-proof in any case. Colin Curtis recalls his surprise when early house DJ Graeme Park arrived at a gig in Nottingham's Rock City armed only with 12-inches. 'There were no LPs in there. That was it. That was the start of the mixing.'

TV mix-up – Greg Wilson shows Jools Holland a thing or two.

George Powers at Crackers

If David Mancuso's Loft was the spiritual birthplace of disco, the primeval soup of acid house started bubbling in a scruffy little dump of a club in a basement just off Oxford Street. It had grotty carpeting, a modest dancefloor, a rickety DJ set-up and a shrieking sound system. Chewing gum pocked the floor, the leather seats were sticky and cracked, and the whole place smelled of sausage and chips – a crafty licensing hours swerve. You'd have serious problems seeing how anyone could be proud of the place.

But for a generation of London DJs and tastemakers, Crackers was where they first got hooked. By the magnetism of its DJ, the quality of its music, and the loyalty and intensity of its dancers, through the second half of the seventies this unprepossessing jazz-funk club inspired scores of future London faces to devote themselves to dance music. The roll call is deep: Jazzie B, Fabio, Norman Jay, Terry Farley, Paul 'Trouble' Anderson, Ashley Beedle, Colin Dale, Trevor Nelson, Carl Cox, Barry K Sharpe, Johnny Walker, Cleveland Anderson, to name only the most well-known. As dedicated soul boys they all prided themselves on having the best threads, the best tunes and, with particular arrogance, the best club. Soul boys loved – *lived for* – Crackers. At 203 Wardour Street the attitude that would culminate in acid house was born. As Norman Jay wrote, 'This was our Wigan Casino, our Loft, our Paradise Garage.'

On Sunday evenings, and later on Friday afternoons, Crackers would jump to the most spectacular dancing. On the floor was a select group of sinewy supermovers, whirling, stomping and flying their way through phenomenal jazz-dance routines. (One of Jonathan Ross's earliest TV jobs was recruiting dancers there for a UK version of *Soul Train*.) They practised hard, many took classes, some were professionals, all were famous within the club's extended family: Olly, Horace Carter, Bassey, John O'Reilly, Clive Clarke, Eon Irving, Tommy Mac, Gary Haisman, Trevor Shakes, Bevis Pink, Jabba from Ealing . . .

Lesser mortals knew to stay near the bar. 'You couldn't even stand on the floor unless you could dance,' explains Terry Farley. Even good dancers feared being drawn into an embarrassing battle. 'You'd have some guy who was fuckin' amazing come right up in your face and throw all these moves and then you'd have to walk away.'

All sorts of stunts were pulled for supremacy. Cleveland Anderson recalls a night when Horace secured himself fame.

'He walked in halfway through the night with this hot bird, put his leather bag down, and started freaking out until everyone just backed off. He grabs a chair, puts it right in the middle of the dancefloor and starts dancing with it. He was on it, around it, flicking it up. The record finished, he put the chair back, grabbed his bag and walked out of the club. Next day he was the talk of the scene. That was how much a dancer meant in London then.'

As the capital's most upfront soul/jazz-funk club when imports were becoming more readily available, Crackers was a forum for a new breed of collector, the first place to hear the hottest tunes (key imports store Contempo had opened close by on Hanway Street). It was also an early focal point for the radical clothes-horses who drove London street fashion through its punk-and-after heyday. From PVC bondage gear, via plastic sandals and carpenter jeans, right up to the Pringle sweaters of the casuals, Crackers managed to set the tone.

Perhaps more significantly, the club also presided over the dawn of black Britishness. Smack in the centre of town, multiracial, and with a scorching soundtrack, Crackers offered a generation of London-born black youth the identity they'd been missing. Leaving the neighbourhood to go 'up west' and dance there symbolised your transition from immigrant offspring to modern Londoner. Forget the island your parents came from, forget the police stop-and-searching you, forget National Front graffiti telling you to go back somewhere you'd never been. You were black, you were British, you were the future, you went to Crackers.

On the other hand, if you were white, you'd found a place with black music and black people that didn't feel like you were trespassing. For many, it was a foretaste of a colour-blind society. 'What was so great was going into a place and it was mixed,' reflects drum and bass don, Fabio. 'Reggae parties you didn't meet any white people in there. But this was fifty-fifty. That was the first time I'd ever seen that. The first time I saw colour didn't really matter.'

For West Indian kids it was musical rebellion too. Even if you loved reggae, it hung heavy on you like a birthright, a taste imposed by your elders. But to dance in a soul club was to announce your independence, a defiant badge of honour all the more attractive because you got stick for it.

'They used to say if you like soul music you were gay,' laughs Fabio, who kept his Crackers visits highly secret. One weekend at a local reggae party, a girl insisted she'd seen him there.

'Everybody was like, "Boy, I hope that weren't you!"

' "– Nah, in a soul club? Are you crazy?" '

'There was no mistaking the fact that you were a soul boy,' attests Cleveland Anderson, chest puffing out proudly. 'The reggae boys wouldn't hesitate in telling you 'batty boy' because the girls might have loved the soul boys, but the reggae boys hated them.'

Crackers had gone through more than a few DJs in its first year – Pepe, Andy Hunter, Mickey Price, the cool-as-ice Mark Roman (a sixties pirate radio heart throb), even leading suburban soul jock Chris Hill had taken a turn – so when a new resident was brought in from Bumbles in Wood Green it was seen as the last throw for a failing venue. George Power's Sunday evening session, however, was an instant success. Though Power was Greek-Cypriot, his following was black. His sets incorporated jazz-funk imports, the best of Philly, Latin-influenced jazz, and soul, most of it months ahead of UK release: Barry Waite's dubbed-out funk 'Sting'; the driving French disco of Crystal World's 'Crystal Grass' and Reuben Wilson's 'Got To Get Your Own' – now regarded as a rare groove classic, then brand new.

In the burning hot summer of 1976, Power arrived with his mixed/gay crowd and proceeded to tear up the place. With camp excitability, he charged the atmosphere and egged on the dancers, shouting, 'It's time to get *jazzay!*' or, 'Shake your *poussez*, laydeez!' In response you'd hear Zulu whoops from the floor.

'He was totally on the button, understood what black kids were about. He became a legend,' enthuses Norman Jay. 'In our eyes – inner city urban kids – George Power was more important than any Chris Hill or Robbie Vincent. They weren't as cutting edge, or as up-to-the-minute. They didn't mean anything to us.'

At first glance this scruffy, rather naff Greek guy had little to recommend him to his teenage disciples. 'George was ten years older than everyone, at least,' remembers Terry Farley. 'He had terrible clothes – and it was really important then how you looked – he used the mic when no one else did. George had everything wrong about him. You think "why do these kids accept him, he's so wrong?" But he was *fantastic*, and people had a real passion about him.'

'We'd just come from black and white tellies, one phone on the street . . . and now it was our day,' relates Jazzie B of Soul II Soul. 'The 2 Tone thing was out, ska was huge, they had the relief teachers in school that everyone was shagging 'cos they was the same age as you, everyone was wearing Kickers. We were into being a bit smarter. Now we had royalty: we had George Power for Christ sake!'

With its tough dykes, hard-as-nails gay boys, fashion-freak Bowie kids, and a deadly reverential attitude to music, Crackers was not a flippant place. Indeed, its uncompromising take on looking good and having fun was no doubt what made it so inspiring.

'There certainly weren't no peace or love in there,' asserts Farley. 'Crackers wasn't fun, it was very serious, but it was great because it was your thing.'

'It was an anorak scene; it wasn't where you came to meet people,' insists Jazzie. 'It was mainly for dancers, because it was where they came to burn.'

Crackers wasn't the only show in town. The central London soul-boy circuit included Global Village with Pepe and Norman Scott, Gullivers in Mayfair – swisher and older, with Graham Canter and James Hamilton – and the 100 Club where Ronnie L played. But thanks to its music and its energy, until its demise in 1981, Crackers was the one. 'It was the first club

I went to where it was, "Wow, this is just amazing!" ' says Farley. 'Crackers was the first club for that generation.' Between them, the ruffians, movers, stylers and wannabe DJs who danced to George Power would have a profound effect on British dance music; from rare groove to house, to drum and bass and techno, all inspired by the leftfield jazz and tricky disco of a badly-dressed Greek guy from North London.

Jazz-funk

The West End soul circuit had a little white cousin in the suburbs. He drove a Ford Cortina with go-faster stripes and had a girlfriend called 'Chelle. He was jazz-funk. Like ripples in a particularly large pond, London's waves of cultish soul, jazz and proto-disco lapped gently into Essex, Surrey and Kent. Jazz-funk, as the soul scene in the south became known, would dominate British club culture – for better or worse – from its early seventies origins right until acid house finally laid it to rest. This was Britain's closest equivalent to an American-style disco scene, the arena from which dance music rose as a commercial force. And it was from here that many of acid house's evangelists would emerge – soul boy renegades almost all of them.

In the mid seventies Britain was not a pleasant place to be. An oil crisis had reduced the country to a three-day week, with power cuts as an added bonus. With constant confrontation between government and unions, and IRA bombs almost monthly, paranoid right-wingers even talked of staging a military coup. The country was brown, as if colour had been rationed. In fact everything seemed to be in short supply: petrol, sugar, jobs, fun.

In stark contrast, jazz-funk's early aficionados were colourful, brash and stylish. Many of them were Bowie kids and early punk rockers; sharp and street-wise. Mohair sweaters, peg trousers, wedge haircuts, cap-sleeved T-shirts – these were all sure signifiers that the wearer knew how to dance and probably owned some Kool & the Gang and BT Express albums.

The scene's landmark venues read less like citadels of glamour than a particularly ribald pub crawl: Lacy Lady, the Orsett Cock, Frenchies, the Rio, Flicks, the Belvedere. If suburban jazz-funk was born anywhere, it was in Canvey Island, an ugly lump on the Essex coastline with an oil refinery for a view. Canvey's best-known musical export, pub rockers Dr Feelgood, dubbed it (only half joking) the Thames Delta. Here, in a club called the Goldmine, a former worker at Dagenham's Ford car plant named Chris Hill combined an encyclopaedic knowledge of black dance music with the tacky showmanship of a mobile DJ cranked up to eleven.

Hill played upfront soul (and later, disco) imports, some judiciously chosen rock, and more than anyone else, opened up the world of contemporary jazz to the dancefloor. In contrast to its immediate forebear northern soul, jazz-funk looked forward, prizing the latest P&P import rather than crackly Detroit oldies; an ethos seen when Hill broke tracks like the Patrick Adams-produced 'Just Let Me Do My Thing' by Sine, the mellow jazz of Grover Washington's 'Sausalito' and Razzy's country-soul 'I Hate Hate' (later covered by Danny Rampling as Sound Of Shoom). He'd also drop the occasional off-the-wall choice like Glenn Miller, which sparked a craze for forties forces' threads – just one of the club's many fashion fads.

In the early seventies Hill's constituency was fairly black, since his nights were promoted in *Blues & Soul*. 'You'd get a lot of black guys coming down from east London,' relates DJ Bob Jones, a contemporary of Hill's. 'People were wearing suits, with canes and spats, gloves, real dandified. They were so cool and they'd know all the latest dance moves.' At its height in the later seventies the Goldmine attracted travelling fans from all over the country. Coaches would come down from Scotland and the dancers would sleep in the car park overnight. It was a magnet for fashion-oriented youth, with future stars like Spandau Ballet, Depeche Mode and Culture Club present, as well as punk vanguard the Bromley Contingent (including Siouxsie Sioux and Billy Idol). Punk's future wardrobe was clearly in evidence.

Something of a backwater, Canvey Island didn't take kindly to the Goldmine's early clientele of black youth (and a significant gay minority, too). Hill received poison pen letters, even death threats. The door staff were employed expressly to keep local people *out*. 'Nobody too old,' owner Stan Barrett told David Johnson in *The Face*. 'And only people with style – which means their own style, not Gary Numan's.' Justifying his approach, Barrett argued, 'People have never come to the Goldmine for a good drink up, always the music and the scene.'

'It was electric,' enthuses Crazy Beat record store owner Gary Dennis, then a teenage clubber. 'It was amazing. The music was incredible and the people were so friendly. It was so new to me, I couldn't believe this was going on – and in *Canvey Island*.'

Other clubs opened in the wake of the Goldmine's success – the Rio in Didcot, Frenchies in Camberley, Dante's in Bognor, and Ilford's Lacy Lady, to which Hill moved, and which *Blues & Soul* columnist Dave Godin rated among his top five clubs: 'a dead natural place'. Hill's reputation spread rapidly, and he became the best-paid club DJ in the country, earning £1,000 a week. Capitalising on this earning power, a cartel of similarly minded DJs coalesced around him, including Robbie Vincent, Froggy, Tom Holland, Sean French and Chris Brown – aka the

Soul Mafia. Younger lieutenants Johnny Walker, Jeff Young and future acid house mogul Pete Tong joined them in the early eighties.

Chris Hill's influence grew such that he could single-handedly propel tunes into the pop charts. 'Chris was – by his own admission – very populist,' explains Essex DJ Mark Cotgrave (aka Snowboy), relating how he once heard him get on the mic at an all-dayer to demand his crowd buy 'Turn The Music Up' by Players Association. 'It was almost like a political rally.' The record duly entered the chart at no.8 (UK). Hill's power was cemented further when he formed Ensign Records, signing the cream of home-grown jazz-funk and crossing many of them to pop: Phil Fearon, Light Of The World, Eddy Grant, Incognito (and he later discovered Sinead O'Connor).

The north

Outside the capital the uptempo northern soul sound remained dominant. But this wasn't the whole story. There had always been pools of slower funkier music – fall-outs from the splits and disagreements of the early northern scene. In Manchester there were the Ritz all-dayers, promoted by Neil Rushton (later instrumental in breaking techno in the UK), where jazz-funk and northern soul sat side-by-side, and also black clubs like the Reno, where Haçienda jock Hewan Clarke played originally, and the Nile, which had been providing pure black music for Moss-siders since the fifties.

In 1974 the Timepiece opened in Toxteth, Liverpool, a grand all-night affair with a restaurant, where Les Spaine dropped a soundtrack of heavy duty funk and reggae for a mixed salad of a crowd that included plenty of black American servicemen. Such was Spaine's reputation that many would drive up to Liverpool from bases as far away as Lakenheath, Alconbury and Upper Hayford, bringing with them the latest moves.

'These guys would turn up in their Thunderbirds. We were hot, man, *we were hot*,' beams Spaine. 'It was like a little island on its own, every dance step was droppin'.'

Spaine, along with Birmingham DJ Pat Martin, incorporated the ill-fated National Association of DJs, broadly based on the same concept as David Mancuso's Record Pool, with the intention of creating a dialogue between record company and DJ. Although they managed to attract a number of DJs the idea never really took off, but it brought Spaine to the attention of Tamla Motown, who hired him as a promoter (he went on to manage Aswad and Heatwave).

Manchester, too, had its funk adepts, thanks to the Yanks record store run by American Ed Balbier, and to the all-nighters at Rafters featuring John Grant and Colin Curtis, newly liberated from the northern scene.

Rafters, where punk bands like Warsaw (who later became Joy Division) had played a few years earlier, established Curtis's legendary position among northern DJs, as he moved effortlessly from the sweet soul of his younger days through jazz-funk and then to disco, pure jazz and early house. Curtis also recalls with great affection his later club Berlin, opened in 1979, though like most Manchester venues, it was a hovel. 'The dancefloor was like something out of a Dennis Wheatley film, with a really low roof. You had black guys, rastas, famous people, such a mixture. I met this Brazilian dancer who was at college in Manchester. These guys would just come in and jazz dance to me. Fantastic freestyle jazz dancing.'

Some of these DJs had enough of a draw to entice a few curious soul boys up from London. Ashley Beedle remembers piling into a mate's van to go and hear Colin Curtis: 'He turned me on to a lot of harder, trippier stuff than the jazz-funk scene.' Cleveland Anderson made regular trips up to Angels in Burnley, in Norman Jay's bumpy blue Escort van. 'It was a serious soul place,' he says. 'We used to get up there, dance all night and then come straight back and be in school for nine o'clock next morning. We used to do that every Wednesday.'

Froggy at the Royalty

For its original fans, jazz-funk was a treasured secret. 'It was something that no one else was into,' beams DJ Gilles Peterson. 'It was a little like listening to pirate radio, which was also a bit elitist. It was difficult to explain to anyone else, which is what made it so special; it had that tribal element.' Shunned by the mainstream media, it was sustained by word-of-mouth and the enthusiasm of specialist magazines. '*Blues & Soul* was the *Mixmag* of the day and you couldn't buy it anywhere,' recalls Pete Tong. 'You had to subscribe to it. So you felt like you were in a secret society.'

But what began as a little-documented scene of enthusiasts soon multiplied into thousands. In 1977 jazz-funk staged a coup against the northern soul sound that prevailed in the rest of the country. At a Reading all-dayer Chris Hill led his disciples from their small back room onto the main dancefloor and demanded that the northern DJs give way and play funk. In retaliation a northern fan smashed Hill's copy of Idris Muhammad's 'Could Heaven Ever Be Like This?' (The pieces were later framed with the inscription 'Remixed by a northern DJ'). The next year the tables had turned and Chris Hill and the Soul Mafia were enthroned in the main room with a thousand London-based soul boys.

At its height, jazz-funk approached the fervour, credibility and inclusiveness of the underground American disco scene. At the Royalty in Southgate black met white and urban met suburban, as Froggy, newly fired up about mixing, cranked up his behemoth sound system and played fabulously sequenced music.

'Where Froggy had the edge was he had a sound system which most black kids could relate to,' explains Norman Jay. 'Which is why, out of all the Mafia DJs he had the biggest black following.'

Using a variety of Soul Mafia guests, the Royalty created a cross-Atlantic amalgam, where leftfield US productions like Peech Boys, Loose Joints, Sharon Redd and D-Train met the jazz-funk of Willie Bobo and Lonnie Liston Smith, and rising British bands like Level 42 and I Level.

When Froggy met Larry – Soul Mafia hipster Froggy trades notes with New York legend Larry Levan.

Jazz-funk grew into a huge youth phenomenon, but still retained its essential cultishness. As disco made its presence felt in the UK, it was the jazz-funk DJs whose style and tastes were followed in all the new carpet-and-chrome nightspots that sprang up (especially Robbie Vincent, whose radio rise culminated in 1983 in a Radio One show where he tickled the whole nation's 'rhythm buds'). Disco's crash, keenly felt in the US, had its landing cushioned in the UK by the jazz-funk scene, which was peaking just as its American counterpart was declared dead, and which regularly forced records into the charts right through the 1980s. In suburban Britain jazz-funk ensured that disco never went away, it merely added a touch of fusion, a blond wedge, and carried on.

As the scene grew, its early sense of playfulness got out of hand. By the eighties, dancefloors were filled with (heterosexual) men wearing alarmingly tight satin shorts, deck shoes and singlets, and often brandishing cannon-sized air-horns. Customised T-shirts alerted you to an endless army of club crews and raving posses: the Dunstable Soul Disciples, the Dalston Soul Patrol, Brixton Frontline, Funkmaster Generals, the Black Kidney, the Pre-Clones, the Souldiers and the enigmatically named Worried. Conga lines and party games crept in. Danny Baker observed it all in the *NME*. 'I stood in the Royalty a few weeks ago and soaked up the oddest, most anarchic, craziest daftest scenes since 1977. The only way to get more people in is with goose-grease and a hot shoe-horn.'

This zany behaviour might have been more acceptable if the music had retained its edge, but the Soul Mafia's latter-day sound headed steadily towards the elevator. Here was a scene that raised the smooth boogie of Kleeer and the bland soul of Maze to mythic status. And if things got out of hand at the Royalty, imagine what happened when they went to the beach. In April 1979, inspired by a gig at a Club 18-30 resort, Froggy and Robbie Vincent came up with the idea of soul all-dayers and weekenders; clubbing mini-breaks fondly remembered as much for the sauciness in the chalets as the music on the dancefloor. The formula, which continues to this day, was put into action first at Caister, then Bognor and various other seaside towns (in recent years Southport weekenders have incorporated house DJs). The 1980 Knebworth Soul Weekender – described by *The Face* as 'a much more agreeable use of Hertfordshire than heavy metal,' demonstrated how large jazz-funk had become, with an event as big as anything the rave scene would later generate: 'Whoever decreed disco defunct forgot to tell 15,000 tribal conscious dancers.'

Such dominance was undermined only when the new genres arrived. The Soul Mafia's myopic definition of black music made splits inevitable. Chris Hill wouldn't play rap or electro, claiming, 'Just because it's popular with the black youth doesn't make it any good,' and clung stiffly to a uniform sound of 'real' soul. Pete Tong was one of the younger jocks who left the scene as a result: 'It seemed mad to me,' he says. 'They were quite happy to keep regurgitating old soul records. When rap came along, me and Jeff Young became the embarrassment on the bill at those weekenders. Chris was like, "Oh, fucking hell, here they are with that old racket!" '

Through 1986 and '87 Nicky Holloway's influential parties – the Special Branch and Rockley Sands weekenders – managed to combine house and jazz-funk, but it was soon clear that the soul boys had had their day. Pete Tong recalls Chris Hill's reaction: 'When house music came along, that was the last straw.'

Electro

Blues & Soul northern club correspondent Frank Elson employed asterisks when writing the word 'electro'. 'It was like when punk arrived,' says Mark Cotgrave. 'They talked about electro as though it was the anti-Christ.'

But such antipathy was a red rag to a bull when it came to the younger DJs, the ones who would embrace hip hop, and then house, with the revolutionary fervour they deserved. Greg Wilson, one of this new breed, remembers the recriminations: ' "What are you playing that electronic shit for? It's not black music. It's not soul." The people saying this were usually middle-aged white guys.' (Greg is white.) 'It was as though they thought I was leading the black crowd astray.' In fact, as the jazz-funk scene leant towards over-produced quiet storm fodder from Luther Vandross and Alexander O'Neal, Greg saw more soul in electro. 'The music they thought was soul: beautiful voices, great production . . . bland as fuck! It was like black cabaret. It wasn't the raw, gritty soul of Otis Redding, and I felt that this electro-funk had more in common with that.'

Gerald Simpson (aka A Guy Called Gerald), felt the same. 'Early kinds of synth music seemed to be always trying to mimic traditional instruments or songs, whereas this new sound was definitely not trying to hide the fact that it was electronic. There was something raw and exciting about it.'

Like many, Fabio was converted by particular records. 'We were soul boys, and at first we were like, "Man this electronic thing's taking away the soul of it . . ." But "Riot In Lagos", "Planet Rock" and all the early Tommy Boy stuff was just irresistible. I caught the bug and felt honoured to be part of the early electro scene.'

' "Planet Rock" was the one that split the scene,' confirms Wilson. 'No self respecting jazz-funk DJ was gonna play that.'

Electro was a real phenomenon in the UK. Many a British DJ has roots breakdancing to 'Johnny The Fox' in an Arndale shopping centre on Auntie Glynis's kitchen lino. Some DJs, like Wilson at Legend in Manchester, or future hip hop supremo Tim Westwood at Spats in London switched wholesale to this new sound; many others adopted it as part of their broadening musical menu. By breaking with the past and welcoming the future, it was these renegades of funk who laid the groundwork for both acid house and the UK hip hop scene.

Meanwhile, jazz-funk was descending into all-out comedy, complete with foam fights, a stale playlist and a guaranteed half-hour finale of novelty records. The sartorial precision of the early soul boys had given way to some of the worst-dressed clubbers ever (when they could keep their clothes on). Chris Hill, connoisseur that he was, had a hit with 'Bionic Santa', and insisted on singing along (badly) to 'Bring The Family Back' at the end of each Caister weekender. What had begun with the coolest kids on the block now had a gang of Timmy Malletts line dancing to 'Oops Upside Your Head'. The committed took refuge in the back room, where Bob Jones played: 'People would stick in the jazz room, because the main room crowd became a bit of a monster: shaving foam, very beery,' recalls Jones.

This ignoble ending made it easy to forget the contribution jazz-funk made to British club culture. In its network of clubs, parties and pirate radio, it built an infrastructure that would eventually benefit acid house. Most of house's original DJs either learnt their trade on its dancefloors or defected directly from jazz-funk's DJ booths. In addition it brought jazz and jazz fusion to a far wider audience than they would normally have enjoyed (or in some cases, deserved). It handed down many of its dancers, and bequeathed its virulent obsession with US imports.

We didn't take the satin shorts, though.

Rare groove

The other great precursor to acid house was the 'rare groove' warehouse scene, the culmination of the early eighties explosion in fashion and music. After punk had detonated British pop culture into bloom, flamboyant self-expression was the order of the day and misfits and style pioneers no longer felt hindered by the need to look in any way normal. The New Romantics, as the fabulous freaks from clubs like Billy's, Hell and Blitz were named, took dressing up to extremes and plundered history for ruffled shirts, kilts, spats and other heroic one-night styles. At Taboo, where Boy George held court, Australian giant Leigh Bowery became clubland's proud queen mother, with his escalating outfits that matched polka dot make-up with plastic pig noses, or six pairs of specs and an inflatable frock, and turned dressing up into performance art. (His ideas would later be stolen wholesale by New York's Club Kids.)

Nightclub tribes sprouted almost monthly, and all this creative energy was chronicled in the new 'style' magazines, *The Face*, the short-lived *Blitz*, and *i-D*, which avoided models and pioneered street-fashion reportage. In their mad finery – from flat-top psychobillies to zoot-suited jazz dancers to hard times ragamuffins and psychedelic skinheads – ordinary kids were outclassing established designers by miles.

Of course, there was a nightlife to match. There were weekend-long punk parties in docklands, loft nights thrown for the fashion set, and the chi-chi extravagance of big-ticket one-offs like the Westworld productions. The idea of independent club promotion was catching on keenly, lighting up little venues with a wealth of one-nighters and mini scenes. Every second person snapped in *i-D* gave their profession as 'club runner'.

Like the colourful costumes in attendance, music was grabbed from everywhere. There was synth pop, industrial, and danceable post-punk to throw in the pot, along with the fiddles and steel guitars of a thriving western revival. Hip hop and electro were making waves, early house was getting played, and even go-go, Washington DC's percussion-crazy funk spin-off, had its moment. Underpinning all this was the sound that gradually won out: the retro funk and soul that became known as 'rare groove'. The name came from Norman Jay's 'Original Rare Groove Show' on Kiss FM – then a pirate station – on which Jay reintroduced seventies funk tracks to an attentive audience.

New Romantic DJ *du jour* was Rusty Egan, the former Rich Kids' drummer, who played everywhere that mattered from Billy's to the Camden Palace, mixing stark European electronica with rabid rock and camp disco. At Taboo, DJ Jeffrey Hinton pushed good taste to its limits with bizarre pop, while future jocks Princess Julia and Malcolm Duffy worked the coat-check. Le Beat Route with Steve Lewis (immortalised in Spandau Ballet's 'Chant No. 1') added politically charged music to this weird mix, with tracks like Brother D's 'How We Gonna Make The Black Nation Rise'. Black Market at the Wag followed the same continuum, promoted by northern soul veteran Rene Gelston and featuring Barry K Sharpe as DJ, while spinners like Jay Strongman, star DJ of the era, drew from the same pool of styles, throwing in rockabilly to freshen the soup.

The first warehouse parties catered to the fashionable club set. Chris Sullivan, who later owned the Wag club, threw Mayhem all-nighters in Battersea as early as 1978. Bowler-hatted Phil Dirtbox, who'd been throwing in-crowd parties since 1982, scaled them up and made Dirtbox events a fixture for over a decade. Titanic, a posh warehouse party run by former Funkapolitan bass player Tom Dixon (later head of design at Habitat), attracted a glitzy west London crowd, including hot designers like Scott Crolla, to hear early hip hop DJ Newtrament spin. Jazzie B remembers their parties with affection: 'Movies showing in one half, disco lights in the other, the DJ in the middle in a boxing ring. First time I saw two chicks DJing. The scene was off the hook. Proper scene, proper New York, it was all American, it was all fashion.'

By the mid eighties, the warehouse scene was unassailable. Rare groove filled the style mags with pimpin' seventies fashions and exaggerated Afros, new bands like Push and the Brand New Heavies played the retro sounds live, and record companies jumped on it as a trendy way to market their back catalogue material, getting hits out of reissued songs by Vicki Anderson, Bobby Byrd and the Jackson Sisters.

And despite the era's emphasis on pose, the spirit that would be taken up by acid house was peeking through. At one party clubbers took to crunching empty drink cans round their feet to insulate them from the freezing concrete. People were already calling them raves. London's *Evening Standard* even rehearsed the moral indignation that would later accompany acid house, declaring the warehouses 'hell-holes of junk, funk and sex'.

The number and popularity of these all-night parties was a reaction to conventional clubs. Antiquated licensing meant early closing, and door policies were often racist. Many applied limits on black youth. Jazzie B recalls being turned away many times after travelling to hear Robbie Vincent. 'There'd be literally four black guys in there and that was the quota.'

Rare groove was acid house's Cape Kennedy. It was the launch pad towards a democratic and liberated nightlife: the warehouses had no door policies, anyone with a fiver and a bit of weed was welcome. Rare groove provided the structures needed to run large-scale underground events – unlicensed venues, clued-up sound systems and an event-hungry population. It also founded an effective communications network – pirate radio audiences had grown significantly and magazines were now writing seriously about clubs, DJs and dance music. Thanks to rare groove, *i-D* and *The Face* left you in no doubt that clubbing was the centrepiece to life in London. 'You already had everything there,' says Terry Farley. 'They just switched the music and, instead of there being a thousand people, suddenly there were ten thousand.'

However, for a long time, because it was so strong, rare groove prevented house gaining a foothold in London. 'It wasn't that they didn't like house,' says Terry Farley, 'they just didn't *need* it. London was probably the best it had been since Crackers.'

Gay London

As house music was steadily added to the stew of sounds rocking London, it found many early champions on the gay scene.

It hadn't been until Freddie Laker's cheap flights in 1977 that gay London had seen gay New York at first hand. The result had been an explosion of bushy moustaches, check shirts and Levi 501s, as the 'clone' look crossed the Atlantic. Before then, however, few of London's gay clubbers had any idea just how far behind New York and San Francisco they lagged. Although London had a thriving community and an assortment of bars, many clustered around Earl's Court, there was no purpose-built gay dance club until 1975, when Bang opened on Charing

Cross Road, with resident DJs Gerry Collins, Norman Scott and Tallulah. 'The minute it came on the scene, it was a *huge* success,' relates Tallulah. 'The *queues*! It went right round past the 100 Club.'

In Alkarim Jivani's history *It's Not Unusual* door picker Peter Burton recalls the trouble his less-than-clued-up doorman gave him on opening night. 'He used to say, "Do you know what kind of club this is?" And I'd leap from behind my desk and say, "Oh Mr Warhol, do come in, it's absolutely free for you and your five hundred friends." Rock Hudson and Rod Stewart, and Elton and all those people used to come because it was something so unusual.' Others opened in Bang's wake, including the standard-setting Embassy, the Copacabana in Earl's Court, and Maunkberry's, which brought the fashionistas to Jermyn Street with great music. Then there was Heaven, of course, which dominated the eighties with hi-energy guru Ian Levine at its helm.

But while Levine shook those Charing Cross arches to Miquel Brown and Divine, DJs at the more alternative gay nights were eagerly adding Chicago and Detroit records to the mix. Pyramid (Wednesdays at Heaven) and Jungle (Mondays at Busbys) were very influential; both were promoted by Kevin Millins and Steve Swindells (whose brother Dave wrote the clubs' section in *Time Out*). As clone-free zones, they managed to avoid the generic homo soundtrack of cheesy Eurobeat, and the residents at both clubs, Mark Moore and Colin Faver, were two of the country's first DJs to play house: 'We didn't *know* we were playing it,' admits Moore. 'It was just another electronic import that we played along with Koto and the Italo-disco stuff.'

Ian Levine called Pyramid the 'freaks night'. It was very mixed, with lots of straight people, full of wild costumes and characters. 'We were definitely the black sheep of the gay scene,' laughs Moore. Like the New York club of the same name, Pyramid dragged drag into new realms of irony and artiness. Promoter Steve Swindells recalls the wild shows he saw there. 'It was so different from stupid old tart drag. People like Matthew Glamorre in a twenty-foot dress with people popping out of it. Fat Tony used to do a whole Bollywood routine, deliberately miming badly, with Princess Julia as a man. Very cool, very alternative.'

Moore – who as S-Express (with vocalist Sonique) would later make one of the first UK house tracks – worked hard to get more records from Chicago and dedicated himself to breaking house. 'I was on a mission because most people *hated* house music and it was all rare groove and hip hop. All my friends were like, "Why do you have to keep playing this house music?" I'd play "Strings Of Life" at the Mud Club and clear the floor. Three weeks later you could see pockets of people come onto the floor, dancing to it and going crazy – and this was without ecstasy. They turned out to be people like DJ Harvey, guys like that.' Moore would use 'Al-Naafiysh' by Hashim, an uptempo electro record, as a way of tricking the homeboys into dancing to house. He delighted in such minor triumphs, but for a long time playing house was far from rewarding. 'I remember many times thinking, "this is hard work; I hope no one shoots me!" '

Playing house

In 1987 change was in the air. It actually felt like an era was coming to a close. Gorbachev's glasnost was starting to defrost the cold war. Democracy movements were thriving all over eastern Europe. Margaret Thatcher's Conservative government, exhausted and exhausting, spluttered to another election victory while the country was still in turmoil from industrial conflict. The stock market crash in October signalled a massive downturn in the economy and a collapse in the housing market, leaving many with mortgages higher than their homes were worth. Celebrating her third term with the callousness that would make it her last, Thatcher claimed, 'There is no such thing as society. There are individual men and women, and there are families.' The implication was that to succeed you had to detach yourself from any collective spirit. No U-turns, no sympathy, no soul.

The snobbery of London's club scene was also breeding opposition. Working-class casuals like Terry Farley resented being forced to adopt the styles of the ruling St Martins art-school cliques. 'To get into the clubs at night we would have to change the way we looked completely. We couldn't go straight from the football, we had to go home and get changed. It did piss us off. I knew loads about records, I knew as much as they did, but I could only come in if I got changed.' Many of the scene's power brokers and door pickers weren't even Londoners. 'I didn't mind the clothes they were wearing in these places,' says Farley, 'but it was the inconvenience of being told what to do in your city, by people who were . . . *Welsh.*'

Determined to have a voice, at the end of 1987, inspired by Peter Hooton's Liverpool FC fanzine *The End*, Farley and some similarly cultured hooligans from Slough and Windsor (Andrew Weatherall, Steven Mayes and Cymon Eckel) put together a fanzine called *Boys Own.* 'We are aiming at the boy (or girl) who one day stands on the terraces, the next day stands in a sweaty club, and the day after stays in reading Brendan Behan whilst listening to Run DMC,' it declared. *Boys Own* was filled with astute pop-culture critiques, like reviews of crap flyers ('This one's so moody I had a niggling suspicion it could be a very well perpetrated situationist type hoax . . .') or state-of-the-nation pieces bemoaning 'the lack of proper bumbles' (work it out). As Farley and his mates were drawn into the growing house movement, *Boys Own* evolved into the scene's chronicle.

It wasn't yet clear that house music would rescue nightlife from its pervasive cliquishness, but among those who had discovered it, a community feeling was growing. Spin Offs, a record store opened by Greg James in Fulham, was a favourite haunt, and a small group of DJs were forming whose common bond was house. They'd been turned on by early tastemakers like Mark Moore and Colin Faver and Eddie Richards who were playing an increasing amount of house at Camden Palace.

The Palace was a baroque Edwardian music hall which had benefited from a top-shelf sound system in 1982, making it one of London's few venues with sound powerful enough to show house off to full advantage. Faver, who had begun DJing by playing between bands in his time as a high-profile post-punk gig promoter, was an early house convert, not least because he also played at many gay nights where crowds were more receptive. Together with 'Evil' Eddie Richards (who isn't evil at all; the nickname stuck after a Halloween party), Faver would mix up house and hip hop next to synth groups like New Order, Kraftwerk and Depeche Mode.

Another important missionary was Jazzy M who was spreading house across the capital via his Tuesday and Thursday night 'Jackin' Zone' shows on LWR, and his Mi Price record store in Croydon. Eager listeners would send him pages of heartfelt poetry, simply because he was playing records by Master C&J and Sleezy D. Among the correspondents were nascent stars like Underworld's Darren Emerson and the Hartnoll brothers (Paul and Phil), from Kent, whose M25 classic 'Chime', as Orbital, began as a demo tape played on Jazzy's show.

The most influential house evangelists were two Irish brothers, Noel and Maurice Watson. Their entry into clubland's dandified fashion milieu had been instant, thanks to Maurice's credentials as a master tailor. He secured a job with fashion company Demob and, accompanied by Noel, was DJing at prestigious Demob parties from 1982.

The following year the pair joined forces with Rip, Rig & Panic bassist Sean Oliver to throw their own parties in a disused school on Battle Bridge Road in Kings Cross (later the scene of infamous Mutoid Waste Company raves). These weekly all-nighters lasted unbusted for a full seven months. Oliver's sister Andrea and a young Neneh Cherry ran the bar, the Watsons scratched their way through the latest hip hop and electro. The Clash hung out, along with the ex-Pistols, Jazzie B and Nellee Hooper of Soul II Soul, and Malcolm McLaren, who brought white labels of

'Buffalo Girls' down for the duo. Terry Farley got a major break warming up for the Watsons and was stunned by the music they played. 'They came on and played two hours of records I'd never heard. They were all new labels like Sleeping Bag, that real sort of tribally sound. I asked them where they'd got them from and they were like, "oh we got them from New York".'

As their star rose they took their crowd into the West End and launched Delirium at the Astoria on Saturdays, with a mostly hip hop menu. The opening night was a Def Jam showcase, with Run DMC, Beastie Boys and Whodini performing, while Jam Master Jay played with Maurice and Noel. Maurice's regular transatlantic record buying kept them well ahead of the pack and they were soon turning away up to 2,000 people every week.

In 1986 Maurice returned from New York with a record bag full of house. 'You're not going to believe what I've got,' he told Noel, excitedly. 'There's another new thing going on, wait till you hear this!' Noel was initially unimpressed. 'It's too gay orientated. I don't really like it.' But he was gradually swayed by his brother's enthusiasm.

When they started playing these house tracks, however, the reactions of their hip hop crowd were so violent the management had to build a cage around the booth to protect the DJs. Although a few of the white kids got it, the black kids most definitely didn't. 'It cleared the floor,' says Noel. 'People booed us. Bottles and cans were thrown.' Defiantly, Maurice insisted, 'They're going to have to learn to dance to this. They're going to have to learn what this music is and we're gonna have to be the ones who break this because it's cutting edge.'

House continued to ruffle feathers. Soul Mafia DJ Johnny Walker was told, 'You've gone right off the rails,' when he introduced it to his jazz–funk crowd. 'They just didn't understand it. A few people actually said, "I really like this", but the majority of the crowd, especially the older ones who had grown up with this purist attitude, were like, "Oh my god!" '

When Mike Pickering DJed at Fever at the Astoria he got booed off. 'There were a lot of black guys there, and they were shoving notes into my face saying, "Stop playing this fucking homo music." ' At an LWR event Jazzy M, was pulled off stage and threatened with a broken bottle for putting on house tracks. 'What are you playing this gay music for, what are you doing? I wanna dance with my girl,' shouted his attacker.

At the start of 1987, house was still just another fad, like go-go had been the year before. There was little to suggest it would be anything more. The rush of UK producers to adopt the Chicago techniques hadn't happened yet. There had been several house compilations, notably *Jack Trax* and London Records' *The House Sound Of Chicago* series (the

Elementary – the Watson brothers, Noel and Maurice, at Delirium, January 1987.

cornerstone of Pete Tong's fortunes), and house had even spawned two chart hits: 'Love Can't Turn Around' by Farley Jackmaster Funk featuring Darryl Pandy, which reached no.10 (UK) in September 1986 and Steve 'Silk' Hurley's 'Jack Your Body', which hit the number one slot in January 1987. However, these came and went and didn't look much like a trend. If anything, the latter – thanks to its oddball cartoon video – was seen as a novelty record.

Delirium closed and Maurice relocated to New York before the Watson brothers could see the results of their dogged evangelising. But Danny Rampling for one, believed in the spark the club had started. 'In Delirium there was a crowd of maybe thirty to fifty people that were in tune with the feeling that was developing, and there was a real strong spiritual feeling that was there,' he says. 'It was a brand new energy.' As it turned out there was only one element holding things back. Mark Moore was convinced he knew what this was. 'I remember when I did my first S-Express interview they asked me why they thought house hadn't taken off in London. I said it was because the drugs were all wrong.'

The north

While the south was violently divided over house, the north had no such hesitancy. DJs adopted it swiftly, as did their clubbers – DJs like Graeme Park at Nottingham's Garage, DJ Parrot and Winston Hazel at Sheffield's

Jive Turkey, Tim Lennox at Manchester gay club Number One, and Mike Pickering and Jon Dasilva at Manchester's Haçienda.

'They were more on it,' says Pete Tong. 'The day a house record came in, they chucked all the old ones out. They were looking at us, going, "You fucking southern soul tossers!" '

Northern tastes, notably a love of post-punk electronica, meant that the aesthetic leap required to appreciate house was much smaller than in London. The scene could already claim close musical kinship with Chicago and Detroit in any case. Northern soul had made earlier ties, and more recently electronic bands from northern industrial cities – Human League, Cabaret Voltaire, New Order – had provided crucial inspiration for the pioneers of house and techno. The New Romantic movement is often derided for its chronic narcissism and overuse of Max Factor, but many of its records endure as darkly electronic slices of futurism. Producers Richard Burgess, Trevor Horn, Zeus B Held and Mute founder Daniel Miller fashioned proto-house and gleaming funk from huge machines that make today's synths look like pocket calculators. Mike Pickering's projects Quando Quango and T-Coy were among the arty experiments and pop confections, as were acts like Fashion, Soft Cell, Visage and Shock. As a result, in the north, where the majority of this electronic pop had originated, there was a continuity to the new music that London couldn't hear. To clubbers in Manchester, Liverpool and Sheffield, house completed a circle; it was their own music sent back to them with an injection of black funkiness. In the south by comparison, rare groove, hip hop and the short-lived go-go craze all but killed any love for the early eighties synth-pop bands.

'In nightclubs, those records – and electronic music generally – sounded so much better than other music,' insists DJ Parrot (Richard Barrett), an early adopter of house. 'But I don't think I'd have been ever drawn to electronic music if I didn't think it had something to do with Sheffield. I listened to the Cabs and the Human League *because* they came from Sheffield.'

Also in contrast to London, the new crowd that house attracted was largely black. 'With the advent of electro and the early garage and house records the ratio between black and white changed,' says Jonathan Woodliffe, a regular DJ on the all-dayer scene. 'It was very noticeable.' Records like Warp 9's 'Nunk', Orbit's 'And The Beat Goes On', Hanson & Davis's 'Tonight', and 'You Don't Know' by Serious Intention, became huge. 'It went nuts,' laughs Colin Curtis. 'The whole dancefloor became like a sea of bodies – it was like one nation under a groove. The music became an identity for black kids right across the Midlands.' This was replicated all over the north, from the Blue Note in Derby right up to

Legend and the Haçienda in Manchester, until ecstasy's arrival whitened the scene dramatically.

In Sheffield, where DJ Parrot's Jive Turkey was mixing up Cabaret Voltaire, breakneck samba, electro, and Bo Diddley, the addition of house brought jazz dancers to the fray (led by future DJ Winston Hazel). 'You'd be buying these Chip E records thinking "what the fuck is this?" but it seemed to fit perfectly with the vibe of Cabs' records,' says Parrot. 'Then we started getting black kids coming down – and at the time black and white crowds didn't really mix – but the Foot-workers were really into these records.' Jive Turkey managed to hold on to its older more musically sophisticated crowd even after ecstasy. 'For a while we got the energy from one scene and the ears from another,' Parrot reflects.

They hired out Sheffield's City Hall ballroom to throw early raves, cramming 2,000 people into a 700-capacity venue – until the council found out. Jive Turkey became an important lodestone for the new sound of Sheffield, the distorted and distended rumble of bass that the city's Warp label was founded on.

Nearby Nottingham was another early house city. Graeme Park, a shop worker in Selectadisc, was DJing at the Garage there, mixing Mantronix with indie records and house. 'Graeme, technically, was miles ahead of everyone else,' remembers Parrot, who brought him to play at Jive Turkey. 'He was doing all this wicky wicky stuff over the top of the records. And the crowd were really going with it.'

The Ibiza visit

In 1585 Sir Walter Raleigh returned from the New World with tobacco and the potato; 402 years later in 1987, though fags and chips were still popular elements of a good night out, Britain was ready for another nightlife-enhancing discovery.

'You've gotta come over and see the place, it's going mental!'

Speaking these words from Ibiza to London, Trevor Fung made sure the last crucial piece in the acid house jigsaw was about to drop into place.

1987 had been an amazing summer for Fung. He and his cousin Ian St Paul had taken over a little upstairs bar in San Antonio and renamed it the Project Club. They'd attracted a large portion of the many Brits who were in Ibiza working the season, among them future DJs Nancy Noise (Nancy Turner) and Lisa Loud (Lisa McKay). And by selling tickets for the big clubs on the island, they'd ensured the Project became a packed meet-up place. Through each hot Spanish night crowds spilled out into the street as Trevor dropped a kicking combination of London club favourites like Mantronix and the wild Balearic tunes he was learning about from Alfredo at Amnesia.

Fung had been partying on the island since 1979, able to fly over as often as weekly thanks to a day job in the travel industry. Entranced by the bizarre constituency of visiting celebs, Eurotrash, wily Brits and international gay party monsters, he was now assiduously gathering contacts on the island, especially since he was bringing tunes over from the promotion departments of London record labels and selling them to the island's key DJs.

Back home in Streatham he ran a small club also called the Project (previously the Funhouse, originally Ziggy's wine bar), with good friend Paul Oakenfold. The two had met on the jazz-funk scene on a coach trip to Slough where the bus had its windows smashed in (a strange incident of London/Slough soul-boy rivalry). Fung was DJing jazz-funk in the shadow of the Soul Mafia, and Oakenfold was a chef with a lot of questions about how you became a DJ. The Streatham Project Club ran from 1981-89, with a sound system brought in each Friday by their warm-up DJ, Carl Cox from Brighton (who Fung claims started on a fee of £30 for his trouble).

In Ibiza Fung had gradually cottoned on to ecstasy. He first tried it in 1986, an orange and white capsule strong enough to make him throw up, bought from a dealer who now owns one of the most famous clubs on the island. At the end of August 1987, he was about to share Ibiza's party secret with the whole of London.

The first time Trevor invited him to Ibiza, Paul Oakenfold decided he didn't like the place and went home early. But now he wanted to come out and celebrate his birthday. Ever the wily operator, Oakenfold had shot up the nightlife pecking order – he was plugging records for Def Jam and doing well as a hip hop DJ. He asked Trevor to find a place to stay for him and his friends: DJs Danny Rampling and Johnny Walker and party promoter Nicky Holloway.

'When the boys arrived, I took them to the bar,' says Fung. They were immediately struck by the current buzz in Ibiza compared with the sniffy rare groove scene back home. 'They were like, "Fucking hell, can't believe this".' Smiling to himself that his adopted island was already working its magic, Trevor reached in his pocket and prepared to really impress them.

'I didn't want to say too much, so I just said, "Try this, it don't do too much to you".' He laughs uproariously as he remembers it.

They ended up at Amnesia. 'Johnny was sitting in a speaker. Danny was jumping up and down. Paul was like, "It's changed since I last been here." Chaos!'

'I was very hesitant at first,' recalls Walker. But having seen Paul and

Danny and Nicky do one and then go skipping and hopping around the club holding hands, going "I *love* you", I thought, "well, this doesn't look too bad, I'll try one". And suddenly the whole night just turned into this fabulous, sparkling, colourful night. I just felt so wonderful. I remember walking into this high white-walled sort of building, through the gates and into this fabulous open-air club with palm trees and a mirrored pyramid and dazzling light show going on, and all these wild crazy flamboyant colourful people dancing about.'

They found themselves dancing furiously to joyously eclectic music, much of which would have been an anathema to the self-consciously cool club scene back in London: pop-dance like George Michael's 'I Want Your Sex', followed by Chicago house like Ralphi Rosario's 'You Used To Hold Me', followed by an obscure indie record like 'Jesus On The Payroll' by Thrashing Doves. The lightbulbs went on. 'Hearing Alfredo play, it was *completely* mindblowing compared to what we were used to in London. We were like, "Wow! What the fuck is *this*?" '

By the end of the week, they'd resolved to introduce this life-affirming experience to London. Walker recalls the sense of mission they all felt. 'Soon as we got back, "You've got to try this!" Every club we went into, we were like, "Have you tried this? You gotta have some of this, it's unbelievable." '

Ecstasy

E, X, MDMA, methylenedioxymethylamphetamine. Ecstasy, the chemical compound which changed everything. It's hard to imagine a drug more conducive to the club experience. It gives you energy, it enhances light and sound and it can make a roomful of people drop their defences, forget their insecurities and feel a sense of intense togetherness. Not for nothing is it classified as an empathogen, as in empathy, as in appreciating other people.

Britain was hardly a place to have expected an explosion of drug-taking. These were Thatcher's Children: hard-working, council-house-buying, share-speculating bores. Weren't they? Yet this creeping materialist conformity was probably the precise reason its impact was so huge. (Britain now has the highest incidence of youth drug-taking in Europe.)

Ecstasy started appearing in the UK around 1985, just after it was made illegal in the US ('E' was outlawed in Britain in 1977). Originally synthesised in 1912, it made a resurgence as a psychotherapy tool, and spread as a recreational drug via Texan hippies and international quasi-Buddhist sex communes.

It was on the floors of the New York gay scene that ecstasy first met dance music. People would dissolve it in the free coffee at the Saint in

1981, although some clubbers preferred its more sexual sister drug MDA. A celeb-heavy Dallas club called the Starck grew to fame in 1984, the last year ecstasy was legal, by selling it over the bar or from drug waiters wearing T-shirts that read 'BUY MY XTC'. It was introduced to London scenesters by transatlantic party animals like Boy George and Marc Almond, whose band Soft Cell has the distinction of making the first ecstasy-influenced record, 1981's 'Memorabilia'. In its remixed version on their album *Non Stop Ecstatic Dancing* this insistent proto-techno groove featured their dealer Cindy Ecstasy rapping.

Before house music, though, the UK didn't see it as a dance-enhancer, more a 'designer drug' for swank cocktail parties. Here were people dressed in polo necks and MA1 jackets being very aloof listening to Sadé. When they tried E, it just didn't fit. 'The music was the wrong backing track to it,' agrees Dave Dorrell, one of a small inner circle in London who had tried ecstasy then. 'Everyone was just kind of wobbling around like jellies on a chair.'

However, the marriage of ecstasy and house would prove nothing short of seismic. The club scene cool was about to be blown. Noel Watson, who'd played house at Delirium to empty dancefloors, folded arms and flying bottles, vividly remembers the change after they moved the night to Heaven, switched it to an all-house playlist, and ecstasy appeared. 'Suddenly everybody who was anti-house music loved it. They were hugging each other. It was amazing. I played "Strings of Life" there and people would go mad.'

Much of the drug was initially supplied by globetrotting football casuals.

'A lot of people fucked off about 1983 or 1984,' says DJ Parrot. 'People who'd previously been faces around town and football games, they just disappeared. The term was 'International Tourist Thieves'. A lot of 'em ended up in Ibiza. When that contingent started coming back is when the ecstasy started coming in.'

Ian St Paul told *Once In A Lifetime* author Jane Bussmann how he fell in with some of these young scallies.

'They were going round Europe on InterRail cards robbing. We called them the Boccy Boys, because they used to sit outside the Café Del Mar living off boccadillo sandwiches because they had no money.' St Paul gave up his bar to hang out with them. 'I found myself driving my jeep as their getaway car while they were robbing hotel safes and petrol stations. They never got caught; they were professionals.'

Parrot recalls the first time he was offered E. 'Black Paul he was called. He asked if I wanted to buy some eggs. I was like, "what the fuck are you on about?" They were £25. I was just laughing at him. I thought, "there's no way you're gonna sell any of that in here." That was more than some people were getting on the dole! Obviously, though, what the fuck did I know?'

As a psychoactive drug that had treated marriage breakdown and soldiers' shell shock, it was an unusual choice of dancefloor intoxicant. But the way it affected groups rather than just individuals made it unprecedented. Capsules, pink calis, white burgers, rhubarb and custards, if it was real MDMA it would make you feel profoundly comfortable with yourself, followed by a craving for company. In a room full of users smiles became infectious and you felt confident that everyone was in the same great mood. Ecstasy was nothing if not party-shaped. In Push and Mireille Silcott's *The Book Of E*, record distributor Nick Spiers relates the moment it first 'clicked' for him: 'On E it seemed like you became a cog in the big wheel of the whole room you were in, this churning energy thing, and you became a part of it, you gave yourself over to the experience. That's what acid house was about.'

In economic terms the combination of house music and ecstasy would prove to be a uniquely potent proposition, exported globally, generating billions. As we'll see in later chapters, the illegal side of this nightlife economy has earned dance culture more than its share of government disapproval.

While our parents thought E was one step down from heroin, we thought it was one step up from beer. Eventually, ecstasy became an almost universal peak experience for young people, as much a part of growing up as your first cigarette, ushering in a youth culture where drug-taking is considered normal. And while the long-term mental health implications of this remain dauntingly unknown, the social effects have been profound. You'd expect nothing less from a drug taken by as many as half-a-million people every weekend. Anything that can get murderous football hooligans skipping round a dancefloor holding hands with transvestites must be viewed with a certain respect.

The return

When Paul Oakenfold, Johnny Walker, Nicky Holloway and Danny Rampling returned home from Ibiza, they worked hard to re-enact the magical atmosphere they'd witnessed at Alfredo's Amnesia. They had a fully tested nightlife package – it could almost be a franchise. There were the clothes (loose, casual, democratic, holiday), the drug (ecstasy), the records (Chicago house and Balearic classics) and, courtesy of Danny Rampling's skinny arms and their wavey floppings, there was even a dance.

Fung, Oakenfold and St Paul threw parties in Streatham for the scallies and bar-workers they'd met on the island, even flying Alfredo in to play. Scouring indie record shops like Rough Trade, Oakenfold quickly appropriated a big chunk of the Spaniard's playlist. Nicky Holloway immediately flipped his rare groove/hip hop Special Branch nights onto the new formula. The new vibe hardly needed much promotion. 'I suppose people saw us running about having a good time, big smileys, you know,' recalls Walker. 'And everyone thought, "Mmm, this looks interesting, what are they up to?" And it gradually started to happen.'

At the first major jazz-funk event after their return, their appearance caused consternation. Gilles Peterson, a rare spliffhead in what was essentially a beer-boy scene, remembers being surprised to see behaviour more eccentric than his own. 'It was a bit of a shock at Rockley Sands when they all came back and were suddenly sitting in speakers on ecstasy!'

'Johnny Walker was playing George Kranz's "Din Daa Daa" and Rampling jumped on the stage and started doing his funny dance,' chuckles Terry Farley. 'People were going, "He's took one of them E things! You know them Es? They've got them in Ibiza." '

Almost immediately, the cool London club scene, carefully cultivated since the birth of *The Face* and the days of the New Romantics, was irrelevant. Now you no longer had to dress like a Regency dandy or a polka-dot Humpty Dumpty. You didn't have to pretend you liked Blue Rondo A La Turk, or cultivate an angular moustache or strategically rip your jeans. Now you could shake off all these stylish shackles and release your inner child. No more VIP Rooms, no more velvet ropes, and certainly no more velvet jackets.

Paul Oakenfold recalled inviting the *Boys Own* crew to come and hear Alfredo after a night at the Wag. 'They turned up in their floppy rare groove hats and I said, "No, no, no: that's not it any more".'

'*Boys Own* magazine was totally rare groove,' admits Terry Farley. 'I had the big trousers and the hat. Then suddenly I was like, "right we're changing".'

Club culture was now reborn. But for almost a year the infant was swathed in secrecy, its adherents fiercely protective of this new Age of Aquarius. Early press coverage only hinted at how different things were getting, and cryptically referred to 'ecstatic dancing'. In the summer of 1988, this new way of having fun would explode into mainstream consciousness, as the rave movement was splashed all over the papers, but for now its devotees wanted it for themselves. Farley confesses he kept it secret even from friends of ten years' standing, because he knew they wouldn't fit. 'Everyone was like that. "This is our thing. This is us." It was so amazing you didn't want anyone else to get it.'

The Shoom

'Happy Happy Happy . . .' read the flyers, with a scattering of tumbling grinning pills, starting a craze for yellow smiley faces. Sch-oom, later Shoom, named after the feeling of coming up on an E, was run by Danny Rampling and his future wife Jenni. It started in October 1987 at the Fitness Centre in Southwark Street, a gym with mirrored walls, lots of strawberry-flavoured smoke and room for only about 200. 'Everyone would turn up at midnight on a Saturday night,' recalls Johnny Walker. 'In, lock the doors, on with the smoke machines and strobes and the Balearic classics, and the party would just go on until about six or seven in the morning.'

'That first night was *the* defining, life-changing moment of my life,' the Beloved's Helena Marsh told Sheryl Garratt in her acid house history *Adventures In Wonderland*. 'All my values, my opinions, everything changed. I went down there in my designer clothes and by the end of the evening they had gone. I was wearing wool Gaultier pants and it was so hot in there I had to take them off. So I went into the toilet with my friend, we ripped off our trousers, he took off his polka dot boxer shorts and I put them on. They were all sweaty, but it felt right.'

'It was the maddest place I'd ever been to, laughs Pete Heller, who became resident DJ alongside Danny. 'It suited my aesthetic completely, because all I did was take acid, and lots of it. I'd go straight to the dancefloor and that was it.'

'Everyone told me it was such a friendly place,' remembers Mark Moore, 'but I remember walking in and there's smoke everywhere and everyone was walking around like *Night Of The Living Dead*. Then, about an hour later, suddenly people are coming up and hugging you and "What's your name? I love you, you're great!" They're *all* on ecstasy!'

Though its small size necessitated some fairly ruthless doormanship, Shoom welcomed a democratic mix. Style journalists and off-duty pop stars chatted with roofers and plasterers. More than a few of these 'loved-up' clubbers were well-known football hooligans. 'A lot of kids used to be quite bad, a lot are from the terraces,' admitted Rampling in *i-D*. 'Five years ago these kids were having punch ups. But all that has gone out of the window.' Now they were trance-dancing to Fingers Inc's 'Distant Planet' while dressed like Mexican bandits. What was going on?

Shoom set the tone for the clubs that would follow. Chicago stars Marshall Jefferson, Larry Heard, Bam Bam and Robert Owens all DJed or performed. And it was at Shoom that the house DJ started his rise to messiah status. 'At the end they come up and shake my hand,' a puzzled Colin Faver told John Godfrey in *i-D*, after guesting there. 'It just doesn't happen anywhere else.' When Rampling was due to play, people would run round the club whispering, 'Danny's on in five minutes'. And everyone would crowd the dancefloor in anticipation, because it *mattered that much*. This had never happened in the UK before, not even in northern soul clubs (where clubbers generally worshipped the 45s rather than their owners). 'During the rare groove thing you wouldn't acknowledge the crowd,' relates Terry Farley. 'There was no connection. Suddenly Danny's standing there and he's waving his record around, shouting and people are shouting at him and hugging.'

Future and Spectrum

When Ian St Paul told friends he was starting a new Monday night at Heaven, they thought he was mad. He and the rest of the Ibiza clique had been doing well in Sanctuary (Heaven's little annex) with Future, their Thursday night Amnesia reunion, where since November 1987 (two weeks after Shoom opened) Oakenfold, Noise and East End soul DJ Tony Wilson had trotted out the Alfredo Top 40. Future had come about after Fung and St Paul brought a huge group of pilled-up Ibiza mates to a gay night in Heaven when their own party had fallen through. 'All the gays in the club were going, "What the fuck?!" ' laughs Trevor Fung, relating how the sight of all these nutters dancing on E immediately led to a night of their own. But while Future had been doing great, filling the vast space of Heaven next door was far more daunting.

Spectrum opened on 11 April 1988 and its first few weeks were nearly empty. 'But I knew something which everyone didn't,' says Oakenfold, 'which was ecstasy. So I knew Spectrum was going to go off. I knew it in my heart. That's why I stuck with it.' Sure enough, by the fourth week it was rammed. 'All the Ibiza workers, they'd come from everywhere: Aberdeen, Glasgow, Manchester, Leeds,' explains Fung.

This wasn't the sweet sunshine sound of Amnesia. Although upstairs Terry Farley and Roger The Hippie (Roger Beard) played Balearic beats and reggae, downstairs was house. Acid house. It was hard, insistent and driving. Lasers zapped off walls and over an oscillating sea of sweat and sinew. There were epic decorations – giant spiders, the Statue of Liberty, a floor full of fake snow. Coolly standing around was a thing of the past – the point of being there was now the music and the dancing. As with Shoom, the DJ was increasingly venerated, especially since Heaven's DJ booth was positioned like a pulpit.

Even seasoned clubbers were astonished at the energy now being released. Fabio recalls walking into Spectrum with a couple of mates. 'They were like, "What the hell is going on here?" We saw everyone with smiley T-shirts, big eyes, chewing their teeth, and just walking around in another world. My friends fucked off and left me in there. They told me,

"It's like we've walked into hell. We're going back to Brixton." ' But Fabio was hooked, not least by Oakenfold's theatrical five-minute entrance routine. 'I remember looking up, seeing Paul Oakenfold and this smoke, and him being like a fucking god up there. I was like, "My god, this is absolutely amazing." '

Spectrum was later renamed Land of Oz after a tabloid story implicated Heaven's owner Richard Branson in the unthinkable crimes of acid house. Here Gary Haisman, once a dancer at Crackers, now a party promoter, started the acid house war cry of 'Aciieeed'. It was also the club where Rampling's acid house wavy-pointy-hands dance took off. As more clubbers got 'sorted', the ecstasy experience took on a mystical importance, with people finding cosmic messages in the most unlikely music. When Farley played Barry White's 'It's Ecstasy When You Lay Down Next To Me' it became an anthem. 'I used to play Jackie Wilson's "The Sweetest Feeling" every week at Spectrum and people would go, "That record! Fuckin' hell, I never thought this was about E!",' he laughs.

The old guard, still obsessed with style, missed the point. Mark Moore took promoter Philip Sallon to Future and told him, 'This is the future, literally the future. It's what's gonna happen next.' Sallon pooh-poohed him, 'Don't be silly – they're just kids from the suburbs.'

Hedonism

'Free drugs! Free party!' Who wouldn't by tempted by a flyer like that? Hedonism was the first event to take the rare groove warehouse party blueprint and switch it to house. A series of free one-off parties held in various far-west London locations between February and May 1988, this was where the rave template came together. Thanks to a monstrous sound system, Hedonism was awash with chest-concussing bass. Many recall that this was where they first heard house music through the kind of speakers it was made for. Add to this plenty of happy drugs, beaming faces, a wildly diverse crowd and friendly interaction and openness. Anyone who went to Hedonism was going to want more.

Danny and Jenni Rampling arrived straight from their wedding. 'It was like nothing I'd ever seen,' said record promoter Nicky Trax. 'People were taking Es and speed and smoking spliff, but what struck me about it was it was much more open. In Hedonism, they were telling people they were on drugs or were sharing them. But most of all, people were all talking to each other.'

Hedonism marks the start of what would become rave culture. But for Leslie Lawrence (of pioneering UK house act Bang The Party), in common with others who'd been on the house and Balearic scenes since their inception, it was when the movement peaked. 'I think by the time Hedonism came, that was the icing on the cake. It was supposed to be the elements coming together after the mad explosion. It was supposed to be the ultimate. And that was the end I think. After that it was just too big.'

There was a sense of belonging that previously hadn't been present on the warehouse scene. The new spirit manifested itself most memorably in the half-hour gap between one sound system shutting down and Soul II Soul's cranking up. The break was filled with a cacophony of percussion as the clubbers beat out their own monster rhythm on walls, floors, bottles, anything that came to hand. In *Pump Up The Volume* DJ and Shamen frontman Mr C confessed to Sean Bidder that this moment was what drove him to make music. 'That was really instrumental in showing me the power of hypnotic rhythms . . . this is why I'm into this music, this is why I really want to be a house producer and a DJ.'

Clink Street

The Hedonism vibe found a more permanent home in some dank Dickensian catacombs that now house London's prison museum. The weekly RIP parties, or Clink Street as they are universally known, embodied a far tougher and more multiracial version of the acid house epiphany than Shoom just around the corner. Instead of flower power and strawberry smoke it had stark strobes and camouflage netting, and a crowd whose heart lay in the ruggedly working class East End. Like Hedonism it owed less to Ibiza, and more to the underground sound system network. If Shoom was a jazz-funk club taking a trip, Clink Street was the acid house inheritor of the 'blues party' tradition of illegal reggae speakeasies.

Fittingly then, the sound was provided first by Soul II Soul, and then by Shock, a funk and hip hop sound system that had recently added house to its playlist, and which included Ashley Beedle (later of X-Press 2) and Ricardo Da Force, rapper for the KLF. The resident DJs were recruited from Mr C's party, Fantasy – Lawrence 'Kid' Bachelor, 'Evil' Eddie Richards and former milkman Mr C himself (Richard West).

It was the lovechild of Lu Vukovic and Paul Stone, an anarchist punkette and a dub promoter from Portsmouth. After a first night in a Euston shop basement they found their London Bridge home at the start of May 1988. Clink Street's importance has often been overlooked, most likely because while Shoom ended up as quite the media darling, Vukovic's politically charged idealism extended to banning cameras and dissuading journalists from writing about it (fittingly, RIP stood for 'Revolution In Progress'). 'Clink Street was slummier, dodgier,' Eddie Richards told Matthew Collin in *Altered State*. 'Dodgier characters on the door, dodgier characters inside, a dodgier feeling about. I think it was a bit frightening. Really frightening sometimes.'

These characters included some serious football hard-cases, who wouldn't have hesitated to raise a Stanley knife to each other if they'd met outside this acid house cocoon. Inside they were chatting and sharing pills. At the other end of the scale visitors included composer Philip Glass and lisping violinist Nigel Kennedy; the rest of the crowd was simply every type of person in between.

RIP became so popular during the summer of 1988 that the Saturdays spread to Fridays and then Sundays. Some people wouldn't go home all weekend. Every weekend. And there was something pagan and sinister about Clink Street, evoked by the earthy smell of damp and sweat. One night, when Ashley Beedle played 'Bring Down The Walls' by Fingers Inc, the crowd took Robert Owen's lyrics at their word and started clawing away at the crumbling cladding on the walls until they'd demolished four layers of it down to the brick. Sheryl Garratt was among many there that night who were struck by the symbolism. 'There were no longer any barriers holding us back. The old elitism was finished. The walls were coming down.'

The Dungeon

The snowball rolled on and in 1988 house events sprang up all over. Kid Bachelor, who had DJed with Soul II Soul and was making early house tracks as a third of Bang The Party, started throwing his own Sunday-nighter, Confusion, after the demise of Soul II Soul's famous Africa Centre rare groove parties. There was Love at the Wag, Enter The Dragon in Kensington, Slam in Glasgow, Bristol's Vision, Frenzy in Brighton, Hooch in Edinburgh, Leeds's Warehouse and Club Havana in Middlesborough.

The Dungeon, a club in far-east London, offers a perfect example of how the do-it-yourself virus infected people. Rob Acteson and Linden C (Linden Cambridge), two DJs who'd recently switched from rare groove to house, started throwing parties in spring 1988 in a weird network of vaulted cellars under a pub in Leyton. They were so energised by the new music they worked like dogs to turn this 'damp wet hole' into a serviceable venue for the owner, shelling out thousands and even excavating seven feet of concrete to lower some floors. In Acteson's mind it was a continuation of the local outlaw parties they were used to, like the rare groove nights that had filled abandoned houses along the route of the A12 extension. 'The government had compulsory-purchased massive amounts of property and left the houses derelict for years. I could leave my house, travel five minutes down the road and listen to Norman & Joey Jay, Trevor Nelson, Derek Boland, Jay Strongman etc – in a house!'

The first night was a birthday party for a friend who'd found the place. 'That night, more than anything, changed my life. It really did. It was the first time I'd seen a proper house environment. It all went mad for me after that.' There were 300 at the first night, a week later 1,000. Within a couple of months they had expanded into the pub upstairs and even had marquees in the car park, and were putting perhaps 7,000 people through the place over each weekend. And since it was one of the few illegal parties that was never busted (thanks to its layout the Dungeon was unbustable) they even welcomed coaches from Liverpool.

Calling their sound system crew Hypnosis, Acteson and Linden C were joined by Eddie Richards, Steve Proctor and later by Rhythm Doctor (Chris Long), with MC Noise whipping the crowds to a frenzy. Mr C, however, was the star of the show. 'Mr C was the man in there,' laughs Acteson. 'He had a lot of skills, and he was good on the mic as well. People loved it. He played beautiful Jersey vocals, and he'd know where all the breakdowns were in the track and he'd be rapping over the breaks.'

The Dungeon exemplified the power of acid house to switch ordinary suburban wage slaves on like light bulbs. 'You could see life-changing experiences every week. It really was like that. A lot of people had shown no interest in music before. Their lives would have been going to the pub on a Saturday night; at a push they might have listened to a bit of Run DMC or LL Cool J, and that was the extent of their musical knowledge. Then within two or three weeks of coming down to the Dungeon, it was their entire life.' The club also illustrates how drug-taking quickly became accepted. 'A lot of the people down my way used to look down their noses at me for smoking a spliff. Within the space of a year they'd be going there and dropping pills every week.'

The Haçienda

The club which famously ignited house in the north was Manchester's Haçienda. It had been opened on 21 May 1982 by stone-age funnyman Bernard Manning. His bigoted jokes didn't go down too well and he returned his fee, saying, 'Take my advice, never hire a comedian.' At its start the forward-looking musical policy was similarly out of sync with the clientele's expectations. The original resident DJ, Hewan Clarke, programmed a mix of black funk, soul and disco, while sullen students mooched around the cavernous space in raincoats waiting in vain for Echo & the Bunnymen to be played. 'I just remember it being like a private club for about fifty people,' reflects writer Jon Savage, who also DJed there. 'And on the few nights when they had bands, all these other people would come in.'

The club was the brainchild of a group of Manchester music folk including Tony Wilson, supremo of Factory Records, and Rob Gretton, New Order's manager. It even had a Factory catalogue number, FAC 51. And it was modelled unashamedly on the big clubs of New York: the Paradise Garage, Funhouse and Danceteria. As Wilson put it: 'I just thought, "Why hasn't Manchester got one of those? Fucking New York's got one, we should have one."'

New Order were also among the club's directors, and as the band was regularly over in New York recording with Arthur Baker, they formed the lynchpin of the Manc–Yank connection. 'There's always been this big underground link with New York, because of New Order's and Factory's early success there,' Mike Pickering told Jon Savage in *The Haçienda Must Be Built*. 'The most important thing about the Paradise Garage was that Larry Levan used to mix these underground New York records with records on Rough Trade or Factory. As far as I was concerned, the dream was that the Haçienda would be like that.'

'Manchester had no glamour prior to the house scene,' insists DJ/producer Danny Dware. 'If you weren't an indie kid and into the Smiths there was nothing. It seemed like everything was happening in London.' But then 'Bus Dis' and 'Souled Out', Stu Allen's enormously popular shows on Radio Piccadilly, which had championed hip hop and streetsoul, began featuring the new sound of Chicago and the city's dance scene started taking off.

The Haçienda's dancefloor finally filled around 1986 when the club's Nude night – having started two years earlier – switched to a playlist heavily weighted with house. With the recruitment of Jon Dasilva (Jonathan Hibbert) and later Graeme Park from Nottingham, together with a batch of ecstasy courtesy of a gang of Salford scallies, the touchpaper was lit. Another night, Hot, despite only running for a few months in 1988, was also hugely influential. The sullen students were now replaced by a combustible tribal mix of dancers, many fuelled by the strange new empathetic hug-drug. 'I loved the year or so leading up to the ecstasy explosion,' beams Mike Pickering. 'We had a fire limit of twelve hundred but we were getting sixteen hundred, and the thing about it was they were complete music fans.'

Graeme Park couldn't believe the atmosphere when he first played there in July 1988, 'It was three of the most incredible weeks I've ever had in my life,' he told Sheryl Garratt. 'I was playing the records I'd been playing for the past few months, but getting this unbelievable response.' Instead of the slow filling up he was used to in Nottingham, the Haçienda had them queuing to get in as early as 9pm. 'At ten the club was full and the atmosphere was so intense. It was electric. Every time I went to light a cigarette, I was worried I was going to make the place ignite.'

The Trip

Back in London, the Trip was where the explosive acid house experience started to emerge from the underground. Clubbers here were so fired up that when the night ended they'd dance round someone's car stereo or in the fountains across the street, shouting 'Acieeeeed' at passers by. On one occasion, a police van arrived, siren blaring, and the crowd in Charing Cross Road chanted as one, 'Can you feel it?' since the siren sounded just like the sample in Royal House's 'Can You Party?'. Nicky Holloway once set up a sound system in a nearby car park. Just to extend the party by twenty minutes.

Coinciding neatly with an *i-D* story on the acid house phenomenon, the Trip opened at the Astoria on 4 June 1988 to queues round the block and pandemonium inside. 'I'm absolutely knocked out by this,' declared Nicky Holloway to *Update* after the first night. 'I've done some promoting of gigs over the years but this is THE BUSINESS!' The mayhem continued for a further ten weeks and then ended as tumultuously as it began, with thousands in the street and in Trafalgar Square and scores of police looking on, bamboozled.

It showed how out of control things were going to get – and how quickly the wildfire would spread. 'I remember going to the Trip and it blew my mind,' smiles Gilles Peterson. From a couple of mates back from Spain looking daft at Rockley Sands, acid house could now cause a roadblock outside one of London's biggest clubs. 'Within a few months the whole thing had just totally changed.' What craziness was due next?

House was poised to become mainstream, and everyone knew that once out of the bag it would be huge and unstoppable. The more snobby among the pioneers started calling themselves 'Balearic' rather than 'acid house' fans in an effort to distance themselves from the inevitable masses now climbing aboard the bandwagon wearing smiley T-shirts and day-glo surfwear. Nick Spiers voiced a widespread view: 'The sheep . . . there were many. So acid house became rave, so all the sheep could fit.' *Boys Own* christened them 'Acid Teds', but the rest of the world would know them as ravers. They were the shouting, grinning, second wave who would take acid house out of these few London clubs and propel it into a national, and then international, youth culture.

For the vast majority, acid house began in a field or an aircraft hangar or an empty film studio. They remember driving into the uncharted green and brown beyond London to follow rivers of brake lights down country lanes in search of a bassline. Raves were the greatest expression of the acid house ideal of togetherness, and DJs soon found themselves at the heart of parties of unprecedented size. However, as huge unlicensed events where thousands of young people took illegal drugs, they also generated serious political implications. You can read the full rave story in a later chapter.

Revolution

Acid house bulldozed youth culture, razing everything in its path and dominating music in Britain, for an unprecedented fifteen years. Subsequent pop revolutions have been rather cursory in comparison. Grunge, Britpop, boy bands, the Spice Girls – any takers? Though there are currently some scorching guitar rebels making a play, it's hardly a

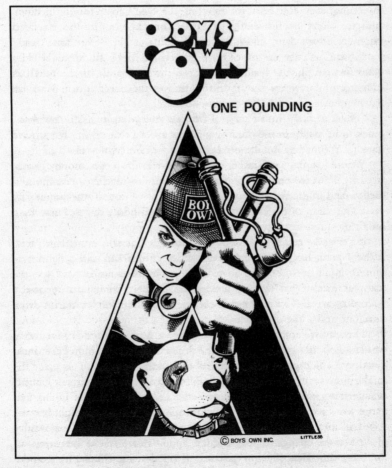

ONE POUNDING

© BOYS OWN INC.   LITTLE 88

Like Clockwork – Boys Own, the voice of the early acid house scene.

sound we've never heard before. And millions of teenagers still give their all to a weekend of house.

A youth culture isn't really convincing unless it generates some actual hatred. And house was the last time music really polarised people. 'I thought it was so fucking brilliant and I couldn't understand why no one else thought it was brilliant,' declares Mark Moore. 'I just thought, "This music is fucking great!" But no one else agreed with me at the time.

'I'm actually *proud* of the times I've cleared dancefloors,' he adds, smiling.

The comparison has to be with punk – for making enemies, for sweeping away dinosaurs, for resetting the clock, for releasing creativity and for sheer energy expended. Pete Tong agrees. 'It was a seminal moment. It was dance music's punk rock. It was like Before and After.'

Fiona Cartledge, creator of the Sign of the Times boutique and parties, goes further. Having lived through the thrill of punk, as she told Jane Bussmann, for years she found nothing that could live up to the excitement.

'Then, with the house scene, I felt that energy again: *this is now.* And I knew from being in the punk scene how special that feeling is, and how rare . . . You had to just experience it and *fuck* everything else.'

Where punk proclaimed an anyone–can–do–it philosophy, house actually delivered on the promise. Certainly it provided the necessary self-belief. And in the way it heightened our sense of now, in the way it gave us a succession of perfect moments, it rammed home the fact that life is not a dress rehearsal.

It certainly made music-making more democratic even than punk. Where punk had told you to learn three chords and start a band, acid house didn't even ask you to pick up an instrument. As we'll see, the sampler meant that the DJ needed no further training to become a recording artist. Now you didn't even need a studio, just an Atari, a drum machine and a bag of records.

The way we enjoyed music changed, too. With its more minimal song structures, house greatly lessened the importance of each individual track, making the dancers succumb instead to a continuous mix. This made the night more focused, more singular, and let the DJ play with the hypnotic, trance-inducing qualities of music – the shamanistic side of DJing. The Americans had experienced this approach since Francis Grasso, but the UK had always prized the integrity of individual songs more. Jon Dasilva described the change to Sean Bidder: 'People mirrored the long mixes in the way they danced; they just stayed on the floor. It wasn't just the chemicals, it was the music as well and the way the music was played, the intensity of the whole experience.' In this way, house gave the DJ much greater control over the dancefloor.

This change was an important reason why acid house was such a cataclysmic year zero – it was a whole new way to party, incompatible with the older ways of clubbing.

'House only worked when you went, "right: this is a house club",' says Terry Farley. 'You went there in your house clothes, you did the house dance – 'cos you couldn't do your old dance. You did a totally different drug. So you had all these people taking a new drug together, doing a new dance, in their new clothes, with their new mates.'

Madchester

So revolutionary were these changes, they even upset the seemingly distant world of guitar rock. As the eighties closed, Manchester's distinctive take on acid house gave us 'indie dance', when local bands, led by the Happy Mondays, adopted the new dancefloor aesthetic. Frontman Shaun Ryder confessed that in a reverse of accepted tradition the Mondays were a musical habit formed around some serious drug-taking, and their scratchy psychedelic rock-funk proved the point. Remixed by Paul Oakenfold their raucous reading of John Kongos' 'Step On' became their first UK top 10 hit in 1990. 'There was no big secret to indie dance,' claims Oakenfold. 'We'd work on the rhythm to make it a lot more acceptable in nightclubs. And to keep the integrity of the artist you keep the guitars.'

The Stone Roses followed in the Mondays' wake, welding this baggy Mancunian rock to James Brown rhythms, as did bands like the Charlatans, the Inspiral Carpets and the impossibly hopeless Northside. 'All Manchester bands began sounding like "Funky Drummer" played by the Velvet Underground,' said one commentator. Manchester was dubbed 'Madchester', A&R men and rabidly enthusiastic journalists descended on the city in droves, and the sound spread nationally. Scotland's Primal Scream had their 'I'm Losing More Than I'll Ever Have' wrenched apart by *Boy's Own* DJ Andrew Weatherall to produce the supremely twisted remix, 'Loaded', another key indie dance record.

After acid house, this sound was seen as a brief resurgence of band-driven music, but it was actually a clever reconstruction of rock to make it palatable to a market that had learned how to dance. One more indication of the power of the acid house revolution.

Acid jazz

A similar process kept the jazz-funk sphere afloat by giving us 'acid jazz', courtesy of soul boys Gilles Peterson and Chris Bangs. The duo were playing a one-off gig promoted by Nicky Holloway at the Waterman's Art Centre in Brentford. 'I think Paul Oakenfold or Pete Tong was DJing,' recalls Peterson. 'It was all "get on one, matey" and it was banging acid house. They'd just got back from Ibiza, and they were introducing stuff like Phuture's "Acid Trax". Bangsy and I were like, "what the fuck are we gonna play?" ' Aware that something had changed and that their normal set would sound prehistoric after this, they scoured their boxes for the most way-out tracks they had. 'Bangsy pulled out "Iron Leg" by Mickey & the Soul Generation, put the record on, and "Fuck that! If that was acid house, this is acid jazz!" '

Pleased with the reactions, they consolidated this new aesthetic at their Cock Happy parties, in the Cock Tavern in Smithfield meat market, where they pushed jazz-funk to its leftfield limits. 'That's the first, shall we say, acid jazz party, where we mixed the ecstasy spirit with a different musical soundtrack.' Inspired by this new sound, they sought to incorporate it into their sets, playing Phuture's 'Acid Tracks' or 808 State's 'Pacific State' alongside rare groovers like Funk Incorporated's 'Chicken Lickin' or 'Celebration Suite', an Airto batucada.

'I must admit,' confesses Gilles. 'I did need to take an E to know what it was all about. Jazz has never sounded the same since!'

Everyone's invited

The *Independent* reported in 1993 that Prince Charles had recently been told about the friendliness of raves while visiting an unemployment training centre. After a young girl explained how everyone puts their arms around each other, he seemed to understand: 'Ah – one does not have to be introduced.'

Acid house transformed the nation profoundly. 'It wasn't just a club change,' insists Oakenfold. 'It changed the whole culture.' Ecstasy let wallflowers everywhere meet people and have a laugh. And the new clubland democracy meant the person you were happily gabbing to about climbing trees, or Victorian sexual deviancy, or your Aunty Janet's wartime heroism, could be absolutely anyone.

'House was the first time those barriers broke down,' says Terry Farley. 'Suddenly you were talking to people outside of your class and it didn't matter that they were from up north or what clothes they had on.' British kids had long built their identities around opposition – mod or rocker, Liverpool or Everton, black or white, gay or straight, punk or skin, but acid house was different. It had no opposing youth movement. It let people define themselves by similarities rather than differences.

And the pop culture steering wheel had finally been snatched from the usual art school suspects. Acid house was driven by working class football casuals, a direct expression of casual tastes in music and fashion. 'All those people who had spent years grooming their career at *The Face* were surplus to requirements, out on their ear,' said Junior Boys Own label director Steve Hall, 'in favour of some scally football-hooligan types that had good drugs and knew where to get cool records.'

In the face of what had become a very unfriendly world, people now gained formidable support from clubbing. Instead of making you worry whether your trousers were trendy enough, going out made you feel like part of a new family. This new sense of security led people to step bravely forward. Many recall dumping longstanding boyfriends or girlfriends (and falling promptly in love). Others talk of giving up dull jobs to try something more satisfying. Indeed, this impulse was so common that in a Shoom newsletter the Ramplings warned their clubbers against it in gently parental tones. Thousands of people were able to springboard from acid house into creative careers, in music, design, fashion, club promotion and more. Meeting people from very different walks of life opened up possibilities never previously imagined. It was inspiring simply to talk to so many different people.

Youth cultures are about the feeling that you belong to something, and this is precisely what ecstasy heightens so powerfully. No wonder the youth culture it was part of was so enduring. There was no overt philosophy to acid house, but everything about it drove people together – towards community and collective action. Out on the dancefloor, acid house did for ordinary Brits what underground disco had done for black gay Americans twenty-five years earlier – it let them experience the climax and the joy of dancing in a room where everyone is in the same moment, sharing the same experience. This ecstatic communion is the real reason acid house, at least in its early days, was such a powerful force for change. Not just the drugs. Not just the music. These were only the means to an end. The real reason dance culture swept the world was because it let millions of people taste this precious feeling of togetherness for the first time in their lives.

Once you stepped into it, life's drudgery was irrelevant, and only these wonderful feelings, this ticklish flutter in the pit of the belly, the sweat and the smiles of a jumping dancefloor, the people you swapped numbers with at the end of the night, only these things really mattered.

Acid house was when we stopped trying to find a good time and learnt how to be one.

No one was left out.

Everyone was the centre of attention.

SIXTEEN
UK SOUNDS

Keep On Moving

'When people really talk about roots music – this is what it's about, because it's a way of life, it's a part of our culture.'

– Jah Shaka

'I got the big beat,
I hear the sound.'

– Dizzee Rascal

I grew up in Brixton, music was always around me. On a Saturday night you could have five, six parties going on. They were in people's houses, or they'd rig up a sound system in old squats. They'd charge like two pounds on the door, they used to have a little bar set up; the whole thing was about going in and buying drinks. You'd have the guy who hosted the night – the MC – and the guy who used to play music; there was this *narration* and it was brilliant.

'It was all very civilised, but it was really dangerous too, because we were mixing with hardened Brixton criminals. You stepped on someone's lizard-skin shoes, man, and it was curtains. It was like *Goodfellas*. You knew – don't fuck with these guys. There was one dread in particular, he was so smooth. He used to do this slow rubbing dance with girls, and he could dance with a girl and skin up a spliff at the same time. The dangerous thing was a lot of people aspired to be like these guys. I did as well, but luckily I was more into music than wanting to go out on the rob.

'The DJs decided where to set up their sound system and play their music. The guys, the criminals, used to follow them around, 'cos all the girls used to be there, and of course wherever there's nice girls there's criminals. These beautiful women that wouldn't look at you. You never had a chance. We were like fourteen and they were twenty-one. At around eight in the morning they'd slow it down and you had to ask a girl for a dance. I think I had one dance in the three years I was going to blues parties. I was so nervous she walked away half way through it.'

Like most black Britons of his generation, drum and bass pioneer

Fabio took his first clubland steps in neighbourhood 'blues' parties (named not because they played the blues, but after Blue Beat, an early ska label). In British inner-cities, blues have been a fact of life since the first waves of immigration in the fifties.

In 1954 Duke Vin and Count Suckle (Wilbert Campbell) stowed away on a banana boat bound for London. A year later, Vin started the first sound system on British shores, and Suckle turned an old Paddington snooker hall into the Cue Club, which jumped to rhythm and blues and the new ska records coming over from Jamaica. Back home the sound systems were stealing the musicians' thunder in dance halls across the island. And in the black centres of Britain – in St Annes, Handsworth, St Pauls, Chapeltown, Toxteth, in Brixton and Harlesden and Hackney – there was soon a blues party every weekend.

'The blues scene was the original club scene,' insists Fabio. 'Using huge sound systems, having MCs, the whole emphasis on loud sounds. We used to go to regular clubs and the sound was so crap, and you'd get DJs talking shit all night. The sound systems were great. Weren't any money in it; it was strictly about breaking into premises and having a party till one o'clock in the afternoon.'

If you're British, there's a bassline that's part of you. It's the rolling low-end groove that wakes the streets during those few precious weeks of summer, the overdriven thump that soundtracks the country's unbuttoning. The rest of the year it retreats underground and you'll hear it leaking out of lock-ups and pirates, basements and dark cars. It might be the brick-shaking hardcore of a Hackney squat party, or the rumbling undertow of a drum and bass night, or the compressed ungg-chank licking at the heels of a grime MC. The British bass is the note that gets you to your feet at Rampage at Carnival, or Orbital at Glastonbury, or weighs down your eyelids at Jah Shaka in some far-flung community hall.

This bass has boiled and growled and woofed through thousands of speakers into millions of chests, and though it started in forgotten, deprived corners, it's now a national treasure, as much a part of the United Kingdom as patties, naan bread and Belgian lager. The British bass has been a profound and constant influence on the country's DJs and producers, the filter through which all other music styles must pass. In this way it gave us hardcore, jungle, drum and bass, UK garage, breaks, two-step, grime and all their offspring.

Where does it come from, this rogue gene that makes British music different?

The reggae sound system.

The British bass grew fat on music from America – funk, hip hop, house and techno – but it came, originally, from Jamaica.

JA to UK

The story of reggae is at times as British as it is Jamaican, the cold island providing nearly as many innovations as the hot. Even before Nicky Thomas sang about dropping your bus fare when there's snow on the ground, there was a uniquely UK take on the sound. As well as licensing ska tracks to keep skinheads stomping, Lee Gopthal's Trojan label grew mighty by adding strings and orchestration to make British-tuned versions of Jamaican songs, and by remixing records to match the demanding technical standards of the BBC; tactics that propelled tracks like Bob & Marcia's 'Young Gifted And Black' and Jimmy Cliff's 'Wonderful World, Beautiful People' into the UK top ten. Years later, even Bob Marley had his music washed with guitar over-dubs as Chris Blackwell and his Island label worked from London to make him an international star.

Though the black British population came from all over the Caribbean, bringing a wealth of different music, Jamaican reggae won out because, based on records, its culture was most easily imported intact. But it was inevitable that it would evolve differently away from home. The reggae bands were one example, as young British kids who'd grown up hearing the Who as well as the Skatalites turned this studio-based medium into a live one. Instead of itinerant musicians serving a famous vocalist and an all-powerful producer, the British rootsmen were found in autonomous bands, like Matumbi, Steel Pulse, Misty In Roots or Aswad, all of which were built in the standard gigging rock-group mould.

It was dub, with its radical mutations, that would have the greatest lasting influence on British music. Culturally, however, it was lovers' rock that provided the UK's most significant twist. Completely rejected in Jamaica until big stars like Gregory Isaacs and Dennis Brown were deemed part of it, this poppy British reggae was the sound that finally broke free of tradition. Lovers' rock was born in Dalston's Four Aces club, when an enterprising young DJ, Lloyd Coxsone (Lloyd Blackwood), who'd been dropping a few soul tracks into his sets, saw that the eager schoolgirls singing sweetly over dubplates at his weekly talent contest could easily be turned into little pop stars, and he roped in leading producer Dennis Bovell to make it happen. A masterstroke, given that women outnumbered men when it came to buying reggae singles, and would naturally prefer chirpy ballads about wayward boyfriends to righteous laments filled with bible prophecies and police brutality. Fifteen-year-old Louisa Mark's 'Caught You In A Lie' on Safari was the first – a hit in 1975 – and scores more followed. Though these tunes were as sugary as the 'stringsinged' remixes that Trojan had crafted a few years earlier, they were finally looking forward rather than back. Lovers' rock, with one foot on a Caribbean speaker stack and the other in a Streatham school disco, reminded a generation of black British youngsters that it was about time they had their own identity.

British sound systems (or 'sounds') were fiercely conservative; many were in such thrall to their Jamaican forebears that they didn't even bother to think of new names: London had its own King Tubby's, Duke Reid's and Sir Coxsone International; not counterfeits so much as homages. Given the value of its record market the UK scene was well served by the Jamaican producers, with the biggest sounds, like Fatman, Coxsone and Jah Shaka, receiving dubplate 'specials' as exciting and as exclusive as the big guns in Kingston.

This old-boy network provided a solid foundation for apprentice soundmen, and most learnt their craft under the wing of an uncle or older brother. However, in other ways the sounds would prove severely limiting. Their music was stuck in Jamaica: few would play British records, and to consider anything beyond heavy dub and roots or rockers' reggae was heresy. The records belonged to the sound, not a particular selector, so individualism was kept in check, and in keeping with dubplate culture, more value was placed on exclusivity than freshness.

More alienating perhaps was that, like their records, their idea of blackness was imported whole from Trenchtown, and centred on the Rastafarian militancy of dreadlocks and 'conscious' protest songs. That the British sounds were heard indoors in a fog of ganja instead of under Caribbean stars, made this politicised and serious music even more moody and oppressive. So when British-born black kids began tasting the delights of mainstream discos and the vitality of the soul scene it was inevitable they'd start building a healthy distance. The UK might be as much a Babylon as JA, but you could easily forget it watching Pan's People dance to Stevie Wonder on *Top Of The Pops*.

'We moved out of the radical scene when it became lovers' rock, when the British started to make their own music,' says Jazzie B of Soul II Soul. 'There were girls at those parties, where there were never girls at these things before.' The only women on the roots scene were as hard as nails. 'Knock into them and you'd be into getting stabbed up. And that was by them, not their boyfriends.' But lovers' rock, full of girly vocals, changed things dramatically. 'It brought that calmness and lovingness back into it again. Plus it was an English style of music, and the real hard reggae boys couldn't stand it, because it wasn't Jamaican.'

Good Times

By the mid seventies, when dub was laying the thunderous foundations of the British bassline, there were quite a few youngsters who could solder a crossover circuit and turn building site plywood into speaker cabinets just as well as the dreadlocks who'd taught them, but whose hearts beat to Atlantic, Stax and Motown rather than dread, beat and blood.

'Being part of a sound was the done thing,' says Norman Jay. 'It was almost like a gang. My brother Joey was into building sound systems. All the kids round my way were.' Initially, Jay, now a veteran London DJ, and pillar of the Notting Hill Carnival, saw nothing in it to interest him. 'I'd already tasted West End life, so I didn't wanna go and stand in a bloody church hall and get kicked out at ten thirty. I was never into the whole soundclash culture. My brother, being a Rasta, it's tradition, but really it wasn't for me.'

Norman was a soul boy, snappily turned out in pegged trousers and a mohair sweater. Instead of worrying about the apocalypse due to fall when the 'Two Sevens Clash', he went to Crackers and danced to Roy Ayers' 'Running Away'. He travelled widely to the white soul clubs across the south, and sampled the northern scene while following his beloved Tottenham Hotspur FC. In 1979, thanks to Freddie Laker's £99 return flights to New York, he even saw a Brownsville disco-funk block party in action, while staying with relatives in Brooklyn. He put up with the jibes thrown at him back in the Grove: 'You know, soul boy, gay boy. That's the association they made.' Finally, Norman persuaded his brother to let him throw a soul blues for his birthday using Joey's sound, Great Tribulation. 'I told him: "It's gonna be a soul party. Everywhere I go it's reggae, reggae, reggae, and now, in my own house, no." About two hundred people turned up, mainly West End kids, dressed in the height of sartorial elegance. It was like having a West End club in your mum's house. I was playing soul funk, disco, everything – basically my whole collection up to that point. Our lot was loving it. And all these reggae boys were going "What the fuck music is this?" '

Norman continued the idea of soul blues as did his friend Cleveland Anderson. 'We'd go spotting empty houses,' remembers Cleveland. 'Then we'd go back there, nudge the window, change the locks, make sure there's electric. In those days, you were so brazen, you'd turn up at ten o'clock in the morning offloading massive speakers and the neighbours aren't even asking any questions. We'd walk around the area, and invite pretty girls with flyers, and come ten o'clock, BAM!'

Other early soul sounds included east London's Good Groove and Funkadelic; there was Mastermind and Hard Rock SS. Paul Anderson, a star dancer on the scene, had risen to fame as the first black DJ to play at Crackers, and later built his own sound, Trouble Funk. Froggy, a white soul DJ, put together a formidable system (based on the old roadshow rig for Radio One's Dave Lee Travis) with advice from reggae soundmen Jah Tubby and Jah Whoosh, and along with Derek Boland, he famously used it to rock Bentley's at the Bridge House in Canning Town. (Boland would later become Brit-rapper Derek B, and still later move into jungle). Later, in 1982, Rapattack joined the fray.

Serious sound systems had started playing at the annual Notting Hill Carnival, bringing the British bass to a new public arena. Notting Hill's 1976 riots , sparked by racist policing, had upped the carnival's credibility considerably, turning it from calypso-driven island nostalgia into an arena for defiant dreadlocks. From 1980 Norman and Joey staked out an annual pitch in Cambridge Gardens. Gradually Norman's Philly 12-inches took over from Joey's roots music, making theirs one of the first carnival sounds to play funk and soul. Eventually Norman renamed the sound to match: symbolising not only the musical move, but also a change in identity from oppressed Jamaican to optimistic black Briton, Great Tribulation became Good Times.

Soul II Soul

The next great sound system to move from reggae to soul would get to play on a global stage, and by putting a uniquely British spin on an essentially American music, would take the British bass all the way to the Grammies.

Beresford Romeo was born into the business, with five older brothers who were all soundmen to some degree, starting with the eldest, Johnson, who played ska and rocksteady on a north London sound called Count Barry's back in the sixties. As Jazzie B, Beresford and his Soul II Soul sound system would epitomise British black music's rising confidence.

'I learnt a lot from being around my brothers: carrying the boxes, being pinched in the back of the Transit van, surfing on the top of the gear.' Jazzie's first paying gig was playing lovers' rock at a school party on the Queen's Jubilee weekend in 1977 with his friend Philip 'Daddae' Harvey. They carried their gear, borrowed from his brother's sound, on the bus. Back then, as Jah Rico, they had just a single BSR turntable – reggae style – but Jazzie quickly built a case, in woodwork class at school, for the double decks he'd need when he broadened his playlist. 'It was very bad in our day,' he says. 'You was either reggae or soul. There weren't no in between. We were all trying to learn about Rastafarianism, but I was into jazz music, 'cos it had a little edge to it. That's how I got the name Jazzie.'

He was soon studying sound engineering and working at Tannoy, followed by a stint at Theatre Projects (which fitted out the Camden Palace, an early taste for London of a big New York-style system), and work as tape engineer for Cockney warbler Tommy Steele at the Nova studio where the Blues Band and Brit-funkers Central Line recorded. 'I went through all that, cutting the acetates with the guys in the white coats,' says Jazzie. 'They'd be having a laugh at all the darkies who come in to cut their dubs on a Friday. Spend mountains of money, saying "turn up the bass, turn up the bass". And they'd use this term, "cut it flat", which to a Jamaican means you have just the bass and the tops, but when you speak to a technician, "flat" is at zero. They used to take the piss up there.'

All this was in the service of his sound, now a mighty set of six stacks renamed Soul II Soul. '1982. Dougie's Hideaway on a Thursday night. All the birds free,' he remembers, smiling. 'It was this blues place at the back of these flats in Junction Road, Archway. Velvet wallpaper, red carpet, really naff. And it was all school, all our schools, all our mates. We went in there with silly string and streamers and everything. Busiest night the geezer ever had, but he got pissed off 'cos there was all this silly string.'

Jazzie's eureka moment had come when he'd seen Paul 'Trouble' Anderson – who he knew as a leading face from Crackers – playing soul in a Haringey blues on a sound called Galaxy Soul Shuttle (which belonged to latter-day folk devil Winston Silcott). 'Paul gave us hope,' he says, raising Anderson above all his other forebears, including Norman Jay. 'The difference between Trouble and everybody else: Paul was in the ghetto, he was in the black scene, whereas the others were trying to get out of it. He meant more to us because of that.'

Steadily, through christenings, weddings and community centres, Soul II Soul grew, and a distinct attitude developed. They took only what they wanted from sound system tradition and rejected the rest. Not for them a narrow range of music. At a Soul II Soul party you'd hear everything from jazz, soul, funk and hip hop to Tears For Fears' 'Shout' and the Stones' 'Too Much Blood'. Similarly they weren't content to lurk in neighbourhood shadows; they saw themselves as proud businessmen, entrepreneurs, and struck up alliances and travelled, not only across London, but also to Bristol, Nottingham, Derby.

As the Thatcher decade progressed, Jazzie and his cohorts – Daddae Harvey, Q, Aitch B and Sparky D – even opened a pair of Soul II Soul stores, complete with a clothing line and a corporate logo. They began styling themselves as 'funki dreds', their locks sharpened by a buzz-cut back and sides. The look was Filofax-Rasta, a slick mod Afrocentrism that spoke volumes about their ambition. Jazzie confirms: 'The premise of everything I did was to make my sound the biggest in the world.'

Soul II Soul's story was echoed across the country as more and more sounds moved away from their reggae origins. Struck by hip hop, Mastermind from Harlesden turned into an eight-man team of MCs and

WAREHOUSE PARTY
NOTE · TO · NOTE

SOUL TO SOUL

SATURDAY MAY 3rd
47-50 PANCRAS RD N.W.1
⊖ KINGS X

£2½

11 – TILL U Drop

WAREHOUSE PARTY
ON
SAT 12th APRIL

AT
8 Greenland St. NW.1
(off Camden High St and Bayham St
Nearest ⊖ Camden Town

MUSIC BY
soul 2 soul

From 11pm

A FUNKI DRED EVENT

BE SEEN...'IN THE PLACE TO BE'

with 'soul to soul'
HI-TECH ROADSHOW

Valentines Day 1986 IS ....

Moxen & Laurence Presentations First Anniversary

so check it out!

Friday 14th Feb

10 till morning

165 MORTIMER RD.
KENSAL RISE N.W.10
(off chamberlayne rd)

KENSAL GREEN ⊖

SOUL TO SOUL

finsbury park

at 227 seven
sister rd n4.
sat 8th march

from
11p
m

soul party

fee £2-50p

SATURDAY 11th JANUARY '86

COME ON
DARLING

FROM 11pm

CHANGE OF VENUE

"YOU MUST BE JOKING LOVE
SOUL TO SOUL'S PLAYING
AT SEVEN LADIES TONITE"

NEWS FLASH

DUE TO CIRCUMSTANCES
BEYOND OUR CONTROL
TONITES VENUE HAS BEEN
CHANGED TO
No4 PERTH ROAD,
(Off Stroud Green Road)
FINSBURY PARK N. 4

THERE WILL BE A
FUNKY CONVOY
EVERY 15MINS

WE APOLOGISE FOR ANY
INCONVENIENCE CAUSED

DJs, complete with six turntables. In Hackney, Trevor Nelson, a young blade on the soul scene, started Madhatters – the name calculated to discourage reggae lovers. Shock, on which DJ Ashley Beedle learnt his trade, would be the first to play house at Carnival, and went on to power the famous Clink Street parties. 'We started playing a lot of the really early house records because to us they had the same rawness as reggae,' says Beedle.

In Bristol a thriving post-reggae scene, via producers such as Smith and Mighty, gave birth to the loping, ambient hip hop style later christened 'trip hop'. The Bristol sound slowed breakbeats to a narcotic crawl, influenced by oceans of dub, a little Burt Bacharach and a good deal of sweet smoke, and was taken to the world by artists including Portishead, Tricky and Massive Attack. These latter two grew from a sound system which lasted through the eighties called the Wild Bunch, a multiracial crew of DJs and MCs fusing rap, reggae and soul. Such broad playlists were the order of the day as a generation of DJs sought out a mix that might better define black Britishness.

The Africa Centre

In the years before acid house arrived, London had a thriving underground centred on the post-punk collision of fashion and music: the warehouse scene. This, too, favoured a broad mix of music, and since its events were staged in lofts, studios and empty commercial buildings, promoters usually had to arrange their own sound. Inevitably, the new breed of sound system operators moved in, armed with the right experience and plenty of blag. A new constituency was exposed to the British bass as their mostly black crowds became increasingly multiracial. Norman Jay rebranded Good Times as Shake'n'Fingerpop and got stuck in; Soul II Soul did some parties as Serious Shit, and then found themselves providing the equipment for Family Funktion, a north London party collective with a following of trendy students. One of Family Funktion's DJ's was Julian O'Riordan. Adept at bluffing away police with points of law he'd picked up studying at the London School of Economics, he was granted the name Judge Jules.

'He wasn't a very good DJ, but he had a good crowd,' recalls Norman. 'But the main thing was, he was white. His crowd would dilute things, to make it more socially acceptable. Jazzie was astute: "Get in with some white dudes and your party won't get busted." '

Camberwell, Southwark, Old Street, Kings Cross... The venues ranged from disused carpet warehouses and railway depots to old theatres and boarded-up cinemas – anywhere with a floor big enough to dance on. If a place couldn't be hired legally then it would be appropriated for the evening, through either a friendly estate agent or, failing that, a crowbar. At an empty school on Hampstead Heath, Norman did a party called Amityville. 'That was legendary because it was the first time the hoorays, Sloanies and middle-class white people turned up. These lovely looking birds with posh accents, Jeeps, everything. Over two thousand people. The next day it was in *The Sunday Times*.'

Soul II Soul crowned the warehouse movement when they defied central London's backward racial politics and the established rules of turf and took their sound system into the heart of the West End. After two police raids, a Hackney petrol bomb and a night barricaded inside a club in Old Street by the National Front, Jazzie felt they'd weathered enough slings and arrows. It was time for something audacious.

'We totally broke the mould. When we came uptown we brought *everyone* with us. And no one could believe it.' Covent Garden's Africa Centre was a gift to the African people from the Christian Aid Society. As such it enjoyed a complex legal status that kept the party one step ahead of the authorities for most of its existence. On Sunday nights between 1986 and 1988, the centre's little cellar dripped to a packed multiracial crowd grooving to the SIIS ethos of 'A happy face and a thumpin' bass for a lovin' race'. The old soul order, where the crowd would stand and watch a handful of great dancers, was gone; here everyone got on it. 'If you're not dancing, fuck off and make some space,' Jazzie would shout, as Maceo & the Macks' 'Cross The Tracks' or the Meters' 'Just Kissed My Baby' ripped through the room.

'Everybody seemed to be interesting there,' recalls Rhythm Doctor (Chris Long). 'You could feel some real creative energy.'

Jazzie remembers how they'd crank up the heating and tune the sound for hours, leaving the crowd outside to build up steam. 'I'd wait until you could *smell* the atmosphere. And when you opened the door people were so hungry to get in it reminded me of Crackers.'

True to sound system tradition, Soul II Soul made their own dubplates. After teaming up with producer Nellee Hooper from Bristol's Wild Bunch, and vocalists Rose Windross, Do'reen and Caron Wheeler – who were faces from the dancefloor – Soul II Soul's tracks got them a deal and moved quickly from Africa Centre exclusives to international hits. A few years earlier the Brit-funk movement had seen groups like Hi Tension, Loose Ends and Central Line emulating US-style smooth funk, and doing their best to sell it back to where it came from. Now, with 'Fairplay', 'Feel Free' and then the massive 'Keep On Moving', and 'Back To Life' a UK no.1, Soul II Soul had changed the game completely. With insistent, grooving basslines, and unmistakable reggae roots, here was a truly *British* soul sound, a reflection of the rich stew of music and the genuine melting pot of people that rocked their parties. The British bassline had topped the charts. While musicians had been happy to follow well-worn US grooves, the DJ was creating music that really spoke for its time and place.

Nellee Hooper went on to produce his former Wild Bunch mates Massive Attack, and secured global stature working with Björk and Madonna. Soul II Soul sold ten million albums world-wide and collected two Grammies. Jazzie says his proudest moment was taking his sound system to play in Jamaica. In retrospect, however, his group's greatest contribution was giving shape and spirit to the British bassline – giving the UK's black music the balls to speak for itself. They also showed black Britons that it was possible to integrate into the very heart of their nation without abandoning their cultural heritage. As Jazzie says in Lloyd Bradley's sleevenotes to *Soul II Soul At The Africa Centre*, 'In a reggae sound system we faced the wall with our backs to the crowd – that was just how it was done in that world. Now we looked out at the people and they could look at us. We could see each others' faces. It was the difference between looking inward and looking outward. Being exclusive or being inclusive.'

Shut Up And Dance

Clearly, decades of reverence toward black American music were wearing thin. Britain was tired of being the fanatical collector; it wanted to get onstage. Soul, disco and, especially, hip hop had been American revolutions that admitted few foreigners, but when house came along it was an uprising everyone could share. After absorbing the basic US blueprints Britain's supercharged dance scene would throw up a succession of house hybrids and mutations, all built from the British bass, some radical enough to found new genres.

Nowhere did music evolve faster than on the new sound systems. Because they created their own scenes they could play anything they wanted. They didn't need anything more than a social club or an empty basement and a few wised-up older brothers to keep things nice. Away from the established clubs with their more settled music, early closing hours and still-racist door policies, playing to crowds of neighbours and schoolfriends in the poorest parts of the inner cities, the future of music was being written.

In 1982 PJ (Philip Johnson), Smiley (Carl Hymans) and DJ Hype (Kevin Ford) scraped together enough gear to throw their first party, in a church hall near Stoke Newington's Lea Bridge roundabout. 'You had to have a sound system. Back then you couldn't just have a record box. You had to have your own thing if people were going to hear you, take you seriously.' Playing reggae, dub and a little soul on a single turntable, they closely followed the blues party traditions they'd grown up with, 'I'm sure I was conceived in a blues,' laughs Smiley. 'It's life really, the sound thing. You just got to live it.'

Thanks to Hype's place on a young offenders' rehabilitation scheme, the Islington Music Workshop, they put together a demo. This won them enough further studio time to produce their first record, a double A-side of 'Puppet Capers' and 'My Tennents' (a piss-take of Run DMC's 'My Adidas'). Under their sound's name, Private Party, this was released on a label set up as part of the scheme.

By 1986, they were regularly breaking into empty council houses for parties. Their jump-up reggae was moving to the back seat, as they twisted established sound system practice into a very new style. There were two decks now, which Hype was using to scratch up a dust-storm of hip hop for PJ and Smiley's rhymes (Hype would be a DMC finalist in 1989). More than this, they pitched the records up as far as they would go, playing tracks like Mantronix' 'Fresh Is The word' or James Brown's 'The Big Pay Back' and 'Funky President' at a whirlwind 130bpm. 'We wanted to be able to dance to it. Not just nod your head,' says Smiley. They were professional dancers (PJ was also a working stuntman, Smiley a cabinet-maker) and the pitch change was their instinctive way of upping the energy in the parties. As PJ says, 'We always wanted to get people dancing. On a sound system it's about getting the vibes going, having a good time. So the tempo increased as part of that.' Their new name said it all: Shut Up And Dance.

'But still we wanted to take it further,' says Smiley. 'So we made our stuff a lot faster when we started making music properly.' Beyond their parties, though, their revved-up hip hop found no takers. 'No one wanted to know. No major label, no indie. They were all like: "This is too fast; this isn't going with the norm." So we thought "fuck you lot, we're going to do it all ourselves".' In 1989 they found themselves driving round London's record shops with newly-pressed copies of '5,6,7,8' in the back of PJ's Ford Escort. Within a week they were pressing more, and Smiley's younger brother was breathlessly telling them they had to go to the Dungeon, the Hackney acid house epicentre, where the ravers were going wild to their track. Until this point, they claim, they'd had nothing to do with house. 'We're not a rave group, we're a fast hip hop group,' they declared in *Melody Maker*. 'We've moved hip hop on in a way Public Enemy haven't dared to.'

But hip hop wasn't interested, 'The scene we thought we were in didn't want to know,' says PJ. 'And this other scene held out its arms to us. We were like, "But we're this", and they were like "No you're not.

You're coming over here mate".' Rocket-fast breakbeat loops splattered with blatant pop samples (Suzanne Vega, Eurythmics) were exactly what the ravers in the East End's acid caves wanted to hear, and these records were received as 'hardcore house'. There were similar ideas around – the US 'hip house' of Todd Terry, Fast Eddie and Tyree Cooper, as well as techno experiments by Frankie Bones and CJ Bolland – but none of these captured the essence of a dark, smoky, drug-fuelled Hackney blues the way Shut Up And Dance did.

Rough, rugged, clearly unpolished, yet charging with energy; this was the British bass filtering through. 'What made them great was they didn't give a fuck about what they did,' says Rhythm Doctor. 'Usually it's not even in time, it's all mad, it's loose, and they don't care.'

Their humour scored points, too, as Shut Up And Dance gently poked the rave scene with records like '£10 To Get In', and its sequel '£20 To Get In'. In the latter's intro an outraged punter protests that he thought entry was only £10. 'No mate, it's 'ad a remix,' booms the bouncer. Their biggest hit 'Raving I'm Raving', a record that finally (and expensively) awoke the record company sample-police, trod a clever line between endorsing acid house and questioning the E-motions it was based on: 'Do I really feel the way that I feel?' Shut Up And Dance's records were all the stronger for the unusual position they enjoyed – they were in the rave scene but not of it.

Excited by the way their party-bred style had reached this unexpected audience, they introduced the ravers to another sound system element: reggae toasting. They recruited a pair of MCs from a reggae sound called Unity: Demon Rocker and Flinty Badman (who'd gone to PJ's school). Not sure how the results would be received, they took the duo into the studio and had them rhyme over some house-tempo breaks. 'It weren't no holding back thing,' says Smiley. 'It wasn't, "Oh talk a bit more English". They were MCing properly on it. Hardcore reggae people full blasting it.' The Ragga Twins' 'Hooligan 69', with its 'dearly beloved' Prince intro, sent the Dungeon crazy. 'Spliffhead', 'Wipe The Needle' and 'Illegal Gunshot' did the same. It was a portentous sound. With fast breaks and ragga MCing, Shut Up And Dance had laid down a complete blueprint. From here, jungle was inevitable.

Bleep and bass

Another Anglicised form of house had been brewing in Sheffield. Again, its strength came from combining house and reggae, and again it was a sound that flourished in a thriving illegal party scene. Warp Records, started by Steve Beckett and Rob Mitchell, fostered a series of artists and productions that became known as 'bleep and bass'. Unique 3 (who were from Bradford and weren't on Warp), LFO, Forgemasters and Sweet Exorcist (Cabaret Voltaire's Richard H Kirk and DJ Parrot) took up the challenge laid down by the early Chicago and Detroit records and built on their city's synthesiser tradition, updating it with weapons-grade basslines.

Birthplace of stainless steel, a tough industrial town that rang to the constant clang of drop-forges, Sheffield had long produced music ahead of the norm. From the mid seventies, Dadaist youngsters Cabaret Voltaire led the field, experimenting with cut-ups, tape loops, sampled sound and all-out electronic noise assault. With these 'industrial' pioneers in their midst, when punk arrived Sheffield bands picked up, not guitars, but synths and rhythm boxes. So while the rest of the country endured inept rock, Sheffield produced a generation of electronic futurists: Heaven 17, Clock DVA, Human League and ABC.

Warp's pioneering UK techno connected this tradition with the needs of the sound system. In their quest for the ultimate bass, LFO ('Low Frequency Oscillations') would record a note on a cassette recorder with the levels too high, then sample the resulting overdriven boom. On 'Testone', Sweet Exorcist layered together pure sine waves to build body-bashing subsonics. Multiple basslines became the norm, and when it came to mastering the tracks producers would get the engineer to turn off all the protection circuits so the groove cut in the record was as deep and fearsome as possible. They would watch in glee as their basslines overheated the cutting heads to near-destruction. One track, 'Dextrous' by Nightmares On Wax, was originally so heavy it couldn't be turned into vinyl at all until it was remixed with a few knobs turned down. The producers would convene at a club called Kiki's and see whose tunes had enough angry resonance to get its thick glass bar shaking.

Over these slab-cracking basslines danced trebly acid bleeps and plinks. Like dub reggae, which also emphasises the polar extremes of frequencies, this was clearly music designed for fat, scary speakers. Warp's Steve Beckett claims the style came originally from a Leeds sound system called Ital Rockers. He told Simon Reynolds, 'They'd cut just twenty or thirty tracks on acetate, and have sound system parties underneath this hotel. No lights, two hundred people, and they'd play reggae, then hip hop, then these bleep and bass tunes. And they'd be toasting on top of it.'

When Orbital made 'Chime' and took it into the top 20 in 1990, the bleep and bass era had found its anthem. And like scores of records now appearing each week, 'Chime' was home-made. The home studio revolution had ushered in a flood of music, especially since producers were no longer relying on established record labels. Either they'd start their own, or dispense with the idea altogether and just pay to press up tunes with nothing more than a name and a title, lugging them around to sell through the dance stores. DJs had always been excited by imports, now they had a native form of hot, upfront record: the white label.

Hardcore

By the nineties, the DJ could cultivate any sound he wanted. With so many tracks, and so many mixes of each, he could carve out a signature style like never before. And every time the DJ played there were ten little producers in the crowd, gathering musical ideas for the spaghetti of electronics that cluttered their bedrooms. So if the DJ pitched records up, a few weeks later he'd be handed a clutch of records *made* faster. If the DJ found four obscure tracks that shared a quirky drum pattern, this would find pride of place in scores of new tunes. With DJs suggesting directions, and producers twisting the British bass into all manner of surprises, house music spidered into different genres like cracks in glass.

Around 1991 the rave movement displayed the first of these fractures. The slower, more elegant house scene was heading for the comfort of a more intimate club environment, leaving the hardcore ravers to their own devices. Rave companies like Raindance, Rezerection and Amnesia adopted a legal, licensed approach and started throwing regular hardcore events, and rave fashions appeared – including white gloves, Vicks inhalers (to enhance the drug rush), dust masks and light-sticks.

Behind closed doors in raves in the south east, and in Midlands clubs like Eclipse in Coventry and Kinetix in Stoke-on-Trent (where Doc Scott and DJ SS plied their trade), the music underwent a dramatic evolution. DJs pitched records faster and faster (some tampering with their turntables to exceed the maximum +8 pitch change), and showed a predilection for breakbeats. The DJs' palette ranged from hip house records like Renegade Soundwave's 'The Phantom' and Unique 3's 'The Theme', via Frankie Bones' 'Bones' Breaks', to the harsh 'hoover' sounds of Belgian techno.

Hand in hand with the changing music came a change in drugs. As demand for ecstasy climbed, quality plunged. Tablets were likely to be either MDEA, ecstasy's more 'mongy' cousin (like the infamous 'snowballs'), or simply full of amphetamine. People stopped calling them Es; now they were just 'pills'. The dance press derided hardcore as the new heavy metal. After the hip had moved on to handbag house, rave was left to working class suburban kids, arguably those with the greatest need for escapism. At their core were unrepentant 'nutters' who revelled in the ecstasy experience and saw raving as a mission. Martin James described them in *State Of Bass*, his history of jungle. 'People would boast about the amount of Es they'd dropped, in a way reminiscent of the fifteen-pints-a-night lager boys. Living on the edge of reality, the ravers were all or nothing, one hundred per cent hardcore. The music reflected this extremity as beats and noises became more manic.'

By 1992 there were records being made specifically for this scene. Shades Of Rhythm, Bizarre Inc, Altern-8, the Shamen and the Prodigy grew famous by offering stage shows for the ravers, enjoying the largest audiences newly formed bands had ever seen. Cartoon records like the Prodigy's 'Charly' and Smart E's 'Sesame's Treat' pitted familiar children's TV theme tunes against a crashing onslaught of manic rhythms. Break-beats spiralled to 160bpm, and songs became a fly-past of euphoric peaks and Minnie Mouse vocals, these helium divas an attempt to preserve the emotional impact of vocal house in the face of rapidly climbing tempos. Instead of music that might be enhanced by ecstasy, these were tunes *designed* for drugs.

If you weren't fully committed to sweaty, shirts-off nights popping bonkers conkers, the hardcore techno scene wasn't hard to deride; a reaction was inevitable. Mixmag's August 1992 cover showed the Prodigy's Liam Howlett putting a gun to his head, accusing his group of killing rave with their infantilist 'Charly' single. Warp, whose early records had fed the scene, distanced themselves by moving into ambience with their *Artificial Intelligence* album. Lovers of the more thoughtful Detroit sensibility, and the deeper, more austere techno it produced, declared their independence in purist clubs like Steve Bicknell's Lost or Colin Dale and Colin Faver's Knowledge.

Undeterred, the kids revelled in their unfashionability and hardcore rooted itself across the UK: in Ayr's deathly Hangar 13, in east London's Labrynth, in Club UK in Wandsworth and many more. Rave peaked commercially in 1993 with crowds of 25,000 at (legal) Fantazia in Castle Donington, although the previous August a Vision event at Hampshire's Popham airfield boasted a crowd of 38,000 after gatecrashers stormed the fence.

Jungle

'Freight weight bass rolling over me. The rumblism in full effect. Rolling bass that powers over you, assaults the senses in its intensity, rollin' like thunder. From back to front a wave of sound.' Nothing written about jungle is as passionate as *Junglist*, the novel by Two Fingers and James T Kirk (Andrew Green and Eddie Otchere). 'I was there when rave just went too fast,' says the narrator, a DJ who's abandoned the house scene, sick of the 'false consciousness' of ecstasy. 'House: that middle class bullshit. So boring and predictable,' he complains, no longer fooled by the music's escapism. 'Jungle's truer to humanity's real roots. It cuts away the falseness, gives you the ups and the downs, the dark and the light.'

Out of hardcore house came: breakbeat, defined by its rhythms; techno, defined by its level of Detroit purity; and rave, defined by its cartoonishness, or by the fact that it had 'bands' like the Prodigy who could jump around onstage and wave things at you. But the key division in the scene was one of mood. If you took out the 'happy hardcore' tracks you were left with 'dark'.

'The whole night was dark,' writes Brian Belle-Fortune in his jungle history *All Crews*. 'I remember dancing at the front, looking round and noticing there wasn't a smile amongst the people. Not one smile. But everyone was into it. It wasn't a bad vibe. I remember being off my head and thinking that I must remember this. This is different now. It was serious like a military army. People were concentrating, no waving hands in the air.'

Dark, or darkcore was a reaction against the toytown tunes loved by the happy hardcore 'cheesy quavers' ravers. Championed by DJs Grooverider, Jumping Jack Frost, Randall, Kenny Ken and Mickey Finn, it used fear to generate a rush: horror movie samples, edgy, alarming noises, a tempo that crept ever upwards and, always, the breakbeat. Around the start of 1993 this sound began to be singled out – at the Roller Express in Edmonton, where soundclashes were staged in a boxing ring, and in east London raves like Telepathy. As the acid utopia came crashing down to earth – beset by police clampdowns, dodgy pills, and the criminal elements taking the reins – many preferred this gritty urban realism to the fluffiness of the early ecstasy years. And the darker mood coincided with a deluge of new music.

Jungle's approaching footsteps had been heard a few years before. In 1989 Lenny De Ice made 'We Are I:E', a tense foretaste of the sound. There was ragga techno from SL2 (Slipmatt and Lime) and Shut Up And Dance. There was Paul Ibiza fusing bleeps, breaks and reggae basslines. There were labels like Kickin', Living Dream, and Reinforced where, as 4 Hero, Dego McFarlane and Mark Claire conjured defining tracks like 'Mr Kirk's Nightmare', and where, with Goldie and others, they staged three-day sessions of unholy dark arts from which they emerged blinking into the sunshine with DAT tapes full of sonic monsters.

The accelerated breakbeat was the key to this explosion. It was an easy style to work in, as sampling and looping beats is swifter than programming a drum machine. Just as early hip hop rode the primal beats of 'Funky Drummer', jungle endlessly recycled the break from 'Amen Brother' by the Winstons. For producers raised in hip hop and reggae, using breakbeats added a funkiness, a roughness, a 'blackness' to the metronome of house and techno. And breakbeats at house tempo stole hip hop from the Americans and stamped it with a velocity that said 'made in Britain'. Forget trying to rap in the wrong accent, here was a truly home-grown sound system style, the British bass grown strong. As Carl Cox said about the flood of hardcore records in 1991 and 1992, 'It was just fantastic to see that we had our own thing going on right there, that we didn't need Todd Terry to make records for us. We started to create our own empire of our own music, our own record labels, and also our own culture.'

In the West End, a night at Heaven called Rage became the showcase for the sound that some were already calling 'jungle-techno'. The DJs were acid house stalwarts Fabio (Fitzroy Heslop) and Grooverider (Roger Bingham), who teased out the blacker elements of hardcore. Future artists and DJs like Kemistry and Storm, DJ Rap, Photek, Dillinja and Ed Rush were in regular attendance, as was jungle's first star Goldie, a young Midlands graffiti artist fresh back from living in Miami.

On their first visit Kemistry and Storm (Kemi Olusanya and Jane Coneely) queued for over three hours. 'When we finally got in, we only had about an-hour-and-a-half left,' Storm told Martin James. 'But it didn't matter because we knew this was something totally different. A really cutting edge thing.' These Midlands girls were so energised by Rage they dropped everything to become DJs.

'The energy at Rage was unreal,' Goldie wrote in his autobiography. 'The adrenalin was pumping around the place. There was still the late rave stuff but here was a new sound, a mad fusion of the old and the new.'

'Rage was a total experiment,' admits Fabio. 'We didn't have a fucking clue. We were just . . . "it worked, we're doing this". We never used to play like that anywhere else. Everywhere else we still played more soulful stuff. But in that big club where we had carte blanche, it was Fabio and Grooverider's house and we just did what the fuck we wanted.'

With soul backgrounds, the pair had shot to attention DJing at the early acid scene's end-up spot, the after-hours Mendoza's in Brixton. By 1991, with a following from their 'Phase 1 FM' shows and starring roles in Sunrise, Energy and many more of the M25 raves, they were easily ramming out the upstairs Star Bar in Heaven every Thursday, playing the hard techno coming through from Belgium and Germany. When headline DJs Colin Faver and Trevor Fung missed a flight back from LA, Fab and Groove filled in on the main floor and rocked it so hard that Rage's American house sound was clearly on its way out. Pretty soon they were getting dubplates from Detroit heroes May and Saunderson as well as white labels from Joey Beltram and other rising stars of hardcore (Rage was where the UK first heard Beltram's 'Energy Flash'). They accelerated things to unreal levels; pitching things up, even hitting 45 instead of 33. 'It was just the craziest mixture of extreme madness,' says Fabio.

To add further fuel they tried something else: 'We'd get these B-side mixes from Masters At Work, with straight up breaks on, and we used to speed them up and mix them into the techno stuff,' recalls Fabio. The reaction was extreme. 'Anytime we did that we were getting people euphoric. Like this is something really new.'

When the right records reached the speakers the cry would go up: 'Jungle! jungle! jungle!' Fabio remembers a regular, Danny Jungle, punching it out from the middle of the floor; others insist the name came from outside the scene, and that it was a judgement that spoke of racism. Some refer you to 'the Jungle' in Kingston, a place called Tivoli Gardens, and claim this rough Jamaican yard found fame from a sampled shout to its inhabitants – 'alla da junglist' – on a 1991 Rebel MC track; some point to Paul Ibiza who printed 'Junglizm' on his record sleeves and said his tracks were for smoking and chilling 'as if you were deep in a jungle', while others point to hardcore collective Top Buzz who threw the phrase 'jungle-techno' around to describe their style. Whatever the name's origins, the music was an intense alternative to house, and Rage led the way until 1993, when the mood became too much and the promoter pulled the plug.

'We ghettoed out the whole fucking place, man,' beams Fabio. 'The old-school crowd just left and Rage turned from this posey kind of night with loads of girls and loads of well dressed people, to being ghetto. It was so ghetto. It added to the whole vibe of the night though. Until it got to the stage where you didn't know whether you were gonna get killed down there or not.'

AWOL (A Way Of Life) in Islington's Paradise club took the baton after Rage. Here Randall, Mickey Finn, Kenny Ken, Dr S Gachet and Darren Jay presided over a loud, smoke-filled, lighter-flamed hotbox that rang to air-horns and cries for rewinds, and introduced Randall's onslaught of double-dropping – layering two whole tracks over each other.

'With AWOL there was definitely something special,' writes Brian Belle-Fortune. 'The place had all the right ingredients.'

'It was school for me,' agrees DJ Andy C. 'You'd be exposed to all the different wicked styles of music and you used to hear some mad mixing; especially at ten o'clock in the morning. Some weeks it didn't finish until one in the afternoon. It was definitely inspirational.'

'All the DJs would stay there after their sets,' adds AWOL's resident MC, GQ. 'Groove and Fabio would pass by. Goldie would be there with his head in a speaker – Randall would be tearing the arse out of it. Kenny

Ken would snake through the club and plant his hand over the edge of the DJ box, stopping the record for the rewind.'

By 1994, jungle was in the ascendant. Kool FM, Fantasy and Centreforce broadcast jungle across the capital. MCs Navigator, Moose, GQ and MC Det made their names mixing ragga phrasing with rave excitement. DJ Ron took his Sunday Roast parties uptown to the Astoria, the Lazerdrome in Peckham showed the way for the dressy champagne-and-designer-gear attitude, the Midlands scene was thriving with raves attracting thousands, and London's East End was still strong. Jungle Fever's big, well run raves brought the whole scene together.

A 'breakbeat science' was forged as producers pushed their equipment and revelled in mutations and experiments. 'If the breakbeat is the genetic code of digital music, its basic yet complex DNA, then jungle is the secret technology of gene-splicing sound, the unofficial science of rhythm hacking sonic molecules into polypercussive grafts,' wrote grammatical scientist Kodwo Eshun in *i-D*. Breakbeats were doubled, reversed, chopped and multilayered. A digital process called timestretching, where a sound can be speeded up without changing its pitch (and vice versa), was used to the full, fooling dancers with paradoxes of velocity. Drums, woven between cavernous basslines, became texture and melody as well as rhythm. With *Black Secret Technology* Gerald Simpson, aka A Guy Called Gerald, showed the music was capable of album-length expression. The mind behind 'Voodoo Ray' and 'Pacific State' had been playing with breakbeats ever since his disillusionment with house, and had made tracks of ragga-chat jungle long before most.

All jungle needed was a star. Enter Clifford Price, a mixed-race face glinting with gold teeth, whose energy – a mix of charismatic enthusiasm and intimidating aggression – matched the music perfectly. Goldie was a Midlands b-boy whose graffiti writing was a passport to any scene he cared to investigate. In a neat historical twist he'd been a regular at Soul II Soul's parties and even hung out with them in the studio. Having missed acid house, he landed in Rage in a long leather Miami gangster's coat, only to be blown away by the club's multiracial smiles. Almost immediately Goldie set his sights on making music and teamed up with the Reinforced producers as Rufige Cru, later thrusting records like his darkcore masterpiece 'Terminator' at DJs and proclaiming his music's greatness from the stage in endearing/embarrassing displays of self-belief.

Unusually, the music press didn't notice jungle for ages. When rave filled up the hardcore scene with cartoon vocals and children's TV themes, journalists were happy to slag it off as a populist dead-end. They saw much more mileage in the Orb's 'ambient techno', and 'progressive house' – a synthetic and self-conscious evolution of the classic house style. So for once a new genre had space to develop in peace. But when Rob Playford's label Moving Shadow put out distinctive tracks like Omni Trio's 'Renegade Snares' and Deep Blue's 'The Helicopter Tune', media interest was suddenly massive. The press frothed about 'the black punk rock', and had to grudgingly admit that hardcore had produced a new and exciting genre. When Goldie secured a powerful deal with London Records for his *Timeless* album, jungle was the sound of the moment.

But just as it was getting some attention the music was in danger of barrelling itself into a corner marked 'ragga'. In summer 1994 two hits landed in the charts, M-Beat & General Levy's 'Incredible' and Shy FX & UK Apache's 'Original Nuttah'. Both were heavily ragga influenced, indeed General Levy was a reggae MC who had nothing to do with the jungle scene. Jungle had always carried a certain reggae influence, now it was flooded with 'bad bwoy' ragga lyrics encouraging yardie gangsterism.

With a truly British sense of bureaucracy, this change was resisted by a group of concerned citizens calling itself the Drum And Bass Committee, led by the Rebel MC (Michael West, former ska-pop rapper in Double Trouble). With members supposedly including DJ Ray Keith, Goldie, Fabio, Grooverider, A Guy Called Gerald and other leading players, the committee proposed DJ boycotts of certain raves and tried to blacklist the General Levy track. Keith even asked Dave Piccioni, owner of Black Market records, the scene's key store (and his own place of work), not to stock it. Piccioni said that unless Keith cared to pay his mortgage, he'd stock what he liked. But it's hard to overstate how much some people resented these records. DJ Rap claims she received death threats for playing them. She ignored these to rapturous reaction.

Helpfully, the music was evolving fast enough to outrun any mis-associations, and as more sophisticated textural production emerged, using jazz samples in place of ragga toasting, the music's breadth was reasserted. Bristol's Roni Size (Ryan Williams) and former classical pianist LTJ Bukem (Danny Williamson) did much to popularise these mellower, more ambient sounds, and Bukem and a post-Rage Fabio flexed it at a new night, Speed.

'I started bringing my musical background of jazz fusion into hardcore, seeing how tempos could be changed, how we could experiment with sounds,' Bukem told Kodwo Eshun. There was enough of a distinction for a new name, 'drum and bass', to stick, although this inevitably carried its own implications: jungle was still coloured by ragga, while drum and bass nights seemed to attract more than their share of nerdy white students; certainly, plenty of offence was given when the prefix 'intelligent' was occasionally added.

Jungle stands proud as the UK's first genuinely indigenous form of black music, singing its roots loud and clear: its basslines speak of reggae's sound system comradeship, its tempo and energy lead back to the rave movement, the rough, have-a-go production of its early records can even be traced to punk. From a defiantly multiracial underground, jungle synthesised all these strands of modern Britain into a musical history of the last two decades. It also gave a huge boost of confidence to other melting pot sounds, as British-born Asians like Talvin Singh and Nitin Sawhney fused hip hop and drum and bass with traditional Punjabi bhangra to form their own second-generation roots music.

When the world's media declared 1996 the year of 'Cool Britannia' they concentrated on 'Britpop'. Yet while its stars Oasis were failing to dent America with reheated Beatles chords, the real sound of Britain, still pumping from every pirate, was jungle. Although its club scene gradually lost much of its glamour, there is no doubt about jungle/drum and bass's continuing influence. Indeed, led by Sao Paulo DJs Marky and Patife this British style is currently storming, of all places, that land of rhythm, Brazil.

Jungle's importance wasn't about naked patriotism; it lay in the fact that here, finally, was a dance music that related directly to your upbringing, your local scene, your own experience. Gerald Simpson expressed it perfectly in *All Crews*: 'It wasn't important that it was a British thing, more that it was a home thing . . . It's about our generation. We were the kids who watched *Grange Hill*. It's our era. We finally have an identity. This is us.'

UK garage

'In '91 people either wanted it hard or they wanted the other thing.' Timmi Magic, one third of the Dreem Teem DJ collective, recalls the birth of what would become garage – 'the other thing'. 'There was a definite division, where you were either Ce Ce Peniston or you were 'Charly' and the Prodigy. You either went hardcore or you went all US-ey. I went on the US path.'

After acid house peaked, while the hardcore DJs went off into far-flung warehouses and overheated legal raves, those favouring the more soulful and songful house styles took their Strictly Rhythm and Emotive records, pressed their trousers, and grooved towards more seductive environs. Eventually they would reach a promised land of champagne, cocaine, Moschino, and lots of girls in leopard-print satin.

In 1989 Timmi Magic (Timothy Eugene), an east Londoner (from Leyton), evangelised into DJing by acid house, was making his name playing at a club on the south coast called Sterns, in Hastings. Sterns would prove to be a crucible for various styles over the years (including most recently the tech-house of Terry Francis), and the club's three floors showed how the scene was already starting to segment. The top floor had the breakbeat sound that would become drum and bass; the ground floor held the DJs who would nail their colours to the hardcore techno mast, including Carl Cox playing on three decks, and Top Buzz, a hardcore collective that included Mikee B (Michael Bennett) later one of the Dreem Teem. Finally, on the middle floor, gestating garage, you'd find Rhythm Doctor and Femi B (who went on to launch Feel Real together), DJ Harvey and Justin Berkmann – who would found the Ministry of Sound.

'You could tell from their clothing the people that wanted to hang upstairs with the girls and give it some,' says Timmi. 'If you wanted to nut off you was downstairs, you had a bit of Vicks on the back of your neck and, weee, you was off. I moved away from that because I liked to have a shirt that didn't sweat so much.'

This was in many ways a split between those who favoured the new UK sounds and those who still looked to the US. As we've seen, garage takes its name from the New York club Paradise Garage, though its sound came largely from another; Zanzibar, in Newark, New Jersey, where Tony Humphries cultivated 'the Jersey sound'. This was music influenced by the jazz, soul and gospel traditions, a style that loved vocals and melodies, that prized 'real' instruments (and plenty of hi-hats).

Graham Park championed this in the post-Madchester Haçienda, as did Allistair Whitehead in Nottingham's Venus. In London the KCC sound system brought it to carnival, and twins Bobby and Steve Lavinière made it their trademark at Garage City which started in 1991; the same year Feel Real was established by Rhythm Doctor, Rob Acteson and Femi B. These clubs brought over a long succession of US DJs and vocalists: Masters At Work, Inner City, Arnold Jarvis, Robert Owens, Barbara Tucker, DJ Pierre. The 'house and garage' style was what drove the explosion of glamorous, aspirational clubbing. When the Ministry of Sound first opened it was a cathedral to the sound, decorated with giant blow-ups of the US labels the scene revered, and it moved to a DJ calendar of American visitors. They even persuaded godfather of garage Tony Humphries to pack his bags and move to London to become the club's weekly resident. As the glamour quotient rose in UK clubland, this passionate, aspirational, escapist music dominated.

If the original split from hardcore had been about taking the music in a very American direction, the next step was a move back towards the British bass. Certain DJs started favouring records with sharper highs, more intricate percussion and meatier basslines; the same dynamic that drum and bass was making waves with. There was also, as Timmi explains, an increase in tempo. 'Most of the US DJs would play the vocal mix, but we'd turn it over and play the dub mix and pitch it up a little.' Playing dubs avoided the chipmunk effect of sped-up vocals, plus there was space for an MC to rhyme.

A turning point came when Grant Nelson, whose aesthetic had been forged by his time as a hardcore producer, took a Strictly Rhythm tune, 'Blues For You' by Logic and remixed it for his own label, Nice N Ripe, making it perfect for these DJs' dancefloors. 'It was exactly the same tune, it just had different sounds – the British sounds that you'd expect in a bit of jungle and drum and bass. Even though it was still housey, it was a lot brighter and a lot heavier on the dancefloor. And that for me is the defining tune.'

This sound was embraced by the UK DJs as a refreshing alternative to the soulful vocal house they found a little too smooth. Ironically, the early records that matched Nelson's new formula were actually American. For a while, the emerging UK garage scene ran on records by producers like DJ Disciple, Smack Productions, Masters At Work, Todd Edwards and Kerri Chandler. Then UK producers jumped in, going for it with skippy drum patterns and jungle-style bottoms, using production techniques learnt from drum and bass. Melody lines were truncated and stuttered, vocals warped and timestretched, frequencies rationed to cut-crystal highs and trunk-funking lows.

The new UK sound was in direct opposition to the purists who still swooned over their US imports and wouldn't dream of disrespectfully pitching them up. It was a way of appropriating garage – taking what was *theirs* and making it *ours*. Soon the sound was distinct enough to put off the established house and garage nights. 'In 1993 we couldn't get any work on a Saturday night. Ministry? No, out. The house room in Heaven? No! Feel Real? No. And I knew all the guys at these clubs. I was like, "C'mon mate, give us a go." No, no no.' Cut off from the major venues, UK-style garage was relegated to the second room in jungle raves and the smoochier moments on pirate stations.

And so the Sunday scene was born. When promoter Timmy Ram Jam opened his Happy Days after-hours in a pub called the Elephant And Castle down the road from the Ministry of Sound, its 6am opening time was designed to catch the Saturday-nighters whose energy hadn't left them yet (or was hidden in their pocket in powdered form). Hosted by MC Creed in a fairly low-key style, the residents were Mickey Simms, Matt 'Jam' Lamont, a former draughtsman from Luton who'd taken to DJing after redundancy, and later Karl 'Tuff Enuff' Brown, whose roots were in reggae and electro, and who had engineered in Rebel MC's pop breakbeat group Double Trouble. Again the tempo crept higher, as this jittery, high-impact music kept a dancefloor in motion when most of it had been up all night. 'Their sound was a lot moodier. It was an older crowd, loads of birds, a few gangsters, a lot of brandy,' recalls Timmi Magic. The party would go on 'til late afternoon when many would go to chill in Kennington Park.

As the club swelled it moved to the Frog And Nightgown pub on the Old Kent Road, and then in 1995 to the Arches in Southwark. Here, the DJs who would form the Dreem Teem – Timmi Magic, Mikee B and Spoony – as well as Matt Lamont and Karl Brown who were now making tracks together as Tuff Jam, would play in rotation. Spoony (Jonathan Joseph), who'd met the other Dreem Teem DJs on pirate station London Underground, recalls the excitement of the Arches: 'It was electric. You felt it. You could touch the atmosphere, you could bottle it. You took a deep breath and you were hit by hundreds of people dancing five hundred per cent. No one looking around caring who's in there, they're just in there grooving away. And as a DJ that's all you can ask for.' Here one symbolic night, Tony Humphries was booked to play; and as if to demonstrate how far UK garage had moved away from his smooth US soul-house, he bombed badly.

UK garage grew at a phenomenal pace, picking up disaffected refugees from the increasingly testosterone-marred drum and bass scene, which women clubbers had all but abandoned. Miranda Sawyer wrote about UK garage's bounty of womenfolk in the *Observer* in 2000, as the scene reached a peak at the hugely successful Twice as Nice nights at the Coliseum in Vauxhall. 'And what girls they are. Of all shapes, ages, colours, they are united in their rejection of unnecessary clothing. The skimpiest of skirts and the hankiest of tops are uniform, as are glamour heels. Their hair is twisted into works of art. The toilets chatter with compliments – "Lookin' good girl!".' UK garage unashamedly aimed itself at feminine hips. Spoony remembers the female presence as a powerful recruiting force, 'At first people didn't necessarily like or understand the music, but Jesus, they'd never seen so many women in one place.' There was soon Sunday night fever. 'Sunday night became Saturday night,' says Spoony. 'I'm taking Monday off work, getting the car cleaned on Saturday, I'm getting my hair cut as late as I can on Saturday so it still looks brand new on Sunday. If you go looking your part there's a good chance you could be on it.' Garage even got its own Ibiza as the big promotion companies, Twice as Nice and Garage, staked an outpost in Cyprus in the town of Aiya Napa.

Early on, things had been very much centred on England's capital. In reaction to the disliked 'speed garage' tag the scene, which still thought of itself as simply 'garage', became 'the London sound'. As waves spread to other cities, the name gradually settled as 'UK garage'. The media had

Dream team – at Twice as Nice these girls helped kill drum and bass.

started paying attention in late 1996, when records began hitting the charts. New York DJ Armand van Helden, with a stated aim of fusing house and jungle, remixed CJ Bolland's track 'Sugar Is Sweeter' in the garage style and took it to no.11(UK). In 1997 Double 99 had a club hit with 'Ripgroove', Tuff Jam took vocalist Rosie Gaines's 'Closer Than Close' to no.4 (UK), and pianist and oboe player MJ Cole (Matt Coleman) brought his distinctive musicality to the scene.

The same year, a further stylistic change crystallised things as tracks came out which abandoned the four-on-the-floor kickdrum pattern of house and earned the name 'two-step' for the way there were now only two kickdrum thumps in a bar. The first two-step record was 'Never Gonna Let You Go' by Tina Moore. (Incidentally, someone really needs to explain to the garage DJs the difference between '4/4 time' – four beats or *counts* in a bar, which all modern dance music has, and 'four-on-the-floor' – four *kick-drums* in a bar.) Soon, with remixes like Brandy's 'Boys Mind', two-step was giving a much-needed boost to R&B, lending its energy and rhythms to a genre limping along on hip hop's leftovers. The majors jumped at garage mixes as a way to get anodyne American vocalists into the UK charts.

By 2000 UK garage was the national sound. The hits came thick and fast: Artful Dodger introduced singer Craig David on 'Re-Rewind' and 'Fill Me In', which made no.1 (UK); Shanks & Bigfoot also claimed the top slot with 'Sweet Like Chocolate' and DJ Luck & MC Neat showcased the more MC-led side of garage with 'A Little Bit Of Luck'. Dreem Teem took the London sound to the Notting Hill Carnival with twelve acts, including Mystique, Craig David, Elizabeth Troy and Shola Ama. Trevor Nelson, representing the established face of soul, took just two. As if to rub in the triumph of the new, after Dreem Teem played their last record, Nelson came on and it poured with rain.

Grime

UK garage's evolution was played out as much on *Top Of The Pops* as in underground clubs. Major labels quickly moved to sign acts and the biggest DJs were snapped up from the pirates – Tuff Jam and north London stalwart EZ to Kiss FM, and the Dreem Teem to Radio One. Acutely aware of how quickly it had become mainstream, its figureheads became protective. 'We are holding our ground, because when this sound disappears we don't want to disappear with it,' said Tuff Jam in *Muzik* at the end of 1997, expressing concern about the 'jungalistic' elements they saw creeping in; the gunshots, rewinds and angry basslines. 'We have to make sure people keep churning out musical garage instead of this throwaway garage. We're trying to keep it cleansed, to keep the goodness in it so it's not dark and dingy and makes people feel moody. If I go into a record shop and hear something with that wah wah bassline or timestretch vocals I think "no thank you".'

Expressing personal preference is one thing but, as any DJ will tell you, trying to impose your static taste in the face of an evolving scene can be disaster. Tuff Jam were accused of simple snobbery, and Dreem Teem of protecting their turf, as kids embraced exactly the elements the older DJs most disliked. But rather than bow out, the old guard did exactly what the drum and bass DJs had done when they saw their music threatened by renegade ragga elements – they formed a committee. Founded in autumn 1999, the UK Garage Committee included DJs Jason Kaye, Dominic Spreadlove and MC Creed, with Norris 'Da Boss' Windross as chairman and Spoony as spokesman. It was formed largely in reaction to a violent MC-led hit, 'Bound 4 Da Reload' by Oxide & Neutrino, two of the populous Battersea collective So Solid Crew, which the Dreem Teem and Windross refused to play. The committee talked of more recognition in radio playlists, establishing an awards' ceremony and getting specialist garage charts in dance magazines. But given that garage was hardly unsuccessful, their agenda seems more about preventing change. 'Proper UK garage consists of core elements, a certain amount of soulfulness and above all a certain groove,' declared Windross as the waters lapped at his feet.

This was a generation gap, and it was about the rise of the MC. On one side were thirtysomething DJs who'd all come up through the rave years from soul or reggae roots; on the other were teenagers who had little musical heritage beyond recent US hip hop, but an overriding desire to get on the mic and express themselves. Yes, it brought violence to venues, as lyrics about guns and gangs brought the angry, respect-obsessed underside of city life into a previously joyful musical culture. And yes, it changed the music completely, as a parade of MCs spat rhymes over more minimal beats and took what had been a dancefloor-based scene onto the stage. But pontificating wasn't going to stop this music. That would be like the Sugar Hill Gang asking 50 Cent to stick to jolly party tunes.

Though rarely present in more mainstream clubs, MCs had always been a part of underground house – from Chalkie White, who voiced at many of the raves, to E-Mix, who'd rhymed over tracks at Feel Real. But the garage MCs only began to overshadow the music around 2001, the same year So Solid Crew were handed fame.

MC-based garage eventually had its christening and became 'grime', the name derived from the 'grimy style' of American rappers like Wu Tang Clan's Old Dirty Bastard. Grime: the word alone rips the sound from its classy roots and rubs it in dirt and crime. Inspired by So Solid's success (Eminem's unprecedented global domination through 2001 can't have hurt, either), to stripped-down garage rhythm tracks, Britain's kids staged an explosion of rapping. Given that every second hoodie-wearing youth was suddenly an MC, much of this was derivative and lame, but some – that of Dizzee Rascal, Wylie, Roll Deep, Skinnyman and Lady Sovereign, for example – was revealing, poetic and cut through with humour. The original garage DJs, faced with the decimation of their club circuit by violence, both real and imagined, moved back towards the soulful melodies and house rhythms they'd once left behind, leaving teenage UK to embark on a grime wave.

Made in Britain

For years the UK played librarian to the US, cataloguing its canon and rescuing its obscurities. But starting in the eighties, nurtured by sound system culture and energised by acid house, Britain finally laid down a lineage of home-grown dance music.

There had always been a few convincing examples among those Brits who adopted US styles – from Imagination and Loose Ends to the Ruthless Rap Assassins and the Stereo MCs, but when a generation of UK sound systems abandoned reggae roots to blaze their own trails, they freed British music from having to emulate something American. Grime isn't *like* hip hop, and it isn't *copying* hip hop, it *is* hip hop – its British flowering. Like jungle, like drum and bass, like two-step, it's raw, ghetto-bred sound system music, and it reflects the time and place it comes from. The British bassline, born on sound systems, bred by DJs, and fed on vinyl, has triumphed.

And because the new dance music is best made by fans, connoisseurs and collectors, after the eighties, innovation in dance music crossed the Atlantic – decisively – from the US to the UK. And the new, all-conquering producer was the DJ.

SEVENTEEN
ARTIST

Even Better Than The
Real Thing

'1988 saw the latest would-be revolution happen in pop music. The DJ, with his pair of Technics and box of records, can make it to the top with a little help from a sample machine, squiggly bassline and beat box. Yet again this was interpreted as the masses finally liberating the means of making music from all the undesirables.'

– Jimmy Cauty and Bill Drummond (KLF)

'You can't make an omelette without breaking eggs.'

– Lenin

So the DJ germinated rhythm and blues, he christened and disseminated rock'n'roll, he gave shape to reggae and he was the dazzling architect of the disco revolution. And then, from disco's hardy rootstock he single-handedly bred hip hop, house, garage, techno and hi-energy, not to mention all their offshoots and hybrids. But what else did he do?

What else? Not resting for a moment after four decades building radical new musical styles, the DJ set off towards his current position as the most powerful creative force in popular music. He became a producer, and given that he'd devised entirely new ways of conceiving and constructing music, the DJ soon eclipsed the Luddite competition. The new genres the DJ had created were centred on the idea of non-musicians making music. And as the pre-eminent musical non-musician, the DJ found himself heading the field.

His star rose and rose. The music industry, which had never been too sure about the DJ, grew to love him for the way he could remix a song into any market; it adored him for the way his name could be used to sell collections of otherwise anonymous tracks. And when his dance revolution swept all other pop before it, and dramatically changed the way people consumed music, the DJ found himself at the centre of momentous social change.

The DJ's craft and his skills were close to fully formed as long as twenty-five years ago. Disco and hip hop were his moments of true innovation. Most advances since then have come in his role as a producer, and in his possession of a good manager. But with wily representation and clever marketing, the DJ is now the hero of his age; a pop-star, a crowd-draw, a reliable brand name. And he gets paid (like supermodels and movie stars, those other victors of late consumer capitalism) not according to how talented he is, nor by how hard he works, but by the size of his franchise – how many ears he can reach and how many units he can shift.

How did all this happen?

DJ/producer/remixer

Provided you don't let him bore you about artistic expression or musical evangelism, a DJ's job is pretty single minded – he has to make people dance. He has to take the strange, ugly people at this wedding reception, or the lecherous drunks in this bar, or the insane mob of ravers in this warehouse, and turn them into a well-oiled dancefloor. He's done it hundreds of times before and he knows exactly which records do what to people. This one will get their toes tapping at the bar, this one will make that mad blonde drag her mate onto the floor, these will suck in the bystanders and any of those will make them go nuts. Don't play that green one though – it's beautiful but the drums are too quiet. It would clear the floor.

Who would you trust to make better dance records, a DJ with years of experience like this and a vast collection of records to steal ideas from, or a highly strung musician obsessed with writing the perfect love song? Perhaps that's unfair, but you get the picture. Since the DJ is the expert at making people dance, it was inevitable that he would eventually dominate the making of dance music itself.

Most successful DJs now carry the job title DJ/producer/remixer. Making their own records, or reconstructing those made by others, is a natural extension of the club DJ's trade, a way to put his creative stamp on the world. It's a way of distilling the particular sound he favours in his club performances into a more tangible form and, importantly, it's how a DJ can most convincingly claim artist status.

'DJs who don't want to make their own records are soft,' says Sasha, 'because no one knows better than a DJ what creates a buzz on a floor.' Norman Cook agrees: 'Most DJs become DJs because they love the music, and if you love the music, you feel you have some of it in you waiting to come out. You're playing tracks that are really simple. You think, this is just a couple of samples and a drum machine, I bet I could probably do that. And invariably, you can.'

The great advantage a DJ has over a musician is the clarity of his goal. His simple task is to produce a record that will make people dance. He may try to make it beautiful and unique as well, but ultimately he can get away with just being *effective*. Artistic integrity, on the dancefloor, is optional. The first house tracks were little more than drum machines recorded onto vinyl, and they tore the roof off. Of course, when music started being made this way the musicians decried it as unmusical and uncreative. The DJ didn't care because his dancers were going wild.

House and hip hop had both emerged as the DJ's response to the demands of his dancefloor; they were based on the DJ's peculiar understanding of music. And they were conceptual revolutions. They brought amazing new ways of even *thinking* about music. Hip hop fostered the idea of sampling; of stealing rather than emulating, of making patchwork music from a multitude of sources. House showed that music made with drum machines and synthesisers could be as sexy, funky and downright danceable as any made with wood, brass and steel. Giving wings to all this was the new electronic equipment that made it so easy. For a few hundred dollars you could buy a new musical universe, neatly packaged in a silver box with Roland, Casio, Korg or Akai stamped on the side. And these revolutionary machines were child's play to the DJ. Drum machines and samplers deal with music the same way as the DJ does: they play over the top of it, or they steal it and repeat it.

Today, what a producer does in the studio to make a dance record is little different in principle from what a DJ does in a club. When a DJ performs, he will be layering parts of records over each other, weaving and splicing different elements to make an original suite of music. Similarly, making or remixing a dance record is usually a case of playing around with chunks of existing sound – drum patterns and samples – and combining them to make something new. Grab a drum break from an old funk track, add a bassline from another, loop them up into a continuous groove, add some snatches of melody with your one-fingered keyboard playing, and bingo. In practice there can be phenomenal levels of subtlety and complexity, but at its simplest, constructing or reconstructing a dance record is very like a compressed version of DJing.

The new methodology has the added bonus of being technically undemanding. With a good studio engineer to press all the buttons and achieve the desired results, it's perfectly possible for a complete novice to make a great dance record. All they need are workable musical ideas. And a good DJ, even the most technically clueless, will have a steady supply of those.

'When you're DJing, you spend untold hours just standing watching people dance,' explains Cook. 'And you begin to realise which bits of a record people react to and which bits get them going. You just learn what makes people dance.' This experience translates easily into inspiration for remixing and production. 'When I'm in the studio, I think back to the night before and what kind of things worked with dancers. You remember how you felt when you put a tune on and it rocked the crowd; or when you played a groove that the crowd totally got into, even when they'd never heard the record before. It doesn't necessarily mean you make great pop music, but if your music's aimed straight at the dancefloor it gives you a head start.'

Most DJs would agree that the leap from playing records to making them is a small one; few see the move from DJ booth to recording studio as anything other than a natural progression. 'Everything I've learned is through playing records. It triggered everything,' says Kenny 'Dope' Gonzales, one half of Nuyorican duo Masters At Work, one of the most respected remix/production teams of the nineties. 'DJing was our training and it still is,' adds his partner 'Little' Louie Vega. 'Learning the structure of songs, the bars, the breaks, is all through DJing.'

The evolution of the remix
The first tape splicing was done by radio producer Jack Mullin on 'The

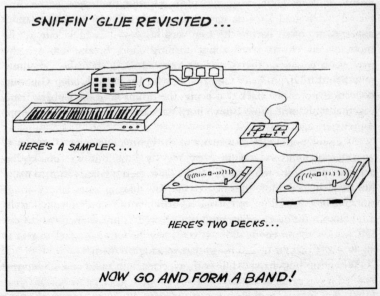

Real gone guitar – *Boys Own* updates the punk rock rallying cry with this music lesson for its readers.

Bing Crosby Show' at the end of the Second World War, using America's first reel-to-reel – previously Nazi technology. Sonic experimentalists like Pierre Schaeffer and Delia Derbyshire (creator of the original *Dr Who* theme) played with tape loops in the late fifties, with The Beatles among the first groups to use them on record. An intriguing precedent for cut-and-paste recording was 'Flying Saucer' in 1956, a million-selling US comedy single made by japesters Dickie Goodman and Bill Buchanan. This took the form of questions to witnesses of a martian invasion, with their answers being snatches of popular songs.

Remixing as we understand it was first done in Jamaica in the sixties when DJ/producers like Bunny Lee, King Tubby and Lee Perry first began to play the mixing desk like an instrument. Pushing two- and four-track recording to its limits, these pioneers unravelled songs into one-off versions and dubplates, emphasising the treble and the bass to make them more effective for outdoor sound systems. The other attraction of these remixes was that they were unique – no other sound system could play them.

A similar creative goal was at work in mid-seventies New York when the disco and hip hop DJs invented the technique of cutting rapidly from one record to another in order to extend the best passages. Walter Gibbons was probably the first to make this technique an important feature of his set. Gibbons often made mixes from two copies of the same record and around 1974 he started using a reel-to-reel to recreate these experiments, often having the tape version pressed as an acetate. While most of his efforts were about turning short breaks into lengthy percussion passages, others combined several songs to make something new. Scottish DJ/producer Colin Gate, who has been through Gibbons' collection, notes one track that brings the drums from the Fatback Band together with some James Brown horn stabs and some cut-up vocals from somewhere else.

As disco's popularity rose, many of the genre's DJs enjoyed careers as commercial remixers and, in New York at least, this was quickly an accepted part of the job – a way for the DJ to feed his dancefloor, to make his performance more distinctive and, by making non-dancey songs suitable for a dancefloor, to enlarge his armoury of records. Danny Krivit, a DJ famous for his re-edits, recalls the change. 'It just seemed that all the DJs who were somebody did it. If you knew how to use a reel-to-reel at all, it wasn't that far of a jump to start splicing on them.'

When hip hop arrived, DJs with experience in radio and advertising realised it was easier to use tape-splicing (or even just a pause button) than learn the imposing skills of Grandmaster Flash or Jazzy Jay. Neil McMillan's epic investigation *Cut Up Or Shut Up*, partially published in

Grand Slam magazine, details pioneers like Chep Nunez (the 'baddest Latin in Manhattan') who worked with Mantronix, as well as the Latin Rascals, Albert Cabrera and Tony Moran – who made a series of influential cut-up records – and also with the best-known sound-stitchers Double Dee & Steinski. All these pioneers helped popularise collage as a method of music-making, as well as showing that the original version of a record needn't be sacrosanct.

At its simplest, remixing is a straightforward process of sorting out a track's good elements from its bad, relative to the dancefloor. As Paul Oakenfold puts it: 'Someone will play you something. You say, "That's wrong, that's wrong, that's wrong." You take all of them out and replace them with this, this, this and this. Rearrange it – and it'll work.' This basic description belies the fact that the concept of the remix has evolved dramatically. A remix can be anything from a slightly different arrangement of a song to a track that bears hardly any relation to the original.

At first the remixer made only structural changes. Strictly speaking these weren't remixes, but re-edits; rather than unravelling a song's sonic fibres, they just chopped up and re-arranged the existing recording. Only with access to the multitrack tapes (the 'parts') could proper remixing take place, where the bassline might be made louder in the mix, or the vocals cut out of a certain passage to leave the accompaniment. Even here, the record companies were very protective of the original song and at first it was all you could do to add a conga.

David Morales, one of the world's best-known remixers, explains how remixing evolved. 'In the beginning, you remixed the original track. You used what was there to create the intro, your body, your break, your tag – the end of the song.' But remixers were soon allowed to add a few new elements. 'You might change the bassline, add percussion, or you added some other things, but you still had the song. You still had the artist intact.'

A third stage came when the vocal track was used intact but the music accompanying it was replaced completely, using music the remixer had made himself. 'You started to put *new* music on remixes. And all you had left from the original was the vocal track. Now people expected to hear something totally different when they bought a remix.'

Finally, remixers were given a free hand to scrap anything from the original and add anything they liked from other sources. In some cases, nothing of the original record remained except perhaps a tiny sampled snatch of vocals or instrumentation. Here, the remixer constructed an entirely new track and incorporated a few yelps from the singer, or a couple of stabs from a guitar. Think of Armand Van Helden's famous reworking of Tori Amos's 'Professional Widow'. Strictly speaking, the remixer was now doing full production (although not getting any royalties or publishing fees for it, because contractually it was almost always only a remix), and this is today's most common form of remixing. 'It's totally leftfield now,' says Morales. 'It's totally in another place. I mean, let's not even call it remixing any more. It's production.'

Now that such radical remixing is so prevalent, the success of a dance record often has very little to do with the original artist or the original song. To a craftsman like Morales who prides himself on respecting the original, this is overstepping the mark.

'Somebody says, "I need a remix." So you take a piece of a vocal: "Bla . . ." and stick it on a rhythm track you have already sitting around. That's a remix? That represents the artist? That doesn't represent the artist, it represents *you*.'

But for many an ambitious DJ/remixer, that is the whole point.

Remix and restyle

Take a painting, cut it into pieces and rearrange the bits. Maybe add some brush strokes of your own, perhaps throw away some of the original. How much do you have to change it before the end result is your work and no longer something made by someone else? Does it help if more people like your collage than liked the original painting? Can the collage be a genuinely new piece of art?

By the end of the seventies, DJs knew that the remix could go further than just make a song more *functional* for the dancefloor. It also offered them a route into the record industry and the means to finally gain recognition as creative artists. By adding stylistic twists, they could give a song the precise musical flavour they wanted, and if the enhancements were individual enough, these would mark out the remixer – rather than the original writer/musician – as the creative force behind a track. If his particular flavour was consistent over a series of records, a remixer could even develop a 'sound', just like any other recording artist. The style of his remixes would match the style of his club performances and all this would work to get him more easily noticed.

When remixes started being more successful than their originals (usually because they'd been made infinitely more danceable), the remixers started taking the limelight away from the original artists. And as remixes strayed further away from their originals stylistically, they started to sound like completely new compositions. By the mid eighties, certain remixers were enjoying name recognition as well as both dancefloor and chart success, and as the DJs' new post-disco genres took hold, the lines between remixing and authorship started to fade.

The idea that a remixer can make something new, that he can do something genuinely creative, has its earliest expression in Jamaica. Here, as early as the sixties, certain dub remixers enjoyed greater recognition than the artists on their records. However, it took a while before this idea gained currency anywhere else. Disco produced several star remixers – pioneers like Tom Moulton, Walter Gibbons, Jim Burgess – but they never enjoyed star billing on their records: appreciation of their artistry was largely confined to the closed world of other DJs. Slightly later, figures such as Shep Pettibone, Jellybean, Larry Levan and François Kevorkian were recognised as having a magic touch, and often when they did a remix their names were fairly prominent on the credits. However, when Epic in the UK emphasised Kevorkian's name above all others on a compilation of his disco remixes, his US label Prelude was incensed that the remixer's name should overshadow the acts themselves.

It was really only with the emergence of house that remixing was widely seen as a genuinely creative activity, when the key DJs of the period – Frankie Knuckles, David Morales, Tony Humphries – made having a reputation as a DJ and a reputation as a dance producer/remixer virtually interchangeable. A DJ's studio work started to become, as it is today, an important means of self-promotion and, in the UK at least, the DJ/remixer had begun his journey towards pop-star status.

Certain American jocks became gods in the UK, not by virtue of their DJ performances, but simply because of their studio work. Brooklyn producer/remixer Todd Terry exemplified this. In the middle of the nineties he commanded a DJ fee higher than anybody, yet his fame came not from playing records but from production and remixing, and his success in this came from marking himself out with a highly distinctive style. By grafting the hard New York hip hop aesthetic onto house, he had brought a richer, stronger percussion palette to the genre in records like Royal House's 'Can You Party' and Todd Terry Project's 'Weekend' and 'Bango' (all 1988). 'That Chicago sound. I took it to the next level,' he says. 'You'd listen to it and say "only Todd would do that, that's Todd's drum pattern, that's his *sound*", the dark, wild hype sound.'

By 1990 the wider music industry felt ready to invest in the idea of the DJ as artist, and there was a signing frenzy in which Robert Clivilles and David Cole, Frankie Knuckles, Blaze and Lil Louis were all awarded album contracts. On the whole, they were marketed as producers who happened to be DJs, with different vocalists and musicians appearing on each track. But most of these album projects bombed commercially (only Clivilles and Cole, as C&C Music Factory, enjoyed any real success) and US major labels once again saw dance music as a risky business, and the idea of the DJ as recording artist as something best left to the independents.

The DJ's rise to artist status was finally ratified in 1993, when a DJ's remix album was released with all the fanfare of a major artist and aimed, in the wake of the UK's dance transformation, squarely at the pop market. Sasha (Alexander Coe), a DJ who had risen to fame as resident at Shelley's in Stoke-on-Trent, released an album made up entirely of remixes (*Sasha: The Remixes*). These weren't songs that he had originated in the studio. He wasn't presented as a producer who was incidentally also a DJ. These were songs originally written and recorded by other artists – many of them well-known, successful artists. Sasha had only *remixed* the tracks: despite this, these reconstructions were on *his* album, with *his* name in the title, and were to be considered *his* pieces of music. But most importantly, unlike the two or three remix albums that had predated it, *Sasha: The Remixes* wasn't a small pressing aimed strictly at connoisseurs and other DJs. It was a major release. 'Sasha is living proof of the dictum that DJs, as dance music's prime movers, are ideally placed to take that music to new levels as producers,' declared Nick Gordon Brown's sleevenotes. 'The lines between DJs and artists, remixers and producers are getting ever more blurred.'

The revolution will be synthesised

Since the sixties, Britain has had the world's most bizarrely knowledgeable music scene, fed by fanatical collectors, a fat pop industry, the world's fastest moving and most diverse charts, and by scores of music magazines – several of them weeklies. Added to this was a wild diversity on radio: city kids in Britain had Radio One, the nation's monolithic (and *non-commercial*) pop station in one ear, and the ever-radical sounds of the pirates in the other. But for all this knowledge, when it came to dance music, Britain spent a quarter-of-a-century completely in thrall to America. It was only with acid house that the UK's rabid dance music connoisseurship finally turned into creativity.

House and hip hop were the vital sparks that fired the DJ's move to production. As long as rare groove ruled the roost there was little pressure to venture into the studio. Unless he was also a talented musician or experienced producer, a DJ in love with old soul records or polished jazz-funk didn't have much hope of making his own music. However, a DJ blown over by the sound collages of hip hop or energised by the synthetic beats of house might perfectly well expect to cook some up for himself. A generation of British DJs became remixers and producers as a result, and in the ever-fertile musical melting pot of urban Britain, a new era of dance music began.

There had been a few earlier experiments with the new methods. Trevor Horn's Art Of Noise project gave us 'Close To The Edit' in 1984, a track which used the Fairlight synthesiser's sampling possibilities to its (rather limited) limits. Before this there had been a warning of how low sampling could go with 1981's Stars On 45 hit singles. The first of these stitched together snatches of all The Beatles' most famous songs over an insistent disco beat (they were actually painstaking copies of the songs rather than true samples). Giving a chilling foretaste of the rule that the more obvious the sample, the more successful the record, this discofied nostalgia was a world-wide hit and spawned several follow-ups.

The Stars On 45 tracks had actually been inspired by a widely available series of bootlegs called *Bits And Pieces* (as well as earlier ones under the name Hollywood). DJs would use these fifteen-minute megamixes of popular disco tracks as warm-up records or as toilet-break standbys. After Stars On 45 took this idea into the charts, in 1983 a former Radio Luxembourg DJ Tony Prince used it as the basis for his DMC (Disco Mix Club) remix service. Paid-up members were sent exclusive DJ-only megamixes of the latest tunes, and because these were for 'promotional use only' Prince didn't have to license the tracks to use them. Similar services had sprung up in the States, the most famous being Disconet, which from 1977 hired DJs including Bobby Guttadaro and Bobby

Vitteriti to reconstruct and combine dancefloor hits for their subscribers.

Prince's DMC organisation also founded a mixing competition – which was quickly hijacked by the hip hop world and remains the pre-eminent forum for turntablists – as well as launching clubbing magazine *Mixmag*, which started life as a members' newsletter (an early issue has a picture of a young Pete Tong dressed as Santa). DMC was joined in the UK remix market by the Leeds-based Music Factory, who in 1989 followed up their DJ-only mixes with a reprise of the Stars On 45 idea – the even more appalling Jive Bunny records.

In more credible environs, jazz-funk DJ Froggy had been experimenting with reel-to-reel re-edits, and in 1985 released a James Brown megamix on Boiling Point. Froggy also worked with future UK hip hop producer Simon Harris on edits for Radio One. Chad Jackson was another young hip hop fan energised by the tracks coming out of New York and he worked on several turntable-based megamixes for DMC.

Double Dee & Steinski

A brief clarification is needed here. While the first hip hop records were hugely exciting mindfucks for most people, the way they were made was far too intimidating to inspire a cavalcade of UK copyists. This role fell instead to the records made by New York sound engineer Douglas DiFranco and advertising copywriter Steve Stein, aka Double Dee & Steinski, who showed that it was possible to make hip hop without having to spend years perfecting supernatural turntable skills.

Already an obsessive record collector, Stein realised that he could emulate a quick-mixing scratch DJ with the studio technology he used to make radio ads. 'I didn't really want to become a scratchy guy, like a turntablist. It obviously took a lot of time to learn how to do, and I had a job.' Instead, at the end of 1983, the duo took six crates of records into the studio, fired up the eight-track recorder, locked the door and emerged with 'Lesson One' (aka 'The Payoff Mix'), a frenzied masterpiece made from a bombardment of cut-up chunks of other records: pieces of 'Adventures On The Wheels Of Steel' and a bit of James Brown; some 'Buffalo Gals', Funky Four's 'That's The Joint' and a little Culture Club; the Supremes, 'Rockit', a snatch of Humphrey Bogart and a hundred more.

The catalyst for this project had been a remix competition sponsored by Tommy Boy records: come up with the best remix of the G.L.O.B.E. & Whiz Kid track 'Play That Beat Mr DJ' and you'd have it broadcast on the radio.

'Six weeks later,' recalls Stein, 'after some meeting at the agency, my secretary goes, "Hey, Tommy Boy just called, Tommy Boy himself". And I went, "Yeah, why?"

' "You won that contest."

' "We *won*???" '

Stein and DiFranco were whisked into hip hop society, they met their DJ heroes – who were all surprised to see they weren't as young or as black as they'd expected – and they recorded more tracks. There was 'Lesson Two', a James Brown megamix; 'Lesson Three (History Of Hip-Hop)', an amalgam of the most ubiquitous old-school breaks; and then Steinski's solo project 'The Motorcade Sped On', a satirical cut-up based on the news soundtrack from the Kennedy assassination. Though these records could never be released commercially, due to their huge volume of illegal samples, Tommy Boy pressed a great many promotional singles and the few which made it to London were gold dust.

As well as the sheer number of different musical sources combined in these records, it was because they were discernibly the result of tape-splicing rather than turntable skills which made them so exciting to British ears. Where Grandmaster Flash had wowed with his dexterity, Steinski's records suggested an easier method of construction. The absence of rapping was another key factor. Here was the green light to make a record for anyone who loved hip hop but, a) couldn't scratch, and b) couldn't rap.

Coldcut and M/A/R/R/S

One group influenced profoundly by the Double Dee & Steinski collages was Coldcut, the musical partnership of ex-art teacher Jonathan More and computer programmer Matt Black – both were DJs.

'They were actually *lessons*,' says Black, explaining that, as the titles suggested, they saw Steinski's records as practical instruction. 'This is how you can go about taking a bunch of old stuff and make it into something new. It wouldn't have happened without those blueprint records.'

Inspired by what they heard, Coldcut became the first UK act to release a sample-built record – 1987's 'Say Kids, What Time Is It?' When the track was released they upped its desirability by pretending it was an American import, even to the extent of scratching off the matrix numbers at the centre of the records.

Another London DJ who couldn't wait to try his hand at the new music was Dave Dorrell. In spring 1987 he was approached by MTV to create some music for a series of video jingles for the channel's European launch. He teamed up with Martin Young from the band Colourbox, who had the necessary studio experience, and set out, as he says, 'to put as many edits into fifteen seconds as possible'. The resulting music – an intense montage of cut-up sounds – graced screens for a few months, but it also whetted their appetites for further production. So, as part of a project involving Colourbox and another band, AR Kane, and with the addition of CJ Mackintosh as their scratch DJ, Dorrell and Young formed M/A/R/R/S. With Coldcut's 'Say Kids...' and Steinski's records as admitted influences, they scraped together as many upfront tunes as they could find and put together 'Pump Up The Volume'. This rapid-fire collage of vocal snatches included Israeli singer Ofra Haza, the Criminal Element Orchestra chanting 'put the needle to the record', Public Enemy shouting 'you're gonna git yours', and some James Brown grunts – all cemented by an insistent dance beat. 'Pump Up The Volume' rocketed to no.1 (UK) in September 1987.

Just before this, Coldcut had put together 'Beats And Pieces', a collage of sampled doorbells plus a bit of Vivaldi. Then, following fast behind M/A/R/R/S and using almost all the same sampled elements, came Coldcut's remix of 'Paid In Full' by US rap group Eric B & Rakim.

'With Eric B & Rakim, we were kind of giggling all the way through it, thinking that we were making it so fucked up, people wouldn't be into it,' confesses Coldcut's Jonathan More. 'We thought, "This'll fuck 'em up. They won't be able to handle this." Eric B & Rakim hated it, but the record-buying public shot it to no.15 (UK) in November 1987. In the wake of their success, Coldcut moved towards a more house-influenced style with records like 'Doctorin' The House' featuring Yazz on vocals and 'People Hold On' with Lisa Stansfield.

There was an explosion of energy as UK dance producers (nearly all of whom were DJs) took up the hip hop and house blueprints – readily fusing elements from the two genres – and made their own readings of the new dance aesthetic. In late 1987 and early 1988 came a score of pop hits, obviously built from these influences. Bomb The Bass with 'Beat Dis', S'Express's 'Theme From S'Express', A Guy Called Gerald's visionary 'Voodoo Ray' and 808 State's 'Pacific State' were some of the key moments. All made the charts.

Bang The Party gained US respect with 'Release Your Body' and 'Bang Bang You're Mine', Baby Ford made the first UK acid record, 'Oochy Koochy', and D Mob gave the country a taste of London's acid club scene with the awful 'We Call It Acieed', which went to no.3 (UK) and caused the BBC to ban all songs containing the word 'acid'.

KLF and the new punk

Another lively impetus was punk, for its still resonating do-it-yourself ideology and its guerrilla approach to the music industry. 'The DIY record thing, that was very important,' says Matt Black. 'In the late seventies, the idea that you could actually make a record yourself was very powerful. I did that with my little band at college. I'm sure hundreds of other people did.' Punk had spawned scores of tiny independent labels as people realised they didn't have to sell their soul to a major label to get a record released; these upstart independents provided a model that hundreds of dance labels would follow.

As well as their punky readiness to put out their own records, another reason for Coldcut's head start had been their familiarity with a piece of simple punk technology, the four-track recorder. 'By the time I got round to doing "Say Kids . . ." I had an advantage, which was that I knew what a four-track was,' says Black. ' "Say Kids . . ." was done on a Portastudio and a cassette machine with an analogue pause button, two turntables and a DJ mixer, and some sound effects.'

New technology was a vital force in Britain, as it had been in Chicago and Detroit. When the first wave of UK house broke, affordable digital sampling was yet to come, but tape sampling was easy enough and drum machines and synthesisers were becoming ever more commonplace. With these digital instruments, the punk manifesto that 'anyone could make music', 'no experience necessary' could be fully realised. John Cage had once written, 'What we can't do ourselves will be done by machines and electrical instruments which we will invent.' Now such machines were a reality and would-be producers were able to sidestep the fact that they had zero musical training (and sidestep studio fees of £1,000 a day) and immediately start putting music together in their bedrooms.

DJ/producer Norman Cook, then playing bass with the Housemartins but already experimenting with cut-and-paste techniques, agrees that the punk DIY ethos was important: 'There was an irreverence to the rules, like you can make a record that's really repetitive and isn't very musical and was made at home in your bedroom and doesn't have chords, drummers, singers, or anyone who can read a musical note.'

Importantly, the sound everyone was chasing was quite lo-fi. Hip hop and Chicago house were all the more inspiring for the very fact that they were far from polished. As Matt Black says, 'There was a nicely ignorant attitude which was that if it sounded fresh, you were in. So just by sampling one bass note off a JB's record into this twenty quid Casio sampler, you could play a bassline. Yeah, it sounded muzzy, but it actually had weight to it and a great sound. There must have been a lot of people that felt as we did at the time – "Hey! Wow! We can do this. We can actually do this ourselves." '

There were certainly plenty of old punks who saw the lure of this new music. Kris Needs, Andy Weatherall and Mike Pickering all had roots in punk, and would all enjoy success with house. Two others, Jimmy Cauty and Bill Drummond, came together as the JAMs (Justified Ancients Of Mu Mu), and later KLF (Kopyright Liberation Front) which, in their mission to annoy, seemed to pick up where the Sex Pistols had left off. Bathing their projects in a rich web of mystic references taken from cult book *The Illuminatus Trilogy*, Drummond and Cauty attacked all that was sacred to the rock-based music industry. Playing the game by all the wrong rules they assaulted the dull notion of originality, took free-for-all sampling to extremes and released a series of outrageously copyright-infringing records. Then, in a blend of eager cynicism and inspired originality, they put a collage record together and took it to no.1 (UK). With a title – 'Doctorin' The Tardis' – that was a piss-take of Coldcut's 'Doctorin' The House', it combined glam rock, rapping and the theme tune from the TV show *Dr Who*. It reached the UK's top slot in June 1988.

After their chart success, Drummond and Cauty wrote a book called *The Manual* (*How To Have A Number One The Easy Way*), which described exactly what its title promised, while giving an incisively amusing insight into the workings of the pop industry. At least one group copied their instructions to the letter and did indeed have a hit record. *The Manual* reminded that talent borrows, but genius steals:

'It is going to be a construction job, fitting bits together. You will have to find the Frankenstein in you to make it work. Your magpie instincts must come to the fore. If you think this sounds like a recipe for some horrific monster, be reassured by us, all music can only be the sum or part total of what has gone before. Every number one song ever written is only made up from bits from other songs. There is no lost chord. No changes untried. No extra notes to the scale or hidden beats to the bar. There is no point in searching for originality.'

This could have been the manifesto for what was underway – nothing less than a revolution, precipitated by the DJ, in the acceptable way to make music.

Commercial remixing

Though it took them a while to recognize the DJ as an artist, the record companies hadn't been slow to turn his remixing skills to their advantage. In the disco era they had quickly realised that having a dance version of a tune originally made for radio allowed them to promote it to a whole new audience via the clubs. In the nineties, when dance music had evolved into highly compartmentalised scenes, this idea of remixing for marketing purposes was taken even further.

In the wake of the acid house explosion, UK remixers such as Darren Emerson, Justin Robertson, Terry Farley and Andy Weatherall were in demand for their ability to nudge guitar bands in the direction of the DJ. The remixer was an intrinsic part of the Madchester explosion of danceable rock, with Paul Oakenfold and others turning shambling beat combos into dancefloor gold. In *i-D*, Weatherall summed up the remixer's role as 'an outside member of the band'. He explained how the remixer's currency was musical knowledge: 'You can't play an instrument, you've just got a big record collection and that's your input.'

A really radical remix could push a track into a whole new genre and make it appeal to a completely new set of fans. A Mariah Carey song which works great as a piece of radio pop could be remixed into a house record, there could be a hip hop version, or you could even get someone to remix it so it worked in a techno club. In an effort to capture each segment of the fragmented dance world, labels started making the remix a vital part of their marketing strategies. Dance singles were issued in double and triple packs as no end of remixes were included. Michael Jackson's 1991 single 'Jam' was released in no fewer than twenty-four different versions.

As a result, certain remixers – those perceived to have a strong style which could be targeted at a particular sector of the market – were in great demand. David Morales was one, a young Brooklyn DJ who had risen to instant fame in fairytale fashion when he had been hired to stand in for the increasingly hazy Larry Levan at the Paradise Garage. Morales soon developed a very distinctive melodic style, influenced in equal parts by the classics of disco and the rawer sounds of Chicago. His first production work was the 1985 dance hit 'Do It Properly' with David Cole and Robert Clivilles (who would later form C&C Music Factory) as Two Puerto Ricans, A Black Man And A Dominican, and this led to a series of remixes starting with 'Instinctual' by Imagination. His Red Zone mixes, named after the Manhattan club where he was resident in the late eighties, sound fresh even when played today.

Through the early nineties, Morales' name could be found on a torrent of remixes, as A&R men treated him as a sure-fire source of elegant vocal house. At times, the industry's marketing-based view of remixing has come into sharp conflict with Morales' artistic judgement, and he's found himself at odds with record company people; they've expected some kind of trademark Morales sound, he's delivered something quite different. 'I've had moments when they've said, "But I wanted this style, I wanted it like this and like that!" ' he admits. 'What some A&R man hears in his head is totally different from what can actually work.'

In 1995 he did what was then the ultimate remix: 'Scream', the first single off Michael Jackson's new album. This was such a high-profile job that rather than send Morales the master tapes to work from (as is standard), he was flown out to Jackson's studio. 'They wouldn't give me the masters. They flew me to LA; flew everybody over, money was no problem. I spent a week in Michael Jackson land.' For three mixes he was paid a rumoured $80,000. Today, even this huge sum has been superseded. Super-commercial hip hop mogul Sean 'P-Diddy' Combs supposedly demands $100,000 and upwards to put his name to a remix.

Artist?

Arguably a DJ doesn't have to make records to be an artist – the greatest can express artistry in their club performances. To hear an awe-inspiring night of music collated from hundreds of different sources, standing on years of collectorship – a sequence of recordings that has never before been imagined and could never be repeated – is to hear nothing less than an artist at work. The argument over the DJ's status is sustained largely by ignorance of what a skilled DJ actually does. If we're happy to award a chef or a conductor or a record producer the accolade of artist we should make room for the DJ, too.

In recent years, technological advances have meant that the DJ can take all sorts of equipment into the booth. In today's digital world everything in a studio can be squeezed into a single laptop, except the coffee machine and the receptionist. Playing digital recordings from a computer lets a DJ split every song he plays into component parts and mix and match these individual elements rather than whole songs. Blurring the line between DJing and musicianship provides further ammunition for those who want to uphold the DJ as an artist. A few years ago several DJs emerged – one of the first being London spinner Pure Science (Phil Sebastian) – who played nothing but their own compositions, tailoring them live using a host of beats, samples and MIDI equipment. This is exactly what dance-based bands like Orbital, Underworld and the Chemical Brothers do when they play 'live'. Instead of having a single finished version of a song, they go onstage and play with its building blocks, maybe pumping the audience with a single growling bass note, then warping that into a creeping bassline and then playing that until the crowd is ready for the onslaught of some drum beats. In this way electronic musicians have exactly the same responsive relation with their audience as any traditional rock musician.

Coldcut, an act who always have the latest toys, believe that the advances in DJing will come in presentation. They talk of ways to make the event more responsive – like having the dancers somehow trigger elements of the music by the way they move (perhaps using floor pads or laser sensors). Their VJamm software allows a DJ to cut and mix video samples while simultaneously playing music. And years before Final

Scratch came along to do pretty much the same thing, they devised a MIDI interface for a turntable – a device they call the 'dextractor' – which allows a DJ to use the back and forth scratch movements of a record to trigger other instruments. With the dextractor, a DJ can scratch any chunk of digital sound he chooses (or even video) – you could scratch a drum beat, a piano riff, a nightingale singing or a film clip of *Debbie Does Dallas*. You can even synchronise a video projection to a record you're scratching.

Even without winning the artist argument, the DJ long ago escaped being seen as just 'someone who puts records on', by virtue of building himself a recording career. Today, thanks largely to this move, the DJ has dance music sewn up. DJs who don't make their own music are rare, as are dance music producers who didn't get their start by playing records. The two crafts are inextricably linked, the one inspiring the other. 'Now I understand records more because I *make* records,' stresses Morales. 'And that just makes you all the better as a DJ because you understand music better.'

Significantly, while the DJ was showing off his new skills as a producer, rock adopted such a knee-jerk anti-technology stance that dance outstripped it in creative terms for many years. Samplers, sequencers and synthesisers were snapped up by the DJ because he was already familiar with the shapes they gave to music (and because he couldn't play any 'real' instruments), while they were heavily criticised by rock-based musicians (who could). Only after artists started embracing dance-derived approaches, did rock start to look innovative again.

In its directions for creating a number one single, Cauty and Drummond's *The Manual* makes it quite clear. 'If you are already a musician stop playing your instrument,' the book insists, '. . . if in a band, quit. Get out. Now.' Over the page, in the authors' list of essential tools, the only thing necessary for pop stardom which comes anywhere near being a musical instrument is a record player and a pile of 7-inch singles.

Since *The Manual* was written in 1988, the revolution it predicted in the way pop music is made has been fought and won. The world's pop has become ever more dance-oriented and the DJ's supremacy has been assured. In 1992, with his star rising, Paul Oakenfold was invited to remix a track by rock giants U2. Retaining the bulk of the song, but sprinkling it with dancefloor magic, Oakenfold's remix was an instant and huge hit in the clubs. The remix shot into the charts a mere three weeks after the original release had slumped from its peak at no.12 (UK). The remix dramatically eclipsed sales of the original and reached no.8 (UK).

Its title?

'Even Better Than The Real Thing'.

EIGHTEEN
OUTLAW

Renegade Snares

'The introduction of a new kind of music must be shunned as imperilling the whole state: since styles of music are never disturbed without affecting the most important political institutions.'

– Plato, *Republic*

'Let us admit that we have attended parties where for one brief night a republic of gratified desires was attained. Shall we not confess that the politics of that night have more reality and force for us than those of, say, the entire US government?'

– Hakim Bey, anarchist philosopher

Dancing is political, stupid. You think you're just having fun, but when you're on the dancefloor you're enjoying a temporary rebellion, rejecting the rules and responsibilities of your daytime life, questioning the values that make you wait for the bus and smile at the boss every morning. A good DJ can use the power of music to suspend reality, making you forget your career struggles and unpaid bills in favour of a few more basic human – even animal – priorities.

As you join the dancefloor you're forging an alliance, however briefly, with hundreds, maybe thousands of people. Dancing is collective action, making you an active participant. You've entered an unspoken agreement to do something *together* – just like protesting or voting. Even in the most commercial club you're not just consuming the event, you're joining with others to create it. This puts the DJ in a powerful position. Politicians have always been wary of people gathering in large numbers, so you can bet they're suspicious of the figure who controls things. If dancing at a rave is breaking the law, then a DJ there is inciting a riot.

The best DJs are cultural outlaws in any case, not content to play what's known and acceptable but always searching out new music to overthrow the old. When this music is particularly inflammable, the DJ will do whatever it takes to get it heard. Add drugs to this and you've really started something.

Acid house was the perfect example, inciting the DJ to all sorts of illegality: whether crashing the locks to play in a Sheffield warehouse, climbing a Hackney tower block to put up a pirate radio antenna, selling pills to finance a record label, or trespassing on farmland to spin for a field of ravers. The desire to take drugs and dance to house music in company with as many people as possible put the DJ right at the centre of a massive law-breaking movement.

The biggest mass arrest in British history? Not striking miners, not poll tax protestors, but a bunch of bemused ravers, victims of the Bright Act, the first law passed against dance culture. In 1990 police violently rounded up 836 clubbers dancing in a warehouse near Leeds and removed them in a fleet of specially-hired coaches. Many were hurt, but only seventeen were charged with anything. The DJ, Rob Tissera, because he'd encouraged the dancers to barricade the doors and carry on partying, was jailed for three months.

So concerned was Parliament about the continuing threat from acid house that to counter it they passed a law overturning the centuries-old right to free assembly. Part of the 1994 Criminal Justice Act, which gives police sweeping powers to control people's movement, refers specifically to people coming together to listen to music, taking particular care to define this so it includes electronic dance music. America, too, has spent much energy concocting laws to use against large dance events, again riding roughshod over long-established legal principles in the process. The infamous RAVE Act makes promoters and venue owners legally responsible for the drug crimes of their clubbers – even when those crimes remain unproven. Penalties can reach $2 million and up to twenty years in prison. And as fear continues to outrun rationality in the United States of Paranoia, even more draconian laws are tabled.

Raves

In 1988 the DJ and his music embarked on an unprecedented project of social change. A new kind of music met a new kind of drug and thousands, eventually millions, of young people discovered a new way of enjoying themselves. House music, having upturned the ways in which music is created, set about transforming the way it is consumed. And acid house, the communal psychedelic culture that grew around it, proved to be an incredibly powerful force.

'We broke down a lot of barriers at the beginning of house music,' says Danny Rampling. 'It broke everything down. It smashed down the walls.' DJing at his acid house club Shoom, Rampling felt that he and his friends had created an alternative community, independent of the outside world. 'When the doors were closed, you could do what you wanted. It was our own state of freedom. It was a free state, as it should be generally anyway. There were no restrictions in that club, at the beginning, whatsoever. All you wanted to do, that was conducive to that atmosphere, you could do it. Like all of the good clubs that have stood the test of time. So, in a sense, yeah, it was an outlaw period.'

As the scene spread, thousands more would share this feeling.

'You felt like a rebel, coming home, midday, with a tie-dyed top on, dripping with sweat, walking into a petrol station with bare feet. You really did feel like an outsider.' To rave DJ and drum and bass pioneer Fabio, house music provided a stark alternative to the nation's grim realities. 'We felt glad to be not part of Thatcher's Britain. We were like, "Fuck Thatcher! Fuck the Tories! We're nothing to do with you." We're going around with bandannas on our heads, dancing in the street. "We don't do nine to fives man. We're fucking outlaws." '

1988 became the second 'Summer of Love' – acid house was happy to compare itself with the hippie idealism of 1967, pleased to be renewing the sixties' mission of rebellion and personal discovery. Flyers copied Grateful Dead posters or used computer-generated fractal patterns to suggest a new psychedelia; loose, colourful, unisex hippie fashions were creeping back. Timothy Leary rekindled his acid evangelism, seeing a psychedelic drug movement emerging on a scale that dwarfed his LSD generation. Acid house was a new year zero for British pop culture, which had spent the last few years telling you to be poised and sophisticated. Now acid house was suggesting you act like a kid and let music and dancing become the centre of your life; other concerns melted away.

House music had introduced the endless beat, bringing a demand for all-night dancing marathons; ecstasy inspired us to do this in large numbers. Legal clubbing simply couldn't cope. Large illegal unlicensed parties were the only way acid house could accommodate its inevitable expansion. This was a culture inspired by the open-air clubs of Ibiza anyway. Like school kids screaming into the playground, we drove out of town and went mad in a field.

The rave scene started with a few fairly spontaneous events thrown by London's acid house movers and shakers. Rare groove had shown the way, and early raves like Hedonism just took the warehouse model, added lots more drugs and switched things to a house soundtrack. These quickly caught the attention of more money-minded promoters and raves expanded in size and ambition until they were huge encampments complete with car parking and fairground rides. For three or four summers, in events like Sunrise, Biology, Energy, you could find yourself sharing the time of your life with thousands of like-minded souls in an aircraft hangar or a muddy cowshed.

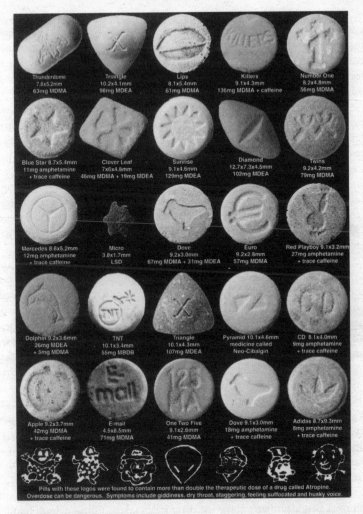

Thunderdome 7.8x5.2mm 63mg MDMA
Triangle 10.2x4.1mm 96mg MDEA
Lips 8.1x5.4mm 61mg MDMA
Killers 9.1x4.3mm 136mg MDMA + caffeine
Number One 8.2x4.8mm 56mg MDMA

Blue Star 8.7x5.4mm 11mg amphetamine + trace caffeine
Clover Leaf 7x6x4.8mm 46mg MDMA + 19mg MDEA
Sunrise 9.1x4.6mm 129mg MDEA
Diamond 12.7x7.3x4.5mm 102mg MDMA
Twins 9.2x4.2mm 79mg MDMA

Mercedes 8.6x5.2mm 12mg amphetamine + trace caffeine
Micro 3.8x1.7mm LSD
Dove 9.2x3.0mm 67mg MDMA + 31mg MDEA
Euro 9.2x2.8mm 57mg MDMA
Red Playboy 9.1x3.2mm 27mg amphetamine + trace caffeine

Dolphin 9.2x3.6mm 26mg MDEA + 5mg MDMA
TNT 10.1x3.4mm 55mg MBDB
Triangle 10.1x4.3mm 107mg MDEA
Pyramid 10.1x4.6mm medicine called Neo-Cibalgin
CD 8.1x4.0mm 9mg amphetamine + trace caffeine

Apple 9.2x3.7mm 42mg MDMA + trace caffeine
E-mail 4.5x8.5mm 71mg MDMA
One Two Five 9.1x2.6mm 41mg MDMA
Dove 9.1x3.0mm 18mg amphetamine + trace caffeine
Adidas 8.7x9.3mm 8mg amphetamine + trace caffeine

Pills with these logos were found to contain more than double the therapeutic dose of a drug called Atropine. Overdose can be dangerous. Symptoms include giddiness, dry throat, staggering, feeling suffocated and husky voice.

Johnny Walker recalls DJing a Biology event in June 1989 at the height of the movement. Here, in an open field in Hertfordshire, the night sky streaked with lasers, gathered an incredible 12,000 ravers. Walker, up on a stage, found himself playing for a churning sea of people, all locked into the groove of his records. 'It was breathtaking, to be onstage and look out and see that many people dancing to what you're playing, it was just incredible.'

Finding a rave was half the fun. As the sun went down, roads would be gridlocked with cars full of people getting ready for a party. Hanging out of windows, blasting music, looking for the right exit or just following a growing mass of traffic until someone actually had a look at a map. Whole motorways were blocked as people approached a party or were turned back from one that had been stopped. People recall one night when all four lanes of the A13, the main eastern artery into London, were jammed with cars all going the same way.

'The raves were an extreme,' Mark Moore told Sean Bidder. 'At the time it was a revolution, you knew things were going to change, you knew music was going to change, everything was going to change. I think it carried on the torch of just this kind of innocence and this kind of freedom of expression – not caring about the rules.

'Getting your car as far as you could, then leaving it in a hedgerow and walking the last bit. Down the muddy lane. Hearing the bass thump get closer, seeing the lights flash through the trees. Meeting people as you go. "Have some water. You been before? Where've you driven from? Are you Jane from Bristol? See you in there." '

A rave was an idealised version of clubbing. It wasn't about visiting some purpose-built venue, it was about creating somewhere new; it was about building a city for a night. A club had a place in space and time, but a rave was made of possibilities. A rave existed in the minds of the people who danced together. Without them it was nowhere, just a field off a motorway exit. While Margaret Thatcher denied the reality of society, in her face were thousands of people making one-night communities. Some commentators put it all down to AIDS; the fear of casual sex had driven a generation to find human warmth in the company of thousands. Others decided it was a longing for a lost innocence – where else did all these childlike fashions come from? Someone even pointed out that this was the first Walkman generation – and now people were desperate for music that was shared. Whatever the underlying forces at work, raves emphasised the ecstatic acid house ideal: it was people that counted above everything.

The first were offshoots of the original acid house clubs. Shoom threw a Brighton barn party for their inner circle, filling it with foam – Ibiza style. And in early 1988 the *Boys Own* crew bussed some Shoomers to a friend's barn outside Guildford. They'd asked Danny Rampling to DJ but he wouldn't miss a night at his club, so Steve Proctor spun while 200 or so scene-makers, celebs included, danced until late morning the next day.

'The bloke who owned the place thought it was the best night of his life,' recalls *Boys Own* founder Terry Farley. 'He was sitting there at about six in the morning playing guitar while Boy George was singing "Karma Chameleon".' Keen to put the big garden to use, one of the *Boys Own* crew, Cymon Eckel, had suggested a fairground inflatable: and so was born the rave cliché of the bouncy castle.

The spirit of acid house was at its height at these happy events. Terry remembers a flock of geese flying out of the dawn mist over a lake. 'All of a sudden everyone started clapping as if we'd organised it. As if they were acid house geese and we'd trained them.' Clubbers would go to great lengths to make the parties memorable: 'There were four cows on a hill about a quarter-of-a-mile away, and someone said, "That cow's dancing". No one believed it, but it really looked like this cow's shaking its leg to the music. Gradually it came closer, down the hill, and it really looks like it's dancing. People are so freaked out they can't look. We watched this dancing cow for a full half-an-hour before we realised... it's Barry Mooncult and a mate inside a pantomime costume.'

As was the case at most early raves, the police were merely bemused. 'They turned up: "What's happening here?",' recalls Farley. 'We said, "Oh, we're from London, we're on these coaches and we're having a party." They went, "There's a few beer cans in the street; can you pick them up." ' These were the innocent times before raves were deemed a threat to a generation. 'A year later they'd be using truncheons,' says Farley.

Larger events soon followed thanks to capitalist prodigy Tony Colston-Hayter. 'Throwing the doors open to everyone became my whole life,' he declared in Sheryl Garratt's *Adventures In Wonderland*. 'Boys Own and Shoom wanted to keep it as their own secret little thing and we wanted to give it to everyone.' Having made money from a video games company, and later from card-counting at blackjack, in 1988 he began organising warehouse parties, including one on Greenwich wasteland (where the battle scenes in *Full Metal Jacket* were shot; now the site of the Millennium Dome), and several in Wembley Studios, which he called Apocalypse Now. But after the scene's first bad press – a Sun newspaper story about Spectrum's 'acid' dealers, and some 'drug-hell' footage on ITN news – resulting in a police raid on his Greenwich party, Colston-Hayter decided to get rural.

On 27 October 1988, ten coaches ferried clubbers from the BBC studios in west London to an equestrian centre in Buckinghamshire for Sunrise, The Mystery Trip. Passengers included most of the acid scene's club promoters, as well as stars including ABC's Martin Fry, Wham!'s Andrew Ridgeley, and Boy George. They arrived to see strobe lights and flaming torches lighting up the sky and then, plunged into darkness except for a single laser, heard Steve Proctor play a set which started with the apocalyptic theme from *2001 A Space Odyssey*. This was the beginning of the 'orbital' or 'M25' parties, named after London's M25 orbital motorway, which had just been completed.

'In the morning, everyone was outside dancing,' recalls Colston-Hayter. 'All the Shoom kids were getting flowers and putting them in their hair and talking to all the horses, like they'd never seen a horse before. Some kids started walking home; they thought they'd get home eventually.'

Raves might well have remained quietly underground had it not been for the tabloids exaggerating things beyond all reason. In between selling its own smiley T-shirts and offering rabid moral condemnation, the Sun told the nation that a few thousand kids were dancing all night on drugs and having sex.

'SPACED OUT! 11,000 YOUNGSTERS GO DRUG CRAZY AT BRITAIN'S BIGGEST EVER ACID HOUSE PARTY.'

The next day, of course, *half a million* kids were asking, 'Where's the party?' With such effective free advertising, in 1989 the rave phenomenon was suddenly of national interest. The drugs aspect was the papers' chief cause for concern, although confused by the name of the music, *acid* house, the newspapers had initially concluded it was LSD they had to fume about. Immediately the fairly accommodating police attitude to raves changed. The BBC banned acid house records from its airwaves and Parliament started brewing up legislation aimed at curbing this evil menace.

Meanwhile, with a scorching summer, 1989 saw the movement explode. The events got larger and more grandiose, with huge sound systems, amazing lasers and lightshows and even funfair rides. The promoters quickly realised the value of new technology, such as mobile phones and reprogrammable telephone message lines, to keep locations secret until the last minute. Incredible scams were pulled off to secure sites and to deflect police interest. There were close links with London's blossoming pirate radio stations. Using messages, which you didn't need to be a wartime code-breaker to figure out, the pirate DJs would advertise the latest secret party rendezvous.

Energy, in May 1989, showed the way. Held in a Shepherd's Bush film studio, it offered dancers the choice of five different rooms, each filled with lasers and built as lavishly as a film set. There was a *Blade Runner* room, Stonehenge, a Greek temple, an Egyptian room and even a sushi bar. Among the DJs were Paul Oakenfold, Trevor Fung, Grooverider, Jazzy M and Nicky Holloway. Jazzy, who was DJing from a twenty-foot-high platform, remembers it as the best gig of his life.

'We were twenty-foot up on the scaffolding that was wobbling about, playing "Strings Of Life" in the middle of the night and everyone going totally mad. Then I stopped it and played it again from the top. Lasers firing everywhere, everyone with their hands in the air. There were probably about five thousand people there. It was amazing.'

East End house crew Hypnosis even took the dance revolution to the 1989 Glastonbury rock festival. Rob Acteson relates how he and fellow DJs Mr C, Linden C and Rhythm Doctor staged their own rave in a car-parking field.

'We wanted to get away with the ultimate outdoor party and spread house music to a new audience at the same time,' says Acteson. 'We had no artist passes or anything . . . we didn't even have a ticket between us.' After a series of scams to gain entry (including moving an entire Portakabin aside) they set up their party.

'By the Friday we'd cranked up the sound system so much we were overpowering the main stage. In the breaks between acts all you could hear across the entire site was our sound.' By the Friday their crowd had swollen to about five hundred people; the next day there were even more. 'Our entire area had become one gigantic rave. Punks, Rastas, hippies, travellers, all going crazy to this weird new music.'

One moment topped off this symbolic invasion. 'The lighting crew from the main stage somehow directed their entire rig to shine on us. It was incredible. It was as if the whole focus of Glastonbury had shifted to us.'

Despite the warmth with which the crowds received them, they were reminded of their outlaw status when the party was broken up in an ugly bust by tooled-up security. But unofficial sound system parties were now a part of the festival.

Sunrise, Biology, Energy, Back To The Future, Genesis, Hypnosis, World Dance – rave companies mushroomed. In the Midlands and the north of England there was Thunderdome, Live The Dream, Joy, Spectrum. As if to put the seal on 1989's year of raving, East End crew Genesis threw a party over Christmas and New Year that lasted five days.

Dance Outlaws

If it feels good, don't do it. That was the message from government. As a knee-jerk reaction to the tabloid horror stories, the Tories passed MP Graham Bright's 1990 Entertainments (Increased Penalties) Act, which drastically upped the penalty for throwing an unlicensed party to £20,000 and six months' imprisonment. Following a series of busts and mass arrests this law did much to curtail the rave phenomenon, but its long-term effect, as it forced the growing scene into properly licensed premises, was to encourage councils to grant clubs later licenses and to bring ecstasy into the mainstream.

Now that raves were clearly illegal, those sections of the great unwashed who thrived on anti-establishment action – travellers, pagans, squatters, eco-warriors – started throwing free parties, the bigger the better, as a continuation of the old hippie festivals. There followed some summer cat and mouse madness as the cops and the travellers played tag, and in 1992, when 25,000 people arrived to dance on Castlemorton Common in Worcestershire to one hundred hours of techno-shamanism from the nation's collected sound systems, the government made it clear they'd had enough. To set an example, members of the Spiral Tribe sound system were arrested and charged with 'conspiracy to cause a public nuisance', only to win their freedom in a court case which cost the taxpayer £4 million. In frustration, John Major's government floored the gas pedal on the passing of their hot new item, the Criminal Justice Act (CJA), a wide-sweeping set of laws which, amongst a hodge-podge of other things, gave police the power to break up a group of people who might be planning a rave and to turn away people traveling to it from as far as five miles away.

This united the outlaws as never before. Travellers, pickets and protesters of any kind all became targets of a single piece of legislation. Although Advance Party, a coalition of sound systems and civil liberties groups, did what they could to bring down the bill, it became law in 1994. The CJA was unique in that it was the first time in Britain that the pop music of a youth culture had been specifically curtailed. That it was compelled to define house and techno, in a famous legal definition, as 'sounds wholly or predominantly characterised by the emission of a succession of repetitive beats', showed just how seriously the government viewed the threat of dance culture, with its combination of music, drugs and hordes of lusty young people. Here was a massive movement over which they had no control.

Meanwhile, it hadn't taken long for things to sour. Some of the original Balearic clubbers had seen raves as a crude cash-in right from the start. 'I hated all that M25 orbital rave shite,' blustered Shoomer Nick Spiers. 'It was too big, too impersonal. Raves were rip-offs! Run by gangsters! Filled with fools!'

At around £15 a ticket and drawing in crowds of up to 20,000, the money soon knocked any lingering idealism out of people. DJs recall asking for their wages and being told to help themselves from a big bag of cash. Promoters remember counting money by simply squeezing it and gauging the thickness of the wedge. Promoters had guns waved in their faces; a Labrynth party saw clubbers attacked by gangsters with machetes. Those motivated by a genuine love of the music were soon overrun by villains either trying to control their doors or putting on their own events purely to make money and sell drugs. Most notorious was the ICF (Inter City Firm), the crime network that had grown out of organised football violence among West Ham supporters. The ICF famously muscled in on most East End parties and many of the raves. They even set up their own (well-known) pirate radio station.

Rob Acteson recalls throwing a rave for about 6,000 people in a Canvey Island property owned by a friend of a high-ranking gangster. Confident they'd cleared about £30,000, after breaking down the sound they went to count the money; it had gone – their host had taken it. 'We went round his house in Canning Town on the Monday,' says Acteson. 'We walked in six-handed. His wife's come out the kitchen with two great big carving knives, "Who the fucking hell do you think you are coming round here?" So we just had to swallow it.'

Wayne Anthony, promoter of the Genesis parties, has written extensively about the seamy side of the raves. He says he paid twenty-five per cent of his takings to 'a well-known firm' as protection money, and claims to have been kidnapped three times by gangs in search of the millions he was supposedly making.

For many, there was quite a wake-up call. DJ Steve Bicknell, who played at Energy, was so wrapped up in the scene's outward idealism, he didn't give money a second thought. 'Then you realise you're playing to twenty thousand people and getting paid £100.' For some, hard commercial reality had dawned much earlier. At an M25 Energy party in 1989 Bicknell recalls watching Paul Oakenfold. 'He was looking at his watch, it was time for him to finish, the other DJ wasn't around. I would have just stood there and carried on DJing, he picked up the phone and negotiated his deal to carry on.'

The police were catching up, too. By the nineties, thanks to the cunning of policeman Ken Tappenden and his specially created Pay Party Unit, promoters found it increasingly difficult to stay a step ahead. Additionally ravers were soon used to paying for tickets to events that delivered a tenth of what they promised, or which didn't exist beyond the promoter's bank account. Also, by this time the club scene had expanded to accommodate the huge numbers of clubbers who had been turned on by the acid house explosion. There was little reason to spend the night driving round unlit highways in search of a party that probably didn't even exist. By the time the Criminal Justice Act was law, the licensing laws had been relaxed a little, and house music had transferred its energy to licensed clubs. Legal, mainstream clubbing was becoming a fact of life

The alcohol interest

Did this shift back to licensed premises come simply from a government's desire to protect its youth, or were there more commercial forces at work? A 1993 report from the Henley Centre estimated the (largely alcohol-free) rave economy at around £2 billion. It also revealed that pub attendance had fallen by 11% between 1982–87, that this decline would double by 1997, and that between 1989–92 the percentage of 16- to 24-year-olds who took illegal drugs had doubled to 30%. This, the report concluded, '. . . poses a significant threat to spending for such sectors as licensed drinks retailers and drink companies.'

As E-takers eschewed alcohol in favour of water or soft drinks like Ribena and Lucozade, the breweries had to fight hard for their market. Enter alcopops, fruit-flavoured alcoholic beverages: potent, colourful new ways of getting drunk, designed and marketed to compete with the psychedelic experience. Starting in 1995 with rival alcoholic lemonades Hooch and Two-Dogs, closely followed by Bacardi Breezers, alcopops became one of the fastest-established product sectors ever: the kings of under-age day-glo vomit.

As well as this marketing masterstroke, the booze barons doubtless fought the threat of ecstasy in more covert ways, perhaps by influencing Parliament's keenness for anti-rave legislation. 'There was a definite boardroom decision taken,' believes Terry Farley, echoing a common attitude among the dance industry. 'They said, "We've gotta get them out of these fields and back into our pubs, how we gonna do this?"' The 1990 Entertainments (Increased Penalties) Act, was proposed by Graham Bright, MP for Luton, home to brewing giant Whitbread.

The UK drinks lobby is certainly powerful enough to get what it wants. At one stage the Parliamentary Beer Club boasted 330 members in Westminster, all keen to further the interests of the nation's breweries and distillers. Who else stood to benefit when the Department of Health raised the recommended weekly levels of alcohol intake by a third, as they did in 1995, despite concerted protest from medical professionals. But perhaps Bright was simply keen to denounce illegal drugs. 'If you're offered cake, just don't take it,' he once advised on spoof TV news programme *Brass Eye* after being told that a new (and fictitious) drug was sweeping the nation.

In 1996 a third law entered the frame when Barry Legg's Public Entertainments (Drug Misuse) Act gave local authorities the power to close nightclubs which didn't prevent drug-taking on their premises. It's easy to see how this again benefited the drinks industry more than any other interests. Now that dance culture was back in the clubs, this act helped ensure that alcohol was the only drug on the menu.

'And now they're the ones that are paying for it with a nation of binge-drinking teenagers,' says Farley. 'Casualties in every major city with glassings and stabbings, when you could have had a nation of loved-up E-takers, not causing any problems.'

Just for the record, official UK Department of Health statistics show that alcohol, a legal drug, kills about 7,000 people a year. Ecstasy, an illegal drug, kills about fifteen.

US rave

Grab your glowsticks, put in your piercings and tie up those pink pigtails. We're going to try some PLUR – Peace Love Unity and Respect. This was the noble slogan adopted by the decade-old American rave movement at the start of our new century. Many were cynical about such innocent idealism – especially from a scene that, in true American style, had grown extremely commodified. Those who'd been involved with US rave in its beginnings were openly contemptuous of the 'candy ravers', many barely into their teens, who espoused PLUR on their sparkling, poetry-filled, jellybean-coloured websites.

But in *The Book Of E*, writer Push argues convincingly that the candy ravers were rebellion incarnate. In the super-consumerist, super-mediated United States, where human contact is most likely to come via a screen, and is probably trying to sell you something, believing in friendliness, kindliness and togetherness is pure teenage rebellion. Hugging someone you've just met is an act of defiance against a cruel, money-driven society. For isolated, anxiety-ridden American youngsters rave was a chance to act their age and play like children.

Ironically, house and techno's pioneers had little to do with the US rave movement. The spread of house into America's suburbs was initially driven by Anglophile American DJs and ex-pat Britons who, having experienced acid house first-hand in the UK, brought it stateside. On the left coast, both Los Angeles and San Francisco found themselves with burgeoning party calendars. The climate and geography encouraged outdoor events and there were lingering psychedelic traditions to draw on. Back east, raves began in New York suburbs as straight white boroughs' kids went crazy over testosterone techno. Here was dance music blasted clean of any lingering gay associations, music Mikey and Vinnie could slam-dance to without looking like fags. 'House is dead, techno lives' read their T-shirts.

The first US house events to borrow the British template were in Los Angeles. In 1988 Orange County DJ Randy Moore – having hung out in London with Paul Oakenfold and Mark Moore earlier that year – put on Sextasy in Los Globos, a Sunset Boulevard dive bar, with fellow promoter Mr Kool-Aid (Steve Enis). Forty clubbers danced to a night of acid house, strobes and fog machines and went home inspired. British ex-pat Michael Cook, realising he'd left Manchester at exactly the wrong time, hooked up with Moore and Enis. 'Personally, I was trying to be part of something that I was hearing about back home, to see if we could make something similar happen there.'Through the nineties Cook would become one of LA's leading DJs.

Sextasy led to a great many larger parties in lofts and derelict warehouses in the south-eastern part of downtown LA, a distinctly cop-free neighbourhood. The promoters set up 'map points' where partygoers could buy directions to the place, effectively the entrance fee. Other 'very druggy' nights were thrown in swish Malibu canyon houses rented out on the side by crafty real estate agents. Things grew ever larger, then on 16 June 1989 Moore, Enis and Cook threw the first of six pioneering parties they called Alice's House. About a thousand people gathered at a huge hall in a community centre called La Casa. 'It was totally mixed. At the beginning in LA it was about fifty per cent gay and fifty per cent straight. A real arty crowd and a lot of Latin kids.' Ecstasy wasn't easily available yet and many clubbers took the name 'acid house' at its word. 'At the very earliest parties it was acid, that was what people took,' laughs Cook. 'They'd heard about "acid house" and they assumed you were supposed to take acid.' There was also a 'paint room' with UV lights and fluorescent paint. 'By four o'clock in the morning, everybody in the party, whether they wanted to or not had paint all over their clothes or their faces.'

Around the same time, OAP (One Almighty Party) started moving their warehouse events from a funk and hip hop soundtrack towards house and rave, and a pair of entrepreneurial Englishmen, the Levy brothers, Steve and Jonathan, did the same with a series of parties called Moonshine and Truth. (They now run Moonshine records, the USA's most successful independent dance label.) With demand growing, in the nineties LA raves expanded into the studios and theme parks of the surrounding counties, later travelling further for desert parties and even for raves on Indian reservations.

New York began emulating acid house in 1989, when DJ DB, newly arrived from London, launched proto-rave night Deep, and then Madchester homage Orange, for the city's homesick Brits. In July 1992, with lighting star Scotto and fellow DJs Soulslinger and Jason Jinx, DB started a weekly rave-in-a-club, NASA. Because it was staged at Manhattan's Shelter (a club fuelled on memories of the Paradise Garage) this was a high-profile assault on New York's original house community. Lasting for just a year, and with a crowd that got younger every week, NASA was a focal point for US rave. It was the setting for the film *Kids* and the place where the infantile candy raver style was born – all those tent-sized trousers, baby's dummies and day-glo furry rucksacks (other atrocities included Mickey Mouse ears and even oven gloves). The music was hard, fast and unrelenting, with 150bpm breaks the order of the day. DB remembers the polarising effect of this new music. 'The English posse that I'd been hanging around with absolutely ditched me. They couldn't handle the fact that the music was full-on rave at this point, banging hard breakbeats. So I got this new generation of kids who were up for anything.' These were the first Americans who grew up on house and techno instead of rock and rap.

In Brooklyn things were a little tougher. Frankie Bones's Storm Raves, set in derelict brickyards and other gritty locations, attracted an older crowd – more working class, largely Hispanic and Italian-American – for nights of unrepentant hardcore. Bones had risen to fame for his 'Bonesbreaks' breakbeat techno tracks which he started releasing in 1988. On the strength of these, in 1989 he'd been flown over to London to play at an Energy rave. Already high from DJing to so many people, a week later he took his first E at Rage and vowed to take the acid house blueprint back home with him. At his first parties he would run videos of British raves as if they were educational films. By 1991 the Storm raves were going full steam, promoted with his brother Adam X and his girlfriend Heather Hart (who started US rave fanzine *Under One Sky*). Bones's store, Groove Records, became the hangout for the city's techno generation: DJs like Lennie Dee, Joey Beltram and Damon Wild. But his wind was taken by a former friend, the sinister Michael Caruso who, as Lord Michael, muscled in with his own events (amid rumours that would have filled a whole *Sopranos* script); by 1992 these were housed in Manhattan's Limelight, quickly the epicentre of US hardcore techno.

Ironically, San Francisco, host to the original Summer of Love, was late to put on raves. Straight clubbers saw house as too gay; the gay scene was still wedded to hi-energy. DJ Doc Martin tried with his Recess nights, as Pete Avila did with Osmosis. But around 1990, having failed to get San Francisco interested in house, Doc gave up and moved to LA. It took a British invasion to get things moving.

The Wicked crew had been part of Tonka, an idealistic Cambridge sound system that spawned DJs including Harvey and Choci. After UK raving turned sour, Tonka's Jenö, Garth, Markie Mark and London promoter Alan McQueen had settled in California where they found themselves treated as cultural gurus. 'We were admired for being English,' Jenö told Mireille Silcott in her book *Rave America*. 'That interest in us allowed us to set down our own blueprint for what became rave in San Francisco. We took the acid house smiley face and had whistles and strobes – things we would never have done in England at that time.' Their Full Moon parties ran from 1991 to 1994, by which time they'd attract as many as 3,000 ravers, all blissed out on a remote beach as the sun came up.

Another Brit, journalist Mark Heley, had his own ideas of what US rave could be, and used his Toon Town parties to promote the esoteric ideas which filled future-gazing magazine *Mondo 2000*. From virtual reality and fluorescent 'smart drinks' to cybersex and group consciousness, Heley didn't just throw parties, he sold people an entire head-bursting lifestyle. As Silcott writes, kids left Toon Town, 'as capital-R Ravers. As in Rave is something you are, not just something you do.'

Understandably there was a backlash against all this British imperialism. In rave mag *XLR8R*, Sunshine Jones of house act Dubtribe wrote, 'House music is a national treasure, a national spiritual treasure. I don't know why this city needed British people to educate them on something that was born here.' The Brits took the rap for everything that had grown wrong with the scene and San Francisco raving was born again, this second wave led by the mouthy and ambitious DJ trio the Hardkiss Brothers (Scott Friedel, Robbie Cameron, Gavin Bieber).

Florida developed its own quirky scene too. In Orlando, a smilingly dull city effectively owned by Disney, DJs Kimball Collins and Dave Canalte and promoter/goddess/nutcase Stace Bass created a house scene at their club Oz which grew in near-perfect parallel to the UK's, heavily influenced by John Digweed and Sasha's frequent trips to the Sunshine State. Orlando was also where the thriving breaks movement emerged around DJ Icey's hybrid of Miami bass hip hop and breakbeat house. They called it 'funky breaks' at first, but when the Hardkiss-led west coasters came up with a similar sound it became 'coastal breaks'. Now it's global we can thankfully just call it 'breaks'.

The birth of US rave was an effective year zero for dance music in America. There were some connections made with the original house scenes, particularly in Chicago and Detroit, but by and large it gained pace by breaking ties with the old centres, instead making stars of suburban outposts like Milwaukee, San Diego, Baltimore, Portland and Orlando. Most of this second generation were ignorant that house had ever worn a black or gay face. Surely this comes from London? Ibiza? Headline visits by Carl Cox, Sasha and Oakenfold only reinforced this impression. But by 2000 there was a generation of home-grown DJs whose skills and music had matured on the US party circuit: DJs like Terry Mullan, DJ Dan, Josh Wink, Derrick Carter, Taylor, Micro, Onionz, Keoki. And after trance took hold the list of indigenous stars grew by the week. The party calendar was filled with huge events, fuelled almost entirely via the internet, which filled with rave sites offering forums, chat rooms, photos and downloadable DJ mixes.

US anti-rave legislation

Then all this exciting energy was squashed. The first moves against DJ culture came in mid-nineties New York. Just as the city's tastes were splintering, and smaller nights with more intriguing styles were flourishing, along came Mayor Rudolph Giuliani. Suddenly 'NO DANCING' signs were the norm in bars, and they weren't kidding. In his mad monk mission to turn the city into a quiet Connecticut suburb, Giuliani dusted off the long-ignored laws relating to cabaret licences. Without such a licence, if more than two or three barflies were seen to be moving rhythmically, the police were quite entitled to raid the place, fine it or even close it down. And they did.

As the rave movement boomed, such extremism went national as the press 'informed' mainstream America about ecstasy. Sensational scare stories were aired until mom and pop were convinced little Jimmy could die from touching a glowstick. Local agencies scrambled for laws they could use to close down anywhere with turntables, and cried out for immediate capital punishment for anyone who uttered the word 'rave'.

In 2001 the owners of Club La Vela in Panama City Beach, the largest club in Florida, faced twenty years in jail and a possible $500,000 fine when they were tried for running parties where drug use took place. Prosecutors attempted to use a 1986 law framed against the owners of crack houses. The case failed since, instead of any seized drugs, as evidence of drug dealing the jury was shown BlowPops candy, chewing gum, glowsticks and a picture of a guy massaging his friend.

In Racine, Wisconsin in 2003 police raided a rave and under local bylaws fined everyone they found in the techno room $968 each. It took the full weight of the American Civil Liberties Union to squash the charges.

Rather than question the absurdity of such cases, or the ethics of a law that criminalises people for the actions of their customers, the Federal legislature pressed on and the RAVE Act (Reducing Americans' Vulnerability to Ecstasy) was the result. This effectively targets not drug dealers, but promoters and venue owners. Not criminals but the musical culture in which they operate. The RAVE Act failed when it was debated in 2002. Undeterred, its sponsors slipped it unnoticed into a Bill about child abduction and it became law, largely without debate, in 2003.

The effect has been to paralyse the dance movement. 'It's had a chilling effect,' says Bill Piper of the Drug Policy Alliance, a pressure group advocating a more rational approach to anti-drug legislation. 'Lots of promoters have said "we're not going to do electronic music events any more; we're going to do other types of events". People would go out to nightclubs and find that glowsticks were banned. You weren't allowed to dance with glowsticks because the venue owners were afraid that that could constitute a rave and they could be arrested.'

A quick online perusal shows the death of a culture. The wild proliferation of rave sites five years ago has disappeared; the few remaining carry eulogies – 'For those of us who were there, raves are a memory that will last forever.'

At first glance it seems the US legislature has wiped out an entire youth culture because of its connections to drugs. What's most worrying is that harm-reduction efforts, like providing a good supply of drinking water, are also seen as evidence that a venue is colluding with drug dealers, so these laws act to make raving more dangerous and *increase* ecstasy casualties. Indeed, showing you've made an effort to prevent drug use at a party is no defence, leaving venue owners stuck in a Catch 22 – alerting the authorities to drug dealing in your club could land you in jail, but so could not telling them about it. In an even more outrageous trampling of civil liberties, Montana Drug Enforcement Agency officials even tried to use the legislation to close down an event before it started. The DEA says it has drafted guidelines for safe, respectable raves, but they won't make these public because evil criminals might turn them to their advantage.

However, some promoters say that while these measures are harsh and unfair, they are not the reason for the dying scene. 'It hasn't affected me one bit,' insists Chris Love, who has promoted some of the biggest parties on the east coast. 'I've always worked closely with the authorities. I never have any loose ends. The only people I know who've had run-ins and problems, they just didn't have their shit together.' Love, who admits he's moving his events more to rock and hip hop, puts it down to commercialisation and a general dance music downturn. 'The rave scene killed itself with the greed coming from a lot of the booking agencies. DJs feel like they're rock stars, signing exclusive deals with clubs. That killed the independent promoter.'

Nevertheless, raves are clear targets for the American authorities' increasingly fascist tendencies. As we're writing, a video clip is making the rounds showing a raid on a desert rave of about 1,000 kids in Utah. It looks like a fairly mild-mannered crowd; the DJs seem remarkably sober. Apparently the organisers believed they had filed all the correct permits, arranging security, ambulance cover and full liability insurance. Despite this the National Guard staged a surprise attack that wouldn't have been out of place in Iraq. The video shows soldiers in full battledress, toting assault rifles, knocking teenagers to the ground and demanding that cameras be turned off, as a helicopter hovers overhead spotlighting the scene. One of the DJs reports that tear gas was released into the crowd, a girl was attacked by a police dog and then kicked in the stomach by three men, while a guardsman shouted 'get the fuck out of here or go to jail'.

When the promoter produced his permit it was allegedly torn up and a gun put to his forehead.

Liberty? Freedom of expression? These are supposedly values worth going to war for.

Women DJs

One cultural side-effect of acid house was the freedom it gave to women to be DJs. In the rushing years at the end of the eighties, anything seemed possible, even the idea that a woman could enter this most male of professions and not be laughed out from behind the decks. DJing's maleness is largely a historical thing and in recent years women DJs have progressed to being, if not sizeable in number, at least a number worth counting. And while some are content to exploit club culture's essential sexism to get ahead, thankfully there are plenty today who are judged on their music rather than their cleavage.

Throughout this book the DJ is 'he' and this is not just a matter of grammatical simplicity. In a century of DJing, women have been largely frozen out of the picture, with precious few exceptions. Until recently the music world has always been very much a boys' club, with women restricted to turning out some vocals for the lads. Like musicianship, DJing has usually been passed on from master to apprentice in an almost masonic manner, making it a tough clique to crack – doubly so for a woman. It's also highly significant that much of early dance culture revolved around gay men, so in most of the important New York and Chicago clubs women were in the clear minority – they were hardly encouraged to step up and play a few tunes. Just look at a few flyers or this month's dance mags to see what skills are sought in female clubbers. And of course the blame must also be levelled at the wider culture. The notion of girls tampering with anything that isn't a typewriter, cooker or cash till is, sadly, relatively new.

The disco era mostly saw women confined to being decorative fixtures on the dancefloor, although New York's Fire Island circuit enjoyed the DJing talents of Sharon White and, latterly, Susan Moribito. In Los Angeles in the early seventies British expatriate Jane Brinton (who became Junior Vasquez's manager) ran a pioneering mobile disco. Later, given the freedoms of post-punk New York, Anita Sarko gained a solid reputation as DJ at Danceteria.

But arguably it was the advent of acid house in the UK, with its have-a-go spirit, that did most to encourage women to take up DJing seriously. Lisa Loud and Nancy Noise, Smokin' Jo, Sister Bliss and Rachel Auburn led the way, and in their footsteps there have been many more. Although the current UK DJ premiership is still a boys-only arena, Lottie is knocking at the door and the championship now includes DJs like Lisa Lashes, Lisa Pin-up and Anne Savage. And even in the far more sexist US, women like Sandra Collins, Jeannie Hopper and DJ Heather are breaking through.

Newer forms of music have less ingrained prejudices and fewer gender barriers. 'Techno and drum and bass – those scenes are more open to female DJs,' says New York's DJ Cosmo. 'These girls grew up with computers and electronics, so it was no big deal to them.' Sure enough, drum and bass gave us Kemistry & Storm, and DJ Rap, who quit her day job as a topless model and became the first female drum and bass producer signed to a major label. Admirably (apart from a pneumatic album cover photo) she blocked any attempts to use her past career as a promotional gimmick. In the US, techno threw up its own stars, with DJ Moneypenny a regular fixture in late eighties New York, while in Chicago there is the fierce duo of Teri Bristol and Psychobitch. And more recently, the UK garage scene has produced its share of talented female DJs, including Donna Dee and DJ Touch. 'Things are changing,' says Cosmo. 'It's not that big of a deal to be a female DJ any more and I think that's great. The less people ask me about it the better.'

'Do whatever you want to do, as long as you can cut it up on the decks,' advises DJ Dazy, who runs an email forum for women DJs. 'Just don't wear a bikini top while you're train-wrecking records. If you don't have the skills, don't embarrass the rest of us women DJs who have worked really hard to get where we are.'

Pirate radio

In pondering the truth of the DJ's outlaw nature, pirate radio offers an intriguing insight. On the one hand, it's the embodiment of his drive to spread music, whatever the consequences. It's a vital underground service, the disseminator of all the tunes too hot and subversive for the legal stations. On the other hand, pirate radio often derives from surprisingly commercial motives, even when its programming is the exact opposite. Pirate radio is all about filling a gap in the market.

'*Call up and put in your code for the reload.*'

Turn on the radio in London (and in most major UK cities) and wedged next to the latest dirge from Coldplay you'll hear a clattering of upfront beats and red-hot street slang: on Rush, Kool, Fresh, Freek, Magic, London Underground or one of about twenty other pirates that spring up and die down daily. Move your dial a whisker and the trebly tones of UK garage will blend into some kicking drum and bass. Move it another millimetre and you'll hear some ragga, or some militant R&B. If it's night time you'll probably hear the urgent grunts of an MC; if it's daylight there'll be some slightly dazed announcements delivered in gapped-out interracial 'cockney'. And whenever the music gets too relaxing, there'll be some girl in an echoey council flat shouting at you to go to some Essex lock-up for a party with fifty different DJs.

The pirate scene is a fast-paced test bed for new music, inextricably linked to whatever underground dance scenes currently have the most momentum. It's here you'll find records belonging to genres that don't even have names yet, broadcast by DJs who are risking a lot to bring you them. If a station gets raided by the authorities, its DJ can face up to six months in jail. Worse, he could have his records confiscated.

Pirate radio takes its name from the outlaw stations of the sixties which actually broadcast from ships moored out in the North Sea and English Channel. These original pirates were started not by rebels, but by entrepreneurs breaking the law to create commercial radio. The airwaves were tied up by the nationalised monopoly of the BBC, so there was ad money in them thar ships.

The first challenger to the BBC was Leonard Plugge's Radio Normandie, which started transmissions to the south coast of England in 1931 from the small French town of Fécamp. In 1934 Radio Luxembourg followed suit, transmitting UK-wide using an aerial hoisted up the Eiffel Tower in Paris. Luxembourg, with Gus Goodwin in the fifties and Tony 'The Royal Ruler' Prince through the sixties, was known for programming a fair amount of black music, and broadcast well into the nineties.

But most famous of them all was Radio Caroline, a ship-based station launched in 1964 by a flamboyant Irishman, Ronan O'Rahilly, who had earlier run the Scene Club in Soho. Such was the unmet demand for a pop music radio station that Caroline received 20,000 fan letters within ten days of its initial transmission and within three weeks had attracted seven million listeners. The station was swiftly followed by a gamut of copyists, among them Radios Sutch, 390, England, Britain, 270, Scotland, and Caroline's more popular and closest rival, Radio London. 'Nobody loves the Pop Pirates – except the listeners,' wrote the *Daily Sketch* in 1965.

The government legislated against the pirates, forcing them to close, and in 1967 the BBC's monolithic pop station Radio One was launched to take the last breath of wind out of the pirates' sails (Radio One hired most of its first DJs from the pirates). But Caroline and London had already shown that the airwaves didn't belong to the government. Anyone with minimal technical ability could broadcast whatever they wanted. In 1971, a schoolboy in Matlock was fined £5 for transmitting pop music to friends at school on equipment which had cost him just 50p to build. He was one of seventy-eight people prosecuted that year for pirate broadcasting.

In the seventies land-based pirates emerged, many serving London's growing black communities. One such station was Radio Invicta, the first to exclusively programme soul. With its slogan 'Soul Over London', Invicta started broadcasting in 1970 from a council maisonette in Mitcham – *Time Out* reported in 1972 that its aim was 'to inform the audience of the freaky deaky discos'. By the start of the eighties there were over two dozen stations operating in the London area alone. As the decade progressed, the number increased and included Rebel Radio, based in Ladbroke Grove, London Weekend Radio (LWR), and Dread Broadcasting Corporation, the city's most popular reggae station.

The acid house years gave a huge burst of energy to pirate radio, which grew inextricably linked to the rave movement. LWR and Kiss FM, an enterprising station broadcasting out of south east London, were the voices of London's clubland through the eighties, and although they were identified more with rare groove, thanks to Colin Faver and Jazzy M, they were also the first stations to play house in London. Things changed dramatically at the beginning of 1989 when Kiss and LWR took themselves off air in attempts to win legal licenses. Immediately a new breed of acid house pirates took over, starting in May 1989 with Centreforce, which broadcast the new music twenty-four hours a day from tower blocks in Stratford. Many point to this as the moment when acid house became unstoppable. Fantasy, Sunrise, Obsession and Dance FM soon joined the throng, as did pirates in Manchester and Birmingham, all advertising the weekend's raves and announcing motorway meeting points on the night. They blasted out the kind of DJ-driven mix shows taken for granted nowadays, but which were then completely new to UK radio.

Danny Rampling has fond memories of broadcasting from a twenty-third-floor flat in a Hackney tower block belonging to dub DJ trio Manasseh.

'It had this magnificent view all over the whole of London. And when house was blowing up, that whole energy and feeling and being twenty-three floors up looking out over the city – that was a very exciting moment for me. And people would be locked into Kiss during that time. It was very popular. I'd made this transition from playing independent soul to playing this wonderful new musical form. Breaking that new music on Kiss, that just felt amazing.' In autumn 1990 Kiss secured a government licence and became fully legal, London's first dedicated dance music station.

In recent years, the pirates have been key to underground music. Jungle and UK garage evolved on the airwaves as much as in the clubs. Dave Stone of jungle label SOUR definitely thinks so. 'Without the pirates I don't think there'd be a scene. Everyone else reviled hardcore. The pirates formed to meet a natural need for people to hear this music.' And despite rising penalties, the pirates remain a serious force. This outlaw medium has defined the way upfront urban music reaches the world. When the BBC launched 1Xtra, a station to cover garage, grime and UK hip hop, it took its entire image and broadcast style, not to mention all its DJs, from the pirates. Just as Radio One had done back in 1967.

Now, of course there is internet radio, making it simple for anyone with a PC, Shoutcast software and decent bandwidth to broadcast whatever they like. But while this is great for specific genres and dedicated music communities, it is narrowcasting, not broadcasting: it's preaching to the converted. Powerful and democratic the internet may

be, but it's hardly going to wake up whole cities to new music like the
pirates did when their outlaw DJs ruled the waves.

Keep it locked.

Outlaw?

After house music put the DJ centre stage, he found himself driving a
whole generation in a way previously known only by revolutionaries and
rock stars. The DJ's ensuing dance revolution has had an undeniable social
impact. In the structures it encouraged, like after-hours clubs, raves and
pirate radio, it was a serious force for lawbreaking. And let's not forget an
enormous trade in recreational drugs. But is the DJ intrinsically an
outlaw? Or is it just coincidence?

The DJ has an envied ability to turn individuals into a collective mass,
but does he ever use it to generate more than just escapist enjoyment?
Well certainly he has in the past. Consider the first radio disc jockeys,
who were seen as a dangerous threat to the music business's status quo.
Or the early black radio DJs who gave their listeners a sense of pride in
their identity a full twenty years before James Brown said 'I'm black and
I'm proud.' Or rock'n'roll propagator Alan Freed, who was scapegoated as
an outlaw by the US government. In Jamaica, amid the island's
tumultuous politics, the sound systems could, and did, turn elections.
Disco's early DJs strove to tell a message with their music, and though
today the dancefloor ideals they propagated – of love, tolerance and
equality – may sound banal after years of repetition, they are remembered
by many as having a potent and tangible force back when racism and
homophobia made them sorely needed. Hip hop, the defiant voice of
black America that is consumed so eagerly by its white youth, has had an
undeniable socio-political agenda ever since the DJ told his MC to rap
about more than just the party. And, when they harnessed the power of
collective action to create whole smiley cities for a night, acid house DJs
were changing people's perspectives forever. Leslie Lawrence sees acid
house as undeniably life-changing: 'House brings change. We've all seen
this. It changes people. Why would anyone in authority support anything
which changes people? Especially music.'

Even without all this, a good DJ is an outlaw in another sense, because
he challenges what is musically safe and accepted. Some have such a
strong desire to evangelise that if established routes aren't available they
will happily break the law to do it. Thinking back to his days as a pirate
DJ, Pete Tong says it didn't even feel illegal.

'It was like a hobby, and the fact that you were so bothered about
doing it, and you would bother to go to such great lengths to do it, it
seemed like, "What do you mean, it's illegal?" '

But now that club culture is an established commercial force in most of the world, it is easy for a DJ to become successful by simply playing the game, without ever taking any risks. Some very famous DJs are content to champion whatever big tune the labels send out, confident that merely by being able to play it months before it's released they will look brave and innovative.

'The majority of DJs are not subversive at all; they're extremely conventional,' asserts Coldcut's Jonathan More, 'because DJing's been completely co-opted by the establishment as a tool, as much as everything else has.' So while DJing has a rich history of subversion, there is much pulling the DJ in the other direction. Some of the most exciting musical revolutionaries end up as boring old farts. Once they taste success, they're happy to let the mainstream snap them up and package them for the masses.

Dom Phillips, former editor of *Mixmag*, agrees. 'They're quite content to stay in with the record companies. They're quite content to stay in with the clubs, because it's their business.' He points out that while the best DJs are cultural outlaws, they are far from rebels when it comes to business. 'Throughout dance music's history it has always been ruthlessly opportunistic, entrepreneurial and capitalist. It's always been about making money.'

'You can join the club or you can stand outside and stick two fingers up,' adds More. 'It just depends which type of DJ you want to be.'

NINETEEN
SUPERSTAR

God Is A DJ

'The DJ for me was literally god. In the ghetto. To be coming of age in a time when that person was such a star was just incredible for me. It's affected my whole life. I can remember looking at a big stack of speakers and going, "Money! – this shit is like some kind of altar!" '

– Fab 5 Freddy

Frank Skinner: 'It's the coolest thing, the guitar.'

Eric Clapton: '*Used* to be. It's DJs now.'

Out of the darkness 400 drummers start beating a curious rhythm based on an ancient folk dance. A crowd of 72,000 sits in rapt attention inside a vast, purpose-built stadium, never used before tonight. The drums echo through the night air, changing their rhythms gradually until they're all marking out a slow thump . . . thump . . . like a giant heartbeat. It's the sound of anticipation. Then lights flame into action, giant sprays of water erupt across the flooded field and sheets of fire and coloured lasers begin to dance. Some ceremonial speeches, then a display of huge, animated sculptures and a group of dancers acting out classical dramas. Finally, an announcer declares, 'The great moment has come.' A muscled figure leads hundreds of smiling young people into the stadium. Up above all this, seen live by four-and-a-half billion people across the world . . . DJ Tiësto puts on his first track.

The Olympic opening ceremony. Not a bad gig if you can get it; Athens 2004 was the first time a DJ had performed. Tiësto played for an hour-and-a-half as the athletes paraded in, dropping several specially created tunes of his own along the way. 'The opportunity to perform my music for billions of people around the globe will be the greatest highlight of my life,' he said beforehand. All in a day's work for Tijs Verwest, former mobile jock and one-time gabber producer from Breda in Holland, now Tiësto – The Best DJ In The World, as voted by the readers of *DJmag* for an unmatched three years in succession.

Steering clear of anything too progressive, which he feels is a little downbeat, Tiësto plays a syrupy blend of universally accessible trance. When he DJs, orchestral melodies sweep around the room like epic film scores, sighing breakdowns give pause enough to put the kettle on, and percussion punches in like a squadron of planes carpet-bombing the dancefloor. It's Disney dance music; uplifting, blissful, a magic kingdom of euphoria. Indeed, to launch his 2005 CD he played in front of Sleeping Beauty's castle.

Tiësto's statistics match any rockstar's. He was the first DJ to fill a 25,000-seater stadium for a solo performance (you can buy the DVD); he recently sold 50,000 tickets for a Dutch gig in an hour and a half; he's won countless awards from dance music organisations worldwide. He is a member of the Order of the Oranje Nassau in Holland, the Dutch equivalent of a British knighthood. There's even a waxwork Tiësto in the Amsterdam Madame Tussauds. Tiësto's website calls him The Best DJ In The World in the same way Michael Jackson was The King of Pop. In 2004 he was discussing arrangements for a US tour promoting his album. He'd had so many requests from promoters he could have played a different town in America every night for a year. Tiësto earns a five-figure sum for a night of playing records. As he said recently, 'It feels like one long orgasm, and it keeps on going. What more could I wish for?'

A star is born

In Britain in the nineties, the DJ became a superstar. The disc jockey has always enjoyed a certain power over the dancers in his club because of the amount of pleasure he can dispense, but away from the dancefloor he had mostly been a rather anonymous figure. Suddenly his status was magnified a thousand-fold and he was treated like a rock god or a pop idol. DJs could play outside of their home town, even overseas, and draw a crowd, they were interviewed in magazines, clubbers began to know what they looked like. People even started describing their musical tastes not in terms of genres or records but by reference to particular DJs.

Capitalising on this change, and indeed encouraging it, were the promoters, who vied with each other to have the most impressive DJ line-ups, often hyping up visiting jocks to godlike status. Soon, the right name on a flyer could make or break a particular club night – and DJs' earnings rocketed accordingly.

'When I started DJing, the DJ was just below glass collector in order of importance in a nightclub,' recalls Norman Cook. 'You were just the bloke who stood in the corner and put records on.' After his chart success as Fatboy Slim, Cook became such a massive draw that promoters often kept his name off a flyer, fearing crowds way in excess of their club's capacity. He's aware that clubbers' response to him has as much to do with his fame as his DJing. 'People go bonkers from the moment I walk on rather than me earning it,' he says. 'You only hope you're worthy of it.'

Around 2000 he was in such demand that he was regularly offered what he considers 'silly money' for a night playing records – figures so high that he found it difficult to refuse. 'Sometimes, the money I get paid I think, "*Fuck*, this is just stupid." I'm worth *some* money, and I've put in the years and paid my dues, but if there's a DJ getting paid £50 and I'm getting paid five grand, I couldn't say I was a hundred times better. I could say I was better than him. I might even say I was twice as good as him, but there's *no* way that I'm a hundred times better than him.'

As we waved goodbye to the last century, the Millennium celebrations showed just how out of hand it had all become – top-rank DJs were demanding fees well into five, even six figures for a single performance. A far cry from the pioneers of the craft, who would play seven nights a week for less money than the bartender. When Francis Grasso was told that today's above-average DJ is paid about a grand he said, confused, 'What . . . a month?'

Like playing a guitar onstage, playing records in a nightclub puts you in the spotlight. However much he might try to submerge his ego and break down the artist/audience boundary, the DJ can't escape being the focus for the dancers' excitement. Clubbers – lost in a world of bodies, music and perhaps brain-altering chemicals – can't help but project their peak experiences onto the DJ. And when a DJ is particularly skilled at steering the emotions in a room, all kinds of heightened feelings can be directed his way.

In the UK, it was the belated arrival of mixing that took the emphasis away from the songs and gave it to the DJ. Danny Rampling remembers how this got a little out of hand at his pioneering acid house night, Shoom. People there were enjoying very powerful new experiences related to the drugs, the sweeping mix of music and the feelings of communion which the club generated. Rampling's role as DJ made him the focus for all this.

'There was a period at Shoom where a group of people was trying to hail me as this new messiah. It quite frightened me, because it was so intense. One guy opened a page in the Bible, and my name – Daniel – was in the Bible in this particular paragraph. And he said, "This is you! This is you! This is what's happening now!" And that completely flipped me out.'

While they are rarely raised to such explicitly messianic status, most DJs have stories about the absurd lengths fans will go to show their awe. David Morales remembers playing in Yellow, one of Tokyo's biggest clubs.

The DJ booth was full of people watching his every move, trying to observe the source of his magic. He remembers feeling slightly embarrassed at the level of worship, wanting to defuse it, wanting to tell them, 'I'm just playing records, I'm not doing anything. *You* can do this.' But later in the evening, things got stranger. As the energy levels rose, the dancers down on the dancefloor started scrabbling at the high wall at the front of the DJ booth: 'They literally wanted to climb over the walls, up to the box. It was amazing.'

Many can report that playing records well has greatly increased their sexual attractiveness. Not a breed famous for their looks, DJs were quick to take advantage of this and welcomed their unlikely new role as sex symbols. Though they never reached the rock monster heights of figures such as Van Halen's David Lee Roth (who at the peak of his fame once took seventeen women to bed with him), DJs started to attract groupies. When DJ-mania was at its peak in the mid nineties, it became the end-of-the-night norm to have a couple of underdressed club vixens carry your records and escort you to your hotel room. Some of these 'jockey sluts' were quite serious about their collecting. A DJ friend admitted that he'd gone back for a night of passion with a British girl in a New York hotel room. In the morning, as she showered, he found a copy of dance magazine Mixmag opened at a page with his face shining out and a felt-tip ring around it. Worse – there was also a handwritten list of British DJs with his name at the bottom.

At Shelley's in Stoke-on-Trent, such was their admiration for the resident DJ's talents that the club's regulars built him into a real hero. At the end of each night, this DJ – a Welshman named Sasha – found a queue of people waiting to shake his hand. Guys even asked him to kiss their girlfriends.

Seeing this kind of DJ adoration, the industry – from record companies to promoters to magazines – sensed a lucrative trend and jumped aboard. In time Sasha would become red hot property as a guest DJ and the first to release a remix album under his own name. In December 1991, *Mixmag* put him on its cover with the line: 'SASHA MANIA – THE FIRST DJ PIN-UP?' The magazine stood to benefit greatly if DJs became stars, and it pulled no punches in promoting Sasha, and others like him, from local nightclub legends towards more stratospheric fame. 'We were accused at the time of creating the idea of a DJ superstar,' recalls Dom Phillips, then the magazine's assistant editor.

Sasha's stardom was quite genuine. His audience reacted as they did because his music – stirring concertos of acappellas and piano-laden house – was generating very powerful emotions. Admittedly, ecstasy was a con-tributing factor, but it was his skill as a DJ, his ability to connect with his dancers, that made Sasha a star. In fact, he resented the way *Mixmag* over-hyped him. In 1994 when the magazine put him on the cover as 'SON OF GOD?', he argued so much with Dom Phillips, by then editor, that the two had an impromptu wrestling match outside Ministry of Sound.

'I was never comfortable on the cover of magazines,' he says. 'Hated it, hated doing that sort of stuff, but it's part of the game isn't it?' Having risen to such fame that he's enjoyed private jets and police escorts (and once even had an impostor playing gigs in his name), Sasha is the first to admit the difference that media hype made to his profile. 'As soon as I was on the cover of *Mixmag* I suddenly started getting people from Australia ringing me up to book me. And touring the world. Without my covers of *Mixmag* I wouldn't have been able to develop my career the way I have.'

There are several precedents for the kind of DJ stardom that happened in the UK. The New York disco DJs were famous in their own closed world, and as hip hop rocked the planet, many DJs, especially Grandmaster Flash, enjoyed considerable recognition; although as Flash points out, most people were utterly confused by the notion of a famous DJ: 'People still didn't know what I did, or thought I was a rapper,' he says.

In the mid eighties, John 'Jellybean' Benitez became the first DJ to be signed as an artist for a major label album deal, after he had shot to world-wide fame for his early eighties remix work. Several other New York star DJs – Shep Pettibone, Tee Scott, François Kevorkian and Larry Levan – had name recognition as remixers, but Jellybean somehow eclipsed them all. Some suggest that it was because he was a rare straight guy in the gay world of New York dance music. Others put it down to the fact that he was Madonna's boyfriend. But most point to his club stardom as DJ at the wild, huge Funhouse. Here he was such a hero that girls would show up wearing T-shirts reading 'LAST NIGHT JELLYBEAN SAVED MY LIFE'. Certainly, anyone who can get James Brown to repeatedly grunt out their name on a record (as Jellybean had managed on James Brown's 'Spillin' The Beans') had to be doing something right.

Even then, the UK was much more accepting of the DJ's fame than was the US. *Billboard*'s former dance editor Brian Chin remembers Jellybean telling him of visiting England and being hounded for auto-graphs. 'And I remember the week I saw his picture on the back of *Number One* magazine, I thought, "Jeez, this would never happen in America." '

Guest DJs and visiting Americans

Perhaps the greatest single factor in making the DJ a star was the practice of hiring guest DJs. Promoters found that a big-name, out-of-town jock could give a considerable boost to a club night's fortunes. To keep up with the demand for their services, the best DJs started playing two, sometimes three gigs a night, eating up thousands of miles of motorway a week, and flying off to Germany, Italy and Japan – where DJ fever was also raging. It was soon standard for a top DJ to roll into a club, play for just two hours, collect his inflated fee and rush off to another engagement.

This was severely damaging to the craft of DJing, as it encouraged jocks to show up with a lot of bombastic tunes, flashy tricks and prepared mixes, rather than develop any real rapport with a crowd. And it severely limited the musical attention span of the average British clubber. How-ever, this was undoubtedly what made the DJ a star. As he took over from the club's resident DJ for a brief couple of hours, the guest spinner was treated like a chart-topping band. The crowd applauded as he came on, watched his every move, and screamed whenever he did anything clever.

Soon there was a national circuit for guest DJs; even the tiniest towns with the pokiest clubs somehow hired a few big names once in a while. Agencies sprang up to organise their bookings, club magazines thrived by offering national listings of who was playing where, and clubbers took to driving to other cities to hear their favourite DJs, something that hadn't much happened since the heyday of northern soul. DJs were regularly earning four-figure sums for each two-hour set they could squeeze in. Some admitted that earning so much money was ridiculous; others began to take themselves very seriously.

The notion of the DJ as guest star was helped in no small part by Britain's fetish for visiting American DJs, which peaked around 1994. In the years after house music established itself throughout UK nightlife, clubbers dug deep into their pockets to hear its founding fathers perform. It was much the same as Chuck Berry playing here in the wake of fifties rock'n'roll fever. Bucketloads of hype were added to the equation – it wasn't cheap to fly someone over and money had to be recouped, so the American DJs were given all the hoopla of the second coming. Naturally, they jumped at the chance to make some real money – even the big guns were still only earning a maximum of $500 a night in their native land.

The biggest were all from New York: Masters At Work, David Morales, Todd Terry, Tony Humphries and Frankie Knuckles. Of these, Todd Terry earned the most money, anything between £7,000 and £10,000. And for this he played a two- or three-hour set composed entirely of his own material. Todd, known by some as 'God', remains ruthlessly sanguine about this, delighting in the fact that he can earn such money while shamelessly promoting his own productions. 'I'm not a DJ. I am a producer,' he says flatly. 'I DJ for money, 'cos I get paid for it.' Lesser stars of American dance music were also able to make a healthy living outside their own country. The leading lights of Detroit and Chicago, revered as they were by the connoisseurs, made occasional trips here and were treated as visiting deities by the trainspotters, as were certain European techno jocks like Sven Väth and Laurent Garnier.

At one stage, such was the draw of an American name on a flyer that several were able to earn money despite being pretty lousy DJs. British audiences knew them solely through their production and remix work, but once the Americans realised how much they could earn in the UK, quite a few producers who had never been DJs hurriedly learned some basic mixing skills and got on a plane.

Conversely, one talented DJ became a legend despite (or maybe because of) refusing to play in the UK. In 1994, Junior Vasquez said, 'I wouldn't ever go over there and play Ministry. It's just stupid, everybody does it.' As a result, to British fans who knew him only by his production work and his mythologised reputation, Vasquez and his club Sound Factory came to represent the ultimate in clubbing. In May 1997 (rather too long after UK fans' interest had peaked) he finally relented and for a large fee played a couple of much-publicised though anticlimactic nights at Cream and Ministry of Sound.

In the twentieth century's closing decade, plenty more Americans made their names on European soil. Armand Van Helden, Danny Tenaglia, Josh Wink, Roger Sanchez, and many more, took advantage of their profession's newly exalted status and found themselves increasingly away from US shores, basking in the booming international dance economy.

In under twenty years the DJ had seen his wages rise from those of a keen hobbyist, happy to earn a little record money, to a level where he could reasonably aspire to banking his first million. Clubland is a supply and demand free-market economy, and the big-name DJs were simply getting paid what they were worth, in audience terms, to the promoters – just like a crap actor gets paid millions to star in a movie because their superstar name ensures ticket sales. Certain DJs began to enjoy such recognition that their marquee value shot up way beyond that of the average rock group. It wasn't necessarily because they worked hard, sometimes it wasn't even because they were any good; it was simply that they could pull in the crowds.

'Do DJs get paid too much money?' asks Pete Tong: 'Well, not really because if they did, you wouldn't book them back, would you?'

'Promoters aren't stupid,' says Norman Cook. 'They aren't running an ageing DJ charity. They're paying you that money because they know they'll make *more*. And they're making it because you're attracting crowds and entertaining them.'

Booking heavyweight DJs became a way of making a particular night seem special or memorable, a promoter's marketing tool. 'One of the ways to give a night a badge of credibility was to put a name on it,' argues Dom Phillips, offering the example of the first *Mixmag*-sponsored night in Bristol in 1990. 'It was the first time Andrew Weatherall had come to town. Nobody had any idea who Andrew Weatherall was. Or what he played. Or what he stood for. But they *did know* that he was a DJ and he'd never been to town before so the whole city went out. It was rammed.'

Marketing the star DJ

The music business revolves around stars. They look good on record sleeves and magazine covers, they can do interviews, they have fans and, most importantly, they have lasting and profitable album-based careers. As DJs acquired star-like attributes, the record industry's ears quickly pricked up.

The first time the major labels bought emphatically into club music was with disco. But they didn't have a clue how to market it, so they had their fingers badly burnt (almost all the disco hits were on independent labels). The majors couldn't get their heads around music which had such a lack of recognisable faces. Disco was constructed by studio producers and session musicians, and with Donna Summer as a notable exception, it failed to produce anyone who could convincingly get teenagers writing teary-eyed, moist-knickered fan letters.

With house it was different. By putting the star DJ at the centre of its dance music marketing efforts, the record industry was able to do with house what, with one or two exceptions, (like the *Saturday Night Fever* soundtrack) it could never do with disco – sell albums of it to the masses, especially since the once-underground activity of intense, drug-assisted nightclubbing was fast becoming a conventional night out.

Here was the guitar hero for the end of the century, a face for all those faceless tunes.

Most early attempts to make the DJ an album artist as a *producer*, such as those by Frankie Knuckles and David Morales, had actually failed quite badly, but in 1992 the idea of the (legal) DJ mixed compilation was born: collections of other people's records mixed by the DJ as if he were playing in a club. With an eye to legitimise the thriving market in bootleg cassettes of club sets from big-name DJs, DMC launched its *Mixmag Live* series with a Carl Cox and Dave Seaman mix album, and *Journeys By DJ* put out a mix album by Billy Nasty. The DJ was on his way to being an album star.

Up until the nineties, young people bought singles. Those 7-inch slices of excitement defined our lives. But then the soundtrack to our youth became the mix CD, the latest *Ministry Annual* or Pete Tong's *Essential Mix* – CDs which sell hundreds of thousands of copies. There is frantic lobbying by the dance labels to have their tunes included; get your track on a big-selling compilation and you might make as much as £35,000 in royalties. When the *Ministry Annual* was selling 500,000 copies, as much as £800,000 went on TV advertising, and there'd still be £1 million profit.

The superstar DJ was a key part of the marketing strategy, earning up to £50,000 for having his name on the cover and endorsing the music. Sometimes his name was all he was selling – in many cases the music was chosen according to complex webs of licensing agreements and mixed by a studio engineer using a computer program called Pro Tools. Here the big name DJ acts as a trusted, recognisable figure who brings together some songs which we'd otherwise never buy – he's a musical *brand*. You buy an *Essential Mix* CD the same way you buy a pair of Nike trainers. 'People buy into trusting the Ministry of Sound logo or trusting Boy George, or trusting me or trusting Sasha,' says Pete Tong.

Superclubs and global brands

We can thank the much-hated 1994 Criminal Justice Act for the rise of mainstream clubbing. With the government intent on outlawing large-scale unlicensed dance events, alternative outlets had to be found for all the young energy that had been unleashed. After the law knocked raves on the head, people flooded into the clubs. They swapped muddy fields for the carpet and chrome of the local Cinderella's and carried on partying. The underground scene was legalised (and largely sanitised), and the money started rolling in. Indeed, cynics have pointed out that ecstasy culture is the ultimate in consumerism – not only do you pay for music and a place to dance, now you can also buy a great party mood whenever you want one. Whatever you think, commercial club culture as we now know it was born out of the ashes of loving, hugging E-culture.

At the start of the nineties, as alternatives to the evil raves, licensing boards had granted permission for later and later club-based dance events, provided alcohol wasn't served (hardly a problem for the E generation). Legal all-night dancing finally arrived at London gay club Trade, and then at the Ministry of Sound in late 1991.

Once dance music was indoors and respectable, it turned glamorous. Club fashion was born – not just trends for practicality's sake like acid house's long-sleeved T-shirts, dungarees and Kickers, but for reasons of fab, decadent flashiness. Fluffy bras and fetish wear, silver miniskirts, daft techno robot gear, and no end of sexy teenage midriffs made their appearance. All were well documented in the pages of *Mixmag*, which was filled with photos of us enjoying our new club-based lifestyle.

Looking back, Dom Phillips insists that, even more than the 1988 acid house revolution, the real turning point in dance culture came in 1994 when clubbing got dressed up and turned its back on the sweaty rave movement that had spawned it. Suddenly, the epitome of UK clubbing was a glamorous mixed-gay club like Leeds's Vague, or Mansfield's opulent Renaissance, filled with neo-classical pillars and girls dressed in satin. In London there was Billion Dollar Babes and Malibu Stacey. 'I remember thinking, "things are really changing",' says Phillips. 'At that point it was suddenly so accessible.' As if to prove his point, club promoters recall 1995 as the year when they made the most money ever.

At this point things had come full circle. Everyone was dancing in the clubs that acid house and rave were supposed to have finished off. 'Clubs started to be Mecca instead of mega,' said 808 State's Andrew Barker. We noticed, with irony, that some of us were dancing round our handbags again. Thus was named 'handbag house' – the easy-cheesy soundtrack to tacky, glitzy nights of Malibu and pineapple. In the UK, clubbing had become an ordinary thing to do. It was suddenly a 'mainstream leisure activity', and it was increasingly at the heart of young people's identities.

Market researchers declared that clubbers were excellent targets for advertising – 'early adopters', 'opinion formers' every one of them – and ad agencies hurried to learn the language of the dancefloor. Clubbers allegedly spent nearly twenty per cent more cash than Miss and Mr Average. As a result, TV ads filled up with rushing techno soundtracks, shiny clubwear babes and barely hidden drug slang. 'Sorted,' shouted the venerable Royal Mail, echoing the cry of a clubber who's just bought his pill.

Alcopops were born, their sugary hit alcohol's attempt to compete with the drug experience. Energy drinks appeared on bar shelves, the jolt of vodka and Red Bull meeting our new desire to get wired instead of drunk. Long-established brands were 'repositioned' (post-clubbing cornflakes anyone?). Drink and cigarette companies patrolled clubs like drug-pushers, giving out free samples to hook those 'early adopters', and in 1994, with Pepsi's Ministry of Sound tour, started actually sponsoring club nights. Graphic designers gave undue emphasis to the letter E, something hilariously evident in the BBC's coverage of the 1997 e-lection. Even the staid world of book publishing tried co-opting club culture. Irvine Welsh showed that the dance generation can actually read, and bookstores were crammed with fluorescent flyer-type book jackets – alcopop fiction!

The commercialisation process triumphed in the superclub, with Liverpool's Cream, the Midlands' Renaissance and London's Ministry of Sound as the leading examples. Originally started with an eye on the grand venues of New York by people who cared about providing the best sound, the best DJs and the finest treatment, the nation's biggest venues soon fell for the lure of money and the power that their 'brands' had accumulated. The superclubs found themselves at the sharp end of the new club-based lifestyle economy. They started deepening their relationship with the nation's clubbers, selling them things other than an occasional night out, and brokered deals with be-suited marketing men based on their magical connection to young people. The most money was to be made from compilation CDs. At first these had been pitched as the latest mixes from superstar DJs, but pretty soon, the clubs' brands were more prominent.

The superclubs also recolonised Ibiza, promoting their own nights in the island's giant venues. By the mid nineties the loved-up post-rave masses knew Ibiza as the birthplace of everything holy, so a pill-popping package trip to San Antonio was now nothing less than a pilgrimage. And it was that much more reassuring if there was a friendly Cream logo waiting for you on the beach. Back home, the summer countryside shook with dance events more massive than any rave, as the superclubs and

Star time – The world's first superstar DJ Jimmy Savile offers a few pointers to Tiësto, the role's latest incarnation.

former rave promoters launched dance festivals, huge two- or three-day encampments based on the rock festival model. Tribal Gathering led the way in 1993, Homelands launched in 1999, and in 1998 the first Creamfields welcomed 50,000 clubbers.

House had become the cornerstone of the pop charts in Britain and much of the rest of the world. As dance music edged its way into the mainstream, the DJ's role was changing to meet new demands: the dance mags needed cover stars, the superclubs needed reliable crowd-pullers. However, to be a household name isn't an ambition that sits well with experimentation, exploration and risk-taking.

As DJs became more famous than their music, one side-effect was the personality jock. At the peak of the DJ's superstar years celebrities were seen turning to DJing as an alternative career. Boy George was often held up as the obvious example, although to be fair, he'd earned his stripes DJing since the early eighties, even if his fame as a pop star gave him a head start. When ex-boxer Nigel Benn announced he was a closet DJ and available for bookings, there were plenty of groans. When big-league footballers David Hughes and Daniele Dichio made the same revelation, they got the same reaction. The cause of female equality in DJing was muddied by a series of dolly-bird DJs, Page Three 'stunnas', at home in both porn mags and dance rags. When porn star Traci Lords hit the decks she hired a real DJ to do all her mixing. In recent years celebs like Paris Hilton and P-Diddy have assumed the DJ's position, no doubt more interested in their centrepiece role at the party than their cueing levels.

The global export of dance culture

'After years of rumour and speculation Sasha's many fans in China are finally getting what they have wished for . . .' reads the press release, going on to detail the various sponsors, media companies, event specialists and tour management firms that make a visit from a superstar DJ possible. After years at the top of his trade, the level-headed Sasha is used to a fair bit of embarrassing idolatry, but nothing prepared him for the reception he received on his first trip to Beijing and Shanghai.

'I've never ever had to do press conferences like I had to out in China. Fifty microphones, and cameras everywhere. I felt like J-Lo or something. It was quite strange.' He laughs, 'I think they were expecting fireworks to come out of my bum or something.' And when the applause for this emissary of western youth culture had died down, what did they actually ask him? 'It's the same all over. The biggest question is always, "How do you find the clubs here? Is it different to the rest of the world?" '

Like pop stars in earlier decades, the superstar DJ was the vehicle that allowed the new dance culture to spread globally. In the wake of the UK's dance explosion, newly wealthy DJs and promoters kept up their tans exploring luxury holiday destinations. Dance outposts sprang up across the world as existing local scenes were energised by regular visits from the new breed of international DJ. Not only this, but the masses expected a house music soundtrack on holiday, and the scruffier, more embroidered elements were busy exporting the neo-hippie rave ideal to places with more beach than soap. Soon much of the world thought house music had been born in the UK.

Britain leads the world in the youth culture export business. Perhaps a hangover of its imperial past, it excels at looting styles from elsewhere, mutating and combining them and then selling them on dressed in a new image. Historically, the country has done well at changing black American styles into forms that appeal to white America. The Stones took the blues and repackaged it with more volume and a psychedelic edge; The Beatles copied the soul sound of the Isley Brothers but gave it a clunking Liverpool thump. And so with post-disco dance music. Having adopted and adapted the black forms of house, techno and hip hop, the British started re-exporting their much-altered versions.

But while house music and UK-style dance culture crossed over into the mainstream in Europe, Australia, South Africa, Asia and parts of South and Central America, the USA was less responsive. Making middle

America dance was not an easy task. While most territories can be won over by charming a few key radio stations and some big-city appearances, the size and insularity of the US makes a musical invasion extremely hard work. In the US house remained underground, preserved and continued by the same marginal big-city scenes which had created it – the black, gay and ethnic club 'families' whose lineage went back to the dancefloors of disco.

Nevertheless, a few Brits were trying their best. In late 1999 the UK dance press was filled with articles describing how DJs such as Oakenfold, Sasha and Norman Cook (Fatboy Slim) were finally making inroads stateside. 'This is the year,' beamed Paul Oakenfold. 'We've been hammering away, and now it looks as if we're going to break it wide open. We're going to take America to the next level.' In 1997 Sasha and John Digweed began their hugely influential residency at New York's Twilo; in 1998 Cream staged an eight-month tour with Dave Seaman headlining.

A few cautious licensing deals had suggested the US majors might start investing in dance music, or 'electronica' as it had become known (a handy industry tag to distance it from its black, gay origins). By 1996 Norman Cook had joined the Prodigy and Chemical Brothers as a recognisable album act and heard his song 'Praise You' all over ads for the Gap. 'Any person I switch off from Hootie And The Blowfish is another soul saved,' laughed Cook as he enjoyed his one-man British invasion.

The common factor of these few British dance acts who saw transatlantic success (as well as home-grown electronica artists like Moby) was arguably that they were examples of dance music made into rock music: bands that were happy onstage, artists who presented themselves in ways the US rock mind could understand. Norman Cook agrees. 'We've all had brushes with rock music,' he says. 'We're not just studio boffins, we're caning rock'n'roll animals that _Rolling Stone_ and _Spin_ can write stories about. There's a couple of guitars in there and that's all the Americans need to latch on to!'

Paul Oakenfold planned to capitalise on this notion. Promoting his Perfecto label, he adapted to the age-old rock methods of tours and live shows. 'We're not interested in the clubs,' he said in 1996. 'We're going straight at it from the college, alternative route. I've got acts who can come out there and tour, just like Oasis.'

Cook, however, refused to repackage himself. 'They're always trying to make me put a band together and play as a band,' he said. ' "This is as far as we can take it where it's still dance music. I don't wanna cross over and be a rock act. I don't wanna play in a band. I don't wanna tour. It's nice that you're promoting me and we're selling albums, but let's not forget that this is what I do." '

Such confusion even led to him having to turn down TV appearances.

'I got offered to do *Letterman* and *Saturday Night Live*, which is a lovely idea, but what would I do? I'm a DJ and it takes two hours to DJ. You can't do it in three minutes.'

House and techno remain insignificant in the US in industry terms – a mere cough compared to the monster contagion of hip hop, rock and country – but in the last few years dance culture has taken significant steps out of the shadows. Home-grown DJ stars like Sandra Collins, Christopher Lawrence and the Crystal Method are gradually building up their fan base (though they usually slip down the bill when the European trance behemoths hit town); after movies like *Go* and *Cruel Intentions* the door has opened to dance-friendly soundtracks; and you'll see plenty of unconvincing headphones and turntables spicing up clothes and drinks ads. Raves may have been largely criminalised, but millions of American kids have danced at one, and perhaps the suppression of the rave movement will have the same effect as it did in Britain and cause US club culture to blossom.

There have been concerted efforts from the dance industry itself. Detroit's annual techno festival is certainly a positive indication. Getting a million people to dance in the streets of the Motor City is no mean achievement. If only they could agree on the same name each year. The DanceStar awards ceremony is another gaudily optimistic force, with a global TV audience of over a billion. 'If any event can root DJ culture out of the underground, it may just be DanceStar USA,' opined the *Miami New Times*; though how much of that audience is in the States?

Another moment came when the Winter Music Conference in Miami, an industry event for the world's dance labels since 1986, was consciously reformatted. It had always been scheduled to coincide with the flamboyant South Beach White Party – a major fixture for the 'circuit queens' – but in recent years it has been shifted by a week, so it coincides neatly with Spring Break, a symbolic move from dance music's gay roots towards more mainstream ambitions. And let's not forget Paul Oakenfold's recent move to a $1.6 million home in the Hollywood hills.

Certainly the make-up of US dancefloors has changed beyond recognition. In contrast to the original American club scenes, the market is resolutely young, white and suburban. As faster, less funky European forms like hardcore and trance took over from indigenous forms of house, there were some painful collisions. Many of the older generation of clubbers looked down on this invasion force, resenting the presence of what they saw as a lot of underage kids wearing impossibly baggy trousers and taking all the wrong drugs. DJs watched their audiences change dramatically. Someone like Junior Vasquez saw his crowd change from being almost exclusively black and gay to being overwhelmingly white, far younger and much straighter. There are few traces of the generation who danced at the American birth of house.

Many believe the US music industry is impervious to dance culture. This far shall it go and no further. Only a handful of house tracks have ever made it into the US top 10, with Sonique's 'It Feels So Good' and Everything But The Girl's 'Missing' as the most recent examples. These were never seen as part of a trend, so there was no push to follow them up. And to have a hit record requires serious investment – for endless plugging to radio stations across the vast continent, and literally hundreds of TV appearances and magazine interviews. European markets are small enough to allow random genius hits by unknown producers to shoot into the charts and be forgotten two weeks later. In contrast it can take up to forty weeks for a record to climb the US hit parade. What credible DJ would play the same track at every gig for that long?'

'There's so much more at stake,' argues Sasha. 'These big record companies aren't going to allow some shitty little record from a nineteen-year-old kid in his bedroom to knock Beyonce off number one when they've invested ten squillion quid in her.'

The consensus is that it will take a massive star before the US industry is ready to get its chequebook out. Maybe it'll be Tiësto. His fans certainly see him as a superstar – they're quite happy to spend $25 on a concert DVD showing three hours of a guy putting records on (a special feature lets you change camera angles for a close up on his hands). As one fan wrote on Amazon.com, 'seeing Tiësto just lose himself was incredible'.

The pedestal

Many who had been involved with clubbing since its 1988 rebirth felt that the rise of the superstar DJ signalled a real loss of innocence, a betrayal of dancefloor unity. As wages rocketed, it seemed that the original goals of equality had been lost. These goals, which were first expressed in David Mancuso's Loft back in seventies New York, were realised most powerfully in Britain in the muddy egalitarianism of the rave movement.

Dave Dorrell, one of the first generation of UK house DJs, admits to being disappointed that the DJ rose so far above his station.

'I bought in wholesale to the "no division, DJ-dancefloor-we're-all-one" unity,' he says. 'I loved all that.'

For Dorrell, one of the best things about the early acid house clubs was the smoke machines. These, he argues, were real levellers. 'Nobody knew what was going on. It was great. You were just all in it together, you were just as much a part dancing in the DJ box as anyone dancing on the floor.'

Nevertheless, he could see the seeds of stardom being sown.

'It was inevitable, of course, that being a couple of feet higher than everyone, on a podium, was going to lead some people's heads to get lost in the clouds. DJs suddenly thought they had to have a Ferrari, a Porsche, you know. And people would be carrying record boxes through the crowd like you're the king . . . Oh please!'

Some see the whole DJ stardom thing as patently ridiculous, pointing out that a guy who plays records is never going to have the same magnetic aura as a traditional performer like, say, James Brown.

'DJs just aren't able to get it up on that kind of level of godhood,' insists Coldcut's Matt Black. 'And yet there's this huge pedestal. We're told, "Here's the new star," and there's this guy standing there looking sheepish, not really doing anything except fiddling with his headphones.

'Name the Jim Morrison of DJs,' he challenges.

TWENTY
TODAY

I Haven't Stopped Dancing Yet

'The super DJ and the superclub game is over.'

– Mark Rodol, chief executive Ministry of Sound

'I'm quite sad about the way it's imploded. It just got big fat and ugly and it needed some air let out of its tyres. It's a shame though, 'cos in Britain they've slashed the tyres completely. The rest of the world is still buzzing.'

– Sasha

Club culture was built on togetherness; on participation, equality, communion. The clubbers are the stars, not the short guy who fiddles with the record player. If we're on a dancefloor but we're all watching the DJ, or in an arena all looking at the stage, we're no longer doing what it's all about: we are once more an audience and no longer the event. After we let the DJ become a superstar, we stopped listening to the music, we believed the hype, we all went crazy for their first record even if was utter rubbish. Instead of memorable parties there were thousands of club nights, all screaming for our attention, all chasing the energy and money the acid house explosion had unleashed. Our precious, underground culture had been stolen from under us, but we hardly noticed. As long as they had us throwing our fists in the air with our eyes monged closed on our Saturday night podiums, we didn't give a fuck. Going clubbing stopped being special; it was just like going to the pub. Dance revolution . . . Where?

As we've seen, by the end of the nineties dance music had become big business, with superclubs, superstar DJs and the dance press wrapped in a sweaty love triangle, their orgy lubricated by pots of marketing money. Never before had a musical culture been so thoroughly infiltrated. Despite being rooted in acid house ideals, the dance world had been built by opportunist entrepreneurs, and it didn't have many qualms about selling out.

While plenty of DJs were happily growing rich off this, financing innovative new drug habits and buying helicopter wax in bulk, the craft of DJing was compromised. A DJ's job is to explore music and break unheard tracks; but a superstar DJ's role was to provide a reliable, familiar climax for the masses. Pete Tong, for one, lamented the pressure to keep things at fever pitch with popular tunes.

'One of the problems of being Pete Tong or Judge Jules or whoever, is that you have that huge responsibility to peak the night,' he said. 'I never forget that – you are there to entertain. When people are queuing to get in and paying their money, they just want to go doolally to their favourite records.'

At his worst, a DJ in a superclub was a corporate whore, the hired power behind the logo. He wasn't there to be creative or innovative, he was there to pull a crowd. Most of the mid-nineties premier league – Sasha, Carl Cox, Paul Oakenfold, Jeremy Healy – rose to prominence by sheer talent. Once famous, however, they entered a spiralling world of high fees, wily agents and persona-hungry magazines. It became hard to book them directly, and many were seen to have priced themselves out of all but the largest venues. As a result, there was a considerable backlash against the superjock. There had been a great many let-downs as promoters falsely advertised big names to fill their clubs. And the honest promoters were paying so much for their star DJs they had no money left for the other elements of a good night out.

'The letters are pouring in to *Mixmag* complaining,' declared the magazine in November 1996, 'from people who spent a brilliant night dancing to DJ Unknown because the £15 queue for DJ Rich Bastard was too long.'

Things looked bad. DJs' fees had shot well past the £1,000 mark: Jeremy Healy was asking £15,000 to play New Year's Eve; Sasha, locked in a studio trying to finish an album, turned down an offer of £50,000 to play for two hours. The superclubs were strengthening their monopolies with the devious idea of the club tour: where a small club pays money for the privilege of hosting a 'visit' by a much bigger club and its much bigger DJs. Then, in a move which summed up just how crazy it had got, magazines reported that a club in Japan had offered Junior Vasquez $150,000 to play. *Mixmag*'s pages were filled with reports on DJs' wages, on whether clubbers were getting value for money, on dance music's creeping commercialism. Among themselves the editors joked about doing a 'self-destruct' issue in which they would print the actual astronomic sums people like Pete Tong were making. Clubs without name DJs started to suffer, dance music was all over TV commercials, and club records were regularly making the pop charts. Things looked sure to crash. 'It was like the eighties before Black Monday,' recalls Dom Phillips.

But dance culture took a cheeky half and carried on unperturbed, not

least the superclubs. They'd grown drunk on the notion that they owned
lifestyle brands: badges that could be stuck on anything. Ministry of
Sound clearly modelled their future on Richard Branson's Virgin as they
launched a record label, a radio station, a national magazine, bottled water,
clothing, a music publishers and a tour-management arm. 'We are
building a global entertainment company,' declared the sign hanging over
its employees' heads. Then, while aiming at a public share offering, they
audaciously offered £30 million for the Royal Yacht Britannia and £6
million to take over the Spirit Zone in the Millennium Dome. They even
paid for a cinema advert to encourage kids to vote, so confident were they
of their place at the heart of youth culture. The Ministry of Sound now
existed as a physical club foremost so that kids worldwide might believe
in the Ministry brand as a reliable indicator of cool. The Old Etonians
who ran the place were making far more money from their portcullis
logo than from having a great dancefloor.

Dance music's march into the mainstream continued. Radio One
brought a new crop of dance DJs into government service, and by 1997
a growing proportion of its output was club music. Yet more superclubs
were born. In 1999 London saw the Scala, Home and Fabric open their
doors, with a combined capacity of 7,000. Liverpool University suggested
that its record number of applications was due to the popularity of
Cream. (Around the same time Cream showed its dedication to the
underground by joining the city's Chamber of Commerce.) The summer
festivals were filling up with dance tents, and house music was spreading
round the world. Berlin's Love Parade attracted over a million people; at
Sydney's Mardi Gras a giant E tablet was paraded through the streets. The
Prodigy and Fatboy Slim were even making inroads stateside, where
dance was creeping into the rock consciousness as 'electronica'.

The internet bubble fed the party, with dance music a key commodity
in the global market in website content. Trustthedj.com paid astonishing
amounts of cash to the world's top DJs for exclusive online rights to their
mixes. WorldPop, another dot.com with vast investment, aimed to beam
dance charts and DJ gossip to subscribers' mobiles twenty-four hours a
day. A wealth of internet radio stations sprang up. Ammo City, the best-
funded of these, boasted unfeasibly glamorous studios – with a business
plan that was glamorously unfeasible.

And in case things started to look too far removed from the Summer
of Love, along came Sheffield's Gatecrasher. A thousand 'Crasher Kids'
were raging weekly in a club where the old '88 ethos of losing it on
ecstasy was, ahem, evident. Fuelled by Mitsubishis, a batch of unusually
strong pills, they spent days before on costumes (*Blue Peter* egg-carton
martians), hours on the dancefloor rushing their eyeballs off to crayola

trance, and days after recovering. The kids were still living it! – proof that house music had escaped a sell-by date. Meanwhile, UK garage was blinging its way into the national consciousness, giving a Moschino'd jolt to R&B and hip hop, tech-house was bubbling through dark cellars everywhere, the breaks scene was thundering along, and Ibiza was the best Ibiza ever . . . again.

In both its mainstream excesses and its more adventurous corners the culture started by acid house looked uncannily like an evergreen force of nature. Explaining that the expected crash had been postponed indefinitely, Judge Jules, DJ at Gatecrasher and the epitome of the superstar system, pointed out insightfully that 'the unique phenomenon of dance culture is the way that commercial and underground clubs coexist'.

However, on the other side of the Millennium things didn't look so rosy.

The crash

For years the superclubs could ignore their many critics, but finally their dancefloors started losing weight. In 2002 Cream closed and Gatecrasher crashed, forced by falling numbers to change to a monthly. Home had shut down the year before – the closure was due to drug dealing in the club, but rumours spoke of dire financial straits. Finally, in 2003 the Ministry admitted the market had changed when it 'relaunched' itself to appeal to an older crowd (ie more tables). Even in Ibiza changes were afoot, and club owners grouped together to move drink tariffs up and price out the undesirables.

As if to signal the end of clubbing-as-lifestyle, the dance press imploded, too. Between 2002 and 2004 *Muzik*, *Ministry* and *Jockey Slut* closed and *Mixmag* lost more than a third of its readers (in the same period, readership of fogey-focused music mags like *Uncut* and *Mojo* rose healthily). The dance generation was growing up and younger readers weren't interested. To add insult to injury, in 2005 the Brit Awards dropped Best Dance Act from its list, and replaced it with a trophy celebrating live music.

The scene had simply grown too huge too fast and couldn't sustain itself. 'It was quantity over quality,' argues Sasha. 'There were too many big nights going on. And the people who were paying their hard-earned money to go into the clubs weren't getting respected. There were so many mediocre nights, so much mediocre music being put out. Everybody jumped on this huge bandwagon.'

Over-loaded, the scene was also guilty of over-commercialisation. 'People are pretty sick of big brand names telling them what to do,' declared *Mixmag*'s Paul French, laying the blame on corporate joyriders. 'The best kind of clubbing is that which feels like it's a secret, feels like you've discovered it,' explained Cream co-owner Darren Hughes to *Night* magazine, without discernible irony. 'People know when they're being sold to, and the backlash has come to bite people's heads off.' In the *Guardian*, Alexis Petridis pointed out, 'It's hard to believe you are taking part in a countercultural happening when it is sponsored by Paco Rabanne and broadcast by the BBC.'

Compounding clubbers' reluctance to dance in a marketing machine was the superclubs' waning interest in what had driven their brands in the first place. Most owned their own venues, and felt little pressure to reinvent themselves. They continued relying on big name DJs and weren't shy of licensing deals which had little to do with their dancefloors. After Ministry launched a clothing label they had to admit you probably wouldn't get into their club if you wore it. An exception which proved this rule was Fabric. Despite its superclub size it maintained its credibility by consistently highlighting new underground DJ talent, and hadn't extended its brand beyond a series of CDs. Fabric rode the clubbing recession largely undaunted.

Commentators declared the end of the ecstasy generation and spoke poetically of a 'comedown'. We'd all partied far longer than the ten years any respectable musical movement is permitted, and now it was time to stay in, eat bananas and turn the phone off. The love-drug that had helped house sweep the world had become a juvenile indulgence; it was commonplace and uncool. The fact that pills cost as little as £2 in some parts of the country only confirmed this. In its place as the club high of choice had come cocaine. Cheaper and more easily available than ever, coke fed the controlled champagne opulence of the UK garage scene and the ruffneck rocks-and-reefer leanings of drum and bass and UK hip hop.

Gatecrasher was perhaps the last gasp of an ecstasy lifestyle. But to join their party, you had to wear kitchen utensils and sweat like a horse. As Alexis Petridis pointed out, after seeing the Crasher Kids in the tabloids the average sixteen-year-old had a clear choice: 'You could either dress like a rapper or one of the Strokes and be in with a chance with the opposite sex, or you could dress like an imbecile and go clubbing.'

And the superstar DJ belatedly faced a good old-fashioned generation gap. There was something creepy about being made to dance by a forty-five-year-old legend who'd soundtracked your parents' E-fuelled gropings. Especially when a crop of skinny androgynes with loud guitars and irrefutable haircuts were making rock rebellion sexy again.

All this is the normal stuff of pop culture shifts. But the 'death' of dance culture in the UK was by no means entirely by natural causes. Other forces were at work, most notably those government-sanctioned drug pushers, the alcohol industry. Whatever you believe about their influence on anti-rave legislation, it is undeniable that the breweries, by revolutionising how and where alcohol is sold, have completely transformed British drinking culture, and it was in the turf war between bars and clubs that dance culture was dealt its hardest blow. Seizing an opportunity to finally see off all-night dancing, the breweries and pubcos added dancefloors, gained late licenses and turned their chain pubs into clubs in all but name. Instead of the place for a pre-club drink, the High Street became the whole night. And instead of a four-hour dancefloor workout drinking mostly water, the hours after 11pm were now for binge-boozing your way into either an overworked ambulance or some unfamiliar knickers. One more pineapple Breezer and that blonde might be pissed enough. With alcopops, with later licenses, with DJ bars, and with relentless government lobbying, the alcohol industry finally regained control of the post-pub leisure economy.

DJing's democratic future

The UK's clubbing recession is best viewed as a return to reality. There aren't the huge sums of money sloshing around any more, and there are far fewer nights capable of supporting an endless parade of international stars, but new talent has done very well out of the changes, and a wonder-fully fragmented underground scene has emerged to make the running. All over the country smaller nights have thrived, manned by no-name DJs just as skilled as the superjocks but more energised and more excited – DJs with a genuine love of music rather than just early access to the hits. Without the pressure to fill vast industrial barns, these clubs were able to start exploring lots of different genres rather than one all-powerful style of music. A night of Brazilian drum and bass, a cellar of New York disco, a community centre filled with angry grime MCs, a warehouse of fashion folk posing to electro-house. Best of all, these are places where people know each other again, clubs that can once again be called parties.

In any case, commercial house, techno and trance remain the lifeblood of the rest of the world's dancefloors. Beyond Britain they're still going nuts for dance music, not least the emerging markets of Asia, Eastern Europe and South America. The new superstar circuit fits together cities like Shanghai, Beijing, Buenos Aires, Moscow. And the superclubs are still with us, having become peripatetic brands, doing what they do best – one-off events for thousands of people, in festivals or in exotic holiday destinations. Someone had to keep those ageing superjocks in villas and Prada.

Even as it crashed the dance boom brought us to a pivotal moment for the DJ's craft. After fifteen years in the spotlight, DJing is no longer some scary and elitist brotherhood; nearly everyone has had a go on some decks and plenty of people have done it in public. As a result, in direct reaction to a decade of over-commercialised nightlife, there's a new punk attitude. Just play your favourite music, find people who share your enthusiasm and start a party. To quote the slogan from London club night It's On, 'Top tunes, shite mixing' is the order of the day. New technologies help democratise DJing, too. Song-recognition service Shazam can do your spotting for you, internet forums keep everyone clued up about new tunes, and online shopping takes the legwork out of tracking down those elusive tracks. All this leaves you to concentrate on the real skill of DJing: having great musical taste and knowing how to share it with people.

The most powerful force making DJing more accessible is the rise of digital music. After years of debating how it would affect the music industry, the digital revolution is here, and in the hands of a few young tearaways it's going to start kicking established methods in the balls. It's still controversial to dare suggest DJing might one day outgrow the 12-inch single. Many DJs will cling to the sexy tactile nature of vinyl regardless, and stress the warmth of its analogue sound, but digital DJing is becoming ever more attractive.

With the arrival of affordable CD burners, and CD players with idiot-proof 'vinyl emulation' controls, CD DJing has finally shaken off its wedding spinner image. CDs mean you can carry far more music, and let you play your own productions burnt straight from the computer. Most DJ/producers now play their work-in-progress from a test CD rather than an expensive (and delicate) acetate. Music is more easily sourced, too. A CD DJ has the world of compilations and reissues open to him, without spending hours lurking around used record stores.

MP3 and other digital formats offer even more possibilities. Even uncompressed you can carry thousands of songs in a laptop, adding years to the life of your spine. You can organise your collection into as many custom playlists as you like, grouping together tracks that fit a certain mood, or suit a particular club; or you can pull up songs by subject, by style, by tempo, by key, by artist, by era. Software such as Traktor or PCDJ lets you find songs, cue them up and mix them however you like, all in the computer. And if you're scared of looking like you're just checking your emails, you can try a clever interface like Final Scratch, which lets you use a normal set of DJ turntables to control the soundfiles: a pair of dummy timecoded records feeds your computer information about every change in speed or direction – so although the songs are just computer files, you can even start scratching them. Add to this the rise of podcasting (DJing on internet radio by uploading iPod mixes) and DJing is now opened up to millions.

The more obvious side of the digital revolution is in the massive quantities of music it makes available and the ease with which this can be transmitted via the internet. As well as downloads, both legal and illegal, it's simple to exchange whole music collections on iPods or hard discs: someone's entire life of collecting music uploaded in minutes.

One DJ who has recently embraced some of the more radical changes that digital DJing has to offer is Sasha. He'll even go so far as to say that it has re-ignited his love of his craft. Having ridden the rocket of superstardom for a decade, DJing was leaving him pretty jaded.

'I'd just had a whole year of touring my ass off and not really enjoying it. I got to 2003 and I was thinking, "What the fuck shall I do now, where shall I go with this?" Then this software came along and it definitely showed me a way to move forward and stay interested.'

The software in question is Ableton Live, a studio program for creating music from scratch and for remixing and re-editing existing tracks. Like several other packages on the market it lets you divide a song into chunks which you can loop and combine however you want, adding effects and other filters as you go. Forget playing something from start to finish as it was originally recorded. Now you can remix everything you play; dropping in endless samples of different tracks, mixing up a unique and unrepeatable patchwork of music. And, as Sasha so enthusiastically explains, all this can be done live.

'When I was DJing with Josh Wink recently, instead of playing whole tracks, he was looping up bits of his set over the top of my bit and sampling bits of mine and we were throwing things backwards and forwards and it became this wall of sound, from just snippets.'

The software keeps everything synchronised on the beat so the DJ can juggle as many elements as his brain can deal with. It's like giving a DJ twenty decks and forty arms to control them. With thousands of songs stored in his laptop, software like this has opened up a whole new world. While the first few hours of Sasha's set will be largely one track after another, the peak hour will be a whirlwind of extreme digital DJ creativity.

It's not just his performance style that's changed; his music is broader too. He now finds himself buying a far wider range of music, because he can tailor every track to suit his set – however short or weird the original. In this way Sasha, probably the world's most obsessively scrutinised DJ, can edge a few steps ahead of his army of stalker-like trainspotters, and play a set of music they can't identify and certainly couldn't emulate.

Sasha offers another glimpse into the future. One of the paradoxes of international DJ superstardom was that all his travelling left no time for the real work of a DJ – listening to new music. Now he is fully digital that problem is solved. With a computer server in his office that an assistant feeds the latest tracks into, Sasha's finger is never off the pulse, wherever he finds himself. 'I can log into my server anywhere I am in the world and

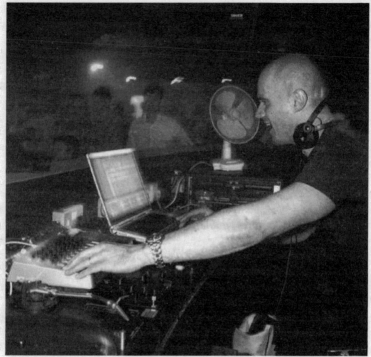

PC world – John OO Fleming rocks the crowd while checking his email.

download in a digital format straight into my laptop and be playing out that night with new music. Before, if I was on tour for a long time I'd have to get sent a box of records from London. I had to make sure I had access to a set of decks. Now stuff goes straight onto my iPod and I'm in a taxi listening to new music and sorting things through. It's definitely allowing me much more freedom to be spontaneous and throw in new music.'

DJs are a surprisingly Luddite bunch, and there is already very vocal opposition to digital DJing. What these people forget is that dance music has always been propelled by technology. By ignoring the digital revolution they may find themselves marooned – as did typesetters with the advent of desktop publishing. It seems almost inevitable that DJing will evolve toward something more akin to live remixing, and there may well be a sharp divide between those who learn the new tricks and those who stick with playing one song after another. For certain styles of music, and that doubtless includes the progressive house scene that Sasha inhabits, the new methods may quickly become required skills. 'Not everyone's going to embrace it. But people are going to get used to hearing these kind of sets, and they're going to start expecting it. In five years time computers in DJ booths will be completely normal,' he predicts.

And just as the advent of amplification, recording, variable speed turntables, drum machines and samplers all changed music dramatically, perhaps these sequencing programs will inspire radical new genres. 'You give this product to an eighteen-year-old kid, who's going to approach it from a completely new sense of musicality, that's when fireworks will happen,' says Sasha. 'That's when the next sound, the next generation of what a DJ performance is, will come.'

The digital revolution will affect the DJ in a broader sense because it makes his job increasingly necessary. With so much music flooding us, we'll need DJs to keep us afloat. They may have cultivated a slightly sexier image but DJs are essentially librarians, and as broadcasting gives way to narrowcasting and a more specialist, more segmented world, and as the music industry abandons everything except the most tried and tested, we need DJs to sift through the shelves and find us the gold – unless we're prepared to spend a large chunk of our time listening to music we might not like.

Instead of radio you'll soon be able to go to the Body & Soul channel, or the tech-step network or the Balearic nostalgia station, and hear the precise style of music you want, on demand. The idea of a music collection will give way to an ever-expanding online jukebox. You'll have your own private radio channel which automatically sequences the music you like best, according to your mood, and even goes out and adds new things according to what it knows you like. And behind all these will be an army of sophisticated buyers, selectors and programmers – DJs.

The torrential flow of information will make an impact in the booth as well. The idea of having 10,000 records on a hard drive sounds daunting to us now but in a couple of years will be the norm. Or maybe the DJ booth will just be a line out to a sound system and a high bandwidth line in from the internet. A DJ will simply plug in his laptop and start playing. He might not even carry tunes in his computer. Perhaps he'll just keep playlists of his favourites and download the actual music as he needs it from a vast website database holding all the recordings ever made: that way he need never own a single track, just pay a license fee for each one he plays. Some DJs will play in a way we recognise today, but others will use music software to twist and shape existing songs out of all recognition, combining elements from ten different tracks, adding their own rhythms, melodies, basslines. They might jam with other DJs or musicians, maybe they'll trigger lights and projections in tandem to the music, or maybe they'll have feedback sensors that let them know which way the audience wants things to go. Maybe the dancers themselves will have some sort of direct control over the music.

Some DJs will gleefully expand their job description. The new software will help blur the lines between DJing and musicianship and take the DJ a little further in his quest to be respected as an artist. Those quick off the mark will probably become famous for it. Other DJs will use these digital possibilities not to change what they do, but to make it easier to play a night of beautiful, moving, well chosen music. Many of the DJ's future toys may actually reduce the amount of technical expertise needed. Then, in the way that fully automatic cameras meant a good eye could beat years of know-how, they will make it far clearer what DJing is about. Your value as a DJ won't hinge on dull technical skills like beatmixing and level control, but on emotion, sensitivity and musicality. Such 'toys' will bring DJing back to the fundamentals of taste and programming. It will be about music rather than machinery.

The buzz remains

Wherever DJing is headed, its history teaches us to keep our eyes on the underground, and in dance music there's *always* an underground. This is at its most creative just after things have become horribly commercial. The mainstream picks up on something, burns it up, and declares it dead. But meanwhile, the pioneers have moved on and are free to push things further, to reclaim the momentum and come up with something new. So however fat and gaudy club culture becomes in your part of the world, rest assured that behind it there's something exciting.

For every cheesy commercial DJ who's happy to play what the record pluggers send him, who charts records he doesn't like just so he stays on the mailing list, who plays records he hates because everyone else is playing them, there's another DJ who searches out rare and unheard tracks in place of promotional freebies, who develops his own style, who throws his own parties, who generates his own following, who creates new music.

There'll always be an underground and it will always be filled with people who love music, not as a job but as the centrepiece to their lives – even if manipulative drug-pop seems to rule the day and even if most clubs are clogged with DJs who have abandoned their missionary zeal to return to the safe job of musical waiter. The exceptions are where the energy lies.

The fragmentation of dance music into scores of specialised genres is another reason for excitement. This works directly against the idea of the superclub and the prostitute DJ, and can only encourage experimentation and creativity. As homogenised stadium-sized dance music continues to sweep much of the world, in its shadow there are already pockets of resistance. Strange after-hours filled with strobes and smoke, in warehouses in bad parts of town, where the DJs are playing amazing music you never heard before: you can bet that sooner or later, out of these devious little scenes will come something interesting, and inevitably something momentous. That's how we got disco, hip hop, house, drum and bass . . .

What's next? Who knows – all that's certain is that something somewhere is busy evolving, just like it's always done.

We spent the last fifty years recording pop music, now we're gonna have incredible fun recycling it into any form we want. No more waiting for the next big thing, let's look forward to the next amazing tweak, the next gut-wrenching new noise, the next unbelievable collision of sampled sound.

And dance music is now truly international, and internationalist. Musical possibilities have become global. The established centres of our story have splintered so much that the next great record might just as likely come from Norway as from New York. And with words losing out to the universal beat, we all speak the same language. French people can finally make music that English people like. In fact you can bet that any really radical new styles of dance music will emerge from somewhere truly bizarre, far away from the intense scrutiny of the dance media and the commentators who swoop on anything novel before it has a chance to spread its wings.

Abetting this dramatic crashing of borders is the rise of digital music. The means of music production have long been in the hands of the masses; now we have the means of distribution too, and record companies – who were only ever banks stupid enough to lend money to musicians – are redundant. Any DJ can create a global community of listeners via the net. A DJ can make music in his own home, transmit it to another DJ across the world in a club in Singapore, who can load it into his laptop in the middle of his set and play it as the next record.

The disc jockey has been with us for exactly one hundred years. In that time he has been ignored, misunderstood, despised, worshipped and adored. He has stayed at the forefront of music; twisting and shaping it into fresh forms, perverting technology and forcing from it stunning new sounds. He has conjured a long series of novel genres in his endless search for material to keep his dancers moving. In the US the DJ created amazing music, then the UK gave him a home and made him a star. He continued his magic and around him there grew a musical culture more revolutionary and more enduring than any before.

After the 1988 Summer of Love, kids in Britain were finally enjoying the transcendent rituals on which the US evolution of dance music had been based. They finally understood the real power of a DJ, and in large numbers. Now, having conquered Europe and much of the southern hemisphere, their dance revolution is spreading back across the Atlantic and east into Asia. Having forged music more truly universal than any preceding it, the DJ is arguably a conduit for celebration and communion on a global scale. It's possible that the DJ is the ultimate expression of the ancient shamanic role; that the DJ is the greatest witch doctor there has ever been, unmatched at shaking us out of the drudge of the day and into the life of the night.

Why do we worship at the knees of the record-slinger? Because he is occasionally capable of divinity. When it all connects in a club, there's nowhere you can have more fun.

'A really great DJ is totally capable of making a bad record sound okay, a good record sound great, and a great record sound fantastic – by the context they put them in, and what they put around them. How they steer them. They can do all kinds of tricks. A great DJ can make people spontaneously cheer just for a little squelchy noise. Which is quite insane really. A little noise like *wha-wha-wha* and people go, "Yeeeaaah!" They can have people clapping along to a cymbal, just by the way they're bringing it in. When it's done well, it's fantastic. If it's done really well, it can be quite transcendental.'

It's a mystic art indeed. It seems so banal, but it holds the potential of phenomenal, inexpressible power. A great DJ can arouse more raw emotion in his audience than the composer of the most bittersweet opera, or the author of the most uplifting novel, or the director of the most life-affirming film.

When you're DJing and you're great at it, you're not playing records, you're playing the dancefloor. You're not just mixing tunes, you're mixing energy and emotions, mixing from surprise into hope and happiness, cutting from liberation to ecstasy to love. When it goes right, you're inside the bodies of everyone in the room, you know what they're feeling and where they're going, and you're taking them there. You're sweeping them off the earthly plane and transporting them to a higher place. You're moving their bodies and their souls with the music that flows from your fingertips.

You're putting them in the moment.

'Sweaty palms. Huge smiles. That kind of intenseness when you're in the zone, when you're in the box on your own. Oh my God! What's the next record? Frantically searching, making sure your instinct's right, changing your mind, then going back to your first choice, and then ripping that out and putting it on at the last minute . . . and it works!

'And seeing people smiling.

'And singing.

'And going crazy.'

CLUB CHARTS

Club Charts

Jimmy Savile original eight

Charlie Barnett Orchestra – Skyliner
Lou Busch – Zambezi
Tommy Dorsey – Sunny Side Of The Street
Harry James – I'm Beginning To See The Light
Stan Kenton – Painted Rhythm
Joe Loss – Tea For Two Cha Cha
Glenn Miller – In The Mood
Glenn Miller – Pennsylvania 6-5000
(compiled by Jimmy Savile)

Wigan Casino 50

The Adventurers – Easy Baby
Lee Andrews – I've Had It
Paul Anka – I Can't Help Loving You
Yvonne Baker – You Didn't Say A Word
Frankie Beverly & the Butlers – If That's What You Wanted
George Blackwell – Can't Lose My Head
Mel Britt – She'll Come Running Back
Doni Burdick – Bari Track
The Carstairs – It Really Hurts Me Girl
The Casualeers – Dance Dance Dance
Johnny Caswell – You Don't Love Me Anymore
Lorraine Chandler – I Can't Change
Freddie Chavez – They'll Never Know Why
The Checkerboard Squares – Double Cookin'
Morris Chestnut – Too Darn Soulful
Connie Clark & Orchestra – My Sugar Baby

Eula Cooper – Let Our Love Grow Higher
Dean Cortney – I'll Always Need You
The Del Larks – Job Opening
The Detroit Executives – Cool Off
The Dynamics – Yes I Love You Baby
Epitome Of Sound – You Don't Love Me
The Four Perfections – I'm Not Strong Enough
Edward Hamilton & the Arabians – Baby Don't You Weep
Joe Hicks – Don't It Make You Feel Funky
Willie Hutch – Love Runs Out
Gloria Jones – Tainted Love
Tamiko Jones – I'm Spellbound
Tobi Legend – Time Will Pass You By
Little Richie – Just Another Heartache
Joe Mathews – Ain't Nothing You Can Do
Jodi Mathis – Don't You Care Anymore
Garnett Mimms – Looking For You
Dean Parrish – I'm On My Way
Jimmy Radcliffe – Long After Tonight Is All Over
Saxie Russell – Psychedelic Soul
The Salvadores – Stick By Me Baby
Larry Santos – You Got Me Where You Want Me
The Sherries – Put Your Arms Around Me
The Silhouettes – Not Me Baby
R Dean Taylor – There's A Ghost In My House
Don Thomas – Come On Train
The Tomangoes – I Really Love You
The Velvet Satins – Nothing Can Compare To You

The Volcanoes – The Laws Of Love
Sam Ward – Sister Lee
Jerry Williams – If You Ask Me
Maurice Williams – Being Without You
Billy Woods – Let Me Make You Happy
The World Column – So Is The Sun
(compiled by Ian Dewhirst)

Loft 100

Andwella – Hold On To Your Mind
Ashford & Simpson – Stay Free
Atmosfear – Dancing In Outer Space
Babe Ruth – The Mexican
Barrabas – Woman
Archie Bell & the Drells – Let's Groove
Blackbyrds – Walking In Rhythm
Black Rascals – Keeping My Mind
Brass Construction – Music Makes You Feel Like Dancing
James Brown – Give It Up And Turn It Loose
Candido – Thousand Finger Man
Cassio – Baby Love
Central Line – Walking Into Sunshine
Code 718 – Equinox
Crown Heights Affair – Say A Prayer For Two
Deep Vibes – A Brand New Day
Alfredo De La Fe – My Favourite Things
Manu Dibango – Soul Makossa
Dinosaur L – Go Bang!
Don Ray – Standing In The Rain
Double Exposure – My Love Is Free
Lamont Dozier – Going Back To My Roots
D Train – Keep On
George Duke – Brazilian Love Affair
Ian Dury – Spasticus Autisticus
Earth Wind & Fire – The Way Of The World
Easy Going – Baby I Love You
Fingers Inc – Mystery Of Love
First Choice – Doctor Love
Forrrce – Keep On Dancing
The Gap Band – Yearning For Your Love
Joe Gibbs – Chapter 3

Eddy Grant – Living On The Frontline
Johnny Hammond – Los Conquistadores Chocolates
Damon Harris – It's Music
Ednah Holt – Serious Sirius Space Party
The Holy Ghost – Walk On Air (Sun & Moon Mix)
Frank Hooker & the Positive People – This Feeling
Instant House – Lost Horizons
Tamiko Jones – Can't Live Without Your Love
Kat Mandu – Don't Stop Keep On
Eddie Kendricks – Girl You Need A Change Of Mind
Gladys Knight – Friendship Train
Bo Kool – Money No Love
Patti Labelle – The Spirit's In It
Lil Louis – Music Saved My Life
Luna – I Wanna Be Free
Man Friday – Love Honey Love Heartache
Janice McClain – Smack Dab In The Middle
Chuck Mangione with Hamilton Philharmonic – Land Of Make Believe
Rita Marley – One Draw
Harold Melvin & the Bluenotes – Wake Up Everybody
MFSB – Love Is The Message
Dorothy Morrison – Rain
Van Morrison – Astral Weeks
Idris Muhammad – Could Heaven Ever Be Like This
Nicodemus – Boneman Connection
Nightlife Unlimited – The Love Is In You (No. 2)
Nuyorican Soul – Nervous Track
Odyssey – Inside Out
The O'Jays – Love Train
The O'Jays – Message In Our Music
Babatunde Olatunji – Jingo-Bah
One Way with Al Hudson – Music
The Orb – Little Fluffy Clouds
Ozo – Anambra
Pal Joey – Spend The Night
Pleasure – Take A Chance

Powerline – Double Journey
Prince – Sexy Dancer
Psychotropic – Only For The Headstrong
Resonance – Yellow Train
Rinder & Lewis – Lust
Risco Connection – Ain't No Stopping Us Now
Demis Roussos – L.O.V.E. Got A Hold On Me
Sandee – Notice Me
Bunny Sigler – By The Way You Dance
Slick – Space Bass
Lonnie Liston Smith – Expansions
Soft House Company – A Little Piano
Larry Spinoza – So Good
Nick Straker Band – A Little Bit Of Jazz
Sun Palace – Rude Movements
Sylvester – Over And Over
Ten City – Devotion
Third World – Now That We Found Love
The Trammps – Where The Happy People Go
280 West featuring Diamond Temple – Love's Masquerade
Miroslav Vitous – New York City
Dexter Wansel – Life On Mars
War – City Country City
Fred Wesley – House Party
The Whispers – And The Beat Goes On
Lenny White – Fancy Dancer
David Williams – Come On Down Boogie People
Winners – Get Ready For The Future
Edgar Winter – Above & Beyond
Jah Wobble, Holger Czukay, Jaki Liebezeit – How Much Are They/
Stevie Wonder – All I Do
Michael Wycoff – Diamond Real
(compiled by DJ Cosmo & David Mancuso)

Gallery 50
Barrabas – Woman
The B-52's – Dance This Mess Around
The B-52's – Rock Lobster
Blue Magic – Look Me Up

Bonnie Bramlett – Crazy 'Bout My Baby
James Brown – Give It Up And Turn It Loose
Jeannie Brown – Can't Stop Talking
Lynn Collins – Think
Dinosaur – Kiss Me Again
Doctor Buzzard's Original Savannah Band – Cherchez La Femme
Double Exposure – Ten Percent
Double Exposure – My Love Is Free
Fantastic Johnny C – Waiting For The Rain
First Choice – Doctor Love
Loleatta Holloway – Hit And Run
Loleatta Holloway – Dreamin'
Loleatta Holloway – We're Growing Stronger The Longer
Isley Brothers – Get Into Something
The Jacksons – Forever Came Today
Margie Joseph – Prophecy
Eddie Kendricks – Girl You Need A Change Of Mind
Eddie Kendricks – Date With The Rain
Labelle – What Can I Do For You
Labelle – Messin' With My Mind
Harold Melvin & the Bluenotes – The Love I Lost
Harold Melvin & the Bluenotes – Bad Luck
MFSB – Love Is The Message
MFSB – TSOP
Midnight Movers – Follow The Wind
Mighty Clouds Of Joy – Mighty High
Dorothy Morrison – Rain
The O'Jays – For The Love Of Money
Teddy Pendergrass – You Can't Hide
Realistics – How Can I Forget
Diana Ross – Love Hangover
Gloria Spencer – I Got It
Southshore Commission – Free Man
The Supremes – Up The Ladder To The Roof
The Supremes – Let My Heart Do The Walking
Sylvester – Mighty Real
Temptations – Law Of The Land

Traffic – Gimme Some Loving (live)
The Trammps – Love Epidemic
The Trammps – Disco Party
The Trammps – That's Where The Happy People Go
Undisputed Truth – Law Of The Land
Martha Velez – Aggravation
War – City Country City
Betty Wright – Where Is The Love
Zulema – Giving Up?
(compiled by Nicky Siano)

Saint 70

ABBA – The Visitors
Beautiful Bend – Make That Feeling Come Again
Blancmange – That's Love That It Is
Brother Beyond – The Harder I Try
Cerrone – Call Me Tonight
Cerrone – Love Is Here
Cerrone – Tripping On The Moon
China Crisis – Wishful Thinking
China Crisis – Working with Fire and Steel
Cock Robin – When Your Heart Is Weak
Communards – Never Can Say Goodbye
Patrick Cowley – Megatron Man
Crystal & the Pink – Back To You
Cut Glass – Without Your Love
Cut Glass – Alive With Love
Deacon Blue – Real Gone Kid
Electronic – Getting Away With It
Eurogliders – Heaven
Eurythmics – Love Is A Stranger
John Farnham – Age of Reason
Frazier Chorus – Typical
Hitlist – Into The Fire
India – Stay With Me
Julius Brown – Party
Yvonne Elliman – Love Pains
Peter Griffin – Step By Step
Rose Laurens – American Love
Amanda Lear – Follow Me
Denis LePage – Hot Wax
Lime – Babe, We're Gonna Love Tonight
Lime – Come And Get Your Love
Limahl – Never Ending Story

Lotus Eaters – You Don't Need Someone New
Menage – Memories
Men Without Hats – I Got The Message
Freddie Mercury – I Was Born To Love You
Midnight Powers – Dance, It's My Life
Miquel Brown – Close To Perfection
Motels – Total Control
Phyllis Nelson – Don't Stop The Train
Nightlife Unlimited – Love Is In You
Passengers – Hot Leather
Pet Shop Boys – Being Boring
Philip Oakey/Giorgio Moroder – Electric Dreams
Oh Romeo – These Memories
Pointer Sisters – Jump
Chris Rea – I Can Hear Your Heartbeat
Sharon Redd – In The Name Of Love
Cliff Richards – My Pretty One
Jimmy Ruffin – Hold On To My Love
Secession – Touch
Teri de Sario – Ain't Nothin' Gonna Keep Me From You
Marlena Shaw – Touch Me In The Morning
Stereo Fun, Inc. – Got You Where I Want You, Babe
Donna Summer – Heaven Knows
Suzy Q – Computer Music
Sylvester – Don't Stop
Sylvester – Band of Gold
Talk Talk – It's My Life
Tantra – Hills Of Katmandu
Tantra – Wishbone
Technique – Can We Try Again
Thompson Twins – Hold Me Now
Time Bandits – Endless Road
USA/European Connection II – There's A Way Into My Heart
USA/European Connection II – I'd Like To Get Closer
USA/European Connection II – Do Me Good
Viola Wills – Stormy Weather
Viola Wills – If You Could Read My Mind

Voyage – Souvenirs
(compiled by Robbie Leslie)

Paradise Garage 100

Affinity – Don't Go Away
Ashford & Simpson – No One Gets The Prize
Carl Bean – I Was Born This Way
Hamilton Bohannon – Let's Start The Dance
Dee Dee Bridgewater – Bad For Me
James Brown – Give It Up And Turn It Loose (live version)
Peter Brown – Do You Wanna Get Funky With Me
David Byrne & Brian Eno – The Jezebel Spirit
Central Line – Walking Into Sunshine
Chicago – Street Player
The Chi-Lites – My First Mistake
Chocolette – It's That East Street Beat
Martin Circus – Disco Circus
The Clash – Magnificent Dance
Company B – Fascinated
Dinosaur L – Go Bang!
D Train – You're The One For Me
Ian Dury – Spasticus Autisticus
ESG – Moody
ESG – Stand In Line
Marianne Faithfull – Why D'Ya Do It
Family Tree – Family Tree
Fingers Inc – Mystery Of Love
First Choice – Let No Man Put Asunder
First Choice – Double Cross
Front Line Orchestra – Don't Turn Your Back On Me
Funk Masters – Love Money
Taana Gardner – Heartbeat
Manuel Gottsching – E2E4
Eddy Grant – Living On The Frontline
Eddy Grant – Nobody's Got Time/Timewarp
Gwen Guthrie – Seventh Heaven
Gwen Guthrie – Padlock
Loleatta Holloway – Love Sensation
Loleatta Holloway – Hit And Run
Ednah Holt – Serious Sirius Space Party

Thelma Houston – I'm Here Again
Imagination – Just An Illusion
Inner Life – Ain't No Mountain High Enough
Instant Funk – Got My Mind Made Up
Jackson 5 – I Am Love
Mick Jagger – Lucky In Love
Marshall Jefferson – Move Your Body
Grace Jones – Slave To The Rhythm
Grace Jones – Pull Up To The Bumper
Tamiko Jones – Can't Live Without Your Love
Kebek Elektrik – War Dance
Eddie Kendricks – Girl You Need A Change Of Mind
Chaka Khan – Clouds
Chaka Khan – I Know You, I Live You
Klein & MBO – Dirty Talk
Kraftwerk – The Robots
Labelle – What Can I Do For You
Patti Labelle – The Spirit's In It
Lace – Can't Play Around
Loose Joints – Is It All Over My Face?
M – Pop Muzik
Man Friday – Love Honey, Love Heartache
MFSB – Love Is The Message
Steve Miller Band – Macho City
Modern Romance – Salsa Rappsody
Melba Moore – You Stepped Into My Life
Alicia Myers – I Want To Thank You
Stevie Nicks – Stand Back
Nitro Deluxe – Let's Get Brutal
Northend – Tee's Happy
Nu-Shooz – I Can't Wait
NYC Citi Peech Boys – Life Is Something Special
NYC Citi Peech Boys – Don't Make Me Wait
Yoko Ono – Walking On Thin Ice
Phreek – Weekend
Pleasure – Take A Chance
The Police – Voices In My Head
Will Powers – Adventures In Success
Rockers Revenge – Walking On Sunshine
Sharon Ridley – Change

Alexander Robotnick – Problèmes d'Amour
Diana Ross – Love Hangover
Salsoul Orchestra – Love Break
Sister Sledge – Lost In Music
Sister Sledge – We Are Family
Sparque – Let's Go Dancing
Cat Stevens – Was Dog A Doughnut
Nick Straker Band – A Little Bit Of Jazz
Strikers – Body Music
Sugar Hill Gang – Rappers' Delight
Donna Summer – I Feel Love
Sylvester – I Need Someone To Love Tonight
Sylvester – Over And Over
Syreeta – Can't Shake Your Love
Talking Heads – I Zimbra
Talking Heads – Once In A Lifetime
Tom Tom Club – Genius Of Love
Touch – Without You
Two Tons of Fun – I Got The Feeling
Visual – The Music Got Me
The Weather Girls – Just Us
Womack & Womack – Baby I'm Scared Of You
Yazoo – Situation
Yello – Bostich?
(compiled by the Committee)

Cosmic Club 50

King Sunny Adé – IRE
Akendengue – Epuguzu
Antena – Bye Bye Papaye (@45)
Antena – Achilles (@45)
Jan Akkerman – Back To The Factory
Area Code 615 – Stone Fox Chase
Azymuth – Young Embrace
Tony Banks – Charm
Bautista – Vida (@45)
Jorge Ben – Ponta de Lanca Africano
Brian Briggs – Aeo
Candido – Jingo
Chris and Cosey – This Is Mee
Gal Costa – Pescaria
Tony Esposito – Pagaia
Fuhrs & Frohling – Happiness (@45)
Gilberto Gil – Toda Menina Baiana
Incredible Bongo Band – Let There Be Drums

Jean Michael Jarre – Magnetic Fields
Killing Joke – Requiem
Kissing The Pink – Mr. Blunt (@33)
Koto – Chinese Revenge
Kowalski – Ultradeterminanten
Toure Kunda – Emma
Fela Kuti – Zombie
Liaisons Dangereuses – Los Ninos Del Parque
Logic System – Unit
Love International – Dance On The Groove
Depeche Mode – Shout (@33)
Monsoon – Wings of the down
Airto Moreira – Parana
Mythos – Terra Incognita (@45)
Nazare' Pereira – O Chero Da Carolina (@45)
Mike Oldfield – Foreign Affair
Osibisa – Raghupati Raghava Rajaram
Ozo – Anambra
Passport – Ju Ju Man
Payolas – Eyes Of A stranger (@45)
Jim Pepper – Ya Na Ho
Rah Band – Electric Fling
Steel Mind – Boss Man
Cat Stevens – Was Dog A Doughnut
Tumblack – Invocation
Jasper Van't Hof's – Pili Pili
Richard Wahnfried – Time Actor
XTC – It's Nearly Africa
Yellow Magic Orchestra – Computer Game
Yellowman – Zungguzungguguzungguzeng (@45)
Zaka Percussion – Le Serpent
Zaza – Dschungel Liebe
(compiled by Daniele Baldelli)

Liaisons Dangereuses 80 (radio show)

Absolute Body Control – Final report
African Head Charge – Off The Beaten track
Wally Badarou – Novela Das Nove
Dave Ball – Strict Tempo
Beat-A-Max – The Caravan
Max Berlin – Elle Et Moi

Zazou/Bikaye/CY1 – Dju Ya Feza
The Bridge – Love Dance
Burundi Black – Burundi Black
Cabaret Voltaire – Yashar
C Cat Trance – Shake The Mind
Chris & Cosey – Walking Through Heaven
Anne Clark – Sleeper in Metropolis
Anne Clark – Our Darkness
Coutain – J'aime Regarder Les Filles
Cramps – Human Fly
Crash Course In Science – Cardboard Lamb
Crash Course In Science – Flying Turns
Cultural Vibe – Ma Foom Bey
Dark Day – Nudes In The Forest
De Dissidenten – De Dissidenten
Brian Eno & David Byrne – Jezebel Spirit
Brian Eno & David Byrne – Regiment
Eurythmics – Monkey Monkey
Executive Slacks – The Bus
Fingerprintz – Wet Job
Serge Gainsbourg – Requiem Pour Un Con
Peter Godwin – French Emotions
Grauzone – Film 2
John Foxx – Underpass
Paul Haig – World Raw
Hard Hats – Tear Down The House
Pierre Henry & Michel Colombier – Psyche Rock
Informatics – Proximity Switch
Information Society – Running
Johnny Harris – Odyssey
Fad Gadget – State Of The Nation
Jansen & Barbieri – Mission
Killing Joke – Turn To Red
Kissing The Pink – Big Man Restless
Kissing The Pink – Footsteps
Liquid Liquid – Optimo
Logic System – Unit
Love & Rockets – Ball Of Confusion
Macattack – The Art Of Drums
Monsoon – Ever So Lonely
The Neon Judgement – TV Treated
Newcleus – Auto-man

Nitzer Ebb – Join In The Chant
Nitzer Ebb – Let Your Body Learn
No More – Suicide Commando
Peech Boys – On A Journey
Carlos Peron – Dropouts
Carlos Peron – Nothing Is True
Dave Pike Set – Mathar
PiL – Death Disco
The Pool – Jamaica Running
Portion Control – The Great Divide
Will Powers – Adventures In Success
Psyche – Eating Violins
Psyche – The Saint Became A Lush
Recoil – Excerpt From Stone
Renegade Soundwave – Cocaine Sex
Eberhard Schoener & Sting – Why Don't You Answer
Section 25 – Looking from the Hilltop
Simple Minds – League of Nations
Simple Minds – Theme For Great Cities
Severed Heads – Dead Eyes Opened
Severed Heads – Goodbye Tonsils
Pete Shelley – Witness The Change
Sisterhood – Finland Red, Egypt white
Snakefinger – The Man In The Dark Sedan
Snowy Red – Euroshima (Wardance)
Unknown Cases – Masimbabele
Jasper Van 'T Hof – Pili-Pili
Vicious Pink – 8:15 To Nowhere
Vicious Pink – The Spaceship Is Over There
Wasch – Heartbeat
West India Company – Ave Maria
Jah Wobble, Holger Czukay, Jaki Liebezeit – How Much Are They?
(compiled by Paul Ward)

Warehouse 50

Ashford & Simpson – It Seems To Hang On
Roy Ayers – Running Away
Peter Brown – Do You Wanna Get Funky With Me
Donald Byrd – Love Has Come Around
Candido – Thousand Finger Man
Change – Paradise

The Clash – Magnificent Dance
Tony Cook & the Party People – On The Floor
Dinosaur L – Go Bang!
Dr Armando's Seventh Avenue Rumba Band – Deputy Of Love
Ecstasy, Passion And Pain – Touch And Go
ESG – Moody
Taana Gardner – Work That Body
Eddy Grant – Timewarp
Gwen Guthrie – It Should Have Been You
Jimmy Bo Horn – Spank
Geraldine Hunt – Can't Fake The Feeling
Imagination – Burning Up
Indeep – Last Night A DJ Saved My Life
Inner Life – Caught Up (In A One Night Love Affair)
Howard Johnson – So Fine
David Joseph – You Can't Hide Your Love
Kat Mandu – The Break
Chaka Khan – Ain't Nobody
Chaka Khan – I'm Every Woman
Klein & MBO – Dirty Talk
Patti Labelle – Music Is My Way Of Life
Loose Joints – Is It All Over My Face?
Machine – There But For The Grace Of God Go I
Gwen McCrae – Funky Sensation
Sergio Mendes – I'll Tell You
MFSB – Love Is The Message
Giorgio Moroder – E=MC2
The Originals – Down To Love Town
Phreek – Weekend
Positive Force – We Got The Funk
Powerline – Double Journey
Prince – Sexy Dancer
Diana Ross – The Boss
Paul Simpson Connection – Use Me, Lose Me
Skatt Brothers – Walk The Night
Slave – Party Lights
Gino Soccio – Dancer
Sparque – Let's Go Dancing

Nick Straker Band – A Little Bit Of Jazz
Tantra – Mother Africa
Harry Thumann – Underwater
Two Man Sound – Que Tal America
Unlimited Touch – In The Middle
Yello – Bostich
(compiled by the Committee)

Music Box 50

Adonis – No Way Back
Armando – 151
Armando – Land Of Confusion
Roy Ayers – Running Away
Brother To Brother – In The Bottle
Brother To Brother – Chance With You
Chip E – It's House
Chip E – Time To Jack
ESG – Moody
Fingers Inc – Washing Machine
Fingers Inc – Mystery Of Love
First Choice – Let No Man Put Asunder
First Choice – Doctor Love
Fun Fun – Happy Station
Dan Hartman – Vertigo/Relight My Fire
Isaac Hayes – I Can't Turn Around
Hercules – Ways To Jack
Loleatta Holloway – Catch Me On The Rebound
Steve Silk Hurley – Jack Your Body
Steve Silk Hurley – Jungle DJ
Jack Master Dick's Revenge – Sensuous Woman
The JBs – Doin' It To Death (Funky Good Time)
Jungle Wonz – Time Marches On
Eddie Kendricks – Going Up In Smoke
Eddie Kendricks – Girl You Need A Change Of Mind
Chaka Khan – I'm Every Woman
Chaka Khan – Clouds
Klein & MBO – Dirty Talk
Frankie Knuckles & Jamie Principle – Your Love
Frankie Knuckles & Jamie Principle – Baby Wants To Ride

Liquid Liquid – Optimo
Cheryl Lynn – You Saved My Day
Harold Melvin & the Bluenotes – The Love I Lost
Harold Melvin & the Bluenotes – Bad Luck
Mr Fingers – Can You Feel It?
Alicia Myers – I Wanna Thank You
On The House – Move Your Body
Phuture – Acid Tracks
Jamie Principle – Bad Boy
Rhythim Is Rhythim – Strings Of Life
Diana Ross – Love Hangover
Sleezy D – I've Lost Control
S.L.Y. – I Need A Freak
Southshore Commission – Free Man
Sylvester – You Make Me Feel (Mighty Real)
Talk Talk – It's My Life
Third World – Now That We Found Love
Visage – Frequency 7
Bobby Womack – I Can Understand It
Stevie Wonder – As
(compiled by Spanky)

Roxy 100

Abaco Dream – Life And Death In G & A
Afrika Bambaataa & the Soul Sonic Force – Planet Rock
Afrika Bambaataa & the Soul Sonic Force – Renegades Of Funk
Afrika Bambaataa And Family – Bambaataa's Theme
The Aleems – Release Yourself
Art Of Noise – Beat Box
Babe Ruth – The Mexican
The B-52s – Mesopotamia
Blondie – Rapture
Kurtis Blow – The Breaks
Chuck Brown & the Soul Searchers – Bustin' Loose
James Brown – Papa Don't Take No Mess
Tyrone Brunson – The Smurf
The Bus Boys – Did You See Me
Bobby Byrd – I Know You Got Soul
Cameo – Flirt

Chic – Good Times
The Clash – Rock The Casbah
George Clinton – Loopzilla
Lyn Collins – Think
Culture Club – Time
Dead Or Alive – You Spin Me Round (Like A Record)
Defunkt – Razor's Edge
Manu Dibango – Soul Makossa
Dominatrix – The Dominatrix Sleeps Tonight
Shirley Ellis – The Clapping Song
ESG – Moody
Fab 5 Freddy with B-Side – Change The Beat
Falco – Der Kommissar
Foreigner – Urgent
Aretha Franklin – Rock Steady
Freeze – I.O.U.
Friend And Lover – Reach Out In The Darkness
'Fusion Mix': Mohawks – Champ, James Brown – Get Up, Get Into It, Get Involved, Dyke & The Blazers – Let A Woman Be A Woman, Let A Man Be A Man
Peter Gabriel – Shock The Monkey
Graham Central Station – Now Do U Wanna Dance
Grand Funk Railroad – Inside Looking Out
Grandmaster Flash & the Furious Five – The Message
Grandmaster Flash – Larry Love
Eddy Grant – California Style
Hall & Oates – I Can't Go For That
Herbie Hancock – Rockit
Hashim – Al Naafiysh (The Soul)
The Incredible Bongo Band – Apache
Jackson 5 – Dancing Machine
Michael Jackson – PYT
Rick James – Superfreak
Joan Jett – I Love Rock'n'Roll
Grace Jones – My Jamaican Guy
Herman Kelly – Dance To The Drummer's Beat
Kool & the Gang – Jungle Jazz
Kraftwerk – Trans Europe Express
Kraftwerk – Numbers

George Kranz – Din Da Da
Fela Ransome Kuti – Shakara
Cyndi Lauper – Girls Just Wanna Have Fun
Liquid Liquid – Cavern
Lisa Lisa & the Cult Jam – Head To Toe
Little Sister – You're The One
LL Cool J – Rock The Bells
Madonna – Everybody
Malcolm McLaren – Buffalo Girls
Man Parrish – Hip Hop Bebop
Vaughan Mason – Bounce Rock Skate
Michigan & Smiley – Diseases
The Miracles – Mickey Monkey
New Edition – Candy Girls
Nicodemus – Boneman Connection
Gary Numan – Cars
The O'Jays – Money
Parliament – Atomic Dog
Phase 2 – The Roxy
Pointer Sisters – Automatic
Prince – Controversy
Queen – We Will Rock You
Ram Jam – Black Betty
Rock Steady Crew – Hey You Rock Steady Crew
Rolling Stones – Start Me Up
Run DMC – It's Like That
The Sequence – Funk You Up
Shalamar – A Night To Remember
Shango – Zulu Groove
Shannon – Let The Music Play
Sister Nancy – Bambam
Sly & the Family Stone – Family Affair
SOS Band – Just Be Good To Me
Jimmy Spicer – Bubble Bunch
Steppenwolf – Magic Carpet Ride
Strafe – Set It Off
Sugar Hill Gang – Rappers' Delight
Donna Summer – I Feel Love
Talking Heads – Once In A Lifetime
Tom Tom Club – Genius Of Love
Treacherous Three – Yes We Can Can
Trouble Funk – Trouble Funk Express
West Street Mob – Breakdance
Yazoo – Situation
Yellow Magic Orchestra – Firecracker
Yellowman – Zuzuzangzang

Zapp – More Bounce To The Ounce?
(compiled by Afrika Bambaataa & Kool Lady Blue)

Soul II Soul at the Africa Centre 50

Steve Arrington – Weak At The Knees
Roy Ayers – One Sweet Love To Remember
Gary Bartz – Music Is My Sanctuary
Big Daddy Kane – Raw
Commodores – Brick House
Eric B – Eric B Is President
Eric B & Rakim – I Know You Got Soul
Cerrone – Music Of Life
Lee Dorsey – Night People
Faze O – Riding High
Fun Boy Three – Faith Hope & Charity
Johnny Hammond – Tell Me What To Do
Willie Hutch – Give Me Some Of That Old Love
Marshall Jefferson – House Music Anthem
Wornell Jones – Must Have Been Love
Curtis Mayfield – What Is My Woman For
JB's – Same Beat
Jomanda – Make My Body Rock
Cymande – Brothers On The Slide
James Mason – Sweet Power Your Embrace
LL Cool J – Rock The Bells
Donna McGee – Mr Blind Man
Mickey & the Soul Generation – Iron Leg
Mighty Ryders – Evil Vibrations
Ultra Naté – It's Over Now
Nolen & Crossley – Salsa Boogie
O'Jays – Give The People What They Want
Oneness Of Juju – Every Which Way But Loose
One Way – Mr Groove
Steve Parks – Moving In The Right Direction
Pleasure – Glide
Jamie Principle – Baby Wants To Ride

Public Enemy – Public Enemy
Ramp – Everybody Loves The Sunshine
Raze – Jack The Groove
Brentford Rocker – Greedy G
Toni Scott – The Chief
Soul II Soul – Fairplay
Spoony G – Spoony's Rap
Stetsasonic – Talking All That Jazz
Foster Sylvers – Missdemeanour
Tommy Stewart – Bump & Hustle Music
Todd Terry – Bango
Voices Of East Harlem – Wanted Dead Or Alive
Dexter Wansell – Life On Mars
Fred Wesley & the JB's – Blow Your Head
Reuben Wilson – Got To Get Your Own
Larry Young – Turn Out The Lights
The Younger Generation – We Rap More Mellow
2 In A Room – Do What You Want
(compiled by Jazzie B)

Jive Turkey 100

Oleta Adams – Rhythm Of Life
Afrodisiac – Song Of The Siren
Anne Marie – Just Waiting
Armando – Land Of Confusion
Atmosfear – Dancing In Outer Space
Bang The Party – Bang Bang Your Mine
Rob Base – It Takes Two
Bas Noir – I'm Glad You Came To Me
Bas Noir – My Love Is Magic
Archie Bell & the Drells – Don't Let Love Get You Down
Regina Belle – Good Lovin'
Blapps Posse – Don't Hold Back
Blue Zone – Big Thing
Russ Brown – Gotta Find A Way
Chanelle – One Man
Chimes – Never Underestimate
Chimes – Heaven
Craig T Cooper – 25 Hours A Day
Dazzle – You Dazzle Me

Wanda Dee – Straight To The Bone
Degrees Of Motion – Do You Want It Right Now
De La Soul – Say No Go
De La Soul – Eye Know
D-Influence – I'm The One
Dionne – Come Get My Lovin'
En Vogue – Hold On
Equation – The Answer
Fallout – The Morning After
Farley Jackmaster Funk – The Acid Life
Mr Fingers – Can You Feel It
Forgemasters – Track With No Name
Paris Grey – Don't Lead Me
A Guy Called Gerald – Voodoo Ray
GTO – Pure
Lalah Hathaway – Heaven Knows
Neal Howard – Perpetual Motion
Ital Rockers – Ital's Anthem
Jade – Don't Walk Away
Arnold Jarvis – Take Some Time Out
Miles Jaye – Heaven
Kechia Jenkins – I Need Somebody
Jolly Roger – Ulysses (The Groove)
Jomanda – Make My Body Rock
Shay Jones – Are You Gonna Be There
Jungle Wonz – The Jungle
K Alexi Shelby – My Medusa
Keynotes – Let's Let's Let's Dance
Landlord – I Like It
Joanna Law – First Time Ever
Debbie Malone – Rescue Me
LFO – Mentok 1
Gwen McCrae – All This Love That I'm Giving
Mantronix – Got To Have Your Love
Master C&J – Dub Love
Master C&J – Face It
Mayday - Sinister
Arthur Miles – Helping Hand
DJ Mink – Hey Hey Can U Relate
Chanté Moore – Love's Taken Over
New Jersey Queens – Party Don't Worry About It
Nightmares On Wax – Aftermath
Nightmares On Wax – Dextrous
Nightmares On Wax – I'm For Real
Steve Parks – Moving In All Directions

Push Pull – Africa
Plez – I Can't Stop
Quazar – Day-Glo
Quazar – Through The Looking Glass
Fonda Rae – Tuch Me
Reese & Santonio – The Sound
Ralph Rosario – Get Up, Get Out
Rhythim Is Rhythim – Beyond The Dance
Rhythim Is Rhythim – It Is What It Is
Rhythim Is Rhythim – Nude Photo
Rhythim Is Rhythim – Strings Of Life
Rhythim Is Rhythim – The Dance
Royal Delight – I'll Be A Freak For You
Rufus – Ain't Nobody (Knuckles Mix)
Ryuichi Sakamoto – Riot In Lagos
Sandee – Notice Me
Shalor – I'm In Love
Soul II Soul – Fair Play
Soul II Soul – Back To Life
Soul II Soul – Keep On Movin'
Soul II Soul – Jazzie's Groove
Smith & Mighty – Anyone
Smith & Mighty – Walk On By
Stereo MC's – Non-Stop
Sterling Void – Runaway Girl
Sterling Void – Alright
Stetsasonic – Talking All That Jazz
Sugar Bear – Don't Scandalize Mine
Liz Torres – Can't Get Enough
Unique 3 – The Theme, Weight For The Bass, Rhythm Takes Control
Virgo Four – In A Vision
Virgo Four – Take Me Higher
Alyson Williams – Sleeptalk
Young Disciples – Apparently Nothin'
808 State – Let Yourself Go
80s Ladies – Turned On To You
(compiled by DJ Parrot)

Haçienda 50

A Guy Called Gerald – Voodoo Ray
Bam Bam – Give It To Me
Bamboo – Bamboo
Coolhouse – Rock This Party Right
Delite – Wild Times
Roberta Flack – Uh Oh Ooh Ooh Look Out

808 State – Pacific State
ESP – It's You
Farley Farley Farley – Give Yourself To Me
Siedah Garrett – K.I.S.S.I.N.G.
Loleatta Holloway – Love Sensation
House Master Baldwin – Don't Lead Me
Inner City – Big Fun
Jago – I'm Going To Go (Knuckles Mix)
Arnold Jarvis – Take Some Time Out
Kenny Jammin' Jason – Can U Dance
Maurice Joshua – I Gotta Big Dick
Landlord – I Like It
Liaisons D – Future FJP
Lil Louis – French Kiss
Mantronix – King Of The Beats
Mark The 45 King – The 900 Number
Nayobe – I Love The Way You Love Me (Dub)
New Fast Automatic Daffodils – Big (Baka)
Nightwriters – Let The Music Use You
Orange Lemon – Dreams Of Santa Anna
Orbital – Chime
Paradox – Jail Break
Phase II – Reachin'
Phuture – Acid Tracks
Phuture – Slam
Precious – Definition Of A Track
Rhythim Is Rhythim – Strings Of Life
Rhythim Is Rhythim – Nude Photo
Risque 3 – Essence Of A Dream
Ce Ce Rogers – Someday
Rusty – Everything Is Gonna Change
Shaker Song – Shaker Song
Sha-Lor – I'm In Love
S.L.Y. – I Need A Freak
Joe Smooth – Promised Land
Sueño Latino – Sueño Latino
Sweet Exorcist – Test Four
T Coy – Carino
Ten City – Right Back To You
The LP – Acid Trax
28th Street Crew – I Need A Rhythm
Unique 3 – The Theme

Virgo – Mechanically Replayed
Sterling Void – It's Alright
(compiled by Jon Dasilva)

Shoom 50

A Guy Called Gerald – Voodoo Ray
Adonis – The Poke
Adonis – No Way Back
Art Of Noise – Crusoe
Bang The Party – Release Your Body
The Clash – The Magnificent Dance
CLS – Can You Feel It?
Code 6 – Drop The Deal
Elkin & Nelson – Jibaro
Fallout – The Morning After
Fingers Inc – Distant Planet
Gentry Ice – Do You Want To Jack
Paris Grey – Don't Lead Me
Richie Havens – Going Back To My Roots
Inner City – Good Life
It's Immaterial – Driving Away From Home
Arnold Jarvis – Time Out For Lovin'
Kenny Jammin' Jason – Can U Dance
Marshall Jefferson – The House Music Anthem
Laurent X – Machines
MFSB – Love Is The Message
Mr Fingers – Stars
Nightwriters – Let The Music Use You
Phase II – Reachin'
Phuture – Acid Tracks
DJ Pierre's Fantasy Club – Dream Girl
William Pitt – City Lights
Jamie Principle – Baby Wants To Ride
Raze – Break 4 Love
The Residents – Kaw Liga
Rhythim Is Rhythim – Strings Of Life
Rickster – The Night Moves On
Ce Ce Rogers – Someday
Rolling Stones – Sympathy For The Devil
Ralphi Rosario – You Used To Hold Me
Paul Simpson & Adeva – Musical Freedom
Joyce Sims – Come Into My Life
Taja Seville – Love Is Contagious

S*Express – Theme From S*Express
Mandy Smith – I Just Can't Wait
Joe Smooth – Promised Land
Split Second – Flesh
Ten City – Devotion
Ten City – Right Back To You
Todd Terry – Black Riot
Mac Thornhill – (Who's Gonna) Ease The Pressure
U2 – I Still Haven't Found What I'm Looking For
Barry White – It's Ecstasy When You Lay Down Next To Me
The Woodentops – Why Why Why
Pete Wylie – Sinful
(compiled by Danny Rampling)

Rage 50

Adamski – Killer
Aphrodisiac – Song Of The Siren
Fierce Ruling Diva – You Gotta Believe
Blake Baxter – Sexuality
Blake Baxter – When We Used To Play
Joey Beltram – Energy Flash
Joey Beltram – Mentasm
Black Dog – Virtual
Blue Jean – Paradise
Fall Out – The Morning After
Flowmasters – Let It Take Control
Arthur Baker feat Robert Owens – Silly Games (Bonesbreak Mix)
LTJ Bukem – Horizons
LTJ Bukem – Music
Centrefield Assignment – Mi Casa
Innerzone Orchestra – Bug In The Bassbin
Lennie De Ice – We Are I.E.
Danny D – That's The Way Of The World (Morales mix)
Johnny Dangerous – Reasons To Be Dismal
Deep Blue – The Helicopter Track
Ego Trip - Dreamworld
Euphony – Just For You London (Bodysnatch remix)
DAL – Strings On A Monster Bass
Fabio And Grooverider – Rage
Fingers Inc – I'm Strong

Fingers Inc – Mr Fingers
Goldie – Terminator
Mr Fingers – What About This Love
Housemaster Baldwin And Paris Grey
  – Don't Lead Me
Neal Howard – To Be Or Not To Be
Jungle Wonz – The Jungle
Marc Kinchen – MK EP
Bobby Konders – The Poem
Leftfield – Not Forgotten
LFO - LFO
Kenny Dope – Petey Wheatstraw
Moby – Go
Voodoo Child – Voodoo Child EP
OB1 – OB1
Jimi Polo – Better Days
Rhythim Is Rhythim – It Is What It Is
Rhythim Is Rhythim – Strings Of Life
Ralphi Rosario – You Used To Hold
  Me
Tronikhouse – Hardcore Techno EP
Smooth And Simmons – 4 Seasons
Sueño Latino – Sueño Latino
Ron Trent – Aftermath
Sterling Void – Runaway Girl
Zero B – Lock up
Zero B – Rumpelstilstkin
(compiled by Fabio)

Sound Factory 50

African Dreams – It All Begins Here
Aphrohead – In The Dark We Live
Black Traxx – Your Mind Is So Crazy
Cajmere – Percolator
Mariah Carey – Dreamlover
Doomsday – Atom Bomb
Doop – Doop
DSK – What Would We Do (Farley &
  Heller's Eight Minutes Of
  Madness)
East Village Loft Society – Manhattan
  Anthem
E G Fullalove – Divas To The
  Dancefloor
Factory Kids – I'm Simian Dammit!
First Choice – Doctor Love
KC Flight – Voices
Rosie Gaines – Exploding All Over
  Europe

Happy Mondays – Stinkin' Thinkin'
  (Junior Style Mix)
Headrush – Underground
Hed Boys – Boys And Girls
Nick Holder – Erotic Illusions
Whitney Houston – I'm Every Woman
Kiwi Dreams – Y?
Kristine W – Feel What You Want
Lectroluv – Dream Drums
Lectroluv – Struck By Love
Lidell Townsell – Nu Nu
Lidell Townsell – Get With You
Livin' Joy – Dreamer
Madonna – all tracks
Billie Ray Martin – Your Loving Arms
Vernessa Mitchell – Reap
Moraes – Welcome To The Factory
Outdance – Reality
Pascal's Bongo Massive – Père Cochon
Karen Pollack – You Can't Hurt
  Me
Roxy – Get Huh
Frank Ski – Tony's Bitch Track
The Soundman – The Factory
Sugarcubes – A Leash Called Love
Danny Tenaglia – Bottom Heavy
Thompson Twins – The Saint (8th
  Street Dub)
Barbara Tucker – Beautiful People
Underground Sound of Lisbon – So
  Get Up
U2 – Lemon
Armand Van Helden – Witch Doktor
Junior Vasquez – X
Junior Vasquez – Get Your Hands Off
  My Man
Waterlillies – Never Get Enough
Melanie Williams – Not Enough
X-Press 2 – Music X-Press
X-Press 2 – London X-Press
Yo Yo Honey – Higher (DJ Pierre
  Mix)?
(compiled by Rob Di Stefano)

Feel Real 50

Bizarre Inc – Took My Love (MK
  dubs)
Bjork – Violently Happy (MAW mix)
The Funky People – Funky People

Darryl James & David Anthony – You Make Me Happy

David Morales & The Bad Yard Band – In De Ghetto

Deee-Lite – Pussycat Meow (Murk remix)

Donnell Rush – Symphony

Equation – I'll Say A Prayer For You

Ethyl Meatplow – Queenie

Funky Green Dogs From Outer Space – Reach For Me

Hardrive – Deep Inside EP

House Of Gypsies – Samba

Jark Prongo – Shake It

Jasper Street Company – A Feeling – Basement Boys

Joe T Vanelli – Play With The Voice (Maw)

Johnny P – For Real

Johnny P – Look Good

Karen Pollack – You Can't Touch Me

Karen Pollock – Reach Out To Me

Leee John – Mighty Power Of Love

Liberty City – Some Loving

Lil Louis – Club Lonely

Logic – Blues For You

Loni Clark – Searchin' (Mood II Swing mix)

Lonnie Gordon – Do You Want It (Smack mix)

Martha Wash – Leave A Light On

MAW/Michael Watford – My Love

MD X-spress – God Made Me Phunky

Melissa Morgan – Still In Love – Maw

Mental Instrum – Bott-ee Rider

Michael Watford – Holdin On

Michael Watford – Michael's Prayer

MK – Burning

Nu Colours – My Desire – Maw Dub 3

Peacetime – The Truth Will Set You Free

Ralph Falcon – Every Now & Then

River Ocean – Love & Happiness

Robinson Wall Project – Family Prayer

Roc & Kato – Jungle Love

Round One – I'm Your Brother

Shanice – I Like

Sole Fusion – We Can Make It (Bass Hit dub)

Solution – Feels So Right

South Stret Player – Who Keeps Changing Your Mind

Step – Tribal Love/One Leg On The Ceiling

Ten City – Fantasy

Tribal Liberation – Afri-kah

Vivian Lee – Music Is So Wonderful

Wall Of Sound – Critical

Wall Of Sound – I Need Your Love

(compiled by Rob Acteson & Rhythm Doctor)

Stealth 50

Air Liquide – Robot War

Tori Amos – God (Joi Remix)

A Reminiscent Drive – Flame One

Atavistic Rhythms – Snackwitch

Boom Boom Satellites – Dub Me Crazy

Coldcut – Atomic Moog

Dr Rocket – (live performance)

The Dust Brothers – Chemical Beats

Fat Boy Slim – The Weekend Starts Here

Fearless 4 – Rockin' It

DJ Food – Turtle Soup (Wagon Christ Mix)

DJ Food – Scratch Yer Head (Squarepusher Mix)

4E – Temple Trax

La Funk Mob – La Doctoresse

Gescom – Mag

Glowball – Frequency

Happy Campers – No Mind

Pierre Henry & Michel Colombier – Psyche Rock

The Herbaliser – (live performance)

Dick Hyman – Give It Up Or Turn It Loose

Innerzone Orchestra – Bug In The Bassbin

Jedi Knights – May The Funk Be With You

Jedi Knights – Ruak Et & Kok-Bah

Jhelisha – Friendly Pressure (acappella mixed over anything)

Kid Koala – (live performance)

Fela Kuti – any track

Derrick Laro & Trinity – Don't Stop Till You Get Enough

Idris Muhammad – Power of Soul

Multiplication Rock – Three Is The Magic Number

Nicolette – No More Government

Ocean Colour Scene – The Riverboat

Photek – Seven Samurai/Hidden Camera

Pointer Sisters – Yes We Can Can

Primal Scream – Don't Fight It, Feel It

Primal Scream – Trainspotting

Red Snapper – Hot Flush

Red Snapper – In Deep

Alex Reece – Jazz Master (Kruder & Dorfmeister remix)

Talvin Singh – (live performance)

Solaris – Slow Burn Dub

Space Time Continuum – Sea Biscuit Pressure

Squarepusher – Male Pills mixed with . . . Dream Warriors – My Definition Of A Boombastic Jazz Style – (acappella)

Squarepusher – (live performance)

Peter Thomas – Chariot Of The Gods soundtrack

Peter Thomas Orchestra – The Obelisk of Karak

Tipsy – Nude On The Moon

2 Player – Extreme Possibilities (Wagon Christ Mix)

Ultra Magnetic MCs – Papa Large

Warp 69 – Natural High (Global Communications Mix)

Witchman – Leviathan?

(compiled by Jonathan Moore & Matt Black)

Twice As Nice 50

Amira – My Desire (Dreem Teem remix)

Anthill Mob – Plenty More

Artful Dodger feat Craig David and Robbie Craig – Woman Trouble

Darryl B – Too Late

Baffled – Over You

Bizzi – Bizzi's Party (Booker T remix)

Brandy – Angel in Disguise (X men remix)

Brasstooth – Celebrate Life

TJ Cases – Dedicated To Love

TJ Cases – Joy

TJ Cases – Do It Again

Shawn Christopher – Make My Love (Kerri Chandler mix)

MJ Cole – Crazy Love

Robbie Craig – Lessons In Love

Roy Davis Junior – Gabriel

Detah – Relax (Grant Nelson mix)

DHL – Favorite Girl

Double G – Twisted Future

Dreem Teem Vs Artful Dodger – It Ain't Enough

Dreem Teem – Dreem Teem Theme

Todd Edwards – As I Am

500 Rekords – Find The Path EP

Lenny Fontana – Spirit Of The Sun (Steve Gurley remix)

Groove Chronicles – Groove Chronicles Theme

Harddrive – Deep Inside

High Times – Feel It

K2 – Bouncing Flow

Kele Le Roc – My Love (10 below mixes)

DJ Luck and MC Neat – Little Bit Of Luck

Masterstepz – Melody

Masterstepz feat Richie Dan – Are you ready

Masters Of Ceremonies – Do You Really Like It

M Dubs – Bump And Grind

M Dubs – Over You

Monsta Boy – Sorry

Mood II Swing – Closer

Peace by Piece – Nobody's Business (Dreem Teem remix)

Tito Puente – Oye Como Va (MAW mixes)

Ramsey and Fen – Love Bug

Reservoir Dogs – What To Do About Us

RIP Groove – Oh Baby

RIP Groove – RIP

Guy Simone – You're Mine,
So Solid Crew – Oh No
Sticky feat Ms Dynamite – Boo
TJR – Just Gets Better
Tuff Jam – History Of House
Norris 'da Boss' Windross – Funky
　　Groove
Wookie – Battle
Wookie – Scrappy
(compiled by Spoony)

Popcorn 50

Jimmy Hughes – My Loving Time
Sam Fletcher – I'd Think It Over
David Coleman – Drown My Heart
Johnny Lytle – Samba Saravah
Joe Torres – Get Out Of My Way
Prince Buster – Dance Cleopatra
　　Dance
Johnnie Taylor – Blues In The Night
Mel Torme – Comin' Home Baby
Edwin Starr – S.O.S. (Stop Her On
　　Sight) aka Scott On Swingers
Manny Corchado – Pow Wow
Lenny O'Henry – Across The Street
Rene Bloch – Harlem Nocturne
The Mighty Marvelows – Your Little
　　Sister
Jackie Mittoo – El Bang Bang
Martinis – Hung Over
Luther Ingram & the G-men – I Spy
　　(For The FBI)
Googie Rene Combo – The Chiller
　　(A Very Short Story)
Billy Larkin & the Delegates – Hole In
　　The Wall
Barbara Lewis – Think A Little Sugar
Marvin Jenkins – I've Got The Blues
　　(Parts 1 & 2)
Gene Chandler – You Can Hurt Me
　　No More/You Threw A Lucky
　　Punch
Sarah Vaughan – Johnny, Be Smart
Jimmy Foster – Stranger In Paradise
Oscar Brown Jr. – When Malindy
　　Sings
The Funky Lloyd Price Orchestra –
　　Ooh Pee Day

Clyde McPhatter – I'll Love You Till
　　The Cows Come Home
Baby Washington – Leave Me Alone
Dave 'Baby' Cortez – Summertime
　　Cha Cha Cha
The Skatalites – Exodus
Johnny Nash – Fallin' In And Out Of
　　Love
Red Tyler & The Gyros – Junk Village
Spooners Crowd – Two In The
　　Morning
The Blues Busters – I Won't Let You
　　Go
South Central Avenue Municipal Blues
　　Band – The Soul Of Bonnie &
　　Clyde
The Temptations –You've Got To Earn
　　It
Hank Levine – Image (Part 1)
Willie Bobo – Trinidad
Hanks Jacobs – Heide
Andre Williams – Rip Tips (Part 1 & 2)
Vernon Garrett – Shine It On
Clay Hammond – Dance Little Girl
Ozzie Torrens – Ozzaboo
Cool Benny – Wobble Cha
Curtis Knight – Voodoo Woman
Little J. Hinton – Let's Start A
　　Romance
Hector Rivera & His Orchestra – I
　　Want A Change For Romance
The J's with Jamie – Yoshiko
Ramsey Lewis – China Gate
The Souljers – Chinese Checkers
Abbe Lane – Whatever Lola Wants
(compiled by Eddie de Clercq)

SOURCES
and Index

Original interviews

All conducted by the authors, except *transcripts lent by Matthew Collin, **audiotapes lent by Drew DeNicola.

Abbatiello, Sal, 5.10.98, 21.3.01
Acteson, Rob, 3.8.05
Ahearn, Charlie, 22.3.01
Allen, Harry, 25.7.01
Aletti, Vince, 12.10.98
Alfredo, 21.7.05
Anderson, Cleveland, 9.9.04
Atkins, Juan, 30.8.04
Baldelli, Daniele, 23.4.04
Bambaataa, Afrika, 21.12.95, 6.10.98,
Baker, Arthur, 25.1.99
Barrow, Steve, 10.9.98
Belolo, Henri, 23.10.04
Bellars, Rob, 25.3.99
Benini, Luca, 17.6.05
Becha, Mo, 15.3.05
Beedle, Ashley, 4.9.96, 15.7.03
Berkman, Justin, 3.10.97
Beysens, Eric, 15.3.05
Bicknell, Steve, 22.3.05
Blow, Kurtis, 27.9.98
Brown, Geoff, 8.9.03
Boy George, 7.1.02
Byrd, Gary, 20.11.98
Carpenter, Kenny, 11.1.99
Carter, Derrick, 24.2.95
Casey, Bob,1.2.99
Cayre, Ken, 11.3.05
Chase, Charlie, 1.10.98
Chin, Brian, 5.10.98
Clinton, George, 17.5.95
Coldcut, 14.4.99

Cook, Michael,
Cook, Norman, 19.3.99
Combs, Sean Puffy, 17.4.95
Cosmo, 25.5.99
Cotgrave, Mark, 3.5.05
Curtis, Colin, 6.9.03
D'Acquisto, Steve, 5.10.98
Damier, Chez, 23.2.95
Darge, Keb, 2.3.05
Dasilva, Jon, 22.6.05
Davis, Rob, 13.11.00
Dene, Farmer Carl, 28.3.99
De Clercq, Eddy, 15.6.05
deKrechewo, Nick, 8.10.98
Dexter, Jeff, 18.2.99
Dewhirst, Ian, 14.9.98, 2.4.99
Digweed, John, 25.2.02
Dorrell, Dave, 3.3.99
Dwayre, Danny, 1.12.00
Dynell, Johnny, 8.10.98
Eagle, Roger, 10.9.98
E, Chip, 30.5.05
Evison, Dave 1.5.99
Fab 5 Freddy, 5.10.98
Fabio, 4.2.05
Farley, Andy, 19.8.05
Farley, Terry, 2.11.94*, 23.2.05
Farley Jackmaster Funk, 22.2.95
Fouquaert, David, 15.3.05
Froggy, 7.9.04
Fung, Trevor, 3.2.05
Gillett, Charlie, 5.3.99
Gomes, Michael, 2.2.99
Godin, Dave, 21.9.98
Grabel, Richard, 2.2.99
Grandmaster Flash, 8.10.98, 22.3.01
Grand Mixer D.ST, 7.10.98
Grand Wizard Theodore, 2.10.98

Stockhausen, Klaus, 26.7.05
Swift, Rob, 20.3.01
Swindells, Steve, 18.8.04
Tallulah, 28.7.04
Tenaglia, Danny 1.10.98
Terry, Todd, 3.11.94, 21.5.96
Tissera, Rob, 14.10.99
Tong, Pete, 13.5.99
Toop, David, 6.6.01
Torrales, Hippie 26.4.03
Tyree, 20.2.95
Van Ennerseel, Koenraad, 16.3.05
Vaughan, Quincy, 23.4.03
Vasquez, Junior, 2.11.95
Verhelst, Frie, 16.3.05
Viteritti, Bobby, 22.3.01
Walker, Johnny, 1.10.97
Ward, Paul, 25.5.05
Watson, Noel, 26.5.05
Wesker, Lindsay, 10.2.99
Wilson, Greg, 8.9.03
Wilson, Mick, 16.11.00
Winley, Paul, 2.10.98
Woodliffe, Jonathan, 23.9.98
Zufo, Gianni, 21.6.05

Books

Adler, Bill – Rap (St Martins, 1992)
Ahearn, Charlie & Fricke, Jim – Yes Yes Y'All (Perseus, 2002)
Anthony, Wayne – Class of 88 (Virgin, 1998)
Anthony, Wayne – Ibiza Highs (Virgin, 1999)
Armstrong, Stephen – The White Island (Bantam, 2004)
Barclay, Eddie – Que La Fête Continue (Robert Laffont, 1988)
Barr, Tim – Techno (Rough Guides, 2000)
Barrow, Steve & Dalton, Peter – The Rough Guide to Reggae (Rough Guides, 1997)
Beadle, Jeremy J – Will Pop Eat Itself? (Faber & Faber, 1993)
Belle-Fortune, Brian – All Crews (Vision, 2004)
Benson, Richard (ed) – Night Fever (Boxtree 1997)
Bidder, Sean – House (Rough Guides, 1999)
Bidder, Sean – Pump Up The Volume (Channel 4, 2001)
Boy George with Spencer Bright – Take It Like A Man (Sidgwick & Jackson, 1995)
Bradley, Lloyd – Bass Culture (Viking, 2000)
Brewster, Bill & Broughton, Frank– The Manual (Headline 1998)
Bromberg, Craig – The Wicked Ways of Malcolm McLaren (Harper & Row, 1989)
Broughton, Frank (ed) – Time Out Book of Interviews (Penguin, 1998)

Burchill, Julie – Damaged Gods (Arrow, 1986)

Bussman, Jane – Once in a Lifetime (Virgin, 1998)

Bussy, Pascal – Kraftwerk (Saf, 2005)

Cale, John & Bockris, Victor – What's Welsh For Zen (Bloomsbury, 1999)

Cantor, Louis – Wheelin' on Beale (Pharos, 1992)

Cauty, Jimmy & Drummond, Bill – The Manual (KLF, 1988)

Chanan, Michael – Repeated Takes (Verso, 1995)

Chapman, Rob – Selling The Sixties (Routledge, 1992)

Cheren, Mel – Keep On Dancin' (24 Hours For Life, 2000)

Chang, Jeff – Can't Stop, Won't Stop (St. Martin's Press, 2005)

Clarke, Donald (ed) – The Penguin Encyclopedia of Popular Music (Penguin 1990)

Cohn, Nik – Awopbopaloobpalopbamboom (Minerva, 1969)

Collin, Matthew – Altered State (Serpent's Tail, 1997)

Cox, Harvey – The Feast of Fools (Harvard University Press, 1969)

Dannen, Frederic – Hit Men (Vintage, 1991)

David, Hugh – On Queer Street (Harper Collins 1997)

Davis, Stephen & Simon, Peter– Reggae Bloodlines (Anchor Press, 1979)

Davis, Stephen & Simon, Peter – Reggae International (R&B New York, 1982)

Dawson, Jim – The Twist (Faber & Faber, 1995)

de Koningh, Michael & Griffiths, Marc – Tighten Up (Sanctuary, 2003)

Diebold David – Tribal Rites (Time Warp Publishing 1988)

Douglas, Susan J – Listening In (Times, 1999)

Eisenberg, Evan – The Recording Angel; (Picador, 1988)

Eure, Joseph & Spady, James G – Nation Conscious Rap (PC International, 1991)

Fernando, SH Jr – The New Beats (Anchor, 1994)

Fleming, Jonathan – What Kind Of House Party Is This? (MIY, 1995)

Floyd, Samuel A – The Power of Black Music (Oxford University Press, 1995)

Flür, Wolfgang – Kraftwerk, I Was a Robot (Sanctuary, 2003)

Fong-Torres, Ben – The Hits Just Keep Coming (Miller Freeman, 1998)

Frith, Simon – Music for Pleasure (Polity, 1988)

Frith, Simon – Sound Effects (Pantheon 1981)

Gamson, Joshua – The Fabulous Sylvester (Henry Holt, 2005)

Garratt, Sheryl – Adventures In Wonderland (Headline, 1998)

George, Nelson – The Death Of Rhythm And Blues (Plume, 1988)

George, Nelson – Hip Hop America (Viking, 1998)

Gilbert, Jeremy & Pearson, Ewan – Discographies (Routledge, 1999)

Gillett, Charlie – The Sound Of The City (Sphere, 1970)

Gillett, Charlie & Frith, Simon (eds) – The Beat Goes On (Pluto, 1992)

Godfrey, John – A Decade of i-Deas (Penguin, 1990)

Goldie – Nine Lives (Sceptre, 2002)

Goldman, Albert – Disco! (Hawthorn, 1978)

Goldman, Albert – Sound Bites (Abacus, 1992)

Green, Jonathon – Days In The Life (Pimlico, 1998)

Guinness Book of British Hit Singles 11th Edition (Guinness, 1997)

Haden-Guest, Anthony – The Last Party (William Morrow, 1997)

Hager, Steven – Hip Hop (St Martins 1984)

Hamblett, Charles & Deverson, Jane – Generation X (Tandem, 1964)

Hammond, Ray – The Musician and the Micro (Blandford, 1983)
Harrison, Melissa (ed) – High Society (Piatkus, 1998)
Haslam, Dave – Manchester, England (Fourth Estate, 1999)
Haslam, Dave – Adventures On The Wheels of Steel (Fourth Estate, 2001)
Hebdige Dick – Cut 'n' Mix (Comedia 1987)
Hibbert, Tom – Who The Hell? (Virgin 1994)
Hilmes, Michelle – Radio Voices (University of Minneapolis Press, 1997)
Hinde, John & Mosco, Stephen – Rebel Radio (Pluto, 1985)
Holleran, Andrew, Dancer From The Dance (Penguin, 1978)
Howard, Roland – The Rise of the Nine O'clock Service (Mowbray, 1996)
Jackson, Hal – The House That Jack Built (Colossus, 2001)
Jackson, John – Big Beat Heat (Schirmer, 1991)
Jahn, Brian & Tom Weber – Reggae Island (Da Capo, 1998)
James, Martin – French Connections (Sanctuary, 2003)
James, Martin – State of Bass (Boxtree, 1997)
Jivani, Alkarim – It's Not Unusual (Michael O'Mara, 1997)
Joe, Radcliffe A. – This Business Of Disco (Billboard, 1980)
Jonas, Gerald – Dancing (Harry N Abrams, 1992)
Kaiser, Charles – The Gay Metropolis (Harcourt Brace, 1997)
Kaski, Tero & Vuorinen, Pekka – Reggae Inna Dance Hall Style (Black Star, 1984)
Katz, David – Solid Foundation (Bloomsbury, 2003)
Keith, Michael C – Voices in the Purple Haze (Praeger, 1997)
Kempster Chris (ed) History of House (Sanctuary, 1996)
Knoedelseder, William – Stiffed (HarperPerennial, 1993)
Krivine, J – Jukebox Saturday Night (Buckleberry Press, 1977)
Larkin, Colin (ed) – Guinness Encyclopedia of Popular Music (Guinness, 1993)
Larkin, Colin – Virgin Encyclopaedia of Reggae (Virgin, 1998)
Lawrence, Tim – Love Saves The Day (Duke University Press, 2003)
Lee, Martin A & Shlain, Bruce– Acid Dreams (Grove, 1992)
Loiseau, Jean-Claude – Les Zazous (Le Sagittaire, 1977)
McLean, Duncan – Lone Star Swing (Vintage, 1998)
McKay, George (ed) – DiY Culture (Verso, 1998)
McKenna, Pete – Nightshift (S.T. Publishing, 1996)
Martin, Linda & Segrave, Kerry – Anti Rock (Da Capo Press, 1993)
Melly, George – Revolt Into Style (Penguin, 1970)
Melly, George – Owning Up (Penguin, 1965)
Middles, Mick – Red Mick (Headline, 1993)
Mietzitis, Vita – Night Dancin' (Ballantine, 1980)
Montague, Magnificent – Burn, Baby! Burn! (University of Illinois Press, 2003)
Morrow, Cousin Brucie – My Life In Rock'n'Roll Radio (Beech Tree, 1987)
Musto, Michael – Downtown (Vintage, 1986)
Nash, Peter – The Human League (Star, 1982)
Needs, Kris – Needs Must (Virgin, 1999)
Noakes, Bob – Last of the Pirates (Paul Harris, 1984)
Norman, Philip – Symphony for the Devil (Dell, 1984)
Perkins, William Eric (ed) – Droppin' Science (Temple University Press, 1996)
Post, Steve – Playing in the FM Band (Viking, 1974)
Pryce-Jones, David – Paris in the Third Reich (Holt, Rinehart & Winston, 1981)

Push & Silcott, Mireille – The Book of E (Omnibus Press, 2000)

Passman, Arnold – The Deejays (Macmillan, 1971)

Regine – Appel Moi Par Mon Prenom (Deutsch 1988)

Rietveld, Hillegonda – This is Our House (Ashgate, 1998)

Romanowski, Patricia & George-Warren, Holly – Rolling Stone Encyclopedia of Rock & Roll (Fireside, 1995)

Rose, Tricia – Black Noise (Wesleyan University Press, 1994)

Reynolds, Simon – Energy Flash (Picador, 1998)

Reynolds, Simon – Rip it Up And Start Again (Faber & Faber, 2005)

Rimmer, Dave – Like Punk Never Happened (Faber & Faber, 1985)

Rutledge, Leigh W – The Gay Decades (Plume, 1992)

St John, Graham (ed) – Rave Culture And Religion (Routledge, 2004)

Savage, Jon – The Hacienda Must Be Built (International Music, 1995)

Savage, Jon – Time Travel (Chatto & Windus 1996)

Savile, Jimmy – As it Happens (Barrie & Jenkins, 1974)

Scott, Ronnie – Some of My Best Friends Are Blues (WH Allen, 1979)

Selvin, Joel – Summer of Love (Plume, 1994)

Shack, William A – Harlem in Montmartre (Berkeley, 2001)

Shapiro, Harry – Waiting for the Man (Quartet, 1988)

Shapiro, Peter – Drum'n'bass (Rough Guides, 1999)

Shapiro, Peter – Hip-hop (Rough Guides, 2001)

Shapiro, Peter (ed) – Modulations (Caipirinha, 2000)

Shapiro, Peter – Turn The Beat Around (Faber & Faber, 2005)

Shaw, William – Westsiders (Bloomsbury, 2000)

Sicko, Dan – Techno Rebels (Billboard, 1999)

Silcott, Mireille – Rave America (ECW Press, 1999)

Smith, Joe – Off the Record (Warner, 1988)

Southern, Eileen – The Music of Black Americans (WW Norton, 1983)

Stanley, Lawrence A & Jefferson Morley – Rap: The Lyrics (Penguin, 1992)

Tee, Ralph – Soul Music, Who's Who (Prima, 1992)

Théberge, Paul – Any Sound You Can Imagine (Wesleyan University Press, 1997)

Thornton, Sarah – Club Cultures (Polity, 1995)

Tilley, Sue – Leigh Bowery (Hodder & Stoughton, 2000)

Toop, David – Rap Attack 2 (Serpents Tail 1984)

Toop, David – Ocean of Sound (Serpents Tail, 1995)

Troy, Sandy – Captain Trips (Thunder's Mouth, 1994)

Two Fingers & Kirk, James T – Junglist (Boxtree, 1995)

Urgell, Ricardo (Ed.) – El Baile, Pacha 66-93 (Nube, 1993)

Vian, Boris – Round About Close To Midnight (Quartet, 1988)

Warburton, John – Hallelujah (Virgin, 2000)

Washington-George, Martha – Black Radio (Xlibris, 2001)

Waterman, Pete – I Wish I Was Me (Virgin, 2000)

Wexler, Jerry & Ritz, David – Rhythm and the Blues (St Martins, 1993)

Whitburn, Joel – The Billboard Book Of Top 40 Hits (Billboard, 1996)

Wilson, Tony – 24 Hour Party People (Channel 4, 2002)

Winstanley, Russ & Nowell, David – Soul Survivors (Robson Books, 1996)

Wolfe, Tom – The Electric Kool-Aid Acid Test (Bantam, 1968)

Wolfe, Tom – The Pump House Gang (Bantam, 1968)
Zwerin, Mike – Swing Under the Nazis (Cooper Square, 2000)

Magazines & periodicals

Billboard, Black Music, Blues & Soul, Boys Own, Cashbox, Club, Collusion, Dance Music Report, Dazed & Confused, Details, Disco, DJmag, Downbeat, Echoes, Evening Standard, The Face, Faith Fanzine, Grand Slam, Guardian, i-D, Independent, Interview, LA City Beat, LA Times, Life, Maclean's, Melody Maker, Melting Pot, Mixmag, Mix/Master, Mojo, Music Technology, Muzik, MX, NME, New York, New York Post, New York Times, New York Sunday News, Night, Nightlife, NY Press, Observer, Out/Look, Paper, Penthouse, Popular Music, Q, Record Mirror, Rolling Stone, San Francisco Bay Guardian, Spin, Streetsound, Time, Time Out, Time Out New York, Togetherness, Variety, Village Voice. Wire, XXL.

Dissertations

Austin, Brian Todd – The Construction And Transformation Of The American Disc Jockey Occupation, 1950-1993. University of Texas at Austin PhD Dissertation, 1994.
Fikentscher, Kai – 'You Better Work!' Music, Dance And Marginality In Underground Dance Clubs Of NYC. Columbia University PhD dissertation.
Hyde, Daniel P – The Search For The Magic Formula, The Success Of Stock/Aitken/Waterman University of Birmingham PhD dissertation, 1999.

Film, radio and television

BBC TV – Dancing In The Street, 1996
BBC TV – Beat This (Arena), 1984
BBC TV – When Louis Met Jimmy, 2000
BBC Radio Two – History Of Ibiza, 2004
DeNicola, Drew – The Original 13 (documentary in progress).
Diverse – Soul Nation, 2004
Granada TV – The Wigan Casino Story, 1998
Tyne Tees – The Tube, 1983
WMAQ-TV (Chicago) – What Is House? 1991
BBC Radio One – One Family, 1997

Sleevenotes

Bradley, Lloyd –Soul II Soul At The Africa Centre (Casual, 2003)
Brewster, Bill – Tony Humphries, Choice (Azuli, 2003)
Chin, Brian –The Disco Box (Rhino, 2000)
Gordon Brown, Nick – Sasha, The Remixes (Stress, 1993)
Jah Shaka – Jah Shaka Presents Dubmasters vol.1 (Island, 1989)
Lawrence, Tim – Acid (Soul Jazz, 2005)
Stone, Jonas – Jeff Mills, Choice (Azuli, 2004)
McLaren, Malcolm – Duck Rock (Charisma, 1983)
Wilson, Frank – Eddie Kendricks: The Ultimate Collection (Motown, 1998)

Websites

http://houbi.com/belpop/
http://members.home.nl/discopatrick
www.bbc.co.uk
www.cerysmaticfactory.info
www.deephousepage.com
www.disco–disco.com
www.discogs.com
www.djhistory.com
www.djtimes.com
www.dmadance.com
www.everythingstartswithe.co.uk
www.faithfanzine.com
www.fantazia.org.uk
www.garagemusic.co.uk
www.intuitivemusic.com
www.jahsonic.com
www.liaisons.be
www.littledetroit.net
www.members.accessus.net
www.nottinghillcarnival.net
www.offshoreradio.co.uk
www.pirateradiouk.com
www.ravelinks.com
www.raves.com
www.rocksbackpages.com
www.rsrecords.com
www.saber.net/~orb/
www.samurai.fm
www.suenomartino.net
www.technotourist.org
www.trustthedj.com
www.ultrave.org

Picture Sources

Page references are in parentheses:

S Weir (v); The Granger Collection, New York (14); courtesy of Donna Halper (31); © BBC (32); Peter Hastings (45); Joe Scherschel/*Life* magazine © Time, Inc. (49); Frank Broughton (54); © Jeff Dexter 1966 (70); Redferns (89); Peter Simon (120); © Dennis Morris/www.dennis morris.com (129); Frank Broughton (142); © 1975 The Estate of Peter Hujar, courtesy James Danziger Gallery, NY (151); from the collection of D Krivit (154); © Bob Casey/Melting Pot (166); from the collection of D Krivit (190); Sonia Moskowitz UPI/Corbis–Bettman (193); Gaslight Advertising Archives, Inc. (197); Robbie Leslie (209); Pete Jones (237); V Richard Haro © Newsday, Inc., 1993 (241); David Corio © Corbis/S.I.N. (250); © KLB Productions, Inc. (271); Laura Levine (275); Tina Paul (298); from the collection of D Krivit (303); from the collection of D Krivit (306); Simon Witter (318); from the collection of C Neal (321); Rip (346); Derrick May (357); Dave Swindells (376); Daniele Baldelli (391); *i-D* (400); Greg Wilson (405); Froggy (413); Dave Swindells (423); The Maoist Republic of Slough (439); Jazzie B (453); courtesy Twice as Nice (471); Boys Own (479); *i-D* (499); © *Time Out* (515); James Quinton/Retna Pictures (533); Chris Davison (548).

INDEX

Note: page references *in italics* indicate illustrations.